Lecture Notes in Computer Science   9798

Commenced Publication in 1973
Founding and Former Series Editors:
Gerhard Goos, Juris Hartmanis, and Jan van Leeuwen

More information about this series at http://www.springer.com/series/7407

Qing Yang · Wei Yu
Yacine Challal (Eds.)

Wireless Algorithms, Systems, and Applications

11th International Conference, WASA 2016
Bozeman, MT, USA, August 8–10, 2016
Proceedings

 Springer

Editors
Qing Yang
Montana State University
Bozeman
USA

Wei Yu
Department of Computer and Information
  Sciences
Towson University
Towson, MD
USA

Yacine Challal
Laboratoire de Méthodes de Conception de
Algiers
Algeria

ISSN 0302-9743   ISSN 1611-3349 (electronic)
Lecture Notes in Computer Science
ISBN 978-3-319-42835-2   ISBN 978-3-319-42836-9 (eBook)
DOI 10.1007/978-3-319-42836-9

Library of Congress Control Number: 2016945113

LNCS Sublibrary: SL1 – Theoretical Computer Science and General Issues

Printed on acid-free paper

This Springer imprint is published by Springer Nature
The registered company is Springer International Publishing AG Switzerland

Preface

This book constitutes the proceedings of the 11th International Conference on Wireless Algorithms, Systems and Applications, WASA 2016, which was held in Bozeman, Montana, USA, during August 8–10, 2016. The 50 full papers presented (including nine invited papers) were carefully reviewed and selected from 148 submissions. The papers cover a wide range of topics including RFID systems, cognitive radio networks, smart mobile applications, wireless network theory, delay-tolerant networks, cyber-physical systems, mobile cloud and social networks, wireless sensor networks, device-to-device communication, wireless network security, big data, wireless mesh networks, vehicle ad hoc networks, MIMO wireless systems, and privacy-preservation systems.

We express our gratitude to the authors for their excellent contributions to this conference and the book. We are also grateful to all the Technical Program Committee members for their efforts in reviewing the submissions and for their valuable comments and suggestions that significantly improved the quality of the papers. We sincerely thank the Steering Committee and general chair for their advice and support, and the publication, publicity, Web, and local chairs for their hard work.

June 2016

Qing Yang
Wei Yu
Yacine Challal

Organization

Steering Committee

Xiuzhen Susan Cheng	The George Washington University, USA (Chair)
Zhipeng Cai	Georgia State University, USA (Chair)
Jiannong Cao	Hong Kong Polytechnic University, Hong Kong, SAR China
Ness Shroff	The Ohio State University, USA
Wei Zhao	University of Macau, SAR China
PengJun Wan	Illinois Institute of Technology, USA
Ty Znati	University of Pittsburgh, USA
Xinbing Wang	Shanghai Jiao Tong University, China

General Chair

Nirwan Ansari	New Jersey Institute of Technology, USA

Technical Program Committee Co-chairs

Qing Yang	Montana State University, USA
Wei Yu	Towson University, USA
Yacine Challal	Université de Technologie de Compiègne, France

Publication Chairs

Houbing Song	West Virginia University, USA
Yantao Qiao	AT&T Labs, Inc. USA

Publicity Chair

Zhou Su	Shanghai University

Web Chair

Lei Chen	Georgia Southern University, USA

Local Organization Chair

Brendan Mumey	Montana State University, USA

Technical Program Committee

Wei Yu	Towson University, USA
Qing Yang	Montana State University, USA
Houbing Song	West Virginia University, USA
Linqiang Ge	Georgia Southwest State University, USA
Yu Cheng	Illinois Institute of Technology, USA
Jian Wang	National Institute of Standards Technology, USA
Wei Cheng	Virginia Commonwealth University, USA
Donghyun Kim	North Carolina Central University, USA
Qun Li	College of William and Mary, USA
Haojin Zhu	Shanghai Jiao Tong University, China
Yanhua Li	University of Minnesota, USA
Sanghwan Lee	Kookmin University, USA
Manki Min	South Dakota State University, USA
Lichen Zhang	Shaanxi Normal University, China
Hongwei Du	Harbin Institute of Technology Shenzhen Graduate School, China
Na Ruan	Shanghai Jiaotong University, China
Zhipeng Cai	Georgia State University, USA
Yingshu Li	Georgia State University, USA
Fan Li	Beijing Institute of Technology, China
Kuai Xu	ASU, USA
Jie Lin	Xi'an Jiaotong University, China
Xiaofeng Gao	Shanghai Jiao Tong University, China
Lifei Wei	Shanghai Ocean University, China
Dongxiao Yu	The University of Hong Kong, SAR China
Minming Li	City University of Hong Kong, SAR China
Xiaoxia Huang	Shenzhen Institutes of Advanced Technology, Chinese Academy of Sciences, China
Minhui Xue	East China Normal University/NYU Shanghai, China
Yuexuan Wang	The University of Hong Kong, SAR China
Hwangnam Kim	Korea University, South Korea
Li Wang	Beijing University of Posts and Telecommunications, China
Hongbin Liang	Southwest Jiaotong University, China
Linwei Niu	West Virginia State University, China
Siyao Cheng	Harbin Institute of Technology, China
Chaokun Wang	Tsinghua University, China
Abdulrahman Alhothaily	The George Washington University, USA
Aziz Mohaisen	Verisign Labs, USA
Jianguo Yao	Shanghai Jiao Tong University, China
Jiguo Yu	Qufu Normal University, China
Zhenhua Li	Tsinghua University, China
Yipin Sun	National University of Defense Technology, China

Zhongli Liu	UMass Lowell, USA
Zhihan Lu	UCL, UK
Jie Lian	University of Virginia, USA
Syed Hassan Ahmed	Kynugpook National University, South Korea
Qinghe Du	Xi'an Jiaotong University, China
Xiali Hei	Delaware State University, USA
Huihui Wang	Jacksonville University, USA
Yu Jiang	Tsinghua University, China
Hanlin Zhang	Towson University, USA

Contents

Randomized Skip Graph-Based Authentication for Large-Scale RFID Systems

Yudai Komori, Kazuya Sakai$^{(\boxtimes)}$, and Satoshi Fukumoto

Tokyo Metropolitan University, 6-6 Asahigaoka, Hino, Tokyo 191-0065, Japan
komori-yudai@ed.tmu.ac.jp, {ksakai,s-fuku}@tmu.ac.jp

Abstract. Private RFID authentication with structured key management securely singulates RF tags in the logarithmic order by having group keys shared by several tags. However, the degree of tags' privacy will decrease should some tags in the system be compromised by correlating tampered group keys. Improving the degree of tags' privacy in keeping with fast authentication speed is equivalent to reducing the correlation probability of group keys. To this end, we propose Randomized Skip Graphs-Based Authentication (RSGA) that significantly improves the tags' privacy in terms of anonymity with reasonable amount of key storage cost. The simulation results demonstrate that the proposed scheme achieves it design goals.

Keywords: Radio Frequency Identification (RFID) · Security and privacy · Skip graphs

1 Introduction

Fast and secure object identification, generally called *private tag authentication*, is critical to efficiently monitor and manage a large number of objects with Radio Frequency Identification (RFID) technologies. In a singulation process, an RF reader queries an RF tag, and then the tag replies its ID or data to the reader. Since the tag's ID itself is private information, the reply must be protected against various threats, such as eavesdropping and compromised attacks, where tags are physically tampered and the keys associated with compromised tags are disclosed to adversaries.

A large amount of efforts have been made to protect tag's replies with low-cost operations, e.g., the XOR operation and 16-bit pseudo random functions (PRFs) [4]. In Hash Lock [9], a tag sends a hashed ID, instead of its real ID, to a reader, and then, the reader searches the corresponding entry in the back-end server. While this approach defends tag's replies against various attacks, the authentication speed is of $O(N)$, where N is the number of tags in the system. Hence, such a straightforward approach is not practical for large-scale RFID systems. In order to efficiently and securely read tags' content, private authentication protocols with structured key management, such as groups [3], a balanced tree [5–7,10], and skip lists [8], have been proposed. In these schemes,

© Springer International Publishing Switzerland 2016
Q. Yang et al. (Eds.): WASA 2016, LNCS 9798, pp. 1–12, 2016.
DOI: 10.1007/978-3-319-42836-9_1

each tag has its unique key and a set of groups keys. Groups keys are shared by several tags and used to confine the search space of a unique key. With efficient data structures, the tag authentication completes within $O(\log_k N)$.

However, private authentication protocols with structured key management unfortunately reduce the degree of privacy, should some tags in the system be compromised. This is because group keys are shared by several tags, and physical tampering of some tags makes the other tags less anonymous. How to remedy this issue is equivalent to reducing the probability that two tags share common group keys (hence after we refer to it as *the correlation probability*). The introduction of random walking over a data structure, e.g., randomized tree-walking [10] and randomized skip-lists [8], significantly reduces the correlation probability. Nevertheless, two tags are still correlated should they have same groups keys at all the levels of in a balanced tree or skip lists.

In this paper, we will further reduce the correlation probability with novel structured key management using one of advanced data structures, called *skip graphs* [1]. The contributions of this paper are as follows. First, we design a private tag authentication protocol, namely Randomized Skip Graphs-Based Authentication (RSGA), in which unique and group keys are maintained with a skip graph. In keeping the authentication speed to be $O(\log_k N)$, where N is the number of tags in the system and k is the balancing factor of a skip graph, RSGA provides higher degree of privacy with the storage cost of $O(N \log_k N)$. Second, we prove that the proposed RSGA results in the correlation probability of $\left(\frac{1}{N}\right)^{\lceil \log_k N \rceil - 1}$, which is much lower than any of the existing solutions. In addition, the number of gates required to implement RSGA at a tag is discussed. Finally, we conduct extensive simulations and demonstrate that the proposed scheme achieves it design goals.

The rest of this paper is organized as follows. Section 2 reviews the related works and provides preliminary. We propose RSGA in Sect. 3. The performance of the proposed protocol is evaluated by mathematical analyses as well as by simulations in Sects. 4 and 5, respectively. Section 6 concludes this paper.

2 Related Works and Preliminary

2.1 Related Works

To protect tag's replies, a number of encryption-based authentication protocols have been proposed in the past. Weis proposes Hash-lock [9] where a tag computes a hashed ID using its unique key, and then, replies the hash to a reader. The reader communicates back-end-server for searching the pair of the tag's ID and unique key corresponding to the tag's reply. The reader must search all the pairs of a tag ID and a unique key, which cases authentication to take a long time. This motivates private authentication to have structured key management.

Private authentication protocols with structured key management [3,5,7,8,10] use one unique key and a set of group keys. A tag's reply contains a set of hash values each of which is computed using the unique key and the set of group keys. In the authentication phase, A reader first scans the group keys to confine the search space of the unique key. As shown in Fig. 1, the tree-based authentication schemes [5,7] use a balanced tree for the key management. The tags in the system is located at leaf nodes in the tree. Each tag obtains the unique key from its leaf node and the set of group keys at the non-leaf nodes on the path to the root. Starting from the root, the reader identifies a tag by traveling the tree toward the corresponding leaf node. Hence, authentication speed of the tree-based protocols are $O(\log_k N)$, where N is the number of tags and k is the balancing factor of the tree. However, should some tags be compromised and group keys are correlated, the system anonymity significantly decreases.

Improving anonymity is equivalent to making the correlation probability as small as possible. To this end, Lu et al. [6] use a sparse tree, where the number of non-leaf nodes are much larger than the number of tags. However, this approach increases the height of a tree causing to unacceptable storage cost to tags. Sun et al. [8] incorporates the idea of random walking over a skip list, which is a probabilistic tree-like structure consisted of a set of lists. By taking random shift at each level of skip lists and incorporate the dependency among levels, two tags are never linked unless they have exactly the same set of group keys.

There exists a faster authentication protocol, e.g., ETAP [2], which runs in $O(1)$ by mapping hashed IDs and real IDs using a hash function. However, their claim is based on *average* performance, and hash-based protocols may take $O(n)$ in the worst case. Hence, this direction is out of our scope.

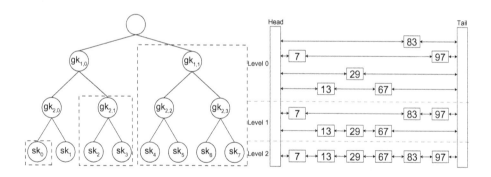

Fig. 1. An example of tree-based protocols.

Fig. 2. An example of skip graphs.

2.2   Preliminary

Anonymity. To quantify of the degree of privacy, anonymity [8] is widely used, which is defined as the state of not being identifiable among an anonymous set. An anonymous set is the set of tags whose replies are indistinguishable from each other.

For example, 8 tags are managed with a binary tree structure in Fig. 1. When no tag is compromised, every tag is identified with probability of 1/8 by random guessing. Assume that tag 1 with unique key sk_1 and group keys $GK_1 = \{gk_{1,0}, gk_{2,0}\}$ is compromised. The replies from the other tags will be partially disclosed from the keys associated with tag 1. Eventually, the adversary learns that the tags are divided into 3 disjoint groups, i.e., $\{0\}$, $\{2,3\}$, and $\{4,5,6,7\}$. As a result, the other tags are anonymous within these groups, i.e., uncompromised tags can be identified with probability of either 1, 0.5, or 0.25.

Skip Graph. A skip graph [1] is a probabilistic data structure, which has the full functionality of a balanced tree and consists of a set of ordered doubly linked lists as shown in Fig. 2. Hence, a skip graph can be seen as a set of trees. Each level, except the lowest level (labeled by Level 2), has one or more lists, and the lowest level has one list containing all the nodes. Every node participates to one of the lists at each level. A node in the list at level i for $i > 0$ appears at level $i - 1$ with probability of $1/k$, where k is the balancing factor. Given the number of inputs N, the number of levels, denoted by η, is defined as $\eta = \lceil \log_k N \rceil$, and there are $k^{\eta-j}$ lists at level j on average. The operations of search, insert, and delete are performed in $O(\log_k N)$. The space complexity is $O(N \log_k N)$.

3 RSGA

3.1 Motivations and Basic Idea

To the best of our knowledge, the use of random walking over a data structure, e.g., RSLA [8], achieves the highest degree of privacy among the existing works. In this approach, the correlation probability depends on the number of levels and the number of internal nodes at each level. In the tree-based and skip lists-based protocols, the number of levels is defined as $\eta = \lceil \log_k N \rceil$. The number of nodes at level i is defined as k^i. Hence, the correlation probability can be obtained by $\prod_{i=1}^{\eta-1} \frac{1}{k^i}$.

One naive approach to decrease the correlation probability is the use of sparse structures [6], i.e., the internal nodes in a data structure is much larger than the number of tags. However, introducing redundant internal nodes is undesirable. The number of group keys that each tag stores increases in proportion to the number of levels of a data structure. In general, the passive tag has 512-bit memory, and the length of a tag's ID is 96 bits. Assuming that the length of a unique key and a group key is 32 bits, the number of levels can be at most 13. The number of tags which can be supported by this approach is much smaller than 2^{13} when the structure is sparse. Thus, this approach is not practical.

To tackle this issue, we propose Randomized Skip Graph-based Authentication (RSGA) which works as follows. First, a skip graph with $\eta + 1$ levels is deterministically constructed in which unique keys are located at the nodes in the list at level η and the group keys are located at the nodes in the list at level j $(1 \leq j \leq \eta - 1)$. Then, each tag is associated with a node of the lowest level list. Starting from the bottom, a tag obtains the unique key and a set of group keys along the path toward the top level list. At each level, random shifting is performed (hence, the protocol is *randomized*). In the singulation process, the reader will find the node corresponding to a tag's reply in the lowest list by traveling from the top. The proposed RSGA differs from RSLA [8] in the initialization, key issuing, and private authentication phases. Note that the key updating and maintenance algorithms in [5,8] can be applied to RSGA. Each phase is elaborated on in the subsequent sections.

Table 1. Definition of notations.

Symbols	Definition
k	The balancing factor of a skip graph
N	The number of tags in the system
η	The number of levels of a skip graph, $\lceil \log_k N \rceil$
$L_{j,l}$	The l-th list at level j in a skip graph ($0 \leq j \leq \eta$)
v_i, V	Node i in a list, and a set of nodes
sk_i	Tag i's unique secret key
GK_i	A set of group keys of tag i, $\{gk_1, gk_2, ..., gk_{\eta-1}\}$
R_i	A set of shift numbers of tag i, $\{r_1, r_2, ..., r_{\eta-1}\}$
ptr	The index of the list at level 1
n_t, n_r	Nonces from a tag and a reader
β, γ	A tag's reply, $\{\beta_1, \beta_2, ..., \beta_{\eta-1}\}$ and γ
$H(.), E(.), D(.)$	The hash, encryption, and decryption functions

3.2 Definitions and Assumptions

We assume that an RFID system consists of N tags and one reader, which is connected to the back-end server. In addition, the reader and back-end server are assumed to be connected via a secure channel. Hence, the reader is the final destination of all the tags.

The nonce is randomly selected by the reader and a tag, which are denoted by n_r and n_t, respectively. The hash function $H(x)$ is assumed to be collision resistant, and an encryption function $E(K, x)$ is implemented by low-cost cryptographic operations [9], where K is given key and x is an input. In addition, the pseudo random family (PRF) is defined as $F(K, x)$ which returns a 96 bits value. We assume that RF reader has enough computational power to run a decryption function $D(K, x)$ with key K and input x. The symbols used in this paper is listed in Table 1.

3.3   The Proposed Authentication Protocol

Construction of a Skip Graph. Given the number of tags N and the balancing factor k, a skip graph with $\eta + 1$ levels is generated, where η is defined as $\lceil \log_k N \rceil$. There exits one list in the lowest level, which contains all the nodes, so that every tag can be allocated. At level j ($1 \leq j \leq \eta - 1$), there are $k^{\eta-j}$ lists and each of them contains $\frac{N}{k^{\eta-j}}$ nodes. To form a list, node v_i has pointers to the right and left nodes in the same list at level j, which are denoted by $v_i.right[j]$ and $v_i.left[j]$. The left pointer of the head node and the right pointer of the last node in the list are null. Let $L_{j,l}$ be the l-th list at the j-th level from the top. For all the level, node v_i belongs to list $L_{j,l}$ where l is computed by $i \bmod k^{\eta-j}$. The level 0 has one list which contains node v_0, and this is used as the entry point for key searching.

Each node has a key for each level. Let $v_i.key[j]$ be the variable to store a key at node v_i. To be specific, $v_i.key[\eta]$ contains unique key sk_i and $v_i.key[j]$ ($1 \leq j \leq \eta - 1$) contains group key $gk_{i,j}$. No key is assigned to the node in level 0 list. Thus, $v_0.key[0]$ is empty.

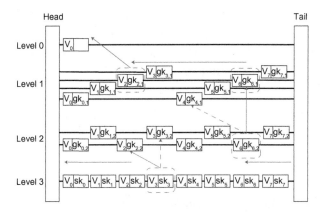

Fig. 3. An example of key issuing.

Since the construction of a skip graph is deterministic, our skip graph with the balancing factor k works in the same fashion to a set of k-balanced trees with the nodes in the lower levels belonging to more than one tree. For example, Fig. 3 shows a skip graph with $N = 8$ and $k = 2$. The corresponding set of binary trees are shown in Fig. 4.

Key Issuing. In RSGA, every tag has four variables, the unique key sk_t, a set of group keys GK_t, a set of random shift numbers R_t, and list index ptr. Tag t is located at one of the nodes, say v_i, in the list at level η, and the unique key at $v_i.key[\eta]$ is assigned to tag t. A set of group keys are assigned to tag t by traveling with random shifting from v_i at level η to the top of the skip graph.

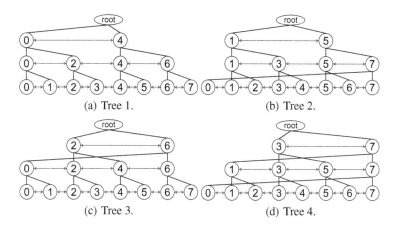

(a) Tree 1.   (b) Tree 2.

(c) Tree 3.   (d) Tree 4.

Fig. 4. The corresponding set of trees.

At level j, node v_i has a set of parents, denoted by $V_{i,j}$, since there are more than one lists at level j $(1 \leq j \leq \eta - 1)$. Here, $V_{i,j}$ includes k nodes, v_p for $p = i - nk^{\eta-j} \mod N$ $(0 \leq n \leq k - 1)$. The key issuer randomly selects one of the node in $V_{i,j}$ and moves to the upper list $L_{j-1,l}$ to which node v_i belongs at level $j - 1$. Then, random number $r_j \in [0, N - 1]$ is generated and the left shift by r_i is token. If the pointer reaches to the head node in the list, it moves to the tail. The value of r_i is added to R_t for the j-th level. The pointer is now at a node, say $n_{i'}$, at level $j - 1$. The group key at $v_{i'}.key[j - 1]$ is added to GK_t. This process repeated until the pointer reaches at the top list. Unlike a tree and skip lists, there are more than one node at level 1. Thus, the entry point of the skip graph, i.e., the ID of list $L_{1,l}$ at level 1, is kept in ptr. At the end of this process, tag t has one unique key, $\eta - 1$ group keys, $\eta - 1$ shift number, and ptr.

Mutual Authentication. After issuing keys, the reader can securely communicate with tags. In the RSGA authentication protocol, the reader first sends a query with nonce n_r, then a tag generates a reply with nonce n_r and sends the reply. The reader receives and decrypts the tag's reply.

The replying process at the tag's side is as follow. Assume tag t has the unique key sk_t, a set of group keys $GK = \{gk_1, gk_2, ..., gk_{\eta-1}\}$, a set of random shift numbers $R_t = \{r_1, r_2, ..., r_{\eta-1}\}$, and the pointer ptr. When tag t receives a query with nonce n_r from the reader, tag t generates a reply message with nonce n_t. The reply message is defined by ptr, $\beta = \{\beta_1, \beta_2, ..., \beta_{\eta-1}\}$, and γ. The value of β_j consists of a hash value $\beta_j.hash$ and encrypted shift number, i.e., $\beta = (\beta.hash, \beta.num)$, where $\beta.hash = H(gk_j || r_{j-1} || n_t || n_r)$ and $\beta.num = E(gk_j || r_j)$.

At level 1, $\beta_1.hash$ is computed with the base $r_0 = ptr$. The reason why the shift number is included at the previous level is to enforce dependency among the levels to preserve high anonymity. The random shift number r_j is encrypted by $E(gk_j || r_j)$ and set to $\beta_j.num$. While component β is computed using a group key at each level i, and γ is computed using a unique key at level η. The value of γ is obtained by $ID_t \oplus F(0||sk_t||r_{\eta-1}||n_t||n_r)$, where ID_t is the ID of a tag and $F(.)$ is the PRF. As the input of $F(.)$, 0 is concatenated with other parameters for the purpose of the mutual authentication. Finally, tag t sends n_t, β, γ, and ptr to the reader. Note that β contains $\eta - 1$ elements.

On receiving tag t's reply, the reader scans k group keys associated to the nodes in list $L_{1,ptr}$. Let v_i be the node whose $key[1]$ contains the corresponding group key gk_1 for $\beta_1.hash$. In addition, $\beta_1.num$ is decrypted by gk_1 to obtain shift number r_1. The pointer moves to v_i in $L_{j,l}$, and then right shift is token by r_1. If the pointer reaches at the tail node in the list, it moves to the head node of the same list. This process is repeated until the pointer arrives in a node in lowest level list. Since the nodes in the lowest list contains the unique key, the reader can identify the corresponding tag based on the information in the signature γ.

After the tag identification, the mutual authentication process is kicked off. At the end of singulation, the reader knows ID_t and sk_t. The reader computes $\pi = ID_t \oplus F(1||sk_t||n_t||n_r)$ and sends it to tag t. On receiving π, tag t computes ID_t' by $ID_t' = \pi \oplus F(1||sk_t||n_t||n_r)$. If ID_t' equals to tag t's ID_t, tag t accepts the reader. By doing this process, tag t also authenticates the reader.

4   Analyses

In this section, security and performance analyses are provided in terms of the system anonymity, the key storage cost at the back-end sever, and the number of gates required at tags. Note that the key storage cost at tags is the same as the existing solutions [7,8].

4.1   Anonymity Analysis

In RSGA, two tags cannot be correlated unless they has the same group keys at all the levels. The correlation probability of RSGA can be deduced by Theorem 1.

Theorem 1. *Given the number of tags N and the balancing factor k, the correlation probability of RSGA is $(\frac{1}{N})^{\eta-1}$.*

Proof: A skip graph has $\eta = \lceil \log_k N \rceil$ levels excluding level 0 with each containing N nodes. Every tag obtains $\eta - 1$ group keys from level j $(1 \le j \le \eta - 1)$, and two tags will the same group key with probability $1/N$ from level 1 to $\eta - 1$. Thus, the two tags are correlated with probability $(\frac{1}{N})^{\eta-1}$. This concludes the proof. ∎

The anonymity of the system is defined as $\frac{1}{N^2} \sum_i |S_i|^2$, where S is the anonymous set consisting of one or more tags. If no tag is compromised, there exists only one anonymous set and $|S| = N$. Should some tags be compromised, the tags in the system are divided into disjoint set and each tag is anonymous within the set.

Let N_c be the number of compromised tags. In RSGA, an uncompromised tag belongs to the anonymous set with size k or $k-1$ only when it has the same group keys as any of the compromised nodes. Such a probability is formulated in Theorem 1. Otherwise, the tag remains anonymous within the set with size $N - N_c$. Therefore, RSGA provides higher anonymity than any of the existing works under the compromised attack.

4.2   Cost Analysis

The key storage cost at the back-end server is obtained by Theorem 2.

Theorem 2. *Given the number of tags N and the balancing factor k, the number of keys in the system is bounded by $O(N \log N)$.*

Proof: A skip graph has $\eta = \lceil \log_k N \rceil$ levels excluding level 0, and there are N nodes from level 1 to η. Note that the list at level 0 does not contain any key, and it is excluded from the consideration. Thus, the total number of nodes containing a key in the skip graph is $N \log_k N$. Therefore, the key storage cost is $O(N \log_k N)$. This completes the proof. ∎

While RSGA requires larger storage cost than the existing solutions, which require $O(N)$ key storage cost, the back-end server has enough storage capacity. In addition, RSGA never sacrifices the authentication speed compared with the tree-based and skip lists-based approaches. Thus, we stress that RSGA provides higher a privacy preserving mechanism with reasonable key storage cost.

The number of gates to implement the proposed RSGA can be formulated by a similar fashion presented in [8]. At the tag's side, compared with RSLA, RSGA requires one additional $\log_2 N$ bits parameter for *ptr* to indicate the entry point of a skip graph. Since 1-bit memory needs 5 gates (D flip-flop), $5 \log_2 N$ gates are required to store $\log_2 N$-bit information. With the same condition as [8], the number of gates to implement RSGA at a tag is formulated by $3576 + 80 \times (\eta - 1) + 5 \log_2 N$. For instance, 4,856 gates for the security mechanism are required to maintain 2^{16} tags when $k = 2$. In other words, the implementation of RSGA increases approximately 5 cents for each tag. However, we claim that additional 5 cents would not be a significant issue in the RFID systems, where each tag has a relatively long life-cycle, such as library RFID systems.

5   Simulation

In this section, the performance of the proposed RSGA is compared with the tree-based [7], AnonPri [3], and RSLA [8] protocols by computer simulations in Java.

5.1   Simulation Configuration

In the simulations, an RFID system contains one RF reader and 2^8 to 2^{14} RF tags. A simulation experiment is initialized by the key issuing process of each private authentication protocol, and then, 1 % to 90 % tags are randomly selected as being compromised. Under the compromised attack, the reader singulates uncompromised tags using a private authentication protocol. As performance metrics, anonymity, authentication speed, and key storage cost are used. These metrics are computed by exactly the same way as [8]. The balancing factor k for the tree-based, RSLA, and RSGA is set to be either 2, 4, 8, or 16. For AnonPri, the number of pseudo ID pools and the number of pseudo IDs that each tag has are set to be 1000 and 10, respectively. For each configuration, 1000 simulations are conducted.

5.2   Simulation Results

Figure 5 illustrates the system anonymity with the respect to the percentage of compromised tags in the case of $k = 2$. Clearly, RSLA and RSGA, which use a random walking over a data structure, outperform the other protocols. The anonymity of RSGA is higher than RSLA by 5 % $\sim$ 10 % when the percentage of compromised tags is between 20 % and 60 %. This is because the correlation probability of RSGA is much smaller than that of RSLA. Hence, RSGA provides the strongest privacy protection mechanism against the compromised attack.

Figure 6 demonstrates the system anonymity with different balancing factors with respect to the number of compromised tags. Since tags have small memory to store keys, and thus, the number of levels of a tree/skip lists/a skip graph is limited. Hence, the balancing factor must be set to be large to support more tags. However, the anonymity of the existing RSLA decreases as the value of k increases. On the other hand, the anonymity of the proposed RSGA is mostly independent from the balancing factor. This implies that RSGA can accommodate more tags in keeping with the higher anonymity and the same number of group keys that each tag maintains.

Figure 7 presents the authentication speed with respect to the number of tags. Since the tree-based, RSLA, and RSGA run in $O(\log_k N)$, all of them can quickly singulate a tag. In contrast, AnonPri takes a much longer time for authentication when the number of tags increases.

Figure 8 shows the number of unique keys and group keys in the system. The key storage cost of RSGA is largest since it requires $O(N \log_k N)$ key storage cost, while the others incur $O(N)$ key storage cost. Although the tree-based, AnonPri, and RSLA do not require as much storage cost as RSGA, the different is not significant. As unique and group keys are stored in the back-end-server, additional key storage cost would not discourage the deploy of RSGA.

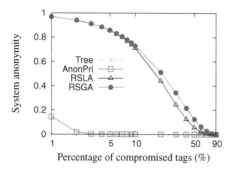

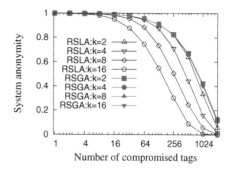

Fig. 5. System anonymity.

Fig. 6. Anonymity with different k values.

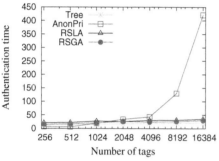

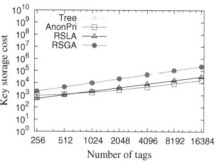

Fig. 7. Authentication speed.

Fig. 8. Storage cost.

6 Conclusion

In this paper, we proposed Randomized Skip Graph-Based Authentication (RSGA) which maintains secret and group keys with a skip graph. The key idea of RSGA is the random shift at each level and dependency among levels of the skip graph. By doing this, two tags are never correlated unless they have exactly the same group keys at all the levels, and the correlation probability is much smaller than any of the existing protocols. Analyses and simulations demonstrate that the proposed RSGA results in the highest anonymity among the tree-based, group-based, and skip lists-based protocols in keeping with reasonable storage cost.

As future works, we would like to investigate efficient key updating and maintenance mechanisms for dynamic systems, where new tags join/leave to/from the system. In addition, formal privacy analyses using the random oracles will be provided.

References

1. Aspnes, J., Shah, G.: Skip graphs. ACM Trans. Algorithms **3**(4), 37 (2007)
2. Chen, M., Chen, S.: ETAP: Enable Lightweight Anonymous RFID authentication with O(1) overhead. In: ICNP, pp. 267–278 (2015)
3. Hoque, M.E., Rahman, F., Ahamed, S.I.: AnonPri: an efficient anonymous private authentication protocol. In: PerCom, pp. 102–110 (2011)
4. Li, Y., Deng, R.H., Lai, J., Ma, C.: On two RFID privacy notions and their relations. ACM Trans. Inf. Syst. Secur. **14**(4), 30 (2011)
5. Lu, L., Han, J., Hu, L., Liu, Y., Ni, L.M., Key-Updating, D.: Privacy-preserving authentication for RFID systems. In: PerCom, pp. 13–22 (2007)
6. Lu, L., Han, J., Xiao, R., Liu, Y.: ACTION: breaking the privacy barrier for RFID systems. In: Infocom, pp. 1951–1961 (2009)
7. Molnar, D., Wagner, D.: Privacy and security in library RFID Issues, practices, and architectures. In: CCS, pp. 210–219 (2004)
8. Sun, M.-T., Sakai, K., Ku, W.-S., Lai, T.H., Vasilakos, A.V.: Private and secure tag access for large-scale RFID systems. IEEE Trans. Dependable Secur. Compt. (in press)
9. Weis, S.A.: Security and Privacy in Radio-Frequency Identification Devices. Master Thesis, MIT (2003)
10. Yao, Q., Qi, Q., Han, J., Zhao, J., Li, X., Liu, Y.: Randomized RFID private authentication. In: PerCom, pp. 1–10 (2009)

Tefnut: An Accurate Smartphone Based Rain Detection System in Vehicles

Hansong Guo[1], He Huang[1,2(✉)], Jianxin Wang[1], Shaojie Tang[3],
Zhenhua Zhao[1], Zehao Sun[1], Yu-E Sun[1,2], Liusheng Huang[1],
and Hengchang Liu[1]

[1] University of Science and Technology of China, Hefei, China
[2] Soochow University, Suzhou, China
`huangh@suda.edu.cn`
[3] University of Texas at Dallas, Richardson, USA

Abstract. Real-time and fine-grained rain information is crucial not only for climate research, weather prediction, water resources management, agricultural production, urban planning and natural disasters monitoring, but also for applications in our daily lives. However, because of the lack of rain detection systems and the high variable attribute of rain, both in time and space, the rain detection today is still not precise enough. In such context, we propose and implement Tefnut (Tefnut is the rain deity in Ancient Egyptian religion.), a novel system that exploits opportunistically crowdsourced in-vehicle audio clips from an alternative, nowadays omnipresent source, smartphones, to achieve precise detection of rain leveraging a supervised recognizer constructed from a series of refined features. We conduct extensive experiments, and evaluation results demonstrate that Tefnut can detect the rain with 96.0 % true positive rate, when deciding with a one-second-long in-vehicle audio segment only.

Keywords: Rain detection · Supervised classification · Signal processing · Smartphone

1 Introduction

According to the information released by the United Nations Office for Disaster Risk Reduction [1], developing countries lack rain detection systems, making them more vulnerable to natural disasters, such as flood, erosion, waterlogging, landslide and debris flow, caused by extreme rain events. Depending on sophisticated and expensive equipments and infrastructures, developed countries can achieve reliable daily and city-wide rain detection. However, rain has high variability, both in time and space, that is to say, the rain may start suddenly, only last for a very short period of time and then stop unexpectedly or within a very small area, the weather conditions may be totally different, in other words, it may be raining on one side, but it is completely sunny on the other side, which is not far away. But on the one hand, even in developed countries, the

© Springer International Publishing Switzerland 2016
Q. Yang et al. (Eds.): WASA 2016, LNCS 9798, pp. 13–23, 2016.
DOI: 10.1007/978-3-319-42836-9_2

rain detection systems are sparsely deployed and can not cover all areas. On the other hand, for most of the cities all over the world, these rain detection equipments and infrastructures are placed far away from the urban centers to avoid the interferences from human activities and only periodically record the rain data. These two situations mentioned above both aggravate the inaccuracy of rain detection. To illustrate that precise rain information also plays an important role in our daily lives, we just provide the following one scenario here, due to the page limitation.

Mr. A likes running. He plans to run to a park several kilometers away this morning. He wants to know whether it is raining there. Because if it is raining, he can change into waterproof shoes and clothes or will not go there. But the rain informations released by all weather apps nowadays are not accurate enough, both with respect to temporal and spatial resolution. The precise rain informations crowdsourced and shared by people whose vehicles are near the park utilizing Tefnut can help him.

Nowadays, smartphones are becoming more and more ubiquitous in our daily lives, which not only just serve as communication devices, but also are equipped with abundant advanced built-in sensors. The development of smartphones stimulates the blooming of mobile sensing researches, such as healthcare [3,31], localization [8,13,20,29], safety [12,16,26,27], human computer interaction [30] and makes our lives more efficient [21,25,28], more intelligent [4,10,22] and more enjoyable [5,9]. However, little attention has been paid to the field of rain detection. In this paper, we explore this area, propose, implement and evaluate Tefnut, which is, to the best of our knowledge, the first rain detection system exploiting opportunistically crowdsourced audio clips from smartphones in vehicles, in both industrial and academic communities.

2   Related Work

In recent years, several other kinds of rain detection systems are proposed. Allamano et al. [2], Roser et al. [19], Gormer et al. [6] and Nashashibi et al. [15] employ images for rain detection. In some literature, Grimes et al. [7] and Wardah et al. [24] leverage satellites and Leijnse et al. [11], Messer et al. [14], Overeem et al. [17], Zinevich et al. [32] and Rayitsfeld et al. [18] exploit microwave links for rain detection.

3   System Design and Implementation

3.1   System Overview

In this part, we provide the system overview of Tefnut (Fig. 1). At the very beginning, Tefnut recognizes the in-vehicle environment adopting the EEMSS proposed in [23]. The microphone will be turned on if and only if the user is in the vehicle.

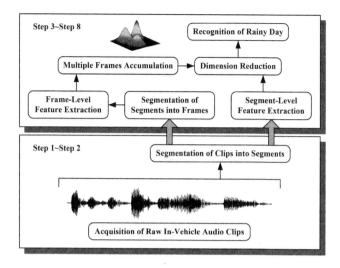

Fig. 1. System overview of Tefnut.

The first step is the acquisition of raw in-vehicle audio clips from smartphone. Then Tefnut divides these audio clips into segments, as presented in Sect. 3.2. In the third step, Tefnut computes several segment-level features in power spectrum, which contain important cues for distinguishing segments generated in rainy and sunny days in vehicles, as reported in Sect. 3.3. In order to study and depict the characteristics of these two kinds of segments more subtly, and then ultimately recognize the segments generated in rainy days in vehicles, Tefnut divides every segment into frames in the fourth step, as given in Sect. 3.4. Based on every frame, Tefnut extracts a series of frame-level features in frequency spectrum and time domain, which are economical but effective, as demonstrated in Sect. 3.5. Then Tefnut accumulates features extracted from different but continuous frames within every segment, as described in Sect. 3.6. In the seventh step, Tefnut conducts the dimension reduction, as outlined in Sect. 3.7. Finally, Tefnut constructs a recognizer, which outputs the recognition results, namely, rainy or sunny day.

3.2 Divide Audio Clips into Segments

The raw audio segments acquisition algorithm we utilized in Tefnut is based on End-Points Detection and Sliding Windows, which are two of the most popular segmentation methodologies. The length of every segment is 1 s in this paper.

3.3 Segment-Level Feature Extraction

In this part, we introduce the features which are selected to detect the rain. These features are all calculated in power spectrum of every segment.

Root Mean Squared Error-Low. This feature measures the smooth degree of power spectrum curve in low frequency part (i.e., less than 7500 Hz). The RMSE-L of segment S_i is calculated as[1]:

$$RMSE\text{-}L_i = \sqrt{\frac{1}{nl_i^p} \sum_{j=1}^{nl_i^p} (a_{ij}^p - \tilde{a}_{ij}^p)^2}$$

where nl_i^p indicates the total number of low frequency components in the power spectrum of segment S_i. a_{ij}^p indicates the amplitude of the j-th frequency component of segment S_i and $\tilde{a}_{ij}^p$ indicates the predicted amplitude of the j-th frequency component calculated by carrying out linear fitting of the power spectrum curve of segment S_i.

Amplitude of Middle Frequency. This feature stands for the amplitude of 7500 Hz in the power spectrum of segment S_i.

Amplitude of Cut-Off Frequency. This feature denotes the amplitude of 15000 Hz in the power spectrum of segment S_i.

Min., Med., Avg. and Var. Amplitude. These features focus on the basic shape of the power spectrum curve.

Energy-Low. This feature pays attention to the signal energy in low frequency part. The E-L of segment S_i is calculated as:

$$E\text{-}L_i = \sum_{j=1}^{nl_i^p} a_{ij}^p$$

Spectral Similarity. This feature describes the similarity degree between power spectrum curves in low and high frequency parts. The SS of segment S_i is calculated as:

$$SS_i = \frac{1}{nl_i^p} \sum_{j=1}^{nl_i^p} |\hat{a}_{ij}^p - \hat{a}_{i(nl_i+j)}^p|$$

where $\hat{a}_{ij}^p$ indicates the modified amplitude of the j-th frequency component calculated by aligning power spectrum curves in low and high frequency parts to x-axis respectively, in other words, by subtracting the average value of all amplitudes in low (high) frequency part from a_{ij}^p if f_{ij}^p is a low (high) frequency component, which corresponds to a_{ij}^p.

3.4 Divide Segments into Frames

In this part, Tefnut divides every segment into frames, whose lengths are 0.032 s in this paper, with an overlap of 50 % between consecutive frames, and then applies Hanning window to every frame to avoid frequency distortion.

---

[1] In this paper, the superscript p, t or f on a variable indicates that this variable is calculated in power spectrum, time domain or frequency spectrum respectively.

3.5 Frame-Level Feature Extraction

The following are several features employed to recognize the sounds generated in rainy days in vehicles, such as raindrops hitting on windows and windshield wipers pivoting, which are all calculated in time domain or frequency spectrum of every frame.

Spectral Centroid. This feature characterizes the barycenter of the frequency spectrum, which is correlated with the perceptual attribute of timbre, i.e., brightness. The SC of frame F_i is calculated as:

$$SC_i = \frac{\sum\limits_{j=2}^{n_i^f} a_{ij}^f \log_2 \frac{f_{ij}^f}{1000}}{\sum\limits_{j=2}^{n_i^f} a_{ij}^f}$$

where n_i^f indicates the total number of frequency components and a_{ij}^f indicates the amplitude of the j-th frequency component f_{ij}^f, in the frequency spectrum of frame F_i.

Spectral Spread. This feature denotes the shape of the frequency spectrum, that is to say, whether it is concentrated in the vicinity of its centroid, or spread out over the frequency spectrum. The SS of frame F_i is calculated as:

$$SS_i = \sqrt{\frac{\sum\limits_{j=2}^{n_i^f} (\log_2 \frac{f_{ij}^f}{1000} - SC_i)^2 a_{ij}^f}{\sum\limits_{j=2}^{n_i^f} a_{ij}^f}}$$

Spectral Roll-Off. This feature captures the frequency below which 95 % of the signal energy is contained. The SR-O of frame F_i is calculated as:

$$SR\text{-}O_i = \min j', \text{ subject to:}$$

$$\sum_{j=1}^{j'} a_{ij}^f \geq 0.95 \sum_{j=1}^{n_i^f} a_{ij}^f$$

Mel Frequency Cepstral Coefficients. These features collectively represent the shape of the spectrum. To calculate the MFCC of frame F_i, Tefnut firstly employs the Hamming window to minimize the maximum side lobe. Then, Tefnut transforms the time domain of frame F_i into frequency domain by performing the DFT (Discrete Fourier Transform). In the third step, utilizing a set of triangular filters, Tefnut computes the Mel scale from the frequency components obtained above. Finally, Tefnut takes the logarithms of powers at all Mel frequencies and conducts the DCT (Discrete Cosine Transform) of these logarithm values. The amplitudes of the output spectrum are the Mel Frequency Cepstral Coefficients.

Avg. Zero-Crossing Rate. This feature counts the average number of occurrences that the sampling points of audio signal pass through the zero axis in time domain within a particular frame. The AZ-CR of frame F_i is calculated as:

$$AZ\text{-}CR_i = \frac{1}{n_i^t - 1} \sum_{j=2}^{n_i^t} [s_{ij}^t s_{i(j-1)}^t < 0]$$

where $[P]$ is the Iverson Bracket, a notation whose numerical value is 1 if the proposition P within square brackets is satisfied, and 0 otherwise. n_i^t indicates the total number of sampling points in time domain of frame F_i and s_{ij}^t indicates the j-th sampling point of frame F_i.

3.6   Multiple Frames Accumulation

In this paper, we put forward a novel approach for describing the distributions of features extracted from different but continuous frames within every segment based on estimating a GMM (Gaussian Mixture Model), which can also be considered as a one-state CDHMM (Continuous Density Hidden Markov Model). Then we employ the parameters of the GMM as new features to conduct the recognition procedure.

3.7   Dimension Reduction

The segment-level features are 9 dimensions and the features output by GMM are 72 dimensions. In order to evaluate the sparseness, maximize the synergies between different features and then reduce the dimension of features, we explore LDA (Linear Discriminant Analysis) and PCA (Principal Component Analysis). Ultimately, according to experimental results, we choose the LDA and integrate it into Tefnut.

4   Evaluation

In this section, we present the results of our experiments. This section consists of three parts. In the first part, we compare the differences in recognition performance among six common recognizers. Then in the following part, we report the experimental results of Tefnut employing two kinds of dimension reduction algorithms. Finally, we demonstrate the time consumption of every step in the recognition process for every segment.

Our experimental dataset contains 5400 rainy day and 5400 sunny day audio segments crowdsourced and labeled by our 25 participants in rainy and sunny days in their vehicles respectively.

4.1   Recognition Performance of Different Recognizers

In this part, we construct six recognizers based on different recognition algorithms, which are Decision Tree, Random Forest, Naive Bayes, Multi Layer Perceptron, k-Nearest Neighbors and Support Vector Machine respectively. Then we conduct a series of 10-fold cross-validation experiments on our dataset. Figure 2 presents the confusion matrixes, Fig. 3(a) illustrates the TPR (True Positive Rate), Fig. 3(b) highlights the FPR (False Positive Rate) and Fig. 4 reports the time consumption for recognition on our experimental dataset of these six recognizers.

a=Rainy Day   b=Sunny Day

	Classified as		Classified as		Classified as		Classified as		Classified as		Classified as	
	a	b	a	b	a	b	a	b	a	b	a	b
a	5138	262	5317	83	5159	241	5347	53	5299	101	5245	155
b	247	5153	264	5136	509	4891	78	5322	298	5102	384	5016
	(a) DT		(b) RF		(c) NB		(d) MLP		(e) k-NN		(f) SVM	

Fig. 2. Confusion matrixes of different recognizers.

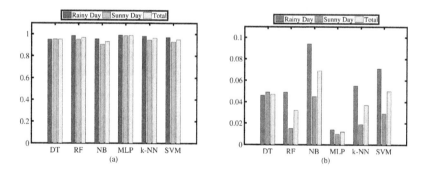

Fig. 3. TPR (a) and FPR (b) of different recognizers. (Color figure online)

We can make two main observations here. Firstly, as presented in Figs. 2 and 3, Multi Layer Perceptron outputs the best recognition performance, namely, 98.8 % TPR, 1.2 % FPR and 131 misrecognition segments, Random Forest achieves the second best recognition performance, that is, 96.8 % TPR, 3.2 % FPR and 347 misrecognition segments and Naive Bayes yields the worst recognition performance, namely, 93.1 % TPR, 6.9 % FPR and 750 misrecognition segments. Secondly, as reported in Fig. 4, we only pay attention to the time consumption of the test process, because the training process can be accomplished offline. k-Nearest Neighbors is the most time-consuming for testing our experimental dataset, 10800 labeled rainy day or sunny day in-vehicle audio segments, which spends 85.69 s. Support Vector Machine is the second most time-consuming and spends 13.84 s. The Decision Tree and Random Forest can both complete the whole test process within 0.4 s.

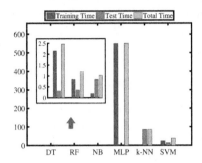

Fig. 4. Total time consumed of different recognizers. (Color figure online)

4.2   Experimental Results

In this part, we construct the recognizer based on Random Forest, in addition, we exploit Principal Component Analysis and Linear Discriminant Analysis to reduce the dimension of features. Then we conduct a series of 10-fold cross-validation experiments on our dataset. Figure 5 illustrates the confusion matrixes, TPR, FPR and feature dimension of these two recognition algorithm combinations.

a=Rainy Day		b=Sunny Day	
Classified as		**Classified as**	
a	b	a	b
a 5209	191	5158	242
b 242	5158	838	4562
TPR: 0.960	FPR: 0.040	TPR: 0.900	FPR: 0.100
Feature Dimension: 1		Feature Dimension: 12	
(a) LDA+RF		**(b) PCA+RF**	

Fig. 5. Confusion matrixes, TPR, FPR and feature dimension of RF along with LDA and PCA.

We can observe that the combination of Linear Discriminant Analysis and Random Forest achieves better recognition performance, namely, 96.0 % TPR, 4.0 % FPR and 433 misrecognition segments, which also reduces the features to 1 dimension and the combination of Principal Component Analysis and Random Forest yields worse recognition performance, that is, 90.0 % TPR, 10.0 % FPR and 1080 misrecognition segments and reduces the features to 12 dimensions.

4.3   Time Consumption of Every Computational Step

In this part, we conduct the recognition experiment on our dataset for ten times and compute the average time consumption for every segment, as shown in Table 1, which is specific to every step. We can observe that Segment-Level Feature Extraction is the most time-consuming, because we need to calculate the power spectrum first, and only then can we extract features. For every segment, the whole recognition process can be accomplished within about 675.93 ms.

Table 1. Time consumption (Avg.±Std.Dev.) of every step in the recognition process for every segment.

Step	Computational Process		Time
1-2	Acquisition of Raw In-Vehicle Audio Clips		(10.40±0.79)ms
	Segmentation of Clips into Segments		
3	Segment-Level Feature Extraction		(578.29±15.85) ms
4-6	Segmentation of Segments into Frames		(46.62±0.74) ms
	Frame-Level Feature Extraction		
	Multiple Frames Accumulation		(40.56±1.17) ms
7-8	Dimension Reduction (LDA)	Train	(0.03±0.01) ms
		Test	0.01 ms
	Recognition of Rainy Day (RF)	Train	0.01 ms
		Test	0 ms
Total			(675.93±16.20) ms

5   Conclusion

Rain detection with high temporal and spatial resolution is significant not only for professional researches and decisions-making, but also for applications in our daily lives. In this paper, we present Tefnut, which is, to the best of our knowledge, the first rain detection system exploiting opportunistically crowdsourced in-vehicle audio clips from smartphones, in both industrial and academic communities. Tefnut utilizes a supervised recognizer constructed from a series of refined features. The evaluation results of extensive experiments demonstrate that Tefnut can detect the rain with 96.0 % true positive rate, when deciding with a one-second-long in-vehicle audio segment only.

Acknowledgement. This paper was supported by National Natural Science Foundation of China under Grant No. 61572342, 61303206 and 61472384, Natural Science Foundation of Jiangsu Province under Grant No. BK20151240 and BK20140395, China Postdoctoral Science Foundation under Grant No. 2015M580470.

References

1. United Nations Office for Disaster Reduction. https://www.unisdr.org
2. Allamano, P., Croci, A., Laio, F.: Toward the camera rain gauge. Water Resour. Res. **51**(3), 1744–1757 (2015)
3. Aminikhanghahi, S., Wang, W., Shin, S., Son, S.H., Jeon, S.I.: Effective tumor feature extraction for smart phone based microwave tomography breast cancer screening. In: Proceedings of the 29th Annual ACM Symposium on Applied Computing, pp. 674–679. ACM (2014)
4. Dhondge, K., Song, S., Choi, B.Y., Park, H.: WiFiHonk: Smartphone-based beacon stuffed WiFi Car2X-communication system for vulnerable road user safety. In: IEEE 79th Vehicular Technology Conference (VTC Spring), 2014, pp. 1–5. IEEE (2014)
5. Gao, X., Tian, J., Liang, X., Wang, G.: ARPP: an Augmented Reality 3D ping-pong game system on Android mobile platform. In: WOCC, pp. 1–6. IEEE (2014)
6. Görmer, S., Kummert, A., Park, S.B., Egbert, P.: Vision-based rain sensing with an in-vehicle camera. In: Intelligent Vehicles Symposium, 2009 IEEE, pp. 279–284. IEEE (2009)
7. Grimes, D., Diop, M.: Satellite-based rainfall estimation for river flow forecasting in Africa. I: rainfall estimates and hydrological forecasts. Hydrol. Sci. J. **48**(4), 567–584 (2003)
8. Gutierrez, N., Belmonte, C., Hanvey, J., Espejo, R., Dong, Z.: Indoor localization for mobile devices. In: ICNSC, pp. 173–178. IEEE (2014)
9. Jing, T., Cui, X., Cheng, W., Zhu, S., Huo, Y.: Enabling smartphone based HD video chats by cooperative transmissions in CRNs. In: Cai, Z., Wang, C., Cheng, S., Wang, H., Gao, H. (eds.) WASA 2014. LNCS, vol. 8491, pp. 636–647. Springer, Heidelberg (2014)
10. Kim, H., Lee, S.K., Kim, H., Kim, H.: Implementing home energy management system with upnp and mobile applications. Comput. Commun. **36**(1), 51–62 (2012)
11. Leijnse, H., Uijlenhoet, R., Stricker, J.: Rainfall measurement using radio links from cellular communication networks. Water Resour. Res. **43**(3) (2007)
12. Li, F., Yang, Y., Wu, J.: CPMC: an efficient proximity malware coping scheme in smartphone-based mobile networks. In: INFOCOM, pp. 1–9. IEEE (2010)
13. Liu, Z., Chen, Y., Liu, B., Wang, J., Fu, X.: Aerial localization with smartphone. In: Wang, X., Zheng, R., Jing, T., Xing, K. (eds.) WASA 2012. LNCS, vol. 7405, pp. 386–397. Springer, Heidelberg (2012)
14. Messer, H., Zinevich, A., Alpert, P.: Environmental monitoring by wireless communication networks. Science **312**(5774), 713 (2006)
15. Nashashibi, F., de Charrette, R., Lia, A.: Detection of unfocused raindrops on a windscreen using low level image processing. In: ICARCV, pp. 1410–1415. IEEE (2010)

16. Novak, E., Li, Q.: Near-pri: private, proximity based location sharing. In: INFO-COM, pp. 37–45. IEEE (2014)
17. Overeem, A., Leijnse, H., Uijlenhoet, R.: Country-wide rainfall maps from cellular communication networks. Proc. Nat. Acad. Sci. **110**(8), 2741–2745 (2013)
18. Rayitsfeld, A., Samuels, R., Zinevich, A., Hadar, U., Alpert, P.: Comparison of two methodologies for long term rainfall monitoring using a commercial microwave communication system. Atmos. Res. **104**, 119–127 (2012)
19. Roser, M., Geiger, A.: Video-based raindrop detection for improved image registration. In: ICCV Workshops, pp. 570–577. IEEE (2009)
20. Tan, G., Lu, M., Jiang, F., Chen, K., Huang, X., Wu, J.: Bumping: a bump-aided inertial navigation method for indoor vehicles using smartphones. IEEE Trans. Parallel Distrib. Syst. **25**(7), 1670–1680 (2014)
21. Tang, Z., Guo, S., Li, P., Miyazaki, T., Jin, H., Liao, X.: Energy-efficient transmission scheduling in mobile phones using machine learning and participatory sensing. IEEE Trans. Veh. Technol. **64**(7), 3167–3176 (2015)
22. Tian, J., Wang, G., Gao, X., Shi, K.: User behavior based automatical navigation system on Android platform. In: WOCC, pp. 1–6. IEEE (2014)
23. Wang, Y., Lin, J., Annavaram, M., Jacobson, Q.A., Hong, J., Krishnamachari, B., Sadeh, N.: A framework of energy efficient mobile sensing for automatic user state recognition. In: MobiSys, pp. 179–192. ACM (2009)
24. Wardah, T., Bakar, S.A., Bardossy, A., Maznorizan, M.: Use of geostationary meteorological satellite images in convective rain estimation for flash-flood forecasting. J. Hydrol. **356**(3), 283–298 (2008)
25. Wen, Y., Shi, J., Zhang, Q., Tian, X., Huang, Z., Yu, H., Cheng, Y., Shen, X.: Quality-driven auction-based incentive mechanism for mobile crowd sensing. IEEE Trans. Veh. Technol. **64**(9), 4203–4214 (2015)
26. Wu, L., Du, X., Wang, L., Fu, X., Mbouna, R.O., Kong, S.G.: Analyzing mobile phone vulnerabilities caused by camera. In: GLOBECOM, pp. 4126–4130. IEEE (2014)
27. Wu, L., Du, X., Wu, J.: MobiFish: a lightweight anti-phishing scheme for mobile phones. In: ICCCN, pp. 1–8. IEEE (2014)
28. Yang, S., Thormann, J.: Poster: crowdsourcing to smartphones: social network based human collaboration. In: MobiHoc, pp. 439–440. ACM (2014)
29. Yoo, S., Kim, E., Kim, H.: Exploiting user movement direction and hidden access point for smartphone localization. Wireless Pers. Commun. **78**(4), 1863–1878 (2014)
30. Yue, Q., Ling, Z., Fu, X., Liu, B., Ren, K., Zhao, W.: Blind recognition of touched keys on mobile devices. In: Proceedings of the 2014 ACM SIGSAC Conference on Computer and Communications Security, pp. 1403–1414. ACM (2014)
31. Zhang, Z., Wang, H., Wang, C., Fang, H.: Cluster-based epidemic control through smartphone-based body area networks. IEEE Trans. Parallel Distrib. Syst. **26**(3), 681–690 (2015)
32. Zinevich, A., Messer, H., Alpert, P.: Frontal rainfall observation by a commercial microwave communication network. J. Appl. Meteorol. Climatol. **48**(7), 1317–1334 (2009)

A New Paradigm for Shortest Link Scheduling in Wireless Networks: Theory and Applications

Fahad Al-dhelaan[1], Peng-Jun Wan[1,2(✉)], and Huaqiang Yuan[2]

[1] Illinois Institute of Technology, Chicago, IL 60616, USA
wan@cs.iit.edu
[2] Dongguan University of Technology,
Dongguan 523808, Guangdong, People's Republic of China

Abstract. Shortest link scheduling (**SLS**) is one of the most fundamental problems in wireless networks. Almost all of the state-of-the-art approximation algorithms for **SLS** in wireless networks are resorted to the ellipsoid method for linear programming exclusively. However, the ellipsoid method can require an inordinate amount of running time and memory even for a moderate sized input, and consequently is often unusable in practice. This paper presents a completely new paradigm for **SLS** in general wireless networks which is radically different from the prevailing ellipsoid method, and is much faster and simpler. The broarder applicability of this new paradigm is demonstrated by its applications to **SLS** in wireless single-channel single-radio networks under the physical interference model, wireless multi-channel multi-radio networks under the protocol interference model, and wireless multi-input multi-output networks with receiver-side interference suppression under the protocol interference model.

Keywords: Link scheduling · Wireless interference · Approximation algorithm

1 Introduction

Shortest link scheduling (**SLS**) is one of the most fundamental problems in wireless networks. Motivated by a unified treatment on **SLS** in single-channel single-radio (SCSR) wireless networks, multi-channel multi-radio (MCMR) wireless networks, and multi-input multi-output (MIMO) wireless networks, we consider the following general formulation of **SLS**. Consider a set of m node-level communication links in a wireless network. Each link l for $1 \le l \le m$ is associated with a finite set E_l of communication primitives. Let E be the union of $E_1, E_2, \cdots, E_m$. A subset I of E is said to be *independent* if all the communication primitives in I can occur successfully at the same time; and let $\mathcal{I}$ denote the collection of all independent subsets of E. In general, $\mathcal{I}$ is specified implicitly by an interference model possibly together with the communication technologies employed at the

© Springer International Publishing Switzerland 2016
Q. Yang et al. (Eds.): WASA 2016, LNCS 9798, pp. 24–36, 2016.
DOI: 10.1007/978-3-319-42836-9_3

physical layer. For each $e \in E$, let $b(e)$ be the data rate of e. Suppose that d is a positive traffic demand function on the m links. A *link schedule* of d is a set

$$\mathcal{S} = \{(I_j, x_j) \in \mathcal{I} \times \mathbb{R}^+ : 1 \le j \le k\}$$

satisfying that for each $1 \le l \le m$,

$$d(l) \le \sum_{j=1}^{k} x_j \sum_{e \in E_l \cap I_j} b(e);$$

the value $\sum_{j=1}^{k} x_j$ are referred to as the *length* (or *latency*) of $\mathcal{S}$, and is denoted by $\|\mathcal{S}\|$. The minimum length of all fractional schedules of d is denoted by $\chi^*(d)$. Then, the problem **SLS** and a closely related problem **Maximum Weighted Independent Set** (**MWIS**) are stated as follows:

- **SLS:** Given a positive demand function d on the m links, find a link schedule $\mathcal{S}$ of d with minimum length.
- **MWIS:** Given a non-negative weight function w on E, find an $I \in \mathcal{I}$ with maximum total weight $w(I) := \sum_{e \in I} w(e)$.

The above formulation is general enough to capture the modeling of various wireless networks:

- **Wireless SCSR network:** Consider a set of m node-level communication links. For the l-th link which is from a node u to a node v, E_l is simply the singleton $\{(u, v)\}$. The independence family $\mathcal{I}$ consists of all subsets I of $E = \bigcup_{l=1}^{m} E_l$ which can transmit successfully at the same time under a specific interference model.
- **Wireless MCMR network:** Suppose that and each node v has $\tau(v)$ radios and there are m node-level communication links and λ channels. For the l-th node-level link which is from a node u to a node v, E_l consists of $\lambda \tau(u) \tau(v)$ radio-level links from u to v. The independence family $\mathcal{I}$ consists of all subsets I of $E = \bigcup_{l=1}^{m} E_l$ which can transmit successfully at the same time under a specific interference model.
- **Wireless MIMO network:** Suppose that and each node v has $\tau(v)$ radios and there are m communication links. For the l-th node-level link which is from a node u to a node v, E_l consists of $\min\{\tau(u), \tau(v)\}$ streams from u to v. The independence family $\mathcal{I}$ consists of all subsets I of $E = \bigcup_{l=1}^{m} E_l$ which can transmit successfully at the same time under a specific interference model and a specific interference suppression scheme.

SLS in wireless SCSR networks under protocol interference model has been studied in [10,12,18]. A polynomial-time greedy constant-approximation algorithm was given in [18]. This algorithm takes advantage of the *unique* binary nature of the protocol interference model: a subset I of E is independent if and only if any pair of elements in I are independent. **SLS** in wireless MCMR networks under protocol interference model in which the radio-level links of each node-level link have *uniform* data rates has been studied in [7,11,22]. A polynomial-time greedy constant-approximation algorithm was given in [22]. However, this algorithm can not be simply extended to **SLS** in wireless MCMR networks under protocol interference model in which the radio-level links of each node-level link have *disparate* data rates. **SLS** in wireless SCSR networks under physical interference model [4,21,24] is notoriously hard due to the non-locality and the additive nature of the wireless interference under the physical interference model. In [21], a polynomial-time approximation-preserving reduction from **SLS** to **MWIS** was developed, and can be extended to arbitrary wireless networks. However, such reduction utilizes the ellipsoid method for linear programming, which is quite inefficient in practice [16]. **SLS** in wireless MIMO networks under protocol interference model [13,25] is also known for its significant technical challenge due to that the complicated constraints on independence. Except for [25], all existing studies are purely heuristic without any provable performance guarantees. In [25], constant-approximation algorithms based on the ellipsoid method for linear programming were proposed for **SLS** in wireless MIMO networks with receiver-side interference suppression. Again, these algorithms are quite inefficient in practice [16].

This paper develops a completely new paradigm for **SLS** problems in general wireless networks which is radically different from the prevailing linear programming based paradigm. The paradigm is effective in terms the approximation bound and efficient in terms of the running time. In addition, it is transparent to the interference model and the communication technologies at the physical layer. We first establish the weak duality between **SLS** and **MWIS** and a simple yet powerful game-theoretic framework. Upon them we design a practical approximation algorithms for **SLS** which offers nice trade-off between accuracy and efficiency. Specifically, let $\mathcal{A}$ be a μ-approximation algorithm for **MWIS**, and $\varepsilon \in (0, 1/2]$ be an accuracy-efficiency trade-off parameter. The approximation algorithm for **SLS** developed in this paper produces a $(1 + \varepsilon)$ μ-approximate solution by making only $O\left(\varepsilon^{-2} m \ln m\right)$ calls to $\mathcal{A}$. Finally, we apply this general algorithm to derive effective and efficient approximation algorithms for **SLS** in wireless SCSR networks under the physical interference model, in wireless MCMR networks under the protocol interference model, and in wireless MIMO networks with receiver-side interference suppression under the protocol interference model. We remark that the new paradigm developed in this paper also has wide applications to general minimum fractional covering problems, which is both faster and conceptually simpler than the known algorithms such as that given in [8].

The remainder of this paper is organized as follows. Section 2 presents a weak duality of **SLS**, which reveals an intrinsic relation between **SLS** and **MWIS**. Section 3 introduces a generic adaptive zero-sum game with retirement. Section 4 describes the general design and analyses of the approximation algorithm for **SLS**. Section 5 presents the applications of this general algorithm to **SLS** in specific wireless networks. Finally, we conclude this paper in Sect. 6. The following standard notations will be adopted in this paper. For any positive integer k, we use $[k]$ to denote the set of first k positive integers $\{1, 2, \cdots, k\}$. For a real-valued function f on a finite set A and any $B \subseteq A$, $f(B)$ represents $\sum_{a \in B} f(a)$.

2 Weak Duality

In this section, we present a weak duality of **SLS** revealing the intrinsic relation between **SLS** and **MWIS**.

Consider an instance of **SLS** specified by m non-empty disjoint subsets $E_1, E_2, \cdots, E_m$, an independence family $\mathcal{I}$ of $E = \bigcup_{l=1}^m E_l$, a positive rate function b on E, and a positive demand function d on $[m]$. Suppose that w is positive weight function on $[m]$. Let $\overline{w}$ be the function on E defined by

$$\overline{w}(e) = \frac{w(l)}{d(l)} b(e)$$

for each $e \in E_l$ and each $l \in [m]$. For any non-empty subset S of $[m]$, denote

$$E_S = \bigcup_{l \in S} E_l,$$
$$\mathcal{I}_S = \{I \subseteq E_S : I \in \mathcal{I}\}.$$

Then, the problem **SLS** has the following weak duality.

Theorem 1. *For any non-empty subset S of $[m]$,*

$$\chi^*(d) \geq \frac{w(S)}{\max_{I \in \mathcal{I}_S} \overline{w}(I)}.$$

Proof. Let $\{(I_j, x_j) : j \in [q]\}$ be a shortest fractional coloring of d. Then,

$$w(S) = \sum_{l \in S} w(l) = \sum_{l \in S} \frac{w(l)}{d(l)} d(l)$$

$$\leq \sum_{l \in S} \frac{w(l)}{d(l)} \sum_{j \in [q]} x_j \sum_{e \in E_l \cap I_j} b(e)$$

$$= \sum_{j \in [q]} x_j \sum_{l \in S} \sum_{e \in E_l \cap I_j} \overline{w}(e)$$

$$= \sum_{j \in [q]} x_j \overline{w}(E_S \cap I_j)$$

$$\leq \left(\max_{I \in \mathcal{I}_S} \overline{w}(I) \right) \sum_{j \in [q]} x_j$$

$$= \left(\max_{I \in \mathcal{I}_S} \overline{w}(I) \right) \chi^*(d).$$

Thus,

$$\chi^*(d) \geq \frac{w(S)}{\max_{I \in \mathcal{I}_S} \overline{w}(I)}.$$

So, the lemma holds.

We remark that by using the strong duality theory of linear programming we can prove the following strong duality of **SLS**: There exist a non-empty subset S of $[m]$ and a positive weight function w on E such that

$$\chi^*(d) = \frac{w(S)}{\max_{I \in \mathcal{I}_S} \overline{w}(I)}.$$

However, such strong duality of **SLS** is not needed in this paper.

3   An Adaptive Zero-Sum Game with Retirement

In this section, we introduce an adaptive zero-sum game with retirement, which generalizes the problem considered by Auer et al. [2], Vovk [17], Cesa-Bianchi et al. [3], Freund and Schapire [5,6], Khandekar [9], and Arora et al. [1] in the context of learning or game theory. The game playing strategy to be described in this subsection makes both the algorithm designs and analyses proposed later in this paper fairly modular and clarifies the high-level structure of the argument. We believe that our general treatment on the game playing strategy will help to facilitate its application to other settings easily.

In the adaptive zero-sum game with retirement, a sequential game is played in rounds between a set A of m profit-making (female) agents and a loss-incurring (male) adversary. At the end of the round, some agents may retire themselves *permanently*, and the set of agents not yet ret retired are said to be *active* agents. Initially, all agents are active. At the beginning of each round, the agents declare an *adaptive* binding strategy in terms of probabilistic distributions on active agents. Then, the adversary generates the profits of active agents in this round subject to the **Normalization Rule**: The maximum value of the individual profits is exactly one. The loss incurred by the adversary is determined by the **Zero-Sum Rule**: The loss of the adversary is *equal* to the expected profit of *active* agents with respect to the binding strategy on active agents. At the end of the round, some agents may decide to retire themselves to prevent the adversary from keeping a single agent overly wealthy while keeping other agents in poverty. The objective of the agents is to make it happen as early as possible that the cumulative profit of *every* agent is at least $\frac{1}{1+\varepsilon}$ times the cumulative loss of the adversary for some pre-specified $\varepsilon \in (0, 1/2]$; the objective of the adversary is exactly the opposite. The game has to be terminated whenever all agents are retired.

Now, we introduce the strategies for the **agents**, while leaving the strategy for the adversary to specific applications. It would be natural for the agents to facilitate a **threshold-based retirement policy**: An agent will be retired permanently after making a cumulative profit at least some threshold $\phi > 0$. The choice of ϕ is essential for the agents to accomplish the objective, and we choose

$$\phi = \frac{\ln m + \varepsilon}{\varepsilon(1 + \varepsilon) + \ln(1 - \varepsilon)}.$$

Since for $\varepsilon \in (0, 1/2]$,

$$\frac{1}{5} < \frac{\varepsilon (1 + \varepsilon) + \ln (1 - \varepsilon)}{\varepsilon^2} < \frac{1}{2}.$$

we have $\phi = \Theta \left(\varepsilon^{-2} \ln m \right)$. In order to expedite the pace, the binding strategy on the active agents would give a greater probability to an active agent with smaller profit. To facilitate such binding strategy, each agent a maintains a positive weight $w(a)$, which is initially one. In each round, the binding strategy on active agents sets the probability of each active agent a proportional to its weight $w(a)$; after observing the profits generated by the adversary, the agents adopt the **Multiplicative Weights Update (MWU)** strategy to update the weights: if an agent a earns a profit $p(a)$, then $w(a)$ is updated by a multiplicative factor $1 - \varepsilon p(a)$.

An implementation of the game playing with these strategies is described as follows. Let S be the set of active agents, which is initially A; let $P(a)$ and $w(a)$ be cumulative profit, and weight of each agent a, which are initially 0, and 1 respectively. Repeat following rounds while S is non-empty:

1. **Generation of profits:** The adversary determines a non-negative profit $p(a)$ for each $a \in S$ subject to the **Normalization Rule**. As the result, for each $a \in S$,

$$P(a) \leftarrow P(a) + p(a);$$

and by the **Zero-Sum Rule** the loss incurred by the adversary is

$$\frac{\sum_{a \in S} w(a) \, p(a)}{w(S)}.$$

2. **Multiplicative Weights Update:** The agent updates $w(a)$ for each $a \in S$ by setting

$$w(a) \leftarrow w(a) (1 - \varepsilon p(a)).$$

3. **Retirement of agents:** For each agent $a \in S$, if $P(a) \geq \phi$ then the agent a is retired (i.e., removed) from S.

The effectiveness of above implementation of the game is asserted in the theorem below.

Theorem 2. *The total number of rounds is at most $m \lceil \phi \rceil$; and at the end of the last round the cumulative profit of each agent is at least ϕ and the cumulative loss of the adversary is at most $(1 + \varepsilon) \phi$.*

Due to the space limitation, the proof of the above theorem is omitted here. We remark that the **MWU** strategy may have the following alternative implementation in each round: for each $a \in S$,

$$w(a) \leftarrow w(a) (1 - \varepsilon)^{p(a)}.$$

With this alternative implementation, each agent a maintains its weight $w(a) = (1 - \varepsilon)^{P(a)}$; in other words, the weight $w(a)$ of each agent a is an exponential function of its cumulative profit $P(a)$, which is conceptually simpler. Theorem 2 still holds with this alternative implementation. However a disadvantage of this implementation is that it requires the computation of an exponential function. In contrast, the **MWU** strategy described in this section only requires multiplication.

4 Approximation Algorithm for SLS

Let $\mathcal{A}$ be a μ-approximation algorithm for **MWIS**, and $\varepsilon \in (0, 1/2]$ be an accuracy-efficiency trade-off parameter. This section presents a purely combinatorial $(1 + \varepsilon) \mu$-approximation algorithm **LS**(ε) for **SLS**.

Let

$$\phi = \frac{\ln m + \varepsilon}{\varepsilon (1 + \varepsilon) + \ln (1 - \varepsilon)}.$$

The algorithm **LS**(ε) outlined in Table 1 first builds up a link schedule $\mathcal{S}$ of ϕd from scratch with successive augmentations by a pair (I, x) in each iteration and then returns $\frac{1}{\phi} \mathcal{S}$ as the output link schedule of d. The design of **LS**(ε) is based on the general framework of an adaptive zero-sum game with retirement introduced in the previous section. Each link $l \in [m]$ corresponds to an agent, and and each augmenting iteration of the **LS**(ε) corresponds to a game round. The agents plays exactly with the strategies described in Sect. 3. For each agent $l \in [m]$, $P(l)$ is its cumulative profit, which is initially 0; ϕ is the retirement threshold of the agents; and S is the set of active agents, which is initially $[m]$. In addition, each agent $l \in [m]$ *implicitly* maintains a weight $w(l)$ which is is initially 1, and *explicitly* maintains a weight $\overline{w}(e) = \frac{w(l)}{d(l)} b(e)$ for each $e \in E_l$ as suggested by Theorem 1. The profit generation strategy of the adversary is coupled with the link schedule augmentation: In each round of the game, the profit of each agent is the *proportion* of its demand served by the augmentation pair. Consequently, at the end of each round the cumulative profit of each agent is the *proportion* of its demand that has been served by the present $\mathcal{S}$. Specifically, at the beginning of each round the adversary computes an IS I of E_S by the algorithm $\mathcal{A}$ with respect to the weight $\overline{w}$. The length x of I is determined by the **Normalization Rule** as follows. Due to the augmentation (I, x), each $l \in S$ earns a profit $x \frac{\delta(l)}{d(l)}$, where $\delta(l) = \sum_{e \in E_l \cap I} b(e)$. The **Normalization Rule** dictates that

$$x = \min \left\{ \frac{d(l)}{\delta(l)} : l \in S, \delta(l) > 0 \right\}.$$

This completes the specification of the adversary's strategy on generating losses in each round. After augmenting $\mathcal{S}$ with the pair (I, x), $P(l)$ for all $l \in S$ and $\overline{w}(e)$ for all $e \in E_S$ are explicitly updated accordingly (and $w(l)$ for all $l \in I$ are implicitly updated accordingly); and if $P(l) \geq \phi$ then l is retired from S. By Theorem 2, the number of rounds is at most $m \lceil \phi \rceil = \left(\varepsilon^{-2} m \ln m \right)$.

After the last round, the proportion of the demand by each $l \in [m]$ served by $\mathcal{S}$ is at least ϕ. Thus, $\frac{1}{\phi}\mathcal{S}$ is a link schedule of d and is returned as the output.

Table 1. Outline of the algorithm $\mathbf{LS}(\varepsilon)$.

Algorithm $\mathbf{LS}(\varepsilon)$.
// **initialization**
$S \leftarrow \emptyset, P \leftarrow \mathbf{0}, S \leftarrow [m]; \phi \leftarrow \frac{\ln m + \varepsilon}{\varepsilon(1+\varepsilon)+\ln(1-\varepsilon)};$
for each $l \in S$ do
for each $e \in E_l$ do $\overline{w}(e) \leftarrow \frac{b(e)}{d(l)};$
// **link schedule augmentations**
while $S \neq \emptyset$ do
// **augmentation**
$I \leftarrow$ the IS of E_S output by $\mathcal{A}$ w.r.t. $\overline{w}$;
for each $l \in S$ do $\delta(l) \leftarrow \sum_{e \in E_l \cap I} b(e);$
$x \leftarrow \min\left\{\frac{d(l)}{\delta(l)} : l \in S, \delta(l) > 0\right\};$
$S \leftarrow S \cup \{(I, x)\};$
// **updates**
for each $l \in S$ do
$P(l) \leftarrow P(l) + x\frac{\delta(l)}{d(l)};$ // **update the profit**
for each $e \in E_l$ do $\overline{w}(e) \leftarrow \overline{w}(e)\left(1 - \varepsilon x\frac{\delta(l)}{d(l)}\right);$ // **MWU**
if $P(l) \geq \phi$ then $S \leftarrow S \setminus \{l\};$ // **retirement**
// **scaling**
return $\frac{1}{\phi}\mathcal{S}.$

The theorem below analyzes the performance of the algorithm $\mathbf{LS}(\varepsilon)$.

Theorem 3. *The algorithm* $\mathbf{LS}(\varepsilon)$ *has an approximation bound* $(1 + \varepsilon)\mu$.

Proof. Consider a specific round in which $\mathcal{S}$ is augmented by a pair (I, x). Let I^* be a maximum $\overline{w}$-weighted independent set of E_S. Then, $\overline{w}(I) \geq \frac{1}{\mu}\overline{w}(I^*)$. By the **Zero-Sum Rule**, the loss of the adversary in this round is

$$\frac{1}{w(S)}\sum_{l \in S} w(l) x \frac{\delta(l)}{d(l)} = x\frac{\sum_{l \in S}\sum_{e \in E_l \cap I}\frac{w(l)b(e)}{d(l)}}{w(S)}$$

$$= x\frac{\sum_{l \in S}\sum_{e \in E_l \cap I}\overline{w}(e)}{w(S)} = x\frac{\overline{w}(I)}{w(S)} \geq \frac{x}{\mu}\frac{\overline{w}(I^*)}{w(S)} \geq \frac{x}{\mu\chi^*(d)},$$

where the last inequality follows from Theorem 1. So, the cumulative loss of the adversary at the end of last round is at least $\frac{\|\mathcal{S}\|}{\mu\chi^*(d)}$. On the other hand, by Theorem 2 the cumulative loss of the adversary at the end of last round is at most $(1 + \varepsilon)\phi$. Thus,

$$\frac{\|\mathcal{S}\|}{\mu\chi^*(d)} \leq (1 + \varepsilon)\phi.$$

Hence, the output link schedule has length

$$\frac{\|\mathcal{S}\|}{\phi} \leq (1 + \varepsilon)\, \mu \chi^* (d).$$

So, the theorem holds.

5   Applications

In this section, we apply the general algorithm $\mathbf{LS}(\varepsilon)$ to derive effective and efficient approximation algorithms for $\mathbf{SLS}$ in wireless SCSR networks under the physical interference model, wireless MCMR networks under the protocol interference model, and wireless MIMO networks with receiver-side interference suppression under the protocol interference model.

5.1   Wireless SCSR Networks Under Physical Interference Model

Consider an instance of wireless SCSR network under the physical interference model. In the setting of no power control, an assignment of transmission power to links is pre-specified, and a set I of links is independent if and only if all links in I can communicate successfully at the same time under the physical interference model. A power assignment is said to be *monotone* if the transmission power of a link is non-decreasing with the link length, to be *sub-linear* if the received power by a link is non-increasing with the link length, and to be a *linear* if all links have the same received power. In the setting of *power control*, a set I of links is independent if and only if there exists a transmission power assignment to I at which all links in can communicate successfully at the same time under the physical interference model. With linear power assignment, constant-approximation algorithms for $\mathbf{MWIS}$ have been developed in [24]; with any other fixed monotone and sublinear power assignment or with power control, logarithmic approximations algorithms for $\mathbf{MWIS}$ have been developed in [14,15,19,21,24]. By utilizing these approximation algorithms for $\mathbf{MWIS}$, the algorithm $\mathbf{LS}(\varepsilon)$ produces constant approximate solutions for $\mathbf{SLS}$ respectively with linear power assignment, and logarithmic approximate solutions for $\mathbf{SLS}$ with any other fixed monotone and sublinear power assignment or with power control.

5.2   Wireless MCMR Networks Under Protocol Interference Model

Consider an instance of wireless MCMR network on a set V of networking nodes with λ channels. Each node v has $\tau(v)$ antennas. Along each node-level communication link $l = (u, v)$, a set E_l of $\lambda \tau(u) \tau(v)$ different radio-level links can be supported. Let E denote the set of radio-level links of all directed node-level communication links. Under an interference model, a set I of radio-level links in E is independent if the following two properties are satisfied:

1. **Radio-Disjointness:** All radio-level links in I are radio-disjoint.
2. **Co-Channel Independence:** All radio-level links in I with the same channel are independent.

Suppose that a protocol interference model is adopted. If all the radio-link in each E_l have the *same* transmission rate, then a greedy constant-approximation algorithm for **SLS** was developed in [22]. However, the algorithmic approach in [22] cannot be extended to the general setting in which the radio-link in each E_l have disparate. But the constant-approximation algorithms for **MWIS** developed in [23] can be extended to this general setting. Indeed, let G be the conflict graph on E. It was shown in [20] that G has an orientation D whose inward local independence number defined by $\max_{e \in E} \max_{I \in \mathcal{I}} |I \cap N_D^{in}[e]|$ is bounded by a constant. Thus, for any nonnegative weight function w on E, the approximation algorithms in [23] can be applied to compute a constant-approximate solution for maximum w-weighted independent subset of E. By utilizing these approximation algorithms for **MWIS**, the algorithm **LS**(ε) produces constant approximate solutions for **SLS** efficiently.

5.3 Wireless MIMO Networks Under Protocol Interference Model

Consider an instance of wireless MIMO network on a set V of networking nodes. Each node v has $\tau(v)$ antennas and operates in the half-duplex mode, i.e. it cannot transmit and receive at the same time. Along each node-level directed communication link $l = (u, v)$, a set E_l of $\min\{\tau(u), \tau(v)\}$ streams can be multiplexed. Let E denote the set of streams of all directed node-level communication links. Under a protocol interference model, each node-level communication link is associated with an interference range and all its streams inherit the same interference range from it. When a set I of streams in E transmit at the same time, the transmission by a stream $e \in I$ from a sender u to a receiver v succeeds with the receiver-side interference suppression if all the following three constraints are satisfied:

1. **Half-Duplex Constraint:** u is not the receiver of any other stream in I, and v is not the sender of any other stream in I.
2. **Sender Constraint:** u is the sender is at most $\tau(u)$ streams in I.
3. **Receiver Constraint:** v lies in the interference range of at most $\tau(v)$ streams in I.

A set I of streams is said to be *independent* if all streams in I succeed when they transmit at the same time. Let $\mathcal{I}$ denote the collection of all independent subsets of E. Constant-approximation algorithms for the problem **MWIS** have been developed in [25] in the following three settings:

– Constant bounded number of antennas at all nodes.
– Uniform interference radii but arbitrary number of antennas.
– Uniform number of antennas but arbitrary interference radii.

By utilizing these algorithms, the algorithm **LS**(ε) produces constant approximation solutions for **SLS** in the above three settings as well.

6   Conclusion

This paper presents a purely combinatorial paradigm for **SLS** in general wireless networks computes a link schedule by a sequence of calls to be a μ-approximation algorithm $\mathcal{A}$ for **MWIS**. This paradigm is radically different from the prevailing approximation-preserving reduction from **SLS** to **MWIS** based on the ellipsoid method for linear programming. On one hand, it shares with the greedy method the simplicity that in each iteration the link schedule is augmented by a pair of independent and duration. On the other hand, in contrast to the greedy method which computes a link schedule of the give traffic demand function d directly, it employs a scaling strategy to first compute a link schedule of up-scaled traffic demand ϕd and then scale down of the link schedule by the factor ϕ. The computation of the link schedule follows a simple yet powerful framework of the adaptive zero-sum game with retirement introduced in Sect. 3. This framework together with the weak duality established in Sect. 2 leads to the proper adaptive maintenance of the weight function on E, which serves as the input to the approximation algorithm $\mathcal{A}$ for **MWIS**. The retirement strategy excludes fully-served links from further scheduling. With these techniques, our paradigm produces a $(1 + \varepsilon)$ μ-approximate solution for for **SLS** by making only $O\left(\varepsilon^{-2}m\ln m\right)$ calls to $\mathcal{A}$. Thus, it offers nice trade-off between accuracy in terms the approximation bound and efficiency in terms of the running time, and is much simpler and faster. The boarder applicability of this new paradigm is demonstrated by its applications to **SLS** in wireless SCSR networks under the physical interference model, wireless MCMR networks under the protocol interference model, and wireless MIMO networks with receiver-side interference suppression under the protocol interference model.

Acknowledgements. This work was supported in part by the National Science Foundation of USA under grants CNS-1219109 and CNS-1454770, and by the National Natural Science Foundation of P. R. China under grants 61529202, 61170216, and 61572131.

References

1. Arora, S., Hazan, E., Kale, S.: The multiplicative weights update method: a meta-algorithm and application. Theor. Comput. **8**(1), 121–164 (2012)
2. Auer, P., Cesa-Bianchi, N., Freund, Y., Schapire, R.: Gambling in a rigged casino: the adversarial multi-armed bandit problem. In: Proceedings of IEEE FOCS, pp. 322–331 (1995)
3. Cesa-Bianchi, N., Freund, Y., Helmbold, D., Haussler, D., Schapire, R., Warmuth, M.: How to use expert advice. J. Assoc. Comput. Mach. **44**(3), 427–485 (1997)
4. Chafekar, D., Kumar, V., Marathe, M., Parthasarathy, S., Srinivasan, A.: Approximation algorithms for computing capacity of wireless networks with SINR constraints. In: IEEE INFOCOM, pp. 1166–1174 (2008)
5. Freund, Y., Schapire, R.: A decision-theoretic generalization of online learning and an application to boosting. J. Comput. Syst. Sci. **55**(1), 119–139 (1997)

6. Freund, Y., Schapire, R.: Adaptive game playing using multiplicative weights. Games Econ. Behav. **29**, 79–103 (1999)
7. Han, B., Kumar, V.S.A., Marathe, M.V., Parthasarathy, S., Srinivasan, A.: Distributed strategies for channel allocation and scheduling in software-defined radio networks. In: Proceedings of the IEEE INFOCOM, pp. 1521–1529 (2009)
8. Jansen, K., Porkolab, L.: On preemptive resource constrained scheduling: polynomial-time approximation schemes. SIAM J. Discrete Math. **20**(3), 545–563 (2006)
9. Khandekar, R.: Lagrangian relaxation based algorithms for convex programming problems, Ph.D. thesis, Indian Institute of Technology, Delhi (2004)
10. Kodialam, M., Nandagopal, T.: Characterizing achievable ratesin multi-hop wireless networks: the joint routing and scheduling problem. In: Proceedings of the ACM MobiCom (2003)
11. Kodialam, M., Nandagopal, T.: Characterizing the capacity region in multi-radio multi-channel wireless mesh networks. In: Proceedings of the ACM MobiCom (2005)
12. Kumar, V.S.A., Marathe, M.V., Parthasarathy, S., Srinivasan, A.: Algorithmic aspects of capacity in wireless networks. SIGMETRICS Perform. Eval. Rev. **33**(1), 133–144 (2005)
13. Liu, J., Hou, Y.T., Shi, Y., Sherali, H.: Cross-layer optimization for MIMO-based wireless ad hoc networks: routing. IEEE J. Sel. Areas Commun. Power Allocation Bandwidth allocation **6**, 913–926 (2008)
14. Ma, C., Al-dhelaan, F., Wan, P.-J.: Maximum independent set of links with a monotone and sublinear power assignment. In: Ren, K., Liu, X., Liang, W., Xu, M., Jia, X., Xing, K. (eds.) WASA 2013. LNCS, vol. 7992, pp. 64–75. Springer, Heidelberg (2013)
15. Ma, C., Al-dhelaan, F., Wan, P.-J.: Maximum independent set of links with power control. In: Ren, K., Liu, X., Liang, W., Xu, M., Jia, X., Xing, K. (eds.) WASA 2013. LNCS, vol. 7992, pp. 474–485. Springer, Heidelberg (2013)
16. Schrijver, A.: Combinatorial Optimization. Algorithms and Combinatorics., vol. 24. Springer, Heidelberg (2003)
17. V. Vovk. A game of prediction with expert advice. In: Proceedings of the 8th Annual Conference on Computational Learning Theory, pp. 51–60 (1995)
18. Wan, P.-J.: Multiflows in Multihop Wireless Networks, In: ACM MOBIHOC, pp. 85–94 (2009)
19. Wan, P.-J., Chen, D., Dai, G., Wang, Z., Yao, F.: Maximizing capacity with power control under physical interference model in duplex mode. In: IEEE INFOCOM, pp. 415–423 (2012)
20. Wan, P.-J., Cheng, Y., Wang, Z., Yao, F.: Multiflows in multi-channel multi-radio multihop wireless networks. In: IEEE INFOCOM, pp. 846–854 (2011)
21. Wan, P.-J., Frieder, O., Jia, X., Yao, F., Xu, X.-H., Tang, S.-J.: Wireless link scheduling under physical interference model. In: IEEE INFOCOM, pp. 838–845 (2011)
22. Wan, P.-J., Jia, X., Dai, G., Du, H., Wan, Z.G., Frieder, O.: Scalable algorithms for wireless link schedulings in multi-channel multi-radio wireless networks. In: IEEE INFOCOM, pp. 2121–2129 (2013)
23. Wan, P.-J., Jia, X., Dai, G., Du, H., Frieder, O.: Fast and simple approximation algorithms for maximum weighted independent set of links. In: IEEE INFOCOM, pp. 1653–1661 (2014)

24. Wan, P.-J., Wang, L., Ma, C., Wang, Z., Xu, B., Li, M.: Maximizing wireless network capacity with linear power: breaking the logarithmic barrier. In: IEEE INFOCOM, pp. 135–139 (2013)
25. Wan, P.-J., Xu, B., Frieder, O., Ji, S., Wang, B., Xu, X.: Capacity maximization in wireless MIMO networks with receiver-side interference suppression. In: ACM MOBIHOC, pp. 145–154 (2014)

CO_2: Design Fault-Tolerant Relay Node Deployment Strategy for Throwbox-Based DTNs

Wenlin Han and Yang Xiao$^{(\boxtimes)}$

Department of Computer Science, The University of Alabama,
342 H.M. Comer, Box 870290, Tuscaloosa 35487-0290, USA
whan2@crimson.ua.edu, yangxiao@ieee.org

Abstract. Delay Tolerant Networks (DTNs) are not like the Internet, where contemporaneous connectivity among all nodes is always available. We need to design a new relay node deployment strategy, which can make DTNs more reliable and fault-tolerant. In this paper, we propose a fault-tolerant relay node deployment strategy for throwbox-based DTNs. It employs an approximation algorithm to choose throwbox placement locations, and to construct a 2-COnnected DTN, called CO_2, where each mobile node can communicate with at least two relay nodes within its activity scope. Simulation results based on Tuscaloosa bus transit system have shown its effectiveness and high efficiency when compared to two types of popular relay node deployment strategies in the literature.

Keywords: DTNs · Throwbox · Fault-tolerance · Relay strategy · Intermittent connection · Reliability

1 Introduction

Delay Tolerant Networks (DTNs) [1] are a class of emerging networks attracting various interests. The history of DTNs can date back to late 1990 [2] with the growth of interest in mobile ad-hoc networks and interplanetary Internet [3]. Other popular applications of DTNs include vehicular ad-hoc networks, rural village networks, underwater acoustic networks, disaster recovery networks, and social networks.

DTNs are not Internet-like networks. They are networks, where contemporaneous connectivity among all nodes does not always exist. Because of long and variable delay, relay nodes, such as throwboxes, are needed to increase contact opportunities and to reduce delay. Relay node deployment strategies can be classified into three categories: contact-oblivious deployment, contact-based deployment, and customized deployment [4]. In the contact-oblivious deployment, throwboxes are deployed without considering the contact opportunities between mobile nodes and throwboxes, such as regularly deploying throwboxes in an area to form a grid. In the contact-based deployment, throwboxes are placed to maximize contact opportunities between nodes, such as placing throwboxes in the areas mostly visited by mobile nodes. In the papers [5,6], learning from primates' scent marking, the authors use sensors nodes or RFID (Radio Frequency

© Springer International Publishing Switzerland 2016
Q. Yang et al. (Eds.): WASA 2016, LNCS 9798, pp. 37–46, 2016.
DOI: 10.1007/978-3-319-42836-9_4

Identification) tags left for messages or traces for other mobile robots for information. However, all the traditional deployment strategies have not addressed the problem of fault-tolerance. We need a novel strategy to deploy relay node that can achieve the fault-tolerance purpose, which means when some of the relay nodes fail, the network can still work properly without performance loss.

Fault-tolerant relay strategy has been studied in wireless sensor networks (WSNs) [7,8]. In the paper [9], the problem of deploying relay nodes to provide the desired fault-tolerance through multi-path connectivity (k-connectivity) is studied, and they propose an algorithm, which is based on an evolutionary scheme to place an optimum number of energy-constrained relay nodes. It can achieve the desired connectivity between homogeneous wireless sensor nodes with the same communication range of each sensor node.

In this paper, we propose a novel strategy, called CO_2, which can deploy relay nodes in DTNs to achieve the fault-tolerance purpose while maintaining a relatively small number of relay nodes. From a set of potential locations of relay throwboxes, CO_2 chooses some nodes to construct a 2-connected graph. These throwboxes cover all the mobile nodes in a DTN letting each mobile node connect with at least two relay nodes. Every node in the 2-connected DTN can reach another node via two node disjoint paths so that it can guarantee fault-tolerance. When some of the relay nodes are out of work, the DTN can still work properly and maintain high performance. Our experiments simulate real bus transit system in Tuscaloosa, Alabama, USA, and the experimental results show that the relay nodes chosen by the proposed CO_2 strategy can make DTNs fault-tolerant with relatively small number of relay throwboxes. The main contributions of this paper include:

- It is the first strategy addressing fault-tolerant relay node deployment problem in DTNs, to the best of our knowledge;
- We analyze the impact of different routing protocols and mobility models working with CO_2;
- We compare performance among three deployment strategies: the contact-oblivious deployment, the contact-based deployment, and CO_2.

The rest of the paper is organized as follows: Sect. 2 outlines and models the problem of fault-tolerant relay node deployment. Section 3 presents the strategy of CO_2 and the related relay node selection algorithm. In Sect. 4, we simulate the real world bus transit system in Tuscaloosa and conduct experiments based on it to show performance improvement. Finally, we conclude the paper and propose future work in Sect. 5.

2   Problem Statement

In this section, we will present the main problem that the proposed CO_2 strategy aiming to address.

The intermittent connection is the most prominent feature of DTNs, and it is also a very challenging problem whenever we need to design a new protocol, algorithm or scheme for DTNs. To increase contact opportunity, throwboxes are employed to enhance network performance. As shown in Fig. 1, it is a simple scenario of a Vehicular DTN. Each bus moves within its range of activity - the oval area, follows its certain route. Contact and message delivery can happen when two buses meet each other, but the contact opportunity is rare when the buses are very few. Some throwboxes are placed in the oval areas, so that a bus can transfer its messages to a certain throwbox, and waits for another bus to pick them up. In this way, buses can communicate with each other. For example, Bus Group G1 can communicate with Bus Group G7 via multiple hops between throwboxes and other buses. However, throwboxes are resource-constrained mobile devices with limited battery capacity. They are deployed outdoor, even in rural areas, baring harsh environment, which means that they stand big chances of failure. If some throwboxes are out of work, some buses may not be able to communicate with each other. For example, if Throwboxes x1, x4 and x5 fail, Bus G1 will lose communication with Bus Group G7.

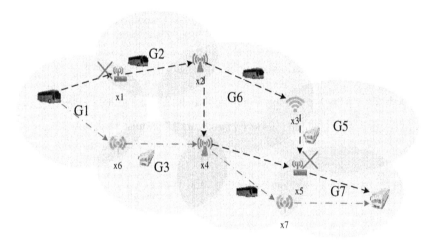

Fig. 1. Fault-tolerance problem scenario of a simple throwbox-based DTN.

We need to design a new relay node placement strategy, which can work well when some of the throwboxes fail, while the number of the throwboxes deployed is the minimum. Here, we define a set of throwboxes as 2-connected if they can still communicate with each other within one or multiple hops when one of them fails.

3 CO_2: Relay Node Placement Strategy

CO_2 is to construct a 2-connected DTN with a reasonable number of relay nodes. The basic idea is to maximize node availability and link availability, while maintaining two disjoint paths with minimum hops. In this section, we will introduce the proposed relay node placement strategy, CO_2, in details.

Let's define:

T is the total number of time segments, where $t = 0, 1, \cdots, T$;

B is the set of mobile nodes, such as buses;

U is the set of possible unchosen locations of relay throwboxes;

R is the set of already chosen locations of relay throwboxes, and it is $\emptyset$ initially;

$label[b]$ is the number of times that a mobile node b is covered by relay throwboxes, $b \in B$;

$C(u)$ is the set of mobile nodes, which can be covered by a relay throwbox u.

Now the problem is to select an appropriate R from U. To observe the links, we assume that we have placed a throwbox v in each possible location in U. Moreover, we name the set of these throwboxes as V. We observe the links between each pair of two throwboxes in V, and name the set of the links as E. Correspondingly, the link states set is named as S. Now we get a graph $G(V, E, S, P)$, where P is the same as defined previously.

To make it concise, we mix the concepts of a throwbox and the location of this throwbox. Thus, when we talk about "pick up a node from U", we mean "pick up a location where we can place a throwbox", and further examine the connections between this throwbox and other throwboxes or mobile nodes. The algorithm mainly includes four steps.

Step I. Pick a node u_0 from U satisfying the following four conditions:

1. At least at sometimes, the node u_0 can work normally, that is

$$p_{u_0} \neq 0. \tag{1}$$

2. The node u_0 has at least one available link, that is

$$\bigvee_{\forall v \in V} \bigvee_{t=0}^{T} s_{u_0 v t} = 1, \tag{2}$$

where $s_{u_0 v t}$ is the link state of Link $e_{u_0 v}$ during time period t and v is a node in V, $u_0 \neq v$.

3. The number of nodes in V that u can communicate with is calculated as $\sum_{\forall v \in V} \bigvee_{t=0}^{T} s_{uvt}$. Moreover, p_u is the probability of working normally. In this step, we pick up a node that can maximize node availability. Let us define W_{1u_0} as:

$$W_{1u_0} = \max_{\forall u \in U} \left\{ p_u \sum_{\forall v \in V} \bigvee_{t=0}^{T} s_{uvt} \right\}, \tag{3}$$

where $u \neq v$.

4. Let us denote the set of nodes satisfying Eq (3) as U_1. If there are more than one nodes in U_1, pick the one of the maximum link availability, that is:

$$W_{2u_0} = \max_{\forall u \in U_1} \left\{ p_u \sum_{\forall v \in V} \sum_{t=0}^{T} s_{uvt} \right\}, \tag{4}$$

where $u \neq v$.

Mark each node $b \in B \cap C(u_0)$ as 1, that is $label[b] = 1$. Put the relay node u_0 into the set R, and remove u_0 from U.

Step II. In the new set U, find a relay node u' that satisfies the following three conditions:

1. u' can reach u_0 through two node-disjoint paths. If there are more than two node-disjoint paths, select the two paths with the minimum number of hops. Define the set of nodes in the two paths as $Q_{u'}$, where $u' \in Q_{u'}$ and $u_0 \notin Q_{u'}$. A similar definition for a node u is Q_u.
2. In this step, we choose u', which makes $Q_{u'}$ mostly cover the nodes in B that already covered by u_0, and the number of relay throwboxes in $Q_{u'}$ is relatively small. Let us define $c(b, Q_u)$ as the number of times that b is covered by the relay throwboxes in the set of $Q_u \cap U$, that is

$$c(b, Q_u) = |\{q' \in Q_u \cap U : b \in C(q')\}|. \tag{5}$$

Also, we need to consider node failure probability. It satisfies:

$$W_{3u'} = \max_{\forall u \in U} \left\{ \frac{p_u \sum_{b \in B} \min(c(b, Q_u), 2 - label[b])}{|Q_u \cap U|} \right\}. \tag{6}$$

3. Let us define the set of nodes satisfying Eq. (6) as U_2. If there are more than one nodes in U_2, pick the one that can maximize the link availability when considering the links between the nodes in Q_u and all other nodes in V.

$$W_{4u'} = \max_{\forall u \in U_2} \left\{ \sum_{\forall u^* \in Q_u} \sum_{\forall v \in V} \sum_{t=0}^{T} p_{u^*} s_{u^* vt} \right\}, \tag{7}$$

where $u^* \neq v$ and $u \neq v$.

Mark each node $b \in B \cap C(Q_{u'} \cap U)$, e.g.,

$$label[b] = label[b] + \min(c(b, Q_{u'}), 2 - label[b]). \tag{8}$$

Put all relay nodes in $Q_{u'}$ into the set R, and remove all nodes in $Q_{u'}$ from U. For all b in B, if $label[b] = 2$, remove b from B.

Step III. Add an artificial node v' into G to construct a graph G', and connect each node in R with v'. Pick a node u'' from U, which meets the following three conditions:

1. u'' can reach v' via at least two node disjoint paths. Define two of these disjoint paths with minimum number of hops as $Q_{u''}$, where $u'' \in Q_{u''}$ and $v' \notin Q_{u''}$.

2. $Q_{u''}$ can mostly cover the nodes in B that already covered by R, and has relatively smaller amount of nodes. u'' satisfies:

$$W_{3u''} = \max_{\forall u \in U} \left\{ \frac{p_u \sum_{b \in B} \min(c(b, Q_u), 2 - label[b])}{|Q_u \cap U|} \right\}. \tag{9}$$

This equation is similar to Eq. (6), but the values of the variables have already changed.

3. Let us define the set of nodes satisfying Eq. (9) as U_3. If there are more than one nodes in U_3, pick the one achieving the maximum link availability of the links between the nodes in Q_u and all other nodes in V.

$$W_{4u''} = \max_{\forall u \in U_3} \left\{ \sum_{\forall u^* \in Q_u} \sum_{\forall v \in V} \sum_{t=0}^{T} p_{u^*} s_{u^* vt} \right\}, \tag{10}$$

where $u^* \neq v$ and $u \neq v$.

Mark each node $b \in B \cap C[Q_{u''} \cap U]$, e.g.,

$$label[b] = label[b] + \min(c[b, Q_{u''}], 2 - label[b]). \tag{11}$$

Put all relay nodes in $Q_{u''}$ into the set R, and remove all nodes in $Q_{u''}$ from U. For all b in B, if $label[b] = 2$, remove b from B.

Step IV. If $B = \emptyset$, we get the solution R; otherwise, repeat Step III.

4 Performance Evaluation

In this section, we will present some experiments to show the effectiveness of the CO_2 strategy.

4.1 Experimental Settings

We simulate bus transit system at Tuscaloosa, Alabama, USA. There are six routes represented by different colors: gold is for Greensboro Route; amaranth represents Stillman Route; University Shuttle Route is red; green represents Shelton State Route; blue is for Holt Route; and V.A./University Route is crimson [10].

Figure 2 illustrates the experimental settings. The simulation tool is Opportunistic Network Environment Simulator (ONE) [11].

4.2 Experimental Results

We evaluate CO_2 performance working with Epidemic [12], a multi-copy routing protocol. We choose delivery ratio, contact time and fault-tolerance as criteria, and compare CO_2 with the contact-oblivious deployment and the contact-based deployment strategies.

Group	Type	ID	Number	Speed/FR	Route/Location
1		b1_	4	10-40 km/h	StillmanRoute
2		b2_	4	10-40 km/h	University Shuttle Route
3		b3_	4	25-60 km/h	Shelton State Route
4		b4_	4	10-40 km/h	Greensboro Route
5		b5_	4	25-60 km/h	Holt Route
6		b6_	4	10-50 km/h	V.A./University Route North
7		b7_	4	25-60 km/h	V.A./University Route South
8		x1	1	80%	G1,G2
9		x2	1	0%	G2,G6
10		x3	1	40%	G6,G5
11		x4	1	0%	G3,G4
12		x5	1	80%	G5,G7
13		x6	1	20%	G1,G3
14		x7	1	20%	G4,G7

Fig. 2. Experimental settings based on real Tuscaloosa bus transit system. FR is the failure rate of a throwbox. (Color figure online)

Delivery Ratio. Figure 3 shows delivery ratio comparison among three strategies. The routing protocol in Fig. 3 is Epidemic routing. Regular deployment is contact-oblivious, and it performs the worst among three strategies. The contact-based deployment works better than the regular deployment. CO_2 achieves the best delivery ratio performance. It improves delivery ratio from less than 50 % to over 80 %.

Fault-Tolerance. Figure 4 shows the comparison of fault-tolerance performance among three strategies, and the routing protocol is the Epidemic routing protocol. When the other strategies cannot deliver any message, CO_2 can still work properly, and the delivery ratio can reach over 40 %.

Contact Time. Figure 5 shows accumulated contact time comparison among three strategies. The routing protocol is the Epidemic routing protocol in Fig. 5. Since the regular deployment strategy is contact-oblivious, the contact opportunities among nodes are not considered during the relay nodes placement process. Its contact time performance is the worst. Compared to the contact-based deployment, CO_2 nearly doubles the contact time.

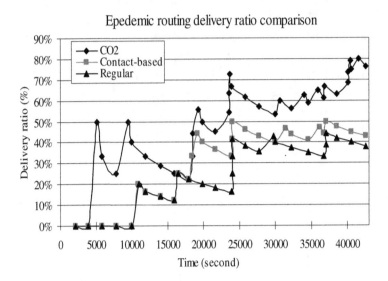

Fig. 3. Delivery ratio comparison among three deployment strategies: Regular deployment, Contact-based deployment and CO_2 deployment. (Color figure online)

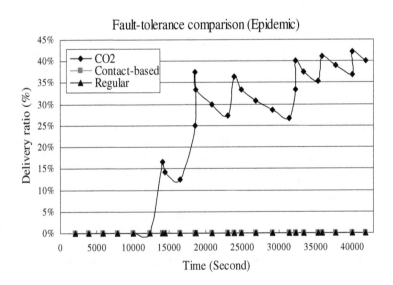

Fig. 4. Fault-tolerance comparison among three deployment strategies: Regular deployment, Contact-based deployment, and CO_2 deployment. (Color figure online)

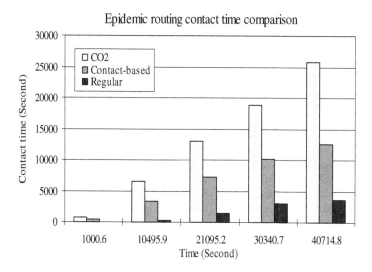

Fig. 5. Contact time comparison among three deployment strategies: Regular deployment, Contact-based deployment, and CO_2 deployment. (Color figure online)

5   Conclusion

In this paper, we proposed a relay node deployment strategy for DTNs, named CO_2. This 2-connected DTN can handle message delivery even when some of the relay nodes fail, and the number of throwboxes deployed is relatively small. We have carried out simulations based on Tuscaloosa bus transit system, and the simulation results have demonstrated that CO_2 achieves much better performance than the contact-oblivious and the contact-based relay node deployment strategies. As a future work, we will further analyse the applicability of CO_2, and its performance working with other routing protocols.

Acknowledgments. This work was supported in part by the National Science Foundation (NSF) under grants CCF-0829827 and CCF-0829828.

References

1. Soares, V., Farahmand, F., Rodrigues, J.: Improving vehicular delay-tolerant network performance with relay nodes. In: Proceedings of Next Generation Internet Networks (NGI 2009), pp. 1–5, July 2009
2. Ivancic, W.D.: Security analysis of DTN architecture and bundle protocol specification for space-based networks. In: Proceedings of 2010 IEEE Aerospace Conference, pp. 1–12, March 2010
3. Boucher, M.: Generation InterPlanetary Internet. http://www.spaceref.com/news/viewnews.html?id=87. Accessed Jan 2013

4. Zhao, W., Chen, Y., Ammar, M., Corner, M., Levine, B., Zegura, E.: Capacity enhancement using throwboxes in DTNs. In: Proceedings of IEEE International Conference on Mobile Adhoc and Sensor Systems (MASS), pp. 31–40, October 2006
5. Xiao, Y., Zhang, Y., Liang, X.: Primate-inspired communication methods for mobile and static sensors and RFID tags. ACM Trans. Auton. Adapt. Syst. **6**(4), 1–37 (2011). Article no. 26
6. Zhang, Y., Xiao, Y.: Primate-inspired scent marking for mobile and static sensors and RFID tags. In: Proceedings of 18th International Conference on Computer Communications and Networks (ICCCN 2009), pp. 1–5, August 2009
7. Wu, Z., Xiong, N., Han, W., Huang, Y.N., Hu, C.Y., Gu, Q., Hang, B.: A fault-tolerant method for enhancing reliability of services composition application in WSNs based on BPEL. Int. J. Distrib. Sens. Netw. **2013**(2013), Article ID 493678, 11 pages (2013). special issue on Fault-Tolerant and Ubiquitous Computing in Sensor Networks
8. Li, J., Pan, Y., Xiao, Y.: Performance study of multiple route dynamic source routing protocols for mobile ad hoc networks. J. Parallel Distrib. Comput. **65**(2), 169–177 (2005). Special issue on Theoretical and Algorithmic Aspects of Sensor, Ad Hoc Wireless, and Peer-to-Peer Networks
9. Dandekar, D.R., Deshmukh, P.R.: Fault-tolerant relay placement in wireless sensor networks using particle swarm optimization. Intell. Soft Comput. **130**, 749–757 (2012)
10. Tuscaloosa Bus Transit Routes Map (2011). http://www.tuscaloosatransit.com/nssfolder/scrapbook/Overlaying%20Route%20Map.pdf
11. Kernen, A., Ott, J.: Increasing Reality for DTN Protocol Simulations. Helsinki University of Technology, Networking Laboratory, Technical Report (2007)
12. Vahdate, A., Becker, D.: Epidemic Routing for Partially-connected Ad-hoc Networks, Duke University, Technical Report CS-2000-06, June 2000

CNFD: A Novel Scheme to Detect Colluded Non-technical Loss Fraud in Smart Grid

Wenlin Han and Yang Xiao$^{(\boxtimes)}$

Department of Computer Science, The University of Alabama, 342 H.M. Comer, Box 870290, Tuscaloosa, AL 35487-0290, USA
whan2@crimson.ua.edu, yangxiao@ieee.org

Abstract. We newly discovered a potential fraud in Smart Grid, called colluded non-technical loss fraud. Different from the traditional non-technical loss frauds where there is only one independent adversary, a colluded non-technical loss fraud happens when a smart meter is tampered by one or more co-existing or collaborating adversaries. The behavior of one adversary may be covered by others and cannot be detected easily by the traditional detection methods. We propose Colluded Non-Technical Loss Fraud Detection (CNFD), a scheme to detect colluded non-technical loss frauds in Smart Gird. CNFD adopts recursive least squares to identify a tampered meter and then to differentiate adversaries based on their mathematical features. Experimental results show that CNFD can detect colluded non-technical loss frauds and can differentiate different adversaries on the same meter.

Keywords: Smart Grid security · Smart meter · Non-technical Loss · Colluded fraud

1 Introduction

Non-Technical Loss (NTL) fraud in Smart Grid [1] is a fraud that a customer illegally gains unpaid electricity via a tampered meter. Utility companies lose billions of dollars due to the NTL fraud annually. According to a recent study [2] from northeast group, LLC, the top 50 emerging market countries lose \$58.7 billion per year due to the NTL fraud. Moreover, these countries will invest \$168 billion over the next decade cumulatively to improve the reliability of Smart Grid infrastructure and to combat the NTL fraud.

A Colluded NTL (CNTL) fraud is a potential fraud that we newly discovered in our recent research. Different from traditional NTL fraud where a meter is tampered by only one adversary, a colluded NTL fraud is where a meter is tampered by one or more co-existing or collaborating adversaries so that a customer can use extra electricity without paying for it. In other words, multiple adversaries collude an NTL fraud on one meter to gain illegal benefit. Adversaries may not cooperate on an NTL fraud on purpose. An NTL fraud can be committed by a single adversary without any support of others. However, the behavior of

© Springer International Publishing Switzerland 2016
Q. Yang et al. (Eds.): WASA 2016, LNCS 9798, pp. 47–55, 2016.
DOI: 10.1007/978-3-319-42836-9_5

one adversary could be covered by other adversaries, and not be detected easily by the traditional methods implemented in detectors.

Many existing schemes have been proposed to deal with NTL fraud [3–6]. They can identify a tampered meter or trace the corresponding adversary. However, none of them can accurately differentiate behaviors' of different adversaries and thus trace all these adversaries on a single tampered meter. In our previous research, we have proposed NFD [7] and FNFD [8] to detect the NTL fraud in Smart Grid. Both of them can identify the meter that tampered by multiple adversaries. However, none of them can differentiate these adversaries.

In this paper, we propose Colluded Non-Technical Loss Fraud Detection (CNFD), a scheme to deal with the colluded NTL fraud in Smart Grid. CNFD employs Recursive Least Squares (RLS) [9] to identify a tampered meter quickly using a small amount of meter reading data. Then, CNFD models the behaviors' of adversaries on this meter mathematically. According to different parameters of these models, CNFD can differentiate and locate different adversaries. The adversaries themselves may not realize that their behaviors have such features. Thus, CNFD can even predict adversary's behavior. To show the effectiveness of CNFD, we conduct several experiments. The experimental results show that CNFD can detect the CNTL fraud in Smart Grid and clearly describe different behaviors of different adversaries on the same meter.

The main contributions of this paper include:

- We find a potential fraud, the CNTL fraud in Smart Gird;
- We design a novel scheme, CNFD to detect the CNTL fraud in Smart Gird;
- We conduct experiments to show the effectiveness of CNFD.

The rest of the paper is organized as follows: In Sect. 2, we introduce the problem and the attack model of the CNTL fraud. The working process and the related algorithm of CNFD are presented in Sect. 3. We conduct experiments to show how CNFD detects the CNTL fraud in Sect. 4. Related works are introduced in Sect. 5. Finally, we conclude the paper in Sect. 6.

2   Colluded NTL Fraud

In this section, we will introduce the problem and the attack model of the CNTL fraud.

2.1   Problem Definition and Attack Model

We have N households in a community. All households are served by the same power company, and each of them has a smart meter installed. These smart meters are responsible for recording power consumption of the households, and these meter readings are sent to the power company for the purpose of billing. However, the summation of these meter readings is much smaller than the amount that the company supplied to the community. After eliminating technical loss, the non-technical loss is highly suspected.

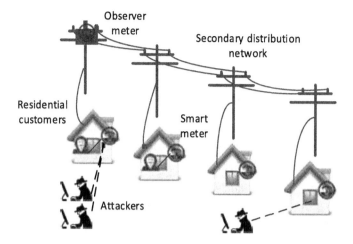

Fig. 1. The conceptual framework of how CNTL works. Some of the meters are normal, and some of the meters are tampered either by the customers themselves or attacked by outside attackers. Some of the tampered meters only has one adversary, while some meters are manipulated by multiple adversaries. The total billing amount of electricity is much less than the total amount supplied to this community.

Among these meters, one or more than one of them are tampered to gain free electricity. As shown in Fig. 1, the meters are either tampered by the customers themselves inside these households, or they are remotely controlled by attackers from outside, or these meters are tampered by both the customers and the attackers. At this time, both the customers and the attackers are adversaries. Some of these meters might be normal. Some of these meters might be tampered by only one adversary. Some of these meters might be tampered by multiple adversaries at the same time. To solve the problem, we have to find out which meters have been tampered. Moreover, we have to learn the adversaries' behaviors and differentiate them.

The CNTL fraud is where a meter is tampered by more than one adversaries so that the meter records less electricity than the household consumed, and the customer gains illegal benefit by paying less money.

3   CNTL Fraud Detection

In this section, we will introduce the theory and the working process of CNFD and its related algorithm.

3.1   Observer Meter

As shown in Fig. 1, a central observer meter is installed in the same secondary distribution network where $n(n \leq N)$ households are connected. This observer is to monitor the n meters and to record the total amount of power supplied to these households.

Each smart meter is responsible for recording power consumed by each household, but some of the readings are less than the consumed amounts. We read these meters at a fixed time interval, e.g. 15 min. The only two things we know are the values reported by each smart meter and the total amount supplied to them in each time period. How do we get to know which meters have been collusively tampered?

3.2   Tampered Meter Detection

We adopt the detection method we previously proposed in the paper [8]. S_i is the coefficient set of all different adversaries on Meter i, and e is the user defined error. Other notations are the same as defined in [8]. Here, we omit the introduction of this part due to the limited space.

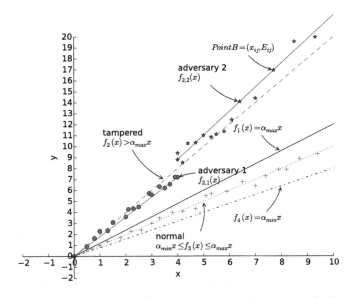

Fig. 2. Understanding the CNTL fraud and the working process of CNFD mathematically. Each point on the coordinate corresponds to a value pair of a meter, that is *(the recorded amount of electricity, the actually consumed amount of electricity)*. Each meter has a line to represent it. All lines above the line of $f_1(x) = \alpha_{max}x$ are tampered meters. All lines between the lines of $f_1(x) = \alpha_{max}x$ and $f_4(x) = \alpha_{min}x$ are normal meters. Among those tampered meters, some of the lines can be better shaped into several different lines. (Color figure online)

As shown in Fig. 2, a tampered meter has a line above the line of $f_1(x) = \alpha_{max}x$, and a normal meter has a line between the lines of $f_1(x) = \alpha_{max}x$ and $f_4(x) = \alpha_{min}x$. A line below the line of $f_4(x)$ is a sign of working error. We can figure out which meters are tampered and obtain the coefficient vector A.

3.3 Adversary Differentiation

We have obtained the coefficient vector A and have identified the tampered meter, Meter t. Now, the problem is how we can differentiate different adversaries on this meter. For example, as shown in Fig. 2, the red dot points and the red star points are value pairs of the same meter. We find that it is a tampered meter which is represented by the line of $f_2(x)$. However, the red dot points relate to adversary 1 which is represented by $f_{2,1}(x)$, and the red star points relate to adversary 2 which is represented by $f_{2,2}(x)$, after further analyzing.

Algorithm 1. CNFD: CNTL fraud detection

1: Initiation: set initial values of e, n, m, α_{min}, α_{max}, A_{j-1}, λ and k. Set $P_{j-1} = kI$. j starts from 1. Set $S_t = \{\}$, $t = -1$.
2: **repeat**
3:     record the value of observer meter E_j in each time period j,
       record the value array of all other meters X_j in each time period j,
       $W_j \leftarrow P_{j-1}X_j^T(\lambda + X_jP_{j-1}X_j^T)^{-1}$,
       $A_j \leftarrow A_{j-1} + W_j(E_j - X_jA_{j-1})$,
       $P_j \leftarrow (I - W_jX_j)P_{j-1}/\lambda$
4: **until** $\mathbf{A_j}$ doesn't change
5: **for** each a_i in $\mathbf{A_j}$ **do**
6:     **if** $a_i > \alpha_{max}$ **then**
7:         identified as tampered
8:         $t \leftarrow i$
9:     **if** $\alpha_{min} \leq a_i \leq \alpha_{max}$ **then**
10:         identified as normal
11:     **else**
12:         report error and exit
13: **if** $t = -1$ **then**
14:     report normal and exit
15: **for** each $j \leq m$ **do**
16:     $a_{tj} = \dfrac{E_j - \sum_{i=1}^{n} a_i x_{ij}}{x_{tj}}(i \neq t)$
17:     **for** each a_k in S_t **do**
18:         **if** $a_{tj} \geq a_k + e$ **or** $a_{tj} \leq a_k - e$ **then**
19:             $S_t = S_t \cup \{a_{tj}\}$
20: Output: S_t.

As shown in Algorithm 1, e is the user defined error to differentiate adversaries' behaviors. S_t is the output set with different coefficients of all adversaries on Meter t, and it is an empty set initially. The basic idea is to isolate the tampered meter and calculate its coefficients in each time period. After getting these coefficients, we analyze their similarity within the error of e and tie them to different adversary behaviors. In other words, we use consumed-electricity/billing-electricity to differentiate slopes of different adversaries.

4   Experiments

We conducted various experiments to test the performance of CNFD, and the experimental results show that CNFD can detect TNTL frauds. However we only introduce one experiment to show the effectiveness of CNFD, due to the limited space.

Table 1. Registered electricity consumption (kWh) in the experiment: 10 m and 1 observer meter

Meter 1	2	3	4	5	6	7	8	9	10	Observer
2920	3590	6470	2300	3490	9550	5530	4110	5830	6310	54397.5
3560	3710	6980	3930	2650	9070	6280	2920	5440	6320	54941.5
3100	4540	7140	3160	3230	9600	6380	2210	6020	6540	56240
2660	4350	6860	3230	3540	10410	6800	6200	8210	7430	64374.5
3380	4430	6100	3060	5220	9330	7380	3800	6510	5510	56492.7
2240	5260	7360	4110	6740	10370	7270	4740	5820	6770	70842.6
3670	3500	7920	4300	2570	9590	6260	4040	6330	6850	64428.2
3000	4530	6250	2940	3760	9740	6500	4530	3280	7590	53970.6
4590	4600	5600	3560	4270	9230	5980	4130	6650	7140	57503.7
2920	4210	5150	3430	3190	10260	5460	4680	6910	5710	53869.4
3640	3260	6150	3270	6430	9200	5860	4740	6540	5630	63736
3050	3680	5430	3440	6470	8020	7190	3560	6610	4610	59919.6
2220	3140	5930	4180	4940	8550	6760	2890	3710	3700	54399
2720	4710	5990	2380	6340	10090	7620	3900	5160	4680	63478.2
3480	3870	7280	4670	5270	9500	8380	3980	5220	6920	67880
4228	3948	6678	5348	4780	10188	8088	3668	4818	7480	68976.4
3840	3750	6090	4710	4870	9570	6840	3110	6270	7350	65778.6
3740	5100	6410	4850	5570	9770	7430	4310	5670	6920	69344.6
3060	5520	7180	3630	3900	10590	6920	4240	5580	6480	67478.2
3630	3790	6820	3520	4580	9850	6670	5740	6130	7280	67663

In this experiment, we employ 10 m and an observer. Table 1 shows their recorded data in 20 measurements.

We get the tampered meter detection result as shown in Fig. 3. The coefficient of Meter 6 converges to 1.972 finally, while other 9 m converge to 1, showing that Meter 6 is tampered. After CNFD's analyzing the data of Meter 6, there are three adversaries who colluded this fraud. Mathematically, their behaviors are represented by $y = 1.45x$, $y = 1.19x$, and $y = 1.98x$, respectively, shown in Fig. 4.

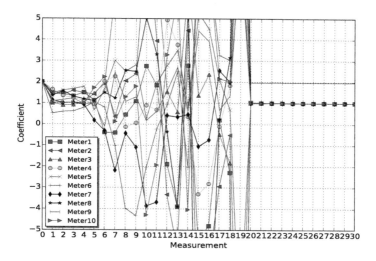

Fig. 3. Tampered meter detection process: the converging process of the coefficients of 10 m. Among these 10 m, the coefficient of Meter 6 converges to 1.972 while others converge to 1, and this means Meter 6 is tampered.

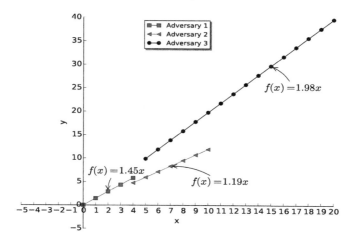

Fig. 4. The final detection result of CNFD. CNFD detection shows that there are three different adversaries who collude the fraud on Meter 6.

5   Related Work

Many physical methods have been proposed to detect NTL frauds [10]. In the papers [11,12], power line impedance techniques are employed to determine the location of a tampered meter based on the impedance values and phase angle of the transmission lines measured at two different operating frequencies. Traffic anomaly detection [13] is a typical method to identity abnormal behaviors, however existing systems [14,15] built on these methods are not designed specially detect the NTL fraud.

User behavior analysis is a typical method to identify the NTL fraud. Some common techniques include data mining, machine learning, pattern recognition, etc. The authors in [16] train support vector machines with data representing all possible forms of thefts in Smart Grid, and develop a dataset of the pattern of customer energy consumption based on customers' historical data. The main problem of user behavior analysis is that it requires a large amount of user data, and it can only identify known fraud behaviors.

Different from the existing methods, we have proposed NFD [7] and FNFD [8] which employ a mathematical approach to detect NTL fraud. NFD and FNFD only need user's meter reading data and a small amount of historic data. Both NFD and FNFD can predict adversary's behavior by generating a functional relationship between the recorded amount of electricity and the actually consumed amount of electricity. However, NFD is more precise than FNFD and FNFD is much faster than NFD. Both of them can identify the meter that tampered by multiple adversaries. However, none of them can differentiate these adversaries.

6   Conclusion

In this paper, we introduce our recently discovered fraud in Smart Grid, the Colluded NTL (CNTL) fraud. The CNTL fraud happens when a meter is tampered by more than one adversaries, and traditional detectors cannot differentiate these adversaries easily. Based on the analysis of the CNTL fraud, we design CNFD to deal with the CNTL fraud. The experimental results show that CNFD is effective in dealing with the CNTL fraud. As a future work, we will study the applicability and performance of CNFD in real-world applications.

Acknowledgements. This work was supported in part by the National Natural Science Foundation of China under the grant 61374200, and the National Science Foundation (NSF) under grant CNS-1059265.

References

1. Han, W., Xiao, Y.: IP^{2}DM for V2G networks in smart grid. In: Proceedings of the 50th International Conference on Communications (ICC 2015), pp. 782–787, June 2015
2. Northeast, Group, and LLC: Emerging markets smart grid: outlook 2015, December 2014. http://www.northeast-group.com/reports/Brochure-Emerging%20Markets%20Smart%20Grid-Outlook%202015-Northeast%20Group.pdf
3. Xiao, Z., Xiao, Y., Du, D.: Non-repudiation in neighborhood area networks for smart grid. IEEE Commun. Mag. **51**(1), 18–26 (2013)
4. Xiao, Z., Xiao, Y., Du, D.: Exploring malicious meter inspection in neighborhood area smart grids. IEEE Trans. Smart Grid **4**(1), 214–226 (2013)

5. Xia, X., Liang, W., Xiao, Y., Zheng, M., Xiao, Z.: Difference-comparison-based approach for malicious meter inspection in neighborhood area smart grids. In: Proceedings of the 50th International Conference on Communications (ICC 2015), pp. 802–807, June 2015

6. Xia, X., Liang, W., Xiao, Y., Zheng, M.: BCGI: a fast approach to detect malicious meters in neighborhood area smart grid. In: Proceedings of the 50th International Conference on Communications (ICC 2015), pp. 7228–7233, June 2015

7. Han, W., Xiao, Y.: NFD: a practical scheme to detect non-technical loss fraud in smart grid. In: Proceedings of the 50th International Conference on Communications (ICC 2014), pp. 605–609, June 2014

8. Han, W., Xiao, Y.: FNFD: a fast scheme to detect and verify non-technical loss fraud in smart grid. International Workshop on Traffic Measurements for Cybersecurity (WTMC 2016) (2016). doi:10.1145/2903185.2903188

9. Hayes, M.H.: Recursive least squares. In: Hayes, M.H. (ed.) Statistical Digital Signal Processing and Modeling, p. 154. Wiley, New York (1996). Chapter 9.4

10. Liu, J., Xiao, Y., Li, S., Liang, W., Chen, C.L.P.: Cyber security, privacy issues in smart grids. IEEE Commun. Surv. Tutorials **14**(4), 981–997 (2012)

11. Wijayakulasooriya, J.V., Dasanayake, D., Muthukumarana, P.I., Kumara, H., Thelisinghe, L.: Remotely accessible single phase energy measuring system. In: Proceedings of the 1st International Conference on Industrial and Information Systems, pp. 304–309, August 2006

12. Pasdar, A., Mirzakuchaki, S.: A solution to remote detecting of illegal electricity usage based on smart metering. In: Proceedings of the 2nd International Workshop on Soft Computing Applications, pp. 163–167, August 2007

13. Han, W., Xiong, W., Xiao, Y., Ellabidy, M., Vasilakos, A.V., Xiong, N.: A class of non-statistical traffic anomaly detection in complex network systems. In: Proceedings of the 32nd International Conference on Distributed Computing Systems Workshops (ICDCSW 2012), pp. 640–646, June 2012

14. Gaushell, D.J., Darlington, H.T.: Supervisory control and data acquisition. Proc. IEEE **75**(3), 1645–1658 (2005)

15. Berthier, R., Sanders, W.H.: Monitoring advanced metering infrastructures with amilyzer. Cyber-security of SCADA & Industrial Control Systems (2013)

16. Depuru, S.S.S.R., Wang, L., Devabhaktuni, V.: Support vector machine based data classification for detection of electricity theft. In: Proceedings of IEEE/PES Power Systems Conference and Exposition (PSCE), pp. 1–8, March 2011

SUO: Social Reciprocity Based Cooperative Mobile Data Traffic Communication

Kaichuan Zhao[1], Chao Wu[1(✉)], Yuezhi Zhou[1], Bowen Yang[1],
and Yaoxue Zhang[2]

[1] Tsinghua University, Beijing, China
{zhaokc13,cwu12,ybw12}@mails.tsinghua.edu.cn, zhouyz@mail.tsinghua.edu.cn
[2] Central South University, Changsha, China
zyx@csu.edu.cn

Abstract. The widespread of mobile applications tightens wireless users' social relationships and encourages them to generate more data traffic under network effects. This boosts the demand for wireless services yet may challenge users' limited wireless capacities and budgets. In this paper, we employ collaborative communication services to address this challenge, by considering the network effect in a social-aware environment. Specifically, we develop an optimization model, namely *SUO*, for the problem formulation. Furthermore, we then propose a distributed update algorithm for users to reach the optimal decisions. We evaluate the performance of our proposed algorithm by numerical studies using real data, and thereby draw useful engineering insights for the operation of wireless providers.

Keywords: Mobile social networking · Wireless data communication · Social reciprocity

1 Introduction

Data traffic through mobile network is predicted to grow further by over 100 times in the next decade [4], which, however, brings an emergent challenge for the existing cellular network infrastructure. To address the challenge of the conflict between the increasing traffic demands and limited resources of cellular networks, it is promising and effective to promote cooperation using direct communications between hand-held devices [15], especially among users who are familiar with each other.

To embrace direct communications between hand-held devices and benefit users with a lower cost, a very recent study in [3] proposes a novel social trust and social reciprocity based framework to promote efficient cooperation among devices for cooperative communications. By projecting communications in a mobile social network onto both physical and social domains, it introduces the physical-social graphs to model the interplay therein while capturing the physical constraints for feasible cooperation and the social relationships among

© Springer International Publishing Switzerland 2016
Q. Yang et al. (Eds.): WASA 2016, LNCS 9798, pp. 56–67, 2016.
DOI: 10.1007/978-3-319-42836-9_6

devices for effective cooperation. However, it poses the users group to compete for the limited resource from one provider. Indeed, each user may have a data flow budget which is not influenced by others (social neighbours). Users with sufficient resources can assist their neighbours to improve their satisfaction of Internet access.

Based on this fact, in this paper, we propose a novel social-aware utility optimization (SUO) model for the cooperative mobile network connections, which takes both self-benefit maximization and users' social relationships into consideration. In addition, we design an incentive mechanism based on social relationship strength (see Sect. 4) to promote users' participations in this cooperative service. In detail, we design this model with the following components: (1) We utilize the social ties as the input to our algorithm, which, however, has rarely been touched in the homogeneous studies, e.g., [2,13]. Specifically, the proposed model characterises the utility of data transmission with social impacts. (2) We introduce an incentive mechanism, which enhances the willingness of users to join the service and contribute their resources, to ensure the success of this service. (3) To relieve the cost of task schedule, we implement the model design in a distributed manner.

We summarise the contributions of this paper as follows:

- We introduce a novel social-aware utility optimization (SUO) model for the cooperative mobile network connections, considering both the self-benefit maximization and user's social parameters.
- We design an incentive mechanism based on the strength of social friendship for inducing users' participation, which improves the interaction among mobile users in cooperative communications.
- We evaluate the performance of the social-aware cooperative connection service. The evaluation results show that our solution can improve the performance of users with social connections than without consideration of social friendships.

The rest of the paper is organized as follows. In Sect. 2, we give a brief review of the related work in the literature. In Sect. 3, we introduce the social-aware system model considered in this paper. In Sect. 4 we present the incentive mechanism for the service and provide a Nash solution for this distributed optimization objects. We present extensive experimental results in Sect. 5. Finally, we conclude this paper in Sect. 6.

2   Related Work

In this section, we review related works from three directions which relate to our work, i.e., cooperative communications, incentive mechanisms and game theory. Moreover, we highlight the key differences between SUO and the existing works.

Mobile Cooperative Communications: Cooperative communications have been extensively studied in the past decade. In [12], the author summarises the mainstream cooperative communication approaches. To boost the participant of mobile content sharing, [7] proposes a video content propagation architecture by using D2D communication and caching strategy. Along another side, in this paper, we are aiming to encourage users with a network incentive effect, which, however, is not addressed in the studies above.

Incentive Mechanisms: Recent studies, e.g., [19], surveys the existing incentive mechanisms in cooperative Communications. Specifically, [10] proposes a resource exchange-based scheme to quantity the amount of data that contributed by each user. On this basis, [9] uses a feedback-based scheme for the D2D systems by means of earning reputation analogous from their contributions to others. Different from these works, in this paper, we are going to take both social relationship and self-benefit limit into consideration, and focus on optimizing the utility of each user subject to Pareto fairness.

Game Solution: Game theory has been widely applied to study cooperative communications in the past decades. For instance, in [16], the author employs a cooperative game to analyze the scenario that users with mobile communications seek to agree on a fair and efficient allocation of spectrum. For P2P systems, [1] studies the interaction of strategic and incentive scheme to improve the system's performance. In contrast with these works, the cooperative game in this paper is integrated with the impact of social connections, and we employ the Nash bargaining solution (NBS) to address the problem of resources sharing and users' fairness in the social-aware cooperative network.

3   System Model

As mentioned above, with the daily increasing of data consumption, bandwidth of the network, especially the mobile network, can not satisfy users with a good quality of experience (QoE). Many solutions have been proposed to address the problem of how to improve the QoE. To embrace a good experience and relieve the hardware cost, one promising solution is the cooperative communication among users.

Figure 1 illustrates a scenario that real-life mobile users can either download their demanding data by cellular connections, or do favor to neighbours[1] by transmitting data blocks through WiFi or Bluetooth approaches. As a result, users who take part in this process can get payments after helping others. The payment feedback is related to the strength of friendships between users, where higher friendships mean lower payments for assistance (see Sect. 4).

3.1   Social-Aware Utility

We consider the cooperative communications in mobile social networks, (i.e., social-aware cooperative networks), where mobile users are willing to cooperate

---

[1] Note that, in this paper, we mainly consider geographical social friends nearby.

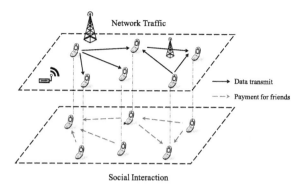

Fig. 1. Social-aware cooperative communications

in providing ubiquitous Internet access to each other. The cooperative network can be defined as a graph $\mathcal{G} = (\mathcal{N}, \mathcal{E})$, where $\mathcal{N}$ is the set of mobile users, and $\mathcal{E}$ is the set of physical directed links connecting them through WiFi or Bluetooth technology. Mobile users $(i \in \mathcal{N})$ can get access to the Internet through base stations. A time-slotted system is considered in this paper, and during each time slot the channels are fixed. We assume that each user can act as a helper node, a client node respectively or simultaneously during each time slot. And users can use their cellular and wireless connections simultaneously.

Let W denote the set of social friendships among direct-connected users. Thus we have $w_{i,j}$ which indicates the social friendship from user i to user j. Since, in real-life, we have the *ground-truth*: each user i's social friendship to herself is $w_{i,i} = 1$, and the strength of social friendship from user i to user $j \neq i$ is normalized as $w_{i,j} \in (0,1]$, with a higher value of $w_{i,j}$ being a stronger social friendship. $w_{i,j} = 0$ denotes no social friendship existing from user i to user j. Specially, $w_{i,j}$ may be not equal to $w_{j,i}$, which is practical in a social network. A user can learn her social friendship with others through the details of social information [6].

A user i may download some data $y_i^t \geq 0$ (in bytes) from the Internet for her own consuming at time slot t. Also, she may download data $x_{i,j}^t \geq 0$ (in bytes) from the Internet as a helper and deliver it to neighbour j, or receive data $x_{j,i}^t \geq 0$ from neighbour j as a client. We represent the maximum data capacity of the link from a base station to user i at time slot t as $C_i^t \geq 0$. And $C_{i,j}^t \geq 0$ denotes the maximum data capacity of the link between user i and user j. Each user will satisfy her own interest demand by consuming data. We denote the function $F_i(\cdot)$ with the utility of user i from satisfying her own need by obtaining data, which is a differentiable, strictly concave, positive, and non-decreasing function of the total bytes she receives during this time slot. In this paper, each user also cares about the utility of her neighbours related to their friendships. Hence, the social-aware utility of each user is defined as follows.

Definition 1. *Considering of a social network* $\mathcal{G} = (\mathcal{N}, \mathcal{E})$, *$W$ is the set of social friendships among direct users. The social-aware utility of a user $i \in \mathcal{N}$ is defined as,*

$$S_i\big(y_i^t, \overrightarrow{x_i^t}, \overrightarrow{x_{-i}^t}\big) = F_i\Big(y_i^t + \sum_{j \in in(i)} x_{j,i}^t\Big) + \sum_{j \in out(i)} w_{i,j} F_j\big(x_{i,j}^t\big) \tag{1}$$

where $\overrightarrow{x_i^t} = \big(x_{i,j}^t : j \in out(i)\big)$ is the vector of her helping decisions, and $\overrightarrow{x_{-i}^t} = \big(x_{j,i}^t : j \in in(i)\big)$ is the helping decisions of her upstream friends.

3.2 Consumptions in SUO Services

Downloading data through the cellular connections can cost some money for mobile users. Let p_i denote the price that a user i pays for downloading one byte using cellular connections, depending on her data plan. The users consume energy while downloading or relaying data. e_i^c and e_i^w are denoted as the energy consumption of user i to receive one byte through cellular and WiFi connections respectively. Hence, the total energy consumption $e_i, \forall i \in \mathcal{N}$ equals,

$$e_i = e_i^c\Big(y_i^t + \sum_{j \in out(i)} x_{i,j}^t\Big) + e_i^w\Big(\sum_{j \in out(i)} x_{i,j}^t + \sum_{j \in in(i)} x_{j,i}^t\Big) \tag{2}$$

Each mobile user $i \in \mathcal{N}$ that takes part in this service concerns about the battery usage of her device. Hence, we use the energy cost function $C_i(e_i)$ to capture this effect, which is strictly convex, and increasing in the total amount of consumed energy e_i (in joules). A function that satisfies these requirements is, such as, $C_i(e_i) = \theta_i^t/(E_i^t - e_i)$, where $E_i^t \geq 0$ is the maximum energy budget of a mobile user i and $\theta_i^t \in (0,1)$ is a normalization parameter indicating user i's sensitivity in energy consumption.

With the parameters introduced above, a user i's benefit is defined as V_i when she participates in this social-aware cooperative network. More specifically,

$$V_i\big(y_i^t, \overrightarrow{x_i^t}, \overrightarrow{x_{-i}^t}\big) = S_i\big(y_i^t, \overrightarrow{x_i^t}, \overrightarrow{x_{-i}^t}\big) - C_i\big(e_i\big) - p_i\Big(y_i^t + \sum_{j \in out(i)} x_{i,j}^t\Big) \tag{3}$$

As the amount of data that user i downloads and transmits to others increases, the benefit V_i may decrease, due to the increase of the credit and energy cost. Mobile users are sensitive of energy battery and data plan usage. As a result, they will have no motivation to participate in this cooperative service, if there is no incentive mechanism. When each mobile user i does not help to download any data and deliver to her downstream users, which is called the independent state, the benefit of user i equals,

$$V_i^S = \max_{y_i \geq 0} F_i\big(y_i^t\big) - C_i\big(e_i^c y_i^t\big) - p_i\big(y_i^t\big) \tag{4}$$

As a consequence, this cooperative service needs to employ an incentive mechanism to encourage users' participations, so as to maximize the service capacity. Meanwhile this mechanism needs to ensure the fairness and efficiency of this cooperative communication service, which is discussed in the next section.

4 Optimal Solution

In this subsection, we design an incentive mechanism with social ties in this system, where the users with higher ties will give lower payments to their friends for assistance. Then we formulate the operation of the service as a Nash bargaining problem based on the incentive mechanism.

Let $h_{j,i} \geq 0$ be the credits that user i pays to j, in order to transmit data over the link $(j, i) \in \mathcal{E}$. Similarly, $h_{i,j} \geq 0$ denotes the price paid by user j to i for delivering data. At the start of the time slot t, each user has a credit budge K_i^t. At the end of the time period, user i's money is:

$$G_i\left(\overrightarrow{h_i}, \overrightarrow{h_{-i}}\right) = \sum_{j \in out(i)} \frac{w_{i,j} + 1}{2} h_{i,j} - \sum_{j \in in(i)} h_{j,i} + K_i^t \tag{5}$$

where the matrices $\overrightarrow{h_i}$ is $\left(h_{j,i} : j \in in(i)\right)$, and $\overrightarrow{h_{-i}}$ is $\left(h_{i,j} : j \in out(i)\right)$.

Finally, the total benefit of each user i is the sum of V_i and G_i. In this cooperating network, each user is not only self-interested, but also value their friendships. We introduce a social-based game theoretic mechanism using the Nash bargaining solution (NBS) to optimize the benefit of all users.

Nash bargain solution is one of the method of axioms bargaining [14]. A Nash bargaining game can be characterized by $\Gamma = \langle \mathcal{I}, (A_i), (u_i) \rangle$, where $\mathcal{I} = \{1, 2, \cdots, n\}$ is the player set, A_i is the strategy set for player i, and u_i is the utility of player i. u_i depends on the strategy profile of all players, $\alpha = (a_1, a_2, \cdots, a_n)$ with $a_i \in A_i$. A pair $(u_i, u_2, \cdots, u_n)$ is called an agreement.

Theorem 1. *Considering of Pareto optimal and fairness, a strategy* $\alpha^* = (a_1^*, a_2^*, \cdots, a_n^*)$ *is called a NBS [18], if it solves the following optimization:*

$$\max \sum_{i \in \mathcal{I}} \ln\left(u_i(\boldsymbol{a}) - u_i^{min}\right), \quad \boldsymbol{a} \in A \tag{6}$$

where u_i^{min} *is the utility that player* i *can get if an agreement is not reached between them.*

Therefore, the bargaining problem for this system is:

$$\max_{x,y,z} \sum_{i \in \mathcal{N}} \ln\left(V_i\left(y_i^t, \overrightarrow{x_i^t}, \overrightarrow{x_{-i}^t}\right) + G_i\left(\overrightarrow{h_i}, \overrightarrow{h_{-i}}\right) - \left(V_i^S + K_i^t\right)\right) \tag{7}$$

$$\text{s.t.} \begin{cases} x_{i,j}^t \leq C_{i,j}^t, \ y_i^t + \sum\limits_{j \in out(i)} x_{i,j}^t \leq C_i^t, \quad \forall i \in \mathcal{N}, \ (i,j) \in \mathcal{E} \\ V_i\left(y_i^t, \overrightarrow{x_i^t}, \overrightarrow{x_{-i}^t}\right) + G_i\left(\overrightarrow{h_i}, \overrightarrow{h_{-i}}\right) \geq V_i^S + K_i^t, \quad \forall i \in \mathcal{N} \\ \sum\limits_{j \in out(i)} \frac{w_{i,j} + 1}{2} h_{i,j} - \sum\limits_{j \in in(i)} h_{j,i} + K_i^t \geq 0, \quad \forall i \in \mathcal{N}, \ (i,j) \in \mathcal{E} \\ y_i^t \geq 0, \ x_{i,j}^t \geq 0, \ K_i^t \geq h_{i,j} \geq 0, \quad \forall i, j \in \mathcal{N} \end{cases} \tag{8}$$

where, $(V_i^S + K_i)$ is the benefit user i can achieve when an agreement is not reached.

The total benefit of each user depends on a local decision variables $\langle y_i^t, \overrightarrow{x_i^t}, \overrightarrow{h_i} \rangle$ and variables of upstream and downstream users' decisions $\langle \overrightarrow{x_{-i}^t}, \overrightarrow{h_{-i}} \rangle$. To tackle the coupled objectives, we introduce the matrices of auxiliary variables for each user and additional consistency constraints for their neighbour users [17]. Thus the coupled objective function is transferred to coupling in the constraints, which can be solved by dual Lagrangian decomposition [17] using the gradient method.

Let $\overrightarrow{\epsilon_i^t} = \left(\epsilon_{j,i}^t : \epsilon_{j,i}^t = x_{j,i}^t, \forall i \in \mathcal{N}, j \in in(i) \right)$ and $\overrightarrow{\zeta_i} = \left(\zeta_{i,j} : \zeta_{i,j} = h_{i,j}, \forall i \in \mathcal{N}, j \in out(i) \right)$ be the auxiliary variables matrices of upstream friends and downstream friends respectively. We denote $\rho = \left(\rho_{ji} : i \in \mathcal{N}, j \in in(i) \right)$, $\mu = \left(\mu_{ij} : i \in \mathcal{N}, j \in out(i) \right)$ and $\pi = \left(\pi_i \geq 0 : i \in \mathcal{N} \right)$ be the Lagrange variables for the constrains. Then the Lagrange function of this problem becomes:

$$L = \sum_{i \in \mathcal{I}} \ln \left(V_i\left(y_i^t, \overrightarrow{x_i^t}, \overrightarrow{\epsilon_i^t}\right) + G_i\left(\overrightarrow{h_i}, \overrightarrow{\zeta_i}\right) - \left(V_i^S(y_i^t) + K_i^t \right) \right)$$
$$+ \sum_{i \in \mathcal{I}} \sum_{j \in in(i)} \rho_{ji}\left(x_{j,i}^t - \epsilon_{j,i}^t\right) + \sum_{i \in \mathcal{I}} \sum_{j \in out(i)} \mu_{ij}\left(h_{i,j} - \zeta_{i,j}\right) \qquad (9)$$
$$+ \sum_{i \in \mathcal{I}} \pi_i \left(\sum_{j \in out(i)} \frac{w_{i,j}+1}{2} h_{i,j} + K_i^t - \sum_{j \in in(i)} h_{j,i} \right)$$

From the concavity of the utility function, we know the Lagrangian is a concave function. In each iteration τ, each user $i \in \mathcal{N}$ maximizes the Lagrange function $L_i(\cdot)$ in terms of the primal variables, and uses the obtained values to update the dual variables. And the objective function $L_i(\cdot)$ of the dual problem is:

$$L_i\left(y_i^t, \overrightarrow{x_i^t}, \overrightarrow{\epsilon_i^t}, \overrightarrow{h_i}, \overrightarrow{\zeta_i}\right) = \ln \left(V_i\left(y_i^t, \overrightarrow{x_i^t}, \overrightarrow{\epsilon_i^t}\right) + G_i\left(\overrightarrow{h_i}, \overrightarrow{\zeta_i}\right) - \left(V_i^S + K_i^t \right) \right)$$
$$+ \sum_{j \in in(i)} \left(\mu_{ji} h_{j,i} - \rho_{ji} \epsilon_{j,i}^t \right) + \sum_{j \in out(i)} \left(\rho_{ij} x_{i,j}^t - \mu_{ij} \zeta_{i,j} \right)$$
$$- \pi_i \sum_{j \in in(i)} h_{j,i} + \sum_{j \in in(i)} \pi_j \frac{w_{i,j}+1}{2} h_{j,i}$$
$$(10)$$

Then each user uses the primal variables and the obtained values to update the dual variables by subgradient:

$$\rho_{ji}(\tau + 1) = \rho_{ji}(\tau) - \beta\left(x_{j,i}^t(\tau) - \epsilon_{j,i}^t(\tau)\right) \qquad (11)$$

$$\mu_{ij}(\tau + 1) = \mu_{ij}(\tau) - \beta\left(h_{i,j}(\tau) - \zeta_{i,j}(\tau)\right) \qquad (12)$$

$$\pi_i(\tau + 1) = \left[\pi_i(\tau) - \beta\left(\sum_{j \in out(i)} \frac{w_{i,j}+1}{2} h_{i,j}(\tau) + K_i^t - \sum_{j \in in(i)} h_{j,i}(\tau) \right) \right]^+ \qquad (13)$$

Algorithm 1. Algorithm of Social-aware NBS

Input: $\mathcal{G} = (\mathcal{I}, \mathcal{E})$, W;
Output: y^*, x^*, h^*; # the optimal solution

 1: **bool** Convergence = **false**;
 2: **while** Convergence is **false do**
 3:    **for** each user $i \in \mathcal{I}$ **do**
 4:       Update $y_i^t, x_i^t, \epsilon_i^t, h_i, \zeta_i$ in (10) and calculate max L_i;
 5:    **end for**
 6:    **for** each $(i, j) \in \mathcal{E}$ **do**
 7:       Update $\lambda_i, \rho_{ji}, \mu_{ij}$ by solving (11), (12), and (13);
 8:    **end for**
 9:    **if** $Conv(\pi, \rho, \mu)$ **then**
10:       Convergence = **true**
11:    **end if**
12: **end while**

---

where τ is the iteration index, $\beta > 0$ is a sufficiently small positive step-size, and $[\cdot]^+$ denotes the projection onto the non-negative orthant. Social-aware nash bargaining solution can solve this problem efficiently.

Algorithm 1 illustrates the computation of y_i^t, $x_{i,j}^t$ and $h_{j,i}^t$. Here $Conv$ (π, ρ, μ) is a test function to determine whether the dual variables (π, ρ, μ) are convergent or not. This algorithm is executed in a synchronous fashion. After finishing the interactions, we can get the final benefit of user i by setting the final values of y_i^t, $x_{i,j}^t$ and $h_{j,i}^t$ to (3) and (5).

5   Performance Evaluation

In this section, we conduct simulations in the Matlab environment to evaluate the performance of our social-aware cooperative connectivity service, and compare this system with the optimal solution in the case of not participating cooperative communications, referred to the self-reliance solution.

5.1   Simulation Setup

Our simulations consider a social graph using the Erdös Rényi (ER) model in [5], where a social connection between two users exists with a probability of P. If a pair of users has a social connection, the weight of the social friendship will be uniformly distributed in $(0, 1]$, with a higher value being a stronger social connection. We set the default number of users as 5, and $P = 0.5$. To evaluate the performance in practice, we also simulate the social graph according to the real data trace from [11]. As Fig. 2 shows, we plot the probability of social connections existing between two users versus the number of users.

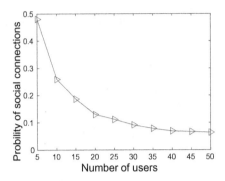

Fig. 2. Probability of social friendship versus number of users in data trace [11]

The utility function of each user $i \in \mathcal{N}$ is $F_i(y_i, x_{-i}) = \log(1 + y_i + \sum_{j \in in(i)} x_{j,i})$ for receiving data. The Internet access method of each user is different, which occurs to different communication capacity and energy cost. For example, [8] has measured the actual average speed for LTE is 12.7 Mbps, with an average energy consumption of 4.65 J/Mbyte. We assume that users communicate with each other using WiFi, and the capacity of each connection is depended on its distance. Finally, we assume that users have different data flow prices, depending on their data plans and service providers.

We consider two different optimization goals, the self-reliance solution and social-aware NBS. In self-reliance solution, the users maximizes their own performance without participating cooperation and social connections. While in social-aware NBS, the social friendships between users are taken into account.

5.2   Simulation Results

In Fig. 3 we simulate the total benefit of users with $N = 5$, where social connections exist between each pair of users with high probability ($P = 0.5$). It depicts that the social-aware solution always improve upon the self-reliance benefit. What's more, social-aware bargaining solutions can achieve more benefit than the selfish solution for most mobile users, which is not considered with social friendships, i.e., $w = 0$. The aggregate total benefit improve 39.7 % with the social-aware solution (compared to the self-reliance solution).

In Fig. 4, we evaluate the impact of N on the average benefit of users with the real data trace from [11]. As expected, we observe that the average benefit decreases with the number of users, for that there is less probability of social connections among a larger number of users. As the users' number increases, the benefits of users gradually converge.

The performance benefits of social-aware cooperative communication service depend on the weight of friendships between users. Figure 5 shows the impact of friendships on the traffic usage between users. It depicts that as the social friendship becomes closer, the traffic usage also increases, which means mobile

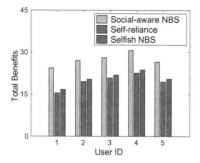

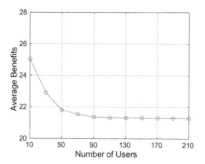

Fig. 3. Total benefits in the case of 5 users. (Color figure online)

Fig. 4. Average optimal benefits versus number of users N.

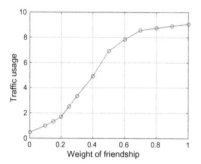

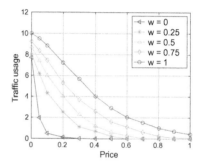

Fig. 5. Traffic flow versus weight of friendship.

Fig. 6. Traffic usage versus price

users would rather help their friends for communication demands. This reveals that the service benefits are larger for users who consider their friendships among their neighbour users.

Apart from the weight of friendships, data price and energy consumption are two factors that influence users' decisions. In Fig. 6, we investigate how the data price affects users' transmission decisions. It depicts that the amount of traffic usage decreases, when the data price for downloading data to herself and neighbours increases. However, the users with higher friendship would like to deliver more data to their friends than the ones not considering social relationship, e.g., for the price of 0.2, the users with $w = 1$ can consume 7 units data more. Besides, for the same price, users with higher friendships are more willing to delivery data, which can give benefits to users and their neighbours. The same results can be seen for energy consumption's impact on transmission decisions in Fig. 7. As energy consumption per unit increases, users may reduce the demands for data. Yet, users with high friendship will transmit more data than the ones with low friendship, e.g., for the users with $w = 1$ can consume data 27.3 % more than users of $w = 0.5$. As a result, in the same condition of price

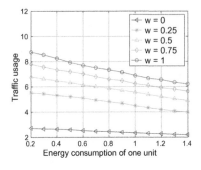

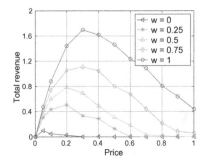

Fig. 7. Total traffic usage versus energy consumption

Fig. 8. Revenue versus price

and energy cost, the social-aware solution can promote more data delivering and satisfy users' demands.

We also consider the revenue of network providers in Fig. 8. It shows that as the price increases, the revenue of the provider also improves. Until an optimal value, the revenue will decrease with price increasing further. For a higher weight of friendship, the optimal value is higher too, e.g., the optimal price can reach 0.3 unit for $w = 1$, when it is 0.05 unit for $w = 0$. The reason is that, users with closed social ties have more attempts to consuming data. This can help providers to make strategies of pricing.

6 Conclusions

In this paper, we consider the problem of sharing network resources among mobile users with the consideration of social ties between them, and propose a social-aware utility optimization (SUO) model for the cooperative mobile network connection. In order to induce mobile users' participations, we design an incentive mechanism based on the weight of social friendships. The reported simulation results show that our method can improve the performance of the participating users. In the future work, we will investigate how to update the weight of friendships fairly, and consider the interests of users to efficiently schedule the routing decisions.

Acknowledgement. We would like to thank the reviewers for their helpful comments. This work is supported by the Tsinghua University Initiative Scientific Research Program (Grant No. 20161080066).

References

1. Buragohain, C., Agrawal, D., Suri, S.: A game theoretic framework for incentives in p2p systems. arXiv preprint cs/0310039 (2003)

2. Chen, K., Shen, H., Zhang, H.: Leveraging social networks for p2p content-based file sharing in mobile ad hoc networks. In: Proceedings of IEEE MASS 2011, pp. 112–121. IEEE (2011)

3. Chen, X., Proulx, B., Gong, X., Zhang, J.: Social trust and social reciprocity based cooperative d2d communications. In: Proceedings of ACM MobiHoc 2013, pp. 187–196. ACM (2013)

4. Cisco Visual Networking Index: Global mobile data traffic forecast update. 2014–2019 (white paper) (2015)

5. Erdös, P., Rényi, A.: On the evolution of random graphs. Publ. Math. Inst. Hung. Acad. Sci. **5**, 17–61 (1960)

6. Gilbert, E., Karahalios, K.: Predicting tie strength with social media. In: Proceedings of the SIGCHI Conference on Human Factors in Computing Systems, pp. 211–220. ACM (2009)

7. Golrezaei, N., Molisch, A.F., Dimakis, A.G., Caire, G.: Femtocaching and device-to-device collaboration: a new architecture for wireless video distribution. IEEE Commun. Mag. **51**(4), 142–149 (2013)

8. Huang, J., Qian, F., Gerber, A., Mao, Z.M., Sen, S., Spatscheck, O.: A close examination of performance and power characteristics of 4g lte networks. In: Proceedings of ACM MobiSys 2012, pp. 225–238. ACM (2012)

9. Iosifidis, G., Gao, L., Huang, J., Tassiulas, L.: Enabling crowd-sourced mobile internet access. In: 2014 Proceedings IEEE INFOCOM, pp. 451–459. IEEE (2014)

10. Janzamin, M., Pakravan, M., Sedghi, H.: A game-theoretic approach for power allocation in bidirectional cooperative communication. In: Proceedings of IEEE WCNC 2010, pp. 1–6. IEEE (2010)

11. Leskovec, J., Krevl, A.: SNAP Datasets: Stanford large network dataset collection (2014). http://snap.stanford.edu/data

12. Li, Q., Hu, R.Q., Qian, Y., Wu, G.: Cooperative communications for wireless networks: techniques and applications in lte-advanced systems. IEEE Wirel. Commun. **19**(2), 22–29 (2012)

13. Liu, G., Yang, Q., Wang, H., Lin, X., Wittie, M.P.: Assessment of multi-hop interpersonal trust in social networks by three-valued subjective logic. In: 2014 Proceedings IEEE INFOCOM, pp. 1698–1706. IEEE (2014)

14. Peters, H.J.: Axiomatic Bargaining Game Theory, vol. 9. Springer, The Netherlands (2013)

15. Sofia, R., Mendes, P.: User-provided networks: consumer as provider. IEEE Commun. Mag. **46**(12), 86–91 (2008)

16. Suris, J.E., DaSilva, L.A., Han, Z., MacKenzie, A.B., Komali, R.S.: Asymptotic optimality for distributed spectrum sharing using bargaining solutions. IEEE Trans. Wirel. Commun. **8**(10), 5225–5237 (2009)

17. Tan, C.W., Palomar, D.P., Chiang, M.: Distributed optimization of coupled systems with applications to network utility maximization. In: Proceedings of IEEE ICASSP 2006, vol. 5, p. V. IEEE (2006)

18. Yaïche, H., Mazumdar, R.R., Rosenberg, C.: A game theoretic framework for bandwidth allocation and pricing in broadband networks. IEEE/ACM Trans. Networking (TON) **8**(5), 667–678 (2000)

19. Yang, D., Fang, X., Xue, G.: Game theory in cooperative communications. IEEE Wirel. Commun. **19**(2), 44–49 (2012)

Piggybacking Lightweight Control Messages on Physical Layer for Multicarrier Wireless LANs

Bing Feng[1($\boxtimes$)], Chi Zhang[1($\boxtimes$)], Lingbo Wei[1($\boxtimes$)], and Yuguang Fang[2($\boxtimes$)]

[1] Key Laboratory of Electromagnetic Space Information,
Chinese Academy of Sciences,
University of Science and Technology of China, Hefei, China
fengice@mail.ustc.edu.cn, {chizhang,lingbowei}@ustc.edu.cn
[2] Department of Electrical and Computer Engineering,
University of Florida, Gainesville, USA
fang@ece.ufl.edu

Abstract. Piggyback is an effective scheme to transmit control messages in wireless local area networks (WLANs). In traditional approaches, the piggyback scheme is achieved by redefining or adding control fields in the MAC frame header, i.e., MAC layer piggyback scheme. However, this method has shortcomings. In this paper, we design and present PhyPig (Physical Piggyback), a cross-layer design for lightweight control channel. In the newly proposed communication strategy, the control messages are piggybacked on OFDM-based physical layer so that PhyPig does not consume extra channel resources, and does not harm the normal data throughput. Specifically, PhyPig modulates control messages (or sequences of binary bits) into null or non-null (i.e., normal) data symbols, the minimum 2-D time-frequency resource unit in OFDM. The thus-transmitted messages can be interpreted by checking the patterns of data symbols on OFDM subcarriers. Our extensive results validate the feasibility of PhyPig and show that PhyPig delivers control messages with close to 100 % accuracy on a channel with practical SNR regions. Further, based on our simulation results, we demonstrate that PhyPig outperforms traditional piggyback scheme with significant performance improvements in different scenarios.

Keywords: OFDM · Lightweight control channel · Cross-layer design · Piggybacking · WLANs

This work was supported in part by the Natural Science Foundation of China (NSFC) under Grants 61202140 and 61328208, by the Fundamental Research Funds for the Central Universities of China, by the Innovation Foundation of the Chinese Academy of Sciences under Grand CXJJ-14-S132, and by the Program for New Century Excellent Talents in University of China under Grant NCET-13-0548. The work of Y. Fang was also partially supported by the US National Science Foundation under grants CNS-1409797 and CNS-1343356.

Q. Yang et al. (Eds.): WASA 2016, LNCS 9798, pp. 68–79, 2016.
DOI: 10.1007/978-3-319-42836-9_7

1   Introduction

Control messages are essential to design efficient WLANs. However, there is no dedicated control channel in WLANs. The piggyback scheme is widely adopted in many studies targeted towards improving performances of various applications such as medium access control (MAC) coordination [1,2], rate control [3], and quality of service (QoS) [4]. Due to the broadcast nature of wireless channels, the control messages piggybacked by MAC frames can be received by neighboring nodes. Traditionally, the control messages are piggybacked on MAC layer by redefining or adding control fields in the MAC frame header.

However, the MAC layer piggyback scheme has a lot of disadvantages. First, the MAC layer piggyback scheme still consumes some channel resources that are originally used to transmit data, and it needs to change the MAC frame structure defined in original 802.11 standards. Second, with MAC layer piggyback scheme, neighboring nodes needs to decode the received frame to get control messages even through the destination address is not itself, which results in extra overhead. Third, the transmission of control messages piggybacked by the data frames lacks robustness. The control messages should be transmitted at lowest data rate so that the delivery is robust. In MAC layer piggyback scheme, the control messages are transmitted at the same data rate with the MAC frame. However, the channel conditions of neighboring nodes may be worse than the intend receiver, so the received frames at neighboring nodes may not be decoded successfully to obtain control messages.

In this paper, we design and present PhyPig (Physical Piggyback), a novel technique that piggybacks lightweight control messages on the OFDM-based physical layer. In PhyPig, the key concept is a novel communication strategy that takes advantage of the underlying OFDM technique to convey information on the physical layer. Instead of being transmitted by actual data symbol values, the control messages are modulated into the pattern of data symbols (null or normal) on the physical layer in PhyPig. More specifically, a null data symbol represents bit "1" while a normal (i.e., non-null) data symbol represents bit "0". A null data symbol is achieved straightforwardly by loading zero power on the corresponding data symbol, and the thus transmitted control messages can be interpreted by symbol level energy detection.

The idea of the proposed communication strategy is simple, but the key challenge is how to ensure the transmission of control messages does not destroy the original data transmission. The feasibility of PhyPig is based on the intuition that if we carefully design the number and distribution of deliberately generated null data symbols, they can be recovered by the existing channel coding in WLAN systems. We obtain the correction capability by two methods. Since the weak data subcarriers produce most of the erroneous data symbols in OFDM systems due to frequency selective fading, we design PhyPig on those weak data subcarriers so that more null data symbols are fallen on the positions of erroneous data symbols. By this way, we can intentionally exploit the correction capability that is originally utilized to correct erroneous data symbols to recover our inserted null data symbols. The second method is to leverage the existence of extra redundancy in the channel coding in current WLAN systems. Our measurements verify the existence of extra decoding capability and are in line with previous studies [5,6] that utilize this phenomenon to design control channel by intend interference in wireless networks. PhyPig is inspired by their works. However, some problems exist in the schemes proposed in [5,6]. It is easy to corrupt the original data transmission due to the uncontrolled contention in control plan. It is a challenge to accurately place a intend signal onto a data symbol due to non synchronization, which adds the system complexity. In addition, these schemes consume significant energy to send interference signal. Compared to [5,6], PhyPig is used for a different communication scenario, which avoids the above problems. Moreover, PhyPig takes frequency selective fading into account to improve the capacity of control messages.

The reset of this paper is organized as follows. Section 2 presents the overview of PhyPig. Section 3 analyzes the feasibility of PhyPig based on our key observations. Section 4 describes the detailed system architecture of PhyPig. Section 5 evaluates the performances of PhyPig and presents corresponding analysis. We conclude this paper in Sect. 6.

2   Overview of PhyPig

The design of PhyPig relies on OFDM that has been widely adopted as the physical technique in modern WLANs (e.g., 802.11a/g/n). We extend 802.11a to design PhyPig in our practical implementation. OFDM divides wireless channel into 64 orthogonal subcarriers of which there are 12 guard subcarriers, 4 pilots, and 48 data subcarriers. The modulated data symbols are mapped onto all data subcarriers to transmit in parallel, and an OFDM symbol is the composite signal of all 64 subcarriers. As shown in Fig. 1(a), a modulated data symbol is the smallest resource unit in OFDM, i.e., a 2-D time-frequency resource block. The time duration of a data symbol (i.e., a time slot) equals to 4 us in 802.11a/g.

There are two system parameters m and n in PhyPig. The m denotes the number of subcarriers selected as control subcarriers from all 48 data subcarriers

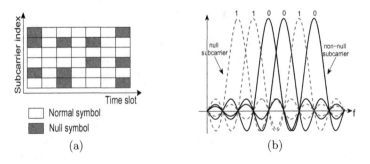

Fig. 1. (a) An illustration example of PhyPig based on OFDM-based physical layer. (b) Power spectrum of control subcarriers in time slot 3. (Color figure online)

to transmit control messages, and the n denotes the interval between time slots where control messages are transmitted. For example, $m = 6$ and $n = 1$ in Fig. 1(a). The rate of control messages depends on the values of m and n. How to select the values of m and n so that the transmission of control messages does not affect the correct decoding of received data frame will be discussed in Sect. 4. Taking Fig. 1(a) for an example, when the transmitter needs to convey a value of 50, it maps the sequence of bits $(1,1,0,0,1,0)$ to corresponding data symbols in a time slot (here is time slot 3). A null data symbol is used to represent bit "1" while a normal data symbol is used to represent bit "0". Figure 1(b) shows the power spectrum of those control subcarriers in time slot 3, and the receiver interprets the transmitted control message by symbol level energy detection. Obviously, the conveyed control bits is "110010" in time slot 3.

Compared to the conventional MAC layer piggyback scheme, we need to understand the benefits of the proposed physical layer piggyback scheme. First, PhyPig transmits control messages without consuming any extra channel resources, and it dose not change the existing MAC frame structure. Second, after receiving the MAC frame, neighboring nodes can directly interpret the conveyed control messages by symbol level energy detection without the conventional decoding of MAC frames, which avoids extra overhead. Third, the physical piggyback scheme is robust. Since symbol level energy detection requires lower SNRs than conventional decoding procedure, neighboring nodes can extract the control messages as long as the physical preamble is received correctly, even if the MAC frame is corrupted and can not be successfully decoded.

3   Feasibility of PhyPig

The feasibility of PhyPig depends on how to obtain correction capability to recovery those inserted null data symbols. In this section, we present our ideas to demonstrate the feasibility of PhyPig based on our observations.

3.1   Frequency Selective Fading

In addition to signal attenuation and noise, frequency selectively fading widely exists in realistic wireless communication scenarios due to multi-path propagation [7,8]. In OFDM systems, different subcarriers have very different channel conditions owing to frequency selectively fading. For example, Fig. 2(a) shows measurements of signal-to-noise-ratio(SNR) across 52 subcarriers in a 20 MHz 802.11a channel. We observe that the SNR of different subcarriers can differ by 9.2 dB or more.

3.2   Symbol Error Pattern

The existing data rate adaption scheme defined in 802.11 standard ignores frequency diversity and treats all subcarriers as the same, i.e., all subcarriers adopt the same channel coding, modulation, and power allocation. As a result, certain subcarriers undergo deeper fading and have higher symbol error rates. The errors will be repeated for each data symbol in those deep fading subcarriers. Therefore, the number of erroneous data symbols within a received frame is dominated by those deep fading subcarriers.

Based on this observation, PhyPig selects those deep fading subcarriers as control subcarriers to design the proposed communication strategy so that more inserted null data symbols fall on the positions of erroneous symbols. Thus the correction capability that is originally used to recover the erroneous data symbols is now utilized to recovery those deliberately inserted null data symbols.

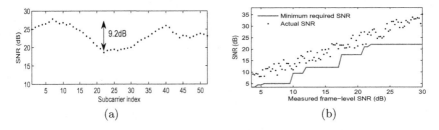

Fig. 2. (a) Measured SNRs of different subcarriers in a 20 MHz frequency selective fading channel. (b) The measured SNR gap between the actual channel SNR and the minimum required SNR in 802.11a.

3.3   Extra Coding Redundancy

To combat bit errors induced by wireless transmissions, Forward Error Correction (FEC) is adopted to correct certain bit errors by adding redundant bits to each data frame. The level of coding redundancy is depend on the code rate, and 802.11 a/g have three types of code rates: 1/2, 2/3, and 3/4. The selection of code rates is accord to the data rate that is selected by SNR-based rate adaptation schemes. A question is that how much redundant bits should be accurately added. In our measurements, we will show that the selected redundancy in channel coding is always higher than the minimum required redundancy to successfully decode the received data frame in current WLAN systems, and the extra redundancy is wasteful.

The gap between the actual decoding capability at the intend receiver and the minimum required decoding capability to decode the received data frame stems from two factors. One is the inaccurate estimation of channel condition at the intend receiver, and the other one is the stair-case rate selection. In SNR-based rate adaptation schemes, the data rate is selected based on the estimated channel condition of the intend receiver. A lower data rate corresponding to a more robust code rate is picked when the channel condition becomes weaker. The current 802.11 a/g Network Interference Cards (NICs) evaluate channel conditions by the metric of SNR. However, the previous measurements [8] have show that SNR-based channel evaluation is a frame-level metric and does not reliably reflect the actual channel condition due to frequency selective fading. Those weak subcarriers lower the value of frame-level SNR. As a result, a low data rate is selected, but in practice the receiver can support higher data rate transmissions due to better channel condition, which means the receiver has extra decoding capability that is under-utilized.

In addition to inaccurate channel estimation, the stair-case rate selection also leads to the gap. The data rate provided by 802.11 standards is discrete while the SNR is continuous. Thus, even if the channel condition is estimated perfectly, the perfect one-to-one matching from channel conditions to data rates can not be obtained. The non-prefect matching results in the under-selection of data rates [9]. For example, when the feedback of SNR is 8 dB, the transmitter will pick the data rate of 12 Mbps whose minimum required SNR is 5 dB, rather than the data rate of 18 Mbps whose minimum required SNR is 9.5 dB.

Based on above analysis, we conduct detailed experiments to measure the gap between the minimum required SNRs to correctly decode received data frame and the actual SNRs at the intend receiver. The typical SNR-based rate adaptation scheme RBAR [3] is adopted in our measurements. The result is shown in Fig. 2(b) including measured frame-level SNRs, minimum required SNRs, and actual SNRs. For example, when the measured frame-level SNR is 11 dB, the required minimum SNR corresponding to data rate of 18 Mbps is 9.5 dB while the actual SNR is 13.2 dB. Thus, the gap is about 3.7 dB in this case. We can clearly see that the gap is significant, which suggests that the extra decoding capability can be utilized to recover those inserted null symbols in PhyPig.

4   PhyPig Design

4.1   Overall System Architecture

PhyPig is a simple extension of the existing OFDM-based WLAN physical layer, and Fig. 3 shows the overall system architecture of PhyPig. We add three new components including loading controller, subcarrier state estimator, and power detector. The loading controller achieves symbol level power allocation at the transmitter. The subcarrier state estimator records SNRs of all data subcarriers and selects m data subcarriers with worst channel conditions.

4.2   Modulation/Demodulation of Control Messages

In standard OFDM-based WLAN architecture, the data bits are modulated into data symbols. Then incoming serial data symbols are converted into parallel data streams by the S/P module. Let $X[k]$ denote the data symbol needed to be transmitted on data subcarrier k. After the Inverse Fast Fourier Transform (IFFT), we obtain the transmitted OFDM signal $x[n]$ at sample time n by

$$x[n] = \frac{1}{N} \sum_{k=0}^{N-1} \sqrt{p_k} X[k] e^{j2\pi \frac{kn}{N}}, \tag{1}$$

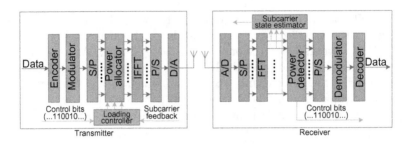

Fig. 3. Architecture of transmitter and receiver in PhyPig. The orange blocks are PhyPig extentions to OFDM-based 802.11. (Color figure online)

where N is the number of OFDM subcarriers, and p_k is the transmission power allocated to the k data subcarrier [10]. In 802.11 standards, the power allocated to each OFDM subcarrier is same, and we have $\sum_{k=0}^{N-1} p_k \leq P_{sum}$, where P_{sum} is the total transmission power of transmitter. The function of loading controller is to control the allocation of power on the selected control subcarriers. If the transmitted bit is "1" on data subcarrier i, it allocates zero power, i.e., $p_i = 0$. Otherwise, it allocates normal transmission power.

The modulated signal is transmitted to the receiver through wireless channel. The received signal is a composite waveform consisting of different subcarriers. Let $y[n]$ denote the received signal at sample time n, and we can obtain the data symbol at data subcarrier k by

$$Y[k] = \sum_{n=0}^{N-1} y[n]e^{-j2\pi\frac{kn}{N}}. \tag{2}$$

The Fast Fourier Transform (FFT) result presents magnitudes of every subcarrier [11], and then the power detector module performs symbol by symbol energy detection on the set of control subcarriers. However, in practical system, the magnitudes of some subcarriers where no power is allocated are not zero due to the existence of noise. Fortunately, the noise energy is same for all subcarriers. Our experiment results show that the magnitude difference between noise and fading signal is large enough to distinguish fading signal from noise.

4.3   Rate Selection of Control Messages

In PhyPig, the null data symbols are deliberately generated, so the key design principle is to carefully select the values of m and n so that the transmission of control messages does not destroy the original data transmission. It is difficult to select the values of m and n by theory analysis. We conduct a large number of experiments in different scenarios with various SNR regions to suggest the selections of m and n.

PhyPig relies on subcarrier level channel conditions to select the set of control subcarriers. However, the commodity 802.11 a/g NICs only provide Received

Signal Strength Indicator (RSSI) that is the total signal power of the received packet and can only be used to obtain per-packet SNR. Thus we can not directly get channel quality at the subcarrier level. To address this issue, we adopt the method used in [8] to obtain channel conditions at the granularity of subcarrier in 802.11 a/g.

Based on subcarrier level channel quality, we select the worst m subcarriers out of 48 data subcarriers as control subcarriers. A bit vector is fed back to indicate the set of selected control subcarriers, and it only occupies one time slot where a null data symbol represents that the corresponding data subcarrier is selected as control subcarrier. In our practical implementation, the parameter m is fixed and is set to 12, and we adjust the rate of control messages by changing the parameter n that is fed back to the transmitter. Note that all information feedbacks are achieved by PhyPig scheme when the ACK frame is transmitting. How to dynamically select the value of n according to channel conditions of the intend receiver is presented in next section.

Now we discuss the capacity of control messages within a frame transmission. Let T_p be the transmission time of packet payload in us, and C_c denote the capacity of control messages within the transmission of a packet payload. When $m = 12$ and $n = 2$, the rate of control messages is 999.996 Kbps. If a frame with 1024 bytes payload is transmitted at 54 Mbps, we get $T_p = 151.7$ us and $C_c = 144$ bits. If this frame is transmitted at 36 Mbps, we can obtain $C_c = 216$ bits. Since the frame aggregation technique has been widely used in modern WLANs, PhyPig can transmit more bits within a frame transmission.

5   Evaluation

In this section, we validate and evaluate PhyPig by extensive simulation experiments written in C++ and Matlab. The implementation of PhyPig is based on the 802.11a PHY layer, and the fixed parameter m is 12 and the parameter n is variable. We conduct our simulations on a wireless channel with frequency selective fading.

5.1   Accuracy of PhyPig Detection

PhyPig interprets control messages by detecting the energy level of the set of selected control subcarriers. We evaluate the detection accuracy of PhyPig under various SNRs. We transmit the pre-defined control message with 60 bits. This experiment was performed by 2000 packets. All 48 data subcarriers are numbered logically from 0 to 48. As shown in Fig. 4(a), 12 contiguous subcarriers, i.e., [16, 17, ..., 26, 27], are selected as control subcarriers due to frequency correlation. After frequency selective fading, different subcarriers have different amplitudes, and the amplitudes of deep fading subcarriers are small. The subcarriers with null data symbols only have noise. We can clearly see that the energy difference between subcarrier with only noise and subcarrier with normal signal is very apparent. Figure 4(b) shows that the detection accuracy is close to 100 % under

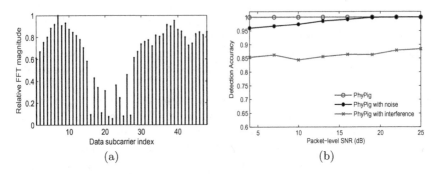

Fig. 4. (a) Relative magnitude of all subcarriers after performing FFT. (b) Detection accuracy of control messages under various SNRs.

ideal channel condition. In a noisy environment, the detection accuracy is above 96 % even at low SNRs. Under a low SNR, the magnitudes of those deep fading subcarriers may be close to null subcarriers. The typical working channel conditions of wireless networks are above 10 dB, so PhyPig works well under practical SNR ranges. Therefore, we conclude that the null subcarriers are easily detected by energy detection after performing FFT. However, when the channel exists strong interference, the detection accuracy is very low for all SNRs. This is due to the fact that interference may active null subcarriers so that it falsely detects a active subcarrier when it is actually absent.

5.2   Rate of Control Messages

In this experiment, given $m = 12$, we test the selection of n to decide the rate of control messages without sacrificing the original data transmission. To get desired packet reception rate (PRR) of the original data frame, we select appropriate value of n with practical SNR regions in our experiments. The data rate is dynamically adjusted by the typical SNR-based rate adaptation scheme RBAR [3]. Both Fig. 5(a) and (b) show the relationship between packet reception rate and measured packet-level SNR. Two modulation schemes including 16-QAM, and 64-QAM are considered in our results. Once the data rate is selected based on the feedback of frame-level SNR, the PRR increases sharply with the increase of SNR. To obtain the desired PRR, larger SNR is needed when smaller value of n is selected. For example, when the modulation is 16-QAM and $n = 2$, if the acceptable PRR is above 98.0 %, the corresponding SNR should be more than 16.2 dB (shown in Fig. 5(a)). Based on our results, we suggest that $n = 4$ is set under small SNRs while $n = 2$ is set under large SNRs.

5.3   Applications of PhyPig

To demonstrate the key features of physical piggyback, we extend the early back-off announcement (EBA) [1] that adopts MAC layer piggyback scheme to a new

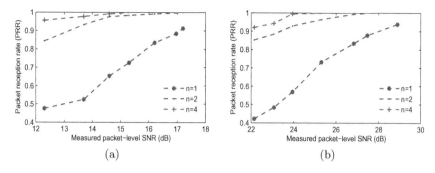

Fig. 5. (a) Packet reception rate versus SNR when 16-QAM and 1/2 code rate. (b) Packet reception rate versus SNR when 64-QAM and 3/4 code rate.

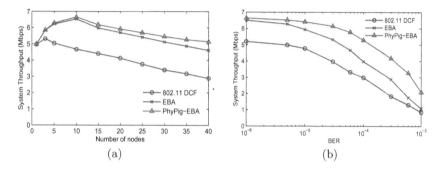

Fig. 6. Simulation results. (a) Comparison of throughput versus number of nodes in error-free channel. (b) Comparison of throughput versus BER.

MAC scheme called PhyPig-EBA that piggybacks the future backoff information on the physical layer. In this distributed MAC scheme, when a node successfully transmits a MAC frame, the next backoff value is piggybacked on the physical layer using PhyPig technique to announce all neighboring nodes. Then all other nodes do not select the same backoff value to avoid collisions. Through exchanging further backoff information, the number of collisions decreases and the network throughput increases significantly.

Figure 6(a) shows the throughput of 802.11 DCF, EBA, and PhyPig-EBA under no channel errors. The result shows that both EBA and PhyPig-EBA outperform 802.11 DCF significantly. Note that PhyPig-EBA is only slightly superior to EBA under this scenario due to the fact that the channel resources are not used in PhyPig-EBA to transmit control information (i.e., next backoff values). To evaluate the robustness of PhyPig, we present the system throughput under various channel error rates. Figure 6(b) shows the comparison of the throughput performance as the BER values vary from 10^{-6} to 10^{-3}. 20 nodes are included in this simulation experiment. It can be observed that the throughput of EBA will be decreased significantly. The reason is that nodes are not likely to receive further backoff information correctly due to channel errors. However, since the obtaining of control messages does not need the decoding of data frame in PhyPig, the proposed scheme works better than EBA under channel with bit errors. Even the received packet is corrupted, PhyPig can still use the received packet to extract control messages.

6   Conclusion

PhyPig is a novel communication strategy that piggybacks lightweight control messages on the OFDM-based physical layer in WLANs. Physical piggyback means the control messages are interpreted on the physical layer without the traditional decoding of received MAC frame. By designing the distribution of inserted null data symbols and utilizing the residual decoding capability existed in current WLAN systems, we obtain correction capability to recover those deliberately generated null data symbols. If we carefully select the rate of control messages, PhyPig doest not destroy the original data frame transmission. Our evaluation results demonstrate the feasibility of PhyPig. As control messages become more necessary in various applications, we believe the proposed physical piggyback scheme can be utilized as a lightweight control channel to address a lot of problems existing in modern wireless networks.

References

1. Choi, J., Yoo, J., Choi, S., Kim, C.: Eba: an enhancement of the ieee 802.11 dcf via distributed reservation. IEEE Trans. Mobile Comput. 4(4), 378–390 (2005)
2. Hosseinabadi, G., Vaidya, N.: Token-dcf: an opportunistic mac protocol for wireless networks. In: IEEE International Conference on Communication Systems and Networks, Bangalore, pp. 1–9 (2013)
3. Holland, G., Vaidya, N., Bahl, P.: A rate-adaptive mac protocol for multi-hop wireless networks. In: ACM International Conference on Mobile Computing and Networking, Rome, pp. 236–251 (2001)
4. Wang, P., Zhuang, W.: A token-based scheduling scheme for wlans supporting voice/data traffic and its performance analysis. IEEE Trans. Wirel. Commun. 7(5), 1708–1718 (2008)
5. Wu, K., Tan, H., Liu, Y., Zhang, J., Zhang, Q., Ni, L.M.: Side channel: bits over interference. IEEE Trans. Mobile Comput. 11(8), 1317–1330 (2012)
6. Cidon, A., Nagaraj, K., Katti, S., Viswanath, P.: Flashback: decoupled lightweight wireless control. ACM SIGCOMM Comput. Commun. Rev. 42(4), 223–234 (2012)
7. Halperin, D., Hu, W., Sheth, A., Wetherall, D.: Tool release: gathering 802.11 n traces with channel state information. ACM SIGCOMM Comput. Commun. Rev. 41(1), 53–53 (2011)
8. Rahul, H., Edalat, F., Katabi, D., Sodini, C.G.: Frequency-aware rate adaptation and mac protocols. In: ACM International Conference on Mobile Computing and Networking, Beijing, pp. 193–204 (2009)

9. Wang, G., Zhang, S., Wu, K., Zhang, Q., Ni, L.M.: Tim: fine-grained rate adaptation in wlans. In: IEEE 34th International Conference on Distributed Computing Systems, pp. 577–586 (2014)
10. Jang, J., Lee, K.B.: Transmit power adaptation for multiuser ofdm systems. IEEE J. Sel. Areas Commun. **21**(2), 171–178 (2003)
11. Dutta, A., Saha, D., Grunwald, D., Sicker, D.: Smack: a smart acknowledgment scheme for broadcast messages in wireless networks. In: ACM SIGCOMM Computer Communication Review, Barcelona, pp. 15–26 (2009)

Multi-focus Image Fusion via Region Mosaicing on Contrast Pyramids

Liguo Zhang[1], Jianguo Sun[1,2(✉)], Weimiao Feng[2], Junyu Lin[1,2(✉)], and Qing Yang[3]

[1] Harbin Engineering University, Harbin 150001, China
{zhangliguo, sunjianguo, linjunyu}@hrbeu.edu.cn
[2] Institute of Information Engineering,
Chinese Academy of Sciences, Beijing 100093, China
[3] Montana State University, Bozeman 59717, USA
Qing.yang@cs.montana.edu

Abstract. This paper proposes a new approach called region mosaicing on contrast pyramids for multi-focus image fusion. A density-based region growing is developed to construct a focused region mask for multi-focus images. The segmented focused region mask is decomposed into a mask pyramid, which is then used for supervised region mosaicing on a contrast pyramid. In this way, the focus measurement and the continuity of focused regions are incorporated and the pixel level pyramid fusion is improved at the region level. Objective and subjective experiments show that the proposed region mosaicing on contrast pyramids approach is more robust to noise and can fully preserves the focus information of the multi-focus images, reducing distortions of the fused images.

Keywords: Multi-focus image · Image fusion · Region Mosaic · Contrast pyramid

1 Introduction

High magnification optical lens, such as microscopes, has a very small depth of field. When capturing an object/scene of depth with optical lens of high magnification typically, only a fraction of the object/scene is in focus. Multi-focus image fusion is a process in which registered images with different focus settings are fused to synthesize an "all-in-focus" image with extended depth of field [1–3]. It plays important roles in microscope imaging [4], optical image de-blurring, shape from focus [4, 5] and image based forensics [6].

Pyramid based approaches have been extensively investigated in the image fusion domain. Some examples include The discrete wavelet transform (DWT) [7, 8], the gradient pyramid [9], the contrast pyramid [10], the Laplacian pyramid [11], the ratio-of-low pass pyramid [12], the shift-invariant DWT [13] and the contour let transform [14–16]. Despite the advantages of pyramid based approaches, they are pixel based and then generally sensitive to noise. Noise pixels often have high contrast, and may be falsely detected as in-focus pixels. Because the fused image obtained by transform domain-based algorithms consider global information, a small change in a

© Springer International Publishing Switzerland 2016
Q. Yang et al. (Eds.): WASA 2016, LNCS 9798, pp. 80–90, 2016.
DOI: 10.1007/978-3-319-42836-9_8

single coefficient of the fused image in the transformed domain may cause all the pixel values to change in spatial domain [17]. Consequently, distortion artifacts and the loss of contrast information are often observed in fused images. Gradient map filtering [8] and multiple coefficient selection principles [18] are proposed to solve this problem, although they need more parameter fine turning to obtain high objective quality.

Compared with pyramid based methods, weighted linear fusion is the most intuitive approach to image fusion [19–21]. When applied to multi-focus image fusion, weights for different regions are calculated to reflect the degree of focus and corresponding pixels from different images and combined with linear weighting. A special case of the weighted linear fusion is region mosaicing, where all the weights in focusing regions are set as 1.0 and other regions as zero. In [22], Agarwala et al. described an interactive framework for combining regions of a set of images into a single composite picture, called "iterative digital photomontage." When it is applied to multi-focus image fusion, it can be regarded as region mosaicing approach with optimized mask segmentation on a graph-cut algorithm. Mosaic algorithms can preserve the original information but they often introduce block artifacts in transitive zones around region boundaries, degrading visual perception quality of fused images.

In recent years, pulse coupled neural network (PCNN) was employed to perform weighted linear fusion with two parallel source images input. Meanwhile focus measurements are carried out for the source images and weighted coefficients are automatically adjusted based on the measurements. The method takes full advantage of neural networks and it also incorporate continuity of focused regions by defining surrounding neurons for pixels, but may be computational inefficient.

It should be noted that most of the existing multi-focus image fusion approaches are derived from general pixel level image fusion methods. The characteristics of multi-focus imaging have not been fully explored. Multi-focus images are often captured frame by frame with a fixed focal length but variant object distances. The continuity of the object surface and the object distance result in multi-focus images having continuous focus regions instead of discrete focus pixels. The traditional pixel level fusion approaches do not necessarily have these characteristics; while region based approaches suffer from deterioration of visual perception [22, 23]. In the classic pixel level CP method, a pixel and its neighbors often do not belong to the same Contrast Pyramid, which introduces fusion errors. When we label the pixels in the fused pyramid according to pixel level measurement, we find that the in-focus regions of different pyramid levels are not similar figures. This suggests that some pixels are reconstructed with pixel values from more than one multi-focus image. As a result, original clear information is lost and distortion is introduced.

In this paper, we propose a simple but effective approach called region mosaicing on contrast pyramids (REMCP) for multi-focus image fusion. The flowchart of our approach is as Fig. 1. It is based on the observation that the in-focus pixels in a multi-focus image form continuous regions. We propose to use density-based region growing (DBRG) to generate a focus region mask for all of the multi-focus images. The DBRG uses both region growing and filtering, and consequently can identify proper focus regions and reduce the impact of noise. A segmented focused region mask is decomposed into a mask pyramid, which is then applied to supervise the region mosaicing on a contrast pyramid. In this way, we improve pixel level pyramid fusion at the region level, where the imaging characteristics of multi-focus images are utilized and the continuity of segmented focused regions is incorporated. In the proposed REMCP approach, decomposition values of a pixel in different pyramid levels but same spatial position are from the same multi-focus image, exactly. This guarantees that distortion artifacts are reduced to the most degree.

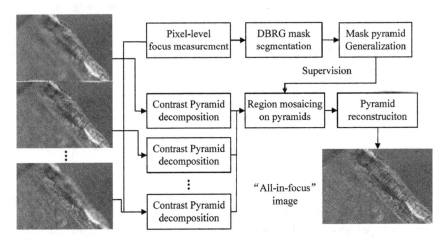

Fig. 1. Flowchart of the proposed REMCP approach. For the limitation of space, three of fifteen multi-focus images are given, while others are omitted for the limited space.

2   Focus Region Segmentation

2.1   Pixel Level Focus Measurement

There are many focus measurements including variance, energy of image gradient (EOG), energy of Laplacian of the image (EOL), sum-modified-Laplacian (SML), and spatial frequency (SF) [1, 7, 8]. In [1], the authors assessed these measurements and reported that SML and EOL measurement can provide better performance than others. For the high computational efficiency, EOL is used in this paper.

We define a neighboring window of size $(-w, w)$ around the pixel $I(x, y)$, then exploit the EOL in the window as the focus measurement. The EOL is calculated as

$$
\begin{aligned}
EOL(x,y) = \sum_{x\in(-w,w)} \sum_{y\in(-w,w)} &[-I(x-1,y-1) - 4I(x-1,y) - I(x-1,y+1) - 4I(x,y-1) \\
&+ 20I(x,y) - 4I(x,y+1) - I(x+1,y-1) - 4I(x+1,y) - I(x+1,y+1)]^2
\end{aligned}
\tag{1}
$$

If a pixel lies in a focused region as well as non-smooth region, its neighboring pixels have large grey value variance, leading to a large EOL. Otherwise, the EOL is small. Assuming that there are multi-focus images to be fused, we define a mask image

M^0 whose pixel values vary in [1, N]. Let $EOL_n(x, y)$ denote the EOL of the nth multi-focus image at pixel (x, y). The pixel-level mask image M^0 is initially labeled with

$$M^0(x, y) = \arg\max_n |(EOL_n(x, y))|, n = 1, 2, 3 \ldots, N. \tag{2}$$

$M^0(x, y) = n$ is EOL of the nth multi-focus image at pixel (x, y), the maximum among all of the N images.

2.2 Focus Region Segmentation

A DBRG segmentation algorithm is based on the analysis of density distribution of pixels of same labels. As illustrated in Fig. 2, the spatial neighborhood $\Omega(x, y)$ of a given pixel is defined as a circle with center at (x, y) and radius R. R is determined experimentally. The density distribution in $\Omega(x, y)$ is defined as

$$D_{\Omega(x,y)}(n) = \left(\frac{1}{\pi R^2} \sum_{(a,b) \in \Omega(x,y)} \delta(M^0(a, b) = n) \right), \tag{3}$$

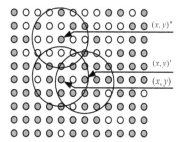

Fig. 2. An illustration of density-connectivity of pixels of same mask label. As pixels marked with the 'gray' label, $(x, y)'$, is density-connected with (x, y), but $(x, y)''$ is not density-connected with (x, y) in terms of the density-connectivity defined below.

where (a, b) indicate a pixel in $\Omega(x, y)$, $\delta(.)$ is a function which returns 1 when the input is true, and returns 0 otherwise.

If the maximum density $\max_n (D_{\Omega(x,y)}(n))$ of $\Omega(x, y)$ is larger than a threshold 0.5, then the pixel (x, y) is called a core pixel and $\Omega(x, y)$ forms a core region. A pixel $\Omega(x, y)'$ is density-connected from pixel (x, y) if $(x, y)'$ is within the spatial neighborhood of (x, y), as shown in Fig. 2.

Based on the above definitions, Table 1 describes the DBRG segmentation algorithm to group discrete label pixels into clusters and form a mask of regions.

Table 1. Mask segmentation via DBRG

Input: Pixel-level mask image M^0
Output: Region-level mask image M

---

1. Create a region-level mask image M, setting all of the pixels to unlabeled;
2. Search the unlabeled pixels in M^0 to find a core pixel (x, y) and core region, $\Omega(x, y)$. If a core pixel (x, y) is found, a new cluster is created with the cluster label

$$M(x, y) = \arg\max_n \left(D_{\Omega(x,y)}(n) \right);\qquad(4)$$

3. Iteratively collect unlabeled pixels in M that are density-connected with (x, y) in M^0, and label these pixels with same cluster label;
4. If there are still existing core pixels in the image, go to 2;
5. For the pixels that are not included in any clusters (noise pixels or pixels from smooth region), merge them with the cluster that has the most adjacent pixels.

---

3   Region Mosaicing on Contrast Pyramids

The focus region segmentation procedure results in a mask that indicates focus regions of all images. This mask is decomposed into a mask pyramid to supervise the fusion process on the contrast pyramid. This procedure is called region mosaicing on pyramid.

3.1   Contrast Pyramid Fusion

According to the definition in [10], the contrast pyramid (CP) and Gaussian pyramid (GP) have the following relationship:

$$C_l(p, q) = G_l(p, q)/V_l(p, q) - U(p, q),\qquad(5)$$

where $C_l(p, q)$, $l = 0,..., L\text{-}1$ denote the pixel value of CP at l^{th} level and location (p, q), $G_l(p, q)$, $l = 0,..., L$ denotes the pixel value of GP at l^{th} level and location (p, q), $V_l(p, q)$, $l = 0,..., L\text{-}1$ denote the low-pass-filtering GP. U denotes a matrix whose elements are all equal to 1.0.

$G_l(p, q)$, $l = 0,..., L$ is calculated by a convolution operation between a Gaussian filter and its up-level GP image as

$$G_l(p, q) = f(p, q) * G_{l-1}(2p, 2q), l = 1, ..., L,\qquad(6)$$

where $f(p, q)$ denotes a Gaussian filter of 5×5 pixels and $*$ is a convolution operation. G_L is the base image and $G_L == I$ denotes an original multi-focus image.

After that, we compute the ratio of the low-pass images at successive levels of the GP. We interpolate new values '0' between the given values of the lower frequency image, and then perform a low-pass-filtering as

$$V_l(p,q) = 4 \cdot f(p,q) * G_{l+1}\left(\frac{p}{2},\frac{q}{2}\right), l = 0,\ldots,L-1, \tag{7}$$

where only integer coordinates contribute to $V_l(x, y)$.

The classical CP algorithm exploits a pixel level competition and fusion on pyramids as

$$RC_l(x,y) = C_{l,\tilde{n}}(x,y), \; l = 0,\ldots,L-1$$
$$\tilde{n} = \arg\max_n \left| C_{l,n}(x,y) \right|, n = 1,\ldots,N \tag{8}$$

where RC_l denotes the level of the fused CP, $C_l(x, y)$ denotes contrast value of pixel (x, y) at l^{th} level of the nth multi-focus image and N denotes the total number of multi-focus images.

3.2 Region Based Contrast Pyramid Fusion

According to (8), the pixel-level fusion pyramid values are selected according to the contrast magnitudes of their source images. In this case, it is found that regions selected for fusion in different pyramid levels are not similar figures. This causes many pixels to be reconstructed with pixel values from more than one multi-focus image, and as a result, the original clear information is lost and distortion is introduced. Therefore, we propose the following region based pyramid fusion scheme.

As shown in Fig. 3, in a REMCP, the segmentation mask $M(p, q)$ is first decomposed into a mask pyramid, $M_l(p, q)$, $l = 0, \ldots, L$, which is then used to supervise a region level fusion of CP, which is formulated as follows.

$$FC_l(p,q) == C_{l,M_l(p,q)}(p,q), \; l = 0,\ldots,L \tag{9}$$

where $FC_l(p, q)$ denotes the Contrast fusion result of pixel (p, q) at the lth level, $M_l(p, q)$ denotes the mask label of the lth level CP, indicating which multi-focus image should be selected for fusion at pixel (p, q).

The base image fusion is performed as

$$FG_L(p,q) = G_{L,M_L(p,q)}(p,q) \tag{10}$$

where $FG_L(p, q)$ denotes the fusion result of pixel (p, q) in the base image at l^{th} level. $G_{L,M_L(p,q)}(p,q)$ denotes the value of (p, q) of the base image. $M_L(p, q)$ denotes the label of pixel (p, q) of the original mask image, calculated by the DBRG segmentation algorithm in Sect. 2.

In the region based fusion procedure, M_{l+1} is the sub-sampling copy of M_l, therefore corresponding regions in them are strict similar figures. Consequently, most of the pixels (except the pixels that lie on region transitive zones) in the fused image are reconstructed with pixel values from the same multi-focus images, and as a result, much of the original clear information is kept reducing distortion.

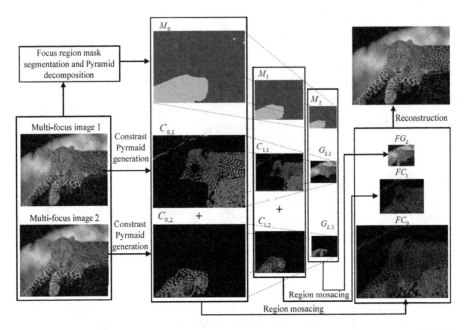

Fig. 3. Illustration of REMCP with two multi-focus images ($N = 2$) and three pyramid levels ($L = 2$). There are two CPs and two base images. The focus label mask is decomposed into a pyramid of three levels as $M_l = 0, 1, 2$. Different colors in M_0 indicate focused regions from different multi-focus images, which are to be reconstructed by fusing the Contrast Pyramids and the base images following the position relationship indicated by the mask pyramid. $C_{l,1} = 0, 1$ denotes the CP pyramid of the first image, and $C_{l,2} = 0, 1$ the second image. $G_{L,1}$ and $G_{L,2}$ denote the base images of two GPs. FC_0 and FC_1 denote the fused CPs. Symbol '+' denotes the fusion operation. (Color figure online)

When reconstructing the boundary areas, information from more than one multi-focus image is used. This is different from the process of reconstructing non-boundary areas. This may induce slight focus information loss in the transitive zones around the boundary areas, while the usage of more than one multi-focus image information guarantees the gradual transformation of a transitive zone, eliminating the block artifacts of the fused images.

Fusion results in the fused CPs ($FC_l, l = 0, ..., L$-1), the low-pass-filtered GPs, ($V_l, l = 0, ..., L$-1), and the fused base GP image, $FG_L(p, q)$, a reconstruction procedure is then carried out with

$$FG_l(p,q) = (FC_l(p,q) + U(p,q)) \times V_l(p,q), \; l = L - 1, ..., 0, \qquad (11)$$

which is derived from (5). A reconstruction starts from the base GP where $FG_L(p, q) = G_L(p, q)$. Then it iteratively calculates the GPs until FG_0 is obtained.

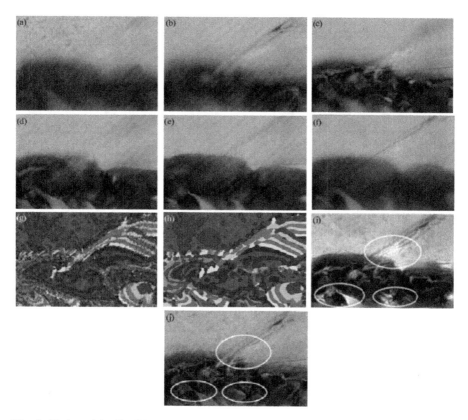

Fig. 4. Fusion of the "bee" image sequence, which contains sixty images in total. (a)–(f) are six sampled examples of the multi-focus images, (g) is the mask image with only EOF measurement, (h) is the mask image with the proposed DBRG segmentation algorithm. (i) is the fusion result of the CP method and (j) of the proposed REMCP approach. (Color figure online)

4 Experiments

Our REMCP was developed for gray image fusion. For RGB color images, the REMCP is carried out on R, G and B channels respectively. In the follows, REMCP approach is evaluated and compared with other approaches. Twelve groups of multi-focus images for quantitative evaluation are prepared. Each group has about 3–70 defocused images of depth variances and textured surfaces. On multi-focus images with ground-truth "all-in-focus" images, we use two statistical variances: root mean squared error (RMSE) and structural similarity (SSIM) [24, 25] to evaluate and compare fusion methods. In Fig. 4, an image sequence of an object with complex 3D shape is shown. The results and comparison in Fig. 4i and j show the advantage of the REMCP approach to pixel level CP approach.

In Fig. 5a and b, it can be seen that when the number of pyramid levels is 6 or 7, the RMSE and SSIM are the highest. A smaller or larger number of pyramid levels cannot take the full advantages of pyramid fusion. This shows that a proper pyramid level is

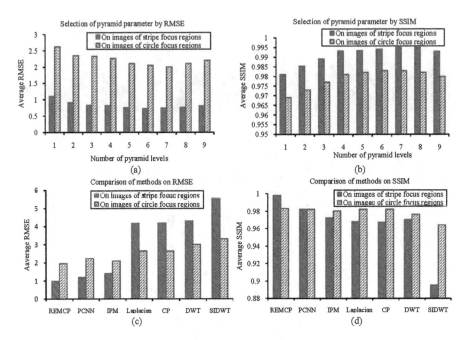

Fig. 5. (a) RMSE and (b) SSIM under different pyramid levels.(c) and (d) are comparisons of REMCP, PCNN [1], IDP [22], CP [10], Laplacian pyramid [11], DWT [7] and shift invariance DWT [26] methods.

significant to the objective quality of the fused image. In Fig. 5c and d, we compared our proposed approach with five typical methods including CP [10], Laplacian pyramid [11], DWT [7], SIDWT [26], IDP [22] and PCNN [1]. PCNN is implemented according to the descriptions in [1].

It can be seen that the RMSE of REMCP is the lowest among all compared methods, indicating its fusion error is also the smallest one. In Fig. 5f, the SSIM index of REMCP approach is the largest among compared methods, indicating that it can preserve the original information of the multi-focus images best. It can be seen in Fig. 5c and d that the proposed REMCP approach performs much better than the classical CP, Laplacian pyramid, DWT and SIDWT methods. Compared with the recently proposed PCNN approach [1] and the iterative photomontage (IDP) approach [22], the proposed REMCP also performs slightly better. This shows that the proposed REMCP approach improves the state-of-the-art. The PCNN method has a much higher computing complexity for its iterative operations, while the proposed REMP approach is much simpler and therefore much more efficient. When performing fusion, our implemented PCNN approach spends about 12.0 s on average to fuse an image of 720×480 pixels with an Intel CORE i5 CPU, while the proposed REMCP approach spends only 1.5 s. In contrast, the IDP approach that uses a graph-cut optimal algorithm to calculate focus region mask spends 2.6 s on average.

5   Conclusions

The new concepts and techniques introduced in this paper include the density-based region growing based focus region segmentation, focus mask image pyramid and the region mosaicing approach on contrast pyramid. An objective and a subjective dataset are also provided for evaluation. Experimental results and comparisons with other methods are also presented, confirming that the proposed method is capable of handling multi-focus images more accurately in various practical conditions. Experiments also show that REMCP can significantly reduce the fusion errors and color distortions as well as preserve the visual perception quality.

Acknowledgement. This work is supported by the National Science Foundation of China with Nos. 61501132, 61202455, 61472096, the Fundamental Research Funds for the Central Universities with No. HEUCFD1508, and the Heilongjiang Postdoctoral Sustentation Fund with No. LBH-Z14055, the National Science Foundation of Heilongjiang with No. F2016009

References

1. Wang, Z., Ma, Y., Gu, J.: Multi-focus image fusion using PCNN. Pattern Recogn. **43**, 2003–2016 (2010)
2. Favaro, P., Soatto, S.: Shape from defocus via diffusion. IEEE Trans. Pattern Anal. Mach. Intell. **30**, 518–531 (2008)
3. Wang, R., Xu, B., Zeng, P., Zhang, X.: Multi-focus image fusion for enhancing fiber microscopic images. Text. Res. J. **82**(4), 352–361 (2012)
4. Tsai, D.C., Chen, H.H.: Reciprocal focus profile. IEEE Trans. Image Process. **21**(2), 459–468 (2012)
5. Hariharan, R., Rajagopalan, A.N.: Shape-from-focus by tensor voting. IEEE Trans. Image Process. **21**(7), 3323–3328 (2012)
6. Peters, T., Bowyer, K.W., Flynn, P.J.: Iris recognition using signal-level fusion of frames from video. IEEE Trans. Inf. Forensics Secur. **4**(4), 837–848 (2009)
7. Pajares, G., Cruz, J.M.: A wavelet-based image fusion tutorial. Pattern Recogn. **37**, 1855–1872 (2004)
8. Tian, J., Chen, L.: Multi-focus image fusion using wavelet-domain statistics. In: 17th IEEE International Conference on Image Processing, pp. 1205–1208 (2010)
9. Petrovic, V.S., Xydeas, C.S.: Gradient-based multiresolution image fusion. IEEE Trans. Image Process. **13**, 228–237 (2004)
10. Toet, A., Van Ruyven, L.J., Valeton, J.M.: Merging thermal and visual images by a contrast pyramid. Opt. Eng. **28**(7), 287789 (1989)
11. Zhang, Z., Blum, R.S.: A categorization of multiscale-decomposition-based image fusion schemes with a performance study for a digital camera application. Proc. IEEE **87**(8), 1315–1326 (1999)
12. Toet, A.: Image fusion by a ratio of low-pass pyramid. Inf. Fusion **9**, 245–253 (1989)
13. Rockinger, O.: Image sequence fusion using a shift-invariant wavelet transform. In: International Conference on Image Processing, vol. 3, pp. 288-291 (1997)
14. Do, M.N., Vetterli, M.: The contourlet transform: an efficient directional multi-resolution image representation. IEEE Trans. Image Process. **14**(12), 2091–2106 (2005)

15. Li, S.T., Yang, B.: Multifocus image fusion by combining curve let and wavelet transform. Pattern Recogn. Lett. **29**(9), 1295–1301 (2008)
16. Li, H., Chai, Y., Li, Z.: Multi-focus Image fusion based on non-sub-sampled contour let transform and focused regions detection. Optik-Int. J. Light Electron Optics **124**, 40–51 (2013)
17. Yang, B., Li, S.T.: Multifocus image fusion and restoration with sparse representation. IEEE Trans Instrum. Measure. **59**(4), 884–892 (2010)
18. Li, H., Wei, S., Chai, Y.: Multifocus image fusion scheme based on feature contrast in the lifting stationary wavelet domain. EURASIP J. Adv. Signal Process. **2012**(1), 1–16 (2012)
19. Li, S.T., Kwok, J.T., Wang, Y.: Combination of images with diverse focuses using the spatial frequency. Inf. Fusion **2**(3), 169–176 (2001)
20. Li, S.T., Yang, B.: Multifocus image fusion using region segmentation and spatial frequency. Image Vis. Comput. **26**(7), 971–979 (2008)
21. Kubota, A., Aizawa, K.: Reconstructing arbitrarily focused images from two differently focused images using linear filters. IEEE Trans. Image Process. **14**(11), 1848–1859 (2005)
22. Agarwala, A., Dontcheva, M., Agrawala, M., Drucker, S., Colburn, A., Curless, B., Salesin, D., Cohen, M.: Interactive digital photomontage. ACM Trans. Graphics (Proceedings of SIGGRAPH 2004) **23**, 294–302 (2004)
23. Hariharan, H., Koschan, A., Abidi, M.: An adaptive focal connectivity algorithm for multifocus fusion. In: IEEE International Conference on Computer Vision and Pattern Recognition, pp. 1–6 (2007)
24. Wang, Z., Bovik, A.C., Sheikh, H.R., Simoncell, E.P.: Image quality assessment: from error visibility to structural similarity. IEEE Trans. Image Process. **13**, 600–612 (2004)
25. Goshtasby, A.A., Nikolov, S.: Image fusion: advances in the state of the art. Inform. Fusion **8**(2), 114–118 (2007)
26. Rockinger O.: Image sequence fusion using a shift-invariant wavelet transform. In: IEEE International Conference on Image Processing, pp. 288–291 (1997)

Distributed Constrained Optimization Over Cloud-Based Multi-agent Networks

Qing Ling[1]([✉]), Wei Xu[1], Manxi Wang[2], and Yongcheng Li[2]

[1] Department of Automation,
University of Science and Technology of China, Hefei, China
[2] State Key Laboratory of Complex Electromagnetic
Environment Effects on Electronics and Information System, Luoyang, China

Abstract. We consider a distributed constrained optimization problem where a group of distributed agents are interconnected via a cloud center, and collaboratively minimize a network-wide objective function subject to local and global constraints. This paper devotes to developing an efficient distributed algorithm that fully utilizes the computation abilities of the cloud center and the agents, as well as avoids extensive communications between the cloud center and the agents. We address these issues by introducing a divide-and-conquer technique, which assigns the local objective functions and constraints to the agents while the global ones to the cloud center. The resultant algorithm naturally yields two layers, the agent layer and the cloud center layer. They exchange their intermediate variables so as to collaboratively obtain a network-wide optimal solution. Numerical experiments demonstrate the effectiveness of the proposed distributed constrained optimization algorithm.

1 Introduction

This paper considers a distributed constrained optimization problem defined over a cloud-based multi-agent network. A group of n distributed agents (also called as nodes) are interconnected via a cloud center, and collaboratively minimize a network-wide objective function subject to local and global constraints. To be specific, every agent i has a local objective function $f_i(x_i)$ and a local constraint $x_i \in \mathcal{X}_i$, where $x_i \in \mathcal{R}^{p_i}$ is a local optimization variable. The network-wide objective function is defined as $\sum_{i=1}^{n} f_i(x_i) + h(x)$, with $h(x)$ being the global objective function depending on the stacked optimization variable $x \triangleq [x_1; \cdots ; x_n] \in \mathcal{R}^p$, $p = \sum_{i=1}^{n} p_i$. The network is also subject to m global constraints on the stacked optimization variable x, denoted as $g_j(x) \leq 0$, $j = 1, \cdots, m$. Therefore, the constrained optimization problem is in the form of

$$\min \quad \sum_{i=1}^{n} f_i(x_i) + h(x), \tag{1}$$
$$s.t. \quad x_i \in \mathcal{X}_i, \ i = 1, \cdots, n,$$
$$g_j(x) \leq 0, \ j = 1, \cdots, m.$$

© Springer International Publishing Switzerland 2016
Q. Yang et al. (Eds.): WASA 2016, LNCS 9798, pp. 91–102, 2016.
DOI: 10.1007/978-3-319-42836-9_9

The formulation of (1) appears in a large number of network applications. For example, every agent can be a robot and the team of cooperative robots are coordinated via a cloud center to monitor an interested area. In this setting, the local optimization variables x_i stand for the positions of the robots. The local objective functions and constraints determine the expected/feasible positions of the individual robots, while the global objective functions and constraints determine the relative orientations of all the robots [1,2]. More examples include networks of smart portable devices [3], smart grids [4,5], large-scale machine learning systems [6,7], to name a few.

One naive approach to solving (1) is letting the cloud center collect all the local objective functions and constraints, and find an optimal solution in a centralized manner. This centralized approach is costly in communication, inflexible to the changes of the network topology and the optimization task, and unreliable due to the danger of leaking local information. A favorable choice is designing distributed algorithms that offload some computation tasks to the agents. That is, every agent processes its own local objective function and constraint while the cloud center processes the global ones; the agents and the cloud center coordinate to guarantee the optimality of the solved argument. The recent works [1,2] propose dual decomposition algorithms to solve (1). However, at every iteration these two algorithms require the cloud center to collect the primal variables from all the agents, compute the dual variables and update the primal variables, and send back the dual variables and all the primal variables to all the agents. Therefore, these algorithms incur heavy communication load.

This paper devotes to developing an efficient distributed algorithm that:

- fully utilizes the computation abilities of the cloud center and the agents;
- avoids extensive communications between the cloud center and the agents.

The main difficulties in solving (1) are that the local and global objective functions are coupled in the cost, as well as that both local and global constraints appear in defining the feasible solution set. We address these issues by introducing a divide-and-conquer technique, which assigns the local objective functions and constraints to the agents while the global ones to the cloud center. The resultant algorithm naturally yields two layers, the agent layer and the cloud center layer. They exchange their intermediate variables so as to collaboratively obtain a network-wide optimal solution.

The rest of the paper is organized as follows. Section 2 develops a distributed constrained optimization algorithm. Implementation issues are discussed in Sect. 3 and numerical experiments are given in Sect. 4. Section 5 concludes the paper and gives future research directions.

2   Algorithm Development

Our main mathematical tool of solving (1) is the alternating direction method of multipliers (ADMM) that is briefly reviewed in Sect. 2.1. The distributed constrained optimization algorithm is developed in Sect. 2.2.

2.1 Brief Review of ADMM

Consider a separable optimization problem

$$\begin{align} \min \quad & c(x) + d(y), \tag{2}\\ s.t. \quad & Ax + By = 0,\\ & x \in \mathcal{X},\ y \in \mathcal{Y}. \end{align}$$

Here $c(x)$ and $d(y)$ are functions of optimization variables $x \in \mathcal{R}^p$ and $y \in \mathcal{R}^q$, respectively; $A \in \mathcal{R}^{s \times p}$ and $B \in \mathcal{R}^{s \times q}$ are two matrices; $\mathcal{X}$ and $\mathcal{Y}$ are the extra constraint sets on x and y, respectively. The two variables are entangled in the linear constraint $Ax + By = 0$, which makes solving (2) a difficult task.

The ADMM operates on the augmented Lagrangian function of (2), which is written as

$$\mathcal{L}_A(x, y, \mu) = c(x) + d(y) + \langle \mu, Ax + By \rangle + \frac{\rho}{2} \|Ax + By\|^2,\ x \in \mathcal{X},\ y \in \mathcal{Y},$$

where $\mu \in \mathcal{R}^s$ is the Lagrange multiplier and ρ is a positive constant. At every iteration, the ADMM first fixes the primal variable y and the dual variable μ, and minimizes the augmented Lagrangian function over the primal variable x. Then it fixes x and μ to minimize the augmented Lagrangian function over y. Finally, the dual variable μ is updated from x and y through a dual (sub)gradient step. At time $k + 1$, the update of x is

$$\begin{align} x^{k+1} &= \arg\min_{x \in \mathcal{X}}\ c(x) + d(y^k) + \langle \mu^k, Ax + By^k \rangle + \frac{\rho}{2} \|Ax + By^k\|^2\\ &= \arg\min_{x \in \mathcal{X}}\ c(x) + \frac{\rho}{2} \|Ax + By^k + \frac{\mu^k}{\rho}\|^2. \end{align}$$

The update of y is

$$\begin{align} y^{k+1} &= \arg\min_{y \in \mathcal{Y}}\ c(x^{k+1}) + d(y) + \langle \mu^k, Ax^{k+1} + By \rangle + \frac{\rho}{2} \|Ax^{k+1} + By\|^2\\ &= \arg\min_{y \in \mathcal{Y}}\ d(y) + \frac{\rho}{2} \|Ax^{k+1} + By + \frac{\mu^k}{\rho}\|^2. \end{align}$$

The update of μ is

$$\mu^{k+1} = \mu^k + \rho(Ax^{k+1} + By^{k+1}).$$

Notice that in this dual (sub)gradient step, the stepsize is the same as the positive constant ρ in the augmented Lagrangian function.

The idea of ADMM can be traced back to the 1970s [8]. When the objective functions $c(x)$ and $d(y)$ as well as the constraints $x \in \mathcal{X}$ and $y \in \mathcal{Y}$ are convex, convergence of the iterates to the optimal primal-dual pair is proved in [9], while its sublinear convergence rate is established in [10,11]. When the objective functions are strongly convex, the ADMM has linear convergence rate [12,13]. The fast convergence speed and the superior computational stability have made the ADMM a popular choice in a large number of applications in recent years; readers are referred to the survey paper [6].

2.2 Distributed Constrained Optimization

Observe that in (1) there is only one group optimization variables $x = [x_1; \cdots ; x_n]$. To apply the ADMM to (1), we introduce another group of auxiliary variables $y \triangleq [y_1; \cdots ; y_n] \in \mathcal{R}^p$ where $y_i \in \mathcal{R}^{p_i}$ for all i. Replacing x in $h(x)$ and all $g_j(x)$ by y and appending a consensus constraint $x = y$ yield

$$\min \quad \sum_{i=1}^{n} f_i(x_i) + h(y), \qquad (3)$$

$$s.t. \quad x - y = 0,$$

$$x_i \in \mathcal{X}_i, \ i = 1, \cdots, n,$$

$$g_j(y) \leq 0, \ j = 1, \cdots, m,$$

which is equivalent to (1). Now (3) is in the form of (2) and the ADMM is hence applicable.

Following the ADMM routine introduced in Sect. 2.1, at time $k + 1$, the update of the primal variable x is

$$x^{k+1} = \arg\min \sum_{i=1}^{n} f_i(x_i) + \frac{\rho}{2}\|x - y^k + \frac{\mu^k}{\rho}\|^2, \qquad (4)$$

$$s.t. \quad x_i \in \mathcal{X}_i, \ i = 1, \cdots, n.$$

Observe that $y \triangleq [y_1; \cdots ; y_n] \in \mathcal{R}^p$ and $\mu \triangleq [\mu_1; \cdots ; \mu_n] \in \mathcal{R}^p$ where $y_i \in \mathcal{R}^{p_i}$ and $\mu_i \in \mathcal{R}^{p_i}$ for all i. Therefore, (4) is separable with respect to all x_i. To be specific, the update of x_i is

$$x_i^{k+1} = \arg\min_{x_i \in \mathcal{X}_i} f_i(x_i) + \frac{\rho}{2}\|x_i - y_i^k + \frac{\mu_i^k}{\rho}\|^2. \qquad (5)$$

The update of the auxiliary variable y is

$$y^{k+1} = \arg\min \ h(y) + \frac{\rho}{2}\|y - x^{k+1} - \frac{\mu^k}{\rho}\|^2, \qquad (6)$$

$$s.t. \quad g_j(y) \leq 0, \ j = 1, \cdots, m.$$

The update of μ is

$$\mu^{k+1} = \mu^k + \rho(x^{k+1} - y^{k+1}). \qquad (7)$$

In the ADMM updates, (7) only involves simple arithmetic operations. Given that $\mathcal{X}_i$ is simple such that projecting onto it is computationally efficient and f_i is convex, (5) can be solved by the projected (sub)gradient method [15]. However, (6) can be nontrivial if the objective function $h(y)$ and the inequality constraint functions $g_j(y)$ are nonlinear. Below we propose to solve (6) with the dual decomposition method [16].

By introducing nonnegative Lagrange multipliers $\nu_j \in \mathcal{R}$ to the inequality constraints $g_j(y) \leq 0$, we have the Lagrangian function

$$\mathcal{L}(y, \nu) = h(y) + \frac{\rho}{2} \| y - x^{k+1} - \frac{\mu^k}{\rho} \|^2 + \sum_{j=1}^{m} \langle \nu_j, g_j(y) \rangle, \tag{8}$$

where $\nu \triangleq [\nu_1; \cdots ; \nu_m] \in \mathcal{R}_+^m$ stacks all the nonnegative Lagrange multipliers. Notice that the Lagrangian function is not augmented, since appending the squares of the nonlinear inequality constraint functions makes the function nonconvex in the primal variable y. At slot $t+1$ in the inner loop of time $k+1$, the dual decomposition method calculates y with (sub)gradient descent, followed by the update of ν from projected (sub)gradient ascent. Denoting $y^{k+1}(t+1)$ and $\nu^{k+1}(t+1)$ as the calculated values of y and μ at slot $t+1$ in the inner loop of time $k+1$, respectively, we have

$$y^{k+1}(t+1) = y^{k+1}(t) - \alpha \frac{\partial \mathcal{L}(y^{k+1}(t), \nu^{k+1}(t))}{\partial y^{k+1}(t)}, \tag{9}$$

where $\dfrac{\partial \mathcal{L}(y^{k+1}(t), \nu^{k+1}(t))}{\partial y^{k+1}(t)}$

$$= \frac{\partial h(y^{k+1}(t))}{\partial y^{k+1}(t)} + \rho y^{k+1}(t) - \rho x^{k+1} - \mu^k + \sum_{j=1}^{m} \langle \nu_j^{k+1}(t), \frac{\partial g_j(y^{k+1}(t))}{\partial y^{k+1}(t)} \rangle.$$

Here α is a positive dual decomposition stepsize; $\partial/\partial y$ is the gradient with respect to y if the function is differentiable, or a subgradient if the function is non-differentiable. For the update of ν, we have

$$\nu^{k+1}(t+1) = \left[\nu^{k+1}(t) + \alpha \frac{\partial \mathcal{L}(y^{k+1}(t+1), \nu^{k+1}(t))}{\partial \nu^{k+1}(t)} \right]_+, \tag{10}$$

where $[\cdot]_+$ denotes projection onto the nonnegative orthant. Due to the separable structure of $\mathcal{L}(y, \nu)$ with respect to all ν_j, for every j the update of (10) yields

$$\nu_j^{k+1}(t+1) = \left[\nu_j^{k+1}(t) + \alpha g_j(y^{k+1}(t+1)) \right]_+. \tag{11}$$

Remark. Given that the objective functions and the constraints in (3) – and equivalently in (1) – are convex, and the subproblems (5) and (6) are accurately solved, the iterates generated by the ADMM updates (5), (6) and (7) guarantees to converge to an optimal solution of (3) for any positive parameter ρ [9, 10]. On the other hand, the dual decomposition updates (9) and (10) also converge to an optimal solution of the convex program (6) when the stepsize α is sufficiently small [16]. The computational stability of the dual decomposition method is favorable due to the existence of the quadratic term in (6), which makes the objective function strongly convex.

3   Implementation Issues

This section discusses issues in implementing the distributed constrained optimization algorithm defined by the updates (5), (6) and (7). The algorithm is outlined in Sect. 3.1. Early termination of the inner loops defined by (9) and (10) is discussed in Sect. 3.2. Section 3.3 compares the proposed algorithm with existing works.

3.1   Algorithm Outline

The proposed distributed constrained optimization algorithm is outlined in Table 1. At time $t = 0$, the cloud center and the agents initialize the variables as $y^0 = 0$, $\mu^0 = 0$ and $x_i^0 = 0$. At time $k + 1$, every agent i updates x_i^{k+1} from (5), using the values of y_i^k and μ_i^k that are known after the communication step in Line 13. Then the cloud center collects all x_i^{k+1} from the agents and solves y^{k+1} from (6) by an inner loop with T slots. The initial values of the inner loop are $y^{k+1}(0) = y^k$ and $\nu^{k+1}(0) = 0$. The primal update of $y^{k+1}(t + 1)$ from (9) requires local variables $y^{k+1}(t)$ and μ^k as well as variables x_i^{k+1} available from the communication step in Line 4. The dual update of $\nu^{k+1}(t+1)$ in (10) requires only local variables $y^{k+1}(t + 1)$ and $\nu^{k+1}(t)$. After the inner loop, the outer-loop primal variable is $y^{k+1} = y^{k+1}(T + 1)$. Both y^{k+1} and x^{k+1} are used in calculating the dual variable μ^{k+1} from (7). Finally, y_i^{k+1} and μ_i^{k+1} are disseminated to every agent i by the cloud center.

Table 1. Distributed constrained optimization algorithm

1. Cloud center initializes $y^0 = 0$ and $\mu^0 = 0$; every agent i initializes $x_i^0 = 0$.
2. **for** $k = 0, 1, \cdots$ **do**
3.   Every agent i updates x_i^{k+1} from (5).
4.   Cloud center collects all x_i^{k+1} from agents.
5.   Cloud center solves (6) by the following inner loop.
6.   Initializes $y^{k+1}(0) = y^k$ and $\nu^{k+1}(0) = 0$.
7.   **for** $t = 0, 1, \cdots, T$ **do**
8.   Updates the primal variable $y^{k+1}(t + 1)$ from (9);
9.   Updates the dual variable $\nu^{k+1}(t + 1)$ from (10).
10.   **end for**
11.   Lets $y^{k+1} = y^{k+1}(T + 1)$.
12.   Cloud center calculates the dual variable μ^{k+1} from (7).
13.   Cloud center sends y_i^{k+1} and μ_i^{k+1} to every agent i.
14. **end for**

3.2   Early Termination of Inner Loops

As we have discussed in Sect. 2.2, the distributed constrained optimization algorithm based on the ADMM converges to the optimal solution of (3) when the subproblems (5) and (6) are exactly solved. When computing the projection on the set $\mathcal{X}_i$ is affordable in agent i, (5) can be efficiently solved by the projected (sub)gradient method. Further, if the local constraints $x_i \in \mathcal{X}^i$ is absent and the local objective function $f_i(x_i)$ has special forms (for example, the ℓ_1 and ℓ_2 norms), the resultant problem has explicit solutions.

Therefore, the main computational bottleneck of the algorithm is the inner loops of solving (6). Theoretically, the dual decomposition subroutine converges to the optimal solution of (6) only when the number of inner iterations T goes to infinity. Though the cloud center is often supposed to have strong computation power, spending a large number of iterations in the inner loops still seems to be inefficient. Fortunately, the ADMM is able to converge to the optimal solution when one subproblem is inexactly solved at every iteration, given that the inexactness is decaying fast enough [14]. Therefore, in implementing the algorithm, we set T to be a fixed small number. Numerical experiments in Sect. 4 show that the solutions of the inner loops will be more and more accurate as the outer loops evolve. We leave the theoretical analysis of the inexact version of the proposed algorithm to our future research.

3.3   Comparisons with Existing Works

The main feature of the proposed distributed consensus optimization algorithm is to utilize the divide-and-conquer technique and assign the computation to two layers, the cloud center layer and the distributed agent layer. The two layers conduct their computing tasks respectively, while collaborate to obtain the global optimal solution through information exchange. To be specific, the cloud center sends the intermediate primal variable y^{k+1} of dimension p and the dual variable μ^{k+1} of dimension p to the agents, while the agents send the intermediate primal variables x_i^{k+1} of dimension p to the cloud center. Notice that y^{k+1} is an estimate of $x = [x_1; \cdots ; x_n]$ from the cloud center's perspective. The two primal variables y^{k+1} and $x^{k+1} = [x_1^{k+1}; \cdots ; x_n^{k+1}]$ shall converge to the same optimal argument as k goes to infinity, and the role of the dual variable μ^{k+1} is to punish the gap between the two vectors. This setting results in affordable communication costs between the two layers.

A naive approach to solving the constrained optimization problem (1) is to let the cloud center collect all the local objective functions and local constraints from the agents. Apparently, this approach is costly in communication, inflexible to the changes of the network topology and the optimization task, and unreliable due to the danger of leaking local information. Contrarily, the proposed algorithm has the advantages of lightweight communication, flexibility to uncertainties, and privacy preservation.

Two notable approaches to solving the constrained optimization problem (1) are the dual decomposition algorithm proposed in [1] and the Tikhonov regularized dual decomposition algorithm proposed in [2]. The two algorithms both work on the primal-dual domain of (1) – instead, our algorithm works on the primal-dual domain of the equivalent form (3). The dual decomposition algorithm in [1] suffers from computational instability when the objective function is not strongly convex and non-differentiable. This issue is addressed in [2] by introducing Tikhonov regularization to both the primal and dual variables, at the cost of yielding a non-optimal solution. However, at every iteration these two algorithms require the cloud center to collect the primal variables from all the agents, compute the dual variables and update the primal variables, and send back the dual variables and all the primal variables to all the agents. Therefore, at every iteration the cloud center collects a p-dimensional primal variable, while sends to every agent an m-dimensional dual variable and an updated p-dimensional primal variable. In comparison, at every iteration in our algorithm, the cloud center collects a p-dimensional primal variables $x = [x_1; \cdots ; x_n]$, while sends to agent i a p_i-dimensional dual variable μ_i and another p_i-dimensional primal variable y_i. In summary, at every iteration these algorithms have the same communication load in collecting information; however, the algorithms proposed in [1,2] have a communication load $n(m+p)$ in sending information that is proportional to the number of agents n, but our algorithm has a communication load $2p$ in sending information that is irrelevant with the network size.

4   Numerical Experiments

In the numerical experiments, we adopt the same benchmark problem as given in [2]. There are eight distributed agents connected via the cloud center. Every agent i has a local decision variable $x_i \in \mathcal{R}^2$, which represents the position of the agent in a two-dimensional plane. The summation of the local objective functions is

$$\sum_{i=1}^{8} f_i(x_i) = x_{1,1}^2 + x_{1,2}^2 + (x_{2,1}+1)^2 + (x_{2,2}-1)^2 + (x_{3,1}-0.2)^2 + (x_{3,2}+0.6)^2$$
$$+ (x_{4,1}+1.4)^2 + (x_{4,2}-1.4)^2 + (x_{5,1}+0.1)^2 + (x_{5,2}-0.5)^2 + (x_{6,1}+0.7)^2$$
$$+ (x_{6,2}-0.7)^2 + (x_{7,1}-0.5)^2 + x_{7,2}-1.1 + (x_{8,1}+0.3)^2 + x_{8,2}^4,$$

where $x_i = [x_{i,1}; x_{i,2}]$ for every i. The global objective function is

$$h(x) = \frac{1}{200}\left(\|x_1 - x_4\|^2 + \|x_1 - x_8\|^2 + \|x_4 - x_8\|^2\right).$$

The agents are subject to five global distance constraints

$$g_1(x) = \|x_1 - x_2\|^2 - 0.6 \leq 0,$$
$$g_2(x) = \|x_1 - x_5\|^2 - 1.2 \leq 0,$$
$$g_3(x) = \|x_7 - x_8\|^2 - 1.8 \leq 0,$$
$$g_4(x) = \|x_1 - x_3\|^2 - 0.4 \leq 0,$$
$$g_5(x) = \|x_4 - x_6\|^2 - 0.9 \leq 0.$$

The variables are also subject to local bound constraints, which are $x_i \in \mathcal{X}_i \triangleq$ $[-1.5, 1.5] \times [-1, 1.5]$ for all the agents i.

We compare the proposed distributed constrained optimization (DCO) algorithm and the Tikhonov regularized dual decomposition (TRDD) algorithm in [2]. The parameters of TRDD are the same as those in [2]: the primal regularization constant is 0.1, the dual regularization constant is 0.1, the primal stepsize is 2.804×10^{-2}, and the dual stepsize is 9.835×10^{-4}. Our proposed DCO algorithm has three parameters: the augmented Lagrangian constant is $\rho = 1.5$, the inner-loop (sub)gradient stepsize is $\alpha = 0.3$, and the number of inner-loop slots T is adjustable, with a default value $T = 5$. The performance metric is relative error, which is defined as the distance between x^k and the optimal solution x^*.

In the first numerical experiment, we compare the performance of DCO and TRDD, as shown in Fig. 1. DCO converges quickly to the optimal solution with an accuracy of 10^{-3} within 20 iterations. As a comparison, TRDD slowly converges to a neighborhood of the optimal solution. The slow convergence is due to the small stepsize that is used to guarantee the computational stability of the dual decomposition method, while the inaccurate estimate comes from the Tikhonov regularization, which essentially yields a new problem to solve with a different optimal solution.

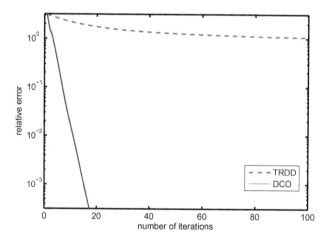

Fig. 1. Performance of the proposed distributed constrained optimization (DCO) algorithm and the Tikhonov regularized dual decomposition (TRDD) algorithm.

In the second numerical experiment, we study the influence of the number of inner-loop slots T on the convergence properties of DCO. Letting all the other parameters unaltered, we vary the value of T as 3, 5, 7, and 10. Figure 2 shows the inner-loop error, which is defined as the distance between the solved result and the optimal solution of (6). Apparently, when we spend more slots in the inner loops, the error shall become smaller. However, for any particular value of T, the error decays to zero along with the evolution of the outer loop,

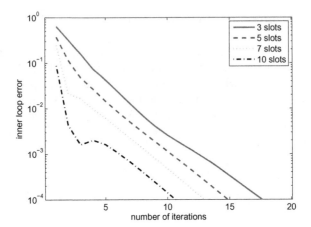

Fig. 2. Inner loop error versus the evolution of outer loop iterations in DCO, under different numbers of inner loop slots T.

which explains the exact convergence of the outer loop iterations demonstrated in Fig. 3. Interestingly, though the inner loop errors are significantly different under different values of T, the outer loop accuracies are quite close. Therefore, we suggest to choose a small value of T so as to save the computation time of solving (6) in the cloud center.

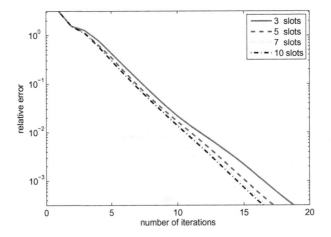

Fig. 3. Outer loop accuracy versus the evolution of outer loop iterations in DCO, under different numbers of inner loop slots T.

5   Conclusions

This paper considers a distributed constrained optimization problem where a group of distributed agents are interconnected via a cloud center, and collaboratively minimize a network-wide objective function subject to local and global constraints. Based on the ADMM, we introduce a divide-and-conquer technique and assign the local objective functions and constraints to the agents while the global ones to the cloud center. This yields a fully distributed constrained optimization algorithm with an agent layer and a cloud center layer. The two layers exchange their intermediate variables so as to collaboratively obtain a network-wide optimal solution. Effectiveness of the proposed algorithm is validated by numerical experiments.

One of our future research direction is to analyze the convergence properties of the proposed algorithm. Of particular interest to us is the effect of the inexact inner loops on the convergence rate and accuracy. Another topic is to consider the impact of communication delays, which are inevitable in the information exchange between the agents and the cloud center, on the performance of the proposed algorithm.

References

1. Hale, M., Egerstedt, M.: Cloud-based optimization: a quasi-decentralized approach to multi-agent coordination. In: Proceedings of IEEE Conference on Decision and Control (2014)
2. Hale, M., Nedich, A., Egerstedt, M.: Cloud-based centralized/decentralized multi-agent optimization with communication delays. In: Proceedings of IEEE Conference on Decision and Control (2015)
3. Armbrust, M., Fox, A., Griffith, R., Joseph, A., Katz, R., Konwinski, A., Lee, G., Patterson, D., Rabkin, A., Stoica, I., Zaharia, M.: A view of cloud computing. Commun. ACM **53**, 50–58 (2010)
4. Giannakis, G., Gatsis, N., Kekatos, V., Kim, S., Zhu, H., Wollenberg, B.: Monitoring and optimization for power systems: a signal processing perspective. IEEE Signal Process. Mag. **30**, 107–128 (2013)
5. Li, X., Scaglione, A.: Robust decentralized state estimation and tracking for power systems via network gossiping. IEEE J. Sel. Areas Commun. **31**, 1184–1194 (2013)
6. Boyd, S., Parikh, N., Chu, E., Peleato, B., Eckstein, J.: Distributed optimization and statistical learning via the alternating direction method of multipliers. Found. Trends Mach. Learn. **3**, 1–122 (2011)
7. Mokhtari, A., Koppel, A., Ribeiro, A.: Doubly random parallel stochastic methods for large scale learning. In: Proceedings of IEEE American Control Conference (2016)
8. Gabay, D., Mercier, B.: A dual algorithm for the solution of nonlinear variational problems via finite element approximation. Comput. Math. Appl. **2**, 17–40 (1976)
9. Eckstein, J., Bertsekas, D.: On the Douglas-Rachford splitting method and the proximal point algorithm for maximal monotone operators. Math. Program. **55**, 293–318 (1992)
10. He, B., Yuan, X.: On the $O(1/t)$ convergence rate of the alternating dirction method. SIAM J. Numer. Anal. **50**, 700–709 (2012)

11. Deng, W., Lai, M., Yin, W.: On the $o(1/k)$ convergence and parallelization of the alternating direction method of multipliers. Preprint at http://arxiv.org/pdf/1312.3040v2.pdf
12. Deng, W., Yin, W.: On the global and linear convergence of the generalized alternating direction method of multipliers. Preprint at http://www.optimization-online.org/DB_FILE/2012/08/3578.pdf
13. Hong, M., Luo, Z.: On the linear convergence of the alternating direction method of multipliers. Preprint at http://arxiv.org/pdf/1208.3922v3.pdf
14. Ng, M., Wang, F., Yuan, X.: Inexact alternating direction methods for image recovery. SIAM J. Sci. Comput. **33**, 1643–1668 (2011)
15. Boyd, S., Vandenberghe, L.: Convex Optimization. Cambridge University Press, New York (2004)
16. Bertsekas, D.: Nonlinear Programming, 2nd edn. Athena Scientific, Belmont (1999)

Tensor Filter: Collaborative Path Inference from GPS Snippets of Vehicles

Hongtao Wang[1,2], Hui Wen[1,2], Feng Yi[1,2], Zhi Li[1(✉)], and Limin Sun[1]

[1] Beijing Key Laboratory of IOT Information Security,
Institute of Information Engineering, CAS, Beijing 100093, China
lizhi@iie.ac.cn
[2] University of Chinese Academy of Sciences, Beijing 100093, China

Abstract. Path inference is an essential component for many location based services. In this paper, we study the problem of inferring vehicle moving paths from noisy and incomplete data captured by GPS devices mounted on vehicles. We propose a collaborative filter model to incorporate both static and dynamic context information to achieve highly accurate path inference. A tensor decomposition technique is adopted to extract context-aware spatial and temporal features from the location data with minimal a prior information about the underlying roads such as the path lengths. We evaluated our framework using a large scale real world dataset, which has one-month location data from more than eight thousand taxis in Beijing. The evaluation results show that our method outperforms state-of-the-art techniques.

1 Introduction

Smart vehicles equipped with communication modules and various types of sensors are becoming an important deployment scenario of IoT (Internet of Things) technology. Harvesting the location data collected by GPS devices installed on vehicles has been quite fruitful and a lot of new applications have been proposed. The location data collected by vehicles is often in the form of 'GPS snippets' which is defined as a set of GPS location records [12]. However, many researches such as *VANET* [5,8,9,17], location privacy preservation [7] and traffic monitoring [22], require more fine-grained path of vehicles. Thus an important problem of mining from the vehicle location data is to map the GPS snippets to physical road network, which is often referred to as *path inference* [10,14].

It is very challenging to achieve accurate path inference due to the lack of sufficient dynamic road context information. For example, a road can be *pedestrian only*, *one-way* or *two-ways* at different times of the day. Some road segments may temporarily closed but we didn't know the details. Not only traffic conditions but also driver behaviors are different and dynamic in different times.

Although dynamic context is particularly important in path inference problem, previous works often overlook such information. In this paper we propose a method to exploit information collected from a group of vehicles to collaboratively build the temporal and spatial context for path inference. The basic idea

Q. Yang et al. (Eds.): WASA 2016, LNCS 9798, pp. 103–115, 2016.
DOI: 10.1007/978-3-319-42836-9_10

of our method is to measure the temporal and spatial 'similarities' between vehicles to infer the probability of a vehicle appearing in one specific road segment at a given time slot. In other words, if we observe that a set of other vehicles are on a road segment at a given time slot, a vehicle very similar to those vehicles is likely to be on that road segment at the same time slot as well.

More specifically, let's assume the vehicle v's location at time t needs to be inferred because v's GPS measurement at t is missing from the GPS snippet data. From v's GPS snippets at t' and t'' ($t' < t < t''$), we know that v is at location $l_{t'}$ and $l_{t''}$, respectively. Furthermore, by referring to the map of road network, we know that there are a finite set of road segments (denoted by $r_1 \sim r_n$) linking point $l_{t'}$ with $l_{t''}$. In the meantime, we observe that a set of vehicles (denoted by $V_i, i \in [1, k]$) are on road segment r_i at time t, since their GPS measurements at t present in the GPS snippet data. By measuring the similarity between vehicle v and vehicles in V_i ($i \in [1, k]$), we can infer that v is on road segment r_j if v is most similar to vehicles in V_j.

The idea of collaborative path inference is straight-forward. However, it is not trivial to implement as two challenges need to be addressed properly: *how to incorporate context into path inference*; and *how to find the latent context from sparse snippets data and measure the similarity between vehicles.*

Recent advances in data mining domain, especially the collaborative filter techniques [16], have provided methods of inferring latent context from snippets data. In this paper, we propose a collaborative path inference model which take dynamic context into account. With this model, both static features and dynamic context are fitted in a unified conditional random field. We also adopt tensor decomposition [11] based collaborative filter, which automatically cluster similar items to groups by discovering latent factors from data. Under this technique, we can derive latent context without defining any similarity metrics. We have made the following contributions:

- *Unified path inference.* We incorporate both static features and dynamic context into a conditional random field. The dynamic context can to some extent overcome the problem caused by law-rate and incomplete sampling.
- *Collaborative context learning.* We use tensor decomposition technique to obtain latent context information collaboratively. To tackle the data sparsity problem in the GPS snippets dataset, we exploit several normalization terms, which are robust and can avert over-fitting.
- *Real evaluation.* We evaluate our solution using the real world dataset. Experimental results show that our solutions are effective in path inference especially under large sampling rate between GPS locations.

The rest of the paper is organized as follows. In Sect. 2, we briefly review related work. Section 3 define the path inference problem and presents our unified CRF model. We then propose a collaborative context feature learning method under tensor decomposition in Sect. 4. Finally in Sect. 5, we evaluate our solution using a large-scale dataset and make concluding discussions.

2   Related Work

The problem of mapping GPS points onto a map is first studied in [19], which uses several simple approaches to match GPS points to nearest road segments. We categorize existing methods into two class: deterministic and probabilistic. Deterministic approaches associate each observation to a segment in road network. They utilize geometric information of road network by considering the shape of the roads [4], or the connectivity and contiguity information [20]. In [2], frèchet distance is used to match partial trajectories to road segments. All those algorithms are very fast, however, they are sensitive to noisy GPS observations.

To overcome the uncertainty of observations, many probabilistic algorithms have been proposed by adopting the idea of particle filter [6], Kalman filter [13] and Interactive-Voting [21]. Under the assumption of *Markov* independence relations, Hidden Markov Model (HMM) [14] and Conditional Random Fields (CRF) [10] have been explored in inferring paths vehicle passed. Both HMM and CRF need to utilize various features for designing the transition probability of states, which encourage the weight learning algorithm using inverse reinforcement learning [15]. However, these algorithms show that the performance is poor when the intervals of GPS observations exceed 5 min [14].

One of the problems of HMM and CRF is that they use context-unaware features when computing the transition probability. These features could not reflect the real traffic condition spatially and temporally. In this paper, we introduce the collaborative method [16] to extract context-aware features from observations. Two influential collaborative filter techniques are matrix factorization and tensor decomposition [11], which have become increasingly popular recently. Tensor decomposition is adopted to process mobile network data for a number of data mining tasks, such as travel time estimation [18], demographic attributes inference [23], and link pattern prediction [3], to name a few. This paper focus on solving the path inference problem under noise and incomplete GPS snippets using tensor decomposition techniques.

3   Probabilistic Path Inference Model

In this section, we firstly define concepts and the problem used in this paper. Then we propose a CRF based model to incorporate both static road features and dynamic context features. Figure 1 shows an example to explain related concepts.

3.1   Problem Definition

We firstly introduce related concepts in this subsection.

GPS Observation and Snippet. A real data set contains millions of GPS measurements, which can be organized by vehicles within a time slots $[1, T]$. A GPS observation g is represented as a triple: $(latitude, longitude, timestamp)$.

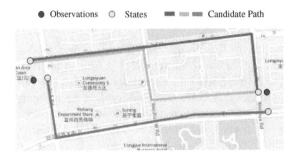

Fig. 1. An example to illustrate concepts (Color figure online)

For a given vehicle, we denote a GPS snippet with n observations as $G = \{g^1, g^2, \cdots, g^n\}$.

State. Due to the inaccuracy in GPS measurements, state $x = (l, o)$ is a projection of observation g to a road segment l, where o is the offset of projection from the start node of l. As one observation g^t can be projected to a number of roads, we can get I^t different candidate states $\mathbf{x}^t = \{x_1^t, x_2^t, \cdots, x_{I^t}^t\}$.

Trajectory. Between two adjacent states $x_i^t \in \mathbf{x}^t$ and $x_{i'}^{t+1} \in \mathbf{x}^{t+1}$, only a small number J^t of paths can be taken by a vehicle. We denote the set of candidate paths between two consecutive observations g^t and g^{t+1} as $\mathbf{p}^t = \{p_1^t, p_2^t, \cdots, p_{J^t}^t\}$. Then a *trajectory* is a sequence of latent states and paths, starting and ending with a state, denoted as $\tau = x^1 p^1 x^2 p^2 \cdots p_{t-1} x_t$, where x^i and p^i are element of $\mathbf{x}^i$ and $\mathbf{p}^i$ respectively. We denote the trajectory space as $\mathcal{T}$, whose dimensions are $I^1 \times J^1 \times I^2 \times J^2 \cdots J^{t-1} \times I^t$.

Finally, the path inference problem then can be defined as:

Given the raw GPS snippets G, Path Inference aims to find the most likely trajectories τ^* in the trajectory space $\mathcal{T}$ for the vehicle with G.

3.2 Unified Inference Model

We build a CRF model to encapsulate both observed and unobserved variables, as shown in Fig. 2. For a specific vehicle, given a sequence of observations $g^{1:T} = g^1, \cdots, g^T$ and an associated trajectory $\tau = x^1 p^1 \cdots x^T$, the most likely trajectory can be inferred by

$$\tau^* = \underset{\tau}{\operatorname{argmax}} \, \pi(\tau | g^{1:T}) \qquad (1)$$

where $\pi(\cdot)$ represents the conditional probability of trajectory τ. $\pi(\cdot)$ consists of multiplications of potential functions over cliques in the graph. For more details of potential functions, please refer to [10]. One of the potential functions in $\pi(\cdot)$ is driver model $\eta(p)$. $\eta(p)$ assigns a weight to any possible path p in latent path variable $\mathbf{p}^i$. We consider the driver model to be an exponential function defined as

$$\eta(p) \propto \exp\left(\mu_1 \phi(p) + \mu_2 \varphi(p)\right) \qquad (2)$$

Where ϕ, φ are static and dynamic feature functions respectively. μ_1 and μ_2 are parameters.

Previous works [10,14] usually use static feature function ϕ with static features such as the length of road segments, the turns of a path, the speed limit of roads, etc. There are two problems in using static features. First, it may be difficult to get those features. Second, those features are context-unaware, making the probabilistic inference not reliable especially on large sampling intervals. Unlike these works, we add dynamic feature function φ in Eq. (2) such that both static features and dynamic context features can be utilized.

Once we determine the feature functions ϕ and φ, the potential function $\pi(\cdot)$ is defined. Then Eq. (1) can be optimized by a standard *Viterbi* algorithm [10]. We omit the details of the algorithm. We next show how dynamic context features are extracted and how we define dynamic feature function in next section.

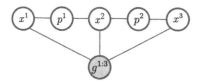

Fig. 2. A CRF model with 3 observations

4   Collaborative Tensor Filter

Previous section has proposed a unified CRF model to incorporate both static and dynamic features. In this section, we first introduce Tensor Filter, a collaborative dynamic feature learning model. Then we propose an effective algorithm to optimize the objective for tensor decomposition. Finally we extract the context-aware features into our unified CRF path inference model.

4.1   Tensor Construction

We firstly illustrate the key idea of collaborative feature learning model. To start with, note that most vehicles are influenced by traffic conditions spatially and temporally. We believe that a vehicle's appearance is determined by some latent factors not only from the vehicle's routine behavior, but also from the road traffic conditions and time slots. Vehicles may select different paths according to the road context at different time.

Based on this intuition, we exploit a large number of vehicles GPS snippets to reveal latent factors of road segments, time and vehicles in a collaborative way. Unlike using matrix, we propose a tensor filter, which converts the GPS raw data into a three-order tensor $\mathcal{A}$ to represent the relationship between road segments, time and vehicles. Specifically, we first assign a unique index to all vehicles, roads and time slots. Then we fill the tensor $\mathcal{A}$ by values under rules: (i) an entry (i, j, k) is set to 1 if a vehicle i appeared in road segment j at time slot k, and (ii) the value is set to 0 otherwise. The rest entries are missing and thus the original tensor $\mathcal{A}$ is incomplete.

The reason we assign 0 or 1 to an entry is that we consider the value of entry (i, j, k) to be the probability of vehicle i appears in road j at time slot k. Under the latent factors, the missing value of $\mathcal{A}$ can be assigned a probability between 0 and 1. As shown in Fig. 3, the original tensor is sparse and a complemented tensor is derived by a tensor decomposition procedure.

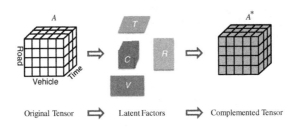

Original Tensor ⇨ Latent Factors ⇨ Complemented Tensor

Fig. 3. Tensor decomposition

4.2   Tensor Decomposition with Regularization

To get the latent factors and complement the missing values, we conduct a tensor decomposition method as well as dealing with the data sparse problem. Assume the original three-order tensor $\mathcal{A} \in \mathbb{R}^{I_1 \times I_2 \times I_3}$, where I_1, I_2 and I_3 are the number of vehicles, roads and time slots respectively. We assign random initial value between 0 and 1 to all the missing entries of $\mathcal{A}$ and latent matrices. Then $\mathcal{A}$ can be factorized by minimizing the objective function below

$$\mathcal{L}(C, V, R, T) = \frac{1}{2} \parallel \mathcal{A} - C \times_V V \times_R R \times_T T \parallel^2 + \mathcal{R}_1 + \mathcal{R}_2 \qquad (3)$$

where $C \in \mathbb{R}^{d_V \times d_R \times d_T}$ is the core tensor reflecting the link between vehicles, roads and time slots. $V \in \mathbb{R}^{I_1 \times d_V}, R \in \mathbb{R}^{I_2 \times d_R}, T \in \mathbb{R}^{I_3 \times d_T}$ are three latent factor matrices representing the low dimensional structure of vehicles, roads and time slots respectively. $\parallel \cdot \parallel^2$ denote the $\mathcal{L}_2$ norm. The symbol $\times_R$ is introduced to tensor-matrix multiplication, and the subscript R indicates the direction of multiplication. $\mathcal{R}_1$ and $\mathcal{R}_2$ are regularizations.

To deal with data sparseness, reasonable regularizations need to be considered for Eq. (3). We introduce the widely used $\mathcal{L}_2$ norm on all latent factor matrices, which encourage the values of factor matrices decay to zero unless supported by data:

$$\mathcal{R}_1(C, V, R, T) = \frac{1}{2} \left(\parallel C \parallel^2 + \parallel V \parallel^2 + \parallel R \parallel^2 + \parallel T \parallel^2 \right) \qquad (4)$$

In addition, we notice the observation that adjacent road segments always experience similar traffic conditions. Under this observation, a vehicle which appeared in road r at time t, would be likely to appear in the neighbors of r at next time slot $t + 1$. Thus we normalize the topology of road network as a regularization term denoted by

$$\mathcal{R}_2(C, V, R, T) = \frac{1}{2} \sum_{r_i \sim r_j} \| R_i - R_j \|^2 \tag{5}$$

where $r_i \sim r_j$ means road segments r_i and r_j are linked directly.

As Eq. (3) is non-convex and there is no closed-form solution, we adopt a gradient descent method to compute a local optimum. The details are shown in Algorithm 1.

Algorithm 1. Tensor Decomposition Procedure

Input: tensor $\mathcal{A}$ and an error threshold ϵ
Output: core tensor C, latent factor matrices V,R,T
1: Initialize C,V,R,T with small values between 0 and 1
2: **while** loss$> \epsilon$ **do**
3:     **for** $\mathcal{A}_{ijk} \neq 0$ **do**
4:         Update C,V_{i*},R_{j*},T_{k*}
5:     **end for**
6:     loss $\leftarrow$ norm($\mathcal{A},C,V,R,T$)
7: **end while**
8: **return** C,V,R,T

In Algorithm 1, line 4 update the initial values to the new one that towards the direction of gradient descent. We can easily compute the derivatives of $\mathcal{F}$ with respect to C,V,R and T. Note that from line 3, we use an element-wise estimation instead of a batch gradient descent for efficiency [18]. The *norm* function from line 6 calculate the $\mathcal{L}_2$ norm, denoted by the loss, of original tensor $\mathcal{A}$ and the new updated tensor. The procedure stops unless the loss exceed the threshold ϵ. Moreover, in every iteration of the procedure, tensor-matrix and tensor-vector multiplications are needed for computing intermediate tensors and we use an open tensor toolbox [1] to get the results.

4.3   Dynamic Feature Extraction

From tensor decomposition, latent factor matrices are derived. We can not directly use these matrices to infer path as it could not reflect vehicle's driver preference. Instead we utilize the complemented tensor $\mathcal{A}^* = C \times_V V \times_R R \times_T T$, whose entry (i, j, k) are the probability that vehicle i may pass segment j at time slot k.

For vehicle i, let a possible trajectory $\tau = x^1 p^1 \cdots x^T, p^k \in \tau$, and k is time slot index. We denote by $p^k = r_1^k | r_2^k | \cdots | r_n^k$ where r_i^k is the ith segment composing the path p^k. We define the context-aware feature function of p^k as

$$\varphi(p^k) = \frac{1}{N} \prod_{r_j^k \in p^k} \mathcal{A}_{ijk}^* \tag{6}$$

where N is the normalization term. In fact, $\varphi(p^k)$ in Eq. (6) can be expressed by the probability that vehicle i appeared in path p^k at time slot k. Take Eq. (6) to Eq. (2), we derive a collaborative method for path inference problem. Using dynamic programming algorithm like Viterbi, which is presented in detail by [10], the most likely path τ^* can be fixed effectively.

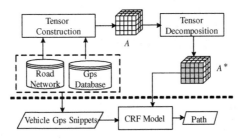

Fig. 4. Overview of our framework

4.4   System Framework

Figure 4 shows the framework of Tensor Filter. We separate the path inference process into two phases. In the first phase, road network and raw GPS measurements are filled into a three order tensor $\mathcal{A}$. Note that $\mathcal{A}$ is a sparse tensor. To deal with data sparseness, reasonable regularization terms are added to run the tensor decomposition procedure. After tensor decomposition, the latent factor matrices are extracted to construct a integrated tensor $\mathcal{A}^*$. In the second phase, context-aware features are computed from the complemented tensor into a CRF model, as well as the specific vehicles, to run the path inference algorithm.

5   Experiments

Our experiments consist of three parts: (1) experimental settings including the data set and experimental environment; (2) baselines and evaluation metrics which are used to evaluate the performance; and (3) the results and discussion of our proposed method.

5.1   Settings

We use a benchmark GPS dataset, the 2009 Beijing Taxi Cab dataset which collected GPS data from 8602 taxi cabs in Beijing, China, during one month period in May, 2009. The sampling intervals of these trajectories are 30 s and 1 min. However, for many reasons many trajectories have non-uniform intervals ranging from 30 s to 10 min. The distribution of intervals and trajectory coverage are shown in [21].

In the map data, there are more than 226,000 road segments in the whole Beijing area. We separate Beijing into several rectangle sub area and fix two area as our test regions, where each region is a 10×10 miles rectangle. We filter trajectories by the selected regions and by time between 8am to 10am. After that, the number of road segments and time slots are fixed to 500 and 120 respectively. If we want to reconstruct the whole path for vehicles which have run across several rectangles, it is not complex connecting the sub paths to a complete inferred path.

Our implemented algorithm run on a desktop machine with Intel Core I5-3380 2.90 GHz dual core CPU. It would cost about 5 min to carry out the tensor decomposition and once the context features are computed, the cost time of inference often take 2–5 min for all trajectories in our test set, each of them taking several seconds.

5.2   Evaluation Approach

We firstly clean the map data by removing and merging some neighboring road segments to construct an undirected road network for each selected region. Then we pick out vehicles which have GPS measurements in those region to build a GPS snippets database. We divide the GPS snippets into two subsets: a training set that all trajectories are sampled within 1 min, and another test set for testing. The test set have non-uniform intervals and we have manually labeled the ground truth for them. In our model, both training trajectories and test trajectories are used to construct the tensor. We will test the effects by adjusting the proportion of training trajectories versus test trajectories in Subsect. 5.3.

We evaluate the performance of tensor filter by three typical metrics: *error*, *precision* and *recall*. The error is defined as the route mismatched fraction, which refers to the ratio of the number of different segments both in inferred path τ and in the true path P, against the total number of the true path in P. The precision of a path τ refers to the ratio of the number of true segments in τ against the total number of all road segments in τ. While the recall refers to the ratio of the number of true road segments in τ against the total number of true road segments P.

We use previous static CRF (SCRF) model and HMM model for path inference as baseline algorithms, both adopting the length of road segment as feature for feature function. For our tensor filter, we set λ_1 and λ_2 to 0.01 for Eq. (3). Next we fix the value of dimensions of latent matrices as $d_V = d_T = d_R = 10$. For Eq. (6) we set N to be the number of road segments a trajectory have. In the end, we adjust parameters μ_1 and μ_2 in Eq. (1) to get the best performance.

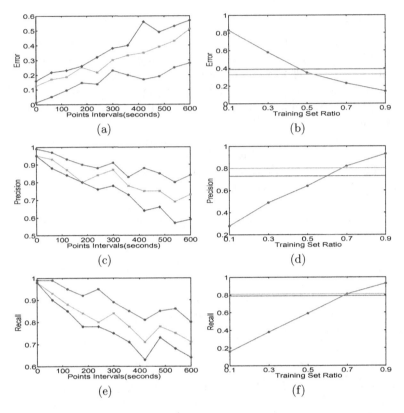

Fig. 5. Experimental results. (The blue line, the bluish yellow line and the red line represent the results of Tensor Filter, SCRF and HMM respectively.) (Color figure online)

5.3   Results

As the ratio of trajectories in training set can severely effect the result of experiments, we first fixed ratio to 90 % by selecting 450 trajectories in training set and 50 trajectories in test set. We use 5 round cross validations to get the average of results. Figure 5(a)(c)(e) shows that as the intervals between two observations grows, the performance of both methods reduce. But our tensor filter outperforms two other methods by all metrics. In detail, we can see that when intervals are lower than 2 min, the error can be within 90 % while other methods can only achieve 80 %. Both precision and recall are more than 95 % for our method, outperforming SCRF and HMM. But the difference is small for three methods, which represents that the performance is influenced slightly by methods, as the higher sampling rate of GPS measurements, the higher entropy they have. However, when intervals are increasing to more than 300 s, our tensor filter greatly outperforms others because it has considered the context spatially and temporally. Even the intervals are 10 min, the error is lower than 30 %, and the precision and recall are higher than 80 % for our tensor filter. Note that if more features are used for training SCRF or HMM, they can have a better performance than depicted by Fig. 5. However, our tensor filter use context features automatically extracted from observations, with none of other redundant features needed.

We next evaluate the performance by changing the number of trajectories in training set. As the trajectories in training set have small intervals, generally 30 or 60 s, it would affect the results of our tensor filter deeply. But they have no effect to the baseline, as shown in Fig. 5(b)(d)(f) where both the HMM and SCRF are a horizonal line. We can see that when training set ratio decrease, the error grows greatly to 80 % as well as the precision and recall dropping to 0.2. When training set ratio is lower than 0.7, the precision and recall of our method could be worse than the baseline. However, if the training set ratio is larger than 0.7, our method performs better. That's because with the 'help' of more high-sampling trajectories in training set, the collaboration of all vehicles could do better for discovering the latent factors.

6   Conclusion

In this paper, we develop a model, Tensor Filter, for collaborative path infer-ence from large GPS snippets data. Unlike previous works which overlook road context, Tensor Filter can incorporate both static features and dynamic con-text features into a unified model, based on conditional random field. To learn the latent context features, we design a tensor factorization algorithm with rea-sonable regularization. In view of real-world experimental results, we discovered that road context can help improve the precision of path inference tasks, and our tensor filter outperforms state-of-the-art methods. We believe that our work will not only advance the research on path inference in mobile data mining, but also benefit many real-world location-based applications.

Acknowledgments. This work was supported in part by the National Natural Sci-ence Foundation of China (Grant No. U1536107), Xinjiang Uygur Autonomous Region Science and Technology Project (Grant No. Y3V0021402), and the "Strategic Priority Research Program" of the Chinese Academy of Sciences (Grant No. XDA06040101).

References

1. Bader, B.W., Kolda, T.G., et al.: Matlab tensor toolbox version 2.6, February 2013. http://www.sandia.gov/~tgkolda/TensorToolbox/
2. Brakatsoulas, S., Pfoser, D., Salas, R., Wenk, C.: On map-matching vehicle tracking data. In: Proceedings of the 31st International Conference on Very Large Data Bases, VLDB 2005 (2005)
3. Gao, S., Denoyer, L., Gallinari, P.: Link pattern prediction with tensor decom-position in multi-relational networks. In: Proceedings of the IEEE Symposium on Computational Intelligence and Data Mining, CIDM 2011, pp. 333–340
4. Greenfeld, J.S.: Matching gps observations to locations on a digital map. In: Trans-portation Research Board 81st Annual Meeting (2002)

5. Guan, X., Huang, Y., Cai, Z., Ohtsuki, T.: Intersection-based forwarding protocol for vehicular ad hoc networks. Telecommun. Syst. **62**(1), 67–76 (2016)
6. Gustafsson, F., Gunnarsson, F., Bergman, N., Forssell, U., Jansson, J., Karlsson, R., Nordlund, P.: Particle filters for positioning, navigation, and tracking. IEEE Trans. Signal Process. **50**(2), 425–437 (2002)
7. He, Y., Sun, L., Li, Z., Li, H., Cheng, X.: An optimal privacy-preserving mechanism for crowdsourced traffic monitoring. In: 10th ACM International Workshop on Foundations of Mobile Computing, FOMC 2014, pp. 11–18 (2014)
8. Huang, Y., Chen, M., Cai, Z., Guan, X., Ohtsuki, T., Zhang, Y.: Graph theory based capacity analysis for vehicular ad hoc networks. In: 2015 IEEE Global Communications Conference, GLOBECOM 2015, pp. 1–5 (2015)
9. Huang, Y., Guan, X., Cai, Z., Ohtsuki, T.: Multicast capacity analysis for social-proximity urban bus assisted vanets. In: Proceedings of IEEE International Conference on Communications, ICC 2013, pp. 6138–6142 (2013)
10. Hunter, T., Abbeel, P., Bayen, A.: The path inference filter: model-based low-latency map matching of probe vehicle data. IEEE Trans. Intell. Transp. Syst. **15**(2), 507–529 (2014)
11. Karatzoglou, A., Amatriain, X., Baltrunas, L., Oliver, N.: Multiverse recommendation: n-dimensional tensor factorization for context-aware collaborative filtering. In: Proceedings of the 2010 ACM Conference on Recommender Systems, RecSys 2010, pp. 79–86 (2010)
12. Li, M., Ahmed, A., Smola, A.J.: Inferring movement trajectories from GPS snippets. In: Proceedings of the Eighth ACM International Conference on Web Search and Data Mining, WSDM 2015 (2015)
13. Najjar, M.E.E., Bonnifait, P.: A road-matching method for precise vehicle localization using belief theory and kalman filtering. Auton. Robots **19**(2), 173–191 (2005)
14. Newson, P., Krumm, J.: Hidden markov map matching through noise and sparseness. In: 17th ACM SIGSPATIAL International Symposium on Advances in Geographic Information Systems, ACM-GIS 2009, pp. 336–343 (2009)
15. Osogami, T., Raymond, R.: Map matching with inverse reinforcement learning. In: Proceedings of the 23rd International Joint Conference on Artificial Intelligence, IJCAI 2013 (2013)
16. Su, X., Khoshgoftaar, T.M.: A survey of collaborative filtering techniques. Adv. Artif. Intellegence **2009**, 1–19 (2009)
17. Wang, X., Guo, L., Ai, C., Li, J., Cai, Z.: An urban area-oriented traffic information query strategy in VANETs. In: Ren, K., Liu, X., Liang, W., Xu, M., Jia, X., Xing, K. (eds.) WASA 2013. LNCS, vol. 7992, pp. 313–324. Springer, Heidelberg (2013)
18. Wang, Y., Zheng, Y., Xue, Y.: Travel time estimation of a path using sparse trajectories. In: The 20th ACM SIGKDD International Conference on Knowledge Discovery and Data Mining, KDD 2014 (2014)
19. White, C.E., Bernstein, D., Kornhauser, A.L.: Some map matching algorithms for personal navigation assistants. Transp. Res. Part C Emerg. Technol. **8**(1–C6), 91–108 (2000)
20. Yin, H., Wolfson, O.: A weight-based map matching method in moving objects databases. In: Proceedings of the 16th International Conference on Scientific and Statistical Database Management, SSDBM 2004, pp. 437–438 (2004)
21. Yuan, J., Zheng, Y., Zhang, C., Xie, X., Sun, G.: An interactive-voting based map matching algorithm. In: Eleventh International Conference on Mobile Data Management, MDM 2010 (2010)

22. Zheng, X., Cai, Z., Li, J., Gao, H.: An application-aware scheduling policy for real-time traffic. In: 35th IEEE International Conference on Distributed Computing Systems, ICDCS 2015, pp. 421–430 (2015)
23. Zhong, Y., Yuan, N.J., Zhong, W., Zhang, F., Xie, X.: You are where you go: inferring demographic attributes from location check-ins. In: Proceedings of the Eighth ACM International Conference on Web Search and Data Mining, WSDM 2015, pp. 295–304 (2015)

NFC Secure Payment and Verification Scheme for Mobile Payment

Kai Fan[1(✉)], Panfei Song[1], Zhao Du[1], Haojin Zhu[2], Hui Li[1],
Yintang Yang[3], Xinghua Li[1], and Chao Yang[1]

[1] State Key Laboratory of Integrated Service Networks, Xidian University,
Xi'an 710071, China
{kfan,lihui,xhli,chaoyang}@mail.xidian.edu.cn,
jarvan_song@sina.com, 734324582@qq.com
[2] Department of Computer Science and Engineering,
Shanghai Jiao Tong University, Shanghai 200240, China
zhu-hj@cs.sjtu.edu.cn
[3] Key Laboratory of Ministry of Education for Wide Band-Gap Semicon.
Materials and Devices, Xidian University, Xi'an 710071, China
ytyang@xidian.edu.cn

Abstract. As one of the most important techniques in IoT, NFC (Near Field Communication) is more interested than ever. NFC is a short-range, high-frequency communication technology well suited for electronic tickets, micro-payment and access control function, which is widely used in the financial industry, traffic transport, road ban control and other fields. However, NFC is becoming increasingly popular in the relevant field, but its secure problems, such as man-in-the-middle-attack, brute force attack and so on, have hindered its further development. To address the security problems and specific application scenarios, we propose a NFC mobile electronic ticket secure payment and verification scheme in the paper. The proposed scheme uses a CS E-Ticket and offline session key generation and distribution technology to prevent major attacks and increase the security of NFC. As a result, the proposed scheme can not only be a good alternative to mobile e-ticket system but also be used in many NFC fields. Furthermore, compared with other existing schemes, the proposed scheme provides a higher security.

Keywords: NFC · Electronic ticket · Verification · Mobile payment · Security

1 Introduction

IoT [1] consists on various information sensing devices and the Internet. As a short-range, high-frequency communication technology, NFC (Near Field Communication) is one of the core technologies of IoT. It is listed as one of the most promising technology.

NFC is a development and breakthroughs of the RFID [2] technology. Compared with traditional identification technology, it can not only provide simple and fast secure wireless connection but also has a good compatibility and low power consumption characteristic. Because it's communication distance is less than 10 cm and it has a

© Springer International Publishing Switzerland 2016
Q. Yang et al. (Eds.): WASA 2016, LNCS 9798, pp. 116–125, 2016.
DOI: 10.1007/978-3-319-42836-9_11

secure element for storing data (SE), NFC has a higher secure performance and can be applicable to the payment and verification field which needs a higher security demand such as electronic train ticket, electronic movie ticket and other fields [3]. Though it has lots of advantages, NFC faces many secure problems. Especially in the open wireless communication environment [4, 5], the information exchange between the device and the device will make it easier to suffer any kinds of secure attacks, such as man-in-the-middle attack, brute force attack and so on, which will lead to disclosure of user privacy. These secure problems have become one of the bottlenecks NFC to promote development.

On the current research status, researchers at home and abroad don't put forward a universal applicability scheme. In NFC mutual authentication phase, Yun-Seok et al. [6] propose a scheme that uses the asymmetric encryption and hash function to try to eliminate the secure and privacy thread. Although the solution can solve the problem of mutual authentication and prevent replay attack and the man-in-the-middle attack, it lacks some necessary secure attributes, such as the message authentication. Ceipidor et al. [7] propose a scheme which uses the symmetric encryption. This scheme implements the mutual authentication between the NFC mobile device and mobile POS device, but it can't guarantee the integrity of the message.

In recent years, with the application field of electronic ticket become wider and wider, secure and privacy problems that exist in ticket purchase and verification process are paid attention to more people. In the purchase process, Ceipidor et al. [8] put forward a scheme using symmetric encryption, asymmetric encryption, calibration values and other technology. For the possible secure problems in the purchase ticket process, this solution is able to achieve mutual authentication, message integrity function and resist the man-in-the-middle attack to some extent. However, because of using the fixed symmetric key encryption, this scheme not only increases the complexity that mobile devices purchase tickets on the internet but also leads to the secure performance reduced greatly. Furthermore, the solution can't cope with "spike refund" malicious ticket transactions behavior.

Meanwhile, in the verification process, some scholars believe that we can use infrastructure treatment scheme that is based on PKI system, the solution adopts asymmetric public key way to generate a digital signature. E-ticket holders and mobile verification devices can ensure its security through the random number verification mode under the PKI system. But this solution needs very complex calculation, and can't achieve necessary secure attributes. At the same time, there are many other shortcomings, for example the poor user experience and ticket clone issue, so the solution can't solve secure and privacy thread in the verification process. In order to better promote the NFC technology, a scheme is needed to be proposed to solve the secure and privacy thread.

Therefore, in this paper we propose a new NFC mobile electronic ticket payment and verification system. Compared with the old NFC system, this system not only solves problems exist in purchase and verification process of e-ticket but also designs a CS E-Ticket, making entire system resist stronger attack with greater security.

The rest of this paper is organized as follows. In Sect. 2, the NFC mobile electronic ticket system is provided including scheme structure, CS E-Ticket, CS E-Ticket secure payment and verification schemes. In Sect. 3, the performance analysis of the system is evaluated in terms of security and practicality. Finally, concluding remarks are provided.

2   NFC Mobile Electronic Ticket System

In this section, in order to better describe the system which we proposed, we will introduce it from the scheme structure, CS E-Ticket, CS E-Ticket secure payment and verification schemes.

2.1   Scheme Structure

The system consists of server, mobile device, mobile POS terminals and mobile verification terminals. There are four stages: registration, booking, purchase and verification. The communication in e-ticket registration and booking process is done in a wireless way. In order to make the whole system more convenient and secure, the communication between mobile devices will be done via the NFC. Structure of the proposed scheme is shown in Fig. 1.

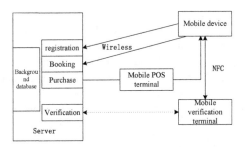

Fig. 1. Scheme structure

(1) **Registration**: The user signs up to an online service. Server will store user's personal information, user's bank information and sensitive information into its own database. Sensitive information includes the serial number of mobile device secure element (IC) and shared key (K_0, DK, m) that K_0 is initial key, DK is distribution key and m is random number. Later both user mobile device and Server can create a set of session key, SK_{MD-Sj}, $j = 1, 2, ..., m$, by using the key generation technology.

(2) **Booking**: User will use mobile device to book tickets on the ticket platform which service providers provide.

(3) **Purchase**: After booking process is finished, the user will use mobile device to complete payment operation via the mobile POS device. Later the mobile device will get e-ticket information. The communication between Server and mobile POS terminal is realized by wireless way.

(4) **Verification**: The mobile verification terminal can communication with the user mobile device by NFC and easily verify the validity of the e-ticket stored in mobile device.

2.2   CS E-Ticket

This CS E-Ticket consists of the context part and secure part [9]. The context part mainly consists of some ticket certification information that ticket providers provide. The secure part mainly includes some confidential information.

As shown in Fig. 2, the content part of ticket has title, location, seat number, time and Mark. Among them, the Mark is used to indicate whether or not the ticket has been locked. The secure part contains of ID_{ticket}, $ID_{company}$, IC, and R. ID_{ticket} is one time certification for ticket, IC is a serial number. IC is unique number built in the SE IC that can't be modified or erased. $ID_{company}$ represents service provider. R denotes a random number of tickets for each transaction.

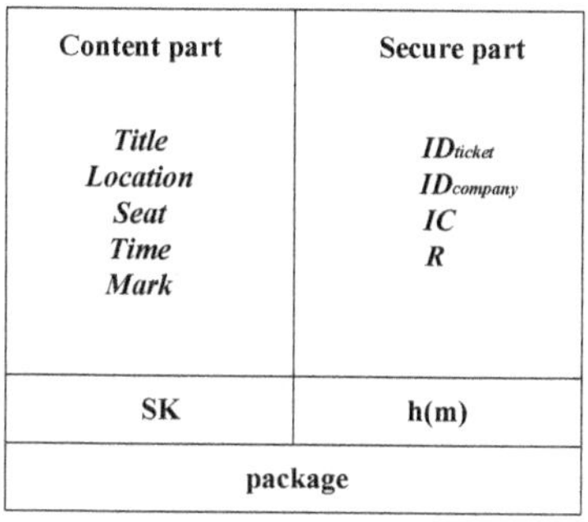

Content part	Secure part
Title Location Seat Time Mark	ID_{ticket} $ID_{company}$ IC R
SK	h(m)
package	

Fig. 2. CS E-ticket

The content part is encrypted by symmetric key. The secure party is stored by using the calculated hash values. The CS E-Ticket style could be various depends on the service providers, take bus ticket for example, it might not have the seat information. Finally, the CS E-Ticket providers will package the context and secure part of ticket which has been encrypted.

This scheme clearly classifies the ticket information. On the one hand it uses symmetric encryption encrypt the content part to prevent information leakage, on the other hand it adopts hash values to keep the ticket information confidential, making CS E-Ticket has stronger security.

2.3   CS E-Ticket NFC Payment Scheme

In this section, there are three entities involved in our payment scheme: the Mobile Device (MD from now on), the Mobile POS terminal (MD_{POS} from now on), and the Server (S from now on). Description of symbols used in the program is shown in Table 1.

The user holds mobile device (MD) containing the necessary data information to achieve the certification of MD_{POS}. MD_{POS} is responsible of the transaction process. The server as a trusted third party shares symmetric key and each entry ID with MD.

Table 1. The Explanation of symbols

Symbol	Description	Symbol	Description
SE	Security Element	$P1, P2$	The content part and secure part of CS E-Ticket
MD	User mobile device	$\{m\}SK$	The message m encrypted by the key SK
MD_{POS}	Mobile POS device	$h(m)$	The hash of the message m
ID_{MD}	User mobile device id	$S1, S2$	The number of times purchase and refund with a certain time
n	Random number	SK_{MD-Sj}	Shared session key between MD and Server
O	Payment information	$\{h(m)\}SK$	The hash of the message m encrypted by key SK

All communication between MD and MD_{POS} is done via NFC. The communication between the Server and MD_{POS} is done via the wireless communication which is based on the wireless secure transport layer protocol (WTLS). Both sides of communication transfer payment information, key information and entry id information in a safe way.

When session key needs to be updated, we can take the offline session key generation technology [10] to update the session key.

In order to start the payment process, user has to move MD closer the RF field of the MD_{POS} by using NFC multimodal features. Considering the e-ticket information security, we can store e-ticket information in NFC SE. Specific steps are as follows in Fig. 3.

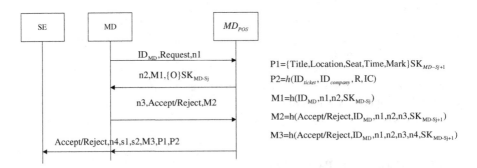

Fig. 3. CS E-Ticket NFC payment scheme

Step 1: $MD \rightarrow MD_{POS} : ID_{MD}, Request, n1$

(1) MD sends MD_{POS} request of e-ticket payment, ID_{MD} and random number $n1$ that is generated by MD. This step will start the payment process.

Step 2: $MD_{POS} \rightarrow MD : n2, h(ID_{MD}, n1, n2, SK_{MD-Sj}), \{o\}SK_{MD-Sj}$

(1) MD_{POS} sends the inquiry information $h(ID_{MD}, n1, n2, SK_{MD-Sj})$ to MD. Then MD will query itself whether there is a stored key SK'_{MD-Sj} that meets the requirements of the conditions.

   a. If the $h(ID_{MD}, n1, n2, SK'_{MD-Sj})$ that MD calculates by using SK'_{MD-Sj} is equal to the receive $h(ID_{MD}, n1, n2, SK_{MD-Sj})$, MD successfully achieves authentication for MD_{POS}. The program will continue.

   b. If not equal, authentication for MD_{POS} fails and MD will ignore this received message.

(2) MD_{POS} sends payment information $\{0\} SK_{MD-Sj}$ and random number $n2$ generated by itself to MD.

   a. MD will use the key to view payment information O, if the payment information is consistent with request information, MD will agree and finish payment. If not, MD refuses to pay.

Step 3: $MD \rightarrow MD_{POS}$:
$n3, Accept/Request, h(Accept/Reject, ID_{MD}, n1, n2, n3, SK_{MD-Sj+1})$

(1) MD sends MD_{POS} a message authentication code $h(Accept/Reject, ID_{MD}, n1, n2, n3, SK_{MD-Sj+1})$ to respond to the challenge. Then, MD_{POS} will find itself whether the next symmetry key satisfies the requirements of the conditions.

   a. If $h(Accept/Reject, ID_{MD}, n1, n2, n3, SK'_{MD-Sj+1})$, which is calculated by MD_{POS} using the next symmetry key $SK'_{MD-Sj+1}$ is equal to the received $h(Accept/Reject, ID_{MD}, n1, n2, n3, SK_{MD-Sj+1})$, the authentication for MD is success. Then the program will continue.

   b. If not equal, the authentication for MD fails and MD_{POS} will ignore the received message.

(2) MD sends MD_{POS} the result of payment and n3 generated by MD.

   a. If MD pays successfully, the scheme continue. Otherwise, MD_{POS} will ignore this message.

Step 4: $MD_{POS} \rightarrow MD$:

   $Accept/Request, n4, s1, s2,$
   $h(Accept/Reject, ID_{MD}, n1, n2, n3, n4, SK_{MD-Sj+1})$
   $\{Title, Location, Seat, Time, Mark\} SK_{MD-Sj+1}, h(ID_{ticket}, ID_{company}, R, IC)$

(1) MD_{POS} sends MD the message authentication code $h(Accept/Reject, ID_{MD}, n1, n2, n3, n4, SK_{MD-Sj+1})$ to notify that this payment has been finished. Then MD will use the current key to verify whether it is satisfied for requirements of the conditions.

   a. If $h(Accept/Reject, ID_{MD}, n1, n2, n3, n4, SK'_{MD-Sj+1})$, which is calculated by MD using the current key $SK'_{MD-Sj+1}$ is equal to the received $h(Accept/Reject, ID_{MD}, n1, n2, n3, n4, SK_{MD-Sj+1})$, the integrity and authenticity verification of received message is success and the scheme will continue.

b. If not equal, the integrity and authenticity verification of received message is failed and *MD* will ignore the message.

(2) MD_{POS} sends *MD*, s1 and *s2*. When s1 and *s2* reach a certain threshold, the user will be blacklisted.

(3) *MD* will receive all ticket information and store it in NFC secure element.
   a. For the encrypted content part information of CS E-Ticket $\{Title, Location, Seat, Time, Mark\}SK_{MD-Sj+1}$, *MD* can use the key $SK_{MD-Sj+1}$ to decrypt and view the CS E-Ticket information.
   b. The secure part of CS E-Ticket will be stored in NFC secure element for verification.

2.4   Offline CS E-Ticket Secure Verification

In the verification process, There are two entries: user mobile device (*MD*) and the mobile verification device (MD_{POS}).

The verification process is similar to the payment process. Firstly, *MD* and MD_V need to complete the mutual authentication by using MAC, then *MD* will send MD_V CS E-Ticket information which MD_{POS} sends *MD* in the payment process. Finally, the MD_V will verify whether the content and secure part of CS E-Ticket information are right.

3   Security Analysis of NFC Mobile Electronic Ticket System

3.1   Security Analysis

In this section, we will analyze our proposed system scheme from the point of view of security and practicability.

1. Mutual authentication

The scheme uses message *sssss* to implement the authentication for mobile POS device, and then use again h($Accept/$Reject, ID_{MD}, $n1, n2, n3, SK_{MD-Sj+1}$) to implement the authentication for mobile device. So the scheme can implement mutual authentication.

2. Confidentiality

In the proposed scheme, all exchange information will use the hash function or symmetric key to ensure that the message is in the cipher state.

3. Non-tracking

The response message generated by the same devices is different in each session. So the attacker could not assure the tracking attack successfully because there is no the fixed messages [11].

4. Brute force attack

According to the proposed system scheme, it is difficult to find the correct session key as session key change every time at the completion of transaction. In addition, applying an offline key generation technology can increase resistance to brute force attacks [12].

5. Forward security

Because the session key is different in each session, the attacker cannot obtain the previous interactive information.

6. Replay attack prevention

By using nonce and limited-use session keys, the proposed system scheme can prevent replay attack as the session keys used in this scheme are used only once.

7. Man-in-the-middle-attack

An attacker who pretends to be an authorized party is not able to analyze the transmitted message since the session keys used in our scheme are changed constantly by using strong encryption technique.

8. The "spike refund" attack

The scheme will calculate the times of purchase and refund within a certain period of time. If the times reach the upper limit, the user will be pulled into the blacklist. By this way, the system scheme we proposed can prevent "spike refund" attack.

9. The e-ticket clone attack

For the system scheme we proposed, on the one hand the secure part information is displayed to user in the form of hash value. On the other hand we bind the IC serial number to user mobile device. By this way, the cloned e-ticket can't finish the authentication and verification process, which prevent the e-ticket clone attack.

Table 2. The analysis of Practicability

	Symmetric encryption	Symmetric decryption	Non Symmetric encryption	Non Symmetric decryption	Hash function	Message number
Yun-Seok et.al	4	4	1	1	3	6
Ceipidoret.al	-	-	2	2	3	6
León-Coca et.al	7	7	-	-	-	7
E -ticket NFC payment scheme	2	2	-	-	4	4
Offline e-ticket verification scheme	2	2	-	-	4	4

3.2   Practicability Analysis

For the train stations, airports and other places where the flow of people is large and the security needs is higher, the proposed scheme has a strong practicability comparing with other schemes in Table 2.

According to this table, the proposed scheme has fewer operations and spends less time to complete the transaction. The scheme only adopts the hash function, symmetric key and MAC technology with a lightweight.

4   Conclusions

Firstly, this paper designs an electronic ticket system and introduces from the registration, booking, ticketing and verification four aspects. This system is composed of servers, mobile device, mobile POS device and mobile verification terminals. For the problems existing in ticketing process, this paper proposes an e-ticket NFC payment scheme. This scheme not only can give the user good experience but also protect the user e-ticket secure information. For the problems in the verification process, an offline session key generation and distribution technology is introduced. On the one hand, this technology increase the security of the communication between each entity. On the other hand, it can cope with the "spike refund" issue so that the system we proposed can applied to train tickets, air tickets and other fields which need higher requirements.

Acknowledgment. This work has been financially supported by the National Natural Science Foundation of China (No. 61303216, No. 61272457, No. U1401251, and No. 61373172), the National High Technology Research and Development Program of China (863 Program) (No. 2012AA013102), the China Postdoctoral Science Foundation funded project (No. 2013M542328), and National 111 Program of China B16037 and B08038, and the Xian Science and Technology Plan funded project (CXY1352WL30).

References

1. Ning, H., Wang, B.: RFID major projects and the state Internet of Things. Mechanical Industry Press (2008)
2. Fan, K., Gong, Y., Liang, C., et al.: Lightweight and ultralightweight RFID mutual authentication protocol with cache in the reader for IoT in 5G. In: Security and Communication Networks. Published online in Wiley Online Library (wileyonlinelibrary. com) (2015). doi:10.1002/sec.1314
3. Pasquet, M., et al.: Secure payment with NFC mobile phone in the Smart Touch project. In: Proceedings of International Symposium on Collaborative Technologies and Systems, pp. 121–126 (2008)
4. Su, Z., Xu, Q., Qi, Q.: Big data in mobile social networks: A QoE oriented framework. IEEE Network **30**(1), 2–57 (2016)
5. Xu, Q., Su, Z., Han, B., Fang, D., Xu, Z., Gan, X.: Analytical model with a novel selfishness division of mobile nodes to participate cooperation. Peer-to-Peer Networking and Applications (2015). doi:10.1007/s12083-015-0330-6

6. Lee, Y.S., Kim, E., Jung, M.S.: A NFC based authentication method for defense of the man in the middle attack. In: Proceedings of the 3rd International Conference on Computer Science and Information Technology (2013)
7. Ceipidor, U.B., Medaglia, C.M., Marino, A., Sposato, S., et al.: KerNees: A protocol for mutual authentication between NFC phones and POS terminals for secure payment transactions. In: Proceedings of 9th International ISC Conference on Information Security and Cryptology (ISCISC-2012), pp. 115–120 (2012)
8. Ceipidor, U.B., Medaglia, C.M., Marino, A., et al.: Mobile ticketing with NFC management for transport companies problems and solutions. In: Proceedings of 5th International Workshop on Near Field Communication (NFC), pp. 1–6 (2013)
9. Wei, J.W., Wei, H.L.: An NFC e-ticket system with offline authentication Information. In: Proceedings of 9th IEEE International Conference on Communications and Signal Processing (ICICS), pp. 1–5 (2013)
10. Kayser, S., Bewernick, B.H., Hurlemann, R., et al.: A secure offline key generation with protection against key compromise. Physi. Rev. B, Condens. Matter **51**(4), 2550–2555 (2009)
11. Fan, K., Li, J., Li, H., Liang, X., Shen, X., Yang, Y.: RSEL: Revocable secure efficient lightweight RFID authentication scheme. Concurrency Comput. Pract. Experience **26**(5), 1084–1096 (2014)
12. Thammarat, C., Chokngamwong, R., Techapanupreeda, C., et al.: A secure lightweight protocol for NFC communications with mutual authentication based on limited-use of session keys. In: Proceedings of 2015 International Conference on Information Networking (ICOIN), pp. 133–138 (2015)

Multi-path Reliable Routing with Pipeline Schedule in Wireless Sensor Networks

Jinbao Li[1,2], Li Zhang[1], Longjiang Guo[1,2(✉)],
Qianqian Ren[1,2], and Yahong Guo[3]

[1] School of Computer Science and Technology,
Heilongjiang University, Harbin, China
longjiangguo@hlju.edu.cn
[2] Key Laboratory of Database and Parallel Computing, Harbin, Heilongjiang, China
[3] School of Information Science and Technology,
Heilongjiang University, Harbin, Heilongjiang, China

Abstract. To solve the problem of data missing caused by communication collision in Wireless Sensor Networks (WSNs), this paper proposes a multi-path reliable routing protocol. This protocol combines the technique of pipeline with multi-path reliable routing, and uses Markov chain to predict the period of using pipeline in order to schedule pipeline dynamically. Therefore, the combined techniques improve the network throughput. In the case that data congestion occurs, and the protocol can keep the data transmission rate unchangeable, and the proposed routing protocol can choose other path to transmit data in order to reduce the number of data missing. Simulation results indicate that the proposed protocol can deal with congestion and improves the network throughput effectively.

1 Introduction

The restriction of resources poses a severe challenge to improve the network performance in WSNs [1–4]. It is important to improve the reliability of data transmission for wireless sensor study under the prerequisite of network throughput.

Compared with the single-path routings, it can improve throughput of the network using multi-path routing. Data transmission have concurrency in multi-path routing, as the data transmitted by more than one path at the same time

L. Guo—This work is supported by the National Natural Science Foundation of China under grant No.61370222, 61300225, Heilongjiang Province Science and Technique Foundation under Grant No. F201324, Program for Group of Science and Technology Innovation of Heilongjiang Educational Committee under grant No.2013TD012, Harbin Municipal Science and Technology Innovation Talent research special funds outstanding academic leaders funded project under Grant No.2015RAXXJ004, Program for New Century Excellent Talents in University under grant No. NCET-11–0955, Programs Foundation of Heilongjiang Educational Committee for New Century Excellent Talents in University under grant No.1252-NCET-011.

Q. Yang et al. (Eds.): WASA 2016, LNCS 9798, pp. 126–138, 2016.
DOI: 10.1007/978-3-319-42836-9_12

[5–8]. Different sending rates will affect the network throughput directly when the source node sends data to multiple neighbors. The high sending rate of the source node will cause data congestion, conversely, the network link can't fully be exploited.

In recent years, there are many researches in control congestion in the wireless network [9–12]. Popa et al. proposed IPS [9] which uses two paths to transmit data simultaneously. When data congested at a node, they can be transmitted to the destination node through a new temporary path, thus reducing the data missing caused by network congestion. Sridevi et al. [10] use the sensor nodes with a variety of perceived parts and assign priorities based on the type of transmitted data to ensure the important data forwarded earlier. Wang et al. [11] use the sequence length to monitor the network congestion, transmit the congested data when the congestion occurs, and thereby control the degree of congestion. Pham [12] use the strategy that allocate rate to different paths at the source node to achieve load balancing and avoid data congestion. The general processing strategies of the above works are adjusting the sending rate of source node in order to reduce data congestion. However, the throughput will be affected by the reduce of sending rate at the source node.

Therefore, it is important to study how to deal with data congestion effectively under the condition of keeping the sending rate of the source node when data congestion occurs. To address the problem, this paper introduce pipeline, and combine it with multi-path routing. this strategy can scheduling data transmission between multiple paths effectively, while keeping the sending rate of the source node. The contribution of this paper is as follows: combining pipeline with multi-path routing based on the data conversion relationship between multiple paths; Proposed a predict method based on Markov chains, predict the appointment time of the multi-path pipeline and schedule it dynamically. Simulation results show that combine pipeline with multi-path can improve network throughput effectively and make the data transmission more reliable.

The remainder of the paper is organized as follows, Sect. 2 proposed the protocol of multi-path reliable routing based on pipeline; Sect. 3 introduced how to select pipeline scheduling time; Sect. 4 is the simulation experiment and result; The final section is conclusion.

2   Protocol Design

This paper make the following assumptions: there exist a ordered path set $Path(s,t) = \{\mathcal{P}_1, \mathcal{P}_2, \ldots, \mathcal{P}_n\}$ from any source node s to destination node t, which contains n disjoint paths and sorted from short to long according to the path length. T_i is the total number of nodes except source node and destination node on path $\mathcal{P}_i$.

2.1   Establish Conversion Relationship Between Multi-paths

In this paper, we use the bridge chain establishment algorithm which proposed in literature [13] to establish the data conversion relationship between multiple paths.

Algorithm 1. Selection algorithm of multi-path.

Input:

1: $Path(s,t) = \{\mathcal{P}_1, \mathcal{P}_2, \ldots, \mathcal{P}_n\}$;

Output:

2: k disjoint paths $OP(s,t) = \{\mathcal{P}_1, \mathcal{P}_2, \ldots, \mathcal{P}_n\}$;

3:

4: select m paths from the input set randomly;

5: **if** $m < 2$ **then**

6:     Goto step 1;

7: **else**

8:     **if** $m = 2$ **then**

9:         Build-Bridge;

10:     **else**

11:         $i = 1$;

12:         **while** $i < m$ **do**

13:             Establish the bridge chain between P_i and $P_{(i+1)}$, $i{+}{+}$;

14:         **end while**

15:         Calculate the reliability of these m paths and goto step 1 until m have selected every data in $\{2, 3, \ldots, n\}$. Then select the combination with maximum reliability from multi-path combination;

16:         **if** the combination is unique **then**

17:             Output all paths in $OP(s,t) = \{\mathcal{P}_1, \mathcal{P}_2, \ldots, \mathcal{P}_n\}$;

18:         **else**

19:             Select the combination with the minimum numbers of paths;

20:         **end if**

21:     **end if**

22: **end if**

If data congestion occurred, data can be transmitted to other path through bridge chain to ensure the reliability of data transmission.

For $\forall \mathcal{P}_i \in P(s,t)$, set $t=1$ if data can be transmitted through bridge chain when data congested at node t, otherwise $t=0$. Therefore the transmit rate of path $\mathcal{P}_i$ is:

$$Transfer_i = \sum_{k=1}^{T_i} t_k p_k / T_i \tag{1}$$

where $Transfer_i$ is the transmit rate of path $\mathcal{P}_i$. T_i is the total number of nodes except source node and destination node on $\mathcal{P}_i$, p_k is the failure(or data congested) probability of the k-th node on the path. Then we can get the reliability of $P(s,t) = \{\mathcal{P}_1, \mathcal{P}_2, \ldots, \mathcal{P}_m\}$

$$R_{i,j} = (Transfer_1 + \cdots + Transfer_m)/m \tag{2}$$

Algorithm 1 is the multi-path selection algorithm. There exist n disjoint paths from source node s to destination node t in the network after s and t have been determined. Algorithm 1 can determine the number of final routing paths $m(m \leq n)$.

2.2   Conversion Between Multi-paths and Pipeline

We use the Algorithm 1 that can select routing paths and regard m disjoint paths as a pipeline which has m pipeline segments with different functions. Assuming that the data congested paths are selected to be the start segment of the pipeline, we can get a dynamic pipeline graph with feed forward and feedback connections through regarding the conversion relationship as processing sequence between pipeline segments. At last, combine the multi-path with pipeline, and guidance the routing schedule by pipeline scheduling scheme.

For example, the network showed in Fig. 1, using the Algorithm 1 to establish bridge chains and determine routing paths. In Fig. 2, the data on P_1 can be transferred to P_2 through $b_{P_1,P_2}(1,7), b_{P_1,P_2}(3,9), b_{P_1,P_2}(4,10)$. When data congested on P_1, they can be transferred to P_2, and then transferred to P_3. P_2 would have output port if the data that transferred from P_1 to P_2 can be sent in time by P_2, otherwise the data will be transferred to P_3.

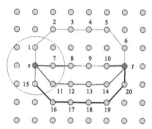

Fig. 1. Network topology

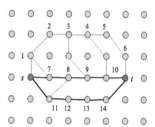

Fig. 2. Routing path

Definition 1. Reservation table is a two-dimensional table which satisfied the following three conditions. (1) Transverse is ordered by time, represented by unit time. (2) Longitudinal represents each path. (3) The cell that row a and column b is set 1 if path b is scheduled at time a, otherwise empty.

When data congestion occurs in the network, we can obtain the reservation table according to the dynamic pipeline graph from the previous section. Monitoring the network throughput at destination node with 10 unit time, and convert the pipeline when the value of the throughput is less than the threshold. As the reservation table is not unique, we can choose different reservation table based on the state of each routing. A row of a reservation table can contains multiple 1 which means a path can be called at different moments. Multiple 1 in a column means that at some point, the data in a path can be transferred to more than one path simultaneously. Figure 4 are several reservation tables without repeated cycle which come from Fig. 3.

Definition 2. The time interval between two starts of pipeline called **waiting Time** w. In waiting time, it will cause resource conflict if start a pipeline segment two or more times so the original congestion path couldn't transfer more congested data to other paths.

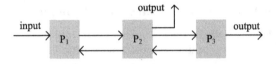

Fig. 3. Pipeline

Definition 3. banned waiting time is the waiting time that cause conflict.

Corresponding to banned waiting time is the allowed waiting time which cause no conflict. For a reservation table with t columns, the max banned waiting time is $p \leq t - 1$, allowed waiting time is $1 \leq q \leq p$, and the smaller allowed waiting time, the higher efficiency of the pipeline. Literature [14] points out through checking the distance between any two "1" in a row, we can obtained the banned waiting time. Such as the banned waiting time is 2 and 4 in the third reservation table of Fig. 4, and the allowed waiting time is 1 and 3.

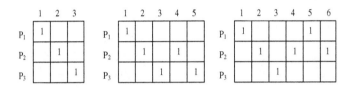

Fig. 4. Network topology

In the mechanism of pipeline, we can use the conflict vector to represent the banned waiting time and allowed waiting time simultaneously.

Definition 4. Conflict vector is a binary vector with p bits, represented by $C = (C_p, C_{p-1}, \cdots, C_2, C_1)$. where $C_p = \{0, 1\}$, $1 \leq p \leq (t - 1)$. Waiting time i is banned waiting time if $C_i = 1$; and allowed waiting time if $C_i = 0.C_p = 1$ indicates the highest bit in conflict vector is always equal to $1^{[10]}$. The vector is (1010) in the third reservation table in Fig. 4.

According to the pipeline mechanism, we can use the conflict vector to construct a **state graph** [14] to explain states change, and then get the minimum waiting time of the pipeline. The method to get conflict graph from conflict vector is as follows: The initial conflict vector shift one bit to right, and the vacated one of the extreme left padded with 0. After shifting k times, k is a allowed waiting time if the digital shifted out is 0, then do bitwise OR between the new vector and the original conflict vector. The purpose of bitwise OR is to avoid conflict that start from $k + 1$ and after. Therefore, conflict graph contains all the allowed state changes without conflict. All the waiting time which is larger than the maximum banned waiting time is the allowed waiting time. Although the scheduling conflicts can always be avoid in a sufficiently long period of time, waiting a long time would lose the meaning of pipeline, no matter the view from industrial demand or network requirements.

For the third reservation table in Fig. 4, the conflict vector is (1010), and the conflict graph is showed in Fig. 5. Shifting 1 bit to right, then get the new vector (0101). (1111) is the result of (1010)OR(0101), and at the third shift (1010) get to (1011), (1011) go back to itself after the third shift. We can obtain some waiting loops from the state graph, such as (1, 5), (3, 5), (3) and (5), then calculating the average waiting time of them, and guiding the schedule of the pipeline by choose the waiting loop with the minimum waiting time.

3   The Selection of Scheduling Time in Assemble Line

In this paper, we proposed a prediction algorithm based on the Markov chain-MAPA. MAPA divide the network into different states according to the current network throughput, and use Markov chain theory to predict the using time of the current pipeline.

3.1   Pipeline State's Classification

Assuming packet reception ratio R is the ratio of the number of packets successfully received by the destination node to source node sends. Before the congestion occurs, R is R_{high} at the monitoring node and regard R_{high} as the R of the network in a good state. When the congestion occurs, let R_{low} as the R at the destination node without taking any congestion handling strategy. Part of the congested data is lost as the forward isn't timely, so $R_{low} < R_{high}$.

To sum up, the pipeline can be divided into three states. when $R \geq R_{high}$, the pipeline is in the valid state; available state if $R_{low} \leq R < R_{high}$, and invalid state if $R < R_{low}$.

Figure 6 shows an example of the three kinds of states of the pipeline, denoted by A, B, and C. Assuming that the packet reception ratio at the destination node changed from top to down, then the states that the pipeline experienced are A-B-C, that is turn to the available state from the valid state and turn to the invalid state lastly.

For a pipeline, saying that the pipeline is in state i at time t if $X_t = i$, $i = \{1, 2, 3\}$ indicates the pipeline is in the valid state, available state, and invalid state respectively. Assume that there is a probability $P_{i,j}$ make it in the state j at the next time if the pipeline is in state i. Assume for any state i, if $n \geq 0$,

$$P\{X_{n+1} = j | X_n = i, X_{n-1} = i_{n-1}, \cdots, X_1 = i_1\} = P_{i,j} \qquad (3)$$

Given the past state and current state, the conditional distribution of the future state is independent of the past state, only depends on the current state.

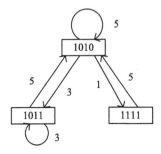

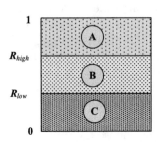

Fig. 5. State graph   **Fig. 6.** 3 kinds of states in pipeline

We can regard the converting process of pipeline as a three-state Markov chain process. As Markov chain process must be converted from one state to another state, and the probability is non-negative, so:

$$\sum_{j=1}^{3} P_{i,j} = 1, i = 1, 2, 3 \tag{4}$$

M is a one-step transfer probability matrix, like Fig. 7. If we use state 1, state 2 and state 3 denote invalid state, available state and valid state respectively, and assume that the current state of pipeline is in valid state, then $M_{3,1}$ indicates that the probability of the pipeline is in failure state at next time.

$$M = \begin{Vmatrix} P_{11} & P_{12} & P_{13} \\ P_{21} & P_{22} & P_{23} \\ P_{31} & P_{32} & P_{33} \end{Vmatrix}$$

Fig. 7. One-step transfer matrix

On the basis of one-step transfer probability, we study n-step transfer probability $P_{i,j}^n$ in this section. $P_{i,j}^n$ is the probability that the current state is i and in state j after $n(n > 0)$ moments, namely:

$$P_{i,j}^n = P\{X_{n+t} = j | X_t = i\} \tag{5}$$

Clearly, $P_{i,j}^1 = P_{ij}$, that is the current state is i and reach to the state j after one-step transfer. According to the approach to calculate n-step transfer probability offered by C-K [15] equation,

$$P_{i,j}^{n+m} = \sum_{k=0}^{\infty} P_{i,k}^n P_{k,j}^m \tag{6}$$

Formula (6) denotes the pipeline of the current state which is i, and reach to state k after n times transfer, then it reach to state j after transfer m times. Let $M^{(n)}$ indicates the transfer probability of $P_{i,j}^n$ after n times transfer, formula (6) can also denoted as follows:

$$M^{(n+m)} = M^{(n)} * M^{(m)} \tag{7}$$

The $*$ in formula (7) indicates matrix multiplication as follows, and formula (8) is determined by induction. $M^{(3)} = M^{(2+1)} = M^{(2)} * M^{(1)} = M^{(1+1)} * M^{(1)} = M^{(1)} * M^{(1)} * M^{(1)} = M * M * M = M^3$.

$$M^{(n)} = M^{(n-1+1)} = M^{n-1} * M = M^n \tag{8}$$

3.2   Prediction Algorithm Based on Markov Chain

This paper uses the pipeline transfer matrix to predict the time slot of the reservation table. The purpose using transfer matrix is to predict the next state of the pipeline according to the current state, and thus predict the state n times later. Suppose the current time is t, stop calculate if the pipeline transfer to invalid state with a high probability at sometime k when calculate the pipeline transfer matrix. Then take the time slot $(k - t)$ as appointment time of current pipeline. In appointment time, Scheduling pipeline in accordance with its current schedule. Convert pipeline if the time reach to k, as current pipeline is in invalid state with a high probability after k.

Now, concrete the one-step transfer matrix in Fig. 7, and then calculate the n-step transfer matrix. Assume that the current packet reception ratio of the pipeline is R, and the biggest change value of packet reception ratio is Δ. For pipeline, this section is concerned on whether the state will eventually reach to the invalid state, convert the pipeline immediately if it happens, so $P_{11} = 1$, $P_{12} = 0$, $P_{13} = 0$.

P_{21} is the probability that the pipeline transfer from available state to invalid state. Such as Fig. 8 shows, the packet reception ratio is R when the pipeline is in available state. At next time, the biggest change value of the packet reception ratio is Δ, so there exist a cycle, R is the center, Δ is the radius, and the packet reception ratio ranging from point a to point b at next moment. P_{21} is the radio of the length of pink line in Fig. 8(a) and 2Δ, $P_{21} = \frac{\Delta - (R - R_{low})}{2\Delta}$.

P_{23} is the probability that the pipeline convert from available state to valid state. Shows as the Fig. 9, P_{23} is the radio of the length of pink line in Fig. 8(b) and 2Δ, $P_{23} = \frac{\Delta + R - R_{high}}{2\Delta}$. Then $P_{22} = 1 - P_{21} - P_{23} = \frac{R_{high} - R_{low}}{2\Delta}$.

P_{31} is the probability that the pipeline convert from valid state to invalid state. Shows as the Fig. 10, P_{31} is the radio of the length of pink line in Fig. 10 and 2Δ, $P_{31} = \frac{\Delta - (R - R_{low})}{2\Delta}$.

P_{32} is the probability that the pipeline convert from valid state to available state. Shows as the Fig. 11, P_{32} is the radio of the length of pink line in Fig. 11 and 2Δ, $P_{32} = \frac{\Delta - (R - R_{high})}{2\Delta}$. Then $P_{33} = 1 - P_{31} - P_{32} = \frac{2R - R_{high} - R_{low}}{2\Delta}$.

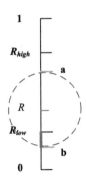

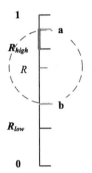

Fig. 8. Available state to invalid state   **Fig. 9.** Available state to valid state

We can calculate the n-step transfer matrix after get the one-step transfer matrix. If $M_{3,1}^{(n)}$ is larger than a certain threshold, stop the calculation and record the matrix order number n as a prediction time of the reservation table. During that period, select an pipeline schedule to guide the congested data transfer, convert the pipeline after n units of time. Should be noted, After $P_{21}, P_{22}, P_{23}, P_{31}, P_{32}$, and P_{33} have been determined, Learned by observation and calculation, there is a limiting probabilities making $M_{3,1}^{(n)}$ values are no longer change. The proposed prediction algorithm based on Markov chain can be calculated in the finite number of steps.

Based on the above thoughts, this section presents a prediction algorithm based on Markov chain (MPRR). The basic idea is as follows: monitoring packet reception ratio R at the destination node if congestion occurs. According to the probability of the packet reception ratio decreases, construct the one-step transfer equation, and then construct the n-step transfer equation. If the probability that the pipeline convert to invalid state is larger than threshold Q or reach to the limiting probabilities of $M_{3,1}^{(n)}$, stop calculate. Output the order of the matrix, and regard it as the length of the appointment time of the pipeline reservation table, then obtained the data transmit between the multiple paths through pipeline.

4   Experiment and Analysis

This section verifies the performance of the proposed method through simulation experiments. 1000 sensor nodes are evenly deployed in a 100 m*100 m network, we use the grid structure network in order to make experiment more convenient. Assume that the transmission period of each node is 50 ms, and the length of each packet is 32 Bytes, the running time is 60 s, a pipeline segment converts its state with the 7th and 33th seconds which are unable to transmit data in time. Experiments investigate four aspects: the sampling period affected the network throughput, the sampling period affected the loss of the transferred data, the

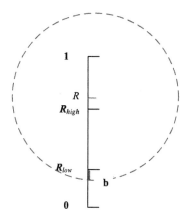

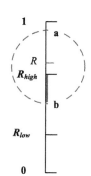

Fig. 10. Valid state to invalid state   **Fig. 11.** Valid state to available state

number of pipeline segments affected the throughput and the number of pipeline segments affected the loss of the transferred data.

4.1   The Impact of Sampling Period

Figure 12 is the impact of execution time on the throughput when the shortest path is 5 hops. F is the sampling period and we set the time of real-time monitoring is one second. From Fig. 12, we can see that with the increase in execution time, the number of packets received by the destination node is on the rise no matter how the sampling period changes. However, from the Fig. 12 we can clearly observe, the network throughput was reduced with the increase of the sampling period. This is because the changes of the pipeline can be found by real-time monitoring in a timely manner, when a pipeline is no longer suitable to continue to use for some reasons, real-time monitoring can convert the pipeline in time to ensure that the network has a larger throughput.

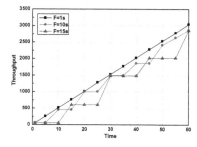

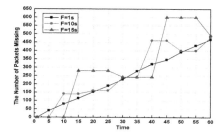

Fig. 12. Sampling period vs through-   **Fig. 13.** Sampling period vs the num-
put   ber of packets missing

Figure 13 is the impact of the sampling period on the transfer of data missing when the shortest path is 5 hops. From Fig. 13 we can observe that with the increase of the sampling period, the loss of transferred data is also increased. When F = 10 s or F = 15 s, transferred data missing remain unchanged in some moments for the periodic sampling, more data loss in some moments for the state of pipeline changes, and once this phenomenon was discovered by periodic monitoring, it convert the pipeline to declined the loss of transferred data.

4.2   The Impact of the Number of Pipeline Segment

When the shortest path length is 5 hops, the sampling period is 10 s, the number of pipeline segments affected the network throughput was shown in Fig. 14. ALN is the number of pipeline segment, as the number of pipeline segment is the number of routing path, so when increase the former, the number of paths in the network can be used in parallel is increased, thus the network throughput is also increased. When increasing the number of pipeline segment, the transferred data can be transmitted to other more paths, which led to the growth of the transfer path, so as the number of data missing.

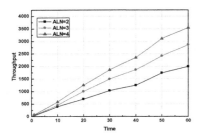
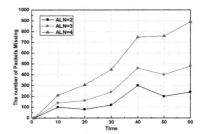

Fig. 14. Numbers of pipeline segment vs throughput

Fig. 15. Numbers of pipeline segment vs data missing

Figure 15 shows the number of pipeline segment affected the transferred data missing when the shortest path length is 5 hops and the sampling period is 10 s. The loss of transferred data increases with the time increase. For periodic sampling, data loss can't be found timely at the destination node, just be found in the periodic time. What's more, as the increase of ALN, data missing get seriously for the elongate of transfer path.

4.3   The Impact of Predicting Time

Assuming when the program is running, the threshold is set to 0.735, and the others don't change. F is the fixed sampling period, F = 1 is real-time monitoring. PF is the prediction period, more flexible than fixed period. From Fig. 16 we can see that the throughput of periodic monitoring is close to the throughput of real-time monitoring which explain the feasible of the periodic monitoring approach.

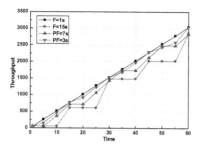 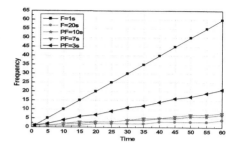

Fig. 16. Prediction time affected the network throughput

Fig. 17. Prediction time affected the frequency of monitoring

When the shortest path length is 5 hops, Fig. 17 illustrates the impact of the prediction time on the frequency of monitoring. In sensor networks, there is a direct relationship between frequency of monitoring and energy consumption, monitoring the more, the greater energy consume. Therefore, ensuring the network throughput and reducing the frequency of monitoring is of great significance for extending the network life cycle.

5   Conclusion

Aiming at data missing caused by data congestion in WSNs, the paper proposes a pipeline based multi-path reliable routing protocol. The protocol establishes the conversion relationship in multiple paths to reduce data missing and improve the reliability of data transmission. Combining multi-path routing with pipeline based on the conversion relationship to improve network throughput. Proposed predict method based on Markov chains for the lack of real-time monitoring and periodic monitoring at the destination node, predict the appointment time dynamically, and convert pipeline in time to ensure the network throughput. Experiments show that the proposed routing can handle data congestion effectively, improve the network throughput, and reduce the number of monitoring.

References

1. Cai, Z., Lin, G., Xue, G.: Improved approximation algorithms for the capacitated multicast routing problem. In: Wang, L. (ed.) COCOON 2005. LNCS, vol. 3595, pp. 136–145. Springer, Heidelberg (2005)
2. Cai, Z., Chen, Z., Lin, G.: A 3.4713-approximation algorithm for the capacitated multicast tree routing problem. Theor. Comput. Sci. Elsevier, Amsterdam (2009)
3. Cai, Z., Goebel, R., Lin, G.: Size-constrained tree partitioning: a story on approximating the multicast k-tree routing problem. Theor. Comput. Sci. **412**, 240–245 (2011). Elsevier, Amsterdam
4. Cheng, S., Cai, Z., Li, J.: Curve query processing in wireless sensor networks. IEEE Trans. Veh. Technol. **64**, 5198–5209 (2015). IEEE Press, New York

5. Gao, D., Yang, O., Zhang, H., Chao, H.C.: Multi-Path routing protocol with unavailable areas identification in wireless sensor networks. J. Wireless Pers. Commun. **60**, 443–462 (2011). Springer, Berlin
6. Lee, S.W., Choi, J.Y., Lim, K.W.: A reliabke and hybrid multi-path routing protocol for muli-interface tactial ad hoc networks. In: Militray communications Conference, pp. 2237–2242. IEEE Press, New York (2010)
7. Teo, J.Y., Ha, Y., Tham, C.K.: Interference-minimized multipath routing with congestion control in wireless sensor network for high-rate streaming. IEEE Trans. Mobile Comput. **7**, 1124–1137 (2008). IEEE Press, New York
8. Ren, F., He, T.: Traffic-Aware dynamic routing to alleviate congestion inwireless sensor networks. IEEE Trans. Parallel Distrib. Syst. **22**, 1585–1599 (2011). IEEE Press, New York
9. Popa, L., Raiciu, C.: Reducing congestion effects in wireless networks by multipath routing. In: International Conference on Network Protocols, pp. 96–105. IEEE Press, New York (2006)
10. Sridevi, S., Usha, M.: Priority based congestion control for heterogeneous traffic in multipath wireless sensor networks. In: Computer Communication and Informatics, pp. 1–5. IEEE Press, New York (2012)
11. Wang, C.G., Sohraby, K.: Priority-based congestion control in wireless sensor networks. In: IEEE International Conference on Sensor Networks, pp. 22–31. IEEE Press, New York (2006)
12. Pham, P.P., Perreau, S.: Performance analysis of reactive shortest path and multipath routing mechanism with load balance. In: International Conference on Computer Communications, pp. 251–259. IEEE Press, New York (2003)
13. Zhang, L., Li, J.B.: A path-transfer based multi-path reliable routing in wireless sensor networks. J. Integr. Plant Biol. **58**, 171–175 (2011). Wiley, New York
14. Wang, K.: Advanced Computer Architecture(The front page). Tsinghua University, Beijing (1995)
15. Ross, S.M.: Applied Stochastic Processes(The ninth edition). Posts Telecom press, Beijing (2007)

A QoE-Aware Adaptive Spectrum Allocation Framework for Secondary Mobile Networks

Liu Cui[1]([⊠]) and Taieb Znati[2]

[1] Department of Computer Science, West Chester Unviersity, West Chester, USA
cuiliu1231@gmail.com
[2] Department of Computer Science, University of Pittsburgh, Pittsburgh, USA

Abstract. Recent statistics show that mobile wireless broadband penetration has exceed that of fixed broadband, with 96.2 % of the world's population subscribing to wireless services and over 40 % of US citizens carry smartphones. This trend is expected to continue in the future at much faster growth rates, and spectrum scarcity becomes a problem. Dynamic spectrum allocation has been proposed as a solution to improve spectrum efficiency and increase the spectrum access opportunities for wireless devices. However, the majority of the research focus on fixed usage. In this paper, we aim at providing high Quality of Experience for mobile devices, whose services cannot be finished within one coverage. We propose an adaptive spectrum allocation framework that optimizes spectrum utilization based on spectrum users' hierarchy, requirements, as well as mobility. The simulation results show that the proposed adaptive spectrum allocation model lead to higher spectrum utilization efficiency, shorter average waiting time and lower probability of call dropping.

1 Introduction

The work in [1] points out that the expected three-orders-of magnitude capacity improvement of next generation wireless networks requires seven fundamental changes in visualizing, modeling, analyzing, simulating, and designing cellular network. Cognizant of the need to improve network capacity, dynamic spectrum access (DSA), enabled by sensing devices and software defined radio, has been proposed to address the spectrum scarcity [2,3]. Several approaches for spectrum sharing have been proposed, including opportunistic sharing and cooperative sharing. Research in opportunistic sharing focuses on increasing spectrum access opportunities, maintaining fairness in spectrum sharing, and avoiding interference to incumbents [4]. Research in cooperative sharing focuses on improving utilities (profits) for all spectrum users, increasing social welfare, and game theory based analysis on bidding schemes and allocation strategies [5]. There are two problems with existing approaches related to this work. First, the majority of the research assumes static spectrum usage, which means the wireless service can be accomplished within one cell's coverage. Second, static allocation that differentiates among spectrum users based on assigned priorities may not fully utilize the spectrum.

© Springer International Publishing Switzerland 2016
Q. Yang et al. (Eds.): WASA 2016, LNCS 9798, pp. 139–148, 2016.
DOI: 10.1007/978-3-319-42836-9_13

Dynamic sharing of spectrum increases spectrum availability, but may lead to interference among users, with potential of service degradation. Moreover, while DSA has potential to increase the effective bandwidth available to mobile users, it also increases the frequency at which hand-off events occur due to small coverage areas [6, 7]. As mobile computing continues to evolve and the access to computing clouds becomes ubiquitous, mobile users will grow to expect highly-reliable, anywhere and anytime multimedia services. Many research effort has been put on mobile computing. [8] proposed a window regulator and a TCP-aware scheduling mechanism to optimize TCP performance in 3G wireless network. [9] presents an epoch-by-epoch framework framework to fairly allocate wireless transmission slots for streaming videos with an aim to improve Quality of Experience (QoE). [10] proposes a novel rate adaptation algorithm for HTTP streaming that detects bandwidth changes due to TCP congestion control and bandwidth changes. However, majority of research in mobile network, so far, has mainly focused on the problem of maintaining connectivity at the network and transport layer in spite of the mobility of the hosts.

The support of QoE requirements in UDHH wireless networks can only be achieved if the need resources remain available during the entire itinerary of the mobile unit. Spectrum allocation in secondary mobile networks, however, is difficult in wireless environment characterized by a high degree of uncertainty in both resource availability and user mobility. These challenges result in the conservative strategy which reserves spectrum resources in a massive coverage for extended period of time, such as static allocation. It protects QoE while sacrifices spectrum utilization efficiency.

Meanwhile, the heterogeneity of next generation wireless networks, coupled with the massive number of communicating devices, gives rise to dynamics and dependencies among the different components of the networks, at different levels of the hierarchy. Instead of the two level spectrum access model, primary users (PUs) and secondary users (SUs), the newly proposed Spectrum Access System (SAS) adopts three their spectrum access hierarchy: incumbents (also called PUs) and two tiers of SUs–Priority Access License (PALs) and General Authorized Access (GAAs). Higher tier receives interference protection from lower tier(s). Consequently, in order to support a QoE aware secondary mobile network, we propose an adaptive spectrum allocation framework that optimizes spectrum utilization based on spectrum users' hierarchy, requirement, as well as mobility. The proposed framework provides the:

- Mechanisms to predict mobile units' path, the arrival and departure times to and from each cell along the path.
- Mechanisms to allocate spectrum to mobile users based on mobility information, spectrum utilization environment, application and importance of the application.

The rest of the paper is organized as following. Section 2 introduces the adaptive framework from service model to spectrum allocation strategies. Section 3 illustrates criteria for for system evaluation. Section 4 provides simulation results. Finally, Sect. 5 concludes the paper with future research directions.

2   Adaptive Framework for Spectrum Allocation in Secondary Mobile Network

The proposed QoE-aware service model and predictive mobility framework use the spectrum database to adaptively allocate spectrum to mobile devices, taking into consideration their mobility profile and QoS requirements. The predictive mobility model is based on three main attributes: earliest arrival time (EAT), latest arrival time (LAT), and latest departure time (LDT). These attributes are used as the basis for a leasing scheme that extends over the interval time between the EAT and LAT. The service model allows mobile devices to specify their spectrum requirements, namely time, bandwidth, location and hierarchy. This section first introduces the service model and then specifies the spectrum allocation schemes.

2.1   Service Model

The service model describes the type and level of QoE that can be supported in the current cell where the mobile unit resides in, and in a cluster of future cells that the mobile may visit. Resource, spectrum, will be allocated predictively to mobile users according to their hierarchy, demand, and spectrum utilization situations. Noted here, the term cell does not only means the coverage by one cellular tower. Rather, it means the effective area covered by any type of wireless transmitter.

The service model is characterized by three factors:

- Time guarantee period, T_G, describes the time duration for which the required resources predictively guaranteed. The time duration is primarily impacted by mobile unit's priority and moving speed. The challenge is to determine T_G that balances both spectrum utilization efficiency and QoE.
- Cluster reservation threshold τ, specifies the minimum percentage of cluster reservation. For example, the most likely cells are ranked according to their probability of being visited by the mobile unit, and then spectrum in the top τ percent will be allocated to the mobile unit. The value of τ depends on users' mobility characters and priority.
- Bandwidth reservation threshold, γ, defines the minimum percentage of the required bandwidth that must be reserved in each future region. Given that the required bandwidth is b_{max}, the network must support at least $b_{min} = b_{max} * \gamma$. Without loss generality, this paper assumes that each mobile unit requires one channel at a time and it will get the entire bandwidth for one channel or nothing. In the future, more adaptive model will be applied considering both bandwidth and power metrics.

The adaptive spectrum allocation strongly depends on an accurate prediction of the mobile's path and the time of arrival to and departure from all cells along the predicted path. The cell residence time within cell j for a mobile unit currently in cell i is characterized by three parameters, namely, expected earliest arrival time, EAT(i, j), expected latest arrival time, LAT(i, j), and latest departure time, LDT(i, j). Consequently, [EAT(i, j), LDT(i, j)] is the expected residence time of the mobile unit within cell j. [12] proposed a framework to predict EAT, LAT, and LDT for users with different mobility categories. It is assumed that these three parameters are available at the spectrum allocation server.

2.2   Adaptive Spectrum Allocation Strategies

The objective for this adaptive spectrum allocation is to maximize spectrum utilization efficiency. Therefore, as expressed in Eq. 1, the objective function is the spectrum utilization (U) which is defined as total number of utilized resource block (U_{RB}) over total number of resource block (T_{RB}). In constraints, the total number of frequency assigned to PALs $i \in [1, n]$ plus the total number of frequency assigned to GAAs $j \in [1, m]$ is less than or equal the total number of available bandwidth B.

$$max \ \ U = \frac{U_{RB}}{T_{RB}}$$
$$s.t. \ \ \sum_{i=1}^{n} b_i + \sum j = 1^m b_j \leq B \tag{1}$$

It is assumed that spectrum is allocated to mobile units as resource blocks defined by time and frequency. In future research, we will further include power level as an additional dimension for spectrum allocation. Queueing network with priority resume can be used to formulate this problem as a utility maximization problem. However it cannot capture the inefficiency brought by resource reservation for mobile unit, which does not arrive due to inaccurate prediction of service demand and mobility.

Therefore, we developed an algorithm to allocate resource blocks to mobile units adaptively considering mobile units' mobility, priority, and spectrum utilization. In this paper, we only focus on secondary mobile networks that consist of PALs and GAAs. It is assumed that a total number of bandwidth B can be assigned to PALs and GAAs.

PALs always have the higher priority in access the spectrum. They revoke GAAs transmission whenever spectrum is not available. In other words, the only cases that PALs need to be delayed is all frequency bands are occupied by other PALs. GAAs are assigned only to available spectrum, since they have the lower priority and are served as FCFS within the same priority. Algorithm 1 determines the spectrum allocation matrix, S. $S[c][t]$ is defined by two dimensions: channel c (frequency) and time slots t.

We focus on the analysis of one cell. The mobility prediction model provides mobility parameters: EAT, LAT, and LDT. When PALs $(P == 2)$ is expected arrive between [EAT,LAT], S find the next available spectrum $(S[c][EAT] == 0)$ and assign it to $S[c][EAT] == 2$. If there is no available spectrum, SAS finds $S[c][EAT] == 3$ or $S[c][EAT + D_t] == 3)$ and assign it to PALs. D_t is the delay for PALs. Then, if PALs arrived during [EAT,LAT], spectrum is further allocated to them for [LAT,LDT].

Algorithm 1. Adaptive Spectrum Allocation

---

initialization: EAT (Poisson), duration between EAT and LAT (Uniform), service time (Exponential), priority (P), arrival (A);
loop: i=1:T
if P==2 then
    find (S[c][t]==0 || S[c][t]==3), t=EAT:T, c∈[0,B];
    S[c,t:t+(LAT-EAT)]=2;
    if A==1 then
        S[c,t:t+(LDT-LAT)]=2;
else
    find (S[c][t]==0), t=EAT:T, c∈[0,B];
    S[c,t:t+(LDT-EAT)]=3;

We compare this adaptive spectrum allocation algorithm with two other algorithm. The first one is static allocation that is currently utilized by the Federal Communications Commission (FCC), where 50 % of the spectrum is allocated to PALs and the other half is allocated to GAAs [11]. Within each static allocated spectrum bands, PALs and GAAs are served as First Come First Service (FCFS). In other words, each type of user has exclusive usage right on their own bands, and they cannot use their counterparts' bands even if it is idle. In order to achieve mobile communication, we apply the same adaptive spectrum allocation scheme. Algorithm 2 illustrates this process.

Algorithm 2. Static Spectrum Allocation

---

initialization: EAT (Poisson), duration between EAT and LAT (Uniform), service time (Exponential), priority (P), arrival (A);
loop: i=1:T
if P==2 then
    find (S[c][t]==0), t=EAT:T, c∈[0,B^P];
    S[c,t:t+(LAT-EAT)]=2;
    if A==1 then
        S[c,t:t+(LDT-LAT)]=2;
else
    find (S[c][t]==0), t=EAT:T, c∈[0,B^G];
    S[c,t:t+(LDT-EAT)]=3;

The second one is a blend of adaptive approach and static allocation. It adaptively allocate spectrum to PALs and GAAs while the entire residence duration [EAT,LDT] are reserved for potential PALs. Therefore, PALs have lower uncertainties in spectrum access while the spectrum utility efficiency may decrease due to the inaccurate prediction of mobile units' mobility. Algorithm 3 illustrates this process.

Algorithm 3. Spectrum Allocation with Reservation

---

initialization: EAT (Poisson), duration between EAT and LAT (Uniform), service
time (Exponential), priority (P), arrival (A);
loop: i=1:T
if P==2 **then**
    find (S[c][t]==0 ‖ S[c][t]==3), t=EAT:T, c∈[0,B];
    S[c,t:t+(LDT-EAT)]=2;
else
    find (S[c][t]==0), t=EAT:T, c∈[0,B];
    S[c,t:t+(LDT-EAT)]=3;

---

3 Determining System Performance

This section provides the matrix that evaluate the efficiency of the adaptive
spectrum allocation strategy, assuming there are m PALs and n GAAs during
time period T. The evaluation metrix includes (1) spectrum utilization efficiency,
(2) probability of call dropping, and (3) average waiting time. In Sect. 4, the
adaptive spectrum allocation framework is compared with other schemes: (1)
static allocation for PALs and GAAs; and (2) adaptive spectrum allocation with
reservation.

The main goal of adaptive framework for spectrum allocation is to increase
spectrum utilization efficiency by allowing more spectrum access for mobile users.
Therefore, two criteria is applied: spectrum occupancy rate and spectrum utilization efficiency. The former one measure the rate that spectrum is reserved
for both arrived and unarrived mobile units, and the later one is defined as total
utilized resource block over total available resource block.

The second evaluation matrix is total number of call dropping (N_d), also
called call dropping rate, is one important criteria to measure QoE for inelastic
services. In inelastic services, service demand cannot tolerate delay. Therefore, if
the spectrum is not available when the mobile unit arrives at the cell, the service
demand is dropped.

Last but not least, average waiting time (delay) is one important criteria
to measure QoE for elastic services. Delay occurs whenever spectrum is not
available, or cannot be revoked from other users. Average waiting time for PAL
(W^P) and average waiting time for GAAs (W^G) will be compared to show the
importance of spectrum access hierarchy.

4 Numerical Results

Simulation is performed in Matlab to obtain numerical results. The simulation
is initialized by service demand SD, each service demand is defined by five randomly generated parameters: (1) EAT follows Poisson process, duration between
EAT and LAT follows uniform distribution with range [0,6], service time follows
exponential distribution, priority $(P = 2)$ indicates PALs and priority $(P = 3)$
indicates GAAs, and arrival $(A = 0, 1)$ describes whether mobile unit arrives

between [EAT,LAT] or not. In the bench mark analysis, the arrival rate is 50 %. In this simulation, we focus on one cell and analyzes the system performance for all mobile devices come in and leave from this cell. Number of mobile devices vary with service arrival rate that ranges from [0,10].

The system performance of adaptive spectrum allocation algorithm will be compared with (1) static allocation spectrum allocation for PALs and GAAs and (2) adaptive spectrum allocation with full reservation for PALs based on the evaluation matrix illustrated in Sect. 3.

Figure 1 depicts the percentage of resource blocks that have been occupied. It includes both resource blocks that utilized by GAAs and PALs and spectrum reservation for PALs that do not arrived due to inaccurate mobility prediction. When the arrival rate is relatively low, adaptive spectrum allocation framework occupies less number of resources blocks than two other approaches. The high occupancy rate for reservation strategy is because it reserves the entire [EAT,LDT] for PALs with any probability of arrival. The high occupancy rate for static allocation is because the limited number of frequency bands for each type of user may lead to uneven utilization.

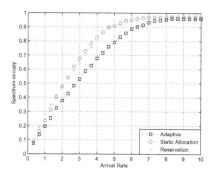

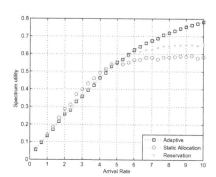

Fig. 1. Spectrum occupancy rate   **Fig. 2.** Spectrum utilization efficiency

Figure 2 depicts the utilization of resource block, since it only measure resource blocks that are utilized by PALs and GAAs over total available resource blocks. While the occupancy rate for adaptive is the lowest one among the three, it provides the highest utility rate. When we use occupancy rate divided by utility rate, it gives the effectiveness of spectrum reservation (probability of reserved resource blocks are used by PALs and GAAs). For example, when the arrival rate is 10, the occupancy rate for all three methods are above 95 %. However, 84 % of the reservation in "Adaptive" method is used by mobiles units, 66 % of the reservation in "Reservation" method are used by mobile units, and only 60 % of reservation in "static allocation" is used by mobile units. In other words, the resource is more effectively utilized under adaptive spectrum allocation framework.

Figure 3 provides total number of call dropping. Call dropping happens when PALs mobile unit comes and all spectrum are allocated to other PALs, and when GAAs mobile unit comes and all spectrum are occupies by other spectrum users (PALs and GAAs). Adaptive spectrum allocation algorithm provides the lowest call dropping and adaptvie allocation with reservation leads to the highest call dropping due to the wasted allocation for those PALs who have not arrived.

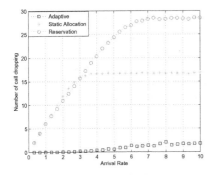

Fig. 3. Number of call dropping

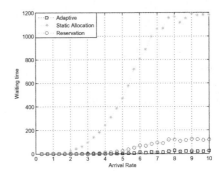

Fig. 4. Average waiting time for PALs

Figures 4 and 5 show the average waiting time for PALs and GAAs, respectively. In both cases, static allocation leads to the highest waiting time, adaptive allocation with reservation leads to the second highest waiting time, and adaptive algorithm leads to the lowest waiting time. Moreover, PALs have lower waiting time than GAAs, since they have higher priority in spectrum access.

Contrast to total number of call dropping, average waiting time measure how long mobile units have to wait until they can be allocated with adequate spectrum. Mobile users with inelastic services should use number of call dropping to choose the appropraite spectrum allocation strategy, while elastic services should use total number of call dropping as criteria.

Figure 6 are sensitivity analysis for spectrum utilization efficiency when all potential mobile units arrives. It is clear that when all mobile units arrive, adaptive allocation and adaptive allocation with reservation lead to the same results, since there is no waste for assign the entire duration [EAT,LDT] to potential PALs. Due to the increase number of arrived mobile units, the spectrum utilization efficiency is higher than Fig. 2 where only 50 % of PALs arrives.

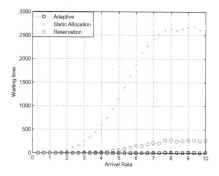

Fig. 5. Average waiting time for GAAs

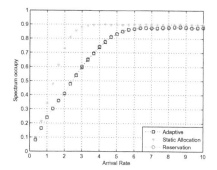

Fig. 6. Spectrum utilization efficiency with 100 % Arrival

5   Conclusion and Future Directions

Mobile network with dynamic spectrum access is the trend for UDHH has not received enough attention as it is entitled to. In order to provide seamless communication along the entire path, resources such as spectrum needs to be reserved ahead of time. This reservation requires an accurate prediction on users' mobility matrix which includes EAT, LAT, and LDT. This paper proposed an adaptive spectrum allocation algorithm which allocate spectrum to mobile units based on their priority and mobility matrix. The simulation compares the adaptive spectrum allocation algorithm with two other approaches: static allocation where PALs and GAAs have their own frequency bands, and adaptive allocation with reservation for all potential PALs on the entire residence duration [EAT,LDT]. It is clear that the adaptive spectrum allocation algorithm has the best performance in terms of both spectrum utilization efficiency and QoE criteria such as average waiting time and number of call dropping.

Future research includes two thrusts. The first one is to increase the accuracy of mobility prediction. In this paper, we provided two scenarios: 50 % of arrival and 100 % of arrival. Based on the simulation results, it is clear that mobility prediction severely impact spectrum utilization efficiency and QoE. In the future research, we will include social data into the mobility prediction to increase the accuracy and provide different spectrum reservation strategies based on mobile units' probability of arrival.

The second thrust is on spectrum allocation algorithm. This paper assumes that all cells have the same. This may not be true when we consider mobile devices that can operate on multiple frequency bands. If that is the case, we also need to optimize spectrum allocation according to mobile units' moving speed. Furthermore, spectrum utilization efficiency can be further improved by allocate mobile users' considering both power level and required bandwidth. More sophisticated algorithm that adaptively increase bandwidth for mobile users when demand is lower than supply and decrease bandwidth when demand is higher than supply can be applied to further improve spectrum utilization efficiency and fairness.

References

1. Andrews, J.G.: Seven ways that HetNets are a cellular paradigm shift. Commun. Mag. IEEE **51**(3), 136–144 (2013)
2. Akyildiz, I.F., et al.: NeXt generation/dynamic spectrum access/cognitive radio wireless networks: a survey. Comput. Networks **50**(13), 2127–2159 (2006)
3. International Telecommunication Union. ICT Facts and Figures. In ICT Data and Statistics Division, Telecommunication Development Bureau, pp. 1-8, February 2013
4. Srinivasa, S., Jafar, S.A.: Cognitive radios for dynamic spectrum access-the throughput potential of cognitive radio: A theoretical perspective. Commun. Mag. IEEE **45**(5), 73–79 (2007)
5. Huang, J., Berry, R.A., Honig, M.L.: Auction-based spectrum sharing. Mobile Netw. Appl. **11**(3), 405–418 (2006)
6. Eng, K.Y., et al.: BAHAMA: A broadband ad-hoc wireless ATM local-area network. In: 1995 IEEE International Conference on Communications, 1995. ICC 1995 Seattle, Gateway to Globalization, vol. 2. IEEE (1995)
7. Agrawal, P., et al.: SWAN: A mobile multimedia wireless network. Pers. Commun. IEEE **3**(2), 18–33 (1996)
8. Chan, M.C., Ramjee, R.: Improving TCP/IP performance over third-generation wireless networks. Mobile Comput. IEEE Trans. **7**(4), 430–443 (2008)
9. Seetharam, A., et al.: On managing quality of experience of multiple video streams in wireless networks. Mobile Comput. IEEE Trans. **14**(3), 619–631 (2015)
10. Liu, C., Bouazizi, I., Gabbouj, M.: Rate adaptation for adaptive HTTP streaming. In: Proceedings of the Second Annual ACM Conference on Multimediasystems. ACM (2011)
11. FCC. Report and Order and Second Further Notice of Proposed Rulemaking, April 17, 2015
12. Aljadhai, A.S.: A Framework for Predictive and Adaptive QoS Support in Wireless Mobile Networks. University of Pittsburgh (1999)

Joint Optimization of Downlink and D2D Transmissions for SVC Streaming in Cooperative Cellular Networks

Guangsheng Feng[1,2,3]($\boxtimes$), Junyu Lin[4]($\boxtimes$), Yongmin Zhang[2,5], Huiqiang Wang[1], Lin Cai[2], Qian Zhao[6], and Hongwu Lv[1]

[1] Harbin Engineering University, Harbin 150001, China
senn.feng@gmail.com
[2] University of Victoria, Victoria V8W 3P6, Canada
[3] Key Laboratory of Complex Systems Modeling and Simulation,
Ministry of Education, Hangzhou Dianzi University, Hangzhou 310018, China
[4] Institute of Information Engineering, Chinese Academy of Sciences,
Beijing 100093, China
linjunyu.hrb@gmail.com
[5] State Key Lab of Industrial Control Technology, Zhejiang University,
Hangzhou 310027, China
[6] Harbin University of Commerce, Harbin 150028, China

Abstract. We study the problem of broadcasting scalable video coded (SVC) streams in cellular networks, where all user equipments (UEs) require the same video content and cooperate with each other. To take the advantage of channel diversity gains, the base station (BS) uses network coding to generate linear combinations of the video packets for broadcasting in the downlink. Once receiving sufficient number of the combinations, a UE can relay packets to others via device-to-device (D2D) connections. To optimize the downlink and D2D transmission arrangement, we first formulate a mixed integer non-linear programming (MINLP) problem, which becomes difficult to solve when the number of UEs increases. Then we convert the MINLP problem to a quasi-convex optimization problem using a continuous step function, and a primal-dual decomposition approach is used to solve it in a distributed way. Simulation results show that the proposed approach achieves a near-optimal solution.

Keywords: Cellular networks · D2D · Scalable video coding · Broadcast

1 Introduction

According to Cisco forecast, mobile video traffic accounts for more than half of all mobile data traffic since 2015. Supporting video streaming in wireless cellular networks is a challenging issue given the large bandwidth consumption, time-varying wireless channels, and heterogeneity of video quality requirements from heterogeneous wireless terminals [1–3]. Recently, the scalable video coding (SVC) technology has been proposed [4,5]. It is quite attractive since one user equipment (UE)

© Springer International Publishing Switzerland 2016
Q. Yang et al. (Eds.): WASA 2016, LNCS 9798, pp. 149–161, 2016.
DOI: 10.1007/978-3-319-42836-9_14

can select an appropriate video quality level based on its individual decoding capabilities, screen size, and channel conditions [6]. However, video streaming is one of the most bandwidth-hungry applications, especially when popular events occur and in a dense location where many people want to access the same video content simultaneously. As a result, a heavy burden will be exerted on the base station (BS), and it is also costly to users.

To address this issue, cooperative transmission of video content has been proposed, where a group of nearby terminals can help each other to achieve a higher transmission efficiency and alleviate the burden of the BS [7,8]. User cooperation implemented via low-cost device-to-device (D2D) connections is a promising technology in cellular networks. To reduce the feedback overhead, network coding is often used in the broadcast/multicast scenarios [9–13]. In our work, we also adopt random linear coding (RLC) for encoding each GoP by the BS or server. Different from the existing work where the BS unicasts videos to users and D2D connections are single-hop only [14–17], we consider a more general case that both BS and UEs take a broadcast strategy.

We will use the terms "node", "UE" and "terminal" interactively in the following. Although we enable all UEs to broadcast, only the UEs received sufficient coded chunks from the BS and their neighbors in advance are allowed to broadcast. The received coded chunks are sufficient to reconstruct an entire layer in one GoP, and we call such UEs are "matured" nodes. After reconstructing a layer successfully, the matured UE can re-encode it for broadcasting to its neighbours.

Although the required amount of SVC traffic is easy known for UEs, the problem of how many video chunks broadcasted by the BS and UEs respectively as well as the total broadcast cost are hardly known without the global information of the whole network. This is the main difficulty that we concern in this work. Since the downlink and D2D traffic have different monetary or energy cost, our objective is to optimize the data traffic allocation between the downlink and D2D in terms of cost. Our main contributions are summarized as follows:

- We formulate the problem of joint downlink and D2D transmissions for SVC streaming in cellular networks as a MINLP problem. By introducing a continuous step function, we convert this problem to a quasi-convex problem.
- A near-optimal solution can be obtained by employing the dual-decomposition approach, and we also propose a distributed algorithm such that each UE can calculate its own broadcast traffic independently.
- We conduct extensive experiments to verify our solution and evaluate the performance of our distributed approach.

The rest of this paper is organized as follows. Section 2 presents the system model and formulates the optimization problem w.r.t. the total cost including both the downlink and D2D costs, and then solve it in a centralized way. Section 3 decouples the proposed optimization problem into subproblems and presents a distributed algorithm for each node to calculate its own broadcast traffic independently, such that all the nodes can adjust their broadcast traffic independently. Section 4 evaluates the proposed approach with extensive simulations, followed by the concluding remarks in Sect. 5.

2   Network Model and Problem Statement

2.1   Network Model

Considering a cellular network scenario, one BS and N UEs are in a cell, where all UEs are equipped with cellular and D2D interfaces, such that they can transmit and receive video streams via the downlink and D2D transmissions. Let $\mathcal{N} = \{1, 2, \cdots, N\}$ denote the set of UEs requesting the same video content simultaneously, which consists of several layer-based GoPs. In this system, the RLC is adopted to encode each layer in one GoP. The BS can broadcast RLC encoded chunks to all the UEs, and each UE can reconstruct and re-encode the matured layer and then broadcast the chunks to its neighbors. Thus, for each layer of a GoP, each UE can receive RLC encoded chunks not only from the BS, but also from other matured UEs by D2D transmission. Due to the different video quality requirements of UEs, different UEs may require different layers, and they only receive and broadcast the layers they request. The data transmission will be stopped when all the required layers for all UEs are received. Considering the different costs of downlink and D2D transmissions, how to meet each UE's video quality requirement with the minimum cost is our main concern.

Generally, the video content consists of a sequence of GoPs, and each GoP includes one base layer and several enhancement layers, denoted by $\mathcal{L} = \{1, 2, \cdots, L\}$. Each layer $l \in \mathcal{L}$ is divided into $C^{(l)}$ original chunks for RLC encoding, and each coded chunk is a linear combination of the $C^{(l)}$ original chunks. According to the RLC scheme, $C^{(l)}$ is also the decoding threshold for layer l. To avoid duplicated RLC-encoded chunks, each node including the BS and UEs will be pre-allocated with an exclusive linear coefficient field, such that each RLC-encoded chunk is unique. Thus, once the number of received encoded chunks for one layer reaches the decoding threshold, i.e., $C^{(l)}$, the corresponding layer can be decoded and reconstructed with these received chunks, no matter which nodes they are generated from. Therefore, there is no packet loss feedback for both the downlink and D2D transmissions, and the BS or UEs simply generate new RLC-encoded chunks for broadcast. To be a D2D broadcast candidate of layer l, there are two necessary conditions for one UE, which are given by

- The UE has been matured with layer l, i.e., it has received enough quantity of coded chunks of layer l, such that this layer can be decoded successfully.
- There exists at least one unmatured neighbor requesting layer l.

Additionally, it is reasonable to assume that each UE only knows its children and parent sets without the knowledge of the whole network topology. Let $\widetilde{\mathcal{N}}_i \subset \mathcal{N}$ and $\mathcal{N}_i \subset \mathcal{N}$ denote the parent set and children set of UE i, respectively[1]. The intersection of $\widetilde{\mathcal{N}}_i$ and $\mathcal{N}_i$ is empty, i.e., one UE cannot belong to another UE's children set and parent set simultaneously. Besides, to avoid serious interference between the downlink and D2D transmissions as well as that among different D2D transmissions, several technologies that can be employed, such as the loosely

---

[1] The set $\widetilde{\mathcal{N}}_i$ only contains UEs, and the BS is not included into it.

controlled D2D mode or fully controlled D2D mode by the BS [18]. In this paper, we adopt the latter one.

2.2 Block Error Rate

Generally, since both of the video server and the BS are connected to the backbone of the Internet, the packet loss rate between them is neglected. In a lossy cellular network, the *block error rate* (BLER), defined as the ratio between the number of chunks in a given message received in error and the total number of chunks transmitted in that message, has a significant influence on the video quality experienced by the UEs and the communication performance of downlink and D2D. In our system, each chunk will be packetized into two M packets for transmission. Only when all the M packets are received, the chunk can be recovered properly.

The Gilbert channel model is used to model the packet loss characteristics in the downlink and D2D transmissions without involving into the details of the underlying link and physical layers [19]. It can be represented by a two-state stationary continuous time Markov chain, and each link state can have one of two values: *Good* or *Bad*. If the link state is *Good*, one packet can be transmitted successfully. Otherwise, it will be lost. Let π_{ij}^{Δ} denote the stationary probability that the state of link (i,j) is Δ, where $\Delta \in \{Good, Bad\}$. According to [20,21], the expected value of π_{ij}^{Δ} can be given by $\pi_{ij}^{\Delta} = \rho_{ij}^{\Delta}/(\rho_{ij}^{Bad} + \rho_{ij}^{Good})$, where ρ_{ij}^{Δ} is the transition probability from *Bad* to *Good* if $\Delta = Good$. Otherwise, it is the transition probability from *Good* to *Bad*. Thus, the BLER from UE i to UE j is

$$p_{ij} = 1 - (1 - \pi_{ij}^{Bad})^M, \tag{1}$$

where UE j is one child of node i. Note that node i may be a UE or the BS, and thus $i \in \{B\} \cup \mathcal{N}$, where, "$B$" means BS. For simplicity, we assume that the BLER will not be changed within one GoP's transmission.

Remark 1. The BLER reflects the average link conditions, by which we only calculate the expected numbers of received and broadcasted chunks by UEs.

2.3 Decoding Requirement

Let $D_i^{(l)}$ ($l \in \mathcal{L}$, $i \in \mathcal{N}$) denote whether layer l is required by UE i, given by

$$D_i^{(l)} = \begin{cases} 1, \text{if node } i \text{ requires layer } l, \\ 0, \text{otherwise.} \end{cases} \tag{2}$$

Note that all the $D_i^{(\ell)}, \ell = 1, 2, \cdots, l$, are equal to 1 if $D_i^{(l)} = 1$, as the higher layer can be decoded only if all lower layer are received. Considering the necessary condition for decoding layer l as discussed in Sect. 2.1, the required quantity of the l-th layer chunks by UE i is calculated by $Z_i^{(l)} = D_i^{(l)} \times C^{(l)}$, where $Z_i^{(l)}$ is equal to $C^{(l)}$ if $D_i^{(l)} = 1$, and to zero otherwise.

The total chunks received by one UE can be come from two parts: from the BS or from its parent UEs. The expected number of the l-th layer chunks received by UE i, denoted by $R_i^{(l)}$, can be calculated by

$$R_i^{(l)} = (1 - p_{Bi})f_B^{(l)} + \sum_{j:i \in \mathcal{N}_j} (1 - p_{ji})f_j^{(l)}, \tag{3}$$

where $f_B^{(l)}$ and $f_j^{(l)}$ are the numbers of chunks broadcasted by BS and UE j, respectively and $f_B^{(l)} > 0$ and $f_j^{(l)} \geq 0$ always hold. $f_j^{(l)}$ can be positive only when UE j is matured with layer l chunks. There is a decoding constraint for UE i, which is given by

$$R_i^{(l)} \geq Z_i^{(l)}, \ \forall i \in \mathcal{N}, \forall l \in \mathcal{L}. \tag{4}$$

It means that quantity of the layer l chunks received by UE i should not be less than its required quantity. UE i will be matured on layer l when the decoding constraint is satisfied.

2.4 Bound for Broadcast Traffic

One of the prerequisites for UE i to be a broadcast candidate is

$$B_i^{(l)} = \begin{cases} 1, & \text{if } R_i^{(l)} \geq C^{(l)} \text{ and } D_i^{(l)} = 1, \\ 0, & \text{otherwise}, \end{cases} \tag{5}$$

where $B_i^{(l)} = 1$ means that UE i has received enough layer l chunks to decode and reconstruct this layer, thus it can re-encode this layer with RLC for broadcast. The traffic volume broadcasted by UE i is possibly positive only when $B_i^{(l)} = 1$.

Due to limited resource and link capacity, there is an upper bound on the broadcast traffic, denoted by $\eta_i^{(\max)}$, such that $f_i^{(l)} \leq \eta_i^{(\max)}$. Since UE i can broadcast the re-encoded chunks only when it is matured, the upper bound on the broadcast traffic of UE i can be given by

$$f_i^{(l)} \leq \eta_i^{(\max)} B_i^{(l)}, \forall i \in \mathcal{N}, \forall l \in \mathcal{L}. \tag{6}$$

Note that the upper bound will be changed as UE i's status varies from unmatured to matured. Constraints (4) and (6) guarantee each matured UE can only broadcast its required chunks. Besides, the amount of each UE's broadcast traffic should be no less than zero, and thus the lower bound on $f_i^{(l)}$ is given by

$$f_i^{(l)} \geq 0, \ \forall i \in \mathcal{N}, \forall l \in \mathcal{L}. \tag{7}$$

2.5 Objective Function

Our objective is to minimize the total traffic cost including the downlink and D2D transmissions. The primal optimization problem can be formulated as:

$$\textbf{P0}: \ \min_{f_B^{(l)}, f_i^{(l)}} \sum_{l=1}^{L} \left(\omega_B U_B(f_B^{(l)}) + \omega_D \sum_{i=1}^{N} U_i(f_i^{(l)}) \right), \tag{8}$$

$$s.t., \quad (4), (6) \text{ and } (7),$$

where $U_B(f_B^{(l)})$ and $U_i(f_i^{(l)})$ are the cost functions of downlink and D2D transmissions, and ω_B and ω_D are their weights respectively, which can be used to adjust the traffic ratio between downlink and D2D. Similar to the existing work [7], the cost functions are convex and twice differentiable.

In the primal optimization problem, the decoding requirement, traffic upper and lower bound are given by constraints (4), (6) and (7), respectively. Constraint (4) guarantees that the quantity of each layer chunks received by each UE should not be less than its required quantity. Constraint (6) guarantees that only matured UEs can broadcast. Constraint (7) guarantees the quantity of chunks broadcasted by each UE is non-negative. It can be found that the constraints (4) and (7) are linear, and the constraint (6) is discontinues due to the binary function of $B_i^{(l)}$. Thus, the primal problem is a MINLP problem and becomes too difficult to solve when the number of UEs increases.

2.6   Approximation of Primal Optimization Problem

The objective function and all constraints to be differentiable is the necessary condition as gradient based solution techniques for convex programming. Because the constraint (6) is discontinuous, Problem **P0** cannot be solved by the gradient based method directly. Inspired by the work [22], we introduce a continuous step function to approximate the binary function in (5), which is a multiplication factor in (6). The continuous step function is given by (as shown in Fig. 1) $g(x_i^{(l)}) = 1/(1 + e^{-kx_i^{(l)}})$ with $x_i^{(l)} = R_i^{(l)} - Z_i^{(l)}$. Obviously, $x_i^{(l)}$ depends on $R_i^{(l)}$ including the chunks broadcasted by BS and its parents.

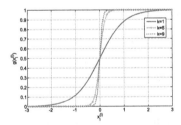

Fig. 1. Step function $g(x_i^{(l)})$, which is sensitive to k. When $k \to +\infty$, $g(x_i^{(l)})$ has a dramatic augmentation from 0.5 to 1 if $x_i^{(l)} \geq 0$, or reduction from 0.5 to 0 if $x_i^{(l)} \leq 0$. Provided $x_i^{(l)} \geq 0$ denotes one UE from the unmatured state to matured one, thus it can immediately become a broadcast candidate once $x_i^{(l)} \geq 0$. (Color figure online)

Correspondingly, constraints (4) and (6) can be rewritten as

$$x_i^{(l)} \geq 0, \ \forall i \in \mathcal{N}, \ \forall l \in \mathcal{L}, \qquad (9)$$

$$f_i^{(l)} - \frac{\eta_i^{(max)}}{1 + e^{-kx_i^{(l)}}} \leq 0, \ \forall i \in \mathcal{N}, \ \forall l \in \mathcal{L}. \qquad (10)$$

Therefore, inequality (6) can be approximated by (10). However, it can incur an unexpected result for two paradox cases when $x_i^{(l)} = 0$. The fist one is $Z_i^{(l)} > 0$, meaning that UE i needs layer l and also receives enough LRC-encoded chunks to reconstruct this layer. In this case, UE i is allowed to broadcast properly. The other case is $Z_i^{(l)} = 0$, meaning that UE i does not needs layer l, and thus the constraint (9) for UE i can always hold. Since the step function $g(x)$ in this case is equal to $1/2$, it results in a positive upper bound of $\eta_i^{\max}/2$ on $f_i^{(l)}$. However, this bound is unreasonable because the UE i is not allowed to broadcast under this case. To resolve this paradox, we replace (10) with the following inequality:

$$f_i^{(l)} - \frac{\eta_i^{(\max)} D_i^{(l)}}{1 + e^{-kx_i^{(l)}}} \le 0, \ \forall i \in \mathcal{N}, \ \forall l \in \mathcal{L}. \tag{11}$$

Since both $D_i^{(l)}$ and $\eta_i^{\max}$ are constants, $x_i^{(l)} \ge 0$, and $f_i^{(l)}$ is convex, constraint (11) is convex. Therefore, Problem **P0** can be converted to the following one:

$$\mathbf{P1}: \ \min_{f_B^{(l)}, f_i^{(l)}} \sum_{l=1}^{L} \left(\omega_B U_B(f_B^{(l)}) + \omega_D \sum_{i=1}^{N} U_i(f_i^{(l)}) \right), \tag{12}$$

$$s.t., \ \ (7), \ (9) \text{ and } (11).$$

Since the step function is concave and all the variables are continuous, the above formulation is a convex optimization problem, which can be solved by the gradient based method [23, 24]. In the following section, we develop a distributed traffic allocation algorithm for downlink and D2D transmissions.

3   Distributed Algorithm Design

To simplify our algorithm design, Problem **P1** can be rewritten as

$$\mathbf{P2}: \ \min_{f_i^{(l)}} \sum_{i=0}^{N} \sum_{l=1}^{L} \omega_i U_i(f_i^{(l)}), \tag{13}$$

$$s.t., \ \ (7), \ (9) \text{ and } (11).$$

Note that the BS is assigned a subscript of 0, and thus $\omega_B = \omega_0$ and $U_B(f_B^{(l)}) = U_0(f_0^{(l)})$. Correspondingly, $\omega_i = \omega_D$, $p_{Bi} = p_{0i}$ and $p_{iB} = p_{i0} = 0$. Let λ and β be the Lagrange multipliers w.r.t. constraint (7) and (9), respectively, and then the Lagrangian function of (13) is given by

$$L(\lambda, \beta) = \min_{f_i^{(l)}} \sum_{i=0}^{N} \sum_{l=1}^{L} \left\{ U_i(f_i^{(l)}) + \lambda_i^{(l)} \left[Z_i^{(l)} - \sum_{j:i \in \mathcal{N}_j} f_j^{(l)}(1 - p_{ji}) \right] - \beta_i^{(l)} f_i^{(l)} \right\},$$

$$s.t., \ f_i^{(l)} - \frac{\eta_i^{(\max)} D_i^{(l)}}{1 + e^{-kx_i^{(l)}}} \le 0, \ \forall i \in \widehat{\mathcal{N}}, \ \forall l \in \mathcal{L}, \tag{14}$$

where $\widehat{\mathcal{N}} = \{0, 1, 2, \cdots, N\}$. Correspondingly, the dual of problem of (14) is

$$\max_{\lambda_i^{(l)}, \beta_i^{(l)}} L(\lambda, \beta),$$

$$\text{s.t., } \lambda_i^{(l)} \geq 0, \beta_i^{(l)} \geq 0, \ \forall i \in \widehat{\mathcal{N}}, \forall l \in \mathcal{L}. \tag{15}$$

To attain a distributed algorithm, we can decompose Problem **P2** such that each node, including the BS and UEs, can figure out its own downlink and D2D traffic. Since the p_{ji} is equal to 1 if there is no link from node j to i, the term of $\sum_{j:i\in\mathcal{N}_j} f_j^{(l)}(1 - p_{ji})$ in (14) could be rewritten as $\sum_j f_j^{(l)}(1 - p_{ji})$. Then, the Lagrangian function (14) can be decomposed into each layer for each node, which is given by

$$L(\lambda_i^{(l)}, \beta_i^{(l)}) = \min_{f_i^{(l)}} U_i(f_i^{(l)}) + \lambda_i^{(l)} Z_i^{(l)} - \sum_{j=0}^{N} \lambda_j^{(l)} f_i^{(l)}(1 - p_{ij}) - \beta_i^{(l)} f_i^{(l)},$$

$$\text{s.t., } f_i^{(l)} - \frac{\eta_i^{(\max)} D_i^{(l)}}{1 + e^{-kx_i^{(l)}}} \leq 0, \ \forall i \in \widehat{\mathcal{N}}, l \in \mathcal{L}. \tag{16}$$

According to the KKT conditions and $e^{-kx_i^{(l)}} \approx 0$, the near-optimal $f_i^{(l)}$ is given by

$$opt(f_i^{(l)})$$

$$= \min \left\{ \min_{f_i^{(l)}} \left\{ U_i(f_i^{(l)}) + \lambda_i^{(l)} Z_i^{(l)} - \sum_{j=0}^{N} \lambda_j^{(l)} f_i^{(l)}(1 - p_{ij}) + \beta_i^{(l)} f_i^{(l)} \right\}, \ \eta_i^{(\max)} D_i^{(l)} \right\}$$

$$\approx \min \left\{ \left\lceil U'^{-1} (\sum_{j=0}^{N} \lambda_j^{(l)}(1 - p_{ij}) - \beta_i^{(l)}) \right\rceil, \ \eta_i^{(\max)} D_i^{(l)} \right\}, \tag{17}$$

where $\lceil \cdot \rceil$ means that '$\cdot$' is rounded up to the nearest integer since the quantity of chunks broadcasted by UE i is integral. The sub-gradient method is employed to update the Lagrangian multipliers λ and β iteratively:

$$\lambda_i^{(l)}(m + 1) = \left[\lambda_i^{(l)}(m) + \alpha(Z_i^{(l)} - \sum_{j:i\in\mathcal{N}_j} f_j^{(l)}(1 - p_{ji})) \right]^+, \tag{18}$$

$$\beta_i^{(l)}(m + 1) = \left[\beta_i^{(l)}(m) - \alpha f_i^{(l)} \right]^+, \tag{19}$$

where m is the iteration number, $\alpha, \alpha > 0$, is a small enough constant step size and $[\cdot]^+ = \max(0, \cdot)$. The pseudo-code for calculating the near-optimal traffic allocation is described in Algorithm 1, in which each node updates its own λ, β and calculate the quantity of chunks to be broadcasted locally. With a small enough step size α, Algorithm 1 can converge after a limited iterations.

Input: $Z_i^{(l)}$, p_{ij}, ω_B and ω_D, $\forall i, j \in \widehat{\mathcal{N}}, \forall l \in \mathcal{L}$
Output: $f^* = \{opt(f_i^{(l)}), \forall i \in \widehat{\mathcal{N}}, \forall l \in \mathcal{L}\}$
1 Initialize α, λ and β ;
2 Flag=true;
3 **while** *Flag* **do**
4   **for** $i = 0; i \leq N$ **do**
5   **for** $l = 1; l \leq L$ **do**
6 | Node i calculates its traffic $opt(f_i^{(l)})$ for each layer using (17)
7   **end**
8   Place $opt(f_i^{(l)})$ into set $F^{(last)}$;
9   Node i updates the Lagrange Multipliers $\lambda_i^{(l)}$, $\beta_i^{(l)}$ using (18) and (19);
10   Node i broadcasts its $\lambda_i^{(l)}$ to its parent nodes j, $j \in \widetilde{\mathcal{N}}_i$, and collects other $\lambda_j^{(l)}$ from its children j, $j \in \mathcal{N}_i$;
11   **end**
12   **if** $(F^{(last)} == F^*)$ & $(F^{(last)} \neq \emptyset)$ **then**
13   Flag=false;
14   Break;
15   **end**
16     $F^* - F^{(last)}$;
17 **end**
18 **return** F^*;

Algorithm 1. Distributed Traffic Allocation (DTA) for downlink and D2D

4 Performance Evaluation

In our simulations, there are nine UEs and one BS in one cell. Considering load balance of the network, we use $U(f) = f^2$ as the objective function, which is convex and twice differentiable. It means that, for each UE, the traffic cost per chunk will be increased much faster with the number of broadcasted chunks increasing. Therefore, each UE will not increase its broadcast traffic even with a lower D2D BLER link. The weights for downlink and D2D transmissions are equally set to 1 except for the simulation in Sect. 4.2. Additionally, each GoP has 6 layers and each layer identically needs 50 coded chunks for reconstruction.

4.1 Influence of Different Link Conditions

Firstly, we conduct two sets of simulations under three cases, and each simulation is repeated 200 times. In each set of simulations, we configure different downlink or D2D BLERs, as Fig. 2 shown, where the x-axis denotes the ranges of "$1 - p_{ij}$" and "$1 - p_{Bj}$" w.r.t. D2D and downlink BLER, respectively. For example, $x = 0.7$ means the "$1 - p_{ij}$" or "$1 - p_{Bj}$" are uniformly distributed in $[0.3, 1.0]$.

    Figure 2(a) shows the minimum traffic cost versus varying p_{ij}, where the downlink BLERs in three cases are uniformly distributed in $[0.05, 0.15]$, $[0.15, 0.25]$ and $[0.35, 0.45]$, respectively. The total traffic cost will be decreased when

p_{ij} is randomly chosen from a lower value x (in x-axis) to 1. In Fig. 2(b), the p_{ij} of D2D are uniformly distributed in [0.05, 0.35], [0.35, 0.70] and [0.55, 0.90], respectively. In all three cases, the traffic costs is decreased when p_{Bj} is randomly chosen from a lower value x (in x-axis) to 1, while the three cases achieve an almost similar traffic cost at different $1-p_{Bj}$ no matter what the p_{ij} is. Therefore, the downlink conditions have more influence on the traffic cost than D2D.

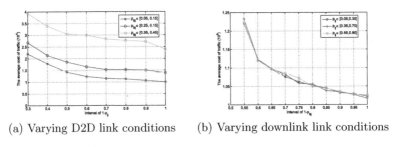

(a) Varying D2D link conditions   (b) Varying downlink link conditions

Fig. 2. The cost of traffic with different BLERs (Color figure online)

Then, to further test the influence of downlink BLER on broadcast traffic, we manually configure two UEs, namely, UE1 and UE2, with lower downlink BLERs in the following simulations, and they can also cover all other UEs within one hop jointly. This simulation is performed under three cases: p_{B1} and p_{B2} are uniformly distributed in [0.05, 0.15], [0.15, 0.25] and [0.35, 0.45], respectively, while other downlink BLERs are uniformly distributed in [0.6, 0.9], [0.7, 0.9] and [0.8, 0.9], respectively. The D2D BLERs are uniformly distributed from 0 to 1. Figure 3 shows the quantity of broadcast chunks versus D2D BLERs. It can be found that UE1 and UE2 broadcast more chunks than other UEs due to their full coverage and lower downlink BLERs. UE1 and UE2 broadcast the least chunks in the first case (Fig. 3(a)) than that in other two cases (Fig. 3(b) and (c)). In contrast, other 7 UEs broadcast more chunks in the first case than that in others. The reason is that, when UE1 and UE1 are matured from BS, the number of chunks received from BS by other 7 UEs is the most on average in first case, and the least in third case due to their different distributions of downlink BLERs. Therefore, UE1 and UE2 will broadcast more chunks to make its neighbors matured in third case than the first two cases.

4.2 Influence of Weight on Traffic Allocation

To test the influence of weight on traffic allocation, we conduct this simulation under different ratio of weights between downlink and D2D. This simulation is performed with one layer, as shown in Fig. 4, where $w_B = 1$ and $w_D = (value\ of\ x) \times 20$. It can be found that the D2D traffic will be decreased with its weight increasing, while the downlink traffic is increased. Therefore, we can give a rationale weight according to their different costs in practice.

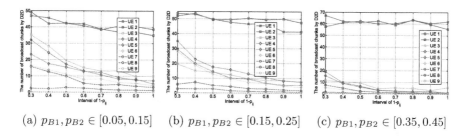

(a) $p_{B1}, p_{B2} \in [0.05, 0.15]$ (b) $p_{B1}, p_{B2} \in [0.15, 0.25]$ (c) $p_{B1}, p_{B2} \in [0.35, 0.45]$

Fig. 3. Traffic allocation under different downlink conditions (Color figure online)

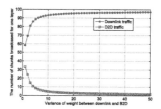

Fig. 4. The influence of weight on traffic allocation (Color figure online)

5 Conclusion

In this paper, we have studied the problem of broadcasting layered video steams in the cellular network. Our objective is to minimize the total traffic cost with consideration of cooperation among UEs. We first construct a MINLP model, in which only the matured UEs can serve as the broadcast candidate. Then, we convert it to a convex model by introducing a step function. Thereafter, we develop a distributed algorithm to obtain its near-optimal value as well as downlink and D2D traffic allocation by employing the theory of convex optimization. Extensive simulations are performed to demonstrate the efficiency of our approach. For the future work, we will focus on investigating the downlink and D2D traffic allocation in consideration of the mobile UEs as well as varying UEs' number.

Acknowledgments. This work is supported by the National Natural Science Foundation of China (No. 61370212, 61402127 and 61502118), the Fundamental Research Fund for the Central Universities (No.HEUCF100601) and the Natural Science Foundation of Heilongjiang Province in China (No. F2016028).

References

1. Zhou, H., Ji, Y., Wang, X., Zhao, B.: Joint resource allocation and user association for SVC multicast over heterogeneous cellular networks. IEEE Trans. Wirel. Commun. **14**(7), 3673–3684 (2015)

2. Bakhshali, A., Chan, W.-Y., Blostein, S.D., et al.: QoE optimization of video multicast with heterogeneous channels and playback requirements. EURASIP J. Wirel. Commun. Networking, 1–21 (2015)
3. He, Z., Cai, Z., Cheng, S., et al.: Approximate aggregation for tracking quantiles and range countings in wireless sensor networks. Theor. Comput. Sci. **607**, 381–390 (2015)
4. Auwera, G.V.D., David, P.T., Reisslein, M.: Traffic and quality characterization of single-layer video streams encoded with the H.264/MPEG-4 advanced video coding standard and scalable video coding extension. Broadcast. IEEE Trans. **54**(3), 698–718 (2008)
5. Condoluci, M., Araniti, G., Molinaro, A., et al.: Multicast resource allocation enhanced by channel state feedbacks for multiple scalable video coding streams in LTE networks. Veh. Technol. IEEE Trans. **65**(5), 1–15 (2015). 10.1109
6. Wang, X., Chen, J., Dutta, A., et al.: Adaptive video streaming over whitespace: SVC for 3-Tiered spectrum sharing. In: 2015 IEEE Conference on Computer Communications (INFOCOM), pp. 28–36 (2015)
7. Keller, L., Le, A., Cici, B., et al.: MicroCast: cooperative video streaming on smartphones. In: The 10th International Conference on Mobile Systems, Applications, and Services, pp. 57–70. ACM (2012)
8. Cheng, S., Cai, Z., Li, J.: Curve query processing in wireless sensor networks. Veh. Technol. IEEE Trans. **64**(11), 5198–5209 (2015)
9. Abedini, N., Sampath, S., Bhattacharyya, R., et al.: Realtime streaming with guaranteed QoS over wireless D2D networks. In: The Fourteenth ACM International Symposium on Mobile ad hoc Networking and Computing, pp. 197–206. ACM (2013)
10. Bethanabhotla, D., Caire, G., Neely, M.J.: Adaptive video streaming for wireless networks with multiple users and helpers. Commun. IEEE Trans. **63**(1), 268–285 (2015)
11. Xing, M., Xiang, S., Cai, L.: A real-time adaptive algorithm for video streaming over multiple wireless access networks. Sel. Areas Commun. IEEE J. **32**(4), 795–805 (2014)
12. Almowuena, S., Rahman, M., Hsu, C.-H., et al.: Energy-aware and bandwidth-efficient hybrid video streaming over mobile networks. Multimedia IEEE Trans. **18**(1), 102–115 (2016)
13. Vukobratović, D., Stanković, V.: Unequal error protection random linear coding strategies for erasure channels. Commun. IEEE Trans. **60**(5), 1243–1252 (2012)
14. Ostovari, P., Wu, J., Khreishah, A., et al.: Scalable video streaming with helper nodes using random linear network coding. IEEE/ACM Trans. Netw., 1–14 (2015). doi:10.1109/TNET
15. Thomos, N., Kurdoglu, E., Frossard, P., et al.: Adaptive prioritized random linear coding and scheduling for layered data delivery from multiple servers. Multimedia IEEE Trans. **17**(6), 893–906 (2015)
16. Wu, J., Cheng, B., Yuen, C., et al.: Distortion-aware concurrent multipath transfer for mobile video streaming in heterogeneous wireless networks. Mobile Comput. IEEE Trans. **14**(4), 688–701 (2015)
17. He, Z., Cai, Z., Wang, X.: Modeling propagation dynamics and developing optimized countermeasures for rumor spreading in online social networks. In: The 35th International Conference onDistributed Computing Systems, pp. 205–214. IEEE (2015)
18. Lei, L., Zhong, Z., Lin, C., et al.: Operator controlled device-to-device communications in LTE-advanced networks. IEEE Wirel. Commun. **19**(3), 96–104 (2012)

19. Gilbert, E.N.: Capacity of a burst-noise channel. Bell Syst. Techn. J. **39**(5), 1253–1265 (1960)
20. Hasslinger, G., Schwahn, A., Hartleb, F.: 2-State (semi-) Markov processes beyond Gilbert-Elliott: Traffic and channel models based on 2nd order statistics. In: 2013 Proceedings IEEE INFOCOM, pp. 1438–1446. IEEE (2013)
21. Wu, J., Yuen, C., Cheung, N.M., et al.: Delay-constrained high definition video transmission in heterogeneous wireless networks with multi-homed terminals. IEEE Trans. Mobile Comput. **15**(3), 641–655 (2016)
22. Gaudette, B., Hanumaiah, V., Vrudhula, S., et al.: Optimal range assignment in solar powered active wireless sensor networks. In: 2012 Proceedings IEEE INFOCOM, pp. 2354–2362. IEEE (2012)
23. Zhang, Y., He, S., Chen, J., et al.: Distributed sampling rate control for rechargeable sensor nodes with limited battery capacity. IEEE Trans. Wirel. Commun. **12**(6), 3096–3106 (2013). Zhou15
24. Zhang, Y., He, S., Chen, J.: Data gathering optimization by dynamic sensing and routing in rechargeable sensor networks. IEEE/ACM Trans. Networking, doi:10.1109/TNET.2015.2425146

Identifying Discrepant Tags in RFID-enabled Supply Chains

Caidong Gu[1(✉)], Wei Gong[2], and Amiya Nayak[3]

[1] Suzhou Vocational University, Suzhou, China
gucaidong6688@163.com
[2] Simon Fraser University, Burnaby, Canada
[3] University of Ottawa, Ottawa, Canada

Abstract. Radio Frequency Identification (RFID) technology is becoming a revolutionary element in supply chain management by providing real-time visibility of goods flows. Across supply chains, one-for-one checking is required at each handover point to discover discrepancies between the physical shipped inventory and receiver's order. This operation is so ubiquitous throughout the product life cycle that its efficiency improvement can prominently optimize the whole supply chain. There are several main challenges, however, in designing efficient solutions for it: inconsistent tag information, high-volume and high-speed RFID data, and high latency in EPCglobal Network. Based on the characteristic polynomial, we propose a tag identification protocol that achieves better almost minimal latency. The most salient feature of our protocol is that its communication complexities scales well with the size of discrepant tags, instead of the size of overall number of tags in traditional methods. Through experimental comparisons, we show that our protocol significantly outperforms previous methods in terms of communication latency.

1 Introduction

Radio Frequency Identification (RFID) that uses radio wave to identify the object, is becoming a revolutionary element in supply chain management around the world [1]. The supply chain usually includes all possible processes involved in the flow of goods: from the supplier to manufacturer to distributor to retailer, and to end-customers. Previously considered as a labor and knowledge intensive process, supply chain management significantly benefits from the adoption of RFID technology in many industries. For example, Wal-Mart gained $287 million benefit from RFID by fixing just a small portion of its inventory problems [2]. There are several compelling reasons of RFID usage for all involved partners in supply chain. First, it improves the efficiency of product pipeline during manufacturing. Since multiple RFID tags can be read simultaneously and automatically without being in the line-of-sight of an RFID reader, many labor intensive tasks can be done in just a few seconds, such as counting. Second, it offers valuable visibility of real-time goods movement and secured transportation during shipping. As active tags are often installed on shipping containers, companies

© Springer International Publishing Switzerland 2016
Q. Yang et al. (Eds.): WASA 2016, LNCS 9798, pp. 162–173, 2016.
DOI: 10.1007/978-3-319-42836-9_15

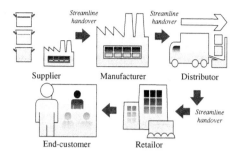

Fig. 1. An example of retail supply chain.

are able to real-time track and manage containers and goods in each handover of supply chain. Third, it increases delivery speed and dispatch accuracy during distributing. As the products reach destination, they are automatically scanned and registered at the entrance, efficiently sorted and put in proper places with the help of RFID.

As shown in Fig. 1, a typical supply chain includes end-customers who buy goods from a retailer. The retailer might have stocked many kinds of goods from distributor, who usually imports goods in large quantities from manufacturer. The supplier provides raw materials to manufacturer. Across the supply chain, all streamline handover points are required for one-for-one checking that is to detailedly compare individual items from two sources to determine if they agree. For example, when products arrive from a distributor, the retailer should perform a physical scan using RFID to collect goods information on pallets and cases. Then these gathered information are used to check against the ship list sent by the distributor. If there are any discrepancies found, the retailer should immediately identify and fixed them. Therefore, one-for-one checking is such a common and frequent operation in streamline handover that its efficiency improvement should prominently optimize whole supply chain.

Despite the importance of one-for-one checking, there are several key challenges in designing efficient solutions for it.

Inconsistent Information: The mismatches between physical shipped inventory and receiver's orders often occur due to many factors, such as theft and inventory errors. According to national retail security survey [3], in 2010 US retailers lost more than \$19.3 billion caused by vendor fraud, administrative errors, shoplifting and employee theft. Therefore resolving these discrepancies is not easy in the presence of possible missing, counterfeit, unread, misplaced tags, or all of them.

Big Data: Since RFID-enabled supply chain is streamlined by automatically monitoring the flow of goods, pervasive RFID readers deployed across supply chain continuously generate real-time data in high-volume and high-speed. For instance, Walmart creates about 7 terabyte RFID data everyday [4]. Thus, getting fast and accurate analytic results from those big RFID data poses a big challenge in time-critical supply chain.

High-latency Network: Except for Electronic Product Code (EPC) that is the unique identification of tag, many other RFID data, e.g., arrival time and location, need to be retrieved through centralized EPCglobal Network infrastructures, leading to considerable network delay. Moreover, performance of online operations suffers from notable network latency due to long distance communication in EPCglobal Network. According to measurements in [5], 65 % of the queries take more than 0.5 s to respond even under nearly ideal network conditions. The response time might be even longer in complex test case.

To address the above issues, we propose an efficient scheme for discrepant tag identification in large RFID-enabled supply chains. First, we abstract discrepant tag identification problem and introduce a deterministic identification protocol based on characteristic polynomial. Then to remove the constraint of a priori known parameter, we propose a randomized protocol that can estimate the size of discrepant tag size. Through experimental comparisons, we show that our protocol significantly outperforms previous schemes.

2   Problem Formulation

We abstract one-for-one checking in supply chain as two sides communication: the sender and receiver. We focus on an important network metrics: communication complexity that is the total bits transferred in network. We assume each item is associated with TagData (t) which is a bitstring of size b_t. It consists EPC and TagInfo which are data need to be retrieved through EPCglobal Network, e.g., keys associated with the product. We do not discuss the situations that TagData can be totally obtained by offline means, since it does not follow the EPCglobal standards which are widely adopted in current industries.

As measurements done in [5], EPCglobal Network does not perform well in real-time tracking and tracing application due to undesirable network latency. As a product moves through the supply chain, it may pass through the fields of view of many different trading partners, each of which may record some observable information about that product. These EPC Information Services (EPC-IS) instances then register their knowledge with the EPC Discovery Service. Notable network delay, thus, is inevitably introduced in information retrieval since each of EPC-IS instances who have information about this product needs to be visited. Therefore, in EPCglobal Network application, we seek to make minimal communication complexity while keeping round complexity as minimum as possible.

Thus, we formalize the problem of discrepant tags identification as follows: given a physical scanned list with size n, $P = \{t_1^p, t_1^p, ..., t_n^p\}$ on receiver and the ship list with size m, $S = \{t_1^s, t_2^s, ..., t_m^s\}$ on sender, how can receiver identify all disagreed tags using minimal communication complexity and round complexity.

3   Deterministic Identification Protocol

The key of Deterministic Identification Protocol (DIP) is to employ characteristic polynomial, which is proposed in [6,7]. It is used to encode both physical list and ship list. Simply put, first, both receiver and sender evaluate their own characteristic polynomials at sample points. Then sender transfers its characteristic polynomial value to receiver, instead of raw RFID data. Finally, receiver discovers all discrepant tags by interpolating corresponding rational function. Here we assume the upper bound of discrepant tag size, d, is known as a priori for both sides. Next, we will describe encoding and decoding processes of DIP using characteristic polynomial.

Encode. By characteristic polynomial definition, a set of tagData, $T = \{t_1, t_2, ..., t_n\}$, can be represented as:

$$\mathcal{P}_T(t) = (t - t_1)(t - t_2) \cdots (t - t_n). \tag{1}$$

We use ΔP to denote the tags that are only on physical list but not on ship list. Similarly, ΔS stands for the tags which are only on ship list but not on physical list. Q denotes the tags that are both on physical list and ship list. Therefore, consider the ratio between characteristic polynomials of P and S:

$$\frac{\mathcal{P}_P(t)}{\mathcal{P}_S(t)} = \frac{\mathcal{P}_Q(t) \cdot \mathcal{P}_{\Delta P}(t)}{\mathcal{P}_Q(t) \cdot \mathcal{P}_{\Delta S}(t)} = \frac{\mathcal{P}_{\Delta P}(t)}{\mathcal{P}_{\Delta S}(t)}. \tag{2}$$

From above we know that efficient computations of the ratio of these two characteristic polynomials is important for recovering ΔP and ΔS. Thus, sender needs to evaluate characteristic polynomial over a collection of d sample points and transmits those polynomial values as codewords.

Note that if a sample point happens to be an element of P or S, then computation of their polynomial ratio becomes hard due to vanishment of corresponding characteristic polynomial. Therefore, we require that all arithmetic operations are taken within finite field $\mathbb{F}_q$ to ensure that d sample points should not coincide with tagData in list, where q is at least $2^{b_t} + d$.

Decode. Although the degrees of $\mathcal{P}_P(t)$ and $\mathcal{P}_S(t)$ are always very high due to large list size, the degrees of numerator and denominator of $\frac{\mathcal{P}_{\Delta P}(t)}{\mathcal{P}_{\Delta S}(t)}$ may be rather small as all common factors cancel out in Eq. 2. Meanwhile, according to standard theorem about rational function interpolation in [8], we know that a support set of size d is adequate to guarantee the uniqueness of rational function. Therefore, we can use Gaussian elimination [9] to completely derive desired rational function with d sample points. The time complexity of Gaussian elimination is $\mathcal{O}(d^3)$.

Analysis. Since the size of finite field q is at least $2^{b_t} + d$, DIP requires one more bit for each evaluation value than TagData size, i.e., $b_t + 1$. In total, DIP is required to transfer d evaluation values and ship list size that is used in decoding. Thus, communication complexity of DIP is $(b_t + 1)d + b_t$ bits.

From above, the advantage of DIP is clearly shown that its communication complexity is linear with the size of discrepant tag size. In other words, the

DIP is highly scalable and thus suitable for large-scale supply chain even with millions of tags.

4 Probabilistic Identification Protocol with Estimation

In order to remove the constraint that assumes the size of discrepant tags is known, we propose Probabilistic Identification Protocol with Estimation (PIP-E). The core of PIP-E is to construct a hierarchical estimator to approximate the number of discrepancies size.

Here we borrow the idea of FM-Sketch [10] to organize the tags in both ship list and physical list. In FM-Sketch, each bit j in data structure is set to 0 or 1. If it is 1, it means that at least one element is sampled with probability 2^{-j}. Intuitively thinking, if there are 8 distinct elements in list, the third bit is set to 1 under sampled probability with $\frac{1}{8}$. Thus, FM-Sketch estimates $2^3 = 8$ as the list size. While FM-Sketch is effective in estimating the set size, it cannot give results of discrepancies size since there is no information about which element is common in this original FM-Sketch. But that is exactly what our hierarchical estimator does.

The hierarchical estimator works as follows. First, we geometrically divide tags in the list into b_t layers. The j-th layer should contain roughly $2^{-(j+1)}$ elements of original list. This partition can be achieved by putting each element to the layer according to the number of leading zeros of its binary form. Then we encode each layer into its corresponding characteristic polynomial (CPi) under θ sample points. An illustration is shown Fig. 2. For example, given $b_t = 4$, element $5 = (00101)_2$ should be assigned to level CP2 and element $8 = (01000)_2$ should be in level CP1.

As shown in Fig. 3, the key of decoding procedure for hierarchical estimator is to run DIP in each level. Therefore, combining discrepancies information in each level would give accurate estimate.

With the help of this hierarchical estimator, it is easy to realize discrepancies identification in one round trip. First receiver sends its hierarchical estimator to sender. Sender then approximates the number of discrepancies (d) from decoding receiver's and its own estimator, and transmits its characteristic polynomials on d points. Finally, receiver interpolates rational function to exactly identify all discrepancies.

Note that geometric partitions discussed before rely on uniformly distributed elements. So some proper hash functions should be properly employed to achieve this, such as t-wise independent hash functions.

Analysis. The bits transferred in each level of hierarchical estimator is θ evaluation points plus one check point:

$$\theta(b_t + 1) + b_t + 1.$$

So the total communication complexity of PIP-E is:

$$(b_t + 1)(\theta b_t + b_t + d + 1) - 1. \tag{3}$$

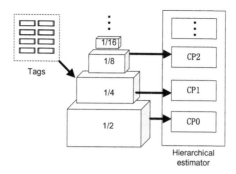

Fig. 2. Hierarchical estimator construction.

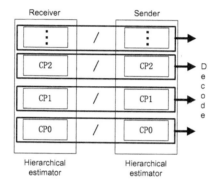

Fig. 3. Hierarchical estimator decoding.

The theoretical results concerning the efficiency of our hierarchical estimator are included in the appendices. According to our experiments, using 96 levels (as typical EPC is 96-bit) of 40 sample points, this hierarchical estimator is accurate to handle discrepancies size up to 2^{96} with high probability. Thus, PIP-E might be able to achieve constant overhead in discrepancies identification.

5 Evaluation

In this section, extensive experiments are conducted to demonstrate efficiencies of our schemes in terms of both communication data and time. We also include the bloom filter based approach as a baseline.

Bloom Filter Based Approach. Another alternative solution for discrepant tag identification may use bloom filter, which is a famous data structure for compressing data set. The bloom filter based solution (BFS) can be executed as follows:

1. Receiver sends its bloom filter BF_1 to sender.
2. Sender discovers ship list's elements not in BF_1 as ΔS, and transfers ΔS and its own bloom filter BF_2 to receiver.
3. Receiver discovers physical list's elements not in BF_2 as ΔP.
4. Elements in ΔP and ΔS are discrepant tags.

5.1 Experimental Comparison

To demonstrate the practicality and effectiveness of our proposed protocols, we develop a simulator using CSIM [11] to emulate an RFID-enabled supply chain. In this section, we will describe our implementation and provide experimental results under different settings.

Table 1. Main parameters in experiments

Parameter	Value
Number of warehouses	5
Pallet injection frequency	10 per second
Cases per pallet	100
Items per case	100
Discrepancies ratio (η)	[0.01, 0.99], default 0.01
Ship list size (N)	[10^7, 10^8], default 5×10^7
Round trip time (RTT)	[1, 1000] ms, default 10 ms
Bandwidth (B)	default 20 Mbits/s
p in bloom filter	default 0.01 %

Experimental Setup. The main parameters are shown in Table 1. The supply chain arranges 5 warehouses in a single-source directed acyclic graph as in Fig. 1. At the source warehouse, pallets of cases are injected and move through warehouses in sequence. At each handover point, we suppose an adversary randomly removes, injects, or replaces tags in original ship list at ratio η. After scanning products, receiver then starts discrepant tag identification process through EPCglobal Network. All experiments are done on a Server with Intel Xeon E5-2620, 32 G memory, and SAMSUNG 1 TB SSD. Since there is no well-known or standard RFID data set, we randomly generate 10^9 96-bit EPCs and store them in MySQL Community Server 5.6.19. We use Victor Shoups Number Theory Library to perform finite field arithmetic [12]. For each result, we take 100 runs and report the average.

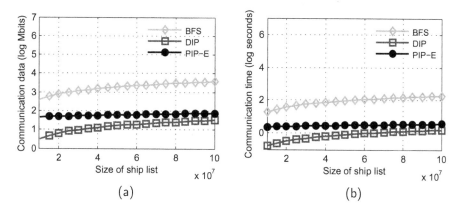

Fig. 4. Communication overhead with RTT=1 ms: (a) Communication data VS varying size of ship list; (b) Communication time VS varying size of ship list.

Varying Size of Ship List. We varies the ship data size from 10^7 to 10^8 with RTT=1 ms and other parameters are default. In this extremely low latency network setting, we make several important observations from Fig. 4. First, DIP and PIP-E achieve much lower cost than BFS in terms of both communication data and time. The main reason for this is that communication complexity of BFS is linear with the size of overall tags, while our probabilistic protocol scales with the size of discrepancy tags. Second, as shown in Fig. 4a, PIP-E is close to lower bound (DIP) for data size. And in the low latency network condition, the advantage of lesser rounds is suppressed, as shown in Fig. 4b. Third, the communication cost of PIP-E is unsensitive to the size of discrepant. The major reason for this is that PIP-E uses fixed-size hierarchical estimator.

Varying Network Latency. Next, we investigate performance of protocols under different latencies: from RTT=100 ms to RTT=1000 ms. The results are shown in Fig. 5. As expected, BFS does not perform well in intermediate latency network as illustrated in Fig. 5a. In high latency network, PIP-E wins over all other protocols. In particular, the communication time of PIP-E is only 25.9 % of BFS, when RTT $= 1000$ ms and $N = 10^8$.

Estimator of PIP-E. Finally, we examine the accuracy of estimator of PIP-E. Here, we use a standard metric relative error (ε),

$$\varepsilon = \frac{\hat{n} - n}{n},$$

where $\hat{n}$ is the estimated value and n is the actual value. Our estimator is evaluated using size of ship list from 10^7 to 10^8 in Fig. 6a and discrepancies ratio from 5 % to 95 % in Fig. 6b. We observe that relative error of our estimator maintains around 0.01 in most of cases. This is another supporting evidence that why PIP-E protocol is so efficient in our previous experiments.

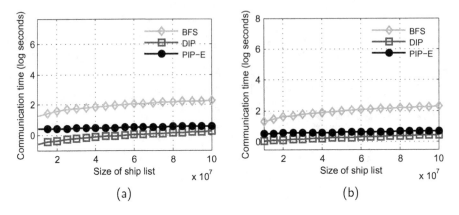

Fig. 5. Communication time under different latencies: (a) intermediate latency network, RTT = 100 ms; (b) high latency network, RTT=1000 ms.

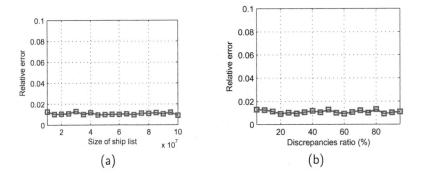

Fig. 6. Relative standard error under different ship size and discrepancies ratio: (a) Relative standard error VS different ship size; (b) Relative standard error VS discrepancies ratio.

6   Related Work

Cardinality estimation, missing-tag identification, and authentication in large-scale RFID systems are closely related to our discrepant tag identification problem.

Recently a number of probabilistic RFID counting schemes are proposed to fast and reliably approximate the count of tags. The first estimation solution, Unified Probabilistic Estimator (UPE), is proposed by Kodialam et al. [13]. Zheng et al. introduce a novel tree structure to encode tag set and improve the estimation efficiency to $\mathcal{O}(\log \log n)$ [14]. Shahzad et al. propose Average Run based Tag Estimation (ART) method based on a new statistical entity, average run length, achieving 7x faster than UPE [15]. While all above schemes work well in estimating the count of tags, it cannot be used in discrepancies identification as it does not discern the tag's genuineness.

Missing-tag is another related problem [16]. Li et al. propose a series of well-designed protocols to efficiently identify all missing-tags in [17]. Trusted Reader Protocol (TRP) and UnTrusted Reader Protocol (UTRP) are introduced to monitor missing tag in both trust and untrust scenarios [18]. While all missing-tag solutions are effective if some tags are indeed absent, they are unable to identify unauthorized tags that are adulterated into original tags without replacement.

To efficiently verify the genuineness of a single tag, many approaches are designed according to various purposes, such as Physically Unclonable Function (PUF) [19], hash based authentication [20], novel tree structure in key management [21]. By distinguishing the difference in single echo observation, the first probabilistic batch authentication scheme is proposed in [22]. Besides heavy computation overhead incurred by those authentication schemes, they cannot discover anything wrong if adversary only takes some tags/products away from ship list without replacement.

In RFID-enable supply chain management, a novel storage model based on bloom filter is proposed for efficient distributed storage and query processing [4]. Lee et al. propose an effective path encoding scheme to encode the flow information for products in supply chain [23]. Cao et al. introduce a scalable and distributed stream processing system for tracking and monitoring products' location and containment [24]. These work, however, do not consider discrepant tag identification problem.

7   Concluding Remarks

In this paper, we propose a protocol that aims to efficiently identify discrepant tags in RFID-enable supply chain. The most prominent feature of our protocol is they scale well to the size of discrepant tags, not the size of overall tags as traditional methods do. Through analysis and experiments, we show that our protocol significantly outperform previous schemes.

Acknowledgments. This work is supported in part by NSFC under Grant No. 61472268 and Natural Sciences and Engineering Research Council (NSERC) of Canada grant no. CRDPJ-476659.

Appendix:

Lemma 1. *Given a level i and a constant $c > 1$, the relative error of estimated cardinality of the union of level j or greater is at most $\mathcal{O}(\sqrt{\frac{c2^i}{M}})$ with probability $(1 - 2^{-c})$, where $j < i$ and M is the size of all tags.*

Proof. In hierarchical estimator, we use Z_j to denote the size of union of level j or greater, and μ_j be its expectation. Thus, we know that

$$\mu_j = \mathrm{E}(Z_j) = \frac{M}{2^j}.$$

Also by chernoff bound, we can get

$$\Pr(Z_j > (1+\varepsilon)) < e^{\frac{-\mu_j\varepsilon^2}{4}}, \Pr(Z_j < (1-\varepsilon)) < e^{\frac{-\mu_j\varepsilon^2}{4}}.$$

Therefore, if we let $\varepsilon = \sqrt{4(c+2)\frac{2^i}{M}\ln 2} \sim \mathcal{O}(\sqrt{\frac{c2^i}{M}})$, we can know that the probability that relative error of Z_j is at most ε is at most $2e^{\frac{-\mu_j\varepsilon^2}{4}}$. Then by a union bound, the probability that the relative error of any Z_j is out of ε is at most

$$\sum_{j=0}^{i} 2e^{\frac{-\mu_j\varepsilon^2}{4}} \leq \sum_{j=0}^{i} 2^{-(c+1)2^{i-j}} \leq 2^{-c}$$

Theorem 1. *Given $0 < \varepsilon, \delta < 1$, the hierarchical estimator is able to estimate the discrepant tag size with relative error ε and failure probability δ.*

Proof. Let α be the constant in the big-O notation in Lemma 1.

If $d^2 \leq \alpha^2\varepsilon^{-2}\log\delta^{-1}$, then the level-0 of hierarchical estimator will decode all discrepant tags with probability at least $1 - \frac{\delta}{2}$.

Otherwise, we use i to be $\frac{d}{2^i} \approx \alpha^2\varepsilon^{-2}\log\delta^{-1}$. Thus, by Lemma 1, the relative error of the number of tags in the i-th and higher level is at most ε with probability $1 - \frac{\delta}{2}$, if we let $c = \lceil\log\delta^{-1}\rceil + 1$.

References

1. Benedetti, D., Maselli, G., Petrioli, C.: Fast identification of mobile RFID tags. In: Proceedings of IEEE MASS (2012)
2. Wal-Mart's RFID Refresh. RFID Journal (2007)
3. Lunn, D.: Employee Theft: Eliminate The Opportunity Guest Series Part 1
4. Liu, J., Xiao, B., Kai, B., Chen, L.: Efficient distributed query processing in large rfid-enabled supply chains. In: Proceedings of IEEE INFOCOM (2014)
5. Ziekow, H., Fabian, B., Müller, C.: High-speed access to RFID data: meeting real-time requirements in distributed value chains. In: Meersman, R., Herrero, P., Dillon, T. (eds.) OTM 2009 Workshops. LNCS, vol. 5872, pp. 142–151. Springer, Heidelberg (2009)
6. Blum, M., Kannan, S.: Designing programs that check their work. J. ACM (JACM) **42**(1), 269–291 (1995)
7. Minsky, Y., Trachtenberg, A., Zippel, R.: Set reconciliation with nearly optimal communication complexity. IEEE Trans. Inf. Theor. **49**(9), 2213–2218 (2003)
8. Stoer, J., Bulirsch, R.: Introduction to Numerical Analysis, vol. 12. Springer, Heidelberg (2002)
9. Zippel, R.E.: Effective Polynomial Computation. Springer, Heidelberg (1993)
10. Flajolet, P., Martin, G.N.: Probabilistic counting algorithms for database applications. J. Comput. Syst. Sci. **31**(2), 182–209 (1985)
11. http://www.csim.com/
12. http://www.shoup.net/ntl/
13. Kodialam, M., Nandagopal, T.: Fast and reliable estimation schemes in RFID systems. In: Proceedings of ACM MobiCom (2006)

14. Zheng, Y., Li, M., Qian, C.: PET: Probabilistic estimating tree for large-scale RFID estimation. In: Proceedings of IEEE ICDCS (2011)
15. Shahzad, M., Liu, A.X.: Every bit counts: fast and scalable RFID estimation. In: Proceedings of ACM MobiCom (2012)
16. Zhang, R., Liu, Y., Zhang, Y., Sun, J.: Fast identification of the missing tags in a large RFID system. In: Proceedings of IEEE SECON (2011)
17. Li, T., Chen, S., Ling, Y.: Identifying the missing tags in a large RFID system. In: Proceedings of ACM MOBIHOC (2010)
18. Tan, C., Sheng, B., Li, Q.: How to monitor for missing RFID tags. In: Proceedings of IEEE ICDCS, pp. 295–302 (2008)
19. Bolotnyy, L., Robins, G.: Physically unclonable function-based security and privacy in RFID systems. In: Proceedings of IEEE PERCOM (2007)
20. Weis, S.A., Sarma, S.E., Rivest, R.L., Engels, D.W.: Security and privacy aspects of low-cost radio frequency identification systems. In: Hutter, D., Müller, G., Stephan, W., Ullmann, M. (eds.) Security in Pervasive Computing. LNCS, vol. 2802, pp. 50–59. Springer, Heidelberg (2004)
21. Lu, L., Liu, Y., Li, X.: Refresh: weak privacy model for RFID systems. In: Proceedings of IEEE INFOCOM (2010)
22. Yang, L., Han, J., Qi, Y., Liu, Y.: Identification-free batch authentication for RFID tags. In: Proceedings of IEEE ICNP (2010)
23. Lee, C.H., Chung, C.W.: Efficient storage scheme and query processing for supply chain management using RFID. In: Proceedings of ACM SIGMOD (2008)
24. Cao, Z., Sutton, C., Diao, Y., Shenoy, P.: Distributed inference and query processing for rfid tracking and monitoring. Proc. VLDB Endowment 4(5), 326–337 (2011)

SHMDRS: A Smartphone-Based Human Motion Detection and Response System

Ke Lin[1], Siyao Cheng[1(✉)], Yingshu Li[2], Jianzhong Li[1], Hong Gao[1], and Hongzhi Wang[1]

[1] School of Computer Science and Technology, Harbin Institute of Technology, Harbin, China
linkehit@163.com, {csy,lijzh,honggao,wanghz}@hit.edu.cn
[2] Department of Computer Science, Georgia State University, Atlanta, GA, USA
yili@gsu.edu

Abstract. Nowadays, the human detection and response system brings convenience to people's daily life, and it also makes many applications of cyber-physical systems (CPS) to be possible. The traditional human detection and response systems always depend on some special devices, so that the prices of such systems are quite expensive. Considering that the widely-used smart phones are embedded many sensors, they provide a new way to construct a low-cost motion detection and response system. In this paper, a new architecture of the motion detection and response system is proposed based on smart phones, and the methods for detecting the human motion and responding accordingly are also given. Comparing with the traditional systems, the newly-proposed motion detection system is server-free and does not require any special devices. Moreover, the location-aware problem is also considered while designing the response module in the system.

Keywords: Human motion detection · Smart phone · Cyber-physical system

1 Introduction

As an important application of cyber-physical systems, the health monitoring and smart home are eagerly required nowadays. For example, many elders are living alone, so that it is very important to obtain their real time health data and detect whether they are falling down immediately for emergency. Thus, efficient and effective systems to detect human motions and respond accordingly are urgently demanded.

Traditional human motion detecting systems are based on body sensor networks (BSNs) [1–3]. The system binds some sensors on the monitoring human, judges the motion of the human based on the collected sensory data, and makes actions according to the judgement. The appearance of BSNs brings much convenience for health monitoring and smart home, however, they also have the following drawbacks, which cannot be ignored. First, the special sensors are

© Springer International Publishing Switzerland 2016
Q. Yang et al. (Eds.): WASA 2016, LNCS 9798, pp. 174–185, 2016.
DOI: 10.1007/978-3-319-42836-9_16

required for a BSN, so that the deployment of such BSN is very expensive. Second, since the sensors always bind to the monitored human's body, it makes the human feel uncomfortable in regular life. Third, since the motions of a human are unpredictable and some motions may break the sensors, the BSNs are also fragile for many cases.

In order to recover the above problems and make motion detecting to be more comfortable for humans, the Kinect [4–6] is developed recently. It has a camera to take the photos or videos of human motions, and the captured motions are classified by comparing the photos (or videos) with the training set. According to the classification results, the responses are made accordingly. It does not require to bind the sensors to human's body, so that the comfortableness and robustness of the systems are largely improved. However, such systems also have their problems. First, the monitoring region of a camera is very limited, so that if a human is moving out of the monitoring region of the camera, then his motions cannot be captured by the system. Second, the multimedia data, such as image or video, are required to be processed in real time, so that the computation complexity is very high in practice. Third, a special server is needed to process the multimedia data, which also increases the costs of the whole system.

Due to the above reasons, designing a low-cost and convenient motion monitoring system is still an open problem for researchers. Considering that the smart phones embedded many sensors, such as accelerometer, digital compass, gyroscope, GPS, microphone and camera [7–10], are widely used currently, the human motion detection and response system can be constructed based on them since many types of sensory data can be acquired and processing ability of the smart phones becomes more and more powerful. Comparing with the Kinect and similar systems, the smart phone based systems are server-free and the data involved in the system are vector data instead of multimedia ones, so that the cost and computational complexity can be largely reduced. Furthermore, the smart phone based system does not require to bind special devices on monitoring human, so that it will be more comfortable if such system is adopted rather than the BSNs. In this paper, we will study such smart phone based system, and the main contributions of the paper are listed as follows:

1. A novel and server-free framework of motion detection and response system is proposed based on widely-used smart phones.
2. Two new modules for motion detecting and responding accordingly are designed based on HTML5 and CSS3. The lightweight detecting and responding algorithms are designed so that they can be applied on the server-free systems.
3. The location-aware algorithm and module are also designed for further improving the performance of the systems.
4. The extensive experimental results are carried out to verify the efficiency and effectiveness of the proposed system.

The organization of the paper is as follows. Section 2 shows the overview of the whole system. Section 3 provides the motion detection algorithm and module. Section 4 gives the response algorithm and module. Section 5 proposes the location-aware algorithm and module. Section 6 presents the experimental results. Section 7 discusses the related works. Finally, Sect. 8 concludes the whole paper.

2   Overview of the System

The overall architecture of the system is shown in Fig. 1, which includes the human motion detecting module, the response module and the location retrieving module.

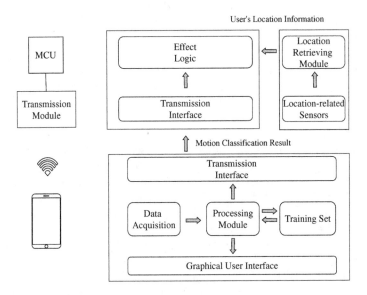

Fig. 1. Overall architecture

The human motion detection module is deployed in a smart phone as an *APP software*. The aim of this module is to recognize the gestures or motions of the user. In order to achieve such aim, the sensory data acquisition and processing components, transmission interface, and graphical user interface should be involved. Besides, the techniques for compressing the training set also should be considered in order to preserve the training set only in the given smart phone and save its storage resource. The details of the human motion detection module is presented in Sect. 3.

The response module is to drive the corresponding reactors according to the motions detected by the first module. We use several micro controlling unit chips to achieve the above aim, and it supports to turn on or off the lights, the doors, the curtains, *etc*. The detailed introduction of such module is given in Sect. 4.

Finally, the location retrieving module is to provide the users' location information to help the reactors to be more accurate. In the human motion detection and response systems, the users always want different reactors to take action even they are doing the same motion. For example, when the user in the lobby, he wants to turn on the light of the lobby by raising his hand. However, the light of bedroom should be turned on when the user in the bedroom by doing the same motion. Therefore, the location-aware motion detection is very important, and user's location information should be carefully considered. In our system, we use several sensors, such as infrared sensors, to collect location information. The detailed information of such module is shown in Sect. 5.

Among all the above modules, no server is involved, so that our system is a server-free system.

3   The Human Motion Detection Module

3.1   Software Architecture

The software module on the smart phone is implemented by HTML5 [11] and CSS3 instead of native programming language for the smart phone platforms (e.g. Java for Android and Objective-C for iOS). That means the detecting system runs on a browser. When the user login to our system for the first time, the local cache will automatically cache the whole system into the smart phone and the server is no longer required. We call it Pseudo-B/S Architecture, which means the software system runs on the browser but it doesn't require a server while using. Choosing such an architecture is based on the following reasons:

1. HTML5 and CSS3 are cross-platform. This allows the system to be deployed on different platforms without recompiling because HTML5 with its JavaScript can be executed on almost all browsers with JavaScript engine (e.g. Safari, Chrome, Firefox for mobile phones).
2. The HTML5 sensor API [12] for ARM platforms is satisfactory for our task. The early applications on mobile phones that collect sensory data are based on native sensor API. This limits the cross-platform scheme. Thanks to the HTML5 sensor API, the sampling rate and data accuracy by browser applications are highly promoted and fine enough for our system.
3. The HTML5 provides application-styled user interface. When an HTML5 page is defined application-styled and fully cached, it can be used without installing and the users never feel they are faced with a web page but a native App.

The graphical user interface is built based on HTML5 with application style and the Bootstrap [13]. The latter is famous as a mobile-device-first frontend framework developed by Twitter. Figure 2 shows the screenshots of GUI, which are so similar to the appearance of native Apps but not web pages.

3.2   Data Acquisition and Collection

The sensory data is collected by the HTML5 sensors API. The 5th generation HTML standard integrates sensors API for mobile phones that runs on

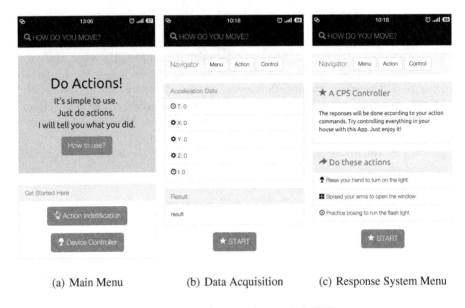

(a) Main Menu   (b) Data Acquisition   (c) Response System Menu

Fig. 2. Examples for App-styled GUI

the browsers instead of on middlewares such as PhoneGap. In our design, each motion sample is described by 20 points, where each point includes a time stamp and 3-axis acceleration data. Each point is sent to the processing module instantly it's collected instead of waiting for the whole sample. The processing module will convert data points into three time series for future uses.

3.3 Data Processing and Machine Learning

The action recognition module is implemented by the machine learning method K-Nearest Neighbours [14,15]. The training set is collected the same way as using the system, and we manually mark those data with the motion type. When the user's new sensory data of motion is collected, the system runs kNN to find the most similar samples in the training set to give the classification of the motion. In order to measure the distance of two samples accurately, the Dynamic Time Warping algorithm (DTW) [16,17], which was firstly used for voice signal recognition is implemented in the module. Algorithm 1 shows its framework. It's a lightweight algorithm calculates the distance (or rather similarity) of two time series [18] considering their warping. Our system firstly calculates the DTW distance of the two samples in x, y and z-axis acceleration, and then the distance of two samples is described by the following equation:

$$d(s_i, s_j) = \sqrt{\frac{dtw(x_i, x_j)^2 + dtw(y_i, y_j)^2 + dtw(z_i, z_j)^2}{3}} \tag{1}$$

where $d(s_i, s_j)$ is the distance of the two samples s_i and s_j that will be used in kNN, $dtw(a, b)$ is the DTW distance between two single-axis time series.

Algorithm 1. Dynamic Time Warping Algorithm (DTW)

Input: Time series x, y with length n

Output: The DTW distance d between x and y

1 Allocate a 2-dimension array named DTW

2 Initialize each $DTW_{i,0}$ with ∞

3 Initialize each $DTW_{0,i}$ with ∞

4 $DTW_{0,0} \leftarrow 0$

5 **for** i *in range (1 to n)* **do**

6   **for** j *in range (1 to n)* **do**

7          $d \leftarrow \sqrt{(x_i - y_j)^2}$

8          $DTW_{i,j} \leftarrow d + min(DTW_{i-1,j}, DTW_{i,j-1}, DTW_{i-1,j-1})$

9 Return $DTW_{n,n}$

3.4 Light-Kernel and Server-Free Design

As Fig. 3(a) shows, when our system was first designed, it was with a processing server (a laptop personal computer), and the function of the mobile phone end was only to collect data and send formalized data to the server, and then the latter dealt with the processing task. Sometimes the user want to try the motion recognition demo when there isn't a computer. We find that running with a server brings so much inconvenience. Besides, The processing ability of a smart phone is high enough to handle the data processing, and the bottleneck of the efficiency is the often the server-client communication complexity. As a result, we improved the motion recognition module to a server-free edition. Figure 3(b) shows the server-free edition of detection system. We reconstructed the recognition module with JavaScript and compressed the training set to save them in the mobile phone. Then we added cache to the system. Those improvements allow the recognition system to run on the smart phone without a server.

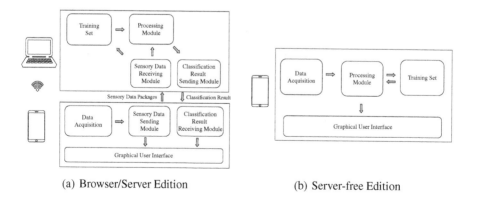

(a) Browser/Server Edition   (b) Server-free Edition

Fig. 3. Architecture of motion detection system

4   The Response and Controller Module

The response module is deployed on micro controlling unit chips. When the motion detection module finishes the classification, it sends a 8-bit controlling signal with the recognition result to the MCU via the transmission module. The MCU works according to the following steps:

Step 1. Wait for interrupts. When the MCU don't receive a interrupt request, it remains idle.

Step 2. Receive the interrupt vector. When the MCU receives the interrupt request from the transmission module, it analyzes the interrupt vector and acquires the classification result from it, and then check whether it's a location-aware command or not. If it's unrelated to location information, jump to step 5.

Step 3. Fetch the user's location. The MCU gets the user's location that is saved in the MCU memory. How the user's location is ascertained will be discussed in Sect. 5.

Step 4. Form the command. The MCU forms the controlling signal based on the interrupt vector and the user's location (if necessary).

Step 5. Send command to the proper reactor. Finally, the MCU sends the controlling signal to the reactors that take effects as the response.

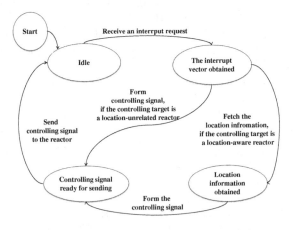

Fig. 4. The state transition diagram of response module

That process can be described by the Fig. 4. The hardware system for response module is deployed on a demoboard and the real household appliances are simulated by LED sets, electric relays, and step motors. Those electric components are connected to the GPIO (General Purpose Input/Output) interfaces of the MCU. For practical uses, the electric relays can be connected to the home appliances, and the step motors can be bound to doors and curtains to control them.

5 The Location Retrieving Module

When the system was firstly implemented, we had to allocate a gesture command for each reactor. We found a problem that if the number of reactors became large, the users would have to remember a long gesture command list, which is no better than a long menu of buttons.

With the progress of our research, we find that some of the reactors have very high similarity. Such as lights and windows in different rooms. If we take locations into consideration, we can control similar reactors in different rooms by the same gesture, which successfully reduces the quantity of gesture commands. For a same gesture the user do, it refers to different reactors when the user is in different places. Such as which light to turn on when the user raises his hands is decided by which room he is in. Thus, we add location retrieving module to the system.

In order to obtain the user's location, we try infrared sensors and pyroelectric sensors to detect the user and the result is desirable. The infrared sensors or laser sensors can be deployed at the doors and send location-changing information when they are sheltered. While the pyroelectric sensors, which can detect infrared rays radiated by the users, can be deployed in certain positions in the room to detect the user's existence.

With the help of those sensors, we can obtain room-level location information of the user. When the user is detected by sensors, the sensors will send an external interrupt signal to the MCU and then save the location information in the memory. When the user do a gesture to control a device, the MCU will take the user's location into consideration to decide which response to take effect.

Considering that not all the reactors need the location information, the reactors in the system can be distinguished into three kinds, which are location-free reactors, location-locked reactors and location-aware reactors. The response module does the following different operations according to the kind it belongs to when receiving interrupt request:

For the location-free reactors, the response is only decided by the motion or gesture the user do. The MCU skips fetching the user's location and sends the controlling signal instantly they receive the classification result. For instance, there is only one air conditioner in your apartment, no matter where you are, your gesture commands related to the air conditioner is surely referring to that one. The system don't have to consider where the user is.

For the location-locked reactors, the controlling command only works when you are at the correct place. The MCU judges the legality of controlling signal by the location information before it takes effect. For example, the system will do nothing if you do the window-controlling gestures at a room without any window, instead of opening the window in other rooms.

For the location-aware reactors, the response is both decided by gesture commands and user's location. The MCU fetches the user's location obtained before and form the controlling signal with a fusion of classification result and location information, and then send to the related reactors.

6   Experimental Results

The first group of experiments is on the human motion data collecting and drawing graphs for several human motions. The data is collected at the sampling rate of 20 Hz with an Android smart phone. The reason for choosing such low sampling rate is considering the sampling ability for HTML5 sensor API and various smart phones. Figure 5 shows some of the sensory data. For each figure, the x-axis is the sampling points # where the interval is 50 ms, while the y-axis is the acceleration data $(m \cdot s^{-2})$, the blue, pink and green lines represent the x, y and z axis for the mobile phone.

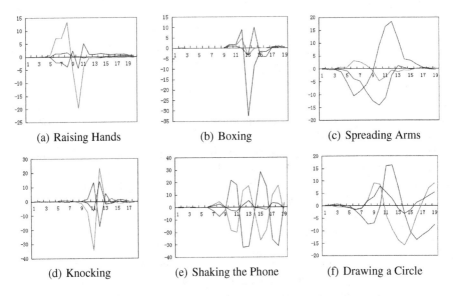

(a) Raising Hands   (b) Boxing   (c) Spreading Arms

(d) Knocking   (e) Shaking the Phone   (f) Drawing a Circle

Fig. 5. Samples of motion sensory data (Color figure online)

We set experiments to test the human motion detection module. For hardware, the tests are done by an Android smart phone (Snapdragon 801, 2 GB RAM, 3-axis accelerometer). For software, Google Chrome is installed and the operating system is Android 4.4. We choose 8 actions to identify, including raising hands, boxing, drawing a circle, shaking the phone, spreading arms, knocking, stretching, lifting dumbbells and the no-treatment control group, doing nothing. When the user do motions, the classification results will be shown by a dialog on the screen. Figure 6 shows part of the experiments and screenshots. As Fig. 7 shows, we get an average accuracy rate of 95 % and the response time (from finishing collecting data to showing the dialog for classification result) is 12.68 ms on average.

The experiments on response and location retrieving module are done on the demoboard. In addition to the two modules, we attach some nixie tubes to the

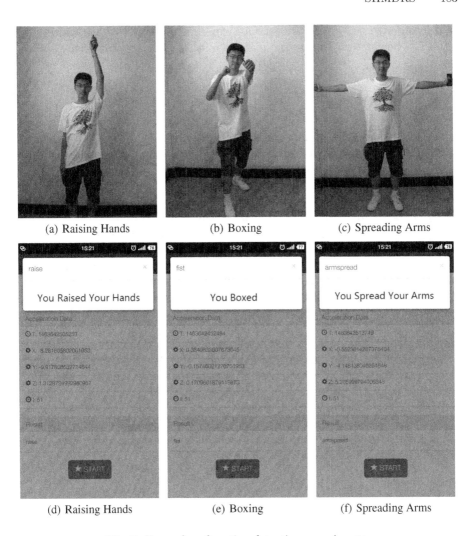

(a) Raising Hands (b) Boxing (c) Spreading Arms

(d) Raising Hands (e) Boxing (f) Spreading Arms

Fig. 6. Examples of motion detection experiments

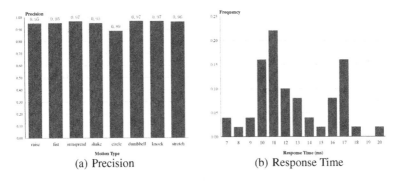

(a) Precision (b) Response Time

Fig. 7. Experimental results

MCU in order to monitor its status. Our experiments show that the controlling signals can be correctly sent to the reactors as long as the classification result is right.

7   Related Works

Up till now, human sensory data collecting and application are widely researched and focused on. Some of the researches use expensive and complex devices for high-quality uses such as medical services. In the paper [1], Darwish et al. implement a smart T-shirt to collect human sensory data based on wireless sensor networks. [2] discusses about making use of RSSI to monitor the movements of patients in order to assist the health care based on WSNs.

Meanwhile, some equipments and devices are designed to collect human sensory data for home users. The most famous devices for motion sensing are Microsoft Kinect and Nintendo Wii. The Kinect is known as a human motion detecting system based on graphical and multimedia data. In the paper [5], the researchers implement a gesture classification system by Kinect image sensors. [6] takes advantage of Max-Entropy Markov Model in motion identification by Kinect image sensors. While the Wii collects human motion data by a hand-held controller. The paper [19] discussed about gesture recognition by the Wii in user's hand based on Hidden Markov Model(HMM). [20] designs a balance bar to monitor the elders' movements to prevent them from falling down.

In conclusion, the above researches are based on special-purpose devices that need purchasing separately. Besides, most of such systems are with a server, which causes high communication complexity. Furthermore, none of them is designed for a home-use cyber-physical controller, and those researches don't consider the user's indoors location, either.

8   Conclusion

This paper studies the smart phone based human motion detection and its application. Firstly, we implement an HTML5-based human motion detection system, giving common users an opportunity to identify their motions by their mobile phones. And then we attach CPS response module to it, which makes it possible to control household appliances via gestures and motions. Then, we improve the architecture of the system to a server-free edition. Eventually, we add the location retrieving module to it. It allows the both the user's location and motion to affect the controlling signals to reactors.

References

1. Ashraf, D., Aboul Ella, H.: Wearable and implantable wireless sensor network solutions for healthcare monitoring. Sensors **12**(9), 12375–12376 (2012)

2. Chakraborty, S., Ghosh, S.K., Jamthe, A., Agrawal, D.P.: Detecting mobility for monitoring patients with parkinsons disease at home using rssi in a wireless sensor network. Procedia Comput. Sci. **19**, 956–961 (2013)

3. Wan, J., Zou, C., Ullah, S., Lai, C.F., Zhou, M., Wang, X.: Cloud-enabled wireless body area networks for pervasive healthcare. IEEE Netw. **27**(5), 56–61 (2013)

4. Zhang, Z.: Microsoft kinect sensor and its effect. IEEE MultiMedia **19**(2), 4–10 (2012)

5. Wang, C., Lai, Z., Wang, H.: Hand gesture recognition based on perceptual shape decomposition with a kinect camera. IEICE Trans. **96**(9), 2147–2151 (2013)

6. Sung, J., Ponce, C., Selman, B., Saxena, A.: Unstructured human activity detection from rgbd images. In: International Conference on Robotics and Automation (2012)

7. Duan, Z., Yan, M., Cai, Z., Wang, X., Han, M., Li, Y.: Truthful incentive mechanisms for social cost minimization in mobile crowdsourcing systems. Sensors **16**(4), 481 (2016)

8. Wang, Y., Cai, Z., Yin, G., Gao, Y., Tong, X., Guanying, W.: An incentive mechanism with privacy protection in mobile crowdsourcing system. Comput. Netw. **102**, 157–171 (2016)

9. Zhang, L., Cai, Z., Wang, X.: FakeMask: A novel privacy preserving approach for smartphones. IEEE Trans. Netw. Serv. Manage. **13**(2), 335–348 (2016)

10. Zhang, L., Wang, X., Lu, J., Li, P., Cai, Z.: An efficient privacy preserving data aggregation approach for mobile sensing. Secur. Commun. Netw. J

11. https://www.w3.org/TR/html5/single-page.html

12. http://w3c.github.io/deviceorientation/spec-source-orientation.html

13. Balasubramanee, V., Wimalasena, C., Singh, R., Pierce, M.: Twitter bootstrap and angularjs: frontend frameworks to expeditescience gateway development. In: IEEE International Conference on Cluster Computing (CLUSTER) (2013)

14. Aslam, M., Zhu, Z., Nandi, A.K.: Automatic modulation classification using combination of genetic programming and knn. IEEE Trans. Wireless Commun. **11**(8), 2742–2750 (2012)

15. Zhang, M., Zhou, Z.: ML-KNN: a lazy learning approach to multi-label learning. Pattern Recogn. **40**(7), 2038–2048 (2007)

16. Mueen, A., Batista, G., Westover, B., Zhu, Q., Zakaria, J., Keogh, E., Rakthanmanon, T., Campana, B.: Searching and mining trillions of time series subsequences under dynamic time warping. In: Proceedings of ACM International Conference on Knowledge Discovery and Data Mining (2012)

17. Petitjean, F., Forestier, G., Webb, G.I., Nicholson, A.E., Chen, Y., Keogh, E.: Dynamic time warping averaging of time series allows faster and moreaccurate classification. In: IEEE International Conference on Data Mining 2014, pp. 470–479 (2014)

18. Ding, H., Trajcevski, G., Scheuermann, P., Wang, X., Keogh, E.: Querying and mining of time series data: experimental comparison ofrepresentations and distance measures. In: Proceedings of The VLDB Endowment (2008)

19. Schlomer, T., Poppinga, B., Henze, N., Boll, S.: Gesture recognition with a Wii controller. In: Proceedings of TEI, pp. 11–14 (2008)

20. Goble, D.J., Cone, B.L., Fling, B.W.: Using the wii fit as a tool for balance assessment and neurorehabilitation: the first half decade of Wii-search. J. Neuroengineering Rehabil. **11**(1), 1–9 (2014)

iRun: A Smartphone-Based System to Alert Runners to Warm Up Before Running

Zhenhua Zhao, Zehao Sun, Liusheng Huang$^{(\boxtimes)}$,
Hansong Guo, Jianxin Wang, and Hongli Xu

School of Computer Science and Technology,
University of Science and Technology of China, Hefei, Anhui, China
{hzq,luciola,guohanso,jacywang}@mail.ustc.edu.cn,
{lshuang,xuhongli}@ustc.edu.cn

Abstract. Running is a good way to keep healthy and relax, while many runners suffer from injuries because of a lack of running knowledge and ignoring the importance of warm-up. Inspired by the fact that more and more people run with smartphones tied up to their arms, we propose a novel system named iRun to alert people to warm up before running. iRun is based on the sensors built in most off-the-shelf smartphones like accelerometers, and it uses human activity recognition (HAR) methods to detect whether the runners warm up or not. The most challenging work is to choose the features that can represent the characteristic of various warm-up actions because different people have different exercise habits. By carefully designing the feature vector which contains features from multi-domains and doing a series of experiments to decide the slide window size and classifier, iRun can achieve 91.4 % true positive (TP) rate in average to distinguish every warm-up action from other movements like running, walk, going upstairs, etc.

Keywords: Human activity recognition · Health · Machine learning · Smartphone sensing

1 Introduction

Running is one of the most popular exercise in daily life, an evidence for this is that China's marathon race has shown a grown spurt. According to statistics in 2014, there are about 75 thousands people who have finished the full marathon, and the number of those who have finished the half marathon or short marathon is 110 thousands and over 600 thousands, respectively. On the other hand, a lot of runners suffer from injuries like joint ligament sprain and muscle sprain because of a lack of running knowledge. A simple but efficient way to avoid the injuries is to warm up before running, because warm-up rises the core and peripheral temperature to get the body ready to roll into the actual pace and effort demand of the given work and get the central nervous system revving, so that the body can contract and relax more efficiently. Hence, alerting runners to warm up before running is a big issues. Since more and more people run with

© Springer International Publishing Switzerland 2016
Q. Yang et al. (Eds.): WASA 2016, LNCS 9798, pp. 186–196, 2016.
DOI: 10.1007/978-3-319-42836-9_17

smartphones tied up to their arms, we can implement this automatic warm-up reminding via smartphones.

Fortunately, as abundant sensors are equipped in most of the off-the-shelf smartphones, the collection of interact measurement data such as accelerometers is convenient, which makes human activity recognition (HAR) one of the core concerns of ubiquitous [11] and wearable computing. Focusing on the automatic detection of specific activities, many works have been done, such as [15] in the medical and health field, [10] about sports. Inspired by all those excellent achievements and the fact that many runners ignore the importance of warm up before running, we propose a novel system named iRun to alert people to do necessary warm-up so that they can really benefit from running without causing injury.

iRun uses the sensors built in the smartphones to detect the runner's actions. The main action recognition chain is shown in Fig. 1. The most challenging work is to choose the features that can represent the characteristic of various warm-up actions because different people have different exercise habits. By carefully designing the feature vector which contains features from multi-domains and doing a series of experiments to decide the slide window size and classifier, the true positive (TP) rate of iRun is 91.4 % in average to distinguish every warm-up action from other movements like running, walk, going upstairs, etc. If the actions in the pre-determined warm-up-action set are not detected in a given time, iRun will try to alert the user to warm up. The main contributions of this work are as follows:

(1) We collect and determine a set of warm-up-action that are common and effective in daily exercise, and those actions are familiar to runners, especially the amateurs.
(2) To distinguish the warm-up actions, we extract a set of discriminative features in different domains, most of which require relatively few computing resource. This ensures that we can get accurate, real-time results.
(3) Unlike other systems that use special wearables, which are difficult to be widely equipped by all runners in short time, iRun is based on the built-in sensors of most off-the-shelf smartphones, making it possible to be immediately put into commission.

2   Background

The first step of our work is to determine the set of warm-up-action. There are various warm-up suggestions. Taking versatility and effectiveness into account, we finally choose nine actions (as is illustrated in Fig. 2). Here are the brief descriptions:

(a) Chest-expanding: arms bend naturally in front of the chest, and then try to pull your elbows backward to expand the chest repetitively.
(b) Shoulder-exercise: put fingertips on the arm, then move the elbows in a circular trajectory clockwise (or anticlockwise).

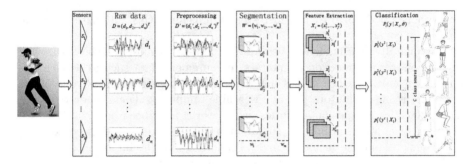

Fig. 1. The action recognition chain of iRun: raw signals(D) are first processed(D') and split into m segments(W_i) from which feature vectors(X_i) are extracted. Given features(X_i), a model with parameters θ scores c activity classes $Y_i = \{y^1, \cdots, y^c\}$ with a confidence vector p_i.

(c) Waist-abdomen-movement: keep your legs tight, then take turns to try to touch your tiptoes as possible as you can.

(d) Lunge-leg: take turns to lunges one leg forward and keep the other tight, then place your hands on the knee and repetitively lean forward.

(e) Shoulder-extension: cross your arms just like the illustration and then try to turn left (or right) with your feet standing still repetitively.

(f) Turning: similar to the shoulder-extension but put your hands up on the head.

(g) Crotch-clap: take turns to skip with one leg then clap below it.

(h) High-knees: maintain a fast cadence as you alternate between bringing your knees up towards your chest.

(i) Knee-joint-movement: place your hands on the knees, then move the knees in a circular trajectory clockwise (or anticlockwise) or just alternate between squat and stand.

After choosing the action set, we concentrate on selecting discriminative features. We first collect some raw data about the warm-up actions, and then observe the data distribution. Combining with the studies in [5,7,12], we finally choose the three-dimensional accelerometer data as our research subjects. According to our survey, the features that can represent the characteristic of various warm-up actions are mainly in time domain and frequency domain. Actually, we extract most of our features from the two domains, but our experimental results show that statistics features like *kurtosis* also help to improve precision. Statistics features can be detected from either time or frequency domain or both.

The last but not least is to decide the proper classification algorithm to detect warm-up actions from other movements like running, walk, going upstair, etc. Taking into consideration the activity recognition and the raw data structure, we choose DTNB (class for building and using a decision table\navie bayes hybrid classifier), AdaBoost, Logistic, SMO, NavieBayes and RandForest as alternatives. After conducting a series of experiments and taking accuracy, time

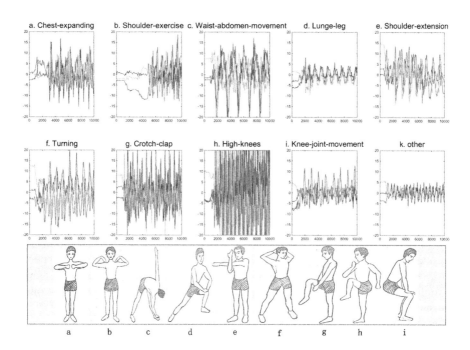

Fig. 2. The warm-up-action set: the ten waveforms are traces of three-dimensional accelerometers data section, which belong to the warm-up-action set we determined and a other record. The pictures are a sketch map of the warm-up-action set and the lowercase letters are corresponding to the descriptions in Sect. 2 (*Background*).

efficiency and computational complexity into consideration, we finally designed a classifier based on Random Forest.

3   Data Collection

Raw data holds an important position in iRun. In order to get pure original accelerometer data of the action set, we designed an application on Android platform. This application produces fifty records of accelerometer data with time stamp per second, and it can also keep running in the background to make sure data collection will not be interrupted by misoperation. Then we recruit fifteen volunteers with different height, weight and, most importantly, different sports habits to carry out the actions in our warm-up-action set. We even do not ask the volunteers to do especial training, which guarantees that the sample raw data is representative. Then, with smartphone tied up to their arms, the volunteers are asked to do warm-up actions one by one, and each action contains at least 4×8 beats (i.e. 32 movements), which ensures that there is enough time to make the actions stable so that we can we can get quality assured features. We also collected some actions data which is out of the warm-up-action set, such as walk, running, going upstairs and so on. Those data are labeled as [others] in our training phase, which is used to indicate that we can distinguish warm-up actions from common running action.

4   System Design

In this section, we detail the workflow of the iRun system, which is also illustrated in Fig. 1. We first introduce how to preprocess the raw data to remove the outliers and DC part. Then, we present the segmentation method and the detailed feature extraction. Finally, we give the algorithm to detect the warm-up phase.

4.1   Preprocess

In this phase, we mainly concentrate on two issues: remove the outliers and direct component (DC) part. We choose Chauvenet-criterion to remove the outliers. We discard the DC part because that it can not carry information. Note that, although normalization is a usual step in preprocess, iRun does not have one, because the original features like peak and amplitude are useful in the feature extraction stage.

4.2   Segmentation

After preprocessing the raw accelerometer data, we use interval-based sliding window [6, 16] which overlap 80 % between neighbored windows to produce segments, which is the unit of features detection. Here, the window size is an noteworthy parameter, since an appropriate window size can significantly improve the TP rate. Besides, as shown in Fig. 2, there is a section in the beginning (the part in the end is similar but not shown) that does not belong to the expected actions, we therefore remove the segments generated by those sections. Here, we adopted a end-points detection [3, 4] based on the short-time-average-energy to get rid of the useless segments (Algorithm 1). In Algorithm 1, S is the segments set and S_i is the ith segment in S, $|S_i|$ is the sample number contained in S_i, γ is a percentage threshold which means we will drop $\gamma\%$ segments from the segment set.

4.3   Feature Extraction

In iRun, features are used to represent the characteristics of raw accelerometer data. A right features set is the most critical factor for a ideal classification result. Referring to [5, 13] and taking computation complexity into consideration, we first focus on time-domain features, then add a few frequency domain features, as well as the statistics features, to improve the TP rate. Actually the time token to calculate features for segments is 0.0252 s in average when the slide window size is 5 s in our experiment. The main features in are presented as follows:

Algorithm 1. The End-points Detection

Input: $S = \{S_1, S_2, \cdots, S_n\}$, γ.
Output: $S' = \{S_1, S_2, \cdots, S_m\}$.
1: **for all** $S_i \in S$ **do**
2:    $k_i = \frac{\sum\limits_j a_{ij}^2}{|S_i|}$, where a_{ij} is the sample point in S_i
3: **end for**
4: sort $\{k_1, k_2, ..., k_n\}$ as $\{k_{l_1}, k_{l_2}, ..., k_{l_n}\}$ in ascending
5: $\theta = \text{round}(n*\gamma)$
6: $S' = S$
7: **for all** $k_{l_j} \in \{k_{l_1}, k_{l_2}, ..., k_{l_n}\}$ **do**
8:    **if** $k_{l_j} \leq k_{l_\theta}$ **then**
9:       remove S_{l_j} from S
10:   **end if**
11: **end for**
12: **return** S'

Time Domain Features. Although time domain features are not sufficient to identify each kind of warm-up action, they can present some intuitive characteristic of the wave form. In iRun, we adopt the *Min & Max & Avg Amplitude*, *ZCR* (zero crossing rate), *RMS* (root mean square), etc. RMS is computed as Eq. 1, where a_k is the k-th sample point in segment S_i and N is the total sample points number in S_i.

$$RMS_i = \sqrt{\frac{\sum\limits_k a_k^2}{N}} \tag{1}$$

Frequency Domain Features. When detecting frequency domain features, we firstly transform the time series accelerometer data into spectrum by FFT (Fast Fourier Transform), then we calculate *Spectral Slope* (Eq. 2) and *Peak Frequency* (Eq. 3).

The spectral slope represents the amount of decreasing of the spectral amplitude and is computed by linear regression of the spectral amplitude. The i-th segment S_i's spectral slope is calculated by Eq. 2, where $a_i(k)$ is the corresponding amplitude of frequency $f_i(k)$ which is the k-th frequency component of S_i. N is the total number of frequency components of S_i.

$$SpectralSlope_i = \frac{1}{\sum\limits_k a_i(k)} \frac{N \sum\limits_k a_i(k) * f_i(k) - \sum\limits_k a_i(k) \sum\limits_k f_i(k)}{N \sum\limits_k f_i^2(k) - (\sum\limits_k f_i(k))^2} \tag{2}$$

The Peak Frequency holds the maximum spectral amplitude in segment S_i. It is calculated by Eq. 3 where $|F_j(a_i)|$ is the amplitude of the j-th frequency component of S_i.

$$\begin{cases} PeakFrequency_i = f_{ij'} \\ j' = \underset{j \in [0,N]}{\text{argmax}} |F_j(a_i)| \end{cases} \tag{3}$$

Algorithm 2. Detect Warm-up Phase

Input: $A = \{a,b,\cdots,i,g\}$, $S = \{S_1,\cdots,S_n\}$, τ, μ.
Output: **True** or **False**.
 1: **for all** $S_i \in S$ **do**
 2:     the classifier mark S_i as s_i, $s_i \in A$
 3: **end for**
 4: $B = \phi$
 5: **for all** $a_i \in A$ **do**
 6:     if   exist j: $s_j = s_{j+1} = s_{j+2} = \cdots = s_{\tau-1} = a_i$ **then**
 7:         put a_i in B
 8:     **end if**
 9: **end for**
10: **return** $|B| \geq \mu$.

Statistics Domain Features. The *kurtosis* gives a measure of flatness of a distribution around the mean value. It is computed from a 4th order moment whose deformation is Eq. 4. Here, a_{ij} is the j-th sample point in segment S_i, and a_i is the mean, N is the total sample points number in S_i.

$$Kurtosis_i = \frac{N \sum\limits_{j=1}^{N} (a_{ij} - \overline{a_i})^4}{(\sum\limits_{j-1}^{N} (a_{ij} - \overline{a_i})^2)^2} \qquad (4)$$

4.4   Detect Warm-Up Phase

After obtaining a classification model, we use the model to mark the segments $\{S_1,\cdots,S_n\}$ that are sorted by time as action series $\{s_1,\cdots,s_n\}$. Then, we deem that action a is done if there exists a continuous sequence $s_j = s_{j+1} = \cdots = s_{\tau-1} = a$. If at least μ actions are done, we deem that there is a warm-up phase (Algorithm 2), and return *True*, otherwise *False*. In Algorithm 2, A is the warm-up-action set, S is the segments set, $|S|$ is the size of S, τ is the lower limit length of a action sequence. Another way to detect the warm-up phase is to check the total warm-up action time (similar to Algorithm 2), while τ means the action's duration time.

5   Evaluation

In this section, we present the experiment results of the evaluation of iRun. We first study the impact of the slide window size, and then we decide the proper multi-class classifier. The main evaluation metrics are TP (true positive) rate (Eq. 5) and FP (false positive) rate (Eq. 6). The time token to calculate features for segments is 0.0252 s in average when the slide window size is 5 s. The final confusion matrix is shown in Fig. 4.

$$TP\ rate = \frac{true\ positives}{true\ positives + false\ negatives} \tag{5}$$

$$FP\ rate = \frac{false\ positives}{true\ negatives + false\ positives} \tag{6}$$

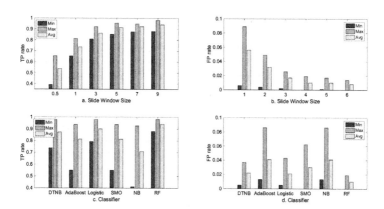

Fig. 3. The results: a and b present TP and FP rate for different slide window sizes and c and d for different classifiers. The unit of the slide window size is *Second*. (Color figure online)

5.1 Slide Window Size

The slide window size, which means the duration time of the segment, is a key parameter in iRun. It should be big enough to hold the properties of the raw data, which makes the segment a good representative. At the same time, obviously, the bigger the slide window size is, the fewer the total number of segments is, and we should ensure the quantity of segments to get a nice classification model. In our experiment, taking the frequency of people's movement into consideration, we choose the slide window size from {0.5 s, 1 s, 3 s, 5 s, 7 s, 9 s}, and the total corresponding instances are {21588, 16172, 5163, 2949, 2007, 1474}. The results are shown in Fig. 3(a and b). The TP rate is under-performing when the slid window size is small, but when it grows up to 5s, the minimal, the maximal and the average of TP rate achieve 85.3 %, 95.5 % and 91.4 %, respectively. Meanwhile, the FP rate is 1.0 % in average, and the maximal is only 1.9 %. When we continue to increase the window size, the TP rate changes little and the FP rate remains still. The time to build model is 2.84 s when slide windows size is 5s. Hence, we set the slide window size 5 s as a good compromise. Here, we emphasize that the classifier used in the experiment is RandForest, and the overlap between segments neighbours is 80 %.

		a	b	c	d	e	f	g	h	i	j
a:Chest-expanding	a	357	2	1	1	2	0	0	1	7	1
b:Shoulder-exercise	b	5	251	2	5	22	0	0	0	0	1
c:Waist-abdomen-movement	c	2	2	289	3	4	0	0	0	0	0
d:Lunge-leg	d	0	0	12	283	14	0	0	0	0	0
e:Shoulder-extension	e	0	6	6	25	281	0	0	0	2	0
f:Turning	f	0	0	0	0	0	147	0	0	0	8
g:Crotch-clap	g	0	1	0	0	0	0	183	0	0	12
h:High-knees	h	0	0	0	0	2	0	0	303	18	4
i:Knee-joint-movement	i	2	4	0	1	5	0	0	29	237	8
j:others	j	4	0	0	0	0	1	0	21	13	359

Fig. 4. The Confusion Matrix with slide window size 5 s and RandForest.

5.2   Proper Multi-class Classifier

We select six classifiers as alternatives, they are DTNB (class for building and using a decision table\navie bayes hybrid classifier), AdaBoost, Logistic, SMO, NavieBayes (NB) and RandForest (RF). With each classifier, we conduct a series of 10-fold cross-validation experiments, which means that we randomly part our data set into ten portions with approximately equal size. Then, we select the k-th portion as the test set and the rest nine as the training set in the k-th fold. After carrying out all of the 10-fold, we obtain a model with the given classifier. The total instances is 2949. As shown in Fig. 3(c and d), the maximum TP rate is at least 92.6 %, while the minimum TP rates are relatively disappointing such as AdoBoost 55.0 %, SMO 54.8 % and NaiveBayes 41.2 %. These results show that not all of the classifier work well on distinguishing the warm-up actions. We choose RandForest, whose TP rate and FP rate is 91.4 % and 1.0 % in average respectively, as the final classifier of iRun and the time it token to build model is 2.84 s. Note that the slide window size in this group of experiments is 5 s and the overlap between segments neighbours is 80 %.

6   Related Work

HAR is one of the core concerns of ubiquitous and wearable computing. A multitude of technical approaches has been proposed to enable applications in diverse domains, for example, [12] recognize smoking gestures by a wristband, [2] capture and reflect on sleep behaviors through Android's widgets, [15] detect sound-related respiratory symptoms using smartphone, [9] come up with novel interaction techniques, [14] concern about automated health assessments and [1] care about healthcare.

With the developing of technical approaches, some researchers are not satisfied with just recognizing the interested activities, they try to assess the quantity of activities. Things become even harder in this field. This is because that quality assessment requires professional knowledge in the specific domain which is usually not the reacher's major, and evaluation metrics are also hard to determine. Despite of these difficulties, there are still some achievements about quality assessments, such as [10] about sports skill assessment. In [8], the author even propose a framework that enables automatic quality analysis, which is based on a hierarchical rule induction technique that effectively abstracts from noise-prone activity data and assesses activity data at different temporal contexts. That work aims to find a general method for quality assessments, which prompts us to add some functions like evaluating running or other actions quality to iRun.

7   Conclusion

In this paper, we propose a novel system, named iRun, which adopts built-in sensors in most off-the-shelf smartphones to detect the warm-up phase before the user do running exercise. If the warm-up phase is not detected, iRun will alert the user to warm up to avoid potential joint injuries. We first choose accelerometer data as the raw materials and determine the warm-up action set, then select appropriate features that can present the characteristics of raw data, after that, we do experiments to decide the right slide window size and classifier. The results indicate that iRun can achieve 91.4 % TP rate in average to detect every warm-up action from other movements like running, walk, going upstairs, etc., which is sufficient for the warm-up detection.

Acknowledgements. This paper is supported by the National Science Foundation of China under No. U1301256.

References

1. Avci, A., Bosch, S., Marin-Perianu, M., Marin-Perianu, R., Havinga, P.: Activity recognition using inertial sensing for healthcare, wellbeing and sports applications: a survey. In: Architecture of computing systems (ARCS). VDE (2010)
2. Choe, E.K., Lee, B., Kay, M., Pratt, W., Kientz, J.A.: Sleeptight: low-burden, self-monitoring technology for capturing and reflecting on sleep behaviors. In: Ubicomp. ACM (2015)
3. Eren, H., Makinist, S., Akin, E., Yilmaz, A.: Estimating driving behavior by a smartphone. In: Intelligent Vehicles Symposium (IV). IEEE (2012)
4. Gu, T., Chen, S., Tao, X., Lu, J.: An unsupervised approach to activity recognition and segmentation based on object-use fingerprints. Data Knowl. Eng. **69**(6), 533–544 (2010)
5. Guo, H., Huang, L., Huang, H., Sun, Z., Peng, J., Yu, Z., Zhu, Z., Xu, H., Liu, H.: Guardian angel: a smartphone based personal security system for emergency alerting. In: UIC-ATC-ScalCom-CBDCom-IoP. IEEE (2015)
6. Győrbíró, N., Fábián, Á., Hományi, G.: An activity recognition system for mobile phones. Mob. Netw. Appl. **14**(1), 82–91 (2009)
7. Hung, H., Englebienne, G., Kools, J.: Classifying social actions with a single accelerometer. In: Ubicomp. ACM (2013)
8. Khan, A., Mellor, S., Berlin, E., Thompson, R., McNaney, R., Olivier, P., Plötz, T.: Beyond activity recognition: skill assessment from accelerometer data. In: Ubicomp. ACM (2015)

9. Kim, D., Hilliges, O., Izadi, S., Butler, A.D., Chen, J., Oikonomidis, I., Olivier, P.: Digits: freehand 3d interactions anywhere using a wrist-worn gloveless sensor. In: Proceedings of UIST. ACM (2012)
10. Ladha, C., Hammerla, N.Y., Olivier, P., Plötz, T.: Climbax: skill assessment for climbing enthusiasts. In: Ubicomp. ACM (2013)
11. Lane, N.D., Miluzzo, E., Lu, H., Peebles, D., Choudhury, T., Campbell, A.T.: A survey of mobile phone sensing. IEEE Commun. Mag. **48**(9), 140–150 (2010)
12. Parate, A., Chiu, M.C., Chadowitz, C., Ganesan, D., Kalogerakis, E.: Risq: recognizing smoking gestures with inertial sensors on a wristband. In: MobiSys. ACM (2014)
13. Peeters, G.: A large set of audio features for sound description (similarity and classification) in the CUIDADO project (2004)
14. Plötz, T., Hammerla, N.Y., Rozga, A., Reavis, A., Call, N., Abowd, G.D.: Automatic assessment of problem behavior in individuals with developmental disabilities. In: Ubicomp. ACM (2012)
15. Sun, X., Lu, Z., Hu, W., Cao, G.: Symdetector: detecting sound-related respiratory symptoms using smartphones. In: Ubicomp. ACM (2015)
16. Wu, W., Dasgupta, S., Ramirez, E.E., Peterson, C., Norman, G.J.: Classification accuracies of physical activities using smartphone motion sensors. J. Med. Internet Res. **14**(5), e130 (2012)

iBeaconing: A Low-Cost, Wireless Student Protection System

Blake Lucas[1], Liran Ma[1(✉)], and Dechang Chen[2]

[1] Department of Computer Science,
Texas Christian University, Fort Worth, TX, USA
{b.g.lucas,l.ma}@tcu.edu
[2] Preventive Medicine and Biometrics,
Uniformed Services University of the Health Sciences, Bethesda, MD, USA
dechang.chen@usuhs.edu

Abstract. For children with autism, normal social stimuli can provoke unpredictable reactions that could place those children in dangerous situations. In most schools, teachers have the two-pronged task of instructing and monitoring these children. In order to simplify this task, we propose integrating new iBeacon technology with the capability of Raspberry Pi computers to construct an entry/exit scanning system. The students will be wearing iBeacon equipped, irremovable bracelets (transmitting on a low power setting), which will be donned when attendance is taken. The Raspberry Pi computers placed above each door will scan for iBeacons continually. Since the iBeacons will be transmitting on a range of -30 to -20 dBmW of power, they have a maximum horizontal range of 2 m. If the iBeacon is within range of the door for more than two seconds, the Raspberry Pi will send a "distress signal" to a server, which is retrieved by the smartphone application, prompting a system-wide alert to be triggered. The benefits of implementing such a system include cost-effectiveness and a decrease in the latent period between alert detection and action.

1 Introduction

For schools with a large population of autistic students, providing individual caretakers for each one is nearly financially impossible. Thus, teachers and a few caretakers have to both instruct the students—an already formidable task, given the different neurological construction of the autistic brain—as well as keep the students safe. If the students become insecure or unhappy, they attempt to leave the building. Unless a teacher or caretaker notices them and takes appropriate action in a timely manner, the student may not be discovered missing for minutes or hours.

Most schools implement a basic "eyes on" policy, empowering faculty to watch for unattended students, but most schools have yet to implement actual monitoring systems, due in part to parental objection and cost. However, Disney Cruise Lines has implemented RFID "checkpointing" for children on its cruise

© Springer International Publishing Switzerland 2016
Q. Yang et al. (Eds.): WASA 2016, LNCS 9798, pp. 197–206, 2016.
DOI: 10.1007/978-3-319-42836-9_18

ships, and parents are very supportive of the new system. The "Oceaneer Bands" have RFID capability and allow children access to the youth areas of the cruise ships. The most important feature of these bands is that they allow the staff to keep an accurate count of the number of children in each area [1]. There are currently no solutions of this nature found in schools. Granted there are some inherent flaws if the system were to be used to monitor children while at school: the RFID tags have to be scanned deliberately, and medium to long range RFID Scanners and transmitters are not inexpensive nor portable. However, with small changes to Disney's checkpoint system—primarily the use of Bluetooth Low Energy, or iBeacon, technology—we can prevent students from wandering away unaccompanied, and thus prevent students from potentially placing themselves in harm's way.

We propose implementing an electronic student protection system similar to the anti-shoplifting systems in stores across the country. The premise is simple: if a student attempts to leave the building without being checked out by a parent or guardian, an alarm is triggered on the smartphone application each teacher installs on their phone.

Mini computer systems called "Raspberry Pi's" [2] will be placed at each entry/exit door in the school. The students, when they are dropped off by their parents, will be marked in attendance and will don an iBeacon-equipped bracelet. When the Raspberry Pi at the door detects an iBeacon for longer than X seconds, it notifies every teacher or administrator via the smartphone application.

Through this project, we wish to establish the prevalence of iBeacon technology over that of its similar RFID counterpart. iBeacon technology is less expensive, more portable, and more customizable than RFID technology, yet it lacks technical support or implementation that comparable RFID solutions have garnered over the years.

The remainder of this paper is organized as follows: Sect. 2 elaborates on the related work in the usage of Bluetooth beacon technology; Sect. 3 discusses the holistic system; Sect. 4 addresses the individual system components; Sect. 5 analyzes implementation and evaluation; and in conclusion, Sect. 6 summarizes the project's progress and potential.

2   Related Work

The idea of a server-controlled entry/exit monitoring system is not a novelty. RFID and server based student monitoring has been discussed and analyzed by Sengar and Sunhare in [3]. This system in [3] does not have an alert component, as it is geared for higher education. Additionally, in a similar fashion to the Disney system [1], the students intentionally scan in and out of classrooms or the library. While this increases accuracy, is does little in the area of safety for our purposes.

RFID systems have been used predominantly in animal tracking and shipping, as explicated by Balch et al. in [4]. The largest issue with this particular type of system is price, and the second is integration. RFID scanners that can reach ranges of 3 meters along with their compatible RFID tags are much more expensive.

The Bluetooth Low Energy solution is structurally similar to the RFID structure. Scanners and tags (in our case, iBeacons) are present. The BLE beacons, however have an advantage in tracking and monitoring. As explained by Papamanthou *et al.* in [5], iBeacons can be ranged based on the reported signal strength, which RFID systems cannot do; RFID scanners only report detection. This ability to approximate distance yields triangulation capability to Bluetooth scanning systems. This allows approximation of physical location instead of just "checkpointing," or monitoring what items or people pass through a certain scanning location.

The largest obstacle to Bluetooth Low Energy implementation is the requirement of an active power source, or battery. Kindt explains a potential power model in [6]. iBeacons and other Bluetooth Low Energy technology transmit a simplified Bluetooth signal, meaning the battery life can last 12–48 months depending on the Transmission Power setting [7].

This project deviates from the typical functionality of iBeacons or Bluetooth through its statically located scanners and dynamic beacons. In typical applications, the beacons represent specific geo-locations and the phone (or scanner) typically uses a special application that queries a server based on the beacon closest to it. Airports are currently using this technology to relay flight information or navigate a patron to their specific gate [8].

3   Overall System Design

The student protection system as a whole is a fairly straightforward network of scanners connected to the central database, which stores student information such as name, grade, a picture, legal guardian contact information, and emergency contact information. This network is connected to the school's "WiFi" network to which each teacher will connect their phones, as illustrated in Fig. 1. This allows direct intranet communication between the Bluetooth scanners (Raspberry Pi's) and the smartphone application. The Central Webserver, which will be hosted on the same computer as the database of student information, processes the data returned to it by the Raspberry Pi scanners and transmits that data to the smartphone application. The smartphone application analyzes the data and, if it determines there is an alert, it activates the alerts protocol. Since every smartphone application does this individually, there is no possibility of a blanket outage, as there would be if the alert detection was handled by the Central Webserver alone. After the application pings the server, it collects all of the necessary information—which sensor triggered the alert, which student is involved, and anything else that needs to be reported—and sends that directly to the teachers and administrators.

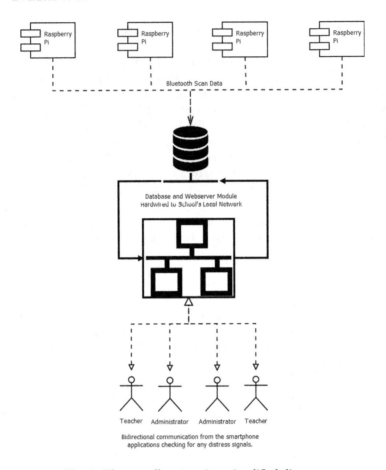

Fig. 1. The overall system in a simplified diagram

3.1   Beacon Scanning

The Raspberry Pi's (Sect. 4.1) continually scan for beacons. The retrieved scan data is taken approximately every 2 s. If a Bluetooth device's UUID does not match the pre-configured UUID, the device will be disregarded. The new scan data is compared to the previous scan data. If there is any overlap, the respective beacon data is uploading to the Raspberry Pi's corresponding data table on the central webserver.

3.2   Alert Data Transmission

The smartphone application (Sect. 4.3) pulls all of the detected beacon data from the corresponding tables of each Raspberry Pi (Table 1, Column 2). The application then performs a binary search through the student information table (Table 1, Column 1). Once it finds the appropriate column, it takes the remainder of the column information (the actual student information), and populates an array of the class *Student* and populates a TableView with all the students that triggered an alert. Separate threads in the application insert information and monitor the array. If the cardinality of the array is every not zero, the alert protocol—lengthy vibrations, buzzer tones, and flashing camera flash—is triggered on the specific personnel responsible for monitoring student safety. These alerts can be put on "Do Not Disturb" mode; however, this mode can only be active for an hour, and if more than 3 alerts are detected in one hour, the "Do Not Disturb" is overridden.

4 System Components

The system can be divided in to three discrete sections: (i) The Bluetooth scanner-equipped Raspberry Pi's, (ii) the central webserver that facilitates communication between the scanners and smartphone application, and (iii) the smartphone application that presents the data in human-readable form to the teachers and administrators.

4.1 The Bluetooth Scanners

The scanners are constructed from a Raspberry Pi running a specialized version of the Raspbian operating system called PiBeacon [9]. A Bluetooth dongle capable of scanning for Bluetooth Low Energy beacons (iBeacons) is plugged in to the USB port of the Raspberry Pi. The Pi can either be hardwired to the network via Ethernet or connected wirelessly via a WiFi adapter. They are configured to start scanning immediately upon restart, so unless a piece of hardware breaks or corrupts, the only maintenance necessary is a reboot of the Pi, performed by unplugging the power cable and plugging it back in to the micro-USB slot.

Figure 2 details the exact methodology of the software. The software program running on the Pi is written entirely in Java [10]. It reads the command line input from the scan command built in to the PiBeacon operating system. This JavaScript Object Notation (JSON) data is parsed by the program and compiled in to an *ArrayList* of custom class *Beacon*. After each scan finishes every X seconds, the ArrayList with the new scan data is compared to the old one. If a beacon is present in both, the program sends the alert trigger to the central webserver, along with the identification numbers of the beacon present. The server finds the student information that corresponds with the identification number of the beacon and forwards that information to the smartphone application to present the alert.

A Note on iBeacons. An iBeacon is a small Bluetooth dongle that transmits five numbers to a Bluetooth scanner: (i) UUID (Universally Unique Identifier), (ii) Major ID, (iii) Minor ID, (iv) RSSI (Received Signal Strength Indicator), and (v) TxPower (Transmission Power) [11]. A critical portion of the project rests on the implementation of iBeacons. The beacons used in the development of this

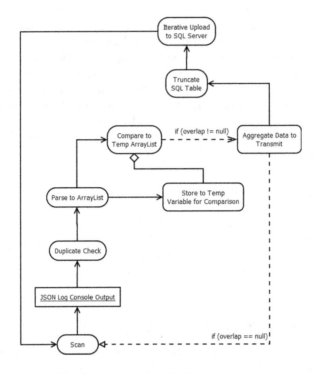

Fig. 2. The flow diagram of the bluetooth scan software

system are Gimbal Series 10 Proximity Beacons. They are broadcasting with a transmission power (TxPower) level of $-23\,$dBmW, giving them an approximate horizontal detection range of 2–2.5 m. If the power is increased, the range will increase as well, but this could lead to more false positives reported by the system.

All of the iBeacons used will have the same UUID, making it easy for the software to filter out irrelevant Bluetooth traffic. The more important information on the iBeacons is the Major ID. This will be the student's ID number, and will vary for each iBeacon. The number will be affixed to the beacon, and the student will always receive the same beacon when they arrive at school.

The only foreseeable difficulty regarding iBeacon usage is the ability to make the iBeacons irremovable by the students but removable by the staff. In order to make this possible, locking mechanisms would need to be in place on each iBeacon bracelet, and the material used must be strong enough to withstand repeated strain, both unintentional and inflicted by the student in a possible attempt to remove the bracelet.

4.2 The Central Webserver and Database

The central server will consist of a Raspberry Pi hosting an SQL Database and an Apache webserver [12]. The SQL Database will contain multiple tables:

1. A table with all relevant student information
2. A table of the beacons detected by each individual Raspberry Pi Scanner
3. A table updated at regular intervals with the status of each Raspberry Pi Scanner

Table 1. SQL table data models

Student information (1)	Detected beacons (2)	Pi statuses (3)
Major ID	UUID	WIFI status
Full name	Major ID	Program status code
Age/Grade	Minor ID	Error messages
Picture	RSSI	
Emergency contact	TxPower	
Medical anomalies		
Legal guardian info		

The central webserver acts as a conduit, facilitating intranet communication between the Raspberry Pi Scanners and the smartphone application, as shown in Fig. 1. Ideally, the central webserver will also host a Java applet that allows an administrator or other IT personnel to view the status of each component and, if needed, use SSH [13] commands to make software changes, reboot scanners, or perform other necessary tasks to ensure the system remains functional.

4.3   The Smartphone Application

The smartphone application, in its rawest form, simply presents a list of students in the "Main Screen" and allows teachers to access particular student information by tapping on a student's name in the TableView. In Fig. 3, the *didSelectRow()* method tells the application which entry to display in the "Individual Student View" page. This method actually displays the alert information for previous alerts when selected in the "Alert Screen".

The only other function present in the basic version is the alert handling technology. When the application detects that an SQL Table is not null, it requests the information about the SQL entries in the table. As referenced in Sect. 4.2, each Raspberry Pi Scanner has its own discrete SQL Table. The smartphone application has a sectioned TableView—one section for each Raspberry Pi Scanner—and when beacon information is sent to the SQL Table, the application includes a "Background SQL Table Monitoring Table Thread" component, as demonstrate in Fig. 3. Every X/2 seconds, or twice as often as the Raspberry Pi Scanners scan, it tells the application to ping the SQL Server and, take the information there and trigger an alert, if necessary. The "Individual Alert Screen" is displayed and the alerts are logged in the "Alert Screen" TableView for the remainder of the school day.

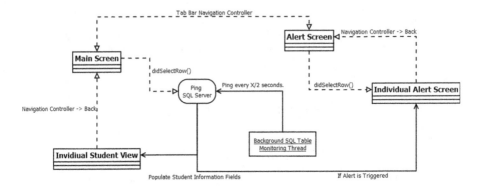

Fig. 3. Illustration of basic application functionality.

5   Implementation

In order for this system to function as intended, it must be installed in a proper fashion, otherwise it will lose accuracy. However, if implemented correctly, this software can perform beyond the rather limited scope of this project.

5.1   Installation

Raspberry Pi's must be connected to the school's local area network. This allows them to inherit the security of the firewall applied by the school, and it also activates intranet access to the scan data. This implies that regardless of active internet connection, the protection system will still be operational.

Additionally, the Pi's need to be tamper-proof, mounted in a similar fashion to thermostats that are not supposed to be adjusted by unauthorized personnel. While this arrangement prevents tampering, it also restricts maintenance. That problem will be corrected when SSH support is added to the webserver, as discussed in Sect. 4.2.

The ideal height the Raspberry Pi Scanners should be mounted is 10 feet, or approximately 3.3 m. By the Pythagorean Theorem, the higher a Raspberry Pi Scanner is mounted, the lower the horizontal detection range becomes, as the maximum total scanning distance, the hypotenuse, does not change.

5.2   Cost

One of the great advantages of Bluetooth Low Energy beacons is the price. The Gimbal Series 10 Proximity Beacons we used in the development of this system cost \$5.00 each. Note that every Unit Price figure in Table 2 is an estimate, along with the quantity figure. Each school or place of implementation would need to determine an appropriate number of each component to purchase. This is a generalized estimate for a small-medium sized center with a large number of students that needed monitoring.

Table 2. The cost model of implementation in a small-medium sized school.

Component	Unit price	Quantity	Total cost
Raspberry Pi	$50.00	5	$250.00
Gimbal beacons	$5.00	40	$200.00
Wristbands	$15.00	40	$600.00
Miscellaneous	–	–	$100.00
Total			$1150.00

It is worth noting that, while the $1150.00 figure from Table 2 seems high, basic RFID scanners sell for over 50 % of the total cost to 150 % of the total cost without eliminating the largest cost to the project: the irremovable wristbands, referenced in Sect. 4.1, that must endure day to day wear without being broken or removed by students.

5.3 Evaluation

Preliminary implementation testing has been underway for approximately a month. The alert system acts in the following manner:

1. The Raspberry Pi Scanners can detect iBeacons from a range of 2–2.5 m after a 2 s scan.
2. The Scanners can clean, analyze, and upload all data found (see Fig. 2) with a proportional efficiency of $O(n\log(n))$.
3. Upon manual SQL table manipulation, the smartphone application (currently developed for iOS) can detect when an alert needs to be triggered.
   3.1 A basic alert can be triggered, but the alert protocol needs to be advanced.
4. The smartphone application can pull student information from the SQL database.
5. The smartphone application can update and retrieve alert information locally, but cannot yet do so in conjunction with the SQL server.

With development progressing at the current rate, we expect to have a fully-operational prototype system active by the end of August, 2016. Implementation of said prototype system should occur in a school specializing in children with autism by the end of the Fall semester, 2016.

6 Conclusion

In this paper, we examined the possibility of introducing Bluetooth Low Energy iBeacons as a plausible low-cost alternative to RFID solutions involving tracking and monitoring. We analyzed the flaws in the implementation of RFID systems as well as the lack of technology utilizing the iBeacon technology in a dynamically located sense. The possibility of using iBeacons to replace RFID solutions and the feasibility of doing so in a more accurate and more cost-effective manner were exhibited in the advancement of this project beyond a theoretical stage and into a developmental reality. The advent of iBeacon technology and the continued prominence of Bluetooth in the mobile device market allows widespread capability for portable, wireless region monitoring systems to flourish.

Through continued research and advancement, we seek to reverse the unilateral nature of iBeacon implementation by demonstrating the versatility of iBeacons compared to their RFID counterparts. We will implement a prototypical system and continue to refine the process of Bluetooth region monitoring. Eventually, we will expand the system's capabilities so that it can be applied across a wider variety of technological landscapes.

Acknowledgment. This research is partially supported by NSF award AST-1443916.

Disclaimer: The views expressed are those of the author(s) and do not necessarily reflect the official views of the Uniformed Services University of the Health Sciences or the Department of Defense.

References

1. Sanders, S.: All New Youth Activities Oceaneer Bands Replacing Mickey Bands. http://disneycruiselineblog.com/2013/11/all-new-youth-activities-oceaneer-bands-replacing-mickey-bands/
2. RaspberryPi: Raspberry Pi. http://raspberrypi.org/
3. Sengar, N., Sunhare, P.: Server operated advance entry-exit monitoring system based on RFID. Int. J. Adv. Res. Electr. Electron. Instrum. Eng. **4**(9) (2015)
4. Balch, T., Feldman, A., Wilson, W.: Assessment of an RFID System for Animal Tracking, Georgia Institute of Technology, October 2004
5. Papamanthou, C., Preparata, F.P., Tamassia, R.: Algorithms for Location Estimation Based on RSSI Sampling (2008)
6. Kindt, P., Yunge, D., Diemer, R., Chakraborty, S.: Precise Energy Modeling for the Bluetooth Low Energy Protocol, Technical University of Munich, March 2014
7. Gimbal: Gimbal Series 10 Proximity Beacons. http://www.gimbal.com/gimbal-beacons/
8. SITA: Sita Shows the Way for iBeacon Technology at Airports. http://www.sita.aero/pressroom/news-releases/sita-shows-the-way-for-ibeacon-technology-at-airports
9. RadiusNetworks: Radius Networks Developer Archives. http://developer.radiusnetworks.com/
10. Oracle: Java programming language. http://docs.oracle.com/javase/7/docs/technotes/guides/language/
11. Townsend, K.: Introduction to Bluetooth Low Energy. Adafruit Learning System, March 2014
12. Wright, S.: Raspberry Pi Web Server. https://www.stewright.me/2015/08/tutorial-install-apache-php-and-mysql-on-a-raspberry-pi-2/
13. Ylonen, T., Lonvick, C.: The Secure Shell (SSH) Protocol Architecture. Network Working Group, January 2006

The Power Control Strategy
for Mine Locomotive Wireless Network
Based on Successive Interference Cancellation

Lei Shi[1]([✉]), Yi Shi[2], Zhenchun Wei[1], Guoxiang Zhou[1], and Xu Ding[1]

[1] School of Computer and Information,
Hefei University of Technology, Hefei, China
shilei@hfut.edu.cn
[2] Bradley Department of Electrical and Computer Engineering,
Virginia Tech, Blacksburg, USA

Abstract. In a mine locomotive wireless network, multiple locomotives move along a tunnel and communicate with access points (APs) on the side of this tunnel. The underground working environment is not safe and thus it is important to maintain high quality communication links. We consider throughput maximization for a mine locomotive wireless network with successive interference cancellation (SIC) and power control. We define time segments such that within each segment, the set of locomotives that can communicate with an AP is fixed and the distance from each locomotive to this AP can be approximated as a constant. To maximize throughput for each segment, we first prove the existence of optimal solutions that satisfy certain features on SIC decoding order and SINR under SIC. Then we can formulate a linear programming problem to obtain optimal solutions. We further propose a concept of the maximum SIC set to reduce problem size and obtain a polynomial complexity algorithm. Simulation results show that our algorithm can increase throughput significantly by comparing with the algorithm using SIC only (no power control) and comparing with the algorithm without using SIC and power control.

Keywords: Mine locomotive · Interference Management · Successive interference cancellation · Power control

1 Introduction

Mine locomotives have been widely used in mining industry for transporting. A typical structure of mine locomotive system is consisted with underground locomotives, access points (APs), and the ground control center, where underground locomotives will transmit their data to APs via wireless communications, and then APs will forward data to the ground control center via a backbone network.

This article is supported by the Natural Science Foundation of China (Grant No. 61370088 and No. 61501161).

© Springer International Publishing Switzerland 2016
Q. Yang et al. (Eds.): WASA 2016, LNCS 9798, pp. 207–218, 2016.
DOI: 10.1007/978-3-319-42836-9_19

A mine locomotive is usually driven by a person to travel along the underground tunnels. However, the underground working environment is not a safe environment and accidents are happened frequently. For example, in China at least 50,000 miners lost their lives from the year 2001 to 2013 [1]. Among all kinds of these incidents, at least 30 % are caused by transporting systems. To build a safe working environment, we should design a robust transporting system. There are two approaches to improve transporting systems: (i) build monitoring systems for mine locomotives [2] and (ii) build unmanned locomotive systems [3]. Under both approaches, the ground control center needs realtime status of locomotives to provide timely response to any incident. Obviously the data collection, transmission and procession in a robust transporting system are largely based on the quality of communications. A robust transporting system can be built only if each locomotive data can be transmitted to APs efficiently and correctly by wireless communications. In this paper, we focus on building a wireless network for underground locomotives.

Though lots of work have been done on unmanned vehicles, such as the Google car [4], there are unique challenges for the underground locomotives. Most of existing work are based on Vehicular Ad-hoc Network (VANET) [5,6] with lots of vehicles, and the IEEE 802.11 is the most common used protocol in VANET [7], which is based on collision avoidance (CA). The CA based protocol may not be the best choice because in the underground tunnel environment, there are limited number of locomotives driving along the railway only with a predetermined schedule.

Recently, many researchers have worked on the Interference Management (IM) based protocols [8]. When several transmitters transmitting simultaneously, the IM based protocols will try to decode and receive all their data while the CA based protocols will not decode any. Among several different IM techniques [9,10], the Successive Interference Cancellation (SIC) technique [11,12] is widely used because of easy implementation and good performance. SIC changes the physical layer behaviors, so new schemes on the upper layer should be designed to fully exploit its capability [13]. For the link layer scheduling, Lv *et al.* [14] designed a greedy scheduling algorithm for multi-hop ad hoc networks with SIC and showed throughput gain from 30 % to 60 % in simulation. Jiang *et al.* [16] designed an optimal algorithm for multi-hop ad hoc networks with SIC. Shi *et al.* [17] proposed a greedy cross-layer algorithm with polynomial complexity for SIC in a multi-hop network. Shi *et al.* [18] also proposed an optimal base station placement algorithm for single-hop wireless sensors networks based on SIC technique. These work all assume fixed transmission power. There is only a few work on applying the SIC technique into the underground environment. In our previous work, we aimed to maximize throughput for the underground locomotives via SIC with power control and designed an optimal locomotive moving schedule [19].

In this paper, we maximize throughput for a mine locomotive network with SIC and power control via optimal scheduling on concurrent transmissions. We make the following contributions. First, we propose a time slot based approach and prove the existence of optimal solution satisfying a particular SIC decoding order. Then we formulate a non-linear programming (NLP) problem to obtain such optimal solutions. Second, we prove the existence of optimal solution satisfying a particular SINR under SIC. Then we formulate a linear programming (LP) problem to obtain such optimal solutions in polynomial time. Third, we propose the concepts of maximum SIC set to further reduce complexity. Finally, we use simulation results to show that our optimal algorithm can achieve much better performance than other two schemes.

The rest of the paper is organized as follows. Section 2 describes the problem and its non-linear programming formulation. We further show how to reformulate it as a linear programming problem. In Sect. 3, we design a polynomial-time algorithm based on the concept of maximum SIC set. In Sect. 4, simulation results show that our algorithm can achieve large throughput improvement than schemes without power control and SIC.

2 Mine Locomotive Wireless Networks

A mine locomotive wireless network provides communication support for locomotives by APs on the side of a straight tunnel (see Fig. 1). These APs are deployed such that there is no overlap of APs' coverage and these APs cover the entire tunnel. Locomotives move along the tunnel and there may be multiple locomotives in an AP's coverage at the same time. APs apply successive interference cancellation (SIC) [12] to receive data from multiple locomotives. We want to maximize throughput for locomotives.

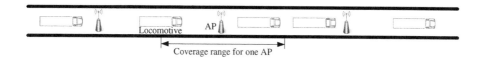

Fig. 1. The straight underground tunnel model.

2.1 Network Model

We focus on the problem for one AP and locomotives within its coverage. The same approach can be applied to other APs. Suppose that each locomotive l_i is in AP's coverage for certain period of time $[t_i^s, t_i^e]$ and all these time periods are within $[0, T]$. Each l_i can apply power control and use power $p_i(t) \in [0, P]$ to transmit its data at time $t \in [t_i^s, t_i^e]$.

To simplify discussion, denote the coordinate of considered AP as zero. Denote $x_i(t)$ as the coordinate of l_i at time t. Then the distance between l_i and AP at time t is $d_i(t) = |x_i(t)|$ and propagation gain $g_i(t)$ is $g_i(t) = \min\{(d_i(t))^{-\lambda}, 1\}$, where λ is the path loss index.

Now we determine the communication range. Denote N_0 as noise and β as the SINR threshold for a successful transmission. The maximum transmission range R_{max} is achieved when the transmission power is P and there is no interference. Then we have $\frac{(R_{max})^{-\lambda}P}{N_0} = \beta$, i.e.,

$$R_{max} = \left(\frac{P}{N_0\beta}\right)^{\frac{1}{\lambda}}. \qquad (1)$$

We define R_{max} as a locomotive's communication range, since the transmission from l_i may be successful only if $d_i(t) \leq R_{max}$. Then the coordinate of l_i is $x_i(t) = -R_{max} + v(t - t_i^s)$, where v is locomotive speed.

A locomotive l_i may not always transmit during $[t_i^s, t_i^e]$. We denote binary variable $\theta_i(t) = 1$ if l_i transmits at time t and $\theta_i(t) = 0$ otherwise. Apparently if $\theta_i(t) = 0$, we have $p_i(t) = 0$, i.e.,

$$\theta_i(t) \cdot P \geq p_i(t) \ (l_i \in N, t \in [0, T]),$$

where N is the set of all locomotives

Under SIC, AP can receive multiple locomotives' data simultaneously and decode them from the strongest signal to the weakest signal [12]. Once a signal is decoded, it will be cancelled from the combined data and thus SINR for the remaining signals are increased. The SINR of l_i at time t under SIC can be written as

$$\gamma_i(t) = \frac{g_i(t)p_i(t)}{N_0 + \sum_{\substack{l_j \in N \\ g_j(t)p_j(t) < g_i(t)p_i(t)}} g_j(t)p_j(t)} \ (l_i \in N, t \in [0, T]).$$

The SINR requirement under SIC is if $\theta_i(t) = 1$, then $\gamma_i(t) \geq \beta$, i.e.,

$$\gamma_i(t) \geq \beta \cdot \theta_i(t) \ (l_i \in N, t \in [0, T]).$$

2.2 Problem Formulation

In Sect. 2.1, we described constraints for a locomotive network with SIC. However, there are infinite number of variables, e.g., $\theta_i(t)$ for $t \in [0, T]$. In this section, we consider a problem based on SIC sets, where SIC set is a set of locomotives that can transmit at the same time under SIC, and prove the existence of optimal solutions that satisfy a particular SIC decoding order. Then we can formulate a non-linear programming (NLP) problem with finite number of variables.

To reduce the number of variables, we divide time $[0, T]$ into m small time segments such that in each time segment, (i) the set of locomotives within AP's coverage does not change, and (ii) the distance between a locomotive in this set and the AP does not change much. Denote the set of time segments as M. By (ii), we can approximate channel gain for a locomotive l_i in time segment k as a constant g_{ik}. Our objective is to maximize throughput in each time segment.

We now formulate an optimization problem for time segment k. Given the set of locomotives within AP's coverage, we can determine all SIC sets (by the approach in the next section). Denote Γ_k as the set of SIC sets in time segment k and S_{kj} as the j-th SIC set in Γ_k. We divide time segment k into $|\Gamma_k|$ time slots and assign one time slot for each SIC set. Denote τ_{kj} as the time slot assigned to S_{kj} and ω_{kj} as the normalized length of time slot τ_{kj}. We have

$$\sum_{j \in \Gamma_k} \omega_{kj} = 1. \tag{2}$$

Since both the set of active locomotives and their channel gains do not change within a time slot, these locomotives do not need to change their transmission powers in a time slot. Denote $p_i(\tau_{kj})$ as the power of l_i in time slot τ_{kj}. The SINR for a locomotive l_i in time slot τ_{kj} is

$$\gamma_i(\tau_{kj}) = \frac{g_{ik} p_i(\tau_{kj})}{N_0 + \sum_{l_h \in S_{kj}}^{g_{hk} p_h(\tau_{kj}) < g_{ik} p_i(\tau_{kj})} g_{hk} p_h(\tau_{kj})} \ (l_i \in S_{kj}, S_{kj} \in \Gamma_k). \tag{3}$$

The SINR requirement under SIC is

$$\gamma_i(\tau_{kj}) \geq \beta \ (l_i \in S_{kj}, S_{kj} \in \Gamma_k). \tag{4}$$

Note that in Eq. (3), the set of terms in $\sum_{l_h \in S_{kj}}^{g_{hk} p_h(\tau_{kj}) < g_{ik} p_i(\tau_{kj})} g_{hk} p_h(\tau_{kj})$ depends on $p_h(\tau_{kj})$ and $p_i(\tau_{kj})$ values. But in a math programming formulation, the set of terms should be fixed. To resolve this issue, it is important to note that optimal solutions are not unique. Instead of considered all optimal solutions, we focus on optimal solutions with a particular SIC decoding order described in the following theorem.

Theorem 1. *There is an optimal solution φ satisfying the following requirement: In each time slot, locomotives are decoded by the decreasing order of their channel gains to AP.*

To prove Theorem 1, we first need the following corollary.

Corollary 1. *Suppose that in an optimal solution $\hat{\varphi}$ and a time slot τ_{kj}, locomotive l_h is decoded right after l_i and l_h's channel gain to AP is larger than l_i's channel gain, where $l_h, l_i \in S_{kj}$. Then there is another optimal solution φ with locomotive l_i is decoded right after l_h in time slot τ_{kj}.*

Corollary 1 can be proved by constructing such a solution φ. The proof is omitted here to save space. Then Theorem 1 can be proved by using Corollary 1 repeatedly to remove any violation on decoding order. By Theorem 1, (3) can be rewritten as

$$\gamma_i(\tau_{kj}) = \frac{g_{ik} p_i(\tau_{kj})}{N_0 + \sum_{l_h \in S_{kj}}^{g_{hk} < g_{ik}} g_{hk} p_h(\tau_{kj})} \ (l_i \in S_{kj}, S_{kj} \in \Gamma_k). \tag{5}$$

Now there are fixed number of terms in $\sum_{l_h \in S_{kj}}^{g_{hk} < g_{ik}} g_{hk} p_h(\tau_{kj})$.

Suppose that the minimum data rate requirement for l_i is r_i. For time segment k, we want to maximize a common scaling factor K_k such that

$$K_k r_i \leq \sum_{S_{kj} \in \Gamma_k}^{l_i \in S_{kj}} W \log_2(1 + \beta)\omega_{kj} \ (l_i \in S_{kj}). \tag{6}$$

Then the optimization problem for time segment k is

$$\begin{aligned} \max \ &K_k \\ \text{s.t.} \ \ &(2),(4),(5),(6) \\ &p_i(\tau_{kj}) \leq P \quad (l_i \in S_{kj}, S_{kj} \in \Gamma_k), \end{aligned} \tag{7}$$

where $p_i(\tau_{kj})$, $\gamma_i(\tau_{kj})$, K_k, and ω_{kj} are variables. This formulation is a NLP problem and is very challenging to solve.

2.3   Reformulation

Problem (7) is non-linear due to p variables in Eq. (5). Thus, we aim to remove these p variables. In this section, we focus on certain optimal solutions that enable us to determine $p_i(\tau_{kj})$ values for a SIC set S_{kj} in each time slot τ_{kj}. Then we formulate a linear programming (LP) problem to obtain such optimal solutions.

As a starting point, we have the following corollary.

Corollary 2. *Suppose that in an optimal solution $\hat{\varphi}$, a locomotive l_i's SINR under SIC is larger than β in time slot τ_{kj}. Then there is an optimal solution φ with l_i's SINR under SIC equal to β in time slot τ_{kj}.*

Corollary 2 can also be proved by construction. Based on Corollary 2, we can further get the following theorem.

Theorem 2. *There is an optimal solution φ satisfying the following requirement: In each time slot τ_{kj}, each locomotive $l_i \in S_{kj}$ has its SINR value under SIC equal to β.*

Theorem 2 can be proved by using Corollary 1 repeatedly, where within each time slot τ_{kj}, locomotives in S_{kj} are checked (and transmission powers are updated if needed) by following the increasing order of their channel gains.

Now we focus on optimal solution described in Theorem 2. For a set S_{kj}, we can determine transmission powers $p_i(\tau_{kj})$ in time slot τ_{kj} as follows.

- From the farthest locomotive to the nearest locomotive in S_{kj}, calculate $p_i(\tau_{kj})$ to make $\gamma_i(\tau_{kj}) = \dfrac{g_{ik}p_i(\tau_{kj})}{N_0 + \sum_{\substack{g_{hk} < g_{ik} \\ l_h \in S_{kj}}} g_{hk}p_h(\tau_{kj})} = \beta$.

Note that (i) $p_h(\tau_{kj})$ values for $l_h \in S_{kj}$ and $g_{hk} < g_{ik}$ are already determined when we calculate $p_i(\tau_{kj})$ and (ii) for a SIC set, the calculated all $p_i(\tau_{kj}) \leq P$, i.e., if any p value is larger than P, the corresponding set is not a SIC set. The complexity to calculate for transmission powers for a SIC set S_{kj} is $O(|S_{kj}|) = O(n_k)$, where n_k is the number of locomotives in time segment k. Once p variables are all determined, problem (7) becomes the following LP.

$$\max K_k$$
$$\text{s.t. } (2), (6), \tag{8}$$

where K_k and ω_{kj} are variables. Note that if we check all non-empty subsets ($2^{n_k} - 1$ subsets) to obtain all SIC sets, the complexity to obtain all SIC sets and transmission powers is $O(2^{n_k}) \cdot O(n_k) = O(n_k 2^{n_k})$ and thus the overall complexity is non-polynomial.

3   Polynomial-Time Algorithm

As we discussed in the last section, a simple algorithm by checking $O(2^{n_k})$ sets to find all SIC sets has an exponential complexity. To reduce complexity, we need to reduce the number of potential SIC sets.

We prove the maximum number of locomotives in a SIC set.

Theorem 3. *The maximum number of locomotives in a SIC set is no more than a small constant* $\alpha_{max} = \min\{1 + \lfloor \log_{(1+\beta)} \frac{P}{\beta N_0} \rfloor, n_k\}$.

Theorem 3 can be proved by following the idea of Theorem 1 in [19], and thus we omit the proof. By Theorem 3, we only need to check subsets with at most α_{max} locomotives to obtain all SIC sets. The number of these subsets is $\sum_{i=1}^{\alpha_{max}} C(n_k, i) = O((n_k)^{\alpha_{max}})$. Then we have the following *SIC-set algorithm*.

- Check all subsets with no more than α_{max} locomotives to find all SIC sets and transmission powers.
- Solve (8) based on identified SIC sets.

The complexity to find all SIC sets and transmission powers is $O((n_k)^{\alpha_{max}}) \cdot O(n_k) = O((n_k)^{\alpha_{max}+1})$. For the second step, since the formulated LP has $O((n_k)^{\alpha_{max}})$ variables, the complexity to solve this LP is $O(((n_k)^{\alpha_{max}})^3) = O((n_k)^{3\alpha_{max}})$ [21]. So the complexity of the SIC-set algorithm is $O((n_k)^{\alpha_{max}+1}) + O((n_k)^{3\alpha_{max}}) = O((n_k)^{3\alpha_{max}})$, which is polynomial.

Note that $(n_k)^{3\alpha_{max}}$ may still be a large number. To further decrease the complexity, we define a concept of maximum SIC set (see Definition 1) and show that we only need to consider solutions with maximum SIC sets.

Definition 1. *A SIC set S is a maximum SIC set if for any locomotive l_i which is closer to the AP than all locomotives in S, $S \cup \{l_i\}$ is not a SIC set.*

Theorem 4. *For a maximum SIC set S_{ki} and a SIC set $S_{kj} \subset S_{ki}$, we have (i) the data rate from each locomotives in $S_{ki} - S_{kj}$ is positive in S_{ki}'s time slot and is zero in S_{kj}'s time slot; (ii) the data rate from each locomotives in S_{kj} is the same in both S_{ki}'s and S_{kj}'s time slots.*

```
1.   //Rename locomotives such that lᵢ has the i-th smallest distance to the AP;
2.   void FindMaxSICSets() {
3.        AddLocomotive(∅, n);
4.   }
5.   //Try to add a locomotive to the current SIC set.
6.   void AddLocomotive(set S, int j) {
7.        bool FindJ=false; //indicate whether we find a locomotive that can be
8.                          //added into the current SIC set.
9.        for (; j > 0; j − −)
10.            if S⋃{lⱼ} is a SIC set {
11.                FindJ=true;
12.                AddLocomotive(S⋃{lⱼ}, j − 1);
13.            }
14.        if (FindJ==false) //the current SIC set is a maximum SIC set
15.            output S;
16. }
```

Fig. 2. Pseudocode for getting all maximum SIC sets.

Theorem 4 can be proved by following the idea of Lemma 2 in [20], thus we omit the proof. Based on Theorem 4, it is easy to see that if we replace S_{kj} by S_{ki} in a solution, the new solution will have a better objective value. Thus, we only need to consider maximum SIC sets in (8) to obtain an optimal solution. We called this approach as the *max-SIC-set algorithm*.

We now show how to find all maximum SIC sets (see pseudocode in Fig. 2). Initially, we have an empty set and then add locomotives to this set while keeping it as a SIC set. We sort the locomotives by their distances to AP, then try to add locomotives from the farthest one to the closest one. During this process, if we cannot find a locomotive l_j that is closer to AP than any locomotive in a SIC set S such that $S\bigcup\{l_j\}$ is a SIC set, then S is a maximum SIC set. Otherwise, S is not a maximum SIC set and we need to further check whether $S\bigcup\{l_j\}$ is a maximum SIC set. The complexity of the algorithm in Fig. 2 is not easy to analyze. Instead, we can compare it with the approach of checking all subsets with no more than α_{max} locomotives to find all SIC sets. This algorithm has much less complexity due to the following two reasons. (i) We do not check all subsets with no more than α_{max} locomotives, i.e., once a set is identified as not a SIC set, we will not add more locomotives to this set and check whether the new set is a SIC set or not (since the new set will not be a SIC set). (ii) When we check a new set, we only need to determine the transmission power for the newly added locomotives (other locomotives' powers are already determined) and compare it with P.

4   Simulation Results

In this section we give simulation results to show the performance of the max-SIC-set algorithm. We compare our results with the other two schemes: SIC

Table 1. Start times and minimum rate requirements of the 20 locomotives.

i	t_i^s(s)	r_i(Kbps)	i	t_i^s(s)	r_i(Kbps)	i	t_i^s(s)	r_i(Kbps)	i	t_i^s(s)	r_i(Kbps)
1	0	480.9	6	57	652.3	11	105	188.4	16	156	237.5
2	12	521.8	7	64	489.2	12	116	713.4	17	165	207.8
3	20	466.2	8	73	197.8	13	126	152.6	18	173	436.3
4	31	469.4	9	79	178.4	14	140	492.4	19	188	396.8
5	44	884.3	10	92	465.4	15	150	641.6	20	195	785.5

only (no power control) and non-SIC (traditional approach). Under these two schemes, each locomotive uses the maximum power to transmit data. Similar algorithms can be designed to obtain optimal solutions under these two schemes.

Table 2. K_k values under different schemes from $k = 21$ to 30

k	time length	K_k (SIC with power control)	K_k (SIC only)	K_k (non-SIC)	k	time length	K_k (SIC with power control)	K_k (SIC only)	K_k (non-SIC)
21	5	1.94	1.14	1.01	26	4	1.73	1.14	1.02
22	5	1.94	1.14	1.01	27	3	1.81	1.09	0.97
23	3	2.10	1.14	1.01	28	5	2.46	1.25	1.10
24	4	1.60	1.02	0.92	29	3	2.46	1.25	1.10
25	5	2.39	1.14	1.02	30	5	1.52	1.17	1.04

Consider wireless networks with 20 to 50 mine locomotives and one AP in a straight tunnel. A locomotive's maximum transmission power is $P = 1$W and the noise power is $N_0 = 10^{-10}$W. The SINR threshold is $\beta = 3$. The path lost index is $\lambda = 4$. Then by (1), a locomotive's communication range is $R_{max} = 240$ m. The channel bandwidth is $W = 22$ MHz. The minimum data transmission rate requirement r_i is between 100 Kbps and 1 Mbps. The traveling speed is $v = 5$ m/s. The maximum length of a time segment is 5 s. The distance between two successive locomotives should be kept at least 30 m for safety reasons. Suppose we have known all start times t_i^s, which are created randomly in our simulations and satisfy the minimum security distance.

We first present detailed results of a wireless network with 20 locomotives in Sect. 4.1. Then we provide complete results for all network instances with different number of locomotives.

4.1 Results for a Wireless Network with 20 Locomotives

Consider a wireless network with 20 locomotives. The start times and the minimum data transmission rate requirement of each locomotive are given in Table 1. The whole schedule time $T = 291$ s, and will be divided into 72 time segments. To show the efficiency of our algorithm, we list the values of K_k from the 21st

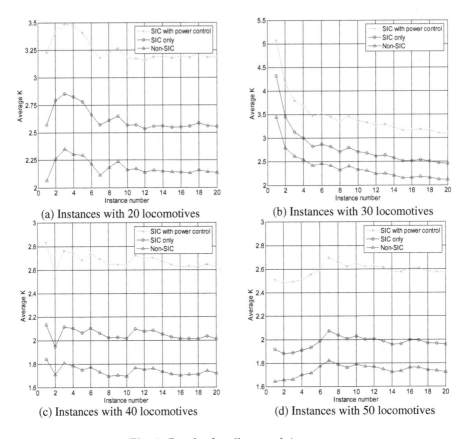

Fig. 3. Results for all network instances.

time segment to the 30th time segment[1] in Table 2 while comparing the values of K_k under the other two schemes. We also list the length of some time segments in Table 2. We can see that SIC with power control can always achieve the best performance while the non-SIC scheme always has the worst performance. To show the overall performance over all segments, we calculate the average K_k values for all segments, which are $K = 3.23$ for the SIC with power control scheme, $K = 2.57$ for the SIC only scheme, and $K = 2.07$ for the non-SIC scheme. That is, the improvement on throughput by the SIC with power control scheme is 125.7 % comparing with the SIC only scheme and is 156.0 % comparing with the non-SIC scheme.

---

[1] We do not show result in the first 10 time slot, since there are only a few locomotives within AP's coverage.

Table 3. K value and improvements for the four group instances.

Number of locomotives	K (SIC with power control)	K (SIC only)	K (non-SIC)	Improvement over SIC only	Improvement over non-SIC
20	3.25	2.62	2.18	123.9 %	148.9 %
30	3.47	2.81	2.38	123.8 %	145.5 %
40	2.68	2.05	1.74	130.4 %	153.7 %
50	2.59	1.98	1.74	131.0 %	148.6 %

4.2 Results for All Network Instances

We consider networks with $20, 30, 40$, or 50 locomotives, and generate 20 different network instances randomly for each network size. Then we calculate the K value for each instance under three schemes, and show the results in Fig. 3. We can see the K value for each instance by the SIC with power control scheme is improved significantly compared with the other two schemes (see Table 3).

5 Conclusions

In this paper, we designed an optimal communication algorithm for underground mine locomotive networks, where an AP receive multiple locomotives' data by using SIC and each locomotive can tune its transmission power to maximize throughput. We proved the existence of optimal solutions that satisfy certain features on SIC decoding order and SINR under SIC, which enable us to have a LP formulation for our problem. We also proposed the concept of the maximum SIC set and used this concept to further reduce problem complexity. The designed max-SIC-set algorithm can obtain optimal solution with polynomial complexity. Simulation results showed that our algorithm can improve the throughput significantly than the other two schemes: SIC only (without power control) and non-SIC (traditional approach). In our future work, we will further design mine locomotive wireless network strategies with complicated underground tunnels.

References

1. Deng, Q.G., Wang, Y., Liu, M.J., Wei, J.J.: Statistic analysis and enlightenment on coal mine accident of China from 2001 2013 periods. Coal Technol. **33**(9), 73–75 (2014)
2. Berglund, T., Brodnik, A., Jonsson, H., Staffanson, M., Croucamp, P.L., Rimer, S., Kruger, C.: Planning smooth and obstacle-avoiding B-spline paths for autonomous mining vehicles. IEEE Trans. Autom. Sci. Eng. **7**(1), 167–172 (2010)
3. Ge, B., Zhang, S.X.: Research on precise positioning technology of mine locomotive unmanned systems. Appl. Mech. Mater. **397**(11), 1602–1605 (2013)
4. Poczter, S.L., Jankovic, L.M.: The Google car: driving toward a better future? J. Bus. Case Stud. **10**(1), 1–7 (2014)

5. Wang, H., Liu, R., Ni, W., Chen, W.: VANET modeling and clustering design under practical traffic, channel and mobility conditions. IEEE Trans. Commun. **63**(3), 870–881 (2015)
6. Hartenstein, H., Laberteaux, K.P.: A tutorial survey on vehicular ad hoc networks. IEEE Commun. Mag. **46**(6), 164–171 (2008)
7. Yao, Y., Rao, L., Liu, X.: Performance and reliability analysis of IEEE 802.11p safety communication in a highway environment. IEEE Trans. Veh. Technol. **62**(9), 4198–4262 (2013)
8. Nabil, A., Hou, Y.T., Zhu, R., Lou, W., Midkiff, S.F.: Recent advances in interference management for wireless networks. IEEE Netw. **29**(5), 83–89 (2015)
9. Andrews, J.G.: Interference cancellation for cellular systems: a contemporary overview. IEEE Wirel. Commun. Mag. **12**(2), 19–29 (2005)
10. Nam, W., Bai, D., Lee, J., Kang, I.: Advanced interference management for 5G cellular networks. IEEE Commun. Mag. **52**(5), 52–60 (2014)
11. Miridakis, N.I., Vergados, D.D.: A survey on the successive interference cancellation performance for single-antenna and multiple-antenna OFDM systems. IEEE Commun. Surv. Tutorials **15**(1), 312–335 (2013)
12. Zhang, X., Haenggi, M.: The performance of successive interference cancellation in random wireless networks. IEEE Trans. Inf. Theory **60**(10), 6368–6388 (2014)
13. Frenger, P., Orten, P., Ottosson, T.: Code-spread CDMA with interference cancellation. IEEE J. Sel. Areas Commun. **17**(12), 2090–2095 (1999)
14. Lv, S., Wang, X., Zhou, X.: Scheduling under SINR model in ad hoc networks with successive interference cancellation. In: Proceedings of the IEEE GLOBECOM, Miami, FL, USA, 6–10 December 2010
15. Lv, S., Zhuang, W., Wang, X., Zhou, X.: Scheduling in wireless ad hoc networks with successive interference cancellation. In: Proceedings of the IEEE INFOCOM, Shanghai, China, 10–15 April 2011
16. Jiang, C., Shi, Y., Hou, Y.T., Lou, W., Kompella, S., Midkiff, S.F.: Squeezing the most out of interference: an optimization framework for joint interference exploitation and avoidance. In: Proceedings of the IEEE INFOCOM, Orlando, FL, Canada, 25–30 March 2012
17. Shi, L., Shi, Y., Ye, Y.X., Wei, Z.C., Han, J.H.: An efficient interference management framework for multi-hop wireless networks. In: Proceedings of the IEEE WCNC, Shanghai, China, 7–10 April 2013
18. Shi, L., Zhang, J., Shi, Y., Ding, X., Wei, Z.: Optimal base station placement for wireless sensor networks with successive interference cancellation. Sensors **15**(1), 1676–1690 (2015)
19. Wu, L., Han, J., Wei, X., Shi, L., Ding, X.: The mine LocomotiveWireless network strategy based on successive interference cancellation. Sensors **15**(11), 28257–28270 (2015)
20. Shi, L., Han, J., Shi, Y., Wei, Z.: Cross-layer optimization for wireless sensor network with multi-packet reception. In: Proceedings of ChinaCom, Beijing, China, 25–27 August 2010
21. Khachiyan, L.G.: Polynomial algorithms in linear programming. USSR Comput. Math. Math. Phys. **20**(1), 53–72 (1980)

ESRS: An Efficient and Secure Relay Selection Algorithm for Mobile Social Networks

Xiaoshuang Xing[1,2]([⊠]), Xiuzhen Cheng[3], Huan Dai[1],
Shengrong Gong[1], Feng Zhao[4], and Hongbin Qiu[4]

[1] School of Computer Science and Engineering,
Changshu Institute of Technology, Changshu, China
{xiaoshuang_xing,daihuanjob}@163.com, shrgong@suda.edu.cn
[2] Provincial Key Laboratory for Computer Information Processing Technology,
Soochow University, Suzhou, China
[3] Computer Science, The George Washington University, Washington DC, USA
cheng@gwu.edu
[4] Guilin University of Electronic Technology, Guilin, China
{zhaofeng,qiuhb}@guet.edu.cn

Abstract. Despite the extensive study on relay selection in mobile social networks (MSNs), few work has considered the fundamental problem of preventing information leakage to non-destination users. To the best of our knowledge, no existing work has taken both transmission latency (i.e. efficiency) and information leakage probability (i.e. security) into consideration for relay selection in MSNs. Therefore we target on designing an efficient and secure relay selection algorithm to enable communication among legitimate users while reducing the information leakage probability to other users. In this paper, a network formation game based relay selection algorithm named ESRS is proposed. We define the payoff functions of the users, design the game evolving rules, and prove the stability of the formed network structure. Extensive simulation is conducted to validate the performance of the ESRS algorithm by using both synthetic trace and real-world trace. The results show that our algorithm outperforms other algorithms by trading a balance between efficiency and security.

1 Introduction

Nowadays, people carry various mobile devices such as smartphones, PADs, and laptops to leverage WiFi, Internet, and 3G/4G cellular networks for pervasive commmunication services [1]. When such infrastructures are unavailable, these devices can form a self-organizing network and enable communication among users by using the opportunistic encounters between them. Such a network is termed as a mobile social network (MSN). Finding appropriate relays and forming suitable routing paths play critical roles for information dissemination in MSNs.

Extensive effort has been taken to design efficient relay selection algorithms and routing protocols for MSNs. Moreover, taking into account the fact that

© Springer International Publishing Switzerland 2016
Q. Yang et al. (Eds.): WASA 2016, LNCS 9798, pp. 219–230, 2016.
DOI: 10.1007/978-3-319-42836-9_20

human social behavior heavily impacts the operation of MSNs, researchers have designed a number of relay selection algorithms by considering human social features such as the visiting frequencies of human beings to certain locations and the encounter frequencies among human beings. However, few literature has considered the fundamental problem of preventing information leakage to non-destination users. Despite the employment of encryption mechanism, reducing the information leakage probability is still critical as encryption mechanism is not "perfectly secure". Therefore, we target on designing an efficient and secure relay selection algorithm to enable communication among legitimate users while reducing the information leakage probability to other users in MSNs.

The main contributions of this paper are as follows: First, both the social relationship among the users and the overhearing probabilities of the users are considered in our design, through which the efficiency and the security of the relay selection algorithm can be ensured. Second, we propose a network formation game based relay selection algorithm. The payoff functions of the information source, the candidate relays, and the information destination are defined, the game evolving rules are designed, and the stability of the formed network structure is proved. Third, extensive simulation is conducted to validate the performance of the proposed relay selection algorithm by using both synthetic trace and real-world trace. The results show that our algorithm outperforms other algorithms by trading a balance between the transmission latency (i.e. efficiency) and the information leakage probability (i.e. security).

In the rest of the paper, we briefly summarize the related work on relay selection in MSNs in Sect. 2. We describe the problem to be solved in Sect. 3. An efficient and secure relay selection algorithm (ESRS) is proposed based on the network formation game in Sect. 4, where we define the payoff functions in Sect. 4.1, design the game evolving rules in Sect. 4.2, and prove the stability of the formed network structure in Sect. 4.3. A simulation study to validate the performance of the ESRS algorithm is reported in Sect. 5. Finally, we conclude the paper in Sect. 6.

2   Related Work

The MSN routing schemes can be classified into four main categories: flooding based schemes, single-copy based schemes, utility based schemes, and quota based schemes. Flooding based schemes maintain low transmission latency at the expense of high storage cost and communication overhead [2,3]. On the contrary, single-copy based schemes reduce the storage cost and the communication overhead by allowing only one copy of an information packet to be transmitted in the network [4]. But they provide no performance guarantee on the transmission latency. To tradeoff between transmission latency and storage/communication cost, utility based schemes and quota based schemes are proposed. In utility based schemes, a user forwards the information only if it encounters another user with higher utility [5]. While in quota based schemes, the number of copies for each information packet is upper bounded by a fixed number [6].

Considering the fact that network operations are heavily impacted by human social behaviors, variants of the aforementioned routing schemes are proposed by exploiting different human social characteristics. [7] takes the rate of encountering other users, or simply the encounter rate, as the main metric for relay selection. A user will forward the information to an encountered user with higher encounter rate with the destination. [8] shares a similar idea with [7] while the encountering duration is taken as the relay selection metric. [9,10], and [11] exploit the mobility properties of the users for relay selection. They intend to predict/assess the encounters among the users through mobility analysis, thus they can be considered as a variant of [7,8].

Despite these efforts to solve the relay selection problem in MSNs, none of them considers the fundamental problem of preventing information leakage to non-destination users [12,13]. Although the encryption mechanism can be employed to protect the information transmission, reducing the information leakage probability is still critical as encryption mechanism is not "perfectly secure". To tackle this challenge, a routing scheme is designed in [14] to reduce information leakage in social networks. However, the social relationship among users is not considered thus the transmission latency (i.e. routing efficiency) can not be guaranteed. To the best of our knowledge, we are the first to take both efficiency and security into consideration for relay selection in MSNs.

3 Problem Description

Consider a mobile social network consisting of a set of users, denoted by $N = \{1, 2, \cdots, n\}$. For each user $i \in N$, a social relationship vector $\Omega_i = \{\omega_{i1}, \omega_{i2}, \cdots, \omega_{in}\}$ is defined to describe its social relationship with others. A higher social relationship $0 \leq \omega_{ij} \leq 1$ indicates a higher frequency that user i meets user j. Moreover, an overhearing probability p_i is defined for each user i to indicate the probability that i intercepts the information not for it. A higher $0 \leq p_i \leq 1$ indicates a higher probability that i overhears others' information.

We study the relay selection problem in the considered mobile social network. We assume that there is an information source $I_s \in N$ trying to share its information with a set of destinations $V_D \subseteq N \setminus I_s$. For each destination $i \in V_D$, we try to find a relay path L_i for it. The relay path can be denoted by $L_i = \{(i_l, i_{l+1}) | l \in \{1, 2, \cdots, l_n^i - 1\}, i_1 = I_s, i_{l_n^i} = i\}$, with (i_l, i_{l+1}) being a relay link from user i_l to user i_{l+1} and l_n^i being the number of users on path L_i. Our objective is to find the relay path L_i with small information leakage probability and transmission latency. To model and solve this problem, we will design an **E**fficient and **S**ecure **R**elay **S**election algorithm (ESRS) in next section.

4 An Efficient and Secure Relay Selection Algorithm

In this section, we model the relay selection problem as a network formation game, where the users, also referred to as the players in the game, have the discretion in forming the relay paths. Each user calculates its payoff as the difference between the benefit and the cost for jointing a specific relay path and decides its strategy that could maximize its own payoff. More specifically, we will define the payoff functions for the information source, the relays, and the destinations in Sect. 4.1, design the game evolving rules (that is the procedure of the ESRS algorithm) in Sect. 4.2, and prove the stability of the network structure formed by the proposed algorithm in Sect. 4.3.

4.1 Payoff Functions

For any game, one basic problem is to inspire the users to participate. In this subsection, we design the payoff functions to capture the incentives for the information source, the relays, and the destinations.

First, we design the payoff function for the information source I_s. Let $N(I_s)$ denote the set of users that are within the transmission range of I_s. Then the destination set V_D could be partitioned into two subsets: $V_D^{in} \subseteq N(I_s)$ and $V_D^{out} = V_D \setminus V_D^{in}$. For any destination $i \in V_D^{in}$, I_s could build a direct transmission link (I_s, i) and gain a unit of payoff through finishing the transmission to destination i. If I_s selects a relay $j \neq i$ for destination i instead of performing the direct transmission, i will not be reached at this time. Thus, we assume that I_s will gain a payoff of $-\infty$ if I_s selects a relay $j \neq i$ for any $i \in V_D^{in}$. For any destination $i \in V_D^{out}$, I_s can either hold the transmission until the destinations move into its transmission range or employ some other users, which are within its transmission range, as relays. For any destination $i \in V_D^{out}$, the probability that I_s will meet i can be denoted by $\omega_{I_s i}$. The probability that destination i will be reached if user $j \in N(I_s)$ is selected as the relay can be denoted by ω_{ji}. Thus, when $\omega_{ji} > \omega_{I_s i}$, the benefit of employing user j as the relay to destination i can be defined as:

$$B_i^s(j) = \omega_{ji} - \omega_{I_s i} \tag{1}$$

However, everything has two sides. Compared with direct transmission, relay transmission may cause a certain probability of information leakage on the relay paths. For a certain relay, the information may be intercepted by itself or be overheard by the users within its transmission range. Therefore, the probability that the information for destination i is leaked at relay $j \in L_i$ can be defined as:

$$C_i^s(j) = \begin{cases} 1 - (1 - p_j) \prod_{k \notin V_D}(1 - \omega_{jk} p_k), & \text{if } j \notin V_D; \\ 1 - \prod_{k \notin V_D}(1 - \omega_{jk} p_k), & \text{if } j \in V_D. \end{cases} \tag{2}$$

where p_j is the overhearing probability of user j.

Calculating the difference between $B_i^s(j)$ and $C_i^s(j)$, we get the payoff earned by I_s for employing user j as a relay to destination i. Taking into account all the discussed cases, we define the payoff function of the information source as follows:

$$U_i^s(j) = \begin{cases} 1 & \text{if } i \in N(I_s), j = i; \\ -\infty & \text{if } i \in N(I_s), j \neq i; \\ B_i^s(j) - C_i^s(j) & \text{if } i \notin N(I_s), j \in N(I_s). \end{cases} \tag{3}$$

Here, the first row indicates the case where destination $i \in V_D^{in}$ and I_s performs the direct transmission; the second row indicates the case where destination $i \in V_D^{in}$ and I_s selects a relay $j \neq i$ for i; and the third row indicates the case where $i \in V_D^{out}$ and I_s selects a relay $j \in N(I_s)$ for i.

When considering the network formation from the view point of the relays, the wages for acting as a relay and the cost for maintianing the relay links are two major concerns. In this work, we assume that each source destination pair $(I_s, i), i \in V_D$, provides a wage budget of α. Each relay j on path L_i earns a wage $B_i^r(j)$ through sharing the total budget according to a predefined rule, which will be detailed in next subsection. As to the cost, we assume that a cost β is needed for user j to maintain each link. Then, the cost of user j for acting as a relay to destination i can be denoted by

$$C_i^r(j) = k_{ij} \cdot \beta \tag{4}$$

where k_{ij} is the number of links that should be added by j to perform the relay function for i.

Therefore, the payoff function of user j for acting as a relay to destination i can be defined as:

$$U_i^r(j) = B_i^r(j) - C_i^r(j) \tag{5}$$

Finally, we define the payoff function for the destinations. For any destination $i \in V_D$, the payoff function U_i^d is defined as:

$$U_i^d = \begin{cases} 1 \text{ if destination } i \text{ is reached}; \\ 0 \text{ otherwise.} \end{cases} \tag{6}$$

That is, destination $i \in V_D$ earns a unit of payoff if i is reached and earns nothing otherwise.

4.2 Relay Selection Based on the Network Formation Game

In the network formation game, the objective of each player (user) is to maximize its payoff [15]. In this subsection, we propose the ESRS algorithm based on the network formation game described above. ESRS consists of M rounds, with M being the maximum number of hops on the relay paths. In the m-th round, $m \in \{1, 2, \cdots, M\}$, the m-th hop relay links for those destinations, which have not been reached, are formed.

For the first round, i.e., $m = 1$, the information source searches within its transmission range for the destinations. For each $i \in V_D^{in}$, I_s forms the relay path $L_i = \{(I_s, i)\}$ and transmits the information to i directly. Then, the following steps are performed to form the first-hop relay paths for those destinations in V_D^{out}:

Step 1. I_s broadcasts an employment information, including the set V_D^{out} and the value of α, to those users belong to $N(I_s)$.

Step 2. Each user $j \in N(I_s)$ feedbacks a relationship list $\Omega_j = \{\omega_{ji} | i \in V\}$ to I_s.

Step 3. After receiving the replies, I_s selects a relay $j_i^* \in N(I_s)$ for each destination $i \in V_D^{out}$ according to the following rule:

$$j_i^* = \arg \max_{j \in N(I_s)} U_i^s(j) \tag{7}$$

where $U_i^s(j) = B_i^s(j) - C_i^s(j)$ can be calculated according to (1), (2), and (3).
Then, I_s constructs an employment list E_j for each $j \in N(I_s)$.

$$E_j = \{i | j_i^* = j\} \tag{8}$$

We should notice that $E_j = \emptyset$, if user $j \in N(I_s)$ is not selected as a relay
for any $i \in V_D^{out}$. For any user $j \in N(I_s)$ with nonempty E_j, I_s sends the
employment list to it.

Step 4. If user j receives a nonempty employment list E_j from I_s, it accepts to
act as relays for a subset of destinations $V_j^* \subseteq E_j$, and feedbacks V_j^* to I_s.
V_j^* is determined according to the following rule:

$$V_j^* = \{\forall i \in V_j^* | U_i^r(j) > 0\} \tag{9}$$

Where $U_i^r(j) = B_i^r(j) - C_i^r(j)$ is the payoff of user j for acting as a relay to
destination i. $C_i^r(j)$ can be calculated according to equation (4) and $B_i^r(j) = \alpha$ in the first round since j is the only relay for destination pair (I_s, i) now.

Step 5. After receiving the feedbacks, I_s constructs the relay links for any $i \in V_j^*$
as $L_i = \{(I_s, j), (j, i)\}$, and modifies the set of destinations need to be relayed
as $V_D^{out} = V_D^{out} \setminus \bigcup V_j^*$. Then, it performs Step 1 to Step 5, until $V_D^{out} = \emptyset$. It
should be noticed that the relays which have rejected the employment of I_s
will not be considered again.

After the first round is finished, the first hop relays of all the destinations
have been employed (if necessary). Denote the set of all the first hop relays by
R_1. The information source I_s sends the information to the relays in R_1. Once
the relays in R_1 have accepted the employment, they have the responsibilities to
transmit the information to the destinations. Otherwise, they will be punished
by a tough punishment mechanism.

Then, our ESRS algorithm selects the second-hop relays in the second round.
In this round, each first hop relay $j \in R_1$, which has the responsibility to transmit the information to the destinations in V_j^*, can be considered as a **virtual
information source** $I_{s_j} = j$ with a set of destinations V_j^*. Each virtual information source I_{s_j} just needs to perform Step 1-Step 5 as in the first round.
The only difference we should notice is that the declared value of α in Step 1 is
changed in the second round. Since relay I_{s_j} has accepted the employment of I_s,
it has the responsibility to relay the information to destination $i \in V_j^*$. When
i is out of the transmission range of j, j is motivated to employ a second hop
relay for help. However, j is a selfish user who has to consider its own benefits.
Therefore, j would not give all the wages it earns from I_s to the second hop
relay. In our work, we assume that j declares a wage budget $\alpha_2 = \frac{\alpha}{2}$ in Step 1.
Therefore, the benefit earned by a second hop relay j_2 will be $B_i^r(j_2) = \alpha_2 = \frac{\alpha}{2}$
in Step 4.

Similarly, the m-th hop relays could be selected independently with the selection of the $(m-1)$-th hop relays. Here, the $(m-1)$-th relays are considered as the virtual information sources, the wage budget α_m is declared to be $\alpha_m = \frac{\alpha}{2^{(m-1)}}$ in Step 1, and the benefit earned by a m-th hop relay j_m is $B_i^r(j_m) = \frac{\alpha}{2^{(m-1)}}$ in Step 4. Finally, the ESRS algorithm ends when all the destinations of the information source I_s are reached.

4.3   Stability Analysis

Performing our ESRS algorithm, a relay path is formed for each destination. The totally $|V_D|$ relay paths construct a network structure, denoted by g. In this subsection, we prove the stability of the formed network structure.

According to [16], there are two kinds of stability, that is, pairwise stability and strong stability, in the network formation game. The definitions of these two kinds of stability are given as follows:

Definition 1. *A network structure g is **pairwise stable** with respective to the payoff function U if*

1. for any edge $(i,j) \in g$, $U_i(g) \geq U_i(g - (i,j))$ and $U_j(g) \geq U_j(g - (i,j))$, and
2. for any edge $(i,j) \notin g$, if $U_i(g + (i,j)) > U_i(g)$ then $U_j(g + (i,j)) < U_j(g)$

Here, $U_i(g)$ denotes the payoff earned by user i in network structure g.

Definition 2. *A network structure g is **strong stable** with respective to the payoff function U if for any other network structure g', which is obtained via deviation from g, there exists at least one player (user) i such that $U_i(g') < U_i(g)$.*

It could be found from the definitions that pairwise stability only considers deviations on a single link at a time, while strong stability allows for more complicated deviations on groups of links. In this paper, we ignore the collusion among users and only consider the deviations on a single link at a time. Based on this assumption, we prove that the proposed ESRS algorithm is pairwise stable as follows.

Theorem 1. *The network structure g formed by the ESRS algorithm is pairwise stable.*

Proof. First, we prove the first condition of pairwise stability. According to the description in Sect. 3, we use edge $(i_{m-1}, i_m) \in g$ to denote the relay link between the $(m-1)$-th hop relay and the m-th hop relay on relay path L_i. Then, we consider four cases.

(1) Case 1: $i_{m-1} = I_s$, $i_m = i$. Edge (i_{m-1}, i_m) indicates that destination $i_m = i$ is within the transmission range of the information source $i_{m-1} = I_s$. Obviously, it is against common sense to break the direct transmission link when i_m is reachable by i_{m-1}. Theoretically, user i_{m-1} earns a payoff of 1 when edge (i_{m-1}, i_m) exists (refer to the first row of equation (3)). If edge (i_{m-1}, i_m) is removed, i_{m-1} should find another user $j \neq i_m$ to relay the message.

According to the second row of (3), i_{m-1} will earns a payoff of $-\infty$ in such a case. Therefore, $U_{i_{m-1}}(g) > U_{i_{m-1}}(g - (i_{m-1}, i_m))$. As for the destination i_m, it earns the payoff of 1, i.e., getting information from i_{m-1}, if edge (i_{m-1}, i_m) exists, and earns nothing if edge (i_{m-1}, i_m) is removed. Thus, $U_{i_m}(g) > U_{i_m}(g - (i_{m-1}, i_m))$.

(2) Case 2: $i_{m-1} = I_s$, $i_m \neq i$. Edge $(i_{m-1}, i_m) = (I_s, i_m)$ indicates that user i_m is a relay selected by the information source. According to (3) and (5), i_{m-1} and i_m earn a payoff of $U_{i_{m-1}}(g) = U_i^s(i_m) = B_i^s(i_m) - C_i^s(i_m)$ and $U_{i_m}(g) = U_i^r(i_m) = B_i^r(i_m) - C_i^r(i_m)$, respectively. It can be seen from (9) that $U_{i_m}(g) = U_i^r(i_m) > 0$. If edge (i_{m-1}, i_m) is removed, user i_m can not earn the payoff $U_i^r(i_m)$ anymore. In other words, we can say that user i_m earns a zero payoff now. Therefore, $U_{i_m}(g) > U_{i_m}(g - (i_{m-1}, i_m))$. As for the information source $i_{m-1} = I_s$, a new relay i'_m should be selected to replace i_m if edge (i_{m-1}, i_m) is deleted. According to (7), $U_i^s(i_m) > U_i^s(i'_m)$. Therefore, $U_{i_{m-1}}(g) > U_{i_{m-1}}(g - (i_{m-1}, i_m))$.

(3) Case 3: $i_{m-1} \neq I_s$, $i_m \neq i$. As described in Sect. 4.2, i_{m-1} can be considered as a virtual information source in this case. Similar to the analysis in Case 2, we find that $U_{i_{m-1}}(g) > U_{i_{m-1}}(g - (i_{m-1}, i_m))$, $U_{i_m}(g) > U_{i_m}(g - (i_{m-1}, i_m))$.

(4) Case 4: $i_{m-1} \neq I_s$, $i_m = i$. In this case, i_{m-1} can also be considered as a virtual information source. Similar to the analysis in Case 1, we have $U_{i_{m-1}}(g) > U_{i_{m-1}}(g - (i_{m-1}, i_m))$, $U_{i_m}(g) > U_{i_m}(g - (i_{m-1}, i_m))$.

Summarizing these four cases, we conclude that g satisfies the first condition of pairwise stability.

Then, we prove the second condition of pairwise stability. For any edge $(p, q) \notin g$, there are two cases.

(1) Case 1: $\forall i \in V_D$, $p \notin L_i$, $q \notin L_i$. This case indicates the situation where neither p or q belongs to any relay path. Forming such an edge is meaningless in the relay selection process. Thus, we do not consider this case in our work.

(2) Case 2: There is a pair of i and $m \in \{1, 2, \cdots, M\}$ such that $p = i_{m-1}$. If $q = i_m$, edge (i_{m-1}, i_m) already exists in the network structure g. Otherwise, adding edge (p, q) means replace relay i_m with another user q. In other words, edge (i_{m-1}, i_m) should be deleted before adding edge (p, q). According to the proof of the first condition, deleting edge (i_{m-1}, i_m) will lead to a decreased payoff for user i_{m-1}. Similarly, the payoff of user i_m will be decreased when there is a pair of i and $m \in \{1, 2, \cdots, M\}$ such that $q = i_m$ and $p \neq i_{m-1}$. Therefore, the network structure g formed by our ESRS algorithm also satisfies the second condition of pairwise stability.

Based on all the above analysis, we draw the conclusion that the network structure g formed by our ESRS algorithm is pairwise stable.

5   Simulation

In this section, we compare the performance of the proposed ESRS algorithm with the random relay selection algorithm (Rand), the relationship based relay selection algorithm (Relation), and the leakage probability based relay selection algorithm (Leakage), in MATLAB, using both synthetic trace and real-world trace. In our simulation, we consider a time-slotted system with a set of users, denoted by $N = \{1, 2, \cdots, n\}$. For each formed relay path, we define the transmission latency as the number of slots cost for reaching the destination, and define the maximum leakage probability as the maximum leakage probability of the users on the relay path. The relay selection algorithms are conducted for 3000 times, the average latency (A-Latency) and the average maximum leakage probability (A-MLP) are used to evaluate the performance of the relay selection algorithms.

The three schemes for comparison are briefly introduced as follows,

- **Rand**: the next hop relay is randomly selected.
- **Relation**: the next hop relay is selected as the user having the maximum social relationship with the destination.
- **Leakage**: the next hop relay is selected as the user with the minimum leakage probability.

5.1 Simulation Study Using the Synthetic Trace

As we know, many human activities in social networks can be modeled by the power law distribution [17]. Therefore, we model the social relationship between users and the probability that a user launches a malicious attack by the power law distribution. For each user i, the social relationship with others is modeled as a power law distribution: $p(x) = C_r x^{-k_r}$, with $x \in N$ being the index of a user, N being the set of users, C_r being a constant indicating the maximum value of $p(x)$, and k_r being the exponent of the distribution. The social relationship vector of user i is generated as $\Omega_i = Randperm\{p(x), x \in N\}$. Similarly, the probability that a user launches a malicious attack, is defined as $p_i = C_l i^{-k_l}$, with $i \in N$ being the user index, C_l being the constant, k_l being the exponent, respectively. The effects of the constant C and the exponent k on the the power law distribution can be shown by Fig. 1. In our simulation, we generate the synthetic trace in a specific case when $N = \{1, 2, \cdots, 50\}$, $C_r = C_l = 0.9$, and $k_r = k_l = 1.1$.

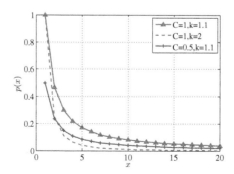

Fig. 1. The power law distribution under different C and k

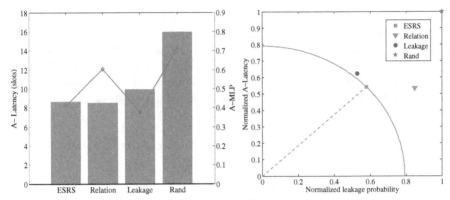

(a) Comparing the latency and leakage prob-   (b) Comparing the ROC performance.
ability.

Fig. 2. Performance comparison in the synthetic trace.

The simulation results using the synthetic trace are shown in Fig. 2. As shown in Fig. 2(a), our ESRS algorithm trades a balance between the efficiency (reflected by A-Latency) and the security (reflected by A-MLP). Furthermore, we normalize A-Latency and A-MLP of the four algorithms with the results of the Rand algorithm and we draw the ROC curves in In Fig. 2(b). Obviously, our ESRS algorithm outperforms Rand, Relation, and Leakage since our algorithm gains a lower transmission latency with a lower leakage probability.

5.2   Simulation Study Using the Real-World Trace

We take the encounter rate obtained from real trace [18], which is conducted at University of St Andrews, as the social relationship between users. To the best of our knowledge, there is no available trace indicating the probability that a user launches a malicious attack. In the real trace simulation, we fix C_l to be 0.9 and change the exponent k_l of the power law distribution $p_i = C_l i^{-k_l}$ from 1 to 3 to investigate the performance of the schemes under different attack probabilities.

The simulation results using the real-world trace are given in Fig. 3. As shwon in Fig. 3(a), Relation always gets the best A-Latency performance as it selects the relays based solely on the relationship (i.e. the encounter rate) among the users. The A-Latency performance of Rand and Leakage are random since the encounter rate is not considered for relay selection. As for the ESRS algorithm, its A-Latency performance approaches that of Relation with the increase of k_l. The reason is explained as follows. According to Fig. 1, the probabilities of users launching malicious attacks decrease with the increasing of k_l. In this case, the relationship among the users play a vital role for relay selection. Therefore, our ESRS algorithm will find the relays with higher encounter rates with the destination and the A-Latency performance will approach that of Relation. The comparison of the A-MLP performance is given in Fig. 3(b). It can be seen

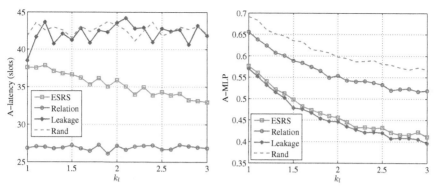

(a) Comparing the A-Latency perfor- (b) Comparing the A-MLP performance.
mance.

Fig. 3. Performance comparison in the real trace.

that the ESRS algorithm maintains a similar A-LMP performance with that of Leakage which selects the relays based solely on the leakage probabilities of the users.

6 Conclusion

This paper tackle the challenge of designing an efficient and secure relay selection algorithm for MSNs. We propose a network formation game based relay selection algorithm named ESRS by defining the payoff functions of the users and designing the game evolving rules. The stability of the network structure formed by our ESRS algorithm is proved and the performance of the ESRS algorithm is compared with other algorithms through extensive simulation study. The simulation results using both synthetic trace and real-world trace show that our algorithm outperforms other algorithms by enabling lower latency and lower information leakage probability communication in MSNs.

Acknowledgment. The authors would like to thank the support from the Provincial Key Laboratory for Computer Information Processing Technology, Soochow University (Grant No. KJS1521 and KJS1522), the National Science Foundation of the US (Grant No. AST-1443858, ECCS-1407986, CNS-1162057 and CNS-1265311), and the National Natural Science Foundation of China (Grant No. 61300186).

References

1. Li, J., Cai, Z., Yan, M., Li, Y.: Using crowdsourced data in location-based social netowrks to explore influence maximization. In: IEEE INFOCOM (2016)
2. He, Z., Cai, Z., Wang, X.: Modeling propagation dynamics and developing optimized countermeasures for rumor spreading in online social networks. In: IEEE ICDCS, pp. 205–214 (2015)

3. Vahdat, A., Becker, D.: Epidemic routing for partially-connected ad hoc networks. Duke University, Technical Report (2000)
4. Wu, J., Wang, Y.: Social feature-based multi-path routing in delay tolerant networks. In: Proceedings of the IEEE INFOCOM, pp. 1368–1376 (2012)
5. Erramilli, V., Crovella, M., Chaintreau, A., Diot, C.: Delegation forwarding. In: Proceedings of the MobiHoc, pp. 251–260 (2008)
6. Spyropoulos, T., Psounis, K., Raghavendra, C.: Efficient routing in intermittently connected mobile networks: The multiple-copy case. IEEE/ACM Trans. Networking **16**(1), 77–90 (2008)
7. Ciobanu, R., Dobre, C., Cristea, V.: Sprint: Social prediction-based opportunistic routing. In: IEEE WoWMoM, pp. 1–7, June 2013
8. Moreira, W., Mendes, P., Sargento, S.: Opportunistic routing based on daily routines. In: IEEE WoWMoM, pp. 1–6, June 2012
9. Wang, S., Liu, M., Cheng, X., Li, Z., Huang, J., Chen, B.: HERO – a home based routing in pocket switched networks. In: Wang, X., Zheng, R., Jing, T., Xing, K. (eds.) WASA 2012. LNCS, vol. 7405, pp. 20–30. Springer, Heidelberg (2012)
10. Wu, J., Xiao, M., Huang, L.: Homing spread: Community home-based multi-copy routing in mobile social networks. In: Proceedings of the IEEE INFOCOM, pp. 2319–2327 (2013)
11. Kim, S.K., Yoon, J.H., Lee, J.Y., Jang, G.Y., Yang, S.B.: A cooperative forwarding scheme for social preference-based selfishness in mobile social networks. Wirel. Netw. **22**(2), 537–552 (2015)
12. Xing, X., Jing, T., Zhou, W., Cheng, X., Huo, Y., Liu, H.: Routing in user-centric networks. IEEE Commun. Mag. **52**(9), 44–51 (2014)
13. Wang, Y., Cai, Z., Yin, G., Gao, Y., Tong, X., Wu, G.: An incentive mechanism with privacy protection in mobile crowdsourcing systems. Comput. Netw. **102**, 157–171 (2016)
14. Cheng, W., Wu, D., Cheng, X., Chen, D.: Routing for information leakage reduction in multi-channel multi-hop ad-hoc social networks. In: Wang, X., Zheng, R., Jing, T., Xing, K. (eds.) WASA 2012. LNCS, vol. 7405, pp. 31–42. Springer, Heidelberg (2012)
15. Li, W., Cheng, X., Jing, T., Xing, X.: Cooperative multi-hop relaying via network formation games in cognitive radio networks. In: IEEE INFOCOM (2013)
16. Jackson, M.O.: A survey of models of network formation: Stability and efficiency (2003)
17. Muchnik, L., Pei, S., Parra, L.C., Reis, S.D.S., Andrade, J.S., Havlin, S., Makse, H.A.: Origins of power-law degree distribution in the heterogeneity of human activity in social networks. Sci. Rep. **3**, 1783 (2013)
18. Parris, I., Abdesslem, B.: Crawdad trace/social network analysis/st_andrews/locshare/2010/sta1. Downloaded from http://crawdad.org//download/st_andrews/locshare/locshare-StA1.tar.gz

Energy Detection of Gaussian Signals Subject to Impulsive Noise in Generalized Fading Channels

José Vinícius de Miranda Cardoso[1,2(✉)], Wamberto José Lira Queiroz[1,2],
Hang Liu[3], and Marcelo Sampaio de Alencar[1,2]

[1] Federal University of Campina Grande, Campina Grande, Brazil
{josevinicius,wamberto,malencar}@iecom.org.br
[2] Institute for Advanced Studies in Communications, Campina Grande, Brazil
[3] The Catholic University of America, Washington, DC, USA
hliu@cua.edu

Abstract. Novel, simple, and accurately approximated expressions for the probability of detection of Gaussian signals in $\eta - \mu$, $\kappa - \mu$, and $\alpha - \mu$ fading channels at the output of an energy detector subject to impulsive noise (Bernoulli-Gaussian model) are presented. The generalized Gauss-Laguerre quadrature is used to approximate the probability of detection as a finite sum. Monte Carlo simulations corroborate the accuracy of the approximations. The results are further extended to cooperative detection with hard decision combining information.

Keywords: Spectrum sensing · Energy detector · Fading · Impulsive noise

1 Introduction

Spectrum sensing is the primary technique to enable dynamic spectrum sharing among primary users (PUs) and secondary users (SUs), such that SUs might access the spectrum opportunistically, without causing interference on PUs' transmissions. To do so, SUs must be able to distinguish (decide) whether or not the spectrum is occupied. Among several techniques for spectrum sensing, the energy detector has attracted widely interests, primarily because of its low-complexity and reasonable performance even in severe fading channels [1].

Hence, this paper presents novel approximated expressions for the probability of detection of Gaussian signals in generalized fading channels, namely, $\kappa - \mu$ [2], $\eta - \mu$ [2], and $\alpha - \mu$ [3], at the output of the energy detector subject to impulsive noise. The assumption for Gaussianity of the transmitted signal occurs in several practical scenarios, such as when the receiver has no prior information about the transmitted signal and in OFDM in which the envelope of the signal weakly converges to a Gaussian process when the number of subcarriers is sufficiently large [4].

© Springer International Publishing Switzerland 2016
Q. Yang et al. (Eds.): WASA 2016, LNCS 9798, pp. 231–240, 2016.
DOI: 10.1007/978-3-319-42836-9_21

The impulsive noise is modeled as a Bernoulli-Gaussian (BG) channel. This channel has been investigated due to its practical importance especially in multi-carrier transmission systems based on orthogonal frequency division multiplexing (OFDM) [5]. Furthermore, Vu *et al.* [6] presented estimators for the ergodic Shannon and constrained capacities of the BG impulsive noise channel in Rayleigh fading.

The probability of detection is approximated by using the generalized Gauss-Laguerre quadrature, which approximates a class of integrals to a finite sum [7]. Additionally, the approximation error quickly goes to zero even for a small number of terms in the sum. In fact, this approximation presents an attractive alternative due to its low computational cost and high accuracy. Moreover, in contrast to the assumption of the Central Limit Theorem, which has been commonly used to approximate the expressions for the probabilities of detection and false alarm [8], the proposed approximation does not require a large number of samples in order to become accurate, and therefore it does not compromise the sensing time. In fact, it works even for a small number of samples and for a wide range of the parameters involved.

The remainder of the paper is organized as follows. Section 2 states the physical assumptions of the spectrum sensing system and describes its underlying mathematical setting. Section 3 presents the generalized fading distributions considered in the proposed analysis. Numerical and analytical results are presented and discussed in Sect. 4. Section 5 presents the conclusions.

2   The Energy Detector

Consider the following hypotheses

$$\mathcal{H}_0 : X_n = W_n + C \cdot U_n, \qquad\qquad n = 1, 2, ..., N \qquad (1)$$
$$\mathcal{H}_1 : X_n = H \cdot S_n + W_n + C \cdot U_n, \qquad n = 1, 2, ..., N \qquad (2)$$

in which $\mathcal{H}_0$ and $\mathcal{H}_1$ stand for the hypotheses that the PU's signal is absent and present, respectively. It is assumed that the channel gain H has probability density function (pdf) f_H, the transmitted signal is Gaussian distributed, *i.e.* $S_n \sim \mathcal{N}(0, \sigma_s^2)$ i.i.d., and so is the noise process $W_n \sim \mathcal{N}(0, \sigma_w^2)$ i.i.d..

The impulsive noise component is modeled according the BG model, i.e. $P[C = 1] = 1 - P[C = 0] = p, p \in [0, 1]$ and $U_n \sim \mathcal{N}(0, \sigma_i^2)$ i.i.d.. Furthermore, it is assumed that C and H are constant during the sensing time, *i.e.* the time for collecting a set of N samples. It is also assumed that $H, S_n, W_n, C,$ and U_n are independent.

Finally, define $\rho_w \triangleq \frac{\sigma_s^2}{\sigma_w^2}$ and $\rho_u \triangleq \frac{\sigma_s^2}{\sigma_u^2}$ as the signal-to-noise ratio (SNR) and the signal-to-impulsive-noise ratio (SIR), respectively, and, without loss of generality, assume that $\sigma_s^2 = 1$ throughout.

The well-known energy detection rule, used to decide between the two aforementioned hypotheses, is defined as follows

$$d_\lambda(Y_N) = \begin{cases} 1, Y_N \geq \lambda, \\ 0, Y_N < \lambda, \end{cases} \qquad (3)$$

in which $Y_N \triangleq \sum_{n=1}^{N} X_n^2$, the threshold λ is a strictly positive real number, and $d_\lambda(Y_N) = j$, $j \in \{0, 1\}$ means that the detector has decided in favor of the hypothesis $\mathcal{H}_j$.

2.1 Hypothesis $\mathcal{H}_0$

Under $\mathcal{H}_0$, the distribution function of Y_N may be written as

$$F_{Y_N}(y) = (1 - p)\gamma\left(\frac{N}{2}, \frac{y\rho_w}{2}\right) + p\gamma\left(\frac{N}{2}, \frac{y\rho_w\rho_u}{2(\rho_w + \rho_u)}\right), \qquad (4)$$

for $y \geq 0$, in which $\gamma(\cdot, \cdot)$ is the lower incomplete gamma function defined as $\gamma(a, z) \triangleq \frac{1}{\Gamma(a)} \int_0^z t^{a-1} e^{-t} \, dt$.

2.2 Hypothesis $\mathcal{H}_1$

Given $H = h$, $h > 0$, the distribution function of Y_N conditioned on H may be written as

$$
\begin{aligned}
F_{Y_N|H}(y|h) =& (1 - p)\gamma\left(\frac{N}{2}, \frac{y\rho_w}{2(h^2\rho_w + 1)}\right) \\
&+ p\gamma\left(\frac{N}{2}, \frac{y\rho_w\rho_u}{2(h^2\rho_w\rho_u + \rho_w + \rho_u)}\right), y > 0, h > 0.
\end{aligned}
\qquad (5)
$$

Given an arbitrarily chosen threshold $\lambda > 0$, the probability of false alarm P_F and the probability of detection P_D may be written as

$$P_F \triangleq P\left(d_\lambda(Y_N) = 1 | \mathcal{H}_0 \text{ is true}\right) = 1 - F_{Y_N}(\lambda), \qquad (6)$$

$$P_D \triangleq P\left(d_\lambda(Y_N) = 1 | \mathcal{H}_1 \text{ is true}\right) = 1 - \int_0^\infty F_{Y_N|H}(\lambda|h) f_H(h) \, dh. \qquad (7)$$

The threshold λ is selected based on the Neyman-Pearson criterion, *i.e.*, λ is the solution of (6) for a given probability of false alarm. Unfortunately, it can not be solved analytically, however, since (6) is a strictly decreasing function in λ, it may be easily inverted numerically.

3 Generalized Fading Channels

3.1 The $\eta - \mu$ Distribution

The $\eta - \mu$ distribution is suitable to model small-scale fading variations in non-line-of-sight conditions. The $\eta - \mu$ distribution includes the following ones as special cases: Hoyt (Nakagami-q), Nakagami-m, Rayleigh, and one-sided Gaussian.

Let H be $\eta - \mu$ distributed. Therefore, its pdf, in its normalized version, may be written as

$$f_H(h) = \frac{4\sqrt{\pi}\mu^{\mu+1/2}h^{2\mu}}{\eta^{\mu-1/2}\sqrt{1-\eta^2}\Gamma(\mu)} \exp\left(-\frac{2\mu h^2}{1-\eta^2}\right)$$
$$\times I_{\mu-1/2}\left(\frac{2\eta\mu h^2}{1-\eta^2}\right), h > 0, \mu > 0, -1 < \eta < 1, \tag{8}$$

in which $I_a(z)$ is the modified Bessel function of first kind and order a.

3.2 The $\kappa - \mu$ Distribution

The $\kappa - \mu$ distribution is a general fading distribution appropriate to model the small-scale fading variations in line-of-sight applications. The $\kappa - \mu$ distribution includes Rice (Nakagami-n), Nakagami-m, Rayleigh, and one-sided Gaussian as special cases. Assuming that H is $\kappa - \mu$ distributed, its density, given in its normalized form, is

$$f_H(h) = \frac{2\mu(1+\kappa)^{\frac{\mu+1}{2}}}{\kappa^{\frac{\mu-1}{2}}\exp(\kappa\mu)} h^\mu \exp\left(-\mu(1+\kappa)h^2\right)$$
$$\times I_{\mu-1}\left(2\mu\sqrt{\kappa(1+\kappa)}h\right), h > 0, \mu > 0, \kappa > 0. \tag{9}$$

3.3 The $\alpha - \mu$ Distribution

The $\alpha - \mu$ fading arises from nonlineries caused by the propagation medium to the transmitted signal, due to multipath propagation in a non-homogeneous environment. The $\alpha-\mu$ distribution includes several others, namely, Gamma, Erlang, Nakagami-m, Chi, exponential, Weibull, one-sided Gaussian, and Rayleigh as special cases. Let H be $\alpha - \mu$ distributed, then its density, in its normalized version, may be written as

$$f_H(h) = \frac{\alpha\mu^\mu h^{\alpha\mu-1}}{\Gamma(\mu)} \exp\left(-\mu h^\alpha\right), h > 0, \alpha > 0, \mu > 0. \tag{10}$$

4   Numerical Analysis

In order to evaluate the performance of the energy detector, it is necessary to solve the integral in (7). As far as the authors are concerned, in case f_H is any of the pdfs considered in this paper (even in simple special cases $e.g.$ Nakagami-m), an analytic solution for the probability of detection (7) does not exist. Therefore, the generalized Gauss-Laguerre quadrature (Appendix) is utilized to approximate the probability of detection (7). By doing so, (7) may be approximated as (11), (12), and (13), $i.e.$

$$P_D^{\eta,\mu}(\lambda) \approx 1 - \frac{\sqrt{\pi}\left(1-\eta^2\right)^\mu \Gamma(M+\mu+\frac{1}{2})}{(2\eta)^{\mu-\frac{1}{2}}\Gamma(\mu)M!(M+1)^2}$$

$$\times \sum_{n=1}^{M}\left\{\frac{r_n I_{\mu-\frac{1}{2}}(\eta r_n)}{\left[L_{M+1}^{\mu-1/2}(r_n)\right]^2}F_{Y_N|H}\left(\lambda\left|\sqrt{\frac{(1-\eta^2)r_n}{2\mu}}\right.\right)\right\} \tag{11}$$

$$P_D^{\kappa,\mu}(\lambda) \approx 1 - \frac{(\kappa\mu)^{\frac{1-\mu}{2}}\Gamma\left(M+\frac{\mu+1}{2}\right)}{M!(M+1)^2\exp(\kappa\mu)}$$

$$\times \sum_{n=1}^{M}\left\{\frac{r_n I_{\mu-1}\left(2\sqrt{\kappa\mu r_n}\right)}{\left[L_{M+1}^{\frac{\mu-1}{2}}(r_n)\right]^2}F_{Y_N|H}\left(\lambda\left|\sqrt{\frac{r_n}{\mu(1+\kappa)}}\right.\right)\right\} \tag{12}$$

$$P_D^{\alpha,\mu}(\lambda) \approx 1 - \frac{\mu^M}{M!(M+1)^2}\sum_{n=1}^{M}\left\{\frac{r_n F_{Y_N|H}\left(\lambda\left|\left(\frac{r_n}{\mu}\right)^{1/\alpha}\right.\right)}{\left[L_{M+1}^{\mu-1}(r_n)\right]^2}\right\} \tag{13}$$

for $\eta-\mu$, $\kappa-\mu$, and $\alpha-\mu$ fading channels, respectively. The parameter M represents both the order of the Laguerre polynomial and the number of terms in the sum.

In the following figures, lines designate theoretical results (approximated using $M = 30$), while markers denote Monte Carlo simulation results with 10^6 realizations. For all figures, it is noted a substantially agreement between the Monte Carlo simulation results and the proposed approximations. Additionally, the number of terms in the sum, which was selected to keep the approximation error below 10^{-4}, is reasonably small.

Figures 1, 2, and 3 show the performance of the energy detector for $\kappa-\mu$, $\eta-\mu$, and $\alpha-\mu$ fading channels, respectively. More precisely, Fig. 1 shows the effect of increasing the signal power (thereafter increasing the SIR) on the probability of detection. Figure 2 illustrates the effectiveness of increasing the number of samples N in overcoming fading, low SIR, and moderate p. Figure 3 compares the performance of the energy detector by either increasing the number of samples or the SIR. Figure 4 depicts the influence of p on the probability of detection for Nakagami-m and Hoyt fading channels for several values of SNR and SIR. Figure 5 presents the complementary receiver operating characteristic (ROC) for the discussed generalized fading scenarios. It may be noted that the performance of the energy detector may be significantly increased if the probability of false alarm is greater than the probability of occurrence of impulsive noise.

4.1   Cooperative Sensing

The performance of the energy detector may be undoubtedly improved when there exist L secondary users that share their local (individual) decisions, and

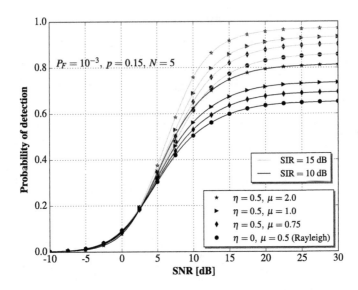

Fig. 1. Probability of detection versus SNR in $\eta - \mu$ fading. Markers represent Monte Carlo simulations with 10^6 realizations, while lines represent (11) for $M = 30$.

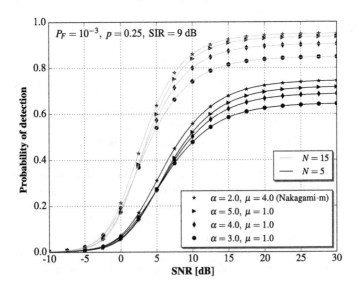

Fig. 2. Probability of detection versus SNR in $\alpha - \mu$ fading. Markers represent Monte Carlo simulations with 10^6 realizations, while lines represent (13) for $M = 30$.

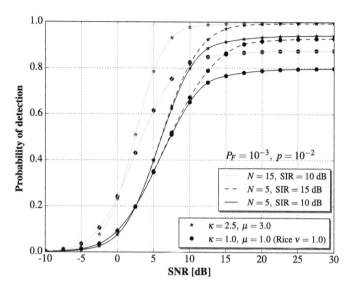

Fig. 3. Probability of detection versus SNR in $\kappa - \mu$ fading. Markers represent Monte Carlo simulations with 10^6 realizations, while lines represent (12) for $M = 30$.

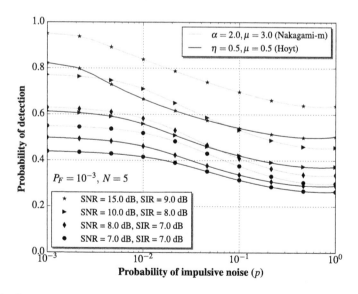

Fig. 4. Probability of detection versus p in Nakagami-m and Hoyt fading. Markers represent Monte Carlo simulations with 10^6 realizations, while lines represent (13) and (11) for $M = 30$.

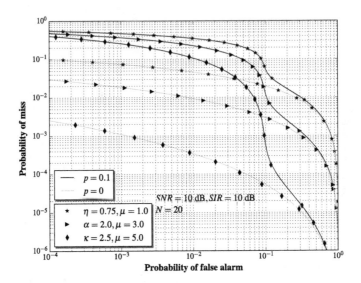

Fig. 5. Probability of miss $(1-P_D)$ versus P_{FA} in generalized fading for different values of the probability of occurrence of impulsive noise (p). Markers represent Monte Carlo simulations with 10^6 realizations, while lines represent (11), (12), (13) for $M = 30$.

thereby jointly decide about the occupation of the channel. In a hard decision cooperative scheme, in which the global decisions are based on a K-out-of-L rule, the detector decides for $\mathcal{H}_1$ if and only if at least K secondary users have decided so.

Therefore, the probabilities of detection and false alarm may be computed as, respectively,

$$Q_D = \sum_{l=K}^{L} \binom{L}{l} P_D^l (1 - P_D)^{L-l}, \tag{14}$$

$$Q_F = \sum_{l=K}^{L} \binom{L}{l} P_F^l (1 - P_F)^{L-l}. \tag{15}$$

When $K = 1$, $K = L$, or $K = \lceil \frac{L}{2} \rceil$, the rules are called OR, AND, and Majority, respectively. It has been shown that the OR rule usually outperforms and Majority rules in many scenarios of practical interest [9]. Therefore, only the OR rule shall be consider henceforth. In particular, when $K = 1$, the probabilities of false alarm and detection may be simplified as

$$Q_D = 1 - (1 - P_D)^L, \tag{16}$$

$$Q_F = 1 - (1 - P_F)^L. \tag{17}$$

Figure 6 depicts the performance of the cooperative energy detector for several values of L under Weibull ($\mu = 1$) and $\kappa - \mu$ fading channels. The performance of the detector improves significantly as the number of cooperative

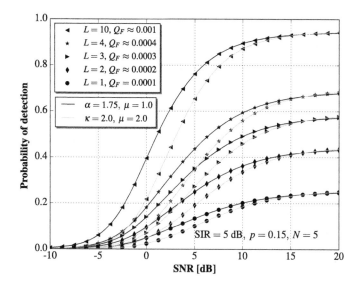

Fig. 6. Performance of the OR-rule in Weibull ($\mu = 1$) and $\kappa - \mu$ fading channels.

users increases. Hence, the cooperative detection may effectively overcome the impairments caused by both low SIR and SNR, and severe fading. In fact, for SNR = 10 dB, the probability of detection increases from 0.2 to roughly 0.9, for the case of no cooperation ($L = 1$) and for a cooperative sensing with ten users ($L = 10$), respectively.

5 Conclusion

This paper has proposed novel, simple, and accurate approximations for the performance evaluation of the energy detector employed to detect Gaussian signals, subject to impulsive noise, in generalized fading channels, namely, $\kappa - \mu$, $\eta - \mu$, and $\alpha - \mu$. The approximations are based on the generalized Gauss-Laguerre quadrature, which approximates the integrals that are required to compute the probability of detection to finite sums, reducing the complexity and ensuring accuracy.

The effects of the probability of occurrence of impulsive noise and the signal-to-impulsive-noise ratio on the performance of the energy detector were described as well. Furthermore, as has been shown, hard decision combining cooperative schemes based on the OR rule effectively overcome the effects of low SIR and severe fading.

The simple form of the proposed expressions provide a tool for design engineers to determine parameters such as the minimum number of samples and the minimum number of cooperating users to achieve a given performance under a variety of fading and impulsive noise scenarios.

Acknowledgment. The authors would like to thank the Coordination for the Improvement of Higher Education Personnel (Capes), Federal University of Campina Grande (UFCG), Institute for Advanced Studies in Communications (Iecom), and The Catholic University of America (CUA) for supporting this research.

Appendix A

The generalized Gauss-Laguerre quadrature [7] states that, for any real number $\beta > -1$,

$$\int_0^\infty t^\beta e^{-t} f(t) \, dt \approx \sum_{n=1}^M v_n f(r_n), \tag{18}$$

in which r_n is the n-th root of the generalized Laguerre polynomial of order M, i.e. L_M^β, and the weight v_n is given as

$$v_n = \frac{r_n \Gamma(M + \beta + 1)}{M!(M+1)^2 \left[L_{M+1}^\beta (r_n) \right]^2}. \tag{19}$$

References

1. Sofotasios, P., Rebeiz, E., Zhang, L., Tsiftsis, T., Cabric, D., Freear, S.: Energy detection based spectrum sensing over $\kappa-\mu$ and $\kappa-\mu$ extreme fading channels. IEEE Trans. Veh. Technol. **62**(3), 1031–1040 (2013)
2. Yacoub, M.: The $\kappa - \mu$ distribution and the $\eta - \mu$ distribution. IEEE Antennas Propag. Mag. **49**(1), 68–81 (2007)
3. Yacoub, M.D.: The $\alpha - \mu$ distribution: A physical fading model for the Stacy distribution. IEEE Trans. Veh. Technol. **56**(1), 27–34 (2007)
4. Wei, S., Goeckel, D., Kelly, P.: Convergence of the complex envelope of bandlimited ofdm signals. IEEE Trans. Inf. Theor. **56**(10), 4893–4904 (2010)
5. Pighi, R., Franceschini, M., Ferrari, G., Raheli, R.: Fundamental performance limits of communications systems impaired by impulse noise. IEEE Trans. Commun. **57**(1), 171–182 (2009)
6. Vu, H., Tran, N., Nguyen, T., Hariharan, S.: Estimating shannon and constrained capacities of bernoulli-gaussian impulsive noise channels in Rayleigh fading. IEEE Trans. Commun. **62**(6), 1845–1856 (2014)
7. Concus, P., Cassatt, D., Jaehnig, G., Melby, E.: Tables for the evaluation of $\int_0^\infty x^\beta e^{-x} f(x) \, dx$ by gauss-laguerre quadrature. Math. Comp. **17**, 245–256 (1963)
8. Horgan, D., Murphy, C.: On the convergence of the chi square and noncentral chi square distributions to the normal distribution. IEEE Commun. Lett. **17**(12), 2233–2236 (2013)
9. Ghasemi, A., Sousa, E.S.: Opportunistic spectrum access in fading channels through coolaboratieve sensing. J. of Commun. **2**(2), 71–82 (2007)

Distance Bounding Protocol for RFID Systems

Yajian Zhou[1] and Jingxian Zhou[2(⊠)]

[1] School of Computer Science,
Beijing University of Posts and Telecommunications, Beijing 100876, China
yajian@bupt.edu.cn
[2] Information Security Evaluation Center,
Civil Aviation University of China, Tianjin 300300, China
jxzhou@cauc.edu.cn

Abstract. A secure mutual distance bounding (SMDB) protocol has been proposed, which employs a combination of slow exchange, bit complement rapid exchange rule and final signature verification mechanisms to guarantee the secure authentication while dramatically reduce success probability of mafia fraud and impersonation attacks. Meanwhile, a particular identifier updating method is introduced to keep the consistency of identifiers between the reader and the database. A comprehensive probabilistic analysis on security properties proves that the proposed SMDB protocol provides ideal resistance against mafia fraud, terrorist fraud and distance fraud attacks.

Keywords: RFID · Distance bounding protocol · Relay attack · Terrorist fraud attack

1 Introduction

The deployment of radio frequency identification (RFID) technologies is becoming widespread in almost all kinds of wireless network-based applications, which can highly benefit from the adoption of RFID solutions. RFID tags store sensitive information and are liable to suffer unauthorized reading, which may lead to some unpredictable activities [1]. RFID tags are also vulnerable to different types of relay attacks, such as distance fraud, mafia fraud, and terrorist fraud attacks, whose object is to suggest a wrong assumption of the distance between a tag and the corresponding reader [2].

During the past decade, a number of distance bounding protocols have been proposed, which are usually classified into two categories, depending on whether

J. Zhou—This work was supported in part by the fundamental research funds for the central universities (3122013C004), the National Natural Science Foundation of China,(61303232), the China Scholarship Council (201406475025), and the National High Technology Research and Development Program('863' Program) of China (2015AA017201).

Q. Yang et al. (Eds.): WASA 2016, LNCS 9798, pp. 241–249, 2016.
DOI: 10.1007/978-3-319-42836-9_22

a final signature is involved. Such protocols differ in terms of the security guarantee capabilities, which can be evaluated by analyzing their resilience to three types of attacks: distance fraud, mafia fraud and terrorist fraud.

In 1994, Brands and Chaum put forward the first distance bounding protocol [3], which features a success probability of distance fraud attacks as low as $(3/4)^n$. Whereas it is not immune to mafia and terrorist fraud attacks. In 2011, Cremers et al. [4] showed that Brands and Chaum's protocol and even all its derivatives following the similar structure were vulnerable to distance hijacking attacks.

As for mafia fraud attacks, the prover is honest, but attackers try to falsify the distance that the verifier establishes by interfering with their communication. For some existing protocols, the probability with which a mafia fraud attack can succeed is bounded by $(3/4)^n$ [5], which is inferior to the optimal value $(1/2)^n$.

Terrorist fraud attacks are similar to those of mafia fraud. The legitimate prover P is dishonest and helps an illegal prover $\tilde{P}$ to cheat the verifier V by a wrong distance without sharing its private key. These attacks can even be fulfilled with probability equals one for some protocols [6], while have not been discussed concerning others [7,8].

Our Contributions. In this paper, we propose a novel secure RFID distance bounding protocol, the SMDB protocol, which provides better security features compared with the existing protocols. The SMDB protocol achieves an ideal security level of $(1/2)^n$ against mafia fraud as well as distance fraud attacks, where n denotes the number challenge/reponse bits during the rapid bit exchange phase.

Outline of the Paper. The organization of the paper is as follows. In Sect. 2, the SMDB protocol is described in detail. In Sect. 3 and 4, we analyze its security and discuss the noise environment, respectively. The conclusion remarking is drawn in Sect. 5.

2   The SMDB Protocol

In order to implement the verification process, the reader has to identify the corresponding tag to access its key information. Unfortunately, this issue is neglected by almost all distance bounding protocols reported in literatures, which merely reveal the fact that the reader and the tag share a secret, without further description on how the reader can locate the secret. In 2007, Reid et al. [9] proposed a distance bounding protocol capable of resistance to terrorist fraud attacks. In this protocol, ID's of both sides are sent in clear form, therefore the privacy can not be preserved and the protocol is vulnerable to tracking attacks. In the protocol from [10], the reader (verifier) has to perform an exhaustive computation and search in its database until a matched secret is found. As a result, it is impractical to deploy the protocol in large-scale RFID systems.

With respect to the aforementioned problems, we propose a secure mutual distance bounding (SMDB) protocol, which works in a uniquely mutual way. The tag responds to the RFID reader's request by transmitting its unique ID, which is then used by the reader to lookup the database for information relevant to the tag. The tag's ID is updated within the database, and the reader keeps both the updated as well as the outdated ID within the database to count for the possible scenario that the tag has not updated its identifier. Meanwhile, for the purpose of providing resistance to attacks in case a tag is impersonated or traced, a distance verification method between the reader and the tag is designed.

The proposed SMDB protocol consists of a slow nonce-exchange, a rapid bit exchange phase, a verification phase and identifier update phase. As shown in Fig. 1, the reader and the tag share an secret x. x and the tag's ID are assumed not to be revealed by neither side. The length of both x and ID is n bits.

2.1 Slow Exchange Phase

Step 1. The reader generates a random n-bit nonce N_R and broadcasts it as a request message.

Step 2. The tag generates a random n-bit nonce N_T, then sends N_T as well as its current identifier ID to the reader.

Step 3. The reader looks up the database for the key x corresponding to the tags's current identifier, ID. If ID is not recognized as a valid identifier, the tag is rejected.

Step 4. Both the reader and the tag compute $2n$-bit sequences $H = f_x(ID, N_R, N_T)$, followed by splitting the value of H into two n-bit sequences d, v.

Where $f : \{0,1\}^* \rightarrow \{0,1\}^{2n}$ is a one-way and collusion resistant pseudo-random function, $d = d_1 d_2 ... d_n$, $v = v_1 v_2 ... v_n$.

2.2 Rapid Bit Exchange Phase

This phase will iterate for n rounds. At the i-th round, the challenge-response delay time will be measured.

Step 5. The reader generates a random bit c_i, initializes the clock to zero and sends c_i to the tag. We denote by c_i' the value received by the tag, which may be unequal to c_i due to errors or fading along the channel.

Step 6. The tag sends a response bit r_i' as follows.

If $d_i = 0 (i = 1, 2, ..., n)$, the tag sends v_i when $c_i' = 0$; when $c_i' = 1$, the tag sends $\overline{v_i}$, where $\overline{v_i}$ denotes the bit complement of v_i.

If $d_i = 1$, the tag sends 0 when $c_i' = v_i$; when $c_i' \neq v_i$, the tag sends 1 as the response bit r_i'.

Similarly, we denote by r_i the value received by the reader.

Step 7. On receiving r_i, the reader stops the clock and stores the delay time $\triangle t_i$.

2.3 Verification Phase

Step 8. The tag concatenates the challenge and response bits to obtain $m = \{c_1' \| c_2' \| \cdots \| c_n' \| r_1' \| r_2' \| \cdots \| r_n'\}$, where m has the length equal to $2n$ bits.

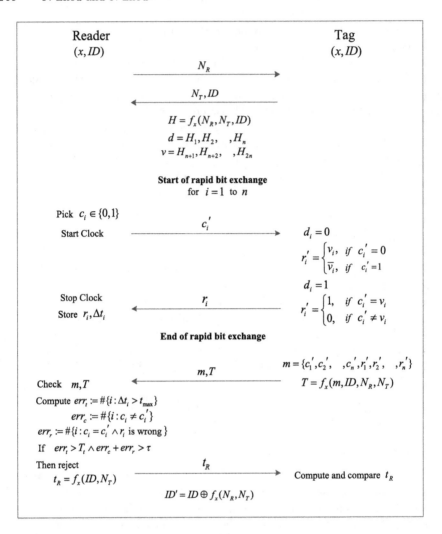

Fig. 1. The Schematic of the SMDB protocol

Then, it computes T by ciphering the concatenation of m, current identifier of the tag and the random numbers involved in the slow exchange phase.

$$T = f_x(m, ID, N_R, N_T) \tag{1}$$

Finally, the tag sends the pair $\{m, T\}$ to the reader.

Step 9. Once received the pair $\{m, T\}$, the reader computes:

$$T' = f_x(m, ID, N_R, N_T) \tag{2}$$

If the equality $T' = T$ holds, the reader goes to the next step; otherwise, it aborts. In the following steps, the reader checks the validity of the responses received during the rapid bit exchange phase.

Step 10. The reader counts the number of rounds immediately when $\triangle t_i$ exceeds $\triangle t_{max}$ and goes to the next step if this number is smaller than or equals to the value T_t; otherwise, it aborts.

Where $\triangle t_{max}$ is a timing bounding; T_t is the number of tolerance that $\triangle t_i$ exceeds $\triangle t_{max}$.

Step 11. The reader computes:

err_c: the number of times that $c_i \neq c'_i$; err_r: the number of times that $c_i = c'_i$ but r_i is wrong according to step 6.

Finally, the reader checks if $err_c + err_r$ is below a fault tolerance threshold τ. If not, the protocol is aborted.

2.4 Identifier Update Phase

In this phase, the reader and the tag update the tag's identifier ID as follows.

Step 12. The reader computes:

$$T_R = f_x(ID, N_T) \tag{3}$$

$$ID' = ID \oplus f_x(N_R, N_T) \tag{4}$$

Subsequently, the reader sends T_R to the tag in order to replace ID with ID' in its database.

Step 13. Upon receiving T_R, the tag checks its correctness as follows:

$$T_R \stackrel{?}{=} f_x(ID, N_T) \tag{5}$$

If the equality holds, the tag replaces ID with $ID'(= ID \oplus f_x(N_R, N_T))$; otherwise, it discards T_R.

Within an environment where it might be possible that the tag does not receive the T_R (because of noise or blocking of the signal by attackers), the reader tends to verdict that the tag has updated its parameter while it actually has not. As a result, the ID value on the tag's side will be different from that stored in the database. A solution to this problem is that the reader should store both the updated as well as outdated ID values in the database to count for the possible scenario that the tag has not updated its identifier.

3 Security Analysis of the SMDB Protocol

Impersonation attacks, mafia, terrorist, and distance fraud attacks are four main security concerns when assessing distance bounding protocols in RFID systems. In this section, security analysis will be delivered to prove that SMDB protocol is capable of keeping RFID tags tamper-proof against any malicious adversaries.

3.1   Analysis on Impersonation Attacks

In impersonation attacks, an attacker has to learn the current identifier ID' or the outdated one of the tag, successfully answer the challenges during the rapid bit exchange phase and guess the final signature T. Let P_{sign} be the probability that the adversary successfully forges the signature T.

In SMDB protocol, a passive attacker can derive the past identifier ID of the tag by eavesdropping the channel over multiple executions of the authentication protocol. In the rapid bit exchange phase, when a challenge is intercepted, the adversary replies with an arbitrary answer. The probability that the adversary offers the correct answer to the reader is $\frac{1}{2}$. The success probability of impersonation attacks is given by:

$$P_{imp} = (\frac{1}{2})^n . P_{sign} \tag{6}$$

Note that depending on the function f, an optimal P_{sign} can be reached by randomly guessing the signature T or by randomly picking x and computing the right T. However, P_{sign} can be neglected if n is large enough.

3.2   Analysis on Mafia Fraud Attacks

For a distance bounding protocol, an attacker is able to exploit three different strategies to conduct her attack, i.e., early-reply, pre-ask and post-ask [11]. The adversary uses either pre-ask or post-ask strategy to implement mafia fraud attacks.

As for the post-ask strategy, the attacker first relays the slow phase reader, trying to guess the right answers. The probability of sending a correct response for a challenge is $\frac{1}{2}$. Then, the attacker queries the legitimate tag with the correct challenges received during the verification phase to obtain the acknowledgment signature T. The success probability of mafia fraud attacks by this strategy is:

$$P_{post-ask} = (\frac{1}{2})^n \tag{7}$$

As concerns the pre-ask strategy, the attacker first relays the slow phase between the reader and the tag, followed by an execution of the rapid bit exchange phase with the tag. The attacker sends predicted challenges c_i'' to the tag and gets the response r_i'' corresponding to her challenges. By this way, the attacker obtains a sequence $\{r_1'', r_2'', \cdots, r_n''\}$. Afterwards, the attacker executes the rapid bit exchange phase with the reader and receives the challenges c_i. There are two equally likely cases, (i) if $c_i = c_i''$, the adversary sends r_i''; otherwise, (ii) she sends $\overline{r_i''}$. Hence, the attacker sends the correct response with the probability equals 1, in the rapid bit exchange phase. In the verification phase, although the attacker receives a signature T from the tag, it can not be used to authenticate herself to the reader, because the sequence m's in two sessions are different.

The attacker can only guess the value of the signature T with the success probability equals $(\frac{1}{4})^n$, or guess the tag's secret x (the success probability is $(\frac{1}{2})^n$) to compute the correct signature T. The success probability of mafia fraud attacks by pre-ask strategy is:

$$P_{per-ask} = 1.max\{(\frac{1}{2})^n, (\frac{1}{4})^n\} = (\frac{1}{2})^n \tag{8}$$

Hence, the success probability of mafia fraud attacks is $(\frac{1}{2})^n$.

3.3   Analysis on Terrorist Fraud Attacks

Suppose the attacker knows $n - v$ bits of the secret key, together with the white-box model [11], it is appropriate to assume the worst scenario in which the dishonest tag transmits the entire n bits of d and v to the attacker without any leakage of its secret x. Under this situation and during the rapid bit exchange phase, the attacker can send the correct response with the probability of 1. Hence, whether the SMDB protocol can provide protection against terrorist fraud attacks depends on the security of the signature T. We assume the dishonest tag does not provide any information about the signature T, which means the attacker must compute the valid signature T required by herself in order to be accepted by the reader.

The attacker can only guess the value of the signature T (the success probability is $(\frac{1}{4})^n$), or guess the tag's secret x (the success probability is $(\frac{1}{2})^v$) to compute the correct signature T. Hence, the success probability of terrorist fraud attacks is :

$$P_{terrorist-fraud} = 1.max\{(\frac{1}{2})^v, (\frac{1}{4})^n\} = (\frac{1}{2})^v \tag{9}$$

3.4   Analysis on Distance Fraud Attacks

In distance fraud attacks, the tag owner herself is fraudulent who attempts to cheat the readers in her proximity. Since the dishonest tag is outside the legal authentication region, she would send the responses earlier in order to pass the proximity check in terms of round trip time measurement. This is called early-reply strategy.

It can be estimated that the success probability of distance fraud attacks towards the SMDB protocol is $(\frac{1}{2})^n$. Let ξ_i be the event that a dishonest tag succeeds in the i-th round. Let Ξ_i be the event defined by $\Xi_i = \xi_i$ and $\Xi_i = \xi_i \mid \xi_1 \wedge \cdots \wedge_{i-1}$ for $i > 1$. When $d_i = 0$, the tag should send the response r_i before receiving the challenge c_i' from the reader in order to cheat the distance. Because $v_i \neq \overline{v_i}$, the tag succeeds with probability $\frac{1}{2}$

$$P[\Xi_i \mid d_i = 0]P[d_i = 0] = \frac{1}{2} \times \frac{1}{2} = \frac{1}{4} \tag{10}$$

When $d_i = 1$, the tag can cheat the distance by sending the response r_i' earlier. Similarly, due to $0 \neq 1$, the tag succeeds with probability $\frac{1}{2}$

$$P[\Xi_i \mid d_i = 1]P[d_i = 1] = \frac{1}{2} \times \frac{1}{2} = \frac{1}{4} \tag{11}$$

From the law of total probability, $P[\Xi_i \mid]$ can be obtained by

$$\begin{aligned} P[\Xi_i \mid] &= P[\Xi_i \mid d_i = 0]P[d_i = 0] + P[\Xi_i \mid d_i = 1]P[d_i = 1] \\ &= \frac{1}{4} + \frac{1}{4} = \frac{1}{2} \end{aligned} \tag{12}$$

Finally, the success probability of distance fraud attacks is given by

$$\begin{aligned} P[\xi_1 \wedge \xi_2 \wedge \cdots \wedge \xi_n] &= P[\xi_1]P[\xi_2 \mid \xi_1] \cdots P[\xi_n \mid \wedge_{i=1}^{n-1}\xi_i] \\ &= P[\Xi_1]P[\Xi_2] \cdots P[\Xi_n] \\ &= (\frac{1}{2})^n \end{aligned} \tag{13}$$

4   Noise Resilience

Our scheme is inspired by the Swiss-Knife RFID distance bounding protocol [5]. At the end of the rapid bit exchange phase, we count the number of misses (errors) ϵ between the transmitted and received challenges and responses. More precisely, we realize that a transmitted challenge c_i might be different from the received one c_i' and similarly a transmitted response r_i' might be different from a received one r_i. These mismatches between c_i, c_i' or r_i, r_i' might be aroused either due to noise in the communicating channel or to the fact that the tag tries to be authenticated is not legitimate (an attacker).

Kim et al. [5] introduces a threshold τ in a distance bounding protocol that can be utilized to avoid the failure of authenticating legitimate tags in consideration that some legitimate errors might be caused due to noise in the communication channel. A detailed analysis of the threshold τ was first provided by Pedro et al. [10], taking into account the probability of having errors due to noise in the communication channel. Their methods are also valid for the SMDB protocol and can be used to select an appropriate value for the threshold τ for a given number (n) of rapid bit exchange challenge-response rounds. For more detailed analysis, we refer readers to [10].

5   Conclusion

In this paper, we proposed a novel and efficient distance bounding protocol, the SMDB protocol, which characterizes in its uniquely mutual authentication procedure, reliable ID consistency mechanism as well as an effective verification method. The protocol has been proved to be capable of providing an ideal resistance against mafia fraud, terrorist fraud, and distance fraud attacks in terms of success probability by means of probabilistic analysis. Furthermore, the SMDB protocol has noise resilience property as well, which is beneficial to alleviate the influence of noise in the channel on the authentication process.

References

1. Jannati, H.: Analysis of relay, terrorist fraud and distance fraud attacks on RFID systems. Int. J. Criti. Infrastruct. Protect. **11**, 51–61 (2015)
2. Guizani, S.: Security analysis of RFID relay attacks. J. Int. Technol. **17**(2), 191–196 (2016)
3. Brands, S., Chaum, D.: Distance bounding protocols. In: Helleseth, T. (ed.) EURO-CRYPT 1993. LNCS, vol. 765, pp. 344–359. Springer, Heidelberg (1994)
4. Cremers, C., Rasmussen, K., Capkun, S.: Distance hijiacking attacks on distance bounding protocols. In: Cryptology ePrint Archive: Report 2011/129 (2011)
5. Kim, C.H., Avoine, G., Koeune, F., Standaert, F.-X., Pereira, O.: The swiss-knife RFID distance bounding protocol. In: Lee, P.J., Cheon, J.H. (eds.) ICISC 2008. LNCS, vol. 5461, pp. 98–115. Springer, Heidelberg (2009)
6. Kim, C.H., Avoine, G.: RFID distance bounding protocol with mixed challenges to prevent relay attacks. In: Garay, J.A., Miyaji, A., Otsuka, A. (eds.) CANS 2009. LNCS, vol. 5888, pp. 119–133. Springer, Heidelberg (2009)
7. Xin, W., Sun, H.P., Chen, Z.: Analysis and design of distance-bounding protocols for RFID. J. Comput. Res. Dev. **50**(11), 2358–2366 (2013)
8. Dowon, H.: Authenticated distance bounding protocol with improved FAR: beyond the minimal bound of FAR. IEICE Trans. Commun. **97**(5), 930–935 (2014)
9. Reid, J., Nieto, J.M.G., Tang, T., Senadji, B.: Detecting relay attacks with timing based protocols. In: Proceedings of the 2nd ACM Symposium on Information, Computer and Communications Security, ASIACCS 2007, New York, USA, pp. 204–213 (2007)
10. Pedro, P.L., Castro, J.H., Tapiador, J., Palomar, E., Lubbe, J.V.: Cryptographic puzzles and distance bounding protocols: Practical tools for RFID security. In: 2010 IEEE International Conference on RFID, Orlando, pp. 45–52 (2010)
11. Avoine, G., Bingol, M.A., Kardas, S., Lauradoux, C., Martin, B.: A Formal Framework for Cryptanalyzing RFID Distance Bounding Protocols. Cryptology ePrint Archive, Report 2009/543 (2009)

Private Weighted Histogram Aggregation in Crowdsourcing

Shaowei Wang, Liusheng Huang[(✉)], Pengzhan Wang,
Hou Deng, Hongli Xu, and Wei Yang

School of Computer Science and Technology,
University of Science and Technology of China, Hefei 230027, Anhui, China
{wangsw,pzwang,dengh}@mail.ustc.edu.cn,
{lshuang,xuhongli,qubit}@ustc.edu.cn

Abstract. Histogram is one of the fundamental aggregates in crowd-sourcing data aggregation. In a crowdsourcing aggregation task, the potential value or importance of each bucket in the histogram may differs, especially when the number of buckets is relatively large but only a few of buckets are of great interests. This is the case weighted histogram aggregation is needed. On the other hand, privacy is a critical issue in crowdsourcing, as data contributed by participants may reveal sensitive information about individuals. In this paper, we study the problem of privacy-preserving weighted histogram aggregation, and propose a new local differential-private mechanism, the bi-parties mechanism, which exploits the weight imbalances among buckets in histogram to minimize weighted error. We provide both theoretical and experimental analyses of the mechanism, specifically, the experimental results demonstrate that our mechanism can averagely reduce 20 % of weighted square error of estimated histograms compared to existing approaches (e.g. randomized response mechanism, exponential mechanism).

Keywords: Differential privacy · Weighted histogram · Local privacy · Crowdsourcing · Randomized response

1 Introduction

For many crowdsourcing tasks (e.g. crowdsourcing voting [17]), histogram is a fundamental intermediate result that summaries statistical information over large number of participants, and can then be postprocessed specifically for crowdsourcing objectives, such as for voting, ranking or averaging. In these cases (e.g. weighted average), each bucket in the histogram maybe assigned with different weights [9], to consensus with the intrinsic importance of each bucket in the task. Hence, as a generalization of the naive histogram, weighted histogram aggregation is an important component in crowdsourcing.

On the other hand, privacy is a crucial issue in crowdsourcing, since the data contributed by participants may reveal identities or activities of individuals [4], especially when crowdsourcing aggregation tasks query about sensitive information, such as genders, ages or locations.

© Springer International Publishing Switzerland 2016
Q. Yang et al. (Eds.): WASA 2016, LNCS 9798, pp. 250–261, 2016.
DOI: 10.1007/978-3-319-42836-9_23

Many efforts have been putted in the area of privacy preserving data aggregation. Specifically, for the task of privacy preserving histogram aggregation, some approaches resort to cryptographic techniques to ensure data computational privacy [13] (e.g. in [3,16]) but usually suffer from high computation costs and are volatile to collusion between the aggregator and other participants, thus may not be suitable for crowdsourcing data aggregation scenarios. In another main branch, by adopting the state-of-art privacy definition of ϵ-differential privacy [6] into the local setting with information-theoretical privacy guarantee, Erlingsson *et al.* [8] and Duchi *et al.* [5] propose randomized response [15] technique on bit map for efficient differential private histogram aggregation, and prove its optimality in the low region of the privacy budget (e.g. $\epsilon = O(1)$). In the high region of the privacy budget, multivariate randomized response technique or exponential mechanism [12] dominates.

Though differential private histogram aggregation has been extensively studied, existing approaches for differential-private histogram aggregation neglected the weighted histogram scenarios, where relatively small noises for heavyweight buckets is preferred from data utility perspective, and may degrades aggregation performance under the metric of weighted histogram error.

In this paper, we propose the bi-parties mechanism for local differential privacy weighted histogram aggregation, it exploits the weight differences of items in the data domain. Basically, our mechanism tries to find the optimal bi-partite cut of buckets in histogram, such that one party of buckets has much higher average weights that the other, and then assign delicate privacy budgets to both parties in a unified way, without waste of privacy budget. The mechanism utilizes both binary randomized response and multivariate randomized response techniques on bit map for achieving local differential privacy. As a result, the weighted histogram error in our mechanism could be significantly reduced. Specifically, this paper makes following contributes:

- We propose a new differential private mechanism, the bi-parties mechanism, for weighted histogram aggregation in crowdsourcing.
- We provide theoretical error bounds of the mechanism under weighted square histogram error, and analyse its advantages over existing approaches.
- We conduct extensive experiments to validate the efficiency and effectiveness of our mechanism, with comparison to existing approaches that are for naive histogram aggregation. The experimental results show that our mechanism averagely reduced 20 % error for weighted histogram estimation.

The remainder of this paper is organized as follows. Section 2 provides preliminary knowledge about local differential privacy definition and the aggregation model. Section 3 describes bi-parties mechanism and the optimal parameters selection. Section 4 analyse computational complexity and error bounds of our mechanism. Section 5 presents experimental results of our mechanism with comparison to existing approaches. Section 6 reviews related work. Lastly Sect. 7 concludes the whole paper.

2   Preliminaries

In this section, we briefly introduce the definition of data privacy: local ϵ-differential privacy, and the privacy preserving weighted histogram aggregation model in crowdsourcing.

2.1   Local Differential Privacy

Local differential privacy [11] is a rigorous data privacy definition in local setting, unlike the original differential privacy definition [6] in centralized setting, it guarantees data privacy relying on no other parties (e.g. database curator, the aggregator, other participants) but the data owner (e.g. a crowdsourcing participant), and hence is quite suitable for preserving participants' data privacy in crowdsourcing scenarios.

Local differential privacy limits the differences in probabilities of sanitized data regardless of the truly data value is. To be precise, let D denote the domain of data (e.g. all possible ages), $d \in D$ be the data value a participant holds and $d' \in Range(\tilde{K})$ be the sanitized data by a privacy preserving mechanism $\tilde{K}$, here the sanitized data d' and the secret data d may not be in the same data domain. The formal definition of local differential privacy is described in Definition 1.

Definition 1 (Local ϵ-differential privacy [11]). *A randomized mechanism $\tilde{K}$ gives local ϵ-differential privacy iff for all possible pairings $d_a, d_b \in D$, and all possible subset $T \subseteq Range(\tilde{K})$,*

$$Pr[\tilde{K}(d_a) \in T] \leq \exp(\epsilon) \cdot Pr[\tilde{K}(d_b) \in T].$$

The ϵ is known as privacy level or privacy budget, and usually be a relatively small value (e.g. $\epsilon = O(1)$) for reasonable protection level of data privacy meanwhile remaining acceptable data utility.

The randomized response [15] technique is the most commonly used technique for preserving local differential privacy, it tells truth with a limited probability, otherwise responses with randomly chosen value from data domain. In this paper, we will present a new mechanism: bi-parities mechanism, that is based on binary and multivariate randomized response technique, and is specially designed for weighted histogram aggregation.

Recall that local ϵ-differential privacy preserving a participant's data privacy locally without trust on any other participants or the aggregator.

2.2   Weighted Histogram Aggregation Model

In a crowdsourcing histogram aggregation task, the aggregator queries participants about the data domain D, in which each participant u_i holds a secret value $d_i \in D$.

To preserve data privacy, each participant randomizes their data d_i independently using privacy preserving randomizer $\tilde{K}$ to obtain a sanitized version data

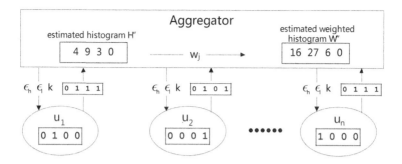

Fig. 1. Aggregation model for differential private weighted histogram estimation in crowdsourcing.

$d'_i \in Range(\tilde{K})$, and publishes d'_i to the aggregator. The aggregator then tries to decode a estimation H'' of histogram over domain D from observed sanitized data list $\{d'_1, d'_2, ..., d'_n\}$, which are received as query results from n participants.

For weighted histogram aggregation, the demonstrative aggregation model is showed in Fig. 1. At first, the aggregator releases or publishes aggregation query to each participant, along with global parameters, including privacy budget ϵ and other mechanism specific parameters, such as the partition bound k and assigned budgets ϵ_h, ϵ_l for two parties in our bi-parties mechanism. In our mechanism, both secrete data d and sanitized data d' are expressed as bit maps, specifically, if a participant's secrete value equals the j-th element D_j in data domain D, then the secrete data $d_i \in \{0,1\}^{|D|}$ is a bit map of length $|D|$ with the j-th bit be set to 1 and other bits be set to 0.

After receiving sanitized data $\{d'_1, d'_2, ..., d'_n\}$ from participants, the aggregator estimate the truly histogram H of $\{d_1, d_2, ..., d_n\}$ as H'', and then assign weights w_j to each bucket in H'' to compose the estimated weighted histogram W'', this is $W''_j = w_j \cdot H''_j$, for $j \in [1, |D|]$. To minimize the error of estimated weighted histogram W'' of the truly weighted histogram W, the mechanism parameters k and ϵ_h, ϵ_l are related to the bucket weights vector $\{w_1, w_2, ..., w_{|d|}\}$, here the truly weighted histogram is $W = \{w_j \cdot H_j \mid j \in [1, |D|]\}$.

3   Mechanism

In this section, we present the bi-parties mechanism and its local ϵ-differential privacy guarantee, then show how to compute optimal choices of the partition bound k and assigned budgets ϵ_h, ϵ_l for two parties in the mechanism.

3.1   Bi-parties Mechanism

The basic idea of optimizing weighted histogram aggregation error is explicit: more privacy budget should be used for heavyweight items than lightweight items in data domain D, but assigning some privacy budget for the data aggregation of participants with heavyweight items and other privacy budget for aggregation of participants with lightweight items violates the privacy constraints in Definition 1, since in such separated way, the privacy adversary would know a participant's secret value is in heavyweight items or lightweight items.

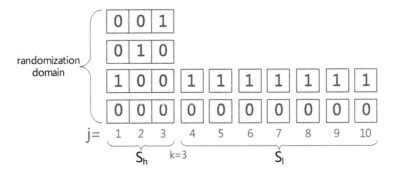

Fig. 2. Example of randomization domain in bi-parties mechanism based on binary and multivariate randomized response technique, the parameter $k = 3, |D| = 10$.

Algorithm 1. Data randomizer for each participant

Input: a secret value $d \in D$ that is represented as a bit map, $d = D_j \in \{0,1\}^{|D|}, j \in [1, |D|]$, partition bound $k \in [1, |D| - 1]$, privacy budgets ϵ_h, ϵ_l that $\epsilon_h + \epsilon_l = \epsilon$.
Output: a sanitized bit map $d' \in \{0,1\}^{|D|}$ that satisfies local ϵ-differential privacy.
1: initialize $d' = \mathbf{0} \in \{0\}^{|D|}$
2: **if** $j \le k$ **then**

3: $j' = \begin{cases} j, & \text{with probability } \frac{\exp(\epsilon_h)}{\exp(\epsilon_h)+k} \\ UniformRandom([1,k]\backslash\{j\}), & \text{with probability } \frac{k-1}{\exp(\epsilon_h)+k} \\ null, & \text{with probability } \frac{1}{\exp(\epsilon_h)+k} \end{cases}$

4:    set $d'_{j'} = 1$ if $j' \ne null$
5:    **for** $r = k+1$ to $|D|$ **do**

6:    $d'_r = \begin{cases} 0, & \text{with probability } \frac{\exp(\epsilon_l)}{\exp(\epsilon_l)+1} \\ 1, & \text{with probability } \frac{1}{\exp(\epsilon_l)+1} \end{cases}$

7:    **end for**
8: **else if** $j > k$ **then**

9: $j' = \begin{cases} UniformRandom([1,k]), & \text{with probability } \frac{k}{\exp(\epsilon_h)+k} \\ null, & \text{with probability } \frac{\exp(\epsilon_h)}{\exp(\epsilon_h)+k} \end{cases}$

10:    set $d'_{j'} = 1$ if $j' \ne null$
11:    **for** $r = k+1$ to $|D|$ **do**

12:    $d'_r = \begin{cases} d_r, & \text{with probability } \frac{\exp(\epsilon_l)}{\exp(\epsilon_l)+1} \\ 1-d_r, & \text{with probability } \frac{1}{\exp(\epsilon_l)+1} \end{cases}$

13:    **end for**
14: **end if**
15: **return** d'

In bi-parties mechanism, the items and privacy budget are partitioned into two parties in a unified way, to take full advantage of the overall privacy budget. The mechanism could be seem as the combination of binary randomized response technique and multivariate randomized response technique.

To separate items into two parties, we firstly sort items of domain D in descent order, which means $w_j \geq w_{j+1}$ for $j \in [1, |D| - 1]$. We then take the first k items as heavyweight item set $S_h \subseteq D$, and the rest as lightweight item set $S_l \subseteq D$. Then we split the overall privacy budget ϵ into two parts: ϵ_h, ϵ_l, where $\epsilon_h \geq 0.5\epsilon$, $\epsilon_l \geq 0.0$ and $\epsilon_h + \epsilon_l = \epsilon$. The ϵ_h will be consumed by S_h and ϵ_l will be consumed by S_l. The concrete choices of k and ϵ_h, ϵ_l according to weight vector w will be presented in the next subsection.

After partitioning domain D and privacy budget, we now present the basic data randomizer with local ϵ-differential privacy. As demonstrated by bit-map form in Fig. 2, if a participant's secret value $d = D_j$ is in S_h, then selects one element from $\{D_1, D_2, ..., D_k, \mathbf{0}\}$ with proper assigned probabilities according to ϵ_h and then independently chooses to select each value in S_l with proper probability according to ϵ_h; if a participant's secret value $d = D_j$ is in S_l, then selects D_j itself with one probability, selects each value in $S_l - \{D_j\}$ independently with another probability, and select one value from $\{D_1, D_2, ..., D_k, \mathbf{0}\}$ with proper assigned probabilities. Formally, the randomizer of bi-parties mechanism is detailed in Algorithm 1.

In concise, the randomizer naturally embeds multivariate randomized response into binary randomized response on bit map, and assigns customized privacy budgets for heavyweight items and lightweight items. This randomizer is evaluated by each participant, its privacy guarantee of the is declared in Theorem 1, proof of which is kind of explicit and will be presented in detail in the longer version of this paper due to limited space here.

Theorem 1. *The randomizer in Algorithm 1 satisfies local ϵ-differential privacy constraints in Definition 1 for domain D.*

Algorithm 2. Histogram decoder for the aggregator

Input: sanitized bit maps $\{d'_1, d'_2, ..., d'_n\}$ from n participants with secret bit maps $\{d_1, d_2, ..., d_n\}$, partition bound $k \in [1, |D|]$, privacy budgets ϵ_h, ϵ_l.
Output: an unbiased weighted estimation H'' of truly histogram $H = sum(\{d_1, d_2, ..., d_n\})$.
  1: $H' = sum(\{d'_1, d'_2, ..., d'_n\})$
  2: **for** $j = 1$ to k **do**
  3:    $H''_j = \frac{H'_j \cdot (\exp(\epsilon_h) + k) - n}{\exp(\epsilon_h) - 1}$
  4: **end for**
  5: **for** $j = k + 1$ to $|D|$ **do**
  6:    $H''_j = \frac{H'_j \cdot (\exp(\epsilon_l) + 1) - n}{\exp(\epsilon_l) - 1}$
  7: **end for**
  8: **return** H''

We now proceed to decoding histogram from the sanitized bit map that is generated by the randomizer in Algorithm 2, it's an unbiased estimator for estimating the truly histogram $H = sum(d_1, d_2, ..., d_n)$. Applying the weight vector $w = w_1, w_2, ..., w_{|D|}$ to unbias estimated histogram H'' finally results in the unbias estimated weighted histogram W'' of truly weighted histogram W.

3.2 Optimal Parameters Selection

In this subsection, we consider the optimal choice of partition bound k and privacy budgets ϵ_h, ϵ_l with the knowledge of weight vector $w = w_1, w_2, ..., w_{|D|}$. The weighted square error WSE of H'' is used as optimization objective here. Formally, the expected weighted square error of H'' given in Algorithm 2 is as follows:

$$
\begin{aligned}
&WSE(k, \epsilon_h, \epsilon_l) \\
&= E[\|W'' - W\|_2^2] = E[\sum_{j=1..|D|} (w_j \cdot H_j'' - w_j \cdot H_j)^2] \\
&= \sum_{j=1..|D|} w_j^2 \cdot E[(H_j'' - H_j)^2] = \sum_{j=1..|D|} w_j^2 \cdot Var[H_j''] \\
&= \sum_{j=1..k} w_j^2 \cdot \frac{H_j \cdot \exp(\epsilon_h) \cdot k + (n - H_j) \cdot (\exp(\epsilon_h) + k - 1)}{(\exp(\epsilon_h) - 1)^2} \\
&+ \sum_{j=(k+1)..|D|} w_j^2 \cdot \frac{n \cdot \exp(\epsilon_l)}{(\exp(\epsilon_l) - 1)^2}.
\end{aligned}
\tag{1}
$$

The weighted square error depends on the truly histogram H, one can use prior knowledge about H as substitution, here we just assume that it's a uniform histogram that $H_j = \frac{n}{|D|}$. As a result, the objective formula in (1) is reduced to:

$$
\begin{aligned}
&WSE(k, \epsilon_h, \epsilon_l) \\
&= \frac{n \cdot |D| \cdot k \cdot \exp(\epsilon_h) + n \cdot (|D| - 1)(k - 1)}{|D| \cdot (\exp(\epsilon_h) - 1)^2} \cdot \sum_{j=1..k} w_j^2 \\
&+ \frac{n \cdot \exp(\epsilon_l)}{(\exp(\epsilon_l) - 1)^2} \cdot \sum_{j=(k+1)..|D|} w_j^2.
\end{aligned}
\tag{2}
$$

For a given privacy budget ϵ, when k is fixed, the objective $WSE(\epsilon_h)$ is strongly convex for the variate $\exp(\epsilon_h) \in (\exp(0.5\epsilon), \exp(\epsilon))$ or variate $\epsilon_h \in (0.5\epsilon, \epsilon)$ when $\exp(\epsilon_l)$ is replaced by $\exp(\epsilon - \epsilon_h)$.

Specifically, the derivative of the objective $WSE(\exp(\epsilon_h))$ in (2) is a quartic-like function and its roots could be expressed in closed-form, though one may also use Newton's method to approximate these roots, so that finding the optimal solution of ϵ_h, ϵ_l for fixed k costs only $O(1)$ time. By iterating over all possible $k \in \{1, 2, ..., |D|\}$, we can get the optimal choice of k as well. In concise, finding the optimal parameters in bi-parties mechanism can be done in $O(|D|)$ computational time.

4   Theoretical Analyses

4.1   Error Bounds

Under the metric of weighted square error WSE as defined in Eq. 1, the estimated weighted histogram in bi-parties mechanism is no less favorable than estimated weighted histogram by state-of-art binary randomized response approaches in [5,8] or multivariate randomized response approaches [12,15], as in bi-parties mechanism, using parameter $(k = 1, \epsilon_h = 0.5\epsilon, \epsilon_l = 0.5\epsilon)$ is equivalent to binary randomized response approaches, and using parameter $(k = |D|, \epsilon_h = \epsilon, \epsilon_l = 0.0)$ is equivalent to multivariate randomized response approaches. Thus, we have:

$$WSE \leq n \cdot \min\{\frac{\exp(0.5 \cdot \epsilon)}{(\exp(0.5 \cdot \epsilon) - 1)^2} \ , \ \frac{|D|^2 \cdot \exp(\epsilon) + (|D| - 1)^2}{|D| \cdot (\exp(\epsilon) - 1)^2}\} \cdot \sum_{j=1..|D|} w_j^2$$

Further more, as detailed in Subsect. 3.2, $WSE(\epsilon_h)$ is strongly convex, thus bi-parties mechanism could do better than binary and multivariate randomized response approaches.

4.2   Computational Complexities

For each participant, the data randomizer of bi-parties mechanism in Algorithm 1 has computational complexity of $O(|D|)$, where D is the domain of participants' secret values and the domain of histogram buckets.

For the aggregator, finding the optimal mechanism parameters k and ϵ_h, ϵ_l as in Subsect. 3.2 costs $O(|D|)$ time, and estimating weighted histogram from observed sanitized data as in Algorithm 2 costs $O(n \cdot |D| + |D|)$ time, where n is the number of participants.

In concise, bi-parties mechanism has only linear complexities with respect to the domain size $|D|$ or number of participants n, for both participants and the aggregator. Hence, bi-parties mechanism is highly efficient for private weighted histogram aggregation in crowdsourcing.

5   Experiments

We evaluate the effectiveness of bi-parties mechanism on extensive weighted histogram aggregation simulations. Each participant's secrete data value is drawn from histogram H that is uniform randomly generated during each aggregation simulation, with privacy budget ϵ ranges from 1.0 to 3.0.

In these simulations, the size of data domain $|D|$ is a moderate number 40, the number of participants is 1000. The weight vector $w = \{w_1, w_2, ..., w_{|D|}\}$ for histograms includes heavy-core-set families and exponential decay families. In heavy-core-set families, a small subset of the data domain is assigned with heavy weights and the rest of the domain is assigned with one unit weights.

In exponential decay families, the weight vector is a exponential decay sequence $\{\exp(-\alpha j) \mid j = [1..|D|]\}$ with decay rate α ranges from 0.25 to 1.5.

We compare our bi-parties mechanism (BPM) with state-of-art approaches for raw histogram aggregation, including binary randomized response (BRR) approaches in [5,8], which beats the classical Laplace mechanism [7] with constant factor improvement, and multivariate randomized response or exponential mechanism (EM) in [12]. The metric we use here is natural logarithm of normalized weighted square error $NWSE = \frac{WSE}{n}$, where WSE is defined in Eq. 1.

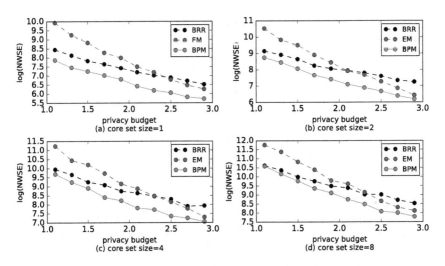

Fig. 3. The simulation results of weighted histogram aggregation with heavy-core-set weight vectors. (Color figure online)

The simulation results with heavy-core-set weight vectors are showed on Fig. 3, the weights for buckets in core set is $|D| = 40$ and the size of core set is in $\{1, 2, 4, 8\}$, each showed in one of the 4 panels in the figure. Compared to the BRR and EM approaches, our BPM approach averagely reduced weighted square error by 20 %.

The simulation results with exponential decay weight vectors are showed on Fig. 4, the decay rate is in $\{0.5, 1.0, 1.5, 2.0\}$, each showed in one of the 4 panels in the figure. Compared to the BRR and EM approaches, our BPM approach averagely reduced weighted square error by 40 %.

In conclusion, our bi-parities mechanism (BPM) outperforms existing approaches for weighted histogram aggregation.

6   Related Work

The work on privacy preserving data aggregation can mainly be categorized into two streams: encryption-based approaches and perturbation-based approaches.

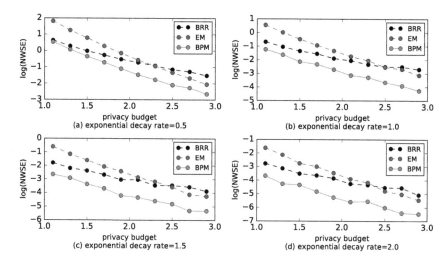

Fig. 4. The simulation results of weighted histogram aggregation with exponential decay weight vectors. (Color figure online)

Encryption-based approaches (e.g. in [1,14,16]) utilize cryptographic tools along with distributed noise generation to ensure computational differential privacy [13]. These approaches may suffer from high computational costs in practice especially when used for histogram aggregation with relatively large data domain. A participant's data privacy in computational differential privacy is also volatile to collusion between the aggregator and other participants.

Perturbation-based approaches perturb truly data locally for privacy preserving. Specifically for local ϵ-differential private raw histogram aggregation, Erlingsson *et al.* [8] and Duchi *et al.* [5] proposed applying binary randomized response technique to bit map, and proves its optimality in the low region of the privacy budget (e.g. $\epsilon = O(1)$). In the high region of the privacy budget, multivariate randomized response technique or exponential mechanism [12] dominates. There are also some work (e.g. [2,10]) focus on private succinct histogram or heavy hitter aggregation.

This paper considers privacy preserving weighted histogram aggregation instead, our bi-parties mechanism is a combination of binary and multivariate randomized response techniques, the multivariate randomized response technique is naturally used for heavyweight buckets with relatively large privacy budget, and the binary randomized response technique is used for lightweight buckets with relatively small privacy budget, hence exploits the complementary advantages of binary and multivariate randomized response techniques.

7   Conclusion

This paper studies privacy preserving data aggregation in crowdsourcing, and propose the bi-parties mechanism for local ϵ-differential private weighted histogram aggregation. The mechanism combines binary and multivariate randomized response techniques for randomizing heavyweight buckets and lightweight buckets in a unified way, hence naturally exploits the imbalances of weights and the complementary advantages of binary and multivariate randomized response techniques. This mechanism is highly efficient as its computational complexity is linear to the data domain or the number of participants, thus is suitable for practical use even in large scale crowdsourcing aggregation. We also provide theoretical and experimental error analyses of bi-parties mechanism, the experimental results shows the mechanism outperforms existing approaches averagely by 20 % for weighted histogram estimation.

Acknowledgements. This paper is supported by the National Science Foundation of China under No. U1301256, 61502443, 61472383 and 61472385, Special Project on IoT of China NDRC (2012-2766), the Natural Science Foundation of Anhui Province in China under No. 1408085MKL08, the China Postdoctoral Science Foundation (No. 2015M570545), the Jiangsu Planned Projects for Postdoctoral Research Funds (No. 1501085C).

References

1. Ács, G., Castelluccia, C.: I have a DREAM! (DiffeRentially privatE smArt Metering). In: Filler, T., Pevný, T., Craver, S., Ker, A. (eds.) IH 2011. LNCS, vol. 6958, pp. 118–132. Springer, Heidelberg (2011)
2. Bassily, R., Smith, A.: Local, private, efficient protocols for succinct histograms. In: STOC. ACM (2015)
3. Chan, T.-H.H., Shi, E., Song, D.: Privacy-preserving stream aggregation with fault tolerance. In: Keromytis, A.D. (ed.) FC 2012. LNCS, vol. 7397, pp. 200–214. Springer, Heidelberg (2012)
4. Christin, D.: Privacy in mobile participatory sensing: current trends and future challenges. J. Syst. Softw. **116**, 57–68 (2015)
5. Duchi, J.C., Jordan, M.I., Wainwright, M.J.: Local privacy and statistical minimax rates. In: FOCS. IEEE (2013)
6. Dwork, C.: Differential privacy. In: Bugliesi, M., Preneel, B., Sassone, V., Wegener, I. (eds.) ICALP 2006. LNCS, vol. 4052, pp. 1–12. Springer, Heidelberg (2006)
7. Dwork, C., McSherry, F., Nissim, K., Smith, A.: Calibrating noise to sensitivity in private data analysis. In: Halevi, S., Rabin, T. (eds.) TCC 2006. LNCS, vol. 3876, pp. 265–284. Springer, Heidelberg (2006)
8. Erlingsson, Ú., Pihur, V., Korolova, A.: Rappor: randomized aggregatable privacy-preserving ordinal response. In: CCS. ACM (2014)
9. Fang, X., Gao, H., Li, J., Li, Y.: Approximate multiple count in wireless sensor networks. In: 2014 Proceedings IEEE INFOCOM. IEEE (2014)
10. Hsu, J., Khanna, S., Roth, A.: Distributed private heavy hitters. In: Czumaj, A., Mehlhorn, K., Pitts, A., Wattenhofer, R. (eds.) ICALP 2012, Part I. LNCS, vol. 7391, pp. 461–472. Springer, Heidelberg (2012)
11. Kasiviswanathan, S.P., Lee, H.K., Nissim, K., Raskhodnikova, S., Smith, A.: What can we learn privately? SIAM J. Comput. **40**(3), 793–826 (2011)
12. McSherry, F., Talwar, K.: Mechanism design via differential privacy. In: FOCS. IEEE (2007)

13. Mironov, I., Pandey, O., Reingold, O., Vadhan, S.: Computational differential privacy. In: Halevi, S. (ed.) CRYPTO 2009. LNCS, vol. 5677, pp. 126–142. Springer, Heidelberg (2009)
14. Shi, E., Chan, T.H., Rieffel, E., Chow, R., Song, D.: Privacy-preserving aggregation of time-series data. In: NDSS (2011)
15. Warner, S.L.: Randomized response: a survey technique for eliminating evasive answer bias. J. Am. Stat. Assoc. **60**(309), 63–69 (1965)
16. Won, J., Ma, C.Y., Yau, D.K., Rao, N.S.: Proactive fault-tolerant aggregation protocol for privacy-assured smart metering. In: INFOCOM. IEEE (2014)
17. Yuen, M.C., King, I., Leung, K.S.: A survey of crowdsourcing systems. In: PASSAT/SocialCom. IEEE (2011)

Minimum Cost Spatial-Temporal Task Allocation in Mobile Crowdsensing

Jiapeng Yu, Mingjun Xiao[✉], Guoju Gao, and Chang Hu

School of Computer Science and Technology/Suzhou Institute for Advanced Study,
University of Science and Technology of China, Heifei, People's Republic of China
xiaomj@ustc.edu.cn

Abstract. With the advances of sensors in smart devices, Mobile Crowdsensing (MCS) is flourishing. In this paper, we focus on Cost-minimizing Task Allocation (CTA) problem with spatial-temporal constraints in MCS. The MCS platform gives a set of tasks with different locations and sensing durations. Meanwhile, the platform hopes to allocate the spatial-temporal tasks to a part of participants with the minimum cost. We prove the NP-hardness of this problem and solve it based on the classical primal-dual algorithm. Moreover, we demonstrate that the approximation ratio is a variable about the scale of the problem. Then, we design a heuristic algorithm based on the Tabu search to solve the CTA problem and point out that the lower bound is guaranteed by the initialization progress. Finally, we conduct extensive simulations to show the significant performance of our algorithm.

Keywords: Mobile Crowdsensing · Task allocation · Heuristic algorithm · Minimum cost

1 Introduction

With the rapid development of smart devices, lots of data can be collected from accelerator, GPS, camera, and other embedded sensors in smart devices [5,15]. Thanks to this, Mobile Crowdsensing (MCS) becomes a new paradigm in which mobile users can utilize their smart devices to perform sensing tasks allocated by an MCS platform [13]. As a necessary component of MCS, task allocation has become one of the most important topics in recent years. In this paper, we mainly focus on the Cost-minimizing Task Allocation (CTA) problem with spatial-temporal constraints. For example, an MCS platform publishes sensing tasks, such as noise pollution mapping, traffic information mapping, temperature measurement [9,12,17]. Each task is related to a location and a sensing duration. On the other hand, a group of users want to participate in the crowdsensing. First, each user tells the MCS platform which tasks it can be performed by itself, the corresponding sensing duration, and the cost that it will charge from the platform. Then, the MCS platform will allocate the tasks with the minimum cost while letting the spacial-temporal constraints be satisfied. Different from existing

© Springer International Publishing Switzerland 2016
Q. Yang et al. (Eds.): WASA 2016, LNCS 9798, pp. 262–271, 2016.
DOI: 10.1007/978-3-319-42836-9_24

works [7,8], we consider that each user will make a deterministic announcement about where it can go and how long it can collect data, especially when the MCS platform introduces some incentive and penalty mechanism. In other words, if a user announces that it can collect sensing data in a place with 5 min length, we assume that this announce is truthful. Besides, each task should be performed by at least one user to satisfy the sensing duration, and each user can perform at least one task, which makes our paper different from the classical set cover problem [4].

We highlight our main contributions as follows:

1. We introduce the Cost-minimizing Task Allocation (CTA) problem with the spacial and temporal constraints.
2. We prove that the CTA problem is NP-hard. A approximation algorithm is given by using the classical duality theory. Then, we demonstrate that the approximation ratio is a variable about the scale of the problem.
3. We design a heuristic algorithm based on the Tabu search, called tCTA, including an initial progress, a weighting scheme, and a tabu rule. Moreover, we show that a lower bound can be guaranteed by the initialization progress.
4. Finally, we conduct extensive simulations to prove that our algorithm has better performances than the compared algorithms.

The remainder of this paper is organized as follows. In Sect. 2, we introduce the model and formulate the problem. In Sect. 3, we prove that this CTA problem is NP-hard. Then, we solve the problem with liner programming and duality theory to show the approximation ratio varying with scale of the problem. In Sect. 4, we design a heuristic algorithm based on Tabu search and we point out that lower bound can be guaranteed by the initialization progress. In Sect. 5, we evaluate the performance of our algorithm through extensive simulations. The related works are mentioned in Sect. 6. Finally, we conclude this paper in Sect. 7.

2   Model and Problem Formulation

2.1   Model

In the CTA problem, we assume that an MCS platform has n tasks, that is, $\boldsymbol{V} = \{\nu_1, \nu_2, \ldots, \nu_n\}$. For each task, the requirement of locations and sensing durations need to be met. We use $\boldsymbol{T} = \{\tau_1, \tau_2, \ldots, \tau_n\}$ to denote the corresponding sensing duration where $\tau_i \geq 0$. In this case, we can put locations and sensing durations together. That is, if τ_i equals 0, user will not pass the location of task i and will not get any useful sensing data about task i.

In MCS, there are m users who wants to perform sensing tasks in $\boldsymbol{V}$, and we use $\boldsymbol{U} = \{u_1, u_2, \ldots, u_m\}$ to denote these users. We use $\boldsymbol{R} = \{r_{ij}\}_{i \in [1,n], j \in [1,m]}$ to denote the available sensing duration of each user in each task. If $r_{ij} = 0$, it means user j can not perform task i. Additionally, we use $\boldsymbol{C} = \{c_1, c_2, \ldots, c_m\}$ to denote the cost of users. In our model, each user can perform more than one task, and each task should be performed by more than one user if necessary, which makes our problem different from classical set cover problem [4]. In this case, the MCS platform will allocate tasks to some users in U with minimum cost while spacial-temporal constraints are satisfied.

2.2 Problem Formulation

In the CTA problem, we need to select a subset of users in U to minimize the allocation cost while ensuring that the sensing time of each task is sufficient. For simplicity, we use a set $\Phi \subseteq U$ to denote a user recruitment strategy and map r_{ij} into $r_i(u_j)$, which means the available sensing duration of user j for task i. Then, the CTA problem can be formulated as follows:

$$Minimize: \quad \sum_{u_i \in \Phi} c(u_i) \tag{1}$$

$$Subject\ to: \quad \Phi \subseteq U \tag{2}$$

$$\sum_{u_j \in \Phi} r_i(u_j) \geq \tau_i \qquad \forall i \in [1, n] \tag{3}$$

$$r_i(u_j) \geq 0, \qquad \forall i \in [1, n], u_i \in \Phi, r_i(u_j) \in \mathbf{R} \tag{4}$$

$$\tau_i > 0, \qquad \forall i \in [1, n], \tau_i \in \mathbf{T} \tag{5}$$

Here, Eq. 3 indicates that the spatial-temporal constraint of each task should be satisfied, that is, allocation strategy must guarantee that the sensing duration of each task should be totally covered by users in Φ. Every task has sensing time length requirement and the available sensing duration of every task differs from users. In this case, the CTA problem is an extension of set cover problem.

3   Algorithm Based on Duality Theory

In this section, we prove that the CTA problem is NP-hard. Then, we adopt a classical algorithm, called dCTA, based on liner programming and duality theory to solve this problem. In the end of this section, we analyze the approximation ratio of dCTA in short.

3.1   NP-hardness of CTA

First, we prove that our CTA problem is NP-hard, as shown in the following theorem:

Theorem 1. The CTA problem is NP-hard.

Proof. To prove the NP-hardness of CTA problem, we consider the classical set cover problem.

$$Minimize: \quad |\Phi_s| \tag{6}$$

$$Subject\ to: \quad \Phi_s \subseteq U_s \tag{7}$$

$$\bigcup_{\mathcal{S} \in \Phi_s} R_s(\mathcal{S}) = T_s \tag{8}$$

where T_s is the universe set with all elements, U_s is a family of whole subsets of T_s, Φ_s is a family of partial subsets of T_s. $\mathcal{S}$ is a subset of T_s, $R_s(\mathcal{S})$ is a set which contains all elements covered by $\mathcal{S}$. The goal of set cover problem is to select the minimum count of subset, that is $|\Phi_s|$, while each element is covered by at least one subset in Φ_s.

Then, we consider a special case of CTA. We set every c_i in C and τ_i in T to be 1. Then, we let $r_i(u_j)$ be a binary variable, that is, each $r_i(u_j)$ will be either 1 or 0. The CTA problem becomes that how to minimize $\sum_{u_i \in \Phi} |1| = |\Phi|$ while every task is performed by at least one user. In this special case, the CTA problem can be converted into classical set cover problem, which is NP-hard. Thus, our CTA problem is at least NP-hard. The theorem holds. ∎

3.2 Design and Performance Analysis of Algorithm

We first give an algorithm using classical duality theory [3,10], called cCTA, as shown in Algorithm 1. In this algorithm, X is a $m - D$ vector which reflects the allocation strategy, where 1 denotes recruitment and 0 otherwise. That is, Φ can map into X. Then, X is relaxed to real field. Y is also a vector similar to X in the dual problem after transformation. More specially, we use $Y = \{y(u_i)\}$ and $X = \{x(u_i)\}$ to denote the variable in dual problem and original problem, respectively. For the simplicity of analysis, we map $c(u_j)$ into c(j). Then, we analyze this algorithm and prove it $|U|$-approximation algorithm.

Algorithm 1. The cCTA Algorithm

Require: C, R, T, U

Ensure: Φ

1: Turn the original problem into a liner programming and find its dual
2: X=0,Y=0,$\Phi = \emptyset$
3: **repeat**
4:     increase dual values in Y until $\sum_{u_i \in \Phi} \frac{r_j(u_i)}{\tau_i} y(u_i) = c(j)$
5:     select some subset of the tight dual constants c(j), and increase the primal variable X corresponding to them by an integral amount.
6: **until** the primal is feasible
7: map X into Φ

Theorem 2. The cCTA algorithm is a $|U|$-approximation algorithm.

Proof. The goal of the dual problem is to maximize $\sum_{u_i \in \Phi} y(u_i)$ while the constraints are satisfied, that is, $\sum_{u_i \in \Phi} \frac{r_j(u_i)}{\tau_i} y(u_i)$ should be no more than $c(j)$ for each j. According to the cCTA algorithm, u_i will be selected when the dual problem hits the bound, that is, $\sum_{u_i \in \Phi} \frac{r_j(u_i)}{\tau_i} y(u_i) = c(j)$. Since the sensing duration is constrained by the task requirement, $\frac{r_j(u_i)}{\tau_i}$ will not be more than 1 for each i and j. We use OPT(IP) and OPT(LP) to denote the optimal solution of the original problem and its relaxed formation [10]. Then, we will have

$$\sum_{u_j \subset \Phi} c(u_j) = \sum_{u_j \in U} c(u_j)x_j = \sum_{u_j \in U} \sum_{u_i \in \Phi} \frac{r_j(u_i)}{\tau_i} y(u_i)x_j \qquad (9)$$

$$\leq \sum_{u_j \in U} \sum_{u_i \in \Phi} y(u_i)x_j \qquad (10)$$

$$\leq |U| \sum_{u_i \in \Phi} y(u_i) \qquad (11)$$

$$\leq |U|OPT(LP) \leq |U|OPT(IP) \qquad (12)$$

Thus, Theorem 2 holds.   ∎

Based on this theorem, we can get the approximation ratio using duality theory and the approximation ratio is a variable related to the scale of users. The cCTA algorithm spends too much time on solving the LP problem. In fact, duality and other method will get similar approximation ratio. In reality, fast and accurate algorithm is necessary. Therefore, in next section we design a heuristic algorithm based on tabu search. We design a greedy algorithm to complete the initial progress with a theoretical approximation ratio.

4   Design Algorithm Based on Tabu Search

In this section, we first design an algorithm based on tabu search including an initial progress, a wighting scheme and a tabu rule. Then, we analyze the performance of tCTA algorithm.

4.1   Design of Algorithm

Tabu search is an extension of local search. The main idea of Tabu search is to avoid past local solutions at each iteration. Tabu search always show its good performance to solve NP-hard problem [1]. In this case, we design Algorithm 2 based on Tabu search. Algorithm 2 mainly consists of three parts: an initial progress, a wighting scheme and a tabu rule. As shown in Algorithm 2, initial progress is from step 2 to step 5. Wighting scheme consists of the scheme of adding elements to strategy set and removing elements from strategy set. The scheme of addition is from step 10 to step 11 and the scheme of removing is from step 12 to step 19. The tabu rule is a set of rules which prohibit some elements adding into strategy set for certain iteration and is also attached with the rule which enables element to be added into strategy set.

We utilize a greedy algorithm to get an initial solution. Ω is denote the temporary optimal solution. We use Δ_i to denote the remain sensing duration that each task requires. $\sum_{i=1}^{n} min\{\Delta_i, r_{ij}\}$ means the contribution of approaching the boundary of constraints from u_j, that is, the sum of all sensing durations required will reduce by $\sum_{i=1}^{n} min\{\Delta_i, r_{ij}\}$ after u_j is recruited. If $\Delta_i = 0$, that is, $task_i$ has been totally covered by users in Ω at current iteration and u_j will contribute nothing to $task_i$. The criterion of greedy algorithm is to select a user to maximize the reduce of all sensing durations in unit cost. Step 6 delete some of $u_j \in \Omega$ which is redundant. Then, Φ memorizes the optimal strategy.

Algorithm 2. The tCTA Algorithm

Require: C, R, T, U
Ensure: Φ
1: $\Omega = \emptyset$, initial k and η
2: **repeat**
3:    Select a user $u_j \in U \backslash \Omega$ to maximize the $\frac{\sum_{i=1}^{n} min\{\Delta_i, r_{ij}\}}{c_j}$
4:    $\Omega = \Omega \bigcup \{u_j\}$
5: **until** Each constraint is satisfied or $|U \backslash \Omega| < 1$
6: Delete u_j from Ω if it can be deleted and all constraints will also be satisfied.
7: Let $\Phi = \Omega$
8: **repeat**
9:    Update tabu length of each element in X and tabu table X
10:   Select a user $u_k \in \Omega$ to maximize the $\sum_{t_i \in T} min\{\sum_{u_j \in \Omega} r_{ij} - r_{ik}, 0\}$
11:   $\Omega = \Omega \backslash \{u_k\}, X = X \bigcup \{u_k\}$, k = k -1, initial η
12:   **while** Ω does not satisfy all constraints and $|U \backslash \Omega| \geq 1$ and $\eta < \theta$ **do**
13:      Select a user $u_k \in U \backslash (\Omega \bigcup X)$ who announce the minimum cost $c(u_k)$
14:      **if** $|U \backslash (\Omega \bigcup X)| < \varepsilon$ and flag ==true **then**
15:         Select a user $u_l \in X$ who announce the minimum cost
16:         let $u_k = min\{u_k, u_l\}$, remove u_k from X when $u_k = u_l$
17:      **end if**
18:      $\Omega = \Omega \bigcup \{u_k\}$
19:   **end while**
20:   **if** $\sum_{u_i \in \Omega} c(u_i) < \sum_{u_i \in \Phi} c(u_i)$ **then**
21:      $\Phi = \Omega$
22:   **end if**
23: **until** $k < 1$

After initialization, a further tabu search will be conducted based on the initial solution. We use k to denote steps of iteration from Step 8 to Step 23. We first update tabu table X and reduce each tabu length by 1 and remove the element from X when the corresponding table length is less than 1. Then, the user in Ω, who will incur minimum lack of the sum of sensing durations required by each task after removing, will be delete, that is, we can remove a safer user from Ω by Step 10. Next, we select users from $U\backslash(\Omega\bigcup X)$ to satisfy constraints again. To avoid the circle of selecting identical element removed from Ω, we select u_k in $U\backslash(\Omega\bigcup X)$ who announces the minimum cost. Additionally, we set a variable, called flag, true with the probability of 0.8 and false with probability of 0.2. We use η as a timer to prevent wasting much time, which should be less than a threshold θ. When $|U\backslash(\Omega\bigcup X)|$ is less than a threshold ε and $flag$ is true, we will select u_l in X who announces the minimum cost and set u_k as the user who announces less cost between u_k and u_l. One thing should be mentioned, Step 16 promises that u_k will be selected from X if $U\backslash(\Omega\bigcup X)$ is an empty set and some constraints are not satisfied. The addition progress will continue until Ω is a feasible solution after addition progress, we will compare the sum of cost from Ω and Φ to get a better solution. Thus, the progress will get an optimal solution from the tCTA.

4.2 Performance Analysis of Algorithm

As shown in Algorithm 2, the computation overhead is dominated by the process from Step 13 to Step 18. Step 12 will be executed no more than $|U| = n$ times at each iteration. Thus, the computation is $O(kn^2)$. Based on the well known analysis in [14], we can obtain the approximation-ratio of initial process. We will select the better solution as optimal solution among the initial solution and other solution. In this case, the lower bound of this algorithm can be promised by initial progress based on greedy algorithm.

5 Evaluation

In this section, we conduct extensive simulations to evaluate the performances of our algorithm. The compared algorithms, the simulation settings, the metrics, and the results are shown as follows.

5.1 Compared Algorithms

We implement two other corresponding algorithms to exactly evaluate the performance of algorithm: MSSC (Minimize Single Step Cost) and MUC (Minimize Unit Cost). Since our problem is different from existing problems. Thus, two algorithms are both based on the greedy algorithm, and MUC is based on the corresponding algorithm in [8]. Specifically, MSSC selects a user with minimum cost when it covers some sensing slots which is not covered by the other recruited users. MUC picks the user u_j who maximizes $\frac{\sum_{i=1}^{n} min\{\Delta_i, r_{ij}\}}{c_j}$. That is, the user who will be selected covers the maximum remain sensing duration which is not covered by the other recruited users in unit cost.

5.2   Simulation Settings and Metrics

We conduct simulation to evaluate the performance of algorithm with various number of tasks, number of users, the most number of task which users can cover and cost range of each user. We fix three variable while changing another one. In this paper, the cost of each user announced is generated from $[\gamma, 10\gamma]$, where γ is selected from $\{1, 2, 3, 4, 5\}$ and number of users is selected from $\{100, 150, 200, 250, 300\}$. Next, the number of task is selected from $\{20, 30, 40, 50, 60\}$. At last, the largest number of task which users can cover is selected from $\{10, 15, 20, 25, 30\}$. In the simulation, we mainly analyze the influence on cost from other variables.

5.3   Evaluation Results

We evaluate our algorithm and two compared algorithm with four variables: number of tasks (n), number of users (m), the most number of task which users can cover (β) and cost range of each (γ). To reduce the influence from random progress, we make three algorithms run together with same parameters ten times and finally analyze the average cost. The result shows that tCTA algorithm has the best performance.

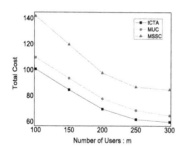   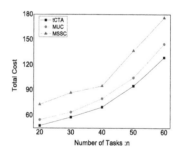

(a) Total Cost vs. Number of Users   (b) Total Cost vs. Number of Tasks

Fig. 1. Performance comparisons: Total cost vs. Number of users m (where n = 40, $\beta = 10$, $\gamma = 2$) and number of tasks n (where m = 200, $\beta = 10$, $\gamma = 2$)

More specially, in Fig. 1(a), the total costs decrease along with the increment of m. It is feasible because increment of number of users will give more better choice to recruit. In Fig. 1(b), the total costs increase with the increments of number of tasks. This is because that tasks usually need more users than before with the increment of number of tasks. In Fig. 2(a), it shows that the most number of tasks which users can perform has little influence on total cost. Finally, along with the increment of cost range of each user, total cost will be more. This is due to the increment of average cost. These results validate our theoretical analysis.

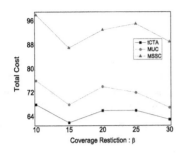 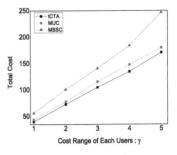

(a) Total Cost vs. Coverage Restriction Upper Bound

(b) Total Cost vs. Cost Range

Fig. 2. Performance comparisons: Total cost vs. Coverage Restriction Upper Bound β (where n = 40, m = 200, γ = 2) and Cost Range γ (where m = 200, β = 10, n = 40)

6   Related Work

In this paper, we study the Cost-minimizing Task Allocation (CTA) problem. There has been much research, focusing on the user recruitment or task allocation in MCS [16]. Some of them focusing on uncertain trajectory such as [8]. But most of researcher study the deterministic trajectory. He et al. in [6] consider allocation with the cost of time budgets. He et al. in [7] design a greedy algorithm and an heuristic algorithm based on GA to separately solve the spatial or temporal coverage by considering both current and future locations of candidate vehicles. Chu et al. in [2] design a data collection system which using integer linear programming to recruit participants to maximize the total explored regions under budget get constrained. Reddy et al. [11] proposed a participants recruitment framework and formulate the location problem as a constrained coverage problem.

Different from others, deterministic performance in our paper does not rely on prediction. Our main goal is to minimize cost while spacial-temporal constraints are satisfied. In our problem, one user can execute more than one task and one task should be executed by more than one user if necessary, which make our problem different from classical set cover problem.

7   Conclusion

In this paper, we introduce the Cost-minimizing Task Allocation problem with spacial and temporal constraints. Then, we merge spatial-temporal constraints to one variable and model this problem. Moreover, we formulate this problem as an extension of set cover problem. Next, we prove that this problem is NP-hard and using classical duality theory to give an approximation ratio. Additionally, we design a heuristic algorithm based on tabu search to solve it. Finally, we give extensive simulations to evaluate the performances of our algorithm.

Acknowledgment. This research was supported by the National Natural Science Foundation of China (NSFC) (Grant No. 61572457, 61379132, 61303206, 61572342, 61502261) and the Natural Science Foundation of Jiangsu Province in China (Grant No. BK20131174, BK2009150).

References

1. Alvarez-Valdes, R., Parreo, F., Tamarit, J.: A tabu search algorithm for a two-dimensional non-guillotine cutting problem. Eur. J. Oper. Res. **183**(3), 1167–1182 (2007)
2. Chu, E.T.H., Chen, Y., Liu, J., Zao, J.: Strategies for crowdsourcing for disaster situation information. WIT Trans. Built Environ. **119**, 257–269 (2011)
3. Du, D.Z., Ko, K.I., Hu, X.: Primal-dual schema and local ratio. In: Du, D.Z., Ko, K.I., Hu, X. (eds.) Design and Analysis of Approximation Algorithms. Springer Optimization and Its Applications, vol. 62, pp. 297–337. Springer, New York (2012)
4. Feige, U.: A threshold of ln n for approximating set cover (preliminary version). In: Proceedings of the Twenty-eighth Annual ACM Symposium on Theory of Computing (1996)
5. Ganti, R.K., Ye, F., Lei, H.: Mobile crowdsensing: current state and future challenges. IEEE Commun. Mag. **49**(11), 32–39 (2011)
6. He, S., Shin, D.H., Zhang, J., Chen, J.: Toward optimal allocation of location dependent tasks in crowdsensing. In: INFOCOM (2014)
7. He, Z., Cao, J., Liu, X.: High quality participant recruitment in vehicle-based crowdsourcing using predictable mobility. In: INFOCOM (2015)
8. Karaliopoulos, M., Telelis, O., Koutsopoulos, I.: User recruitment for mobile crowdsensing over opportunistic networks. In: INFOCOM (2015)
9. Koukoumidis, E., Martonosi, M., Peh, L.S.: Leveraging smartphone cameras for collaborative road advisories. IEEE Trans. Mobile Comput. **11**(5), 707–723 (2012)
10. Rajagopalan, S., Vazirani, V.V.: Primal-dual rnc approximation algorithms for set cover and covering integer programs. SIAM J. Comput. **28**(2), 525–540 (1998)
11. Reddy, S., Estrin, D., Srivastava, M.: Recruitment framework for participatory sensing data collections. In: Floréen, P., Krüger, A., Spasojevic, M. (eds.) Pervasive 2010. LNCS, vol. 6030, pp. 138–155. Springer, Heidelberg (2010)
12. Santis, V.D.: Ear temperature increase produced by cellular phones under extreme exposure conditions. IEEE Trans. Microw. Theory Tech. **60**(6), 1728–1734 (2012)
13. Sherchan, W., Jayaraman, P.P., Krishnaswamy, S., Zaslavsky, A., Loke, S., Sinha, A.: Using on-the-move mining for mobile crowdsensing. In: 2012 IEEE 13th International Conference on Mobile Data Management (MDM) (2012)
14. Wan, P.J., Du, D.Z., Pardalos, P., Wu, W.: Greedy approximations for minimum submodular cover with submodular cost. Comput. Optim. Appl. **45**(2), 463–474 (2010)
15. Xiao, M., Wu, J., Huang, L.: Community-aware opportunistic routing in mobile social networks. IEEE Trans. Comput. **63**(7), 1682–1695 (2014)
16. Xiao, M., Wu, J., Huang, L., Wang, Y., Liu, C.: Multi-task assignment for crowdsensing in mobile social networks. In: INFOCOM (2015)
17. Xu, J., Xiang, J., Yang, D.: Incentive mechanisms for time window dependent tasks in mobile crowdsensing. IEEE Trans. Wirel. Commun. **14**(11), 6353–6364 (2015)

Mining Myself in the Community: Privacy Preserved Crowd Sensing and Computing

Lei Tan, Huiting Fan[✉], Weikang Rui, Zhonghu Xu,
Shuo Zhang, Jing Xu, and Kai Xing

University of Science and Technology of China, Hefei, Anhui, China
{leitan,htfan,jasonrui,xzhh,zshuo,jxu125}@mail.ustc.edu.cn,
kxing@ustc.edu.cn

Abstract. With the raising popularity of online/mobile social applications, many individuals are increasingly attracted to their relative positions when compared to others in terms of emotional mood, travelling location, walking distance, fitness status, etc. These interest can be summarized as one question "where am I in my community?". However, it often forms a deadlock that people are interested in the others' data but are unwilling to disclose their own information (mood, health, etc.).

In order to break the deadlock, we propose a privacy preserving participatory sensing scheme that will not disclose individual's privacy. Specifically, we present a privacy preservation data gathering approach and adopt an improved data mining algorithm to acquire a polynomial approximation function model on distributed user data to provide a privacy preservation method in participatory sensing. Experiments demonstrate that our approach can achieve a valid result comparing with the result without privacy preservation.

Keywords: Privacy · Security · Crowd computing

1 Introduction

Online/mobile social applications and various sensors (mobile phone, tablet PC, ParkNet, pedometer, etc.) have become deeply involved in our daily lives, which consequently triggers a large variety of social participatory sensing applications (Bikenet, DietSense, Ubigreen, etc.). Thus, it's attractive for people to compare with those in the same community in the terms of some private data. For example, one question that can be frequently raised is how well we perform comparing with our friends concerning emotional mood, travelling location, walking distance, fitness status, etc. This can be roughly classified as one question: Where am I in my community? Though adequate evident and underlying data about other participants may immensely help us answer such a question, these data may cause serious leakage of individual privacy (user identity, location, health,

© Springer International Publishing Switzerland 2016
Q. Yang et al. (Eds.): WASA 2016, LNCS 9798, pp. 272–282, 2016.
DOI: 10.1007/978-3-319-42836-9_25

etc.). Consequently there is a surging alert on the conflict between data privacy and participatory social sensing applications.

For the social participatory sensing applications, it is imperative to motivate participations, while at the same time the participatory social sensing process should not violate the privacy of any participating parties (private data). For this purpose, it is essential to develop privacy preserving mining techniques between the users. Specifically, the data analyst (usually the social application server) should be able to extract information about the community (patterns, distributions, etc.), while having no access to any users private data. For the participatory parties, no one can obtain any information about other participants.

In this paper, we propose a privacy preserving computing scheme based on an improved polynomial approximation function model. Each user in the community produces a partial of the overall model's parameters, which can be help to construct the community model. Finally, each user can utilize the community model to compute the probability density function result and find his relative position in the community. In this process, no users' privacy data are disclosed to others, that is, we call the privacy preserving.

Our main contributions can be summarized as follows:

- We propose a privacy preserving design based on an improved data mining algorithm to answer the question "Where am I in my community?" which can help people find their relative statuses in their community.
- We present a privacy preserving method which can get a almost exactly the same data model result without leakage of privacy data as if the original private data were without privacy preserving.
- To the best of our knowledge, there are few methods about privacy preserving participatory crowd sensing and computing the relative position. It is the first work that not only estimating relative position in the community but also ensuring privacy preserving.
- We analyze our approach is robust against collusion attack in theory, which will reveal no privacy information in the existence of a maximum number of collusion parties. The evaluation results corroborate that our approach can help users obtain their corresponding locations as well as break the aforementioned deadlock.

The rest of the paper is organized as follows: Sect. 2 introduces some existing works on privacy preserving methods. Section 3 presents the models and definitions. Details about our privacy-preserving algorithm are presented in Sect. 4. Section 5 is devoted to the method of finding the relative position in my community. Security analyses about our privacy preserving algorithm are reported in Sect. 6. Section 7 reports our experiment results, followed by the conclusion in Sect. 8.

2   Related Work

The first privacy-preserving data mining algorithm was introduced by Agrawal and Srikant [1], which allows parties to cooperate without revealing personal data of any party. He et al. [2] first introduce privacy-preserving data aggregation in WSNs, and present two aggregation methods (CPDA, SMART) for additive aggregation functions. Rahman et al. [3] propose a cluster based additive data aggregation method (REBIVE) using the (k,n) threshold scheme. Feng et al. [4] propose a family of secret perturbation-based schemes that can protect sensor data confidentiality without disrupting additive data aggregation. [5,6] propose privacy preserving data additive data aggregation schemes (AHE, CDA) based on the addition homomorphic encryption. [7,8] use non-encryption technology for data aggregation (GP^{2S}, KIPDA), but they can get an accurate result since the disturbance factor in the real data. Chan et al. [9] present the design and evaluation of PriSense, a new solution to privacy preserving data aggregation in people centric urban sensing systems based on the concept of data slicing and mixing.

Among all the existent privacy preserving solutions, many of them cannot resist against collusion attacks and may leak some intermediate results to potential privacy attacks. In this paper, we propose a robust privacy preserving algorithm which can preserve the privacy of the participating parties in the existence of collusion attacks. Our algorithm can offer savings in processing time through use of inherent parallelism in a distributed system, and would not leak any intermediate computing results that may reveal privacy data to other sensors.

3   Preliminaries, Assumptions and Definitions

3.1   Models and Definitions

We consider a community model consisting of n users $1, 2, \ldots, n$ and a data analyst. Each user i holds his own private information X^j, where X^j has p_i observed data $\{x_1^{(j)}, x_2^{(j)}, \ldots, x_{p_i}^{(j)}\}$. The data analyst is responsible to analyze the data and construct the data model for all the participant users. However, due to the privacy concerns the data analyst cannot access the private information of any participant users.

Our goal is to establish a privacy protection model toward each user. Every user can only know his own privacy data. Our privacy preservation of the proposed protocols is based on semi-honest security model. In this model, each user participating in these protocols has to follow the rules using correct input, and he can collect what he sees during the construction of the model, which is no use to endanger the security. This model is reasonable in many situations since any user who wants to mine others' data will follow these protocols to get the final correct result. Even one user colludes with some other users, which called the collusion attack, he can't obtain anything about others' privacy data.

We assume that:

- All users contribute their own data to participate in the community model construction process, but their data can not be disclosed to others.
- The data analyst in our model is responsible for analyzing the data of all users and constructing a data model for all users.

- The data analyst and all participatory users follow a semi-honest model. Briefly, they are semi-honest and follow the base protocol. Nevertheless, they are interest in others' privacy data, so they may record intermediate information.
- The attacker can be any user. Even there maybe exist some evil users which share their results they have collected and try to deduce private information of other users, the number of these users in collusion is limited.

4   Privacy Preserved Community Modeling

In this section, we present our model in the community for privacy preserving. Basically, there are three steps to construct the community model. Initially, each user uses the polynomial approximation function to build his own data model and generates the parameters of his data model. Thereafter, the data analyst issues a probability coefficient to each user according to the amount of each user's data. Then all users multiply the probability coefficient by their data models, slice them in a certain way and send all the sliced model to other user randomly. Eventually, all the users send the sum of all the received data to the data analyst. As a result, the data analyst can construct the final community model for all users at the community.

4.1   Step 1: Function Modeling and Function Slicing at Each User

Every user in the whole community model should keep his own data X^j secretly and cannot deduce other users' privacy data.

Each user transforms his data into the following form (x_i^j, y_i^j), $i = 1, 2, \ldots, p_i$, where y_i^j is the probability of x_i^j in the user's data set. With the constructed data set, all users can build their own data models with the polynomial approximation function algorithm in a distributed system, which turns user's data model into a polynomial form.

$$f^j(x) = \sum_{i=0}^{m} A_i^j x^i \tag{1}$$

where $f^j(x) = y^j = A^j X$, $A^j = (A_0^j, A_1^j, \ldots, A_m^j)$, $X = (1, x, \ldots, x^m)^T$.

From Fig. 1(a), we can see the Probability Distribution Model of a user's privacy data, which describes the distribution features of the private data. Then we generate the polynomial approximation function model depending on the constructed data set in Fig. 1(b). We can see that the polynomial approximation function can represent the user's data distribution features in the following process, because the approximation function has almost the same features as the private data and will not leak out the real accurate data, which is useful for our proposition to protect the private data.

In addition, the data analyst issues a probability coefficient π^j to each user according to the amount of each user's data, which is the ratio between the

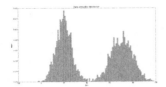 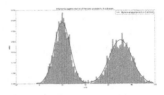

(a) Private data probability distribution (b) Polynomial approximation of the data probability distribution

Fig. 1. Data probability distribution and Polynomial approximation function

number of user's data and the number of the whole community's data. Each user multiplies the probability coefficient by every item of his model.

$$\pi^j f^j(x) = [\pi^j A_0^j \ \pi^j A_1^j \ \pi^j A_2^j \ \cdots \ \pi^j A_m^j] \begin{bmatrix} 1 \\ x \\ x^2 \\ \vdots \\ x^m \end{bmatrix} \tag{2}$$

"Slicing": Each user $j(j = 1, 2, \ldots, n)$ slices his every coefficient $\pi^j A_i^j$ of his function model into c parts: $A_{1i}^j, A_{2i}^j, \ldots, A_{ci}^j$, for which we should make sure that $\sum_{k=1}^{c} A_{ki}^j = \pi^j A_i^j$, where c is a constant and $n/2 \leq c \leq n, i = 0, 1, \ldots, m$ and $A_{1i}^j, A_{2i}^j, \ldots, A_{ci}^j$ can be negative or positive.

Therefore j's model function $\pi^j f^j(x)$ can be written as a new functional form:

$$\pi^j f^j(x) = \mathbb{I}_c \begin{bmatrix} \begin{bmatrix} A_{10}^j & A_{11}^j & A_{12}^j & \cdots & A_{1m}^j \\ A_{20}^j & A_{21}^j & A_{22}^j & \cdots & A_{2m}^j \\ \vdots & \vdots & \vdots & & \vdots \\ A_{c0}^j & A_{c1}^j & A_{c2}^j & \cdots & A_{cm}^j \end{bmatrix} \begin{bmatrix} 1 \\ x \\ x^2 \\ \vdots \\ x^m \end{bmatrix} \end{bmatrix} = \mathbb{I}_c B^j X \tag{3}$$

where $\mathbb{I}_c = [1 \ 1 \ 1 \ \cdots \ 1]_c$ is a c-dimensional unit vector. Take the ith row of the matrix B^j as B_i^j.

$$B_i^j = [A_{i0}^j \ A_{i1}^j \ A_{i2}^j \ \cdots \ A_{im}^j] \tag{4}$$

"Mixing": For each user, one of the coefficient matrix row is kept by himself and the remaining row pieces are sent to other users randomly. We denote B_i^{jk} as a piece of matrix row form user j to user k. If user k does not receive any matrix row from user j, we denote $B^{jk} = 0$.

Since a user j receives the first piece of coefficient matrix row, until to all pieces sent to him are received. Then he aggregates all the received information, mixes them as $U^j = B^{1j} + B^{2j} + B^{3j} + \cdots + B^{nj}$ and sends the result U^j to the data analyst.

4.2 Step 2: Remodeling at Data Analyst

"Collecting and remodeling the final model": All users collect coefficient matrix row and send the result to the data analyst. Upon receiving the first result, data analyst waits for a certain time and ensures all the results are received.

Then the data analyst can obtain the coefficient of the model in the community, thus the final model $F(x)$ can be reconstructed.

$$F(x) = \mathbb{I}_{1 \times n} \left[\begin{bmatrix} U^1 \\ U^2 \\ \vdots \\ U^n \end{bmatrix}_{n \times (m+1)} \begin{bmatrix} 1 \\ x \\ x^2 \\ \cdots \\ x^m \end{bmatrix}_{(m+1) \times 1} \right] = \sum_{i=0}^{m} b_i x^i \tag{5}$$

Figure 2 illustrates the process with $n = 4$ users and slicing size $c = 4$.

5 Mining Myself in My Community

After the previous sections, the data analyst has got the community data distribution model as follow.

$$F(x) = b_0 + b_1 x + b_2 x^2 + \cdots + b_m x^m = \sum_{i=0}^{m} b_i x^i \tag{6}$$

As the model can be built according to some aspect of data in the community, so it can describe the features in this community. Without the need to deliver private data everyone can find his relative position by computing the quantile.

Algorithm 1. Privacy Preserved community modeling

Input: A user's data set with p_j observational data $\{x_1^{(j)}, x_2^{(j)}, \cdots, x_{p_j}^{(j)}\}$, user's data number probability coefficient π^j.

Onput: The user's polynomial approximation function model $\pi^j f^j(x)$, and the coefficient matrix B^j

1: Each user transforms his data into the form (x_i^j, y_i^j), where y_i^j is the probability of x_i^j in the user's data set.

2: All users build their own data models with the polynomial approximation function algorithm in a distributed system,

3: Each user slices his data distribution model by Eq. 3 to obtain the coefficient matrix B^j.

4: For each user, one of the coefficient matrix rows is kept by himself and the remaining row pieces are sent to other users randomly.

5: Each user collects all the received matrix rows, mixes them and send the mixed result to the data analyst, in the same way, the data analyst can reconstruct the final model in the community by Eq. 5

---

6   Security Analysis

Before expounding our security analysis for each stage stated in Sect. 4, we first declare our goals for privacy preserving as follow.

- The private data of each user can only known by the user himself and can't be divulged to any one else.
- Local model $f^i(x)$ can only known to the user i and each user can't deduce other user's model, even some of other participatory users share all what they have collected.
- Though the data analyst is on the basis of sensors' private data to establish the community model, he know nothing about the privacy data of those who deliver data to him at all, neither the user's local function model.
- Do not disclose any midterm calculating outcomes which may reveal private data of users during the process of the community model remodeling.

6.1   Security Analysis for the Stage of Function Modeling at Each User

For the function modeling part displayed in Sect. 4, each user build his own local model over his private data and slices his function model with the polynomial approximation function, which is accomplished by each user. Consequently, no one else, even the data analyst, can obtain the user's private data or function model, unless the user issues the data or function model to others, which is called

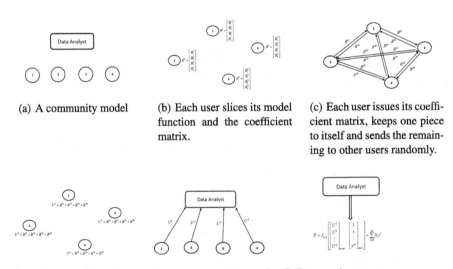

(a) A community model

(b) Each user slices its model function and the coefficient matrix.

(c) Each user issues its coefficient matrix, keeps one piece to itself and sends the remaining to other users randomly.

(d) Each user collects its received data.

(e) All users send the results to the data analyst.

(f) Data analyst reconstructs the model for the community.

Fig. 2. The process of privacy preserved community modeling

collusion attack. Furthermore, we can make these two steps completed by each user in parallel to provide a high efficient procedure for our approach.

6.2   Security Analysis for Stage of Function Slicing at Each User

In slicing and mixing parts mentioned in Sect. 4, firstly, all that are transmitted among users is a kind of particular variant of the coefficient of the users, which means that our approach preserves the model of users, as well as users' private data. After building his local function model, each user slices his function coefficients into a coefficient matrix whose row number is decided by the user himself, that is, others are absolutely ignorant of the row number. Secondly, for purpose of receiving every coefficient matrix row from others each user will schedule a certain time for waiting. Since collecting all the received data, each user mingles and transmits them to the data analyst. Finally, the data analyst rebuilds the community model with the received coefficient matrix rows.

The private data and local model of each user and the global community model of the analyst is protected by the following aspects:

- Since the row number of the coefficient matrix of each user's function model is private, it's impossible for anyone other who collects all data pieces and tries to rebuild the user's function model to deduce the private data. Others have no idea about how many pieces a user have sent out, therefore they couldn't decide how many data pieces should be intercepted.
- No one could collect all the data pieces since there is always one row in the original user. To find out the remain users who had received coefficient matrix information must be impossible in a huge community model.
- Supposed that a user i has received one coefficient matrix piece of user j, he could not rebuild the user j's model with one coefficient piece. Furthermore, even collecting all the data pieces from all the remaining users, user i still can't reestablish the model of user j, because it's impossible for him to distinguish all the pieces of user j from so many different user's pieces.
- The data analyst rebuilds the global model with the received coefficient matrix rows which are intermingled with each other. Hence, the data analyst has no capability to make any user's model distinct from all, not to mention a user's private data.
- When encountering collusion attack, even $n - 1$ users vs 1, our method is robust. There is no way for anyone to infer the private data of someone else, because always one coefficient matrix piece is preserved by the original user.

6.3   Security Analysis for Mining Myself in My Community

In the process of mining myself in my community mentioned in Sect. 5, the data analyst has got the community data distribution model and each user can find his relative position by compute the quantile, which is an easy way and doesn't leak out the user's private information. User can get the answer by himself and do not need to provide any data to anyone else, unless it wants. Therefore there is no risk of data privacy and the privacy results leaked out.

In summary, using above scheme, every user can get an answer to find the relative position in the community without divulging his privacy, which can reach our goal of privacy preservation.

7   Experiment Study

In this section we evaluate the privacy-preserving schemes presented in this paper. Our experiment study is based on three different data sets. The first one is a natural number data set which is generated randomly, The second data set is the Individual household electric power consumption Data Set [10], from which we use the data of household global minute-averaged active power to construct

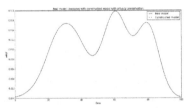
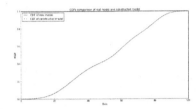

(a) Real model compares with constructed model under privacy preservation.

(b) The CDFs comparison of real model and constructed model.

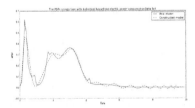
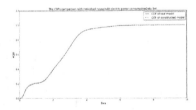

(c) The PDFs comparison with Individual household electric power consumption Data Set.

(d) The CDFs comparison with Individual household electric power consumption Data Set.

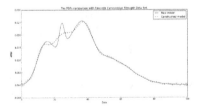
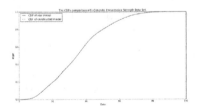

(e) The PDFs comparison with Concrete Compressive Strength Data Set.

(f) The CDFs comparison with Concrete Compressive Strength Data Set.

Fig. 3. The results of each experiment.

the whole community model. In the third experiment, we consider Concrete Compressive Strength [11] as the experiment data set, which contains roughly 1030 instances. The last two data sets can be found in UCI Machine Learning Repository.

Figure 3 exemplifies our results of experiment about the first data set. Figure 3(a) and (b) illuminate the PDFs and the CDFs of the real model which is constructed by all privacy data and the constructed model with privacy preservation. The features of the real model and the constructed model is almost the same, which means that our method can achieve a high accuracy.

To prove our method can be used in real life, we carried out the following experiments. In the second experiment, we use the Individual household electric power consumption Data Set. We divide the whole data set into several parts, each of which represents every user's privacy data. We depict the PDF and CDF of household global minute-averaged active power in Fig. 3(c) and (d) respectively. Each user can get his relative position with the constructed model. In addition, the experiment result substantiates that our scheme can acquire a high accuracy in the real life, which can achieve the goal of mining myself with privacy preserving. Furthermore, Fig. 3(e) and (f) indicate the PDF and CDF of Concrete Compressive Strength Data Set also have a terrific performance.

Eventually, we compare the real model of real private data with the constructed model under privacy preserving. They seem nearly the same as each other, hence we can conclude that our solution performs well from not only in the experiment data set but also in the real life data set, which can be used in the real life to help people mining themselves with privacy preserving.

8   Conclusion

In this paper we propose a privacy preservation data gathering approach and adopt an improved data mining algorithm to acquire a data distribution model on distributed user data to provide a privacy preservation method in participatory sensing. Our algorithm can securely compute the global community model for each participant user without disclosing any privacy information to other participants, which can help users to find the relative position and answer the question "Where am I in my community?" under a privacy preserving scheme. Through the security analysis, we also prove that even in the case of collusion attack, no private information of the participation users will be released.

References

1. Agrawal, R., Srikant, R.: Privacy-preserving data mining. ACM SIGMOD Rec. **29**(2), 439–450 (2000)
2. He, W., Liu, X., Nguyen, H., Nahrstedt, K., Abdelzaher, T.: PDA: privacy-preserving data aggregation in wireless sensor networks. In: 26th IEEE International Conference on Computer Communications, INFOCOM 2007, pp. 2045–2053. IEEE (2007)

3. Rahman, F., Hoque, E., Ahamed, S.I.: Preserving privacy in wireless sensor networks using reliable data aggregation. ACM SIGAPP Appl. Comput. Rev. **11**(3), 52–62 (2011)
4. Feng, T., Wang, C., Zhang, W., Ruan, L.: Confidentiality protection for distributed sensor data aggregation. In: The 27th Conference on Computer Communications, INFOCOM 2008. IEEE (2008)
5. Castelluccia, C., Mykletun, E., Tsudik, G.: Efficient aggregation of encrypted data in wireless sensor networks. In: The Second Annual International Conference on Mobile and Ubiquitous Systems: Networking and Services, MobiQuitous 2005, pp. 109–117. IEEE (2005)
6. Girao, J., Westhoff, D., Schneider, M.: CDA: concealed data aggregation for reverse multicast traffic in wireless sensor networks. In: 2005 IEEE International Conference on Communications, ICC 2005, vol. 5, pp. 3044–3049. IEEE (2005)
7. Groat, M.M., He, W., Forrest, S.: Kipda: k-indistinguishable privacy-preserving data aggregation in wireless sensor networks. In: 2011 Proceedings IEEE INFOCOM, pp. 2024–2032. IEEE (2011)
8. Zhang, W., Wang, C., Feng, T.: Gp^{2}s: generic privacy-preservation solutions for approximate aggregation of sensor data (concise contribution). In: Sixth Annual IEEE International Conference on Pervasive Computing and Communications, PerCom 2008, pp. 179–184. IEEE (2008)
9. Chan, H., Perrig, A., Song, D.: Secure hierarchical in-network aggregation in sensor networks. In: Proceedings of the 13th ACM Conference on Computer and Communications Security, pp. 278–287. ACM (2006)
10. http://archive.ics.uci.edu/ml/datasets/Individual+household+electric+power+consumption
11. http://archive.ics.uci.edu/ml/datasets/Concrete+Compressive+Strength

Exploiting Spectrum Availability and Quality in Routing for Multi-hop Cognitive Radio Networks

Lichen Zhang[1,2], Zhipeng Cai[3,4(✉)], Peng Li[1,2,3], and Xiaoming Wang[1,2]

[1] Key Laboratory Modern Teaching Technology,
Ministry of Education, Xi'an 710119, China
[2] School of Computer Science, Shaanxi Normal University, Xi'an 710119, China
{zhanglichen,lipeng,wangxm}@snnu.edu.cn
[3] Department of Computer Science, Geogia State University, Atlanta 30303, USA
zcai@gsu.edu
[4] College of Computer Science and Technology, Harbin Engineering University,
Harbin 150001, China

Abstract. Cognitive radio networks (CRNs) are considered as a promising solution to the problem of spectrum under utilization and artificial radio spectrum scarcity. The paradigm of dynamic spectrum access allows secondary users (SUs) to utilize wireless spectrum resources which belong to primary users (PUs) with minimal interference to PUs. Due to the dynamic spectrum availability and quality, routing for SUs in multi-hop CRNs is a challenge. In this paper, we introduce novel routing metrics that estimate both the future spectrum availability and the average transmission time. Then, we propose two routing algorithms for multi-hop CRNs that attempt to reduce the probability of spectrum handoff and rerouting upon PU's arrival. Finally, we conduct simulations, whose results show that our proposed algorithms lead to a significant performance improvement over the reference algorithm.

Keywords: Multi-hop cognitive radio networks · Routing · Dynamic spectrum availability · Spectrum-handoff · Average transmission delay

1 Introduction

Recently, the unlicensed portions of wireless spectrums have become increasingly crowded with the rapid growth of wireless communication devices and mobile applications. Meanwhile, a study indicated that the available licensed portion of the spectrums is heavily allocated, but vastly under-utilized [16]. To efficiently utilize the available spectrum resources, cognitive radio has been proposed [8]. Accordingly, cognitive radio networks (CRNs) emerged as a promising solution to the problem of spectrum under utilization and artificial radio spectrum scarcity [18]. In a CRN, there exist two categories of users: secondary users (SUs) and primary users (PUs). By using dynamic spectrum access technology, SUs carrying with cognitive radio devices can sense the surrounding spectrum utilization

© Springer International Publishing Switzerland 2016
Q. Yang et al. (Eds.): WASA 2016, LNCS 9798, pp. 283–294, 2016.
DOI: 10.1007/978-3-319-42836-9_26

and then access spectral holes opportunistically without harmful interference to PUs. During data transmission in a licensed spectrum, an SU has to vacate the spectrum band and conducts spectrum handoff to another spectral hole at once a PU reclaims the spectrum.

Although plenty of routing schemes [13, 19, 21–23] for traditional wireless networks have been proposed, they can not be applied in multi-hop CRNs. In multi-hop CRNs, routing is a challenging problem due to the high dynamic spectrum availability and channel quality [5, 6, 17, 20]. First, there usually does not exist a common available channel in any path between a source and a destination in a multi-hop CRN. Traditional routing approaches in ad-hoc networks which try to find a path with one common channel would fail. In fact, a path may exist in which each segment may share a common channel. Second, the available spectrums change dynamically and frequently, which requires the consideration of both the current available spectrums and the future spectrum dynamics in routing. Since the availability of each channel may change dynamically, in a multi-hop CRN, frequent spectrum handoffs and rerouting may occur. On the other hand, spectrum handoff and rerouting can cause a significant degradation of CRN performance when a data transmission is interrupted by the arrival of PUs. Thus, it is necessary to find a path with less number of spectrum handoffs and rerouting. Third, the different parameters of spectrums such as bandwidths and average idle/busy time influence the quality of the path greatly. Thus, how to utilize these characteristics in routing is important yet difficult.

Recently, a variety of routing approaches have been proposed for CRNs [1, 3, 4, 6, 7, 9, 10, 12], among which there exist two categories of routing schemes in multi-hop CRNs: on-demand routing and opportunistic routing. An on-demand routing scheme (e.g., AODV [14]) involves on-demand route discovery to find spectrum-aware end-to-end routes as well as route maintenance in case of route breaks due to node mobility or dynamic spectrum availability. Chowdhury et al. [6] proposed a geographic forwarding based spectrum aware routing protocol (SEARCH). In SEARCH, route requests are broadcast on every channel using greedy geographic routing, based on which the destination can determine a path with minimal hop count and interference with PUs. However, SEARCH's path optimization is very sensitive to spectrum dynamics due to the lack of consideration of future PUs' arrivals and channel qualities. Badarneh et al. [1] proposed a maximum probability of success (MaxPoS) routing scheme for multi-hop CRNs. In MaxPoS, instant available spectrums and the required transmission time are considered. The transmission probability of success between two nodes by using a common spectrum is defined as the probability that the current available spectrum will remains available for the required minimal transmission time; for two neighboring nodes with a number of common spectrums, the transmission probability of success is defined as the maximal one for all the available spectrums; for a path with several segments, the transmission probability of success is defined as the minimal one for all the segments of the path. In MaxPoS, the path with the maximal transmission probability of success is chosen. However, only one spectrum between two neighboring nodes is considered and chosen, and the other available and currently unavailable spectrums are not taken into consideration. Since the availability of each channel may change dynamically, rerouting has to be conducted on PU's arrival, thus leading to long delivery delay and also decreasing the delivery ratio of packets. Jin *et al.* [10] proposed a geographic routing protocol (TIGHT) for multi-hop CRNs. In TIGHT, the source node tries to select the shortest path along the perimeters of some specific PU regions to avoid the interference with PUs. TIGHT works well in sparse environments especially when there exists a path without PU's activities, and has a poor performance in those scenarios with high dynamic spectrum availability and channel quality.

For the opportunistic routing schemes, a node tries to select a number of candidates from its neighbors based on locally identified spectrum access opportunities, and then broadcasts packets while at the MAC layer only one node is chosen as the actual relay node based on the reception results in a posteriori manner. Liu *et al.* [12] proposed an opportunistic cognitive routing (OCR) protocol for multi-hop CRNs, in which a relay candidate is assigned a higher priority if it has a larger link throughput, a greater relay distance advancement, or a higher link reliability. Although broadcast mechanism decreases the probability of retransmission, opportunistic routing schemes usually fall in local optimization due to the absence of global information such as current or future spectrum availability in other regions.

To fully utilize the instant spectrum availability and future spectrum dynamics, in this paper, we introduce novel routing metrics for multi-hop CRNs. Our goal is to provide a routing approach to increase the delivery ratio of packets and decrease the delivery delay by optimally selecting paths and channel assignments with the above considerations.

The rest of the paper is organized as follows. Section 2 describes the system model and routing metrics. Section 3 presents our routing algorithms, and followed by the simulations in Sect. 4. Finally, Sect. 5 concludes the paper.

2   System Model and Problem Definition

2.1   System Model and Assumptions

We consider a multi-hop CRN consisting of static PUs and SUs. We assume each PU has a licensed channel from a set of orthogonal channels $C = \{c_1, c_2, \ldots, c_m\}$, and each SU can access an unused licensed channel (also called spectrum hole). Furthermore, an SU must vacate the channel and conducts spectrum handoff to another spectral hole at once a PU reclaims the channel.

In a CRN, we assume that a common control channel (CCC) is used by SUs over which the controlling messages are exchanged. Besides the CCC, we assume that each SU is also equipped with a half-duplex cognitive radio, which enables it to switch to any of the available channels [15]. We also assume that each SU has the same fixed maximum transmit power over a given channel.

Furthermore, we model PUs' activities as independent and identically distributed across the available channels. The ON-OFF transitions of PU activity for PU i using channel $c_k \in C$ follows a Poisson model in which ON and OFF periods, namely $T_{\text{on},i}^k$ and $T_{\text{off},i}^k$, are exponentially distributed with rates λ_i^k and μ_i^k, respectively [2]. We assume that all PUs' activities in a channel k are represented by T_{on}^k and T_{off}^k, and each PU uses a single channel k only. SUs track the channel usage pattern, i.e., ON or OFF, and obtain the channel usage statistics through periodic sensing operations. Generally, the statistics of channel usage time change slowly. We assume that each SU has the knowledge about the spectrum usage statistics of PUs by performing spectrum sensing with the operation of neighboring SUs. The parameter estimation is beyond the scope of this paper, and the details can be found in [11].

2.2   Routing Metrics

As described in the system model, the PUs' activities (i.e., active/inactive) can be modeled as an alternating renewal process (ON-OFF model). According to the theory of alternating renewal process, from the point of long-run, the limiting probability that a given channel k possessed by PU i is inactive (i.e., OFF) at any time (denoted by $\mathrm{P}_{\text{off},i}^k$) is equal to

$$\mathrm{P}_{\text{off},i}^k = \frac{\mu_{i,k}}{\mu_{i,k} + \lambda_{i,k}},$$

where $\mu_{i,k}$ and $\lambda_{i,k}$ are the rates of Poisson distributions of PU i over channel k in inactive and active states respectively.

We use Shannon capacity to compute the achievable data transmission rate between two neighboring SUs (denoted by i, j) over a given channel k as follows

$$\nu_k = B + \log_2 \left(1 + \frac{P_{i,j}^k}{B \times N_0} \right),$$

where ν_k, $P_{i,j}^k$, B, and N_0, respectively, denote the data transmission rate, the received power for SU j, the channel bandwidth, and the thermal noise power density. We should note that, the received power $P_{i,j}^k$ is directly proportional to the transmitted power of node i, and inversely proportional to the square of distance between two SUs. Thus, under the assumption that each SU uses the same fixed maximum transmit power over a given channel, we find that the achievable data transmission rate is only related with the distance of two neighboring SUs. Given the size of a packet, the required transmission time over channel k can be computed by s/ν_k, where s is the size of packet, and ν_k is the achievable data transmission rate over channel k.

As we know that the PU's arrival on a channel will interrupt the transmission of SUs and then increases the overall transmission time, the transmission success probability between two neighboring SUs is related with both the required transmission time for a packet and the spectrum availability time on the channel. Thus, like [1], we define the transmission success probability between two neighboring SUs, i and j, over channel k as follows

$$P_{\text{suc}}^{k}(i,j) = P\left(T_k \geq \frac{s}{\nu_k}\right) = e^{-s/(\nu_k \cdot \mu_k)} \tag{1}$$

where s is the packet size, μ_k is the rate of Poisson distribution of channel k in inactive state, and ν_k is the achievable data transmission rate over channel k.

Since both the required transmission time and the spectrum available time are considered in the transmission success probability, it is adopted in various works (e.g., [1]) to improve routing performance. However, from the observation, we know that the above metric does not consider the number and quality of all the available and temporarily unavailable spectrums. Supposing an SU is transmitting data over a channel which is currently the only available channel, rerouting occurs if a PU returns and accesses the only available channel, and thus increasing end-to-end delay and degrading routing performance. Thus, it would be better to consider the number and the quality of all the available and temporarily unavailable spectrums in routing in multi-hop CRNs. In this paper, we introduce novel routing metrics in which the above factors are considered.

Suppose there exist a number of available channels between two neighboring SUs. If we do not limit the end-to-end transmission delay, we could conduct retransmission over other channels when the transmission over one channel failed. In this case, with the number of retransmission increasing, the limiting transmission success probability is 1. Even there is only one channel, the above statement also holds because an SU could wait for the next available time period of channel. However, it is not the case in real scenarios due to the fact that a packet has a limited TTL (time-to-live) and has to be dropped if its TTL expires.

If we restrict the number of transmission over one channel to 1, the transmission success probability over all the available channels is $1 - (1 - p_1)(1 - p_2)\cdots(1 - p_m)$, where $p_k = P_{\text{suc}}^{k}(i,j)$ is the transmission success probability over channel k, and m is the number of available channels. Evidently, the more the number of available channels is, the larger the transmission success probability will be. However, the above computation is under the assumption that all the states do not change, thus not accurate because the states of some channels (available or unavailable) may change during the transmission over a channel.

In order to compute the transmission success probability between two neighboring SUs more accurately, we allow one retransmission between two neighboring SUs if the first transmission fails. The more retransmissions are allowed, the larger the transmission success probability will be, and the much more difficult the above metric is computed, which makes it less feasible in applications. Thus, in this paper, we assume only one retransmission is allowed. Under this assumption, we introduce a novel definition of transmission success probability between two neighboring SUs in which the states and qualities of all channels are considered.

Definition 1. *The transmission success probability between two neighboring SUs, i and j, over all channels under the assumption of one retransmission* *allowed, denoted by $P_{\text{suc}}(i,j)$, is defined as follows,*

$$P_{\text{suc}}(i,j) = p_0 + (1 - p_0) \sum_{k=1}^{n-1} \left(v_k \prod_{m=1}^{k-1} (1 - v_m) p_k \right) \tag{2}$$

where $p_0 = P_{\text{suc}}^{k'}(i,j)$ is the largest transmission success probability over all the available channels between SUs i and j, v_k is the probability that channel k is available when the first transmission fails, $p_k = P_{\text{suc}}^k(i,j)$ is the transmission success probability between SUs i and j over channel k, and n is the number of all the available and unavailable channels between SUs i and j.

From the observation, under the assumption that only one retransmission is allowed, we find that when there exist multiple available channels a higher transmission success probability between two neighboring SUs could be achieved if the channel with the largest transmission success probability is first tried. Thus, in order to increase the transmission probability, when an SU wants to transmit packets to its neighbor, it first attempts to apply the available channel over which the largest transmission success probability is achieved.

In Definition 1, we have to compute v_k, the probability that channel k is available when the first transmission fails. There exist two cases for the state of channel k when the first transmission fails: one is available, and the other is unavailable. Thus, conditioning the state of channel k when the first transmission fails, the probability v_k can be computed as follows,

$$v_k = \max \left(e^{-s/(2v_k \mu_k)}, \frac{\mu_k}{\mu_k + \lambda_k} \right) \tag{3}$$

where s is the size of packet, v_k is the achievable data transmission rate over channel k, μ_k is the rate of Poisson distribution of channel k in available state, and λ_k is the rate of Poisson distribution of channel k in unavailable state.

In Eq. 3, $e^{-s/(2v_k \mu_k)}$ is the probability that channel k remains available when the packet transmission fails with the condition that channel k was available when the first transmission started, and $\mu_k/(\mu_k + \lambda_k)$ is the limiting probability that channel k is available.

Therefore, we define our first routing metric, the transmission success probability over a path under the assumption of one retransmission allowed.

Definition 2. *The transmission success probability over a path p, denoted by TSP_p, is defined as follows,*

$$\text{TSP}_p = \min_{(i,j) \in p} P_{\text{suc}}(i,j) \tag{4}$$

where (i,j) is a pair of neighboring SUs in path p, and $P_{\text{suc}}(i,j)$ is the transmission success probability between two neighboring SUs, i and j.

In order to decrease the end-to-end transmission delay, we consider the average transmission time from source to destination in our routing. With the condition of successful transmission from SU i to its neighboring SU j, the transmission time can be computed.

Definition 3. *The transmission delay between two neighboring SUs, i and j, over all channels under the assumption that the packet transmission succeeds within at most two attempts, denoted by $T_{i,j}$, is defined as follows,*

$$T_{i,j} = \frac{s}{\nu_0} \cdot p_0 + (1 - p_0) \cdot \sum_{k=1}^{n-1} \left(\left(\frac{s}{2\nu_o} + \frac{s}{\nu_k} \right) \cdot v_k \cdot \prod_{m=1}^{k-1} (1 - v_m)p_k \right) \quad (5)$$

where s is the size of the packet, $p_0 = P_{\mathrm{suc}}^{k'}(i,j)$ is the largest transmission success probability over all the available channels between SUs i and j, ν_k is the achievable data transmission rate over channel k, v_k is the probability that channel k is available when the first transmission fails, $p_k = P_{\mathrm{suc}}^{k}(i,j)$ is the transmission success probability between SUs i and j over channel k, and n is the number of all the available and unavailable channels between SUs i and j.

Based on the definition of transmission delay between two neighboring SUs, we can define a metric over a path as the total transmission delay from a source to a destination.

Definition 4. *The transmission delay over a path p, denoted by TTD_p, is defined as follows,*

$$\mathrm{TTD}_p = \sum_{(i,j) \in p} T_{i,j} \quad (6)$$

where (i, j) is a pair of neighboring SUs in path p, and $T_{i,j}$ is the transmission delay between two neighboring SUs, i and j.

3   The Proposed Routing Algorithms

In this section, based on the above routing metrics, we propose two routing algorithms, namely, Maximum Success Probability (MaxSP), and Minimum Expected Transmission Delay (MinETD), respectively.

3.1   Maximum Success Probability (MaxSP) Algorithm

Algorithm 1 describes how the MaxSP algorithm constructs its desired path from a source SU S to a destination SU D. First, S initiates a connection to D by broadcasting an AODV-style Route Request (RREQ) messages over CCC to its neighboring SUs, who forward them on. The RREQ message also accumulates information about the transmission success probabilities using (4) along the path to D. Second, the destination D performs Route Selection and Scheduling by collecting a number of routes and choosing the optimal route based on the transmission success probabilities along the path. After that, D constructs a route reply message, and sends back to S.

Algorithm 1. Maximum Success Probability (MaxSP) Algorithm

Input: source S, destination D, multi-hop CRN
Output: the path with MaxSP
1 S broadcasts RREQ messages to its neighboring SUs over CCC;
2 **for** *each node x receiving RREQ message of S* **do**
3   **if** $x = D$ **then**
4   D computes TSP_p using (4);

5   **else**
6   x computes $P_{\mathrm{suc}}(i,j)$ using (1);
7   x broadcasts RREQ messages to its neighboring SUs over CCC;

8 After a fixed time units on the reception of the first copy of RREQ, node D chooses the best path with maximum TSP_p, and sends back to S.

Algorithm 2. Minimum Expected Transmission Delay (MinETD) Algorithm

---

Input: source S, destination D, multi-hop CRN
Output: the path with MinETD
1 S broadcasts RREQ messages to its neighboring SUs over CCC;
2 **for** *each node x receiving RREQ message of S* **do**
3   **if** $x = D$ **then**
4   D computes TTD_p using (6);

5   **else**
6   x computes $T_{i,j}$ using (5);
7   x broadcasts RREQ messages to its neighboring SUs over CCC;

8 After a fixed time units on the reception of the first copy of RREQ, node D chooses the best path with minimum TTD_p, and sends back to S.

3.2 Minimum Expected Transmission Delay (MinETD) Algorithm

Compared with MaxSP, the main difference in the MinETD algorithm is that the routing metric used in the latter is the minimum expected transmission delay. Algorithm 2 describes how the MinETD algorithm constructs its desired path from a source SU S to a destination SU D.

4 Simulations

4.1 Simulation Settings

In this section, we conduct simulations to evaluate the performance of our proposed routing algorithms by using the NS-2 simulator. In order to compare our proposed algorithms with others, we set the same simulation scenarios as in [1]. In the simulation scenario, the simulation area is $1000 \times 1000\mathrm{m}^2$, in which the numbers of SUs and PUs are assumed to be 50 and 10, respectively. The radio range and the interference range are set to 250 m and 550 m, respectively. The average spectrum busy time of the various PU channels are ranged in $[\,0.5, 25\,]$ms. The bandwidth B, and thermal noise power density N_0 are set to 0.5 MHz, and 0.5×10^{12}W/Hz for all channels. We deploy the locations of SUs and PUs randomly in the simulation area. And then, we run the simulations 100 times, each of which lasts for 300 seconds.

4.2 Simulation Results

Throughput Vs. PUs Availability We first evaluate the throughput of our algorithms with different values of the PUs's availability probability (the limiting probability of the channels in available state, P_{off}). The values of the channels of PUs in available state varies from $P_{off} = 0.1$ to $P_{off} = 0.9$. A larger value of channel availability indicates that a higher usability of channels by SUs. The data transmission power (Ptr) is set to 0.1 W and 0.5 W, and the size of packet is 2 KB. In Fig. 1, we can see that, the throughput of all the algorithms increases with the increase of PUs availability, and both our algorithms outperform Max-Pos [1]. The reason is that, the states of all the available and unavailable channels are considered in our algorithms, while in MaxPos, only one available channel is evaluated between two neighboring SUs in a path, and the state of other channels are not considered. Thus, if there exists only one available channel in some segments of a path, rerouting has to be conducted, leading to a decrease of throughput and delivery ratio. In our algorithms, however, both the number and quality of all available and unavailable channels are evaluated in our routing metrics. Thus, in a routing process, the path with a higher transmission success probability will be chosen. Furthermore, as the transmission power Ptr increases from 0.1 W (Fig. 1(a)) to 0.5 W (Fig. 1(b)), the transmission rate over each channel increases, leading to the increase of the throughput.

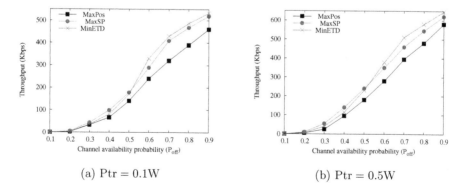

(a) Ptr = 0.1W   (b) Ptr = 0.5W

Fig. 1. Throughput vs. PUs availability.

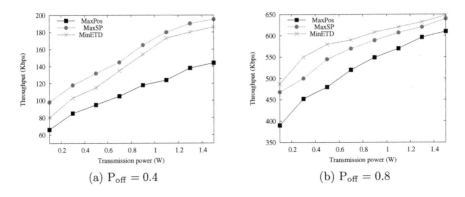

Fig. 2. Throughput vs. transmission power.

Throughput Vs. Transmission Power In this simulation, we compare our algorithms under different transmission power of SUs. The data-packet size is set to 2 KB, and the transmission power varies from 0.1 to 1.5 W. Figure 2 depicts that, the throughput increases with the increase of the transmission power Ptr, and our algorithms perform better. This is because if the transmission power is larger, the transmission range of the signal will be farther, and the received power will be larger, which leads to a higher data transmission rate between two neighboring SUs. Furthermore, from Fig. 2, we can see that in a low channel availability (Fig. 2(a)), MaxSP outperforms MinETD, and in a high channel availability (Fig. 2(b)), MinETD performs best. In a multi-hop CRN with a high channel availability, there exist a number of available channels between two neighboring SUs, thus the probability that all the available channels turn to be unavailable is small during data transmission, which then leads to no or less chances of rerouting. In this case, an SU could choose a channel with a larger transmission success probability and a higher data transmission rate to improve throughput. Thus, in this case, MaxSP outperforms MinETD. On the other hand, in a CRN with a low channel availability, there exist a small number of available channels between two neighboring SUs, which leads to a large probability that all the available channels turn to be unavailable during data transmission. In this case, the transmission success probability dominates the probability of rerouting, which makes MinETD perform better.

5   Conclusions

In this paper, we introduce CRN routing metrics with consideration of both current spectrum availability and future spectrum dynamics. Based on the routing metrics, we proposed routing algorithms, in which an optimal path is chosen by optimally selecting nodes and channel assignments. The simulation results show that our routing schemes have better performance than other CRN routing protocol in terms of throughput. To enhance the usability of the proposed scheme, more works need to be done in the future. Such works include how to determine the best power control to save energy in routing for multi-hop CRNs.

Acknowledgment. This work is supported by the NSF under Grant NO.1252292, the National Natural Science Foundation of China under Grant NOs.61502116, 61402273, 61370084, and 61370217, the Fundamental Research Funds for the Central Universities of China under Grant Nos. GK201401002 and GK201603115.

References

1. Badarneh, O.S., Salameth, H.B.: Opportunistic routing in cognitive radio networks: exploiting spectrum availability and rich channel diversity. In: Proceedings of the IEEE Global Telecommunications Conference (Globecom 2011), pp. 1–5. Houston, USA, December 5–9 2011
2. Bayhan, S., Alagöz, F.: A markovian approach for best-fit channel selection in cognitive radio networks. Ad Hoc Netw. **12**, 165–177 (2014)
3. Cai, Z., Duan, Y., Bourgeois, A.G.: Delay efficient opportunistic routing in asynchronous multi-channel cognitive radio networks. J. Comb. Optim. **29**(4), 815–835 (2015)
4. Cai, Z., Ji, S., He, J., Bourgeois, A.G.: Optimal distributed data collection for asynchronous cognitive radio networks. In: IEEE 32nd International Conference on Distributed Computing Systems (ICDCS 2012), pp. 245–254. IEEE Computer Society, Macau, China, June 18–21 2012
5. Cesana, M., Cuomo, F., Ekici, E.: Routing in cognitive radio networks: challenges and solutions. Ad Hoc Netw. **9**(3), 228–248 (2011)
6. Chowdhury, K., Felice, M.: Search: a routing protocol for mobile cognitive radio ad-hoc networks. Comput. Commun. **32**(18), 1983–1997 (2009)
7. Guan, X., Li, A., Cai, Z., Ohtsuki, T.: Coalition graph game for robust routing in cooperative cognitive radio networks. Mobile Netw. Appl. **20**(2), 147–156 (2015). http://dx.doi.org/10.1007/s11036-015-0589-0
8. Haykin, S.: Cognitive radio: brain-empowered wireless communications. IEEE J. Sel. Areas Commun. **23**(2), 201–220 (2005)
9. Ji, S., Cai, Z., He, J., Beyah, R.: Primary social behavior aware routing and scheduling for cognitive radio networks. In: IEEE 12th Annual International Conference on Sensing, Communication, and Networking (SECON 2015), pp. 417–425. IEEE Computer Society, Seattle, WA, USA, June 22–25 2015
10. Jin, X., Zhang, R., Sun, J., Zhang, Y.: Tight: A geographic routing protocol for cognitive radio mobile ad hoc networks. IEEE Trans. Wirel. Commun. **13**(8), 4670–4681 (2014)
11. Kim, H., Shin, K.G.: Efficient discovery of spectrum opportunities with mac-layer sensing in cognitive radio networks. IEEE Trans. Mobile Comput. **7**(5), 533–545 (2008)
12. Liu, Y., Cai, L.X., Shen, X.S.: Spectrum-aware opportunistic routing in multi-hop cognitive radio networks. IEEE J. Sel. Areas Commun. **30**(10), 1958–1968 (2012)
13. Lu, J., Wang, X., Zhang, L.: Signal power random fading based interference-aware routing for wireless sensor networks. Wirel. Netw. **20**(7), 1715–1727 (2014)
14. Perkins, C., Belding-Royer, E., Das, S.: Ad hoc on-demand distance vector (aodv) routing. In: RFC Editor, pp. 1–5. USA (2003)

15. Salameh, H.B., Krunz, M., Younis, O.: Cooperative adaptive spectrum sharing in cognitive radio networks. IEEE/ACM Trans. Networking **18**(4), 1181–1194 (2010)

16. Salameh, H.B., Krunz, M.: Channel access protocols for multi-hop opportunistic networks: Challenges and recent developments. IEEE Network Spec. Issue Networking Multi-hop Cogn. Netw. **23**(4), 14–19 (2009)

17. Sengupta, S., Subbalakshmi, K.P.: Open research issues in multi-hop cognitive radio networks. IEEE Commun. Mag. **51**(4), 168–176 (2013)

18. Wang, B., Liu, K.: Advances in cognitive radio networks: a survey. IEEE J. Sel. Top. Signal Process. **5**(1), 5–23 (2011)

19. Wei, K., Liang, X., Xu, K.: A survey of social-aware routing protocols in delay tolerant networks: applications, taxonomy and design-related issues. IEEE Commun. Surv. Tutorials **16**(1), 556–578 (2014)

20. Youssef, M., Ibrahim, M., Abdelatif, M., Chen, L., Vasikakos, A.V.: Open research issues in multi-hop cognitive radio networks. IEEE Commun. Mag. **51**(4), 168–176 (2013)

21. Zhang, L., Cai, Z., Lu, J., Wang, X.: Spacial mobility prediction based routing scheme in delay/disruption-tolerant networks. In: Proceedings of International Conference on Identification, Information and Knowledge in the Internet of Things (IIKI 2014), pp. 274–279. Beijing, China, October 17–18 2014

22. Zhang, L., Cai, Z., Lu, J., Wang, X.: Mobility aware routing in delay tolerant networks. Pers. Ubiquit. Comput. **19**(7), 1111–1123 (2015)

23. Zhang, L., Wang, X., Lu, J., Ren, M., Duan, Z., Cai, Z.: A novel contact prediction based routing scheme for dtns. Transactions on Emerging Telecommunications Technologies (2014). http://onlinelibrary.wiley.com/doi/10.1002/ett.2889/abstract

Performance Analysis for High Dimensional Non-parametric Estimation in Complicated Indoor Localization

Yubin Zhao[1(✉)], Xiaopeng Fan[1], and Cheng-Zhong Xu[1,2]

[1] Shenzhen Institutes of Advanced Technology,
Chinese Academy of Sciences, Shenzhen, China
{zhaoyb,xp.fan,cz.xu}@siat.ac.cn
[2] Department of Electrical and Computer Engineering,
Wayne State University, Detroit, MI 48202, USA

Abstract. In this paper, we propose an extended recursive Cramér-Rao lower bound (ER-CRLB) method as a fundamental tool to analyze the performance of wireless indoor localization systems. According to the non-parametric estimation method, the Fisher information matrix of the ER-CRLB is divided into two parts: the state matrix and the auxiliary matrix, which builds a general framework to consider all the possible factors that may influence the estimation performance. Based on this idea, ER-CRLB can fully model the estimation process in the complicated indoor environment, e.g., the sequential position state propagation, target-anchor geometry effect, the NLOS identification, and the related prior information, which are demonstrated in the comprehensive simulations.

Keywords: Indoor localization · Cramér-Rao lower bound · Bayesian estimation · Non-line-of-sight

1 Introduction

The main purpose of the indoor localization system is the position estimation accuracy for a better location based service [2,5]. Cramér-Rao lower bound (CRLB) as the optimal performance indicator for unbiased estimator is widely applied in the localization and positioning systems. Zuo et al. proposed a conditional CRLB which considered the posterior probability is conditioned on the prior probability [12]. For range-based wireless localization system, many researches have provided CRLB results for different scenarios. Qi et al. proposed a generalized CRLB (G-CRLB) of the wireless system for NLOS environment [6]. The hybrid LOS/NLOS

Y. Zhao—This work was supported by the China National Basic Research Program (973 Program, No. 2015CB352400), National Nature Science Foundation of China (Grand No. 61501443, U1401258), Science and Technology Planning Project of Guangdong Province (2015B010129011), and the Research Program of Shenzhen (JSGG20150512145714248).

© Springer International Publishing Switzerland 2016
Q. Yang et al. (Eds.): WASA 2016, LNCS 9798, pp. 295–304, 2016.
DOI: 10.1007/978-3-319-42836-9_27

environment is analyzed and Qi indicated that with a prior knowledge of wireless transmission channel, the estimation performance can be improved [6]. Shen et al. defined an equivalent CRLB (E-CRLB) to a general framework of the wideband wireless network [7]. The multi-path and NLOS effect are both considered and the CRLB with or without prior information are compared in the E-CRLB [7]. A linear CRLB (L-CRLB) is proposed which consider the linearized effect and provided the lower bound for such estimator [9].

Although the above mentioned CRLBs try to provide the general fundamental limits of the localization systems, these CRLBs still cannot analyze the indoor environment precisely since the indoor environment is complicated and influenced by many unknown factors. In this paper, we propose a general analysis method for the complicated indoor localization systems, which is named extended recursive CRLB (ER-CRLB). Instead of other works which employ a specific wireless model, the derivation of the ER-CRLB is based on the proposed abstract function of all the wireless localization system models. The first contribution is that we construct a recursive form of the Fisher information matrix (FIM) according to θ, and we illustrate the calculation rule for the ER-CRLB. The major advantage using the analysis of ER-CRLB is that it is suitable for the complicated and dynamic environment and fully considers the prior information, hybrid unknown factors and the recursive feature of the tracking algorithms.

The second contribution is that we employ the ER-CRLB to analyze the robotic indoor localization system as a case study. The trace-driven simulation is constructed with gathered wireless measurement data from a robotic range-based test-bed. We consider all the possible factors, e.g., the target-anchor geometry effect, the building layout, the relative height differences between the target and anchors, the NLOS transmission channel, the related prior information and the recursive feature of the tracking algorithm. In general, the results demonstrate that ER-CRLB is suitable to exploit all the available information to analyze the performance of the indoor localization systems, and it is not restrict to any specific techniques.

2   Fisher Information Matrix Formulation

The mobile device with unknown position is called target, such as mobile sensor node, smartphone and robot. The position state of the target is denoted as $\boldsymbol{x}_t = [p_t^X \ p_t^Y]^T$, where p_t^X and p_t^Y are the coordinates in the two-dimensional positioning system, and T is the transpose operator. The wireless devices with known positions, which measure the ranges (or distances) to the target are called anchors. For each anchor, the position is denoted as $\mathbf{a}_j = [a_j^X \ a_j^Y]^T$, where a_j^X and a_j^Y are the coordinates. According to the Bayesian estimation framework, the relationship between the estimated state $\boldsymbol{x}_t$ and the measurement $\mathbf{z}_t$ follows:

$$\boldsymbol{x}_t = \mathbf{f}_t(\boldsymbol{x}_{t-1}) + \mathbf{q}_t \tag{1}$$

$$\mathbf{z}_t = \mathbf{h}_t(\mathbf{d}(\boldsymbol{x}_t, \boldsymbol{k}), \ \boldsymbol{l}) + \mathbf{v}_t \tag{2}$$

where (1) is the prediction function and (2) is the abstract measurement function. In (1), the target's movement is based on the transition function $\mathbf{f}_t()$, and $\mathbf{q}_t$ is the prediction noise, which follows normal distribution $\mathcal{N}(\mathbf{0}, \mathbf{Q_t})$. In (2), $\mathbf{z}_t = [z_t^1 \ldots z_t^j \ldots z_t^N]^T$ is the measurement vector, and N denotes the number of anchors; $\mathbf{h}_t() = [h_t^1() \ldots h_t^j() \ldots h_t^N()]^T$ is the nonlinear observation function, which relates to the received waveforms at the target from anchors; $\mathbf{v}_t = [v_t^1 \ldots v_t^j \ldots v_t^N]^T$ is the ranging noise, which is assume as independent noise; $\mathbf{d}() = [d_1() \ldots d_j() \ldots d_N()]^T$ represents the distance vector between the target and anchors. According to the Bayesian theorem, the posterior probability of $\boldsymbol{x}_t$ is expressed as $p(\boldsymbol{x}_t|\mathbf{z}_t, \boldsymbol{x}_{t-1}) = p(\boldsymbol{x}_t|\boldsymbol{x}_{t-1})p(\mathbf{z}_t|\boldsymbol{x}_t)$, where $t-1$ indicates the previous, $p(\boldsymbol{x}_t|\boldsymbol{x}_{t-1})$ is the prior probability [1].

Our analysis fully considers all the possible unknown random factors that may influence the position estimation, hence the parameter vector includes: the current state $\boldsymbol{x}_t$, the previous state $\boldsymbol{x}_{t-1}$, and auxiliary parameter vectors $\boldsymbol{k}$ and $\boldsymbol{l}$. Thus, $\boldsymbol{\theta}$ is expressed as:

$$\boldsymbol{\theta} \triangleq \begin{bmatrix} \boldsymbol{x}_t^T & \boldsymbol{x}_{t-1}^T & \boldsymbol{k}^T & \boldsymbol{l}^T \end{bmatrix}^T \tag{3}$$

If $p(\boldsymbol{\theta}, \mathbf{z}_t)$ denotes the joint probability density function (PDF) of observations $\mathbf{z}_t$ and the state $\boldsymbol{\theta}$, then the FIM, $\mathbf{J}(\boldsymbol{\theta})$, is defined as:

$$\mathbf{J}(\boldsymbol{\theta}) \triangleq \mathbb{E}\left\{ \nabla_{\boldsymbol{\theta}} \ln p(\boldsymbol{\theta}, \mathbf{z}_t) \left[\nabla_{\boldsymbol{\theta}} \ln p(\boldsymbol{\theta}, \mathbf{z}_t) \right]^T \right\}, \tag{4}$$

where $\mathbb{E}\{\cdot\}$ indicates the expectation operator, $\nabla_{\boldsymbol{\theta}} = \begin{bmatrix} \frac{\partial}{\partial \theta_1}, \ldots, \frac{\partial}{\partial \theta_N} \end{bmatrix}^T$ is the operator of first order partial derivatives. And CRLB is just the inverse of FIM, and the estimation covariance can not be lower than it:

$$\mathbf{Cov}_{\boldsymbol{\theta}}(\tilde{\boldsymbol{\theta}}) \succeq \{\mathbf{J}(\boldsymbol{\theta})\}^{-1} \tag{5}$$

where "$\mathbf{A} \succeq \mathbf{B}$" should be interpreted as matrix $\mathbf{A} - \mathbf{B}$ is non-negative define.

Since $p(\boldsymbol{\theta}, \mathbf{z}_t) = p(\mathbf{z}_t|\boldsymbol{\theta})p(\boldsymbol{\theta})$ based on Bayesian theorem, it is easily seen that $\mathbf{J}(\boldsymbol{\theta})$ can be decomposed into two parts:

$$\mathbf{J}(\boldsymbol{\theta}) = \mathbf{J_D}(\boldsymbol{\theta}) + \mathbf{J_P}(\boldsymbol{\theta}) \tag{6}$$

where $\mathbf{J_D}(\boldsymbol{\theta})$ represents the information obtained from measurement data, and $\mathbf{J_P}(\boldsymbol{\theta})$ represents the prior information.

Firstly, we use the notations $\mathbf{h} = \mathbf{h}_t(\mathbf{d}(\boldsymbol{x}_t, \boldsymbol{k}), \boldsymbol{l})$, $h_j = h_t^j(\mathbf{d}(\boldsymbol{x}_t, \boldsymbol{k}), \boldsymbol{l})$, and decompose $\mathbf{J_D}$ using the chain rule as:

$$\mathbf{J_D}(\boldsymbol{\theta}) = \mathbf{H} \cdot \mathbf{J_h} \cdot \mathbf{H}^T \tag{7}$$

where $\mathbf{H} = [\nabla_{\boldsymbol{\theta}} \mathbf{h}]$ and $\mathbf{J_h}$ is the FIM conditioned on $\mathbf{h}$:

$$\mathbf{J_h} = \mathbb{E}\left\{ \nabla_{\mathbf{h}} \ln p(\mathbf{z}_t|\boldsymbol{\theta}) \left[\nabla_{\mathbf{h}} \ln p(\mathbf{z}_t|\boldsymbol{\theta}) \right]^T \right\} \tag{8}$$

The matrix $\mathbf{H}$ is further decomposed into four components:

$$\mathbf{H} = [\mathbf{H}_t \; \mathbf{H}_{t-1} \; \mathbf{K} \; \mathbf{L}]^T \tag{9}$$

where $\mathbf{H}_t = [\nabla_{\boldsymbol{x}_t}\mathbf{h}]_{2\times N}$, $\mathbf{H}_{t-1} = [\nabla_{\boldsymbol{x}_{t-1}}\mathbf{h}]_{2\times N}$, $\mathbf{K} = [\nabla_{\boldsymbol{k}}\mathbf{h}]_{N_k\times N}$ and $L = [\nabla_{\boldsymbol{l}}\mathbf{h}]_{N_l\times N}$. Since $\mathbf{d}$ is independent to the previous state $\boldsymbol{x}_{t-1}$, $\mathbf{H}_{t-1} = 0$. For $\mathbf{J_h}$, we can use diagonal matrices of order N to represent it: $\mathbf{J_h} = \boldsymbol{\Lambda} = \mathbf{diag}(\lambda_1,\ldots,\lambda_j,\ldots,\lambda_N)$, where the diagonal term λ_j depends on $h_t^j()$. Then, $\mathbf{J_D}$ is written as:

$$\mathbf{J_D} = \begin{bmatrix} \mathbf{D}_{11} & \mathbf{0} & \mathbf{D}_{13} & \mathbf{D}_{14} \\ \mathbf{0} & \mathbf{0} & \mathbf{0} & \mathbf{0} \\ \mathbf{D}_{13}^T & \mathbf{0} & \mathbf{D}_{33} & \mathbf{D}_{34} \\ \mathbf{D}_{14}^T & \mathbf{0} & \mathbf{D}_{34}^T & \mathbf{D}_{44} \end{bmatrix} \tag{10}$$

where

$$\begin{aligned} \mathbf{D}_{11} &= \mathbf{H}_t\boldsymbol{\Lambda}\mathbf{H}_t^T; \quad \mathbf{D}_{33} = \mathbf{K}\boldsymbol{\Lambda}\mathbf{K}^T; \\ \mathbf{D}_{13} &= \mathbf{H}_t\boldsymbol{\Lambda}\mathbf{K}^T; \quad \mathbf{D}_{34} = \mathbf{K}\boldsymbol{\Lambda}\mathbf{L}^T; \\ \mathbf{D}_{14} &= \mathbf{H}_t\boldsymbol{\Lambda}\mathbf{L}^T; \quad \mathbf{D}_{44} = \mathbf{L}\boldsymbol{\Lambda}\mathbf{L}^T. \end{aligned} \tag{11}$$

The prior probability for $\boldsymbol{\theta}$ is extended as $p(\boldsymbol{\theta}) = p(\boldsymbol{x}_t|\boldsymbol{x}_{t-1})p(\boldsymbol{k})p(\boldsymbol{l})$, then the prior information is written as:

$$\ln p(\boldsymbol{\theta}) = [\ln p(\boldsymbol{x}_t|\boldsymbol{x}_{t-1})] + \ln p(\boldsymbol{k}) + \ln p(\boldsymbol{l}) \tag{12}$$

where $p(\boldsymbol{k})$ and $p(\boldsymbol{l})$ are independent prior information to $\boldsymbol{x}_t$ and $\boldsymbol{x}_{t-1}$. If we decompose $\boldsymbol{\theta}$ into two sub-vectors: the state vector $[\boldsymbol{x}_t \ \boldsymbol{x}_{t-1}]^T$ and the auxiliary vector $[\boldsymbol{k} \ \boldsymbol{l}]^T$. Then, $\mathbf{J_P}$ can be formulated as:

$$\begin{aligned} \mathbf{J_P} &= \mathbb{E}\left\{\nabla_{\boldsymbol{\theta}}\ln p(\boldsymbol{\theta})\left[\nabla_{\boldsymbol{\theta}}\ln p(\boldsymbol{\theta})\right]^T\right\} \\ &= \begin{bmatrix} \mathbf{J_{P_{11}}} & \mathbf{J_{P_{12}}} \\ \mathbf{J_{P_{12}}^T} & \mathbf{J_{P_{22}}} \end{bmatrix} \end{aligned} \tag{13}$$

where $\mathbf{J_{P_{11}}}$ is the recursive form of $\boldsymbol{x}_t$ and $\boldsymbol{x}_{t-1}$, which is formulated by Tichavsky et al. [8]:

$$\mathbf{J_{P_{11}}} = \begin{bmatrix} \mathbf{M}_{11} & \mathbf{M}_{12} \\ \mathbf{M}_{12}^T & \mathbf{M}_{22} + \mathbf{J}(\boldsymbol{x}_{t-1}) \end{bmatrix} \tag{14}$$

where

$$\begin{aligned} \mathbf{M}_{11} &= \mathbf{Q}_t^{-1} \\ \mathbf{M}_{12} &= \nabla_{\boldsymbol{x}_{t-1}}\mathbf{f}_t(\boldsymbol{x}_{t-1})\mathbf{Q}_t^{-1} \\ \mathbf{M}_{22} &= \nabla_{\boldsymbol{x}_{t-1}}\mathbf{f}_t(\boldsymbol{x}_{t-1})\mathbf{Q}_t^{-1}\left[\nabla_{\boldsymbol{x}_{t-1}}\mathbf{f}_t(\boldsymbol{x}_{t-1})\right]^T \end{aligned} \tag{15}$$

where $\mathbf{J}(\boldsymbol{x}_{t-1})$ is the previous FIM of $\boldsymbol{x}_{t-1}$. And $\mathbf{J_{P_{12}}}$ are $\mathbf{0}$ matrixes since $p(\boldsymbol{k})$ and $p(\boldsymbol{l})$ are independent to $\boldsymbol{x}_t$ and $\boldsymbol{x}_{t-1}$. The prior distribution $p(\boldsymbol{x}_t|\boldsymbol{x}_{t-1})$ is also independent to $\boldsymbol{l}$ and $\boldsymbol{k}$, thus $\mathbf{J_{P_{21}}} = \mathbf{J_{P_{12}}^T} = \mathbf{0}$. Finally, the last element $\mathbf{J_{P_{22}}}$ is expressed as:

$$\mathbf{J_{P_{22}}} = \begin{bmatrix} \mathbf{J_K} & \mathbf{0} \\ \mathbf{0} & \mathbf{J_L} \end{bmatrix} \tag{16}$$

where $\mathbf{J_K}$ and $\mathbf{J_L}$ are the FIMs conditioned on $\boldsymbol{k}$ and $\boldsymbol{l}$ respectively:

$$\begin{aligned} \mathbf{J_K} &= \mathbb{E}\left\{\nabla_{\boldsymbol{k}}\ln p(\boldsymbol{k})\left[\nabla_{\boldsymbol{k}}\ln p(\boldsymbol{k})\right]^T\right\} \\ \mathbf{J_L} &= \mathbb{E}\left\{\nabla_{\boldsymbol{l}}\ln p(\boldsymbol{l})\left[\nabla_{\boldsymbol{l}}\ln p(\boldsymbol{l})\right]^T\right\} \end{aligned} \tag{17}$$

Then, substitute (10) and (13) into (6) and use the form of the Schur complement of the sub-matrix [4], the ER-FIM is attained:

$$\mathbf{J}(\boldsymbol{x}_t) = \mathbf{J}_S - \mathbf{J}_A \tag{18}$$

where:

$$\mathbf{J_S} = \mathbf{M}_{11} + \mathbf{D}_{11} - \mathbf{M}_{12}\left(\mathbf{M}_{22} + \mathbf{J}(\boldsymbol{x}_{t-1})\right)^{-1}\mathbf{M}_{12}^T$$
$$\mathbf{J_A} = [\mathbf{D}_{13}\ \mathbf{D}_{14}]\begin{bmatrix}\mathbf{D}_{33} + \mathbf{J_K} & \mathbf{D}_{34} \\ \mathbf{D}_{34}^T & \mathbf{D}_{44} + \mathbf{J_L}\end{bmatrix}^{-1}[\mathbf{D}_{13}\ \mathbf{D}_{14}]^T. \tag{19}$$

And the formulation of each element can be found in (11), (15) and (17).

Equation (18) only holds when all the elements in $\boldsymbol{\theta}$ are to be estimated and the prior information for the whole $\boldsymbol{\theta}$ is available. In the real analysis, not all the elements are necessary for $\boldsymbol{\theta}$, and some vectors are absent sometimes. For instance, for the non-recursive scenario, the system does not consider $\boldsymbol{x}_{t-1}$. In addition, when the system has deterministic value of the assisted vectors, $\boldsymbol{k}$ and $\boldsymbol{l}$ are not estimated and useless for $\mathbf{J}(\boldsymbol{x}_t)$. Thus, the calculation principle for ER-CRLB is that: when any vector in $\boldsymbol{\theta}$ is absent, the related matrix in (18) turns to $\mathbf{0}$ and we will treat the such $\mathbf{0}$ matrix as the empty matrix, then we mitigate the empty matrix for calculation.

3   Time-of-Arrival Localization System

Let τ_t^j be the time delay of the received signal from anchor j at time t:

$$\tau_t^j = \frac{1}{c}\left[||\boldsymbol{x}_t - \mathbf{a}_j|| + l_t^j\right] \tag{20}$$

where $c = 3 \times 10^8$ m/s is the propagation speed of the signal, and $|| \cdot ||$ denotes the distance between two positions, $l_t^j \geq 0$ is the range drift. The range drift $l_t^j = 0$ for LOS propagation, whereas $l_t^j > 0$ for NLOS propagation. For many indoor systems, the TOA ranging measurement is obtained through the packet transmission time based on the network protocol:

$$z_t^j = c\tau_t^j + v_t^j \tag{21}$$

where the measurement function $h_t^j((\mathbf{d}(\boldsymbol{x}_t, \boldsymbol{k}) + l_t^j)) = c\tau_t^j$, and v_t^j is the measurement noise for anchor j.

3.1   Relative Height

It is assumed that the anchors and targets are on the same plane in many real indoor applications. The goal is to calculate 2D positions, $X - Y$ coordinates of the target. In this case, the height difference between anchor and target is ignored. However, actually, the height difference is involved in the position estimation and has impact on the accuracy. Here, we define the height difference between anchor and target as **relative height** k_t. If the relative height is 0 or assumed to be 0 in the simulation, we define the range measurement as **2D-ranging**. If the relative height between anchor and target is not 0, which is always applicable in the real case, the measurement depends on 3D coordinates, we define the range measurement as **3D-ranging**. The 3D-ranging for each anchor is formulated as:

$$d^j(\boldsymbol{x}_t, k_t) = \sqrt{(p_t^X - a_j^X)^2 + (p_t^Y - a_j^Y)^2 + k_t^2} \qquad (22)$$

The problems of 3D-ranging can be referred in [11]. Then, $\mathbf{K} = [\nabla_k d(\boldsymbol{x}_t, k)]_{1 \times N}$ is expressed as [11]:

$$\mathbf{K} = \left[\begin{array}{ccccc} \frac{\partial d_t^1(\boldsymbol{x}_t, k_t)}{k_t} & \cdots & \frac{\partial d_t^j(\boldsymbol{x}_t, k_t)}{k} & \cdots & \frac{\partial d_t^N(\boldsymbol{x}_t, k_t)}{k_t} \end{array} \right] \qquad (23)$$

where

$$\frac{\partial d_t^j(\boldsymbol{x}_t, k_t)}{k_t} = \frac{k}{\sqrt{(p_t^X - a_j^X)^2 + (p_t^Y - a_j^Y)^2 + k_t^2}} \qquad (24)$$

For the prior information of k_t, the relative height is always nonnegative no matter of the places of the anchors. Thus, we apply the Gamma distribution to indicate the potential distribution of k_t, where $k_t \sim G(\alpha_k, \beta_k)(k_t) = \frac{(\beta_k)^{\alpha_k}}{\Gamma(\alpha_k)} k_t^{\alpha_k - 1} \exp(-\beta_k k_t)$, and α_k is the shape parameter and β_k is the rate parameter. For Gamma distribution, J_k is complicated. To obtain an analytical expression, we assume $\alpha_k > 2$ for simplicity. Then, the Gamma function is $\Gamma(\alpha_k) = \int_0^{+\infty} \exp(-x) x^{\alpha_k - 1} dx$. Thus, $J_k = \mathbb{E}\left(\frac{\partial}{\partial k_t} G(\alpha_k, \beta_k)(k_t)\right)^2$ is derived as:

$$\begin{aligned} J_k =& \beta_k^2 - \frac{2(\alpha_k - 1)\beta_k}{\Gamma(\alpha_k)} \int_0^{+\infty} \beta_k^{\alpha_k} k_t^{\alpha_k - 2} \exp(-\beta_k k_t) dk_t \\ &+ \frac{(\alpha_k - 1)^2}{\Gamma(\alpha_k)} \int_0^{+\infty} \beta_k^{\alpha_k} k_t^{\alpha_k - 3} \exp(-\beta_k k_t) dk_t \end{aligned} \qquad (25)$$

Use the property $\Gamma(\alpha_k) = \alpha_k \Gamma(\alpha_k - 1)$ and substitute it into (25), we obtain:

$$J_k = \frac{\beta_k^2}{\alpha_k - 2} \qquad (26)$$

3.2   NLOS

The vector l can be used as NLOS indicator for TOA ranging. We assume there are $N_l \leq N$ NLOS measurements and the drift for each measurement is independent to others, then $\mathbf{L} = [\nabla_l \mathbf{h}]_{N_l \times N}$ is formulated as:

$$\mathbf{L} = \begin{pmatrix} \mathbf{I}_{N_l} & 0 \end{pmatrix} \qquad (27)$$

where $\mathbf{I}_{N_l}$ is the identity matrix of order N_l, and the rest part is a $N_l \times (N - N_l)$ zero matrix due to the independent condition to the LOS measurement. Since the range drift for the NLOS is also nonnegative, we still use Gamma distribution as the prior information $l_m \sim G(a_m, b_m)(l_m) = \frac{(b_m)^{a_m}}{\Gamma(a_m)} l_m^{a_m-1} \exp(-b_m l_m)$, where $a_m \geq 2$ is the shape parameter, b_m is the rate parameter, and m is the mth NLOS measurement. Similar to (26), we obtain $\mathbf{J_L}$:

$$\mathbf{J_L} = \mathbf{diag}(\frac{b_1^2}{a_1 - 2}, \cdots, \frac{b_m^2}{a_m - 2}, \cdots, \frac{b_{N_l}^2}{a_{N_l} - 2}) \tag{28}$$

4   Simulation

We set up several trace-driven TOA-based indoor localization simulations to evaluate the analytical performance using the ER-CRLB. The simulation environment is constructed according to the data gathered from a robotic test-bed [10]. The parameters in the simulations are obtained from the statistical distribution results of these data. In each simulation, the ER-CRLB considers several different factors, e.g., the recursive process during the target tracking, estimations with and without considering l and k_t. To make the results clear, we mark the CRLBs for different situations by adding superscripts and subscripts, which can be depicted as $\mathbf{CRLB}^{\cdots}_{\cdots}$. The subscripts indicate the considered vectors, including the state vector and the auxiliary vector. The superscripts indicate the available prior information of the considered vectors. For instance, if we want to simulate the estimation with NLOS range drift, the results of the ER-CRLB is marked by $\mathbf{CRLB}_{\boldsymbol{x}_t, \boldsymbol{l}}$. And if the prior information of $\boldsymbol{x}_t$ is attained in the simulation, the results are marked by $\mathbf{CRLB}^{\boldsymbol{x}_t}_{\boldsymbol{x}_t, \boldsymbol{l}}$. For the recursive estimation, we use the notation $\mathbf{CRLB}^{\boldsymbol{x}_{t-1}, \boldsymbol{x}_t, \boldsymbol{l}}_{\boldsymbol{x}_{t-1}, \boldsymbol{x}_t, \boldsymbol{l}}$.

4.1   Spatial Position Error Distribution

In the first simulation, a $100 \times 100\,\mathrm{m}^2$ playing field. There are four big rooms located at four corners of the playing field. The area for each room is $40 \times 40\mathrm{m}^2$. The rest parts of the playing field are the hallways. The anchors are the access points of the WiFi network. We set the relative height as the constant value 1.5m. The range error for each anchor follows zero-mean Gaussian distribution $v_t^j \sim \mathcal{N}(0, R_t^j)$, where R_t^j is 5^2. The range drift for the NLOS measurements is set 2m. For the prior information, the relative height $k_t \sim G(2.5, 2)(k_t)$. The prior information of the NLOS range drift l_m is $l_m \sim G(3.5, 1.8)(l_m)$. For the position state prior information, we assume the prediction function is linear static identity matrix with the zero-mean Gaussian prediction noise $\mathbf{q_t} \sim \mathcal{N}(\mathbf{0}, \mathbf{Q_t})$, where $\mathbf{Q_t} = \mathbf{diag}(\sigma_x^2, \sigma_y^2)$ is the covariance of $\mathbf{q_t}$ and $\sigma_x = \sigma_y = 2\mathrm{m}$. The LOS measurements can only be obtained in one room with four associate anchors, and others measurements are NLOS. For the positions in the hallways, all the measurements are NLOS ranging.

We apply the ER-CRLB to indicate the optimal squared error, which is $\sqrt{\mathrm{tr}(\mathbf{J}^{-1}(\boldsymbol{x}_t))}$. To illustrate the geometrical performance for the 2D localization system in the playing field, we employ $\sqrt{\mathrm{tr}(\mathbf{J}^{-1}(\boldsymbol{x}_t))}$ to depict the spatial position error distribution (SPED) which is defined as the distribution of the position error for every target position [3]. It illustrates how the performance changes from position to position in the playing field. The SPED results are depicted in Fig. 1:

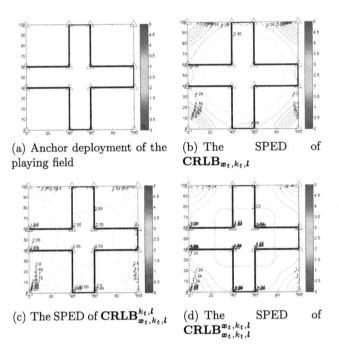

(a) Anchor deployment of the playing field

(b) The   SPED   of $\mathbf{CRLB}_{\boldsymbol{x}_t, k_t, l}$

(c) The SPED of $\mathbf{CRLB}_{\boldsymbol{x}_t, k_t, l}^{k_t, l}$

(d) The   SPED   of $\mathbf{CRLB}_{\boldsymbol{x}_t, k_t, l}^{\boldsymbol{x}_t, k_t, l}$

Fig. 1. The simulation of a building layout (Color figure online)

For numerical comparison, the RMSE in Fig. 1(b) is higher than Fig. 1(c) and (d), which is more than 3.39 m in the central area. And the error become higher and higher when the position is approaching to the corner, which is more than 8m. Due to the lack of prior information, the geometric shape does not have special characters which are related to rooms or corridors. The contours are almost like rectangles located in the center of the playing field. When the prior information of k_t and l is introduced, the accuracy is significantly improved, which is reduced to 2.55m in average. The geometric shapes of the contours are different in the rooms and hallways. It indicates that the localization algorithms using the prior knowledge of NLOS conditions based on the building layout information and the NLOS identification and mitigation methods can reasonably improve the estimation performance. Thus, the layout information in the building map is an important information source for localizations. When the prior information of $\boldsymbol{x}_t$ is introduced in the estimation as indicated in Fig. 1(d), the RMSE is further reduced, which is 1.235 m in almost all the playing field where the target-anchor geometry effect is reduced effectively.

4.2   Bayesian-Based Target Tracking Estimation

In this simulation, we evaluate the performance of the recursive Bayesian estimation for target tracking. We run 1000 Monte-Carlo simulations, and the target moves a separate random path in each simulation. In addition, the target can also be static. Since x_{t-1} can also be estimated in the static scenario and be used for recursive estimation, the analysis results are the same to the dynamic target tracking scenarios. The estimation results are averaged and represented by the RMSE in Fig. 2. There are three solid parallel straight lines which indicate the estimations without prior information: $\mathbf{CRLB}_{x_t,k_t,l}$, $\mathbf{CRLB}_{x_t,k_t}$ and $\mathbf{CRLB}_{x_t,l}$. The three other dash curves illustrate the recursive estimations according to time steps, which are $\mathbf{CRLB}_{x_t,k_t,l}^{x_{t-1},k_t,l}$, $\mathbf{CRLB}_{x_t,k_t}^{x_{t-1},k_t}$ and $\mathbf{CRLB}_{x_t,l}^{x_{t-1},l}$.

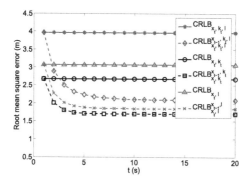

Fig. 2. Sequential estimation lower bound

The Bayesian recursive estimation manner with related prior information effectively reduced the estimation as indicated in Fig. 2. The RMSEs of the three curves gradually converge to low values according to time steps. The impacts of the relative heights and the NLOS drifts still degrade the estimation performance. Even with the recursive estimation, the estimation error can not be further reduced, where the $\mathbf{CRLB}_{x_t,k_t,l}^{x_{t-1},k_t,l}$ is 0.5 m larger than $\mathbf{CRLB}_{x_t,k_t}^{x_{t-1},k_t}$ when $t = 20$.

5   Conclusion

In this paper, we propose a new fundamental analyzing method for the indoor localization system, named ER-CRLB. We draw several conclusions according to the analytical results: (1) the SPED shape of the optimal estimation depends not only on the target-anchors relative positions, but also depends on the building layout and the prior information of the NLOS measurements and the state. (2) Comparing with k_t, l decreases the estimation accuracy more significantly. The prior information of l improves the estimation more effectively than the prior information of k_t. (3) The prior distribution of x_t plays the most important role for the estimation. Such distribution can be attained through the recursive estimation. In general, ER-CRLB is a suitable tool to indicate the optimal estimation bound of the indoor localization systems.

References

1. Arulampalam, M., Maskell, S., Gordon, N., Clapp, T.: A tutorial on particle filters for online nonlinear/non-gaussian bayesian tracking. IEEE Trans. Signal Process. **50**(2), 174–188 (2002)
2. Axel, K.: Location-Based Services: Fundamentals and Operation. Wiely, Chichester (2005)
3. Hillebrandt, T., Will, H., Kyas, M.: Quantitative and spatial evaluation of distance-based localization algorithms. In: Krisp, J.M. (ed.) Progress in Location-Based Services. LNGC, pp. 173–194. Springer, Heidelberg (2013)
4. Horn, R.A., Johnson, C.R.: Matrix analysis. Cambridge University Press, New York (2012)
5. Mao, G., Fidan, B., Anderson, B.: Wireless sensor network localization techniques. Comput. Netw. **51**(10), 2529–2553 (2007)
6. Qi, Y.: Wireless Geolocation in a Non-Line-Of-Sight Environment. Ph.D. thesis, Princeton University (2003)
7. Shen, Y., Win, M.Z.: Fundamental limits of wideband localization part i: a general framework. IEEE Trans. Inf. Theor. **56**(10), 4956–4980 (2010)
8. Tichavsky, P., Muravchik, C., Nehorai, A.: Posterior cramer-rao bounds for discrete-time nonlinear filtering. IEEE Trans. Signal Process. **46**(5), 1386–1396 (1998)
9. Tseng, P.H., Feng, K.T.: Geometry-assisted localization algorithms for wireless networks. IEEE Trans. Mobile Comput. **12**(4), 774–789 (2013)
10. Yang, Y., Zhao, Y., Kyas, M.: A non-parametric modeling of time-of-flight ranging error for indoor network localization. In: 2013 IEEE Global Communications Conference (GLOBECOM), pp. 189–194. IEEE (2013)
11. Zhao, Y., Yang, Y., Kyas, M.: 2d geometrical performance for localization algorithms from 3d perspective. In: 2013 International Conference on Indoor Positioning and Indoor Navigation (IPIN), pp. 1–10, October 2013
12. Zuo, L., Niu, R., Varshney, P.K.: Conditional posterior cramér-rao lower bounds for nonlinear sequential bayesian estimation. IEEE Trans. Signal Process. **59**(1), 1–14 (2011)

Minimum-Delay Data Aggregation Schedule in Duty-Cycled Sensor Networks

Xiaoting Yan[1], Hongwei Du[1(✉)], Qiang Ye[2], and Guoliang Song[1]

[1] Department of Computer Science and Technology, Harbin Institute of Technology Shenzhen Graduate School, Shenzhen Key Laboratory of Internet Information Collaboration, Shenzhen, China
xiaotingyanhit@gmail.com, hwdu@hitsz.edu.cn, sguoliang1221@gmail.com
[2] Department of Computer Science and Information Technology, University of Prince Edward Island, Charlottetown, Canada
qye@upei.ca

Abstract. Data aggregation is one of the challenging issues in Wireless Sensor Networks (WSNs). Traditionally, sensor nodes are assumed to be in the active state all the time, which leads to undesirable energy consumption. Moreover, most of the duty-cycle protocols are proposed to reduce energy consumption. However, the aggregation delay has been ignored during saving energy. This paper focuses on the problem of minimum-delay aggregation schedule in duty-cycled WSNs under the protocol interference model. To solve the problem, we propose an algorithm by firstly construct an aggregation tree based on the connected dominating set (CDS). Then we propose an aggregation schedule algorithm to avoid the interference, which is Leaves Schedule (LS). Different from existing works, we believe that nodes in different layers can transmit concurrently, thus it will greatly increase the number of nodes transmit concurrently and minimize the total transmission times in order to minimize the aggregation delay. Through extensive simulations, we found that the proposed scheduling method outperforms the state-of-the-art schemes.

Keywords: Data aggregation schedule · Minimum delay · Duty-cycled · Wireless Sensor Networks

1 Introduction

With the emergency of better equipped sensor nodes, WSNs have been widely applied in many applications, such as environment monitoring, and data collection [1]. In these applications, battery-powered sensor nodes would be deployed in the target area for a long period of time to sense data, and transmit the sensed data to the base station. According to the fact that neighbor nodes tend to have highly relevant information, data aggregation [2] is usually used during transmission to reduce the total transmission times. In this way, the energy consumption of each node is reduced and the whole network lifetime is prolonged.

© Springer International Publishing Switzerland 2016
Q. Yang et al. (Eds.): WASA 2016, LNCS 9798, pp. 305–317, 2016.
DOI: 10.1007/978-3-319-42836-9_28

To further reduce energy consumption, duty cycle protocols are widely applicable in long-term applications to reduce energy consumption. In duty-cycled networks, nodes switch between active state and dormant state periodically. This kind of mode, undoubtedly, reduce energy consumption to a large extent.

Data aggregation in duty cycled WSNs can greatly reduce energy consumption. However, a node has to wait some certain time for the parent's active state, thus the aggregation delay is largely increased. In some real-time applications, e.g. fire monitoring, people are eager to obtain the aggregated data from WSNs within a short time. Hence the research on how to decrease the aggregation delay in duty-cycled WSNs is of great important. In this paper, we focus on the problem of Minimum-Delay Aggregation Schedule in Duty-Cycled WSNs(MDAS-DC). Our contributions are concluded as follows:

1. We propose an algorithm by firstly construct an aggregation tree based on CDS [3–6]. In duty-cycled WSNs, once the receiver's active time is less than the sender's, the earliest finish time of this transmission is the next duty-cycle period. Thus different from previous construction method, we construct the tree on duty-cycled scenario to minimize the aggregation delay.
2. Based on the aggregation tree, we propose a novel schedule method, which is LS. Different from traditional layer schedule, LS tries to schedule all leaves in each duty-cycled period conflict-free. Thus it minimizes the aggregation delay.
3. Through theoretical analysis, the results show that the proposed algorithm LS is upper bounded by $4R + 11/2 * h + \Delta - 4$ duty cycle periods, where R and Δ are the radius and maximum degree of the network graph G, and h is the height of one node, whose childrens heights are all the same.
4. Through extensive simulations, we found that the proposed scheduling method outperforms the existing schemes for data aggregation in terms of aggregation delay.

The rest of the paper is organized as follows. Section 2 presents the related work. In Sect. 3, we introduce the network model. The minimum-delay scheduling problem is formulated in Sect. 4. The proposed scheduling method is presented in Sect. 5 and the theoretical analysis is included in Sect. 6. The simulation analysis is summarized in Sect. 7. Finally, Sect. 8 concludes this paper.

2   Related Work

Minimizing data aggregation delay in WSNs has been studied over the past decades [7–12]. Under the protocol interference model, it was first introduced by Chen and Xu in [7]. The problem introduced by Chen et al. is proved to be NP-hard and an approximation algorithm was proposed with a delay bound of $(\Delta - 1) \times R$. As the delay bound in [7] would be very high when Δ and R increased, Huang et al. [8] present an approximation algorithm with a delay bound of $23R + \Delta - 18$. Their algorithm is based on CDS and has a significant improvement compared with Chen and Xu [7], especially when Δ is large. After that, CDS has been popularly used in data aggregation. Wan et al. [9] design three aggregation algorithms with latency $15R + \Delta - 4$, $2R + O(\log R) + \Delta$ and $1 + O(\log R/\sqrt[3]{R})R + \Delta$ respectively. It works better when the R is large. Nguyen et al. [10] proposed a new scheduling algorithm based on neighboring dominators and upper bounded by $12R + \Delta - 11$.

However, only a few previous works focus on the duty-cycled WSNs [13–15], and [13,14] study the problem of data aggregation. In [13], Yu and Li work on the collision-free data aggregation scheduling in duty-cycled WSNs. It has two phases as in [8]: data aggregation tree construction and aggregation schedule considering duty-cycle model. In [14], Xiao et al. propose a centralized algorithm for minimizing data aggregation time in duty-cycled WSNs. The construction of the aggregation tree is also based on CDS. However, in the phase of scheduling, both of them schedule nodes layer by layer. It is obviously that so much collision occurred at the parent who has more than one child and that many nodes in different layers can transmit simultaneously. Thus we propose a novel method which schedule all leaves in one iteration to achieve better concurrency and avoid collision at the same time.

To summarize, this paper is the first work to schedule nodes in different layers to transmit simultaneously, to the best of our knowledge.

3 Network Model

Consider a network G consisting of a collection of sensor nodes V along with one sink node V_s. The network topology is represented as a graph $G(V, E)$. V is the set of sensor nodes and E is the set of wireless communication links in the network. If both nodes u and v are within the transmission range of the other, there will be an edge (u, v) between them. Here, we assume that all nodes have the same transmission range r and interference range $\rho \geqslant r$. Under the protocol interference model, two communication links (u_1, v_1), (u_2, v_2) in G are collision-free if both segments $u_1 v_2$ and $u_2 v_1$ are longer than ρ. For simplicity, we further assume $\rho = r$, which is scaled to 1 [9]. Collision occurs differently in duty-cycled WSNs from the traditional WSNs. We generalize the collisions in duty-cycled WSNs into the following cases:

- A sensor node is scheduled to send and receive in the same time slot.
- Different sensor nodes are scheduled to send data packet to the same parent simultaneously.
- Both u and v are scheduled to transmit data packet to different parents in the same period and at the same time slot, and one of the parents is their common neighbor.

In duty-cycle WSNs, the time line of each sensor node is divided into duty-cycle periods P with the same length [16]. The duty-cycle period P is further divided into T time slots with equal length from 0 to $T-1$. Here we assume that the time slot is long enough only for transmitting or receiving one data packet. All nodes work under the duty cycle model, switch between active state and dormant state, and the active state of node u is denoted by $a(u)$. The duty cycle is defined as the ratio between the active time and the whole duty-cycle periods. In this paper, we assume that every node only wakes up once in one period, namely duty cycle is $1/T$. In duty-cycled WSNs, the sender has to wait some time for the receiver's active time slot. Once a(sender) > a(receiver), the earliest finish time of this transmission is the next duty-cycle period. Thus we get the following Eq. 1.

$$DT_{u,v}^{a(v)} = \begin{cases} 0, & a(v) > a(u) \\ 1, & else \end{cases} \tag{1}$$

4   Problem Formulation

Given a sensor network graph $G(V, E)$, the data aggregation schedule S can be represented as a sequence of senders $\{S_1, S_2, ...S_l\}$. Nodes in S_1 transmit data collision-free to $V\backslash S_1$ in their active time slot in the first period. Then nodes in S_2 transmit data to $V\backslash(S_1 \cup S_2)$ in the second period and so on so forth. Finally, nodes in S_l transmit data to V_s. The number l is the data aggregation delay. Thus, data aggregation schedule in duty-cycled WSNs is a sequence of senders $\{s_1, s_2, ...s_l\}$, satisfying that:

1. $S_1 \cup S_2 \cup ... \cup S_l = V\backslash V_s$
2. $S_i \cap S_j = \phi, i \neq j$
3. All nodes transmit in S_i in their corresponding active time slot are conflict-free.

Thus our objective is to assign a transmission time (duty-cycle period) $T_{u,v}^{a(v)}$ to each node and get each element in S_i ($i \leq l, S_i \in S$) such that the aggregation delay l is minimized.

In Fig. 1, one duty-cycle period P is divided into 5 time slots. Three subgraphs in Fig. 1 show the process of data aggregation. At first, both D and E are scheduled to transmit to their parents B and C in the forth time slot of the

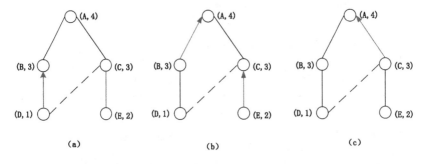

Fig. 1. An example of the data aggregation

first period. In Fig. 1, the dashed line denote that the corresponding nodes are connected in the wireless network graph, while the solid line denote transmission path. Thus, D and C are neighbors, and the segment CD is less than the interference range ρ. There would be a collision between the transmission from D to B and E to C in the first period. Thus in (a), node D transmits in the fourth time slot of the first period, while in (b), node E is put off to transmit in the fourth time slot of the second period. Node B transmits in the fifth time slot of the second period. In (c), node C transmits in the fifth time slot of the third period. Finally, we get $S = \{S_1, S_2, S_3\}$, $S_1 = \{D\}$, $S_2 = \{B, E\}$, $S_3 = \{C\}$, and the total aggregation delay in this example is 3 duty-cycle periods.

5   Data Aggregation Schedule Algorithm

Our proposed solution for minimizing data aggregation delay is composed of two phases: First, Aggregation Tree Construction; Second, Data Aggregation Scheduling. The details will be presented in next two subsections.

Algorithm 1. Aggregation Tree Construction (ATC)

Input: $G(V, E)$;
Output: $T_{AT}(V_T, E_T)$;
1: Transform network graph $G(V, E)$ to a breadth first tree T_{BFS} rooted at the sink node V_s;
2: Divide all nodes into layers: $L_0, L_1, L_2, ...L_j$. L_0: sink node layer;
3: IS $\leftarrow V_s$, CN $\leftarrow \phi$, $E_T \leftarrow \phi$;
4: **for** $i \leftarrow 1$ to j **do**
5:     For nodes in Ele_i, remove the nodes that are neighbored with any node in IS;
6:     **for** each $u \in Ele_i$ **do**
7:         compute the minimum delay from u to v (node in IS and 2-hop distance from u), denoted as $DT_{u,v}^{a(v)}$;
8:     **end for**
9:     **while** $Ele_i \neq \phi$ **do**
10:         find u in Ele_i with minimum $DT_{u,v}^{a(v)}$;
11:         IS $\leftarrow u$, CN $\leftarrow p(u)$, $E_T \leftarrow ((u, p(u)), (p(u), v))$;
12:         $Ele_i = Ele_i/(u \bigcap N(u))$;
13:     **end while**
14: **end for**
15: **for** each $u \in V/(\text{IS} \cup \text{CN})$ **do**
16:     compute the minimum delay from u to v (node in IS and 1-hop distance from u), denoted as $DT_{u,v}^{a(v)}$;
17:     Dominatees $\leftarrow u$, $E_T \leftarrow (u, v)$;
18: **end for**

5.1   Aggregation Tree Construction

In this phase, we present the details of ATC algorithm. First ATC transform the original network graph $G(V, E)$ to a breadth first search Tree (T_{BFS}) rooted at the sink node V_s, and divide all nodes into layers: $L_0, L_1, \cdots L_j$, where L_0 is the sink node and L_1 are its neighbors. Then starting from L_0, it constructs an aggregation tree T_{AT} layer by layer (Algorithm 1). The independent set (IS) is initialize to the sink node at first. Then starting from L_2 to pick up a independent set in each layer. Nodes in L_i is denoted by Ele_i, and remove nodes that are neighbored with any node in IS. Then compute the delays from u to all its 2-hop parents v in IS, and $DT_{u,v}^{a(v)}$ is the minimum delay. Then compute $DT_{u,v}^{a(v)}$ for all nodes in Ele_i. and we find u in Ele_i with minimum $DT_{u,v}^{a(v)}$, and then add u, u's parent node $p(u)$ to sets IS, connector set(CN), and add $(u, p(u))$, $(p(u), v)$ to E_T. Then remove u and its neighbors $N(u)$ in Ele_i. Then find the next u in Ele_i with minimum $DT_{u,v}^{a(v)}$ until there is no node in Ele_i. Till now, the independent set in L_i is obtained. Then we turn to the next layer and repeat this process. Finally, we get $T_{AT}(V_T, E_T)$. Here V_T is equaled to V in G, and composed of IS, CN and dominatees. Nodes in IS and CN constitute dominators.

Algorithm 2. Leaves Schedule (LS).

Input: $T_{AT}(V_T, E_T)$;
Output: aggregation schedule S;
1: transmission period: $P=1$, scheduling period: sdu;
2: **if** $|V_T| \neq 1$ **then**
3:     **for** each $u \in$ leaves **do**
4:         **if** u has not been scheduled in the previous periods **then**
5:             $sdu(u)=P$;
6:         **end if**
7:     **end for**
8:     **for** two nodes $u \in$ leaves, $v \in p(leaves)$, $(u, v) \in E_T$ && $sdu(u)=P$ **do**
9:         **if** $a(v)>a(u)$ **then**
10:             $T_{u,v}^{a(v)}=P$;
11:         **else**
12:             $T_{u,v}^{a(v)}=P+1$;
13:         **end if**
14:     **end for**
15:     **for** nodes $u \in$ leaves, $T_{u,v}^{a(v)} = P$ **do**
16:         find the maximum send set S_p that can transmit collision-free;
17:         for node u not in S_p, $T_{u,v}^{a(v)}=P+1$;
18:     **end for**
19:     return S_p;
20:     remove $u(u \in S_p)$ from V_T, $(u, p(u))$ from E_T
21:     P++;
22: **end if**

5.2   Data Aggregation Schedule

After construct the ATC, the aggregation tree T_{AT} is obtained. Every node in T_{AT} has only one aggregation path to the sink node. Along each path, nodes transmit layer by layer until all data has been transmitted to the sink node. Thus the total aggregation delay is closely related to the layer transmission times. The delay would be considerably reduced, if there are as many as nodes transmit concurrently in one layer transmission. Considering the tree structure, we find that nodes in different layers can transmit concurrently. Based on this phenomenon, we designed LS (Algorithm 2). Every iteration, this algorithm schedules all leaves in T. Their transmission period $T_{u,v}^{a(v)}$ is set to the current period($a(receiver) >$ $a(sender)$), the next period else. Then judge whether these transmissions transmit in the same period conflict with each other and find the largest set that can transmit concurrently. Transmissions not in the set will be set to the next period.

Figure 2 gives an example of leaves aggregation schedule. The number on the link is the transmission period $T_{u,v}^{a(v)}$. In Fig. 2, (a) is the first schedule, node d, k, m, l, e can transmit in the first period. Then find the maximum send set $S_1 = \{d, k, m, l\}$ that can transmit conflict-free in the current period. Because transmissions from k and e to i and b conflict with each other, node e will transmit in the next period. Then remove d, k, m, l from T_{AT}. (b) is the second schedule, nodes i, j, e, f are leaves. Node e has been scheduled in the first schedule, so nodes i, j, f will be set transmission time in this schedule. f will be scheduled to transmit in the third period for $a(c) < a(f)$, and nodes i, j are scheduled to transmitted in the second period. As a result, nodes i, j, e are scheduled to transmit in the second period, and we get $S_2 = \{i, j, e\}$. Repeat this process, until there is only one sink node.

6   Theoretical Analysis

Lemma 1. Given a connected graph G, schedule from dominatees to dominators cost at most $\Delta - 1$ periods.

Proof. Each dominatee, it must be a neighbor of any dominator. For any dominator, it have Δ neighbors at most, one of which is its parent node, so the dominator has at most $\Delta - 1$ dominatees as its neighbors. All these $\Delta - 1$ dominatees nodes send to the dominator node one after another. Thus the total period spent is at most $\Delta - 1$.

Lemma 2. In T_{AT}, a connector is adjacent to at most 5 independent elements [9]. Thus, transmitting from one independent layer to connector layer costs at most 4 duty-cycle periods.

Lemma 3. In T_{AT}, a independent element is adjacent to at most 12 connectors [9]. Thus, transmitting from one connector layer to independent layer costs at most 11 periods, while all neighbors of the sink node transmit to the sink node consume 12 periods at most.

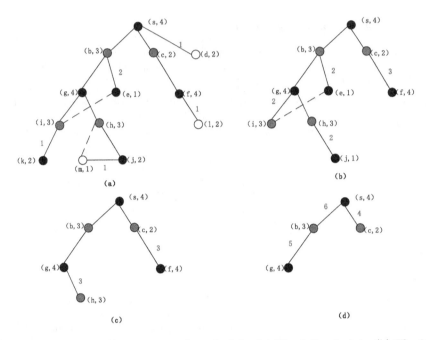

Fig. 2. An example of layer aggregation schedule. (a) The 1-th schedule. (b) The 2-th schedule. (c) The 3-th schedule. (d) The 4-th 5-th 6-th schedule.

Theorem 1. The delay of the schedule produced by LS is upper bounded by $(4R + 11/2 * h + \Delta - 4)$duty-cycle periods, where R and Δ are the radius and maximum degree of the network graph G, and h is the height of node m, whose childrens heights are all the same.

Proof. Considering one node u has many children, and each branch structure rooted at one child constructs a tree with different height, here we first assume that whenever the child node v with the maximum tree height transmit data packet to the parent node, all other child node have already sent data packet to parent node u.

For a dominator u in layer L_i, u is not the sink node, and u is exactly 2-hops distance from its upper level dominator v. u and v are connected by a connector in the middle level. Thus, the height of T_{CDS} (remove dominatees from T_{AT}) can be gotten: $H \leq 2(R-1)$, where R is the radius of the connected graph.

We compute the total aggregation delay by iteration from the sink node. First, we find all children of the sink node. Then compute tree height of the branch structure rooted at each child. Then seek out the node w whose branch structures tree height is the maximum. So the total aggregation delay can be calculated by the delay aggregated to w (denoted as $DT_w^{a(w)}$) plus two period (node w transmit to the sink consumes 2 duty-cycle periods at most). Then the delay aggregated to w is computed in the same method layer by layer until to one node m whose sub-structures all have the same height h.

The delay aggregated to m is at most $(4 + 11) * h/2$ according to Lemmas 2 and 3, thus the total aggregation delay can be obtained by the following formula.

$$\begin{aligned}
DT &= DT_w^{a(w)} + 2 + \Delta \\
&= DT_{w_1}^{a(w_1)} + 2 + 2 + \Delta \\
&= ... \\
&= (11 + 4)/2 * h + 2 * (H - h) + \Delta \\
&\leq 15/2 * h + 2 * [2(R - 1) - h] + \Delta \\
&\leq 4R + 11/2 * h + \Delta - 4
\end{aligned}$$

7   Simulation Analysis

In this section, we evaluate the proposed scheme LS with the most latest and similar scheme GAS [14]. We first introduce the experiment set up. Then in the next part, we simulate LS in randomly deployed sensor networks with different network parameters and compare LS with GAS.

7.1   Simulation Setup

Setup. In this part, we introduce the simulation setup as follows. The sensor nodes are randomly deployed in a 200 m * 200 m area and the sink node is located at the center of the region. All sensor nodes have the same transmission range r and interference range ρ, and $r = \rho$. The active time slot of each node is determined beforehand. The aggregation delay is measured by the number of duty-cycle period. We conduct the experiment 50 times for each setting and the average value is computed as the result.

Showcase. To better analyse the proposed algorithm, we implement the algorithm visualization with a packet of python, called NetworkX. In Figs. 3, 4, 5 and 6,

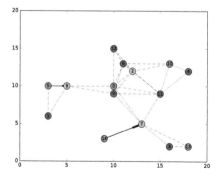

Fig. 3. Data aggregation in the 1-th period (Color figure online)

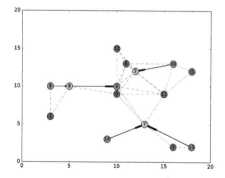

Fig. 4. Data aggregation in the 2-th period (Color figure online)

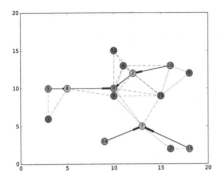

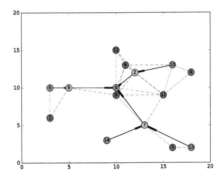

Fig. 5. Data aggregation in the 3-th period (Color figure online)

Fig. 6. Data aggregation in the 4-th period (Color figure online)

we give a specific example, which is the process of aggregation in the dominators. In these figures, nodes in IS are colored red. Nodes in CN are colored yellow and the rest nodes colored green are the dominatees. Node 0 is the sink node. The black dashed lines indicate the communication links in the original network graph, and the black arrowed lines indicate the communications in the corresponding duty-cycle periods. Figure 3 indicates the first period during the process of aggregation in the dominators. Nodes 5, 10, 13 and 14 are scheduled in the first period, but only node 5 and 14 transmit in the first period. For a(10) < a(2) and transmission from node 13 to 7 is conflict with transmission from node 14 to 7. Thus both node 10 and 13 will be put off to transmit in the next period. In Fig. 4, though node 8, 10 and 13 are in different layers (judge from the hops from these nodes to the sink node), we schedule them in the same period in LS. Figures 5 and 6 schedule node 2 and 7 respectively.

7.2   Analysis

Influence of the Network Size. In Fig. 7, the transmission range of each sensor node is fixed to 30 m, and duty cycle is 20 %. Here we measure the aggregation delay with the number of nodes varies from 200 to 800. In Fig. 7, the aggregation delay increases when the number of nodes increase. It is easy to understand that the number of sensor nodes affect the network size. With more sensor nodes sending to the sink node, there will be more time needed. It is obviously that our proposed algorithm increase slower than GAS, and the bigger the number of nodes, the better the improvement of our algorithm in comparison with GAS.

Influence of the Values of Duty Cycle. In Fig. 8, the number of sensor nodes is fixed to 400, and here we measure the aggregation delay when the values of duty cycle are varies in 50 %, 33.33 %, 25 %, 20 %, 12.5 %, 10 %, 6.67 %, 5 %, corresponding to T = 2, 3, 4, 5, 8, 10, 15, 20, respectively. From Fig. 8, when the value of duty cycle increases, correspondingly, the number of time slots in each

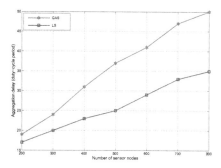 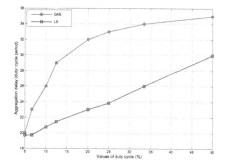

Fig. 7. Aggregation delay with different number of nodes

Fig. 8. Aggregation delay with different values of duty cycle

duty-cycle period decrease. Less time slots lead to less nodes can be transmitted in the same period. Thus the aggregation delay increase with the value of duty cycle increase.

Influence of the Transmission Range. In Fig. 9, the number of sensor nodes is fixed to 400 and the duty cycle is 20 %. We measure the delay with the transmission range varies from 25 to 55. We can observe that the transmission range also influence the average delay. When the transmission range increase, the interference range also increase. Each node will have more neighbors, which will lead to more collisions. Thus the aggregation delay will increase. When the transmission range is large enough, aggregation delay of LS is close to GAS. This is because when the transmission range is large enough, every two node scheduled to transmit in the same period may conflict with each other. Thus all nodes may transmit one after another, then aggregation schedule algorithms may have little affect on the aggregation delay.

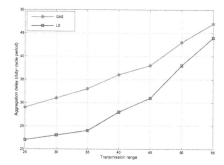

Fig. 9. Aggregation delay with different transmission ranges

8 Conclusion and Future Works

In this paper, we introduce how to minimize data aggregation delay in duty-cycled WSNs. Our proposed scheme is composed of two phases: First, based on CDS, we construct an aggregation tree; Second, data aggregation scheduling. Different from existing works, we believe that nodes in different layers can transmit concurrently, thus greatly minimize aggregation delay. Through extensive simulation, our proposed scheme has a significantly high performance than existing methods. For the future work, on one hand, the restriction in this paper is strong, we will design aggregation schedule algorithm under relaxed restrictions; on the other hand, we will study distributed algorithm on minimum-delay aggregation schedule.

Acknowledgments. This work was supported by the National Natural Science Foundation of China under grant 61370216.

References

1. Ren, M., Li, J., Guo, L., Cai, Z.: Data collection with probabilistic guarantees in opportunistic wireless networks. Int. J. Sensor Netw. (accepted)
2. Du, H., Hu, X., Jia, X.: Energy efficient routing and scheduling for real-time data aggregation in WSNs. Comput. Commun. **29**, 3527–3535 (2006)
3. Du, H., Luo, H.: Routing-cost constrained connected dominating set. In: Kao, M.Y. (ed.) Encyclopedia of Algorithms, pp. 1–5. Springer, New York (2014)
4. Du, H., Wu, W., Ye, Q., Li, D., Lee, W., Xu, X.: CDS-based virtual backbone construction with guaranteed routing cost in wireless sensor networks. IEEE Trans. Parallel Distrib. Syst. **24**(4), 652–661 (2013)
5. Du, H., Ye, Q., Zhong, J., Wang, Y., Lee, W., Park, H.: Polynomial-time approximation scheme for minimum connected dominating set under routing cost constraint in wireless sensor networks. Theor. Comput. Sci. **447**, 38–43 (2011)
6. Du, H., Ye, Q., Wu, W., Lee, W., Li, D., Du, D., et al.: Constant approximation for virtual backbone construction with guaranteed routing cost in wireless sensor networks. In: Proceedings - IEEE INFOCOM, vol. 28, pp. 1737–1744 (2011)
7. Chen, X., Xu, M.: A geographical cellular-like architecture for wireless sensor networks. In: Jia, X., Wu, J., He, Y. (eds.) MSN 2005. LNCS, vol. 3794, pp. 249–258. Springer, Heidelberg (2005)
8. Huang, S.C., Wan, P.J., Vu, C.T., Li, S., Yao, F.: Nearly constant approximation for data aggregation scheduling in wireless sensor networks. In: Proceedings - IEEE INFOCOM, pp. 366–372 (2007)
9. Wan, P.J., Huang, C.H., Wang, L., Wan, Z., Jia, X.: Minimum-latency aggregation scheduling in multihop wireless networks. In: Proceedings - MOBIHOC, pp. 185–194 (2009)
10. Nguyen, T.D., Zalyubovskiy, V., Choo, H.: Efficient Time Latency of Data Aggregation Based on Neighboring Dominators in WSNs. In: GLOBECOM, pp. 1–6 (2011)
11. Du, H., Zhang, Z., Wu, W., Wu, L., Xing, K.: Constant-approximation for optimal data aggregation with physical interference. J. Global Optim. **56**(4), 1653–1666 (2013)

12. He, Z., Cai, Z., Cheng, S., Wang, X.: Approximate aggregation for tracking quantiles and range countings in wireless sensor networks. Theor. Comput. Sci. **607**, 381–390 (2015)
13. Yu, B., Li, J.Z.: Minimum-time aggregation scheduling in dutycycled wireless sensor networks. J. Comput. Sci. Technol. **26**(6), 962–970 (2011)
14. Xiao, S., Huang, J., Pan, L., Cheng, Y., Liu, J.: On centralized and distributed algorithms for minimizing data aggregation time in duty-cycled wireless sensor networks. Wireless Netw. **20**(7), 1729–1741 (2014)
15. Chen, Q., Gao, H., Cheng, S., Cai, Z.: Approximate scheduling and constructing algorithms for minimum-energy multicasting in duty-cycled sensor networks. In: IIKI, pp. 163–168 (2015)
16. Gu, Y., He, T.: Dynamic switching-based data forwarding for low-duty-cycle wireless sensor networks. IEEE Trans. Mob. Comput. **10**(12), 1741–1754 (2011)

Optimal Jamming Attack Schedule Against Wireless State Estimation in Cyber-Physical Systems

Lianghong Peng[1,2], Xianghui Cao[1,2], Changyin Sun[1,2(✉)], and Yu Cheng[3]

[1] School of Automation, Southeast University, Jiangsu 210096, China
{lhpeng,xhcao,cysun}@seu.edu.cn
[2] Key Lab of Measurement and Control of Complex Systems of Engineering,
Ministry of Education, Southeast University, Jiangsu 210096, China
[3] Department of Electrical and Computer Engineering,
Illinois Institute of Technology, Chicago, IL 60616, USA
cheng@iit.edu

Abstract. Recently, the security issues of Cyber-Physical Systems (CPS) have gained a growing amount of research attention. As a typical application of CPS, remote state estimation systems over wireless channels are vulnerable to various cyber attacks, such as channel jamming attacks. Standing on the point of the jamming attacker, this paper investigates the problem of optimal attack schedule under energy constraints against a wireless state estimation system, where two sensors transmit data to a remote estimator over two independent wireless channels. Due to its radio constraint, the attacker is assumed to only launch jamming attack on one of the two channels at a time. We formulate the problem of optimal attack schedule as a nonlinear program which aims to maximize the remote estimation error covariance subjecting to the attacker's energy constraint. We then theoretically derive the optimal schedule and shows that it depends on the attacker's energy budget, the physical system dynamics and the channel properties. Finally, the theoretical results are validated and evaluated through numerical simulations.

Keywords: Cyber-Physical System · Energy constraint · Jamming attack · Optimal attack schedule · Remote state estimation

1 Introduction

The emerging Cyber-Physical Systems (CPS) integrate computation, networking, and control technologies to facilitate intimate interactions between the physical and cyber worlds. CPS have found wide applications in environmental monitoring, building automation, transportation systems, entertainment, consumer appliances, etc. [1–3].

Recently, an increasing amount of research efforts have been devoted to investigating security issues of CPS [4,5]. Malicious cyber attacks can be in various

© Springer International Publishing Switzerland 2016
Q. Yang et al. (Eds.): WASA 2016, LNCS 9798, pp. 318–330, 2016.
DOI: 10.1007/978-3-319-42836-9_29

forms, such as jamming attack [4], replay attack [5] and false data injection attack [6]. Jamming attack aims at blocking the communication between system components by jamming the communication channels [7,8]. The work in [7] proposes four different jamming attack models and evaluates their effectiveness in terms of how each method affects the ability of a wireless node in sending and receiving packets. From a networking point of view, the work in [8] proposes to use honeypots to defend jamming attacks in wireless networks.

Conventional attacks such as those stealing user accounts and files in storage are usually limited to cyber space. However, in the context of CPS, attackers can further cause severe impact to real-time physical systems by cyber attacks. Jamming attack in CPS has attracted some attention of researchers also from the control community [4]. Remote state estimation over wireless channels is a typical application scenario of CPS whose security issues have attracted some attention [9–11]. The problem of optimal zero-delay jamming over an additive noise channel is considered in [9]. The authors in [11] present a methodology to control ground robots under malicious attack on sensors and use a recursive filtering technique that estimates the state of the system. The work in [3] discusses a secure smart grid infrastructure using a Cyber-Physical approach and proposes several countermeasures against various cyber attacks such as replay attacks. However, existing works mainly investigate the attack problem, such as optimal attack schedule, under single sensor and single channel cases [4,12]. In [4], the authors investigate the problem of optimal attack schedule in order to cause highest estimation performance degradation. However, to the authors best knowledge, the problem of optimal attack schedule against state estimation systems with multiple sensors has not been considered in the literature.

In this paper, we consider the problem of optimal jamming attack schedule against remote state estimation in CPS with multiple sensors. In particular, we assume that the sensors monitor multiple physical processes and transmit their sensory data over multiple wireless channels in independent frequency bands. Each sensor firstly runs a local filter to process its measurements about the physical systems, and then transmits the filtered results to a remote estimator through a wireless channel. Due to its radio constraint, the attacker can only jam one of the channels at a time in order to deteriorate the remote estimation quality. Moreover, we assume that the attacker's energy is constrained such that it cannot persistently jamming the channel over time. In the view of the attacker, we aim to find the optimal time schedule for the attacker to maximize the impact of the jamming attack under the attacker's energy constraint. The main contributions of the paper are summarized as follows:

1. We start with two sensors and formulate the optimal jamming attack schedule problem of under the attacker's energy constraint.
2. The optimal jamming attack schedule is theoretically derived. We show that the optimal schedule depends on the physical systems' dynamics, the packet loss rates over the wireless channels and the energy budgets of the attacker. The results are then extended to more general cases with multiple sensors.
3. We validate our results through extensive simulations.

The remainder of this paper is organized as follows. Section 2 formulates the problem. The main results are presented in Sect. 3. Section 4 presents the simulation results, followed by discussion about extension to scenarios with multiple sensors in Sect. 5 and the conclusion in Sect. 6.

Notations. Throughout this paper, we adopt the following notations. $\mathbb{Z}$ is the set of all integers. $\mathbb{R}$ is the set of real numbers; $\mathbb{R}^n$ denotes the n-dimensional Euclidean space and $\mathbb{R}^{n \times m}$ is the set of real matrices of dimension $n \times m$; $\mathbb{S}_+^n$ is the set of n-by-n positive semi-definite matrices. When $X \in \mathbb{S}_+^n$, we simply write $X \geqslant 0$; when X is positive definite, we write $X > 0$. For a square matrix X, denote its trace as $\text{Tr}(X)$. The notation $X \geq Y$ (respectively, $X > Y$), where X and Y are symmetric matrices, means that the matrix $X - Y$ is positive semi-definite (respectively, positive definite). If $Y - X \geqslant 0$, then $\text{Tr}(Y - X) \geqslant 0$. X' is the transpose of X. For functions $f, f_1, f_2 : \mathbb{S}_+^n \rightarrow \mathbb{S}_+^n$, define $f_1 \circ f_2(X) \triangleq f_1(f_2(X))$ and $f^t(X) \triangleq \underbrace{f \circ f \circ \cdots \circ f}_{t \ times}(X)$. For a random variable X, $\text{Pr}[X]$ and $\text{E}[X]$ denote the probability and expected value of X, respectively. $\lfloor \cdot \rfloor$ is the floor function. $\rho(X)$ is the spectral radius of the matrix X.

2   System Model and Problem Formulation

2.1   System Model

Wireless remote estimating the states of dynamic systems is considered in this paper, the dynamic system here can be smart grid and the states of it can be power flow, voltage magnitude and phase angle [3,10]. Consider estimating the states of the following discrete linear dynamic systems [3,10]:

$$x_i(k + 1) = A_i x_i(k) + \omega_i(k), \quad i = 1, 2, \cdots , \tag{1}$$

where $k \in \mathbb{Z}$ is the time indices, $x_i(k) \in \mathbb{R}^n$ is the system state and $\omega_i(k)$ is a white Gaussian noise with covariance matrix $Q_i \geqslant 0$. The initial state $x_i(0)$ is also a zero-mean Gaussian variable with covariance $P_i(0) > 0$. $\rho(A_i) \geq 1$ and the pair $(A_i, \sqrt{Q_i})$ is stabilizable [13].

We consider remotely estimating the states of two dynamic systems of the above form, i.e. $i = 1, 2$. As shown in Fig. 1, two sensors are deployed to take noisy measurements as follows

$$y_i(k) = C_i x_i(k) + v_i(k), \quad i = 1, 2, \tag{2}$$

where $y_1(k) \in \mathbb{R}^{m_1}$ and $y_2(k) \in \mathbb{R}^{m_2}$ are the measurements collected by the two sensors at time k, $v_i(k) \in \mathbb{R}^{m_i}$ are the measurement noises which are zero-mean white Gaussian with covariances $R_i > 0, i = 1, 2$. In addition, $x_i(0), \omega_i(k), v_1(k)$ and $v_2(k)$ are mutually independent. For the problem's tractability, we assume that (A_1, C_1) and (A_2, C_2) are observable [13].

At each time step, each sensor first runs a Kalman filter, which is known as the optimal linear filter, to obtain a local estimate of its corresponding monitored

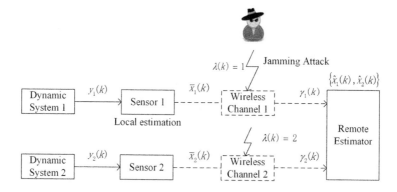

Fig. 1. Remote state estimation under jamming attack.

physical process. Due to space limit, the standard Kalman filtering process is omitted. Interest readers are referred to [14]. Denote $\bar{x}_i(k)$ and $\bar{P}_i(k)$ as the i-th sensor's local state estimate and the corresponding estimation error covariance of i-th system, i.e.,

$$\bar{x}_i(k) = \mathrm{E}[x_i(k)|y_i(1), y_i(2), \cdots, y_i(k)],$$
$$\bar{P}_i(k) = \mathrm{E}[(x_i(k) - \bar{x}_i(k))(x_i(k) - \bar{x}_i(k))'|y_i(1), y_i(2), \cdots, y_i(k)], i = 1, 2. \quad (3)$$

As stated in [14], $\bar{P}_i(k)$ converges exponentially fast to a steady-state value. Therefore, we assume that the local estimates have converged and denote $\bar{P}_i$ as the steady value of $\{\bar{P}_i(k)\}$, $i = 1, 2$.

2.2   Attack Model

The attacker is assumed capable to conduct jamming attack to jam the communication channel between the sensor and the remote estimator, and hence causing random data packet drop outs. In a very similar case where only one sensor is considered, for example in [4], in which the optimal attack schedule is schedule with a consecutive attack sequence n. In our case, it is practical to suppose that the two sensors can explore transmission opportunities over two orthogonal wireless channels corresponding to two interleaving frequency bands [2,15]. Meanwhile, due to the wireless radio can only operate on one channel at a time, each time the attacker can choose only one channel to jam. In order to model the attacker's decisions at time k, define $\lambda(k) = i$, which means the attacker launches jamming attack on channel i, $i = 1, 2$; and $\lambda(k) = 0$ represents that the attacker do not launch attack to the two channels. As mentioned above, $1_{\lambda(k)=1} + 1_{\lambda(k)=2} \le 1, \forall k \in \mathbb{Z}^+$, where 1_{cond} is an indicator function which equals 1 if cond is true and equals 0 if otherwise.

  If the communication channel is jammed, the transmitted packets will be randomly lost. We use a binary random process $\gamma_i(k)$ to describe the packet loss process. That is, $\gamma_i(k) = 1$ indicates that the packet transmitted from sensor i is successfully delivered to the estimator at time k, and $\gamma_i(k) = 0$ if the packet is lost. $\Pr[\gamma_i(k) = 1] = \gamma_i, i = 1, 2$. The remote estimator can know whether a sensor packet is successfully transmitted or not by checking the time stamp and sensor ID of the received packet. The implication of packet loss is that the estimator may fail to generate a stable state estimator. Assume that there will be no packet loss of channel i when channel i is not under attack.

2.3 Problem Formulation

Denote $s = (\lambda(1), \lambda(2), \cdots, \lambda(T))$ as the attacker's schedule.

Average Error: For a given attack schedule s with a time horizon T, define $J_i(s)$ as the average expected estimation error covariance matrix, i.e.,

$$J_i(s) = \frac{1}{T} \sum_{k=1}^{T} \mathrm{E}[P_i(k, \lambda(k))], i = 1, 2. \tag{4}$$

The objective of this paper is to solve the following problem with the energy constraint in the viewpoint of the attacker:

Problem 2.1: Find the optimal attack schedule for maximizing the overall estimation error, i.e.,

$$\max_{s \in \mathcal{S}} \quad \mathrm{Tr}[J_1(s)] + \mathrm{Tr}[J_2(s)], \tag{5}$$

$$s.t. \quad \sum_{k=1}^{T} (1_{\lambda(k)=1} \Psi_1 + 1_{\lambda(k)=2} \Psi_2) \le \Psi, \tag{6}$$

$$1_{\lambda(k)=1} + 1_{\lambda(k)=2} \le 1, \tag{7}$$

where $\mathcal{S} = \{0,1\}^T$ is the set of all possible attack schedules, $\Psi_i > 0$ denotes the consumed energy of attacker to launch once attack to channel $i, i = 1, 2$, Ψ represents maximum total energy of attacker launching T times attack. It is clear that using as much energy as possible to launch jamming attacks can cause the highest estimation performance degradation. Therefore, the total energy Ψ should be utilized as much as possible, i.e.,

$$\Psi - \sum_{k=1}^{T} (1_{\lambda(k)=1} \Psi_1 + 1_{\lambda(k)=2} \Psi_2) < \min\{\Psi_1, \Psi_2\}. \tag{8}$$

3 Optimal Jamming Attack Schedules

Denote $\hat{x}_i(k)$ and $P_i(k)$ as the remote estimator's state estimate and the corresponding estimation error covariance, i.e., $\hat{x}_i(k) = \mathrm{E}[x_i(k)]$, $P_i(k) = \mathrm{E}[(x_i(k) - \hat{x}_i(k))(x_i(k) - \hat{x}_i(k))']$, $i = 1, 2$. Then, we use the local measurements of $x_i(k)$ to compute optimal estimation $\hat{x}_i(k)$ and the corresponding estimation error covariance matrix $P_i(k)$ of the remote estimator. Therefore, the optimal estimation $\hat{x}_i(k)$ and $P_i(k)$ are obtained as follows:

$$\hat{x}_i(k) = \begin{cases} \bar{x}_i(k), & 1_{\lambda(k)=i} = 0 \ or \ 1_{\lambda(k)=i}\gamma_i(k) = 1, \\ A_i\hat{x}_i(k-1), & 1_{\lambda(k)=i}(1-\gamma_i(k)) = 1, i = 1,2, \end{cases} \quad (9)$$

$$P_i(k) = \begin{cases} \bar{P}_i, & 1_{\lambda(k)=i} = 0 \ or \ 1_{\lambda(k)=i}\gamma_i(k) = 1, \\ h_i(P_i(k-1)), & 1_{\lambda(k)=i}(1-\gamma_i(k)) = 1, i = 1,2, \end{cases} \quad (10)$$

where $h_i(X) = A_iXA_i' + Q_i, i = 1,2$.

Next we analysis the optimal jamming attack schedules for Problem 2.1.

Lemma 1. *The function $h_i^k(\bar{P}_i)$ is monotonically increasing in k, where $k \in \mathbb{Z}^+, i = 1,2$ [16].*

For the one-sensor case, it has been proved in [4] that the optimal attack schedule which can maximize the average expected estimation error covariance is any one that belongs to consecutive attack sequences and the block of consecutive attack sequence can be in any position in $[0,T]$. In our case, since the two physical processes are independent, based on [4], it is without loss of generality to assume that the optimal attack schedule is in the following form:

$$s^{\tau_1,\tau_2} : \underbrace{1,1,\cdots,1}_{\tau_1 \ times}, \underbrace{2,2,\cdots,2}_{\tau_2 \ times}, \underbrace{0,0,\cdots,0}_{T-\tau_1-\tau_2 \ times}, \quad (11)$$

where $\tau_1\Psi_1 + \tau_2\Psi_2 \le \Psi$.

Let $E[P_i(k)] = M_i(k)$, and the initial error covariance $E[P_i(0)] = M_i(0) = \bar{P}_i, i = 1,2$. For simplicity, assume that $\frac{\Psi_1}{\Psi_2} = \frac{\alpha}{\beta}$ is a rational number, where α and β are two co-prime integers. Since $\beta\Psi_1 = \alpha\Psi_2$, the energy which can launch β times attack on channel 1 can be used to launch α times attack on channel 2. Then, based on (10),

$$\begin{cases} M_1(k) = \gamma_1\bar{P}_1 + (1-\gamma_1)h_1(M_1(k-1)), \\ M_2(k) = \bar{P}_2, \end{cases} \quad k = 1,\cdots,\tau_1, \quad (12)$$

$$\begin{cases} M_1(k) = \bar{P}_1, \\ M_2(k) = \gamma_2\bar{P}_2 + (1-\gamma_2)h_2(M_2(k-1)), \end{cases} \quad k = \tau_1+1,\cdots,\tau_1+\tau_2, \quad (13)$$

Therefore,

$$TJ(s^{\tau_1,\tau_2}) = TJ_1(s^{\tau_1,\tau_2}) + TJ_2(s^{\tau_1,\tau_2})$$

$$= (T-\tau_1)\bar{P}_1 + (T-\tau_2)\bar{P}_2 + \sum_{k=1}^{\tau_1} M_1(k) + \sum_{j=\tau_1+1}^{\tau_1+\tau_2} M_2(j). \quad (14)$$

Then we have the following theorem.

Theorem 1. *Consider system (1)–(2). The optimal jamming attack schedule that solves Problem 2.1 is $s^{\tau_1^*, \tau_2^*}$, where τ_1^*, τ_2^* are chosen as follows*

1. *if $f_1(\Psi_1, \Psi_2, \bar{P}_1, \gamma_1) \geq f_2(\Psi_1, \Psi_2, \bar{P}_2, \gamma_2)$, then $\tau_1^* = \lfloor \frac{z_1}{\Psi_1} \rfloor, \tau_2^* = \lfloor \frac{\Psi}{\Psi_2} \rfloor$,*
2. *if $f_1(\Psi_1, \Psi_2, \bar{P}_1, \gamma_1) < f_2(\Psi_1, \Psi_2, \bar{P}_2, \gamma_2)$, then $\tau_1^* = \lfloor \frac{\Psi}{\Psi_1} \rfloor, \tau_2^* = \lfloor \frac{z_2}{\Psi_2} \rfloor$,*

where

$$f_i(\Psi_1, \Psi_2, \bar{P}_i, \gamma_i) = (\lfloor \frac{\Psi}{\Psi_i} \rfloor - \lfloor \frac{z_i}{\Psi_i} \rfloor)\bar{P}_i - \sum_{k=\lfloor \frac{z_i}{\Psi_i} \rfloor+1}^{\lfloor \frac{\Psi}{\Psi_i} \rfloor} M_i(k), \tag{15}$$

$$M_i(k) = \gamma_i \sum_{q=0}^{k-1}(1 - \gamma_i)^q h_i^q(\bar{P}_i) + (1 - \gamma_i)^k h_i^k(\bar{P}_i), \quad i = 1, 2, \tag{16}$$

$z_1 = \Psi - \lfloor \frac{\Psi}{\Psi_2} \rfloor \Psi_2, z_2 = \Psi - \lfloor \frac{\Psi}{\Psi_1} \rfloor \Psi_1.$

Proof: According to (14), we have

$$TJ(s^{\tau_1+\beta, \tau_2-\alpha}) - TJ(s^{\tau_1, \tau_2})$$

$$= (T - \tau_1 - \beta)\bar{P}_1 + (T - \tau_2 + \alpha)\bar{P}_2 + \sum_{k=1}^{\tau_1+\beta} M_1(k) + \sum_{j=\tau_1+\beta+1}^{\tau_1+\beta+\tau_2-\alpha} M_2(j)$$

$$-(T - \tau_1)\bar{P}_1 - (T - \tau_2)\bar{P}_2 - \sum_{k=1}^{\tau_1} M_1(k) - \sum_{j=\tau_1+1}^{\tau_1+\tau_2} M_2(j)$$

$$= \sum_{k=1}^{\beta} M_1(\tau_1 + k) - \beta\bar{P}_1 + \alpha\bar{P}_2 - \sum_{k=1}^{\alpha} M_2(\tau_2 - \alpha + k), \tag{17}$$

where $\tau_2 = \lfloor \frac{\Psi - \tau_1 \Psi_1}{\Psi_2} \rfloor$. Denotes

$$G(\tau_1 + \beta, \tau_2 - \alpha) = \sum_{k=1}^{\beta} M_1(\tau_1 + k) - \sum_{k=1}^{\alpha} M_2(\tau_2 - \alpha + k). \tag{18}$$

It follows that

$$G(\tau_1 + \beta) - G(\tau_1) = \sum_{k=1}^{\beta} M_1(\tau_1 + \beta + k) - \sum_{k=1}^{\alpha} M_2(\tau_2 - 2\alpha + k)$$

$$- \sum_{k=1}^{\beta} M_1(\tau_1 + k) + \sum_{k=1}^{\alpha} M_2(\tau_2 - \alpha + k). \tag{19}$$

From (16) and Lemma 1, we know that

$$M_1(k) - M_1(k - 1)$$
$$= \gamma_1(1 - \gamma_1)^{k-1}h_1^{k-1}(\bar{P}_1) + (1 - \gamma_1)^k h_1^k(\bar{P}_1) - (1 - \gamma_1)^{k-1}h_1^{k-1}(\bar{P}_1)$$
$$= (1 - \gamma_1)^k h_1^k(\bar{P}_1) - (1 - \gamma_1)^k h_1^{k-1}(\bar{P}_1) \geq 0. \tag{20}$$

Similarly, we can get $M_2(k) - M_2(k-1) \geq 0$. Therefore, $G(\tau_1 + \beta) - G(\tau_1) \geq 0$ in (19), which implies that the trajectory of $J(s^{\tau_1,\tau_2})$ is a lower convex curve with $\tau_1, \tau_1 \in [0, \lfloor \frac{\Psi}{\Psi_1} \rfloor], \tau_2 = \lfloor \frac{\Psi - \tau_1 \Psi_1}{\Psi_2} \rfloor$. We can conclude that $J(s^{\tau_1,\tau_2})$ can achieve the maximum on both sides of the endpoint, i.e.,

$$\min\{J(s^{0,\lfloor \frac{\Psi}{\Psi_2} \rfloor}), J(s^{\lfloor \frac{\Psi}{\Psi_1} \rfloor, 0})\} \geq J(s^{\tau_1,\tau_2}), \tag{21}$$

for all $\tau_1 \in [0, \lfloor \frac{\Psi}{\Psi_1} \rfloor], \tau_2 = \lfloor \frac{\Psi - \tau_1 \Psi_1}{\Psi_2} \rfloor$. Taking (8) into consideration, we denote $z_1 = \Psi - \lfloor \frac{\Psi}{\Psi_2} \rfloor \Psi_2, z_2 = \Psi - \lfloor \frac{\Psi}{\Psi_1} \rfloor \Psi_1$. Again based on (14), we have

$$TJ(s^{\lfloor \frac{z_1}{\Psi_1} \rfloor, \lfloor \frac{\Psi}{\Psi_2} \rfloor}) = (T - \lfloor \frac{z_1}{\Psi_1} \rfloor)\bar{P}_1 + \sum_{k=1}^{\lfloor \frac{z_1}{\Psi_1} \rfloor} M_1(k) + (T - \lfloor \frac{\Psi}{\Psi_2} \rfloor)\bar{P}_2 + \sum_{j=1}^{\lfloor \frac{\Psi}{\Psi_2} \rfloor} M_2(j),$$

$$TJ(s^{\lfloor \frac{\Psi}{\Psi_1} \rfloor, \lfloor \frac{z_2}{\Psi_2} \rfloor}) = (T - \lfloor \frac{\Psi}{\Psi_1} \rfloor)\bar{P}_1 + (T - \lfloor \frac{z_2}{\Psi_2} \rfloor)\bar{P}_2 + \sum_{k=1}^{\lfloor \frac{\Psi}{\Psi_1} \rfloor} M_1(k) + \sum_{j=1}^{\lfloor \frac{z_2}{\Psi_2} \rfloor} M_2(j).$$

It follows that

$$TJ(s^{\lfloor \frac{z_1}{\Psi_1} \rfloor, \lfloor \frac{\Psi}{\Psi_2} \rfloor}) - TJ(s^{\lfloor \frac{\Psi}{\Psi_1} \rfloor, \lfloor \frac{z_2}{\Psi_2} \rfloor})$$

$$= (\lfloor \frac{\Psi}{\Psi_1} \rfloor - \lfloor \frac{z_1}{\Psi_1} \rfloor)\bar{P}_1 - (\lfloor \frac{\Psi}{\Psi_2} \rfloor - \lfloor \frac{z_2}{\Psi_2} \rfloor)\bar{P}_2 + \sum_{j=\lfloor \frac{z_2}{\Psi_2} \rfloor+1}^{\lfloor \frac{\Psi}{\Psi_2} \rfloor} M_2(j) - \sum_{k=\lfloor \frac{z_1}{\Psi_1} \rfloor+1}^{\lfloor \frac{\Psi}{\Psi_1} \rfloor} M_1(k),$$

therefore,

$$(\tau_1^*, \tau_2^*) = \begin{cases} (\lfloor \frac{z_1}{\Psi_1} \rfloor, \lfloor \frac{\Psi}{\Psi_2} \rfloor) & if \quad J(s^{\lfloor \frac{z_1}{\Psi_1} \rfloor, \lfloor \frac{\Psi}{\Psi_2} \rfloor}) \geq J(s^{\lfloor \frac{\Psi}{\Psi_1} \rfloor, \lfloor \frac{z_2}{\Psi_2} \rfloor}), \\ (\lfloor \frac{\Psi}{\Psi_1} \rfloor, \lfloor \frac{z_2}{\Psi_2} \rfloor) & if \quad J(s^{\lfloor \frac{z_1}{\Psi_1} \rfloor, \lfloor \frac{\Psi}{\Psi_2} \rfloor}) < J(s^{\lfloor \frac{\Psi}{\Psi_1} \rfloor, \lfloor \frac{z_2}{\Psi_2} \rfloor}). \end{cases} \tag{22}$$

The proof is completed. $\square$

Corollary 1. *When $A_1 = A_2, C_1 = C_2, Q_1 = Q_2, \bar{P}_1 = \bar{P}_2, \gamma_1 = \gamma_2, \tau_1^*$ and τ_2^* in Theorem 1 are chosen as follows:*

1. $\tau_1^* = 0, \tau_2^* = \lfloor \frac{\Psi}{\Psi_2} \rfloor$, if

$$\lfloor \frac{\Psi}{\Psi_1} \rfloor - \lfloor \frac{z_1}{\Psi_1} \rfloor \geq \lfloor \frac{\Psi}{\Psi_2} \rfloor - \lfloor \frac{z_2}{\Psi_2} \rfloor \ and \ \lfloor \frac{\Psi}{\Psi_2} \rfloor \geq \lfloor \frac{\Psi}{\Psi_1} \rfloor, \tag{23}$$

2. $\tau_1^* = \lfloor \frac{\Psi}{\Psi_1} \rfloor, \tau_2^* = 0$, if

$$\lfloor \frac{\Psi}{\Psi_1} \rfloor - \lfloor \frac{z_1}{\Psi_1} \rfloor < \lfloor \frac{\Psi}{\Psi_2} \rfloor - \lfloor \frac{z_2}{\Psi_2} \rfloor \ and \ \lfloor \frac{\Psi}{\Psi_2} \rfloor < \lfloor \frac{\Psi}{\Psi_1} \rfloor. \tag{24}$$

4   Illustrative Examples

Consider system (1)–(2) with

$$A_1 = \begin{pmatrix} 1.2 & 0.2 \\ 1 & 0.3 \end{pmatrix}, A_2 = \begin{pmatrix} 1 & 0.1 \\ 1.5 & 0.8 \end{pmatrix}, C_1 = \begin{pmatrix} 0.1 & 0.4 \\ 0 & 0.5 \end{pmatrix}, C_2 = \begin{pmatrix} 0.2 & 0.2 \\ 0 & 0.1 \end{pmatrix},$$

ω_k, v_k^1 and v_k^2 having zero mean and variance $Q_1 = I_{2\times2}$, $Q_2 = 2I_{2\times2}$, $R_1 = 2I_{2\times2}$, $R_2 = I_{2\times2}$. Take $\Psi = 10, \Psi_1 = 1, \Psi_2 = 1, r_1 = 0.1, r_2 = 0.1, T = 20$. Obviously, (A, C_1), (A, C_2) are observable.

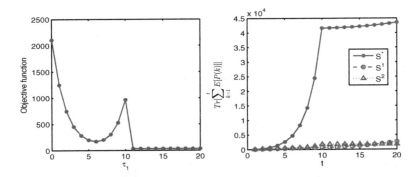

Fig. 2. Left figure shows the performance of $\text{Tr}[J(s^{\tau_1, \tau_2})]$ with $T = 20, \Psi = 10, \Psi_1 = 1, \Psi_2 = 1, r_1 = 0.1, r_2 = 0.1$. Right figure is the performance of $\text{Tr}[\sum_{k=1}^{t} \text{E}[P(k)]]$ under different attack schedule with the same parameters.

Thus according to Theorem 1, we can find the optimal values τ_1^*, τ_2^*. Left figure in Fig. 2 shows the trajectory of $\text{Tr}[J(s^{\tau_1, \tau_2})]$ with the parameters given above. Obviously, when $\tau_1^* = 0, \tau_2^* = 10$, $\text{Tr}[J(s^{\tau_1, \tau_2})]$ arrives the maximum. Then the optimal jamming attack schedule that solves Problem 2.1 is

$$\underbrace{2, 2, \cdots, 2,}_{10\ times} \underbrace{0, 0, \cdots, 0}_{10\ times}. \tag{25}$$

Right one in Fig. 2 represents the trajectories of $\text{Tr}[\sum_{k=1}^{t} \text{E}[P(k)]]$ under different attack sequences with the parameters given above. The curve with s^* is the performance of $\text{Tr}[\sum_{k=1}^{t} \text{E}[P(k)]]$ under following attack sequence

$$s^* : \begin{cases} \underbrace{2, 2, \cdots, 2,}_{t\ times} & while\ t \leq 10, \\ \underbrace{2, 2, \cdots, 2,}_{10\ times} \underbrace{0, 0, \cdots, 0}_{t-10\ times}, & while\ t > 10. \end{cases} \tag{26}$$

The case with s^1 is the trajectory of $\text{Tr}[\sum_{k=1}^{t} E[P(k)]]$ under attack sequence as follows

$$
s^1 : \begin{cases} \underbrace{1,2,1,2,\cdots,1,2,}_{t \ times} & while \ t \leq 10, \\ \underbrace{1,2,1,2,\cdots,1,2,}_{10 \ times}\underbrace{0,0,\cdots,0,}_{t-10 \ times} & while \ t > 10. \end{cases} \tag{27}
$$

The curve with s^2 shows the trace of $\text{Tr}[\sum_{k=1}^{t} E[P(k)]]$ under stochastic attack sequence with attack probability 0.5 to channel 1 and 2. This figure illustrates that $J(s)$ can achieve the maximum under consecutive attack schedule.

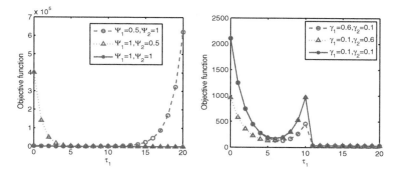

Fig. 3. Left figure is performance of $\text{Tr}[J(s^{\tau_1,\tau_2})]$ under different energy constraint $\Psi_1 = 1, \Psi_2 = 1$, $\Psi_1 = 0.5, \Psi_2 = 1$, and $\Psi_1 = 1, \Psi_2 = 0.5$, respectively. Right figure shows the performance with different rate of packet loss $\gamma_1 = 0.1, \gamma_2 = 0.1$, $\gamma_1 = 0.6, \gamma_2 = 0.1$, and $\gamma_1 = 0.1, \gamma_2 = 0.6$, respectively, the other parameters are same as in Fig. 2.

Left figure in Fig. 3 is the performance of $\text{Tr}[J(s^{\tau_1,\tau_2})]$ with different energy constraint and the other parameters which are the same as in Fig. 2. The trace with $\Psi_1 = 1, \Psi_2 = 1$ is same as the left one in Fig. 2. In the case with $\Psi_1 = 0.5, \Psi_2 = 1$, we have $\tau_1^* = 20, \tau_2^* = 0$. Moreover, in the case with $\Psi_1 = 1, \Psi_2 = 0.5$, the optimal values are $\tau_1^* = 0, \tau_2^* = 20$. The trajectory of $\text{Tr}[J(s^{\tau_1,\tau_2})]$ is different with different energy constraint revealed by this figure. Right one in Fig. 3 shows the traces of $\text{Tr}[J(s^{\tau_1,\tau_2})]$ with different rate of packet loss and the other parameters are same as in Fig. 2. From the three different cases with $\gamma_1 = 0.1, \gamma_2 = 0.1$, $\gamma_1 = 0.6, \gamma_2 = 0.1$ and $\gamma_1 = 0.1, \gamma_2 = 0.6$, we can get that the trace of $\text{Tr}[J(s^{\tau_1,\tau_2})]$ is different with different rate of packet loss.

Figure 4 displays the performance of $\text{Tr}[J(s^{\tau_1,\tau_2})]$ with different system parameters. Case 4 is the same as the left one in Fig. 2. Case 1 shows the trace of $\text{Tr}[J(s^{\tau_1,\tau_2})]$ with $A_1 = \begin{pmatrix} 1.8 & 0.2 \\ 1 & 0.3 \end{pmatrix}$, and the other parameters are same as in Fig. 2. In this case, we can get $\tau_1^* = 10, \tau_2^* = 0$. Case 2 shows the trace of $\text{Tr}[J(s^{\tau_1,\tau_2})]$ with $A_1 = \begin{pmatrix} 1 & 0.2 \\ 1 & 0.3 \end{pmatrix}, A_2 = \begin{pmatrix} 1 & 0.1 \\ 2 & 0.8 \end{pmatrix}$, $\Psi_1 = 0.5, \Psi_2 = 0.5$.

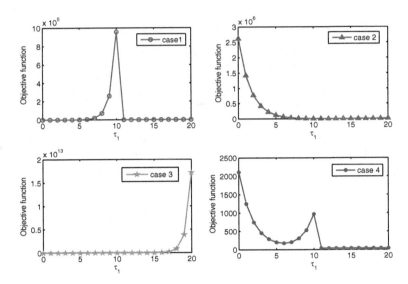

Fig. 4. Performance under four cases with different parameters.

In this case, We can know that $\tau_1^* = 0, \tau_2^* = 10$. Case 3 shows the trace of $\mathrm{Tr}[J(s^{\tau_1,\tau_2})]$ with $A_1 = \begin{pmatrix} 2 & 0.2 \\ 1 & 0.3 \end{pmatrix}, A_2 = \begin{pmatrix} 1 & 0.1 \\ 1 & 0.8 \end{pmatrix}, \Psi_1 = 0.5, \Psi_2 = 0.5$. We can get $\tau_1^* = 20, \tau_2^* = 0$.

5 Discussion on Scenarios with Multiple Sensors

We consider the wireless sensor network with two sensors in the above. However, the application of the network with two sensors has some limitations. Consider the scenarios with multiple sensors, from this paper, we know that the total average expected estimation error covariance matrix $J(s)$ can achieve the maximum under consecutive attack schedule, like

$$\underbrace{1, 1, \cdots, 1}_{\tau_1 \ times}, \underbrace{2, 2, \cdots, 2}_{\tau_2 \ times}, \cdots, \underbrace{i, i, \cdots, i}_{\tau_i \ times}, \cdots, \quad \underbrace{0, 0, \cdots, 0}_{T - \tau_1 - \tau_2 - \cdots, \ times} \quad . \tag{28}$$

Similar to the results above, we can define $f_i(\Psi, \bar{P}_i, \gamma_i)$ which is similar to (15), where $\Psi = (\Psi_1, \Psi_2, \cdots, \Psi_i, \cdots)$, $\Psi_i > 0$ denotes the consumed energy of attacker to launch once attack to channel $i, i = 1, 2, \cdots$. Firstly, from pair-wise comparison of $f_i(\Psi, \bar{P}_i, \gamma_i)$, we will get the maximum, which is denoted as $f_j(\Psi, \bar{P}_j, \gamma_j)$. Then we can conclude that $\tau_j^* = \lfloor \frac{\Psi}{\Psi_j} \rfloor$, where Ψ represents maximum total energy of attacker launching T times attack. Secondly, set $z_j = \Psi - \tau_j^* \Psi_j$, we also can define $f_i^1(\Psi_i, \bar{P}_i, \gamma_i)$, where $\Psi_i \leq z_j, i = 1, 2, \cdots$. Finding the maximum of $f_i^1(\Psi_i, \bar{P}_i, \gamma_i)$ by pair-wise comparison, we achieve the second $\tau_k^* = \lfloor \frac{z_j}{\Psi_k} \rfloor$. Keep going as above, we gain the optimal value $\tau_1^*, \tau_2^*, \cdots, \tau_i^*, \cdots$. The new results about this problem will be given out while we work out.

6 Conclusion

In this paper, the problem of optimal jamming attack schedule against wireless state estimation in Cyber-physical systems has been investigated, where the attacker has energy constraint. We consider there is only one channel jammed by the jamming attack at each time. The optimal jamming attack schedule to maximize the remote state estimation error has been derived. Simulation results demonstrate the optimality of the proposed schedule.

Acknowledgment. This work was supported in part by National Science Foundation of China under grants 61573103 and 61520106009, and by State Key Laboratory of Synthetical Automation for Process Industries.

References

1. Khaitan, S.K., McCalley, J.D.: Design techniques and applications of cyber physical systems: a survey. IEEE Syst. J. **9**(2), 350–365 (2014)
2. Cao, X., Cheng, P., Chen, J., Ge, S.S., Cheng, Y., Sun, Y.: Cognitive radio based state estimation in cyber-physical systems. IEEE J. Sel. Areas Commun. **32**(3), 489–502 (2014)
3. Mo, Y., Kim, T.H.J., Brancik, K., Dickinson, D., Lee, H., Perrig, A., Sinopoli, B.: Cyber-physical security of a smart grid infrastructure. Proc. IEEE **100**(1), 195–209 (2012)
4. Zhang, H., Cheng, P., Shi, L., Chen, J.M.: Optimal denial-of-service attack scheduling with energy constraint. IEEE Trans. Autom. Control **60**(11), 3023–3028 (2015)
5. Mo, Y.L., Sinopoli, B.: Secure control against replay attacks. In: 47th Annual Allerton Conference, Illinois, USA, pp. 911–918 (2009)
6. Teixeira, A., Perez, D., Sandberg, H., Johansson, K.H.: Attack models and scenarios for networked control systems. In: 1st International Conference on High Confidence Networked Systems, pp. 55–64 (2012)
7. Xu, W., Trappe, W., Zhang, Y., Wood, T.: The feasibility of launching and detecting jamming attacks in wireless networks. In: 6th ACM International Symposium on Mobile Ad Hoc Networking and Computing, pp. 46–57 (2005)
8. Thakur, N., Sankaralingam, A.: Introduction to jamming attacks and prevention techniques using honeypots in wireless networks. IRACST - Int. J. Comput. Sci. Inf. Technol. Secur. 3(2) (2013). ISSN 2249-9555
9. Akyol, E., Rose, K., Basar, T.: Optimal zero-delay jamming over an additive noise channel. IEEE Trans. Inf. Theor. **61**(8), 4331–4344 (2015)
10. Manandhar, K., Cao, X., Hu, F., Liu, Y.: Combating false data injection attacks in smart grid using kalman filter. In: 2014 International Conference on Computing, Networking and Communications, pp. 16–20 (2014)
11. Bezzo, N., Weimer, J., Pajic, M., Sokolsky, O., Pappas, G.J., Lee, I.: Attack resilient state estimation for autonomous robotic systems. In: IEEE/RSJ International Conference on Intelligent Robots and Systems, pp. 3692–3698 (2014)

12. Li, M., Koutsopoulos, I., Poovendran, R.: Optimal jamming attacks and network defense policies in wireless sensor networks. In: 26th IEEE International Conference on Computer Communications, pp. 1307–1315 (2007)
13. Rugh, W.J.: Linear System Theory. Prentice hall, Upper Saddle River (1996)
14. Shi, L., Cheng, P., Chen, J.: Sensor data scheduling for optimal state estimation with communication energy constraint. Automatica **47**(8), 1693–1698 (2011)
15. Cao, X., Zhou, X., Liu, L., Cheng, Y.: Energy-efficient spectrum sensing for cognitive radio enabled remote state estimation over wireless channels. IEEE Trans. Wireless Commun. **14**(4), 2058–2071 (2015)
16. Shi, L., Cheng, P., Chen, J.M.: Optimal periodic sensor scheduling with limited resources. IEEE Trans. Autom. Control **56**(9), 2190–2195 (2011)

An Enhanced Structure-Based De-anonymization of Online Social Networks

Hong Li[1,2], Cheng Zhang[2], Yunhua He[2,3],
Xiuzhen Cheng[2], Yan Liu[4], and Limin Sun[1(✉)]

[1] Beijing Key Laboratory of IOT Information Security Technology,
Institute of Information Engineering, CAS, Beijing, China
sunlimin@iie.ac.cn
[2] Department of Computer Science,
The George Washington University, Washington DC, USA
[3] School of Computer, Xidian University, Xi'an, China
[4] School of Software and Microelectronics, Peking University, Beijing, China

Abstract. To protect users' privacy, online social network data are usually anonymized before being sold to or shared with third parities. Various structure-based approaches have been proposed to de-anonymize the social network data. In this paper, we study the limitations of the existing structure-based de-anonymization methods and propose an enhanced de-anonymization algorithm. The basic idea of our algorithm is to leverage the structural transformations of the social graph to de-anonymize the social network data. We also define a new similarity measure that is more robust for de-anonymization. We use the arXiv dataset to evaluate our algorithm, and the experiment results show that our method can significantly improve the de-anonymization rate.

Keywords: Social network · De-anonymization · Network structure

1 Introduction

Online social networks such as Facebook, Twitter, and LinkedIn have been gaining tremendous popularity in recent years as they provide convenient platforms for users to build connections and relationships with each other wherever they are [1,5]. The vast amount of personal and relationship information among the users have become a treasure trove sought by marketers and researchers [7,10,13,19]. A typical approach to protect users' privacy is to anonymize the social network data by removing personally identifiable information before they are made public to academic researchers or third-party companies [4,8,12,14,16,18,20].

Various structure-based approaches have been proposed to de-anonymize social network data [3,6,9–11,17]. Given an anonymized social network structure and an external social network structure with real identities, structure-based de-anonymization algorithms map an anonymous node to its real identity by checking the similarity between its social structures in these two social networks. In

© Springer International Publishing Switzerland 2016
Q. Yang et al. (Eds.): WASA 2016, LNCS 9798, pp. 331–342, 2016.
DOI: 10.1007/978-3-319-42836-9_30

[3], Backstrom *et al.* proposed the first structure-based de-anonymization algorithm that tackles both active attacks and passive attacks. In [10], Narayanan *et al.* extended the de-anonymization attack to large scale directed social networks. In [11], Nilizadeh *et al.* presented an enhanced de-anonymization algorithm by integrating the community structure and the social structure. These existing structure-based methods can de-anonymize the social network data efficiently, but they have the following limitations. First, they cannot differentiate two users that have similar friends in the anonymized social network. Second, the probability of a correct de-anonymization for a user largely depends on the number of common friends the user has in the two social networks. When the user only has a few common friends in two social networks, the success rate of de-anonymization could be very low.

To address the above limitations, we propose an enhanced structure-based de-anonymization algorithm in this paper to de-anonymize the social network data by leveraging the *structural transformation* of a social network, which is a more fine-grained feature of the social network than the network structure. The key insight behind our algorithm lies in that when a user joins a new community, she is likely to build connections with the members of this community in both social networks, which makes her social network graph in one social network evolves in a similar way as that in another social network. If the structural transformation of a user's social network is similar to that of another user's social network, with a high probability they could be the same user. Compared with the existing structure-based schemes, our algorithm can differentiate two users with similar friends by observing the differences in structural transformations. To alleviate the second limitation, we define a new and more generalized similarity measure that takes into consideration all the social neighbors of two unmapped users, instead of only the number of common neighbors as the traditional similarity measure does. The main contributions of this paper are summarized as follows:

- In this paper, we study and identify two major limitations of the existing structure-based de-anonymization algorithms.
- We propose an enhanced structure-based de-anonymization algorithm that employs the structural transformation of the social networks and a new similarity measure to de-anonymize the social network data.
- We use the arXiv dataset that contains co-author relationships to evaluate the performance of our algorithm. The experiment results show that our algorithm can significantly improve the de-anonymization ratio.

The remainder of the paper is structured as follows. In Sect. 2, we introduce the model and definition used in this paper. In Sect. 3, we study the limitations of the existing structure-based de-anonymization algorithms. The basic idea and detailed design of our algorithm are respectively presented in Sects. 4 and 5, followed by an experimental study for the performance validation in Sect. 6. The paper is concluded in Sect. 7.

2   Model and Definition

In this paper, we model two social networks known by an adversary as undirected graphs $G = (V, E)$ and $G' = (V', E')$, where G is an anonymized social graph and G' is a reference social graph with real identities. The vertices V and V' represent the users in G and G', respectively. The edges $E = \{(u_i, u_j, t_{i,j}) | u_i \in V \text{ and } u_j \in V\}$ and $E' = \{(u'_i, u'_j, t'_{i,j}) | u'_i \in V' \text{and} u'_j \in V'\}$ represent the social relationships between users, where $t_{i,j}$ is the time when u_i and u_j become friends in G, and $t'_{i,j}$ is the time when u'_i and u'_j build connections in G'. We will discuss how to get this information in Sect. 4. Given these two social graphs, the objective of the adversary is to de-anonymize the social graph G by mapping the users in G to those in G'. Note that in this paper, we interchangeably use the terms "network", "node", and "link" with "graph", "user", and "edge", respectively.

3   Background and Motivation

3.1   Structure-Based De-anonymization of Social Networks

In general, structure-based de-anonymization attacks consist of two phases: *seed selection* and *mapping propagation* [9–11, 15]. In the seed selection phase, a small number of seeds (i.e. mapped users) are first identified between the anonymized graph and the reference graph. In the mapping propagation phase, the algorithm expands the set of mapped users by iteratively comparing and mapping the neighbors of the previously mapped users. At each iteration, the algorithm randomly picks an arbitrary unmapped node v in V, and then compute a similarity score for each unmapped node v' in V'. The similarity score between v and v' is defined as the number of neighbors of v that have been mapped to the neighbors of v', divided by the square root of their degrees:

$$S(v, v') = \frac{|\{(w, w') : w \in \mathcal{N}(v); w' \in \mathcal{N}(v'); (w, w') \in M\}|}{\sqrt{k_v k_{v'}}} \tag{1}$$

In (1), M is the set of mapped nodes, $\mathcal{N}(v)$ is the set of neighbors of v, and k_v is the degree of v. Then the node with the highest score is mapped to node v if the *eccentricity* of the list of similarity scores exceeds a threshold τ, and the mapping is rejected if the eccentricity is blow the threshold. Eccentricity measures how much a candidate node "stands out" from the rest, and is defined as

$$ecc(L) = \frac{\max_1(L) - \max_2(L)}{\sigma(L)}, \tag{2}$$

where L is the list of similarity scores between v and the unmapped nodes in V', $\max_1(L)$ and $\max_2(L)$ are respectively the highest score and the second highest score in L, and $\sigma(L)$ is the standard deviation of the scores in L.

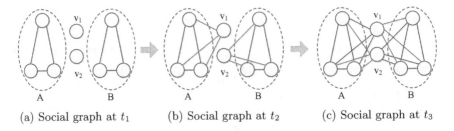

| (a) Social graph at t_1 | (b) Social graph at t_2 | (c) Social graph at t_3 |

Fig. 1. Structural transformations of a social graph.

3.2   Limitations of Existing Structure-Based Approaches

It has been experimentally demonstrated that structure-based de-anonymization attacks can easily break the privacy of the social networks based on only the structures of the corresponding social graphs. However, all the existing structure-based approaches suffer from two major limitations and their de-anonymization rate could be very low in the following situations.

Sharing Similar Friends in One Social Network: As illustrated in Fig. 1(a), v_1 and v_2 are two different users in social network G. They both have connections with all the members in community A and community B; thus the social graph of v_1 is much similar to that of v_2. Therefore v_1 and v_2 could get equal similarity scores if we use the existing structure-based approaches to de-anonymize this social network. However, if we take a closer look at the structural transformations of the social graphs of v_1 and v_2 and take snapshots at different moments, as illustrated in Fig. 1(a)–(c), one can see the differences. Node v_1 first joins community A and builds connections with the members in this community, while node v_2 first builds connections with the members in community B instead. The above observation motivates us to investigate the structural transformations of the social graphs of different users when we de-anonymize a social network. Compared with the structure of a social graph, structural transformation is a more fine-grained feature of the social graph.

Having a Few Common Friends in Two Social Networks: In existing schemes, the similarity score between two users is computed based on the number of common neighbors of the two users in two social networks. Typically, a larger number of common friends yields a higher probability of a successful mapping [11]. However, a user may have different social neighbors in different social networks, which leads to an inadequate number of common friends in two different social networks. To alleviate this limitation, we define a new similarity measure that takes into account all the social neighbors of the two unmapped users, instead of considering only the number of common neighbors. The new similarity measure is a more generalized form of the one defined in (1), which will be discussed in the next section.

4   Basic Idea of Our Algorithm

We propose an enhanced de-anonymization algorithm to address the limitations discussed above. To overcome the first limitation, we leverage the structural transformation of a social graph for more robust and accurate de-anonymization. The key insight behind this consideration is that when a user joins a new community, she is likely to build new connections with the members in this community at different social networks, which makes the social graphs of different social networks evolve in a similar way. Thus, we can de-anonymize a node by checking the similarity between the structural transformations of different social graphs. If the social graph of one node in the social network G is found to evolve in a similar way as that of another node in the social network G', they can be mapped to each other with a high probability. As illustrated in Fig. 2(a), a, b and c are the common friends of v and v'. User v makes friends with a, b, and c at time $t_{v,a}$, $t_{v,b}$, and $t_{v,c}$, respectively, and user v' makes friends with a, b, and c at time $t_{v',a}$, $t_{v',b}$, and $t_{v',c}$, respectively. The similarity between the structural transformations of their social graphs can be defined as follows:

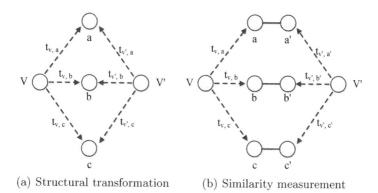

(a) Structural transformation   (b) Similarity measurement

Fig. 2. The basic idea of our algorithm.

$$S\left(v,v'\right) = \frac{1}{\sqrt{k_v k_{v'}}} \left(\frac{1}{e^{|t_{v,a}-t_{v',a}|}} + \frac{1}{e^{|t_{v,b}-t_{v',b}|}} + \frac{1}{e^{|t_{v,c}-t_{v',c}|}} \right) \qquad (3)$$

where k_v and k'_v are the degrees of v and v', respectively. Note that this similarity definition emphasizes that if v and v' make friends with the same node at roughly the same time, with a high probability they are the same user. The time when two users become friends can be obtained via the following approaches:

– In some social networks such as Instagram and LinkedIn, the news that two users become friends is posted on each user's timeline. Moreover, the time when two users become friends is publicly available in some social network data such as DBLP and the arXiv dataset. In this case, we can directly obtain the structural transformations of the social network from the published data.

– If the time at which two users make friends is unavailable, it can be approximated by the time when these two users first interact with each other in the social network.

To alleviate the second limitation discussed above, we compute the similarity score between two unmapped users based on the similarity between their social neighbors, instead of using the number of common neighbors as existing schemes do. We argue that even though a user of G and a user of G' do not have many common neighbors, they could be the same person if their social neighbors are very similar (for example, they are all from the same community). Given a node v in G and a node v' in G', we first compute the similarity between each neighbor of v and each neighbor of v', then pair up the two nodes with the highest similarity score. The similarity score between v and v' is computed based on the identified pairs. Take Fig. 2(b) as an example, v and v' have no common neighbors but their neighborhoods are very similar. We pair up the similar nodes (i.e., a and a', b and b', c and c') and compute the similarity score between v and v' as follows:

$$S\left(v, v'\right) = \frac{1}{\sqrt{k_v k_{v'}}} \left(\frac{S_{sub}(a, a')}{e^{|t_{v,a} - t_{v',a'}|}} + \frac{S_{sub}(b, b')}{e^{|t_{v,b} - t_{v',b'}|}} + \frac{S_{sub}(c, c')}{e^{|t_{v,c} - t_{v',c'}|}} \right) \qquad (4)$$

where $S_{sub}(a, a')$ is the similarity score between a and a'. Note that (4) is extended from (3) to alleviate the second limitation. We will discuss how to compute $S_{sub}(a, a')$ in the next section. Our similarity measure is a more generalized form of (1) used by existing works. When the social neighbors of a user in two different social networks are exactly the same, (4) is identical to (1). However, when the number of common neighbors is small, we can find potential mappings by checking the similarity between their social neighborhood according to (4).

5   The Design of Our Algorithm

Based on the idea outlined in the previous section, we propose an enhanced deanonymization algorithm for social networks. Similar to the existing structure-based methods, our algorithm also consists of two phases: seed identification and mapping propagation.

5.1   Seed Identification

Seed identification intends to identify a small number of "seed" pairs with each containing one vertex in G and one in G' that map to each other. The identified seed pairs will serve as a starting point in the next mapping propagation phase. Seed selection is not our primary contribution in this paper. We can employ the algorithm proposed by Narayanan *et al.* [10] to identify the seeds: given a clique of k nodes in the social network G', the algorithm searches the social network

G for a unique k-clique with matching node degrees and matching number of common neighbors between each of $\binom{k}{2}$ pairs of nodes in the two cliques; if found, the nodes in one clique are mapped to the corresponding nodes in the other clique. We can also adopt Backstrom's algorithm [3], which creates a small number of new user accounts with edges to the seed vertices and creates a special pattern of links among the new accounts such that it is easy to identify the new user accounts and the connected seed nodes in the anonymized graph.

Algorithm 1. Similarity Score Computation

Require:
  Two unmapped nodes: v and v';
  The mapped neighbors: $\mathcal{N}_{map}(v)$ and $\mathcal{N}_{map}(v')$;
  The social graphs: $G = (V, E)$ and $G' = (V', E')$
Ensure: The similarity score between v and v';
 1: Set $V_{sub} = \mathcal{N}_{map}(v) \cup \mathcal{N}_{map}(v')$, $E_{sub} = \emptyset$,
   $pairList = \emptyset$, $Sim_{v,v'} = 0$
 2: **for** each $u \in V_{sub}$ and $u' \in V_{sub}$ **do**
 3: **if** $(u, u') \in E \parallel (u, u') \in E'$ **then**
 4:   $E_{sub} = E_{sub} \cup (u, u')$
 5: **end if**
 6: **end for**
 7: **for** each $u \in \mathcal{N}_{map}(v)$ **do**
 8: Set $max = 0$, $p_u = Null$
 9: **for** each $u' \in \mathcal{N}_{map}(v')$ **do**
10:   // $N_{sub}(u)$: neighbors of u in graph (V_{sub}, E_{sub})
11:   $S_{u,u'} = |N_{sub}(u) \cap N_{sub}(u')| / |N_{sub}(u) \cup N_{sub}(u')|$
12:   **if** $max \leq S_{u,u'}$ **then**
13:    $max = S_{u,u'}$, $p_u = u'$
14:   **end if**
15: **end for**
16: $pairList = pariList \cup (u, p_u)$
17: **end for**
18: // $t_{v,u}$: the time v and u became friends, k_v: degrees of v
19: **for all** $(u, u') \in pairList$ **do**
20: $Sim_{v,v'} = Sim_{v,v'} + S_{u,u'}/e^{|t_{v,u}-t_{v',u'}|}$
21: **end for**
22: $Sim_{v,v'} = Sim_{v,v'}/\sqrt{k_v k_{v'}}$
23: **return** $Sim_{v,v'}$;

5.2 Mapping Propagation

In the mapping propagation phase, we start with the seed pairs obtained in the previous phase and recursively expand such mappings to other nodes in the two social networks. Assume that the set of already-identified mappings is denoted by $M = \{(m, m')|m \in V \text{ and } m' \in V'\}$, the set of mapped nodes in V is denoted by $V_{map} = \{m|\exists m' \in V' \text{ s.t. } (m, m') \in M\}$, and the set of mapped nodes in V' is denoted by $V'_{map} = \{m'|\exists m \in V \text{ s.t. } (m, m') \in M\}$. At each iteration, we randomly pick an already-mapped node pair (m, m') from M, and select a random unmapped node v from the neighbors of m. Then we compute the similarity score between v and each unmapped node v' in the set of unmapped neighbors of m'. The similarity score between v and v' is computed according to Algorithm 1, which are explained as follows.

Building a Sub-Social Graph (line 2–6): We denote the neighbors of v that have been mapped by $\mathcal{N}_{map}(v)$, and the neighbors of v' that have been mapped by $\mathcal{N}_{map}(v')$. We first use the already-mapped neighbors of v and v' to build a sub-social graph $G_{sub} = (V_{sub}, E_{sub})$, where $V_{sub} = \mathcal{N}_{map}(v) \cup \mathcal{N}_{map}(v')$ and $E_{sub} = \{(u, u')|u \in V_{sub} \text{ and } (u, u') \in (E \cup E')\}$. The sub-social graph G_{sub} includes more information since it fuses the nodes and relationships from both social networks.

Paring Similar Nodes (line 7–17): After building the sub-social graph G_{sub}, we compute the similarity score between each node in $\mathcal{N}_{map}(v)$ and each node in $\mathcal{N}_{map}(v')$, and pair each node in $\mathcal{N}_{map}(v)$ with the most similar node in $\mathcal{N}_{map}(v')$. The similarity score between $u \in \mathcal{N}_{map}(v)$ and $u' \in \mathcal{N}_{map}(v')$ is defined as follows:

$$S_{sub}(u, u') = \frac{|N_{sub}(u) \cap N_{sub}(u')|}{|N_{sub}(u) \cup N_{sub}(u')|}, \tag{5}$$

where $N_{sub}(u)$ is the set of neighbors of node u in the sub-social graph G_{sub}. For each node $u \in \mathcal{N}_{map}(v)$, the node $u' \in \mathcal{N}_{map}(v')$ with the highest similarity score is identified as the paired node of u, i.e.:

$$P(u) = \underset{u' \in \mathcal{N}(v')}{\arg\max}\, S_{sub}(u, u') \tag{6}$$

where $P(u)$ is the paired node of u. Note that since $|\mathcal{N}_{map}(v)|$ is not necessarily equal to $|\mathcal{N}_{map}(v')|$, one node could be paired to multiple nodes.

Computing Similarity Score (line 18–22): After pairing the nodes in $\mathcal{N}_{map}(v)$ and $\mathcal{N}_{map}(v')$, we compute the similarity score between v and v' by the following equation:

$$S(v, v') = \frac{\displaystyle\sum_{u \in \mathcal{N}_{map}(v)} \frac{S_{sub}(u, u')}{e^{|t_{v,u} - t_{v',u'}|}}}{\sqrt{k_v k_{v'}}}, \tag{7}$$

where $u' \in \mathcal{N}_{map}(v')$ is the paired node of u, i.e., $u' = P(u)$, $t_{v,u}$ is the time when node v and node u became friends, and k_v is the node degree of v. In the above equation, we use $S_{sub}(u, u')/e^{|t_{v,u} - t_{v',u'}|}$ to capture the similarity between their structural transformations. If v and v' build connections with similar nodes in the same period of time, the similarity score between them should be high.

Similar to the traditional structure-based methods, after computing the similarity score between v and each unmapped node v' in the set of unmapped neighbors of node m', we map the node with the highest similarity score to node v if the eccentricity of the list of similarity scores exceeds a threshold τ. The mapping is rejected if the eccentricity is blow the threshold.

5.3 Discussion

In our proposed algorithm, we employ the structural transformations of the social graph and a new similarity measure to de-anonymize the social network data. Compared with the existing structure-based approaches, our algorithm has the following strengths:

- Our algorithm considers the time when two users became friends in a social network. Existing structure-based de-anonymization schemes can be treated as special cases where it is hardly able to estimate the time when two users became friends or when the social neighbors of a user in two different social networks are exactly the same.
- Our algorithm addresses the two limitations outlined in Sect. 3 that can not be overcome by the existing structure-based de-anonymization schemes. It tackles the limitations by taking into account the structural transformations of a social graph and defining a novel similarity measure to help find more mappings.

In this work, we pair up the neighboring nodes based on the similarity scores. An alternative is to detect communities of the neighboring nodes and then compare the community structures. We will investigate this approach in our future research.

6 Evaluation

We implement our algorithm and the baseline algorithm proposed in [10]. The comparison results are reported in this section.

6.1 Dataset

In our evaluation, we use the arXiv dataset [2] to evaluate the performance of our algorithm. This dataset is crawled from the arXiv Condensed Matter E-Print Archive, and it contains all the e-prints of scientific papers in the category of cs.CR (Cryptography and Security) and cs.NI (Network and Internet Architecture). From the dataset, we construct a social network between scientists, in which the authors are the vertexes, and two authors are connected if they coauthored at least one paper. The network has 17955 nodes and 34976 edges. We replicate the original network and assume that it is anonymized. Then we use a common edge-rewiring method to alter the structure of the original network [11,21]. In our experiments, we use the original network as G and the altered network as G', and the seed nodes are randomly selected.

6.2   Impact of the Number of Seeds

In our evaluation, we first investigate the impact of the number of seeds on the success rate of de-anonymization. In the experiments, we set the eccentricity threshold to 0.1 and the noise rate to 0, and increase the number of seeds from 50 to 250. Figure 3 reports the success rate of de-anonymization when the number of seeds is set to different values. It is observed that the success rate is increased when the number of seeds is varied from 50 to 250. As seen in the figure, our algorithm can de-anonymize more nodes than the baseline algorithm. When the number of seeds is set to 50, the success rates of our algorithm and the baseline algorithm are 0.232 and 0.068, respectively. When the number of seeds is increased to 250, the success rates of our algorithm and the baseline algorithm are improved to 0.429 and 0.165, respectively.

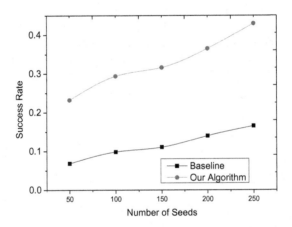

Fig. 3. Impact of the number of seeds

6.3   Impact of Noise

We further evaluate the performances of our algorithm and the baseline algorithm under different levels of noises. In the experiments we set the number of seeds to 300 and the eccentricity threshold to 0.1. Figure 4 demonstrates the impact of the noise rate on the success rate of de-anonymization. It is observed that our algorithm is more efficient the the baseline algorithm. The success rate of our algorithm decreases from 0.462 to 0.297 when the noise rate is increased from 0 to 0.30 while the success rate of the baseline algorithm decreases from 0.206 to 0.153 when the noise rate is increased from 0 to 0.30.

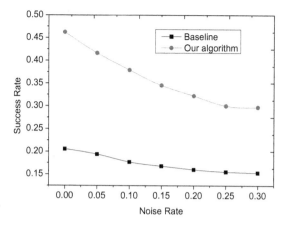

Fig. 4. Impact of noise.

7   Conclusion

In this paper, we identify two limitations of the existing structure-based de-anonymization algorithms for social networks. To overcome these limitations, we propose an enhanced algorithm that leverages the structural transformations of the social networks and a novel similarity measure to de-anonymize the social network data. We use the arXiv dataset to evaluate our algorithm, and the results demonstrate that our algorithm is more efficient than an existing structure-based de-anonymization algorithm.

Acknowledgment. This work was supported by the National Natural Science Foundation of China (Grant No. 61472418), the National Defense Basic Research Program of China (Grant No. JCKY2016602B001), the "Strategic Priority Research Program" of the Chinese Academy of Sciences (Grant No. XDA06040100), and the National Defense Science and Technology Innovation Fund, CAS (No. CXJJ-16-M118).

References

1. Alexa: Top 500 global sites (2016). http://www.alexa.com/topsites. Accessed 2016
2. arXiv: arxiv bibiography (2016). http://arxiv.org/help/api/index. Accessed 2016
3. Backstrom, L., Dwork, C., Kleinberg, J.: Wherefore art thou r3579x?: anonymized social networks, hidden patterns, and structural steganography. In: Proceedings of the 16th International Conference on World Wide Web. pp. 181–190. ACM (2007)
4. Bhagat, S., Cormode, G., Krishnamurthy, B., Srivastava, D.: Class-based graph anonymization for social network data. Proc. VLDB Endowment **2**(1), 766–777 (2009)
5. Deng, D., Du, H., Jia, X., Ye, Q.: Minimum-cost information dissemination in social networks. In: Xu, K., Zhu, H. (eds.) WASA 2015. LNCS, vol. 9204, pp. 83–93. Springer, Heidelberg (2015)

6. Ding, X., Zhang, L., Wan, Z., Gu, M.: A brief survey on de-anonymization attacks in online social networks. In: 2010 International Conference on Computational Aspects of Social Networks (CASoN). pp. 611–615. IEEE (2010)

7. Eagle, N., Pentland, A.: Reality mining: sensing complex social systems. Per. Ubiquit. Comput. **10**(4), 255–268 (2006)

8. Ji, S., Li, W., Gong, N.Z., Mittal, P., Beyah, R.A.: On your social network de-anonymizablity: quantification and large scale evaluation with seed knowledge. In: The 2015 Network and Distributed System Security (NDSS) (2015)

9. Ji, S., Li, W., Srivatsa, M., He, J.S., Beyah, R.: Structure based data de-anonymization of social networks and mobility traces. In: Chow, S.S.M., Camenisch, J., Hui, L.C.K., Yiu, S.M. (eds.) ISC 2014. LNCS, vol. 8783, pp. 237–254. Springer, Heidelberg (2014)

10. Narayanan, A., Shmatikov, V.: De-anonymizing social networks. In: 30th IEEE Symposium on Security and Privacy, 2009, pp. 173–187. IEEE (2009)

11. Nilizadeh, S., Kapadia, A., Ahn, Y.Y.: Community-enhanced de-anonymization of online social networks. In: Proceedings of the 2014 ACM SIGSAC Conference on Computer and Communications Security. pp. 537–548. ACM (2014)

12. ONeill, N.: Senate begins discussing privacy implications of online advertising (2008). http://tinyurl.com/5aqqhe. Accessed 2008

13. Richardson, M., Domingos, P.: Mining knowledge-sharing sites for viral marketing. In: Proceedings of the Eighth ACM SIGKDD International Conference on Knowledge Discovery and Data Mining. pp. 61–70. ACM (2002)

14. Rohan, T., Tunguz-Zawislak, T.J., Sheffer, S.G., Harmsen, J.: Network node ad targeting, May 2013. uS Patent 8,438,062

15. Srivatsa, M., Hicks, M.: Deanonymizing mobility traces: using social network as a side-channel. In: Proceedings of the 2012 ACM Conference on Computer and Communications Security. pp. 628–637. ACM (2012)

16. Wang, Y., Cai, Z., Yin, G., Gao, Y., Tong, X., Wu, G.: An incentive mechanism with privacy protection in mobile crowdsourcing systems. Comput. Netw. **102**, 157–171 (2016)

17. Wondracek, G., Holz, T., Kirda, E., Kruegel, C.: A practical attack to de-anonymize social network users. In: IEEE Symposium on Security and Privacy 2010 (IEEE SP). pp. 223–238. IEEE (2010)

18. Zhang, L., Cai, Z., Wang, X.: Fakeit: privately releasing user context streams for personalized mobile applications. In: IEEE Transactions on Network and Service Management (2016)

19. Zhang, L., Wang, X., Lu, J., Li, P., Cai, Z.: An efficient privacy preserving data aggregation approach for mobile sensing. Secur. Commun. Netw. J. **11**, 980–992 (2016)

20. Zheleva, E., Getoor, L.: Preserving the privacy of sensitive relationships in graph data. In: Bonchi, F., Malin, B., Saygın, Y. (eds.) PInKDD 2007. LNCS, vol. 4890, pp. 153–171. Springer, Heidelberg (2008)

21. Zhou, B., Pei, J., Luk, W.: A brief survey on anonymization techniques for privacy preserving publishing of social network data. ACM Sigkdd Explor. Newslett. **10**(2), 12–22 (2008)

Self-learning Based Motion Recognition Using Sensors Embedded in a Smartphone for Mobile Healthcare

Di Lu, Junqi Guo$^{(\boxtimes)}$, Xi Zhou, Guoxing Zhao, and Rongfang Bie

College of Information Science and Technology, Beijing Normal University,
Beijing, People's Republic of China
guojunqi@bnu.edu.cn

Abstract. Human motion recognition using wearable sensors is becoming a popular topic in the field of mobile health recently. However, most previous studies haven't solved the problem of unlabeled motion recognition very well due to the limitation of learning ability of their systems. In this paper, we propose a self-learning based motion recognition scheme for mobile healthcare, in which a patient only needs to carry an ordinary smartphone that integrates some common inertial sensors, and both labeled and unlabeled motion types can be recognized by using a self-learning data analysis scheme. Experimental results demonstrate that the proposed self-learning scheme behaves better than some existing ones, and its average accuracy reaches above 80 % for motion recognition.

Keywords: Self-learning · Motion recognition · Smartphone

1 Introduction

The wide application of motion recognition technologies has brought a growing number of new solutions to mobile healthcare including nursing care, disease prediction and fitness tracking. For instance, nursing staff may receive a warning message immediately when abnormal actions (e.g. falling down) of postoperative patients are detected, so that sick people can receive prompt medical aid [1]. Besides, some kind of diseases like Parkinson's or epilepsy may be inferred through motion recognition when a person often behaves frequently-occurring actions that deviate from normal ones [2]. Furthermore, motion recognition can be employed to estimate the amount of exercise for sport guidance and diet recommendation [3].

Generally speaking, the existing motion recognition methods for mobile healthcare can be divided into two categories: traditional methods [4, 5] and sensor-based methods [6, 7]. Based on consideration of real-time and cost, the sensor-based methods have currently received more attention than the traditional ones. Moreover, smartphone-based methods [8] have been gradually considered as a simplified implementation of sensor-based methods, since an ordinary smartphone usually integrates several different kinds of inertial sensors. However, there is also a difficulty that may affect the performance of smartphone-based or sensor-based motion recognition methods. It is how to recognize "unseen motions" in the absence of their apriori information in a training dataset. Generally, we define "seen motions" and "unseen motions" as follows: the labeled data

© Springer International Publishing Switzerland 2016
Q. Yang et al. (Eds.): WASA 2016, LNCS 9798, pp. 343–355, 2016.
DOI: 10.1007/978-3-319-42836-9_31

samples of seen motions have already existed in the training dataset, whereas unseen motions are the ones whose labels have been unknown before, so there is no training sample for them. Considering that there are a great number of unpredictable activities in a person's daily life, it is unrealistic to collect sample data of all motion types in advance for training. Therefore, unseen motion recognition is of practical significance due to diversity of human activities and limitation of training datasets. Cheng et al. [9] proposed a zero-shot learning approach to recognize unseen motions. They used semantic attributes to represent patient motions, and then employed an attribute-based learning algorithm for recognition. Although their approach could recognize unseen motions by generalizing knowledge, there was a limitation that semantic attributes of unseen motions should be manually defined before, which implied that there still existed apriori information for unseen motions. Yin et al. [10] presented an approach to detect abnormal and unseen motions using the combination of one-class support vector machine (SVM) and kernel nonlinear regression (KNLR). However, they assumed that there still existed sparse training samples of the abnormal and unseen motions.

To the best of our knowledge, there have been few related studies on smartphone-based motion recognition when there is no apriori information for unseen motions. A similar work is given by Ho et al. [11], in which they proposed an active-learning assisted motion recognition method. However, they did their experiment in an intelligent-home environment where lots of sensors had been deployed before, which greatly increased implementation complexity and cost.

In this paper, we propose a self-learning based patients' motion recognition scheme by using a smartphone for mobile healthcare. Based on a novelty-detection algorithm, the scheme determines whether there are apriori training samples and labeled motion types that well match with sensor data. If not, it automatically assembles these unseen motion data into different clusters and gives them new category labels. These clustered samples combined with the acquired new category labels are then merged into the training dataset to retrain the whole self-learning model for the improvement of its learning ability. Experimental results demonstrate that the proposed self-learning scheme for motion recognition works well for most cases. When there exist several types of unseen activities without any apriori information, the accuracy reaches above 80 % after the self-learning process converges.

The remainder of this paper is organized as follows. In Sect. 2, we describe data acquisition and data processing. In Sect. 3, we propose the entire self-learning framework which contains several algorithms for different purposes. In Sect. 4, experiments are given for performance evaluation and comparison. Finally, we draw conclusions in Sect. 5.

2   Data Acquisition and Processing

2.1   Smartphone-Based Data Acquisition

An ordinary smartphone usually has abundant built-in motion sensors, such as an accelerometer, gyroscope, magnetometer, gravity accelerometer and linear accelerometer.

The sensors involved in our scheme and the corresponding data definition are listed in Table 1.

Table 1. Motion sensors in our scheme

Sensor	Unit	Description
Accelerometer	m/s^2	Acceleration along the three axes (x, y, z)
Gyroscope	rad/s	Angular velocity around the three axes (x, y, z)
Magnetometer	μT	Geomagnetic field intensity along the three axes (x, y, z)
Gravity accelerometer	m/s^2	Gravitational acceleration along the three axes (x, y, z)
Linear accelerometer	m/s^2	Linear acceleration without gravity along the three axis (x, y, z)

As shown in Fig. 1, in order to achieve data collection in a real environment, we develop an application (APP) program based on an Android platform which contains several functions, such as data acquisition and uploading. Meanwhile, we employ a "Java + Spring" framework to develop a set of application programming interface (API) for the user to upload sensor data to the server. Data are finally stored in the MySQL database for motion recognition.

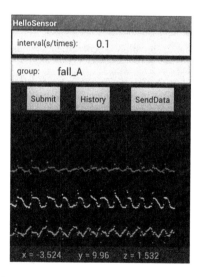

Fig. 1. APP interface for data acquisition

2.2 Data Preprocessing

Note that the sensor data in Table 1 are measured in a smartphone coordinate system instead of an earth coordinate system. As shown in Fig. 2, a smartphone coordinate is the coordinate system relative to the phone screen in its default orientation. The directions of the smartphone coordinate axes change together with the change of screen orientation. Usually, the phone orientation in a pocket is not unsteady because of body movements. Values of sensor data measured in a smartphone coordinate system are inevitably and easily affected by orientation variation. Therefore, all sensor data should be rotated into an earth coordinate system to eliminate differences in orientation variation.

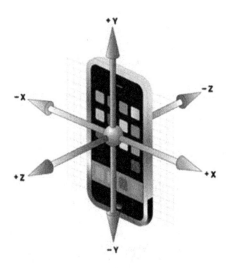

Fig. 2. Smartphone coordinate system

To solve the problem of orientation variation, sensor data are preprocessed using coordinate system transformation to eliminate phone orientation influence. Generally, coordinate system transformation is implemented by using a rotation matrix **R** from one coordinate system to another as follows:

$$\begin{pmatrix} x' \\ y' \\ z' \end{pmatrix} = \mathbf{R} \cdot \begin{pmatrix} x \\ y \\ z \end{pmatrix} \tag{1}$$

Fortunately, the application programming interface (API) for Android application development provides a function "getRotationMatrix"[1] in which the rotation matrix **R** has already been given. Based on this function, data values measured in an earth coordinate system can be obtained as follows:

$$linear\_acc\_earth = \mathbf{R} \cdot (acc - gravity) \tag{2}$$

---

[1] See the help document of Android developer. http://developer.android.com/reference/packages.html.

$$gyro\_earth = \mathbf{R} \cdot gyro \qquad (3)$$

where: *acc*, *gyro* and *gravity* denote the acceleration, angular velocity and gravitational acceleration in a smartphone coordinate system, respectively; *linear_acc_earth* and *gyro_earth* represent the linear acceleration and angular velocity in an earth coordinate system, respectively. Because *acc* contains a gravitational acceleration component, the linear acceleration created only by the patient's movement can be obtained through *acc* minus *gravity*.

We have five types of sensor data (Table 1) by direct measurement and two calculated values (Eqs. 2 and 3). Each of these seven physical quantities contains three-axis components. Considering time sampling, all sensor data over an entire observation duration can be represented as a $21 \times N$ data matrix, where N denotes the sampling number. Then we use a fixed-size sliding window with 50 % overlap to divide the $21 \times N$ data matrix into many small data slices, which will be prepared for feature extraction in Sect. 2.3.

2.3 Feature Extraction

For the purpose of representing motion characteristics and preventing performance degradation, we present a set of robust and effective features which can be extracted from the above data slices, based on several previous studies [12, 13]. The detailed features are listed as follows:

- **Descriptive statistics.** We use seven common statistical indicators: standard deviation, mean, maximum value, minimum value, 50 % quantile, skewness[2] and excess kurtosis[3].
- **Correlation coefficients.** Correlation coefficients describe the correlation between two random variables. We use two common correlation coefficients: Pearson's correlation coefficient[4] and Spearman's rank correlation coefficient[5].
- **Zero-crossing rate.** The zero-crossing rate is given by:

$$zcr = \frac{1}{T-1} \sum_{t=1}^{T-1} \mathrm{sgn}\left\{ s_t s_t - 1 < 0 \right\} \qquad (4)$$

where: s is a signal of length T; the function $\mathrm{sgn}\{w\}$ is equal to 1 or 0 when the value of w is true or false, respectively. Here we calculate the zero-crossing rate of the data for each axis.

---

[2] Wikipedia: skewness. https://en.wikipedia.org/wiki/Skewness.
[3] Wikipedia: Kurtosis. https://en.wikipedia.org/wiki/Kurtosis.
[4] Wikipedia: https://en.wikipedia.org/wiki/Pearson_product-moment_correlation_coefficient.
[5] Wikipedia: https://en.wikipedia.org/wiki/Spearman's_rank_correlation_coefficient.

3   The Self-learning Scheme for Recognition of Both Seen and Unseen Motions

3.1   Framework of the Self-learning Scheme

Traditional data classifiers have no ability to recognize unseen motions accurately. Here we propose a self-learning motion recognition scheme. It adaptively distinguishes "seen motions" and "unseen motions", and then automatically learns new categories from the "unseen motions" to reinforce the ability of motion recognition by itself. The framework of the self-learning scheme is shown in Fig. 3. The self-learning framework contains several main modules as follows:

- *Module 1:* Novelty detection. A kernel null Foley-Sammon transform (KNFST) [14] based novelty detection algorithm is proposed to automatically determine whether test data belong to "seen motions" or "unseen motions";
- *Module 2:* Classification of "seen motions". A random forest algorithm [15] is employed to generate a classifier. Sensor data belonging to "seen motions" can be further classified into several known categories, which also means patients' motions are recognized.

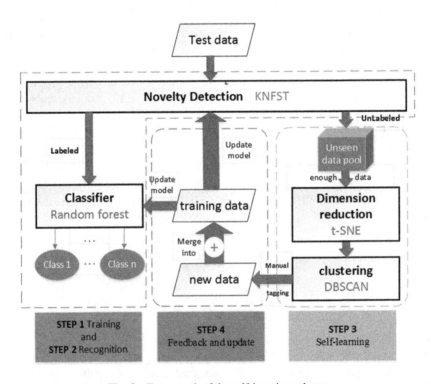

Fig. 3. Framework of the self-learning scheme

- *Module 3:* Clustering of high-dimensional "unseen motions" data. Since "unseen motions" data are usually represented with high-dimensional feature vectors, we employ a t-distributed stochastic neighbor embedding (t-SNE) algorithm [16] for dimension reduction, combined with a density-based spatial clustering of applications with noise (DBSCAN) algorithm [17] for low-dimensional data clustering.

The proposed scheme creatively integrates novelty detection, classification of "seen motion" data, clustering of high-dimensional "unseen motion" data and feedback into a comprehensive self-learning framework. The detailed working procedure can be described as follows:

- *Step1:* Training. Train the KNFST-based novelty detector in *Module 1* and the random forest classifier in *Module 2* according to the training dataset.
- *Step 2:* Recognition. Determine whether the test data belong to "seen motion" types by using the KNFST-based novelty detector. If so, import the data into the random forest classifier for motion recognition; if not, import the data into a data pool of unseen motions for the following self-learning.
- *Step 3:* Self-learning. When the data of unseen motions accumulate enough in the pool, start up a self-learning process. Firstly, reduce the dimension of the data represented with high-dimensional feature vectors by using the t-SNE algorithm. Next, cluster the data with the DBSCAN algorithm. Thirdly, label each cluster manually to give each category of unseen motion a class name.
- *Step 4:* Feedback and update. These sample clusters with new category labels are merged into the original training dataset to retrain the KNFST-based novelty detector and the random forest classifier, so that ability of the self-learning model can be reinforced.

Note that the framework of the proposed self-learning scheme contains four important algorithms: the KNFST-based novelty detection algorithm, random forest, t-SNE and DBSCAN, among which the latter three algorithms are proposed by some previous studies, whereas the first one is proposed by us on the basis of the KNFST. Therefore, we will discuss the KNFST-based novelty detection algorithm below.

3.2   The KNFST-Based Novelty Detection Algorithm

In the field of machine learning, the problem of identifying whether a test sample belongs to a known type or not is defined as "novelty detection". Novelty detection proves to be a complicated problem for high dimensional data [18]. Unfortunately, sensor data are often represented as high-dimensional feature vectors after feature extraction, which makes the design of novelty detection in our scheme more complicated. To solve this problem, we propose a novelty detection algorithm based on the kernel null Foly-Sammon transform (KNFST).

KNFST is a mapping transformation which attempts to map the samples of the same class into a single point, while the samples of different classes are mapped into different points, respectively. Based on this transformation, we implement novelty detection as follows:

- **Step 1:** Training. Relying on the KNFST, find out an optimal transformation matrix **W** according to the training data. Optimization of **W** ensures that the inner-class divergence is equal to 0, while the inter-class divergence is as large as possible. So we can calculate **W** by maximizing the ratio of the inner-class divergence and the inter-class divergence.
- **Step 2:** Definition of novelty score. As shown in Fig. 4, define "novelty score" of an observation sample **y** as the smallest distance from its projection point to central points of all classes, which is represented as follows:

$$NoveltyScore(\mathbf{y}) = \min_{1 \leq i \leq C} distance\{t^*, t^{(i)}\} \tag{5}$$

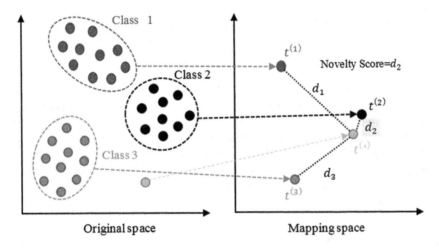

Fig. 4. Geometrical principle of the KNFST-based novelty detection algorithm (Color figure online)

If **y** belongs to a known class, its novelty score is inevitably small. Otherwise, **y** is mapped far away from central points of all classes, which leads to a large novelty score of **y**.

- **Step 3:** Threshold-based Decision. An appropriate threshold δ should be selected for decision. Threshold-based decision is represented as follows:

$$Class(\mathbf{y}) = \begin{cases} unseen & NoveltyScore(\mathbf{y}) > \delta \\ seen & NoveltyScore(\mathbf{y}) \leq \delta \end{cases} \tag{6}$$

Generally, the optimal value of δ is often given by experiments.

4 Experiments

4.1 Data Preparation

To verify the robustness of the proposed scheme under the condition of different smart-phone orientations and positions, we consider 4 different orientations (vertically inward, vertically outward, horizontally inward and horizontally outward) and 2 positions (coat pocket, and trouser pocket). Moreover, we select 6 common types of motions (walking, running, going upstairs, going downstairs, standing and sitting) as the initial "seen motion" types to build a training dataset. All training data in experiments are collected from two postoperative patient volunteers recruited from Beijing KangFu Hospital in China. Volunteers keep doing each type of motions with each orientation and each position for 5 min, so that two volunteers generate the training data with the total amount of 4 (orientations) × 2 (positions) × 6 (activity types) × 2 (volunteers) × 5 (minutes) = 480. In addition, the sampling frequency is set as 25 Hz. Here we selected two elder patients for data acquisition primarily to test the system's ability of learning "unseen motion". If considering individual differences, we need to sample more patients, which will be our future work. After data acquisition, we implement data preprocessing and feature extraction as described in Sects. 2.2 and 2.3.

4.2 Evaluation Criteria

For multivariate classification, accuracy is a typical and common index to evaluate classification performance. It is defined as the percentage of correctly predicted samples in the whole sample set, which is given by:

$$Accuracy(\hat{\mathbf{y}}, \mathbf{y}) = \frac{1}{n} \sum_{i=1}^{n} \text{sgn}\{\hat{y}_i = y_i\} \tag{7}$$

where: $\mathbf{y}$ and $\hat{\mathbf{y}}$ represent real type vector and predicted type vector, respectively.

4.3 Experimental Results

A. Performance of the proposed KNFST-based novelty detection algorithm
   To evaluate performance of the KNFST-based novelty detection algorithm, we compare it with other two common novelty detection algorithms: One-class SVM [19] and Binary SVM [20]. In addition, we employ a "Random" method as the baseline of novelty detection performance. It is considered as the worst novelty detection method, since it determines whether the test data belong to the seen or unseen motions only by the ratio of seen and unseen sample numbers.

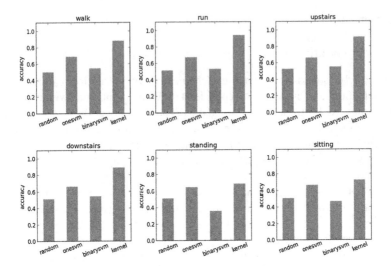

Fig. 5. Accuracy performance of the four novelty detection algorithms (Under only one type of unseen motion)

Figure 5 shows accuracy performance of the four novelty detection algorithms for different types of unseen motions, in which "kernel" denotes our algorithm. From the figure, we can see the detection accuracy of our algorithm is much higher than others in the first four cases and the accuracy of our algorithm is always higher than 80 % except when the unseen category is "standing" or "sitting". The improvement in these two cases is not significant because the body is quiescent under both "standing" and "sitting" states, which makes the algorithm difficult to distinguish them.

B. Performance of the proposed self-learning scheme

Figures 6 and 7 present the distribution of the unseen motion data (Run and Upstairs) after the t-SNE dimension reduction and the DBSCAN clustering, respectively. The

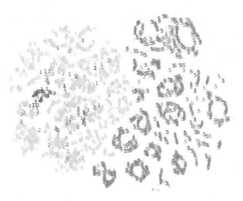

Fig. 6. Dimension reduction result (Color figure online)

samples labeled "5" (red) and "6" (yellow) in Fig. 6 denote the two types of unseen motions: "Run" and "Upstairs", while other samples labeled from "1" to "4" are the seen motion samples. We find that the t-SNE algorithm makes the samples belonging to the same class cluster together. Moreover, the t-SNE can also cluster some seen motion samples together, or scatter them in the region with small sample density, which will be then recognized as noise points (the solid black points) by the DBSCAN algorithm in Fig. 7. Therefore, it reduces the probability that these seen motion samples are mistakenly labeled as the unseen motions.

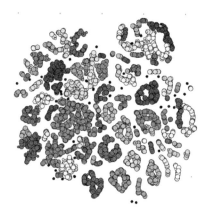

Fig. 7. Clustering result (Color figure online)

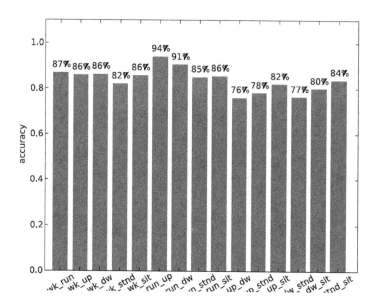

Fig. 8. Accuracy performance of the proposed self-learning scheme

Figure 8 shows the accuracy of the proposed self-learning scheme under the combination of different types of unseen motions. It is obvious that the accuracy reaches above 80 % in most cases after self-learning, which demonstrates the feasibility and efficiency of the self-learning process when there exist several types of unseen motions without any apriori information in the training dataset.

5   Conclusions

We have proposed a self-learning based motion recognition scheme. In our scheme, a patient only needs to carry an ordinary smartphone which contains motion sensors for automatic data collection and uploading. The server preprocesses the sensor data to eliminate orientation influence, and then extracts a set of effective features from the data for further analysis. Moreover, a self-learning framework is proposed for recognizing unpredictable activities without any apriori knowledge in the training dataset. A key functional module in self-learning process is the proposed KNFST-based novelty detection algorithm, which distinguishes unseen and seen motions well. Experiment results demonstrate the feasibility and efficiency of the self-learning scheme for unpredictable motion recognition.

Acknowledgement. This research is sponsored by National Natural Science Foundation of China (No. 61401029, 61171014, 61272475, 61472044, 61472403, 61371185, 11401016, 11401028), the Fundamental Research Funds for the Central Universities (No. 2012LYB46, 2012LYB51, 2014KJJCB32, 2013NT57), Beijing Youth Excellence Program (YETP0296) and Beijing Advanced Innovation Center for Future Education (BJAICFE2016IR-004).

References

1. Győrbíró, N., Fábián, Á., Hományi, G.: An activity recognition system for mobile phones. Mob. Netw. Appl. **14**(1), 82–91 (2009)
2. Morán, A.L., Ramírez-Fernández, C., Meza-Kubo, V., Orihuela-Espina, F., García-Canseco, E., Grimaldo, A.I., Sucar, E.: On the effect of previous technological experience on the usability of a virtual rehabilitation tool for the physical activation and cognitive stimulation of elders. J. Med. Syst. **39**(9), 1–11 (2015)
3. Arif, M., Bilal, M., Kattan, A., et al.: Better physical activity classification using smartphone acceleration sensor. J. Med. Syst. **38**(9), 1–10 (2014)
4. Poppe, R.: A survey on vision-based human action recognition. Image Vis. Comput. **28**(6), 976–990 (2010)
5. Turaga, P., Chellappa, R., Subrahmanian, V.S., et al.: Machine recognition of human activities: a survey. IEEE Trans. Circ. Syst. Video Technol. **18**(11), 1473–1488 (2008)
6. Bao, L., Intille, S.S.: Activity recognition from user-annotated acceleration data. In: Ferscha, A., Mattern, F. (eds.) PERVASIVE 2004. LNCS, vol. 3001, pp. 1–17. Springer, Heidelberg (2004)
7. Grebel, K., Dang, D., Ma, L., Payne, D., Cooper, B.: iSound: a smartphone based intelligent sound fusion system for the hearing impaired. In: Xu, K., Zhu, H. (eds.) WASA 2015. LNCS, vol. 9204, pp. 155–164. Springer, Heidelberg (2015)

8. Incel, O.D., Kose, M., Ersoy, C.: A review and taxonomy of activity recognition on mobile phones. BioNanoScience **3**(2), 145–171 (2013)
9. Cheng, H.T., Sun, F.T., Griss, M., et al.: Nuactiv: recognizing unseen new activities using semantic attribute-based learning. In: Proceeding of the 11th Annual International Conference on Mobile Systems, Applications, and Services, pp. 361–374. ACM (2013)
10. Yin, J., Yang, Q., Pan, J.J.: Sensor-based abnormal human-activity detection. IEEE Trans. Knowl. Data Eng. **20**(8), 1082–1090 (2008)
11. Ho, Y.-C., Lu, C.-H., Chen, I.-H., et al.: Active-learning assisted self-reconfigurable activity recognition in a dynamic environment. In: Proceedings of the 2009 IEEE International Conference on Robotics and Automation, pp. 1567–1572. IEEE Press (2009)
12. Anguita, D., Ghio, A., Oneto, L., et al.: A public domain dataset for human activity recognition using smartphones. In: European Symposium on Artificial Neural Networks, Computational Intelligence and Machine Learning, ESANN (2013)
13. Müller, M.: Dynamic time warping. Inf. Retrieval Music Motion, 69–84 (2007)
14. Foley, D.H., Sammon Jr., J.W.: An optimal set of discriminant vectors. IEEE Trans. Comput. **100**(3), 281–289 (1975)
15. Breiman, L.: Random forests. Mach. Learn. **45**(1), 5–32 (2001)
16. Van der Maaten, L., Hinton, G.: Visualizing data using t-SNE. J. Mach. Learn. Res. **9**(2579–2605), 85 (2008)
17. Ester, M., Kriegel, H.P., Sander, J., et al.: A density-based algorithm for discovering clusters in large spatial databases with noise. In: Kdd, vol. 96(34), pp. 226–231 (1996)
18. Schölkopf, B., Platt, J.C., Shawe-Taylor, J., et al.: Estimating the support of a high-dimensional distribution. Neural Comput. **13**(7), 1443–1471 (2001)
19. Bishop, C.M.: Novelty detection and neural network validation. IEE Proc. Vis. Image Sig. Process. **141**(4), 217–222 (1994). IET
20. Muñoz, A., Muruzábal, J.: Self-organizing maps for outlier detection. Neurocomputing **18**(1), 33–60 (1998)

CrowdBlueNet: Maximizing Crowd Data Collection Using Bluetooth Ad Hoc Networks

Sicong Liu[1], Junzhao Du[2(✉)], Xue Yang[2], Rui Li[2], Hui Liu[2], and Kewei Sha[3,4]

[1] School of Computer Science and Technology, Xidian University, Xi'an, China
[2] School of Software and Institute of Software Engineering,
Xidian University, Xi'an, China
{dujz,rli,liuhui}@xidian.edu.cn
[3] Department of Computer Science,
University of Houston - Clear Lake, Houston, USA
sha@uhcl.edu
[4] Cyber Security Institute, University of Houston - Clear Lake, Houston, USA

Abstract. Crowd management that aims to avoid tragedy like stampede has attracted lots of attention. Crowd management based on crowd traffic data is considered to be one of the most efficient approaches; however, it is challenging to collect accurate and sufficient crowd traffic data in a timely manner. This paper first models the crowd traffic data collection problem with the goals of Minimum Delay and Maximum Throughput (MD-MT); then a Bluetooth based data collection system, CrowdBlueNet is proposed to achieve both goals. CrowdBlueNet consists of novel approaches to construct routing table that enables efficient data transmission in the Bluetooth Ad Hoc network. The prototype based performance evaluation shows the effectiveness and efficiency of CrowdBlueNet.

Keywords: Data collection · Bluetooth · Throughput · Delay

1 Introduction

Crowd management in big events has attracted lots of attention in the last several years, especially after the tragedy happened in Shanghai at the 2015 New Year Celebration [1]. Based on the news report [2], the tragedy happened when the high density flow of people were moving in opposite directions. This tragedy may be avoid with appropriate crowd management. Recent advances in sensor and communication technologies make it possible to develop a system that collect data from the crowd and improve the crowd management based on the collected data. For example, based on the location, people's moving speed and direction, the density of the crowd and the risk of accidents can be evaluated and estimated. Therefore, intelligent strategies to navigate the crowd and avoid the tragedy can be designed and implemented.

Smartphones equipped with various sensors can help collecting basic location, speed and moving direction information [3,4], but it is challenging to collect all

© Springer International Publishing Switzerland 2016
Q. Yang et al. (Eds.): WASA 2016, LNCS 9798, pp. 356–366, 2016.
DOI: 10.1007/978-3-319-42836-9_32

data from each individual device because of the large number and high density of smartphones. On the other hand, it is necessary to collect as much data as possible in a timely manner in order to produce a more accurate picture of the crowd, so that intelligent crowd management strategies and tragedy avoidance mechanisms can be designed and implemented.

Considering different communication modules available in smartphones, most of them lose their capability of transmitting this amount of data to a central place where the data can be analyzed. For example, like the scenario of New Year Celebration in Shanghai, lots of events are organized in an open space area where WiFi is not available [5]. Cellular based communication will lose its capability as well because of the capacity problem [6]. No one could get stable connection when there are a huge number of devices want to get cellular connection at the same time. In addition, Cellular based communication is still expensive in most areas of the world. Near field communication (NFC) is also not applicable because it works only with NFC tags. Fortunately, most smartphones have Bluetooth module installed and the features like low energy consumption (e.g., BLE) make it very suitable for this application. Therefore, we propose to build a Bluetooth Ad Hoc Network, CrowdBlueNet, to collect data from individual smartphones to support crowd management.

CrowdBlueNet makes use of smartphone's Bluetooth channel to build an Ad hoc network. The goals of minimum delay and maximum throughput are achieved based on the design of zone partition, the algorithm of zone head selection, and routing table establishment. The performance evaluation shows that our design brings significant benefits for data collection in a high-density and large-scale area while achieves high throughput. The main contribution of this paper is three-fold. Firstly, we design CrowdBlueNet to collect data from a high density and large scale network. Secondly, we propose algorithms to minimize delay and maximize throughput by optimizing the number of sub-zones in the network initialization stage. Thirdly, a prototype system is developed to validate the efficiency of our design. Extensive experimental results show that the proposed system is effective and efficient.

The rest of this paper is organized as follows. Section 2 provides the challenges, problem formulation. In Sect. 3, we describe the detailed design of Crowd-BlueNet. Prototype based evaluation is presented in Sect. 4. In Sect. 5, we review the related literatures. Finally, we conclude the paper and discuss the future work in Sect. 6.

2   Background and Problem Definition

In this section, we first briefly introduce the Bluetooth protocol. Then crowd traffic data collection problem is formally modeled.

Bluetooth 4.0 [7] is a protocol to connect multiple Bluetooth devices. Although the newer version of Bluetooth (Bluetooth 4.1) can support the device to act two roles (sender and receiver) at the same time, there are still a big amount of Bluetooth 4.0 smartphones in use. In order to ensure the proposed system to be applicable in most devices, we make CrowdBlueNet compatible to the Bluetooth 4.0. Using Bluetooth 4.0, several Bluetooth-equipped devices can form a piconet, in which one device acts as the master and the rest of devices act as the slaves. Slaves can send data to the master. A device can change its role from one to the other based on a schedule. Two or more piconets can form a scatternet. To connect a superior piconet and a junior piconet, there must be a device acting as a relay node that forwards data from the junior piconet to the superior one by switching its role from master to slave [8].

2.1   System Assumption and Problem Modelling

There are several challenges to build CrowdBlueNet. Firstly, in the Crowd-BlueNet initialization phase, participating devices have no prior knowledge of other devices and the communication range of Bluetooth is limited, so it is challenging to construct the routing table in a distributed manner based on Bluetooth communication channel. Secondly, considering the mobility, high density and large scale of the crowd, on one hand, we should collect as much data as possible from massive participating devices even when they are moving. On the other hand, the paring process of multiple devices should be reasonably designed to decrease the delay in multi-hop data forwarding. It is difficult to achieve both goals at the same time.

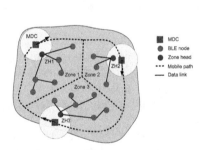

Fig. 1. Topology of CrowdBlueNet.

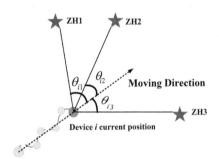

Fig. 2. Destination ZH selection of device i.

The CrowdBlueNet data collection scenario is shown in Fig. 1. We assume there are n participating devices continuously sense their own location, speed and direction information using smartphones. To reduce the delay of forwarding data and improve the throughput, the whole sensing area is divided into n_{ZH} zones and each zone has a Zone Head(ZH). These zones are not connected. Each device is connected to one and only one ZH directly or indirectly. Without loss of generality, in our design we assume the ZHs are fixed. For example, they can be wore by volunteers and polices who are managing crowd traffic at certain road intersections. All ZHs can leverage the Bluetooth Service Discovery Protocol

(SDP) to broadcast their location information to other devices without the need of pairing with them. Because the amount of transferring data is relatively large compared with the SDP messages, we transfer the data by establishing a connection between devices to avoid overwhelming local broadcast. Data received by ZH is send to a Mobile Data Collector (MDC) that is a Bluetooth-quipped device with much higher computation and communication power. The MDC moves along a fixed path periodically with a certain speed to collect data. We can make use of multiple MDCs to collect data, but in this paper, we only consider using only one MDC because the problem is equivalent if we connect the paths of multiple MDCs to form a path of a single MDC. The number of zones is related to the size and the density of the network.

For the purpose of efficient crowd management, it is expected to collect a large amount of real-time data, i.e., to minimize delay and maximize throughput.

Minimum Delay (MD). The delay of data delivering is the time it takes for the data to be transferred from the source device to the ZH. To reduce the delay, we consider device's moving direction, distance and number of hops to ZHs in the routing table construction. As shown in Fig. 2, assuming that the device i is in position X_i at time t, and in X_i' at time t', we can calculate the moving direction o_i of device i as $o_i = \boldsymbol{X_i X_i'}$. Assume the position of ZH_k is Y_k. The vector between the device i and ZH_k is $o_k = \boldsymbol{X_i Y_k}$. Calculating the angle between o_i and o_k, $\theta_{ik} = arccos(\frac{o_i \cdot o_k)}{o_i \times o_k)}$, we select the ZH_{k_i} as the destination ZH of device i based on Eq. (1), because ZH k_i is closest ZH to the moving direction of device i.

$$k_i = \{k | min(\theta_{ik}), k = 1, .., m\}\} \tag{1}$$

After determining the ZH to which the device i will deliver data, each device sets its $ZoneID_i$ to be K_i. During the routing table establishment, each device needs to select its superior device to forward data. When device i received the broadcasting from device j, which contains $ZoneID_j$ and $MinHop_j$, the minimum hop from device j to its ZH. Device i will compare the $ZoneID_j$ with its own Zone ID, $ZoneID_i$. If their $ZoneID$s are the same, i will choose the device who has the minimum $MinHop$, i.e., choosing the closest device to the ZH among the nearby broadcasting devices. Devices will directly transfer data to ZHs if they are within direct communication range of ZHs. In this way, we minimize the data delivering path length and minimize delay.

Considering the dynamics of the traffic, we calculate the moving direction periodically such as every 60 s. Each device updates its destination ZH according to its own moving direction. The update of the routing table is an on demand process. Once the $ZoneID$ of a device is changed, it will broadcast the information to other devices, so they can update their routing table according to the received information. The details of the routing tree construction will be introduced in Sect. 3.

Maximum throughput (MT). In our problem model, we assume that the number of ZHs is fixed and the trajectory of MDC to visit all ZHs is predetermined. It is also assumed that there are n_{ZH} zone heads in the sensing area, and it takes a time interval of T for the MDC to complete a loop that visits all ZHs. The MDC receives data from ZH k when they are within the direct communication range, the time of which is t_i. As shown in Eq. (2), the receiving capability of MDC limits the maximum amount of data that can be collected.

$$N_{maxr} = \sum_{i=1}^{n_{ZH}} V_{ZH} * t_i. \tag{2}$$

where V_{ZH} is the data transmission rate of ZHs and N_{maxr} is the maximum amount of data that can be received by the MDC.

There are K_i member devices in a zone i that continuously sense data and send data to their ZHs. Assuming the sensor's sampling rate of a mobile device to be V_s, the amount of data produced by a zone i in a period T is N_s^i, where $N_s^i = K_i * V_s * T$. N_s^i is in proportion to the number of member devices when the V_s and T are constant. In order to successfully receive all data from ZHs, it is required that $N_r^i \geq N_s^i$, where N_r^i ($N_r^i = V_{ZH} * t_i$) is the amount of data transmitted from ZH_i to MDC during the contact time of t_i. The maximum number of devices that can be in zone i (denoted as K_i^{max}) can be calculated by Eq. (3).

$$K_i^{max} = \frac{V_{ZH} * t_i}{V_s * T} \tag{3}$$

Our objective is to balance the number of devices in different zones so that no zone will have more than K_i^{max} devices. We use the balance ratio in Eq. (4) to evaluate the balance level of different zones' devices amount. The smaller the difference between K_i is, which means a more balanced allocation, the bigger their product will be.

$$\phi(\bar{K}) = \prod_{i=1}^{n_{ZH}} \frac{K_i}{K_i^{max}} \tag{4}$$

where $\bar{K}$ donates the number of devices allocated to each zone. When $\phi(\bar{K}) > 1$, it means that the number of devices in some zones has exceeded the maximum allowed number. In this case, some data cannot be received by the MDC. Therefore, considering the amount of devices n, the maximum throughput problem can be formulated as an optimization problem as follows,

$$max \ \phi(\bar{K})$$
$$s.t. \ \sum_{i=1}^{n_{ZH}} K_i = n \ \& \ K_i < K_i^{max} \tag{5}$$

We follow the above MD-MT optimization goals when we establish the routing tree, which is described in the next section.

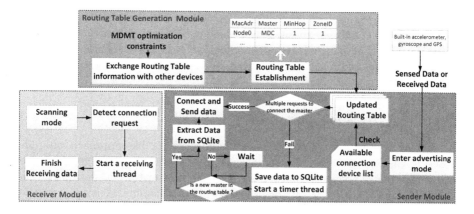

Fig. 3. CrowdBlueNet's module diagram.

3   The Design of CrowdBlueNet

In this section, we illustrate how to establish the Bluetooth ad hoc network to efficiently collect data from massive participating devices, and achieve the MD-MT objectives as defined before.

3.1   Design Overview

CrowdBlueNet consists of three major modules as shown in Fig. 3.

Routing Table Generation Module. This module is used to initialize the CrowdBlueNet and construct the routing table for data delivering. As shown in Fig. 3, each routing table entry contains 4 types of information: $MacAdr$, $Master$, $MinHops$ and $ZoneID$. $MacAdr$ is the MAC address of a device. $Master$ denotes the device's superior device, i.e., the master. $MinHops$ is the hops of this device to the ZH. $ZoneID$ denotes the ID of the zone to which a device belongs. In this module, each device exchanges and updates its routing table to get a converged routing table which contains information of all devices of the current network so that we can calculate the number of devices in each zone.

Sender Module. Devices use this module to send data to their masters. When a device produces a set of new data and has finished its current round of receiving, it turns into advertising mode and tries to get connection with its master. This process stops when either a successful connection is established or a time limitation is reached, which is used to prevent infinite waiting of an unavailable master. The device stores the data that needs to be forwarded in a local SQLite database if it fails in connecting to the master.

Receiver Module. Each device receives data using this module. When a device finishes sending data to its master or stores data in local database as its master is busy, it switches to the scanning mode to detect slaves' connection request. Once it is successfully connected to one slave, the device starts a receiving thread to receive data until all data receiving is completed. It is worth mentioning that a device can receive data from its multiple slaves in parallel by using the frequency-hopping mechanism [9].

3.2 Routing Tree Establishment

The routing tree is constructed using a distance vector like approach, the difference is that we are establishing several trees rooted at different ZHs. We present the rule of how a normal device select its master to send data based on local information so that it satisfies the MD-MT constraints. According to the MD-MT optimization objectives, each device establishes and updates its routing table based on its local and received information in a distributed manner.

At the beginning each device stays in scanning mode and keeps listening to other devices to construct a converged routing table. The tree establishment is started from ZHs of the zone to broadcast the initial routing table. With the process going, each device will finally establish a routing table that contains information of all devices so that the number of zone members can be calculated based on local routing table. For example, from the information in the routing table, we can get the number of devices K_j which have been added to the routing table of zone j based on the $zoneID$. Master selection rules are designed based on two scenarios. When a device A receives advertising packets from several neighboring devices N_A, which contain information such as $ZoneID_i$ of device i ($i \in N_A$) and the minimum hop $MinHop_i$ from i to ZH, two cases are considered as follows.

1. **Have no same-ZoneID devices.** Among all neighboring devices if there is no device having the same $ZoneID$ with device A, i.e., for all i, $ZoneID_i \neq ZoneID_A$. We select the devices that satisfy $\|\theta_{Ak_i} - \theta_{Ak_A}\| \leq \epsilon$ as candidate master devices, where the threshold $\epsilon = 10°$. We choose these devices because their ZHs are close to device A's destination ZH and they are both close to the moving direction of device A. Then by screening the candidates set, it is able to find the devices whose $MinHop_i$ is no more than $(Min(MinHop_i) + 1)$. Here $Min(MinHop_i)$ is the smallest $MinHop$ of all candidates. If a device A selects one candidate i as its master, it will be added to the zone which the candidate i belongs to. We can get the number of devices in each zone from routing table, so after adding the device A to i's zones, the possible number of each zones is $\bar{K}_p$. Then we compare the local balance ratio ϕ based on Eq. (4) and choose the best case $\tilde{K}_p$ with the maximum balance ratio, formally, $\tilde{K}_p = argmax_{\bar{K}_p}\phi(\bar{K}_p)$. The candidate device which meets the above conditions will be selected as the master of device A.

2. **Have same-ZoneID devices.** If there are one or multiple devices whose $ZoneID$ is the same as device A. The device which has the minimum $MinHop$ among the devices is selected to act as the master of device A, as mentioned in Sect. 2.1.

If device B is selected as the master of device A according to above rules, device A will insert a routing entry into its routing table. The value of $MacAdr_A$ is its own Mac address; the $Master_A$ value is $MacAddr_B$; $MinHops_A$ equals to $(MinHops_B + 1)$, and the value of $ZoneID_A$ is the same as $ZoneID_B$. Then device A enters advertising mode and broadcasts the new routing table. Once the routing table is established using above approach, each device can deliver its data to the master which helps to forward the data to the destination ZH.

4   Experiment

We validate the effectiveness of CrowdBlueNet design using a prototype based on Android smartphones. Several types of phones are used in the experiment, including SAMSUNG GALAXY S6, Huawei Honor 6P, MEIZU MX4, MI 4S and the like. The CrowdBlueNet modules and aforementioned protocols are implemented as a mobile APP, which consists of about 2300 lines of Java code. In the experiment, an electric-motorbike equipped with a smartphone acts as the Mobile Data Collector. Our prototype consists of 25 Android devices. A picture of the experiment conducted in the Xidian central plaza is shown in Fig. 4, where all other devices send data to the two ZHs as marked in the picture using the routing scheme described in Sect. 3.

Fig. 4. The real experiment scenario.

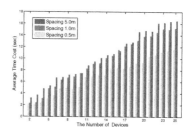

Fig. 5. Average network initialization time. (Color figure online)

4.1   Network Initialization Time

In this subsection, we investigate the relationship between the time of establishing the CrowdBlueNet, i.e., the time for generating the routing table, and the number of participant devices as well as the distance between devices.

In the first experiment, we test different number of participants from 2 to 25 to build the network. The distance between each pair of participating devices randomly ranging from 1.5 m to 5 m. The average time in initializing CowdBlueNet is shown in Fig. 5, which shows that the average delay increases with the number of devices. It validates our design of dividing the network into multiple zones so that each zone could have less number of devices and it can reduce the network establishing time. In the second experiment, we compare the average time for initializing CrowdBlueNet with different spacing distance. As shown in Fig. 5, the average time for initializing a 25-participant CrowdBlueNet increases from 11 s when the spacing distance of participants is 0.5 m to 17 s when the spacing distance is 5.0 m. Generally speaking, the more devices a routing tree have the longer the initialization time is. Therefore zone partition helps routing by connecting close devices to the same zone and limiting the number of devices in each zone.

4.2 Average Data Delivery Time

In this set of experiments, we make all 25 participants send the sensed data to their ZHs, and the MDC continuously receives data from ZHs. We measure the delivery time as the time it takes for the data traveling from the source device to the ZH.

We set our experiment area as a 33 m × 24 m two-dimensional rectangular plane and establish a coordinate system. The ZHs are located at $(3, 3)$ and $(3, 30)$ in the coordinate system. The participating devices are moving randomly in the area. The average data delivery time of each device is shown in Fig. 6. It is shown that the devices located far away from the ZHs take more time to deliver the data to ZH. The largest delivery time is less than 20 s, which is timely enough to satisfy the timeliness requirements considering the fact that an adult takes about 7 s to walk 10 steps.

4.3 Network Throughput

The network throughput is D_{max}/T, where D_{max} is the maximum amount of data successfuly collected by MDC in the period T. We evaluate the throughput of CrowdBlueNet under three experimental settings, zone partition with optimal number of devices, zone partition with random number of devices, and no zone partition.

We conduct the experiment with different number of smartphones ranging from 5 to 25. Each smartphone reads the data from accelerometer, gyroscope and GPS and sends it to the MDC. The sampling frequency of the sensors is set ranging from 1 Hz to 100 Hz, so the size of packets can be small to large. In this way we measure the maximum data amount collected by the MDC. The sampling procedure lasts for about 10 min. The results are shown in Fig. 7, from which we can find that partition in our proposed method can effectively improve the throughput of the network. When the number of devices is less than 9, the throughput of random partition and optimal partition is close, but when the number of devices increases, the advantage of optimal partition is obvious. It shows that the proposed solution is beneficial to large scale networks.

5 Related Work

Bluetooth technology has been widely applied in monitoring systems and used extensively for data collection systems [10, 11]. There are several algorithms [12–14]

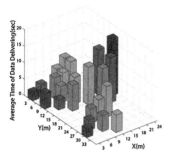

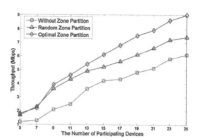

Fig. 6. Average data deliver time.

Fig. 7. Throughput of different number of devices.

for bluetooth scatternet formation. These algorithms are no more optimal in BLE, because they have to consider a limitation in former version of Bluetooth protocol, i.e., one master can maximally have 7 slaves.

Hughes etc. develop a WSN using BLE for construction noise identification and sound locating [15]. The work [16] presents a design of a tree network topology which serves as the network backbone for WSN based on Bluetooth 4.0 technology. In [16], a scatternet formation and multi-hop routing protocol based on the new features in BLE version 4.1 is presented. None of above effort tries to improve the throughput of Bluetooth network or minimize delay by dividing the whole area to zones.

6   Conclusion

In this paper, we propose CrowdBlueNet to efficiently collect information from massive data sources. With CrowdBlueNet, we collect users' movement data from smartphones with two objectives, minimizing delay and maximizing throughput. We use prototype implementation to validate the efficiency of CrowdBlueNet under various experiment settings. In future, we will first design a distributed approach to efficiently get the number of members for each zone. Second, Crowd-BlueNet will be evaluated in large scale systems using more matrices like energy efficiency. Moreover, we plan to study the mobile patterns and the trends of the crowd based on the movement data; therefore, we can provide intelligent crowd management strategies.

Acknowledgments. This work is partially supported by the National Natural Science Foundation of China (NSFC) under Grant No. 61272456,61472312 and 61502374. This work is also supported by the National Science and Technology Pillar Program during the 12th Five-year Plan Period (2014BAJ01B01), the Overall innovation project of Shaanxi province science and technology plan (2012KTZD02-03-03), the Fundamental Research Funds for the Central Universities under project No. BDY041409K5051323005, JB151002 and K5051323003 (Xidian University).

References

1. http://news.baidu.com/z/shanghaicaita/zhuanti.html
2. http://news.sina.com.cn/c/zg/grw/2015-01-01/1843511.html
3. Roy, N., Wang, H., Choudhury, R.R.: I am a smartphone and i can tell my user's walking direction. In: Proceedings of the 12th Annual International Conference on Mobile systems, Applications, and Services, pp. 329–342. ACM (2014)
4. Wang, H., Lai, T.T.-T., Choudhury, R.R.: Mole: motion leaks through smartwatch sensors. In: Proceedings of the 21st Annual International Conference on Mobile Computing and Networking, pp. 155–166. ACM (2015)
5. Maghdid, H.S., Lami, I.A., Ghafoor, K.Z., Lloret, J.: Seamless outdoors-indoors localization solutions on smartphones: implementation and challenges. Acm Comput. Surv. (CSUR) **48**(4), 53 (2016)
6. Breschel, M., Almers, P., Angsmark, F., Arvidsson, A., Bauer, H., van Berkel, K., Canovas, J., Do, M., Ekelund, A., Larsson, T., et al.: 10.8 a multi-standard 2g/3g/4g cellular modem supporting carrier aggregation in 28nm cmos. In: IEEE International Solid-State Circuits Conference Digest of Technical Papers (ISSCC), pp. 190–191. IEEE (2014)
7. Galeev, M.: Bluetooth 4.0: an introduction to bluetooth low energy-part i. EE Times, Design (2011)
8. Paradells, J., Gomez, C., Oller, J.: Overview and evaluation of bluetooth low energy: an emerging low-power wireless technology. Sensors **12**(9), 11734–11753 (2012)
9. Liu, Y., Lee, M.J., Saadawi, T.K.: A bluetooth scatternet-route structure for multihop ad hoc networks. IEEE J. Sel. Areas Commun. **21**(2), 229–239 (2003)
10. Stange, H., Liebig, T., Hecker, D., Andrienko, G., Andrienko, N.: Analytical workflow of monitoring human mobility in big event settings using bluetooth. In: Proceedings of the 3rd ACM SIGSPATIAL international workshop on indoor spatial awareness, pp. 51–58. ACM (2011)
11. Miklós, G., Rácz, A., Turányi, Z., Valkó, A., Johansson, P.: Performance aspects of bluetooth scatternet formation. In: Proceedings of the 1st ACM International Symposium on Mobile Ad Hoc Networking & Computing, pp. 147–148. IEEE Press (2000)
12. Das, A., Ghose, A., Razdan, A., Saran, H., Shorey, R.: Enhancing performance of asynchronous data traffic over the bluetooth wireless ad-hoc network. In: IEEE INFOCOM, vol. 1, pp. 591–600. IEEE (2001)
13. Lee, M.J., Liu, Y.: A bluetooth scatternet-route structure for multihop ad hoc networks. Sel. Areas Commun. **21**, 229–239 (2003)
14. Hughes, J., Yan, J., Soga, K.: Development of wireless sensor network using bluetooth low energy (ble) for construction noise monitoring. Int. J. Smart Sens. Intell. Syst. **8**(2), 1379–1405 (2015)
15. Maharjan, B.K., Witkowski, U., Zandian, R.: Tree network based on bluetooth 4.0 for wireless sensor network applications. In: European Embedded Design in Education and Research Conference (EDERC), pp. 172–176. IEEE (2014)
16. Harris, I.G., Guo, Z.: An on-demand scatternet formation and multi-hop routing protocol for ble-based wireless sensor networks (2015)

An Energy Efficient Multi-hop Routing Protocol for Terahertz Wireless Nanosensor Networks

Juan Xu[✉], Rong Zhang, and Zhiyu Wang

College of Electronics and Information Engineering,
Tongji University, Shanghai, China
jxujuan@tongji.edu.cn, 18862238065@163.com,
wzy_tj90@126.com

Abstract. Wireless nanosensor networks are novel networks where nanonodes can work in Terahertz band. Researches are mainly focused on physical layer while study of routing protocols in this field is still in an initial stage. Consequently, a novel energy efficient multi-hop routing protocol based on network conditions is proposed. In our routing protocol, the area of candidate nodes is narrowed to control the direction of multi-hop forwarding. A link cost function is established to trade off energy consumption, capacity and distance, taking the peculiarities of Terahertz channel into consideration. Several nodes with low link cost have the probability to be selected as a next hop, which prolongs the lifetime of nanosensor networks. Simulation results show that the protocol we proposed can achieve high throughput and low energy consumption, which is a suitable routing for Terahertz nanosenor networks.

Keywords: Nanosensor networks · Terahertz · Multi-hop routing · Molecular absorption · Channel capacity

1 Introduction

Wireless NanoSensor Networks (WNSNs) are novel networks which consists of large numbers of nanosensors. These nanonodes ranging from nano to micro meters in size can perform very specific tasks, such as sensing, computing and transmitting. Compared to nodes in classical wireless sensor networks, nanonodes can detect new types of events at nanoscale. As a consequence, WNSNs will enable a wide range of applications in biomedical, environmental, industrial and military fields, such as health monitoring, drug delivery systems, biological and chemical attack prevention [1].

Graphene-based nano-transceivers and nano-antennas are envisioned to communicate in Terahertz band (0.1–10 THz) which provides very large transmission rates, up to Gb/s or even higher [2]. Furthermore, nano-devices take advantage of the peculiarities of Terahertz band, such as the narrow beam and good directivity which can be used to detect and precisely position smaller targets. Therefore, electromagnetic communication in Terahertz band is a promising approach to develop simple but efficient modulation scheme in the physical layer of WNSNs.

© Springer International Publishing Switzerland 2016
Q. Yang et al. (Eds.): WASA 2016, LNCS 9798, pp. 367–376, 2016.
DOI: 10.1007/978-3-319-42836-9_33

Previous work on energy efficient routing in WSNs is not directly applicable to WNSNs, due to the peculiarities of Terahertz Band communication, in particular the very unique distance-dependent behavior of the available bandwidth and the very high propagation losses. To the best of our knowledge, researches on WNSNs are mainly focused on physical layer [3, 4] while study of routing protocols in this field is still in an initial stage. A Selective Flooding Routing (SFR) is proposed in [5], which limits the direction of flooding to prevent bandwidth waste when concurrent transmissions happen among nanonodes. However, it doesn't capture the peculiarities of Terahertz channel. In [6], a multi-hop and energy harvesting-aware routing protocol for WNSNs is described, which guarantees throughput and enables network lifetime infinite. However, simulation results can only verify a two-hop routing due to complexity, thus limiting its application in practical networks.

This paper proposes an Energy Efficient Multi-hop Routing protocol (EEMR) for Terahertz WNSNs, taking the following two unique aspects of WNSNs into account. On one hand, the peculiarities of Terahertz channel are considered. More specifically, channel capacity is closely related to transmission distances and composition of the medium. Furthermore, Absorption from several molecules in the medium introduces very high molecular absorption loss. On the other hand, routing protocols should not be too complicated due to very limited computational capabilities of nanonodes.

2 System Model

2.1 Network Model

WNSNs are usually designed as cluster-based hierarchical structures including a nanocontroller with more advanced capabilities in each cluster. The nanocontroller is responsible for coordination among nanonodes. All traffic generated by nanonodes will be transmitted to the nanocontroller in a one-hop or multi-hop way. In our protocol, the network topology can be represented as $G = (V, E)$, where $V = \{v_1, v_2, \ldots, v_n\}$ denotes the set of all nanonodes and $E = \{e_{12}, e_{13}, \ldots, e_{ij}\}$, $i, j = 1, 2, \ldots, n$ denotes the set of all possible one-hop links between nanonodes.

2.2 Terahertz Channel Capacity

The whole Terahertz band is divided into different transmission windows due to molecular absorption loss [7], so the total channel capacity can be obtained by computing the capacity within the available bandwidth of each sub-band. According to Shannon formula, Terahertz channel capacity can be written as

$$C_s(d) = \sum^{M} \Delta f_w \log_2 \left[1 + \frac{S(f)}{N_a(d,f) \cdot PL(d,f)} \right] \tag{1}$$

where M is the number of all sub-bands, Δf_w stands for the available bandwidth of different sub-bands, $S(f)$ is the power spectral density of transmitted signals, $N_a(d,f)$ is the noise p.s.d and $PL(d,f)$ is the channel path-loss.

Noise power spectral density $N_a(d,f)$ is shown in [3],

$$N_a(d,f) = K_B T_0 (1 - e^{-k(f)d}) \tag{2}$$

where K_B stands for Boltzmann constant, T_0 is the reference temperature, $k(f)$ stands for the molecular absorption coefficient and d is the total path length.

The total path loss includes spreading loss introduced by a wave's propagation through the medium and molecular absorption attenuation. And the spreading loss can be written as,

$$PL(d,f) = \left(\frac{4\pi f_c d}{c}\right)^2 e^{k(f)d} \tag{3}$$

where f_c is the central frequency of travelling waves.

The available bandwidth Δf_w is defined to meet the following frequency range [8]

$$N_a(d,f)PL(d,f) \le 2N_a(d,f_c(d))PL(d,f_c(d)) \tag{4}$$

where $f_c(d)$ is the central frequency of different sub-bands. Noticed that if a sub-band is sufficiently narrow, molecular absorption is lower than 10 dB/km [9], which is negligible. Each sub-band and noises inside can be considered flat, whereby we can compute the total channel capacity.

2.3   Energy Model

For nanonodes, the energy stored in their nano-batteries is mainly for communications. The energy consumed in forwarding a packet of N_{bit} can be defined as

$$E_c = N_{bit}(E_{tx} + E_{rx}) \tag{5}$$

where E_{tx} and E_{rx} stands for the energy consumption when nanonodes transmit and receive per bit of data, respectively. E_{rx} is usually set as one-tenth of E_{tx} in Terahertz communication systems based on TS-OOK modulation scheme [10]. And E_{tx} can be written as a function of transmission distance d,

$$E_{tx}(d) = \frac{P_{tx}(d)}{C_s(d)} \tag{6}$$

where $P_{tx}(d)$ denotes transmission power, $C_s(d)$ is channel capacity in (1).

To make sure the signal to noise ratio by the receiver reaches SNR_m, the transmission power $P_{tx}(d)$ is defined as

$$P_{tx}(d) = \int_{B(d)} (SNR_m \cdot N_a(d,f) \cdot PL(d,f)) df \tag{7}$$

where $B(d)$ is the available bandwidth of the Terahertz channel.

3   EEMR Protocol

According to the analysis above, an EEMR protocol is proposed based on network conditions. In our protocol, the computational complexity can be reduced by narrowing the areas of candidate nanonodes. In order to trade off energy consumption, channel capacity and distances, a link cost function for each candidate path is established as a standard of selecting a next hop. In addition, several nodes with low link cost have the probability to be selected as a next hop, which prolongs the network lifetime.

3.1   Area of Candidate Nodes

As shown in Fig. 1, the distance between nanocontroller v_c and source node v_s is $d(v_c, v_s)$ and there is a circular area $A_1(v_c, d(v_c, v_s))$ with v_c as the center, $d(v_c, v_s)$ as the radius. Similarly, the area where neighbor nodes of v_s are located can be approximated as a circular area $A_2(v_s, d_s)$ with v_s as the center, d_s as the radius. The area of candidate nodes A_3 can be defined as the intersection of $A_1(v_c, d(v_c, v_s))$ and $A_2(v_s, d_s)$,

$$A_3 = A_1(v_c, d(v_c, v_s)) \bigcap A_2(v_s, d_s) \tag{8}$$

If the candidate nanonode v_i is inside A_3, its position coordinates will meet the following conditions,

$$\begin{cases} \sqrt{(x_i - x_c)^2 + (y_i - y_c)^2} \leq d(v_c, v_s) \\ \sqrt{(x_i - x_s)^2 + (y_i - y_s)^2} \leq d_s \end{cases} \tag{9}$$

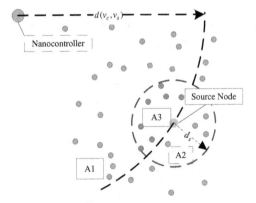

Fig. 1. Area of candidate nodes

where (x_c, y_c), (x_i, y_i) and (x_s, y_s) stands for the position coordinates of v_c, v_i and v_s, respectively. The direction of multi-hop forwarding can be controlled towards the destination node by narrowing the candidate area from $A_2(v_s, d_s)$ to A_3 and computational complexity can be reduced as there's no need to select a next hop among all neighbors.

3.2 Link Cost Function

In our EEMR protocol, a link cost function is established as the basis for selecting a next hop and can be calculated as

$$c(v_i, v_j) = \alpha \tilde{f}(E_c(v_i, v_j)) + \beta \tilde{f}(1/C_s(v_i, v_j)) + (1 - \alpha - \beta)\tilde{f}(d(v_j, v_c)) \qquad (10)$$

where $d(v_j, v_c)$ is the distance between candidate node v_j and nanocontroller v_c, $E_c(v_i, v_j)$ and $C_s(v_i, v_j)$ respectively stands for the energy consumption and channel capacity of candidate path between nanonode v_i and its candidate node v_j, α and β are cost coefficients and range from 0 to 1, $\tilde{f}(\ )$ stands for normalized expression of these three parameters.

Routing strategies usually select a node with the lowest link cost as a next hop, and then establish the optimal transmission path. However, this will result in rapid energy depletion of nodes at the optimal path due to being selected for many times. In order to prolong network lifetime, several nodes with low link cost have the probability to be selected as a next hop, and then forward data to one of those nodes with a certain probability. In other words, after obtaining the link cost of n_h candidate nodes, we can sort them and select the first m nodes with the lowest link cost. The probability of being selected as a next hop among these m nodes can be written as

$$p_{v_j} = \frac{\frac{1}{c(v_i, v_j)}}{\sum\limits_{k=1}^{m} \frac{1}{c(v_i, v_k)}}, \ j \in 1, 2, \ldots, m \qquad (11)$$

where $c(v_i, v_j)$ and $c(v_i, v_k)$ are the link cost of two candidate paths. And the value of m can be expressed as

$$m = \begin{cases} n_h & m \leq \delta \\ \lfloor n_h/\delta \rfloor & m > \delta \end{cases} \qquad (12)$$

where δ is a system parameter. The calculation needed for generating a forwarding list can be further reduced by selecting m in (12). Actually, probability obtained in (11) equals the forwarding probability with which nanonodes forward data and determine a next hop.

Routing Establishment Process. The algorithm of establishing EEMR protocol is shown in Algorithm 1, detailed steps are as follows,

(1) Initialization. Firstly, nanocontroller v_c broadcasts hello messages including its own location within the cluster. Then nanonodes send back their node IDs and

locations after receiving the hello message. At last, v_c records the node ID and corresponding location of every node.

(2) When needing to send data to v_c, a nanonode v_i firstly determines whether v_c is in its one-hop range. If it is, v_i directly forwards data to v_c. Otherwise, v_i broadcasts query messages containing its own location to neighbor nodes within the communication range.

(3) On receiving the query message, neighbor node determines whether it is within candidate area A_3 according to (9). If not, the neighbor node makes no reply to the query message; otherwise, it's a candidate node and denoted as v_j. Then v_j calculates the value of its link cost $c(v_i, v_j)$ and returns an ACK message including the node ID and $c(v_i, v_j)$ to v_i.

(4) v_i sorts all the values of link cost in an ascending order after receiving ACK, selects the first m nodes and calculates the forwarding probability according to (11), then adds the forwarding probability and corresponding node ID into the forwarding list.

(5) v_i forwards data to one of nodes according to the forwarding list. And the one-hop forwarding process is finished after the selected next hop v_l successfully receiving the data. Then v_l will be a new source node and go back to step (2) to establish a routing.

```
Algorithm1
For source code vᵢ
 1: while (nanocontroller v_c does not receive data)
 2:    on receiving hello message from nanocontroller v_c
 3:    if v_c ∈ A₂(vᵢ,d₂)
 4:          forward data to v_c
 5:    else
 6:          broadcast query message
 7:          if candidate node vⱼ ∈ A₃
 8:                compute link cost c(vᵢ,vⱼ)
 9:                reply ACK message to vᵢ
10:          end if
11:    end if
12:    sort all link cost c(vᵢ,vₖ) in ascending order
13:    compute forwarding probability P_vⱼ according to(11)
14:    forward data according to forwarding probability P_vⱼ
15: end while
```

4 Simulation and Performance Analysis

4.1 Statistics Definition

1. Energy efficiency. Energy efficiency is defined as the energy consumption when the destination node successfully receives per bit of data, and can be calculated as

$$e_{con} = \frac{\sum_{i \in V} (E_{ibefore} - E_{iafter})}{N_{bit}} \tag{13}$$

where N_{bit} is the number of bits of a packet, $E_{ibefore}$ and E_{iafter} stands for the energy before and after forwarding a packet of node i, respectively.

2. End-to-end delay. End-to-end delay refers to the time during which a packet are transmitted from the source node and successfully received by the nanocontroller. For a path with m hops, the end-to-end delay can be written as

$$T_d = \sum_{i=1}^{M} \left(N_{bit} T_p + N_{bit} T_q + \frac{d_i}{v} + \frac{N_{bit}}{C_i} \right) \tag{14}$$

where T_p and T_q respectively stands for average processing and queue delay of per bit, d_i and C_i is the path length and channel capacity of the ith hop, respectively, v is propagation speed of the signal.

3. Network lifetime. We define network lifetime as the time length which lasts from the beginning of network operation to the first death of a node in the network,

$$LT = \min\{t | E_v(t) \leq \eta\}, \; v \in V \tag{15}$$

where $E_v(t)$ stands for the energy of node v and η is the threshold of residual energy. A node is considered dead when its energy is below the threshold.

4.2 Parameter Settings

We run some simulations to evaluate the performance of EEMR based on NS-3. As shown in Fig. 2, the simulation scenario is set as a two-dimensional square with $0.1 \times 0.1\,\text{m}^2$ in size, where two hundred nanonodes are independently, randomly distributed. The only one nanocontroller is located in the center of the square. Nanonodes are considered to be operating in an environment with 10 % water vapor and the simplified noise power spectral density equals 1.42×10^{-21}. SNR_m in (7), α and β in (10) is respectively set as 10, 0.5 and 0.3.δ in (12) and η in (15) is respectively set as 2 and 1.4 1.4×10^{-15} J. The packet size and interval time is set as 128 Byte and 0.1 s, respectively.

And the node density is considered constant. Then we study the performance change as a function of the distance between one nanonode and the nanocontroller.

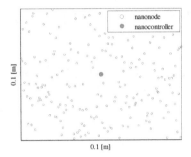

Fig. 2. Topology of WNSNs

4.3   Results

1. Energy efficiency. As shown in Fig. 3, EEMR does better in energy efficiency than SFR. This is because an energy model for Terahertz channel is established in EEMR and energy consumption is taken into account when establishing the link cost function, thus building a transmission path with higher energy efficiency.

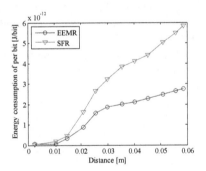

Fig. 3. Energy consumption

2. End-to-end delay. As shown in Fig. 4(a), when the nanocontroller is very close to the source node, the end-to-end delay of these two protocols are almost the same. However, EEMR shows obvious advantage when the distance is above 0.02 m. This is due to the higher achievable information rate in Terahertz channel and the reduction of unnecessary routing hops by limiting the candidate areas.
3. Network lifetime. As shown in Fig. 4(b), network lifetime of both EEMR and SFR are prolonged as initial energy of nanonodes increases. And the former is always longer than the latter. This is because several nodes with low link cost have the probability to be selected as a next hop, which prevents the energy of the same node at the optimal path from rapidly running out due to being selected many times.

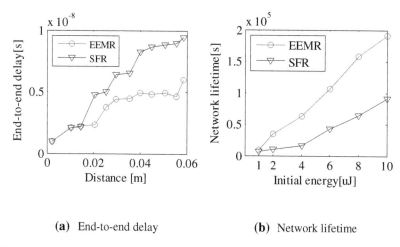

(a) End-to-end delay   **(b)** Network lifetime

Fig. 4. Comparison of end-to-end delay and network lifetime between EEMR and SFR (Colour figure online)

5 Conclusion

In this paper, we propose a multi-hop protocol which limits the area of candidate nodes and controls the direction of multi-hop forwarding to reduce the computational complexity for Terahertz wireless nanosensor networks. Our routing protocol establish a link cost function, taking energy consumption, channel capacity and transmission distance into account, and then select several nodes with low link cost as the next hop with a certain probability to prolong network lifetime. Simulation results show that EEMR gain advantages in energy efficiency, network lifetime and end-to-end delay, thus it prove to be suitable for WNSNs. Considering the value of m involves network lifetime and protocol complexity, a system parameter δ is introduced to reduce the calculation of the forwarding list. We are planning to optimize the value of m to further improve the routing performance. In addition, constructing more simulation scenarios and implementing one more routing scheme as comparison will be included in our future work.

Acknowledgment. This work was supported by in part by the National Natural Science Foundation of China under Grant No.61202384.

References

1. Akyildiz, I.F., Jornet, J.M.: Terahertz band: next frontier for wireless communications. Phys. Commun. **12**, 16–32 (2014)
2. Vicarelli, L., Vitiello, M.S., Coquiuat, D., et al.: Graphene field-effect transistors as room-temperature terahertz detectors. Nat. Mater. **11**(10), 865–871 (2012)

3. Jornet, J.M., Akyildiz, I.F.: Channel modeling and capacity analysis for electromagnetic wireless nanonetworks in the terahertz band. IEEE Trans. Wireless Commun. **10**(10), 3211–3221 (2011)

4. Han, C., Akyildiz, I.F.: Distance-aware multi-carrier (DAMC) modulation in Terahertz Band communication. In: IEEE International Conference on Communication, pp. 5461–5467 (2014)

5. Piro, G., Grieco, L.A., Boggia, G., et al.: Simulating wireless nanosensor networks in the NS-3 platform. In: IEEE International Conference on Advanced Information Networking and Applications Workshops, pp. 67–74 (2013)

6. Pierobon, M., Jornet, J.M., Akkari, N., et al.: A routing framework for energy harvesting wireless nanosensor networks in the Terahertz Band. Wirel. Netw. **20**(5), 1169–1183 (2014)

7. Piesiewicz, R., Kleine-Ostmann, T., Krumbholz, N., et al.: Short-range ultra-broadband terahertz communications: concepts and perspectives. IEEE Antennas Propag. Mag. **49**(6), 24–39 (2007)

8. Wang, P., Jornet, J.M., Malik, M.G.A., et al.: Energy and spectrum-aware MAC protocol for perpetual wireless nanosensor networks in the Terahertz Band. Ad Hoc Netw. **11**(8), 2541–2555 (2013)

9. Jornet, J.M., Akyildiz, I.F.: The internet of multimedia nano-things. Nano Commun. Netw. **3**(4), 242–251 (2012)

10. Jornet, J.M.: A joint energy harvesting and consumption model for self-powered nano-devices in nanonetworks. In: IEEE International Conference on Communications, pp. 6151–6156 (2012)

Stackelberg Game Based Incentive Mechanism for Data Transmission in Mobile Opportunistic Networks

Jianhui Huang[1], Qin Hu[2(✉)], Jingping Bi[1], and Zhongcheng Li[1]

[1] Institute of Computing Technology, Chinese Academy of Sciences,
Beijing, People's Republic of China
[2] College of Information Science and Technology, Beijing Normal University,
Beijing, People's Republic of China
huqin@mail.bnu.edu.cn

Abstract. Mobile opportunistic networks (MONs) can utilize the random contacts among nodes to deliver data, which is a crucial complement of the traditional infrastructure-based communications. However, due to the limited resource and the issues of security and privacy, the selfishness of nodes proves to bring severe negative impact on the data transmission for MONs. Therefore, how to motivate nodes to contribute their transmission capacity turns to be an important topic. Because of the time-varying trait of MONs, it is challenging to incent selfish nodes to help others, because it is hard to control the data forwarding process and the corresponding cost. In this paper, we propose a Stackelberg game based incentive mechanism for data dissemination in MONs, which realizes the optimal resource allocation, including the task assignment and pricing of data forwarding for the relays. In addition, we analyze the existence of the equilibrium state, which theoretically presents some requirements of parameter setting for real deployment of our mechanism. In the end, we demonstrate the effectiveness of our proposed mechanism.

1 Introduction

Mobile Opportunistic Networks (MONs) are a special form of Delay Tolerant Networks (DTNs), which take use of nodes' mobility to realize data dissemination and forwarding through short-distance communications. In most routing protocols of MONs [1–5], there is an ideal assumption that each node is willing to help forwarding messages for other nodes without any charge. As a matter of fact, this ideal assumption cannot always hold in real opportunistic networks. Particularly, because the resources of power, storage, bandwidth and computing capability are limited on each node, the rational individuals will not unconditionally cooperate with other nodes to forward messages for them. While a large number of work have shown that even though a few selfish nodes can bring enormous losses for the network performance [6]. Therefore, it is highly meaningful and valuable to solve the problems of nodes' selfishness and incent them to

© Springer International Publishing Switzerland 2016
Q. Yang et al. (Eds.): WASA 2016, LNCS 9798, pp. 377–388, 2016.
DOI: 10.1007/978-3-319-42836-9_34

contribute transmission capability for improving the transmission performance, resource utilization and practicality of MONs.

At present, the existing data forwarding incentive schemes can be roughly divided into three categories: reputation based, tit-for-tat based and credit based. The reputation based ones utilize the property of human beings who would like to contribute strength to enhance reputation, for motivating nodes to help forwarding data for others. And the tit-for-tat based schemes highlight the reciprocity, where a node receives help from others only after forwarding data for others. While the credit based schemes imitate the economic behavior of human beings, where a node gets reward according to the quantity and quality of data forwarding service for others.

Considering that the network environment of a MON is much complex and variable, the reputation based incentive schemes are hardly efficient to detect and evaluate all nodes' behavior or stimulate the low-reputation nodes to cooperate. The tit-for-tat based incentive schemes can only realize reciprocal transmission among nodes with the similar traffic type. Actually, most of the traffic in MON are different, which results the tit-for-tat based incentive schemes inapplicable in most scenarios. Besides, in the tit-for-tat schemes, all the nodes need to maintain massive state information about the service provision and service usage, which increases the resource consumption of nodes and reduce the scalability of the network. Finally, the above two incentive schemes are only focusing on motivating cooperation among nodes without any consideration about the influence of the nodes' states on their behaviours, such as their resources quantity, service ability and so on.

While the credit based schemes resolve these deficiencies of the above two classes of schemes. This kind of schemes are based on the principles of voluntariness, where each node can decide whether serve or not and how to serve (the transmission amount and the price for forwarding data), according to its actual condition and desired reward of providing services. On account of the time-varying trait of MONs, it is hard to control the data forwarding process and the corresponding cost; besides, it is difficult to implement uniform pricing and task assignment due to the diversity of the traffic types, which brings huge challenges for widely applying the credit based incentive schemes.

To address the above challenges, we propose a Stackelberg game based incentive mechanism for data dissemination, which helps to determine the optimal task assignment and pricing of data forwarding for the relay nodes, realizing the optimal market allocation. In addition, we analyze the conditions of Stackelberg equilibrium. In the end, our extensive simulation study demonstrates that the proposed mechanism can work well under various settings.

2   Related Work

As a crucial research content in MONs, massive studies about the data transmission incentive mechanisms have been presented. In these proposed schemes, incentive mechanisms can be classified into three categories: reputation based, tit-for-tat based and credit based.

The reputation based incentive mechanisms utilize the constraints of reputation on the nodes' behavior. In [7], a reputation-assisted routing scheme was proposed, which evaluated the nodes' competency according to their activity. And research [8] constructed a community and reputation based management model, by which all the nodes' reputation could be managed and demonstrated when necessary.

While tit-for-tat based incentive mechanisms are based on the phenomenon of human beings' mutual benefit, where nodes provide data forwarding services for others as exchange. Upendra Shevade *et al.* [9] proposed an incentive-aware routing protocol, where a node transmits the same amount of data for the node who had provided help to it before. A two-person cooperative game based scheme was proposed in [10] to determine the specific content and quantity when a pair of nodes met.

In fact, credit based incentive mechanisms are closer to human behavior, getting some rewards after contributing efforts. Research [11] employed a virtual currency *MobiCent* to stimulate all the nodes to cooperatively forwarding data for others. By this means, rational nodes would like to contribute more transmission opportunities for others to increase their own rewards and minimize delivery cost or delay by setting different payment schemes. In [12], the client requesting data forwarding paid the forwarding service provider according to the size of access bandwidth, which motivated all the nodes to provide data forwarding services; besides, a pricing model was proposed to manifest the numerical relationship between the payment and the size of access bandwidth.

3   Problem Statement and Utility Functions

In MONs, once encountered with a node, the current relay will negotiate with it on the amount of transmission data and the corresponding price. If they come to an agreement, this node will act as the new relay who is responsible for delivering the data to the destination. After completing the data delivery process, all the nodes forwarding data will receive corresponding rewards. This process is actually a paid crowdsourcing model, where the data holders is the crowdsourcer (requestor) dividing the transmission task into several subtasks and the crowdsourcee (worker) completing the data forwarding task. Once transmission task is finished, each worker will receive proportional payment. Remarkably, the crowdsourcing based model can be adopted by any node on the transmission path from the source to the destination, and each current relay (requestor) can seek one or multiple nodes acting as new relays (worker).

The requestor and the workers decide the price and data forwarding quantity by negotiation. The requestor can evaluate the cost according to several worker's responses and assigns tasks among them, deciding the utility of each worker; while the worker determines its quotation according to the cost of forwarding data, the expected price of the requestor and the estimation of other workers' quotations, affecting the task assignment and the utility. Therefore, the utility is the most significant in the game between the requestor and the worker, then we define them as follows.

The utility function of the requestor is

$$U = M \cdot V - \sum_{i=1}^{N}(m_i \cdot p_i), \tag{1}$$

where M is the overall amount of data need to be transmitted of the requestor, and V is the value per unit amount of data for the requestor, so $M \cdot V$ is the overall value of the data to be sent for the requestor; N is the total number of workers taking part in the data forwarding; m_i is the data amount assigned to worker i, and p_i is the corresponding quotation, so the payment of worker i from the requestor is $m_i \cdot q_i$. Thus, the utility of the requestor U represents the remaining value of data after paying all the workers.

The utility function of the worker i is

$$u_i = m_i \cdot p_i - c_i, \tag{2}$$

$$c_i = \alpha_i \cdot m_i^2 + \beta_i \cdot m_i + \gamma_i, \tag{3}$$

where m_i and p_i are the assigned data amount and the quotation of worker i, respectively; c_i is the cost to complete the task of data forwarding. Considering that the forwarding cost is under the influence of some elements occurring in data forwarding process, such as the transmission distance, the storage capacity, the power consumption and the activity law of nodes, we employ a typical economic model, a quadratic polynomial, to fit the cost c_i. And each worker has a unique set of cost parameters α_i, β_i and γ_i.

Note that the requestor assigns the total amount of data M according to all the workers' quotations, so the task of each worker is a function of the quotations set p and total data amount M.

In summary, the ultimate goal of our mechanism is to complete the negotiation on forwarding price and task assignment between the requestor and the worker, with utility maximization realized simultaneously,

$$\text{Max: } U, \tag{4}$$

$$\text{Max: } u_i, \ (i = 1, \cdots, N), \tag{5}$$

$$\text{s.t., } \sum_{i=1}^{N} m_i = M,$$

where the constraint condition represents that the sum of all the workers' tasks is the requestor's total amount of data to be delivered.

To be clear, each strategy in one trade round is developed independently and has no effect on the subsequent decisions. In other words, the relay node can act as a new requestor after it receives the data and launches a new round of trade. So there is no need to consider the effect of the follow-up data forwarding trades on the utility functions of the requestor and the workers.

4   Stackelberg Game Based Mechanism

4.1   Framework

Based on the Stackelberg game, we design the following framework, which includes several steps (Fig. 1):

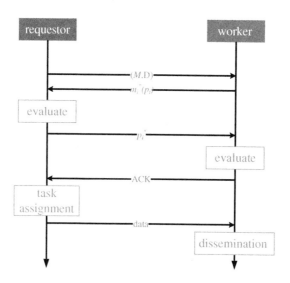

Fig. 1. The framework of trade process between the requestor and the worker.

1. Firstly, the requestor broadcasts its request of forwarding data, including the destination address of the data and the total amount M (optional);
2. Then, after receiving the broadcasting request, the worker calculates the relationship between the optimal assigned data amount m_i^* and the unit price of forwarding data p_i, i.e., $m_i^*(p_i)$, and responses with this function;
3. In the third step, the requestor calculates the optimal bid p_i^* for each worker i after collecting $m_i^*(p_i)$ from all neighbor nodes;
4. Next, once the worker receives the bid of the requestor, it sends back an ACK signal expressing its acceptance of the bid and the corresponding task amount, which indicates the success of this round of trade, and vice versa.
5. In the last step, if the trade runs successfully, the requestor assigns task to each worker and the workers star to implement data forwarding.

During the aforementioned trade process, the requestor bids and assigns tasks on the basis of all the participated workers' quotations, which infers that the requestor can execute task assignment only if all the workers accept the bids of the requestor. Otherwise, any worker's nonacceptance of the bid will result in the failure of this round of enquiry, and the requestor has to launch another round of enquiry. To avoid repeating the same failure in the last round, two methods can be adopted in the new round: (1) the workers who rejected the bid in the last round have no opportunity to participate in this round, or the requestor can directly ignore these worker's quotations; (2) all the workers appears in the new round of enquiry, but both the requestor and the workers should adjust their strategies to promote the success of the trade. The specific algorithms of the requestor and the worker are summarized in Algorithms 1 and 2, respectively.

Algorithm 1. The Algorithm of the Requestor

1: **while** (The trade is failed) $\|$ (The retry number c is below the threshold) **do**
2:     Broadcast the request of forwarding data;
3:     **repeat**
4:         Collect $m_i^*(p_i)$;
5:     **until** Time out;
6:     Calculate the optimal bid p_i^* for each worker i according to the quotations;
7:     **for** Each worker i **do**
8:         Send(p_i^*);
9:     **end for**
10:     **repeat**
11:         Collect the ACK signals;
12:     **until** Time out;
13:     **if** All workers accept the bids **then**
14:         Assign tasks;
15:         **return** ;
16:     **else**
17:         $c++$;
18:     **end if**
19: **end while**

4.2   Calculation of the Optimal Solution

As shown in Fig. 1, the requestor is aiming to calculate the optimal bid and task assignment scheme according to all workers' quotations, which can maximize the utility of both the requestor and the workers. From the perspective of formulas, it is equivalent to seeking the optimal values of m_i and p_i in (4) and (5), supposed to be m_i^* and p_i^*, after which the requestor can get the maximized utility $U(m_i^*, p_i^*)$ $(i = 1, \cdots, N)$, and each worker i can obtain its optimal utility $u_i(m_i, p_i)$, under the constraint condition $\sum_{i=1}^{N} m_i = M$.

Next, we discuss the solving process of (m_i^*, p_i^*). As the utility functions defined in (1) and (2), it is an optimization problem with an equality constraint. To solve this problem, we convert this problem into an unconstrained optimization problem by adding a penalty term, which is on the light of the Lagrange theorem. Now the optimization problems in (4) and (5) are turning into seeking

Algorithm 2. The Algorithm of the Worker i

1: Receive the request of forwarding data;
2: Calculate the reachability of the data according to the destination address;
3: **if** The data can be forwarded to the destination **then**
4:     Calculate the optimal function $m_i^*(p_i)$;
5:     **repeat**
6:         Wait to receive the bid p_i^* of the requestor;
7:     **until** Time out;
8:     **if** p_i^* is received **then**
9:         Calculate the utility u_i^*;
10:         **if** $u_i^* > 0$ **then**
11:             Send back the ACK signal;
12:             Receive Task;
13:             **return** ;
14:         **else**
15:             Reject the bid and end the trade;
16:             **return** ;
17:         **end if**
18:     **end if**
19:     **return** ;
20: **end if**

the optimal (m_i^*, p_i^*) of the following equations,

$$\tilde{U} = M \cdot V - \sum_{i=1}^{N}(m_i \cdot p_i) - \lambda(\sum_{i=1}^{N} m_i - M), \tag{6}$$

$$u_i = m_i \cdot p_i - (\alpha_i \cdot m_i^2 + \beta_i \cdot m_i + \gamma_i), \ i = 1, \cdots, N. \tag{7}$$

In the process of Stackelberg game consisted of the requestor and the worker, it is the worker who firstly submits its relationship between the task amount m_i and the quotation p_i to the requestor, so we find the optimal resolution of u_i by taking the derivation with respect to m_i,

$$\frac{\partial u_i}{\partial m_i} = p_i - 2\alpha_i m_i - \beta_i, \tag{8}$$

and when $\frac{\partial u_i}{\partial m_i} = 0$, u_i is extreme, we have

$$m_i = \frac{p_i - \beta_i}{2\alpha_i}. \tag{9}$$

It is explicit that when u_i is optimized, the task amount m_i is the function of the price p_i. Then we can rewrite the utility function of the requestor with the new form of m_i shown in (9):

$$\tilde{U} = M \cdot V - \sum_{i=1}^{N} p_i \cdot \frac{p_i - \beta_i}{2\alpha_i} - \lambda(\sum_{i=1}^{N} \frac{p_i - \beta_i}{2\alpha_i} - M). \tag{10}$$

Take the derivatives of $\widetilde{U}$ with respect to p_i and λ, respectively, and set the values to zero,

$$
\begin{cases}
\dfrac{\partial \widetilde{U}}{\partial p_i} = -\dfrac{2p_i - \beta_i}{2\alpha_i} - \lambda \dfrac{1}{2\alpha_i} = 0, \\[3mm]
\dfrac{\partial \widetilde{U}}{\partial \lambda} = -(\displaystyle\sum_{i=1}^{N} \dfrac{p_i - \beta_i}{2\alpha_i} - M) = 0.
\end{cases}
\tag{11}
$$

5 Equilibrium Analysis

Using the symbols T_r and T_w to present the strategy sets of the requestor and the worker, we define the equilibrium strategies of both sides as follows.

Definition 1 (The Equilibrium Strategy of the Worker). $m_i^* \in T_w$ *is the equilibrium strategy of the worker i when satisfying,*

$$
u_i(m_i^*(p_i^*), p_i^*) \geq u_i(m_i(p_i^*), p_i^*),
$$

where $p_i^* \in T_r$ is the requestor's optimal strategy for worker i and $m_i(p_i^*) \in T_w$ is an arbitrary strategy of the worker p_i^*.

Definition 2 (The Equilibrium Strategy of the Requestor). $p_i^* \in T_r$ *is the equilibrium strategy of the requestor when satisfying,*

$$
U(m_i^*(p_i^*), p_i^*) \geq U(m_i^*(p_i), p_i) \ (i = 1, \cdots, N),
$$

where $p_i \in T_r$ is arbitrary and $m_i^*(p_i)$ is an optimal strategy of each worker with an arbitrary strategy of the requestor p_i.

Theorem 1. *When the worker i's cost parameter $\alpha_i > 0$, there exist equilibrium strategies between the requestor and the worker.*

Proof. According the above definitions, the equilibrium strategies of the requestor and the worker refer to the strategies maximizing the utility of both sides, which can be converted into dissecting whether the utility functions have optimal values or not, corresponding to the existence of the optimum points m_i^* and p_i^*.

Based on the definition of the worker's utility function, we can know that it is continuously differentiable in its domain, so the existence of m_i^* is up to two factors: (1) u_i has an extreme value in its domain, namely existing m_i enabling $u_i' = \frac{\partial u_i}{\partial m_i} = 0$; (2) the second derivative of the utility function $u_i'' = \frac{\partial^2 u_i}{\partial m_i^2} < 0$. Similarly, the existence of p_i^* also depends the two factors, i.e., the existence of extreme value and the negative second derivative.

Firstly, we testify the first factor. The derivative of u_i with respect to m_i is $u_i' = p_i - 2\alpha_i m_i - \beta_i$. When $u_i' = 0$, the utility function obtains its extreme value, then we have $m_i = \frac{p_i - \beta_i}{2\alpha_i}$. Thus, the utility function of the requestor with the new form of m_i is showing in (10), and in order to get the extreme value, we have the following equation group resulting from (11),

$$
\begin{cases}
2p_i + \lambda = \beta_i, \ (i = 1, \cdots, N), \\
\displaystyle\sum_{i=1}^{N} \frac{p_i - \beta_i}{2\alpha_i} = M.
\end{cases}
\tag{12}
$$

Note that (12) is actually consisted of $N+1$ equations, and the corresponding coefficient matrix is

$$
A = \begin{bmatrix}
2 & 0 & \cdots & 0 & 1 \\
0 & 2 & \cdots & 0 & 1 \\
\vdots & \vdots & \ddots & \vdots & 1 \\
0 & 0 & \cdots & 2 & 1 \\
\frac{1}{2\alpha_1} & \frac{1}{2\alpha_2} & \cdots & \frac{1}{2\alpha_N} & 0
\end{bmatrix}.
$$

When $\alpha_i > 0$, it is easy to calculate the determinant $|A| = 2^N \cdot \sum_{i=1}^{N} \frac{1}{4\alpha_i} > 0$, so the equation group has a unique solution.

Next, it comes to the second factor. The second derivative of the worker's utility function is

$$
u_i'' = \frac{\partial^2 u_i}{\partial m_i^2} = -2\alpha_i,
$$

which implies the trend of the worker's utility change. It is clear that the value of α_i decides the property of the extreme value, i.e., maximum or minimum. When $\alpha_i > 0$, the value of u_i'' is always negative. Therefore, the worker's utility function has a maximum value in the domain. Similarly, the second derivative of $\tilde{U}$ is

$$
\tilde{U}'' = \frac{\partial^2 \tilde{U}}{\partial p_i^2} = -\frac{1}{\alpha_i}.
$$

Considering $\alpha_i > 0$, we have $\tilde{U}'' < 0$, so the extreme value of the requestor's utility function is the maximum value.

Therefore, there exist equilibrium strategies between the requestor and the worker when $\alpha_i > 0$. ∎

According to Theorem 1, the Stackelberg game between the requestor and the worker can reach the equilibrium state when the cost parameter $\alpha_i > 0$.

6   Simulations

In this section, we evaluate our proposed mechanism with some simulations, including the influence of M, α_i, β_i and γ_i on the quotation, task assignment and the utility of both sides. To briefly display the results, we show the situation with three workers and one requestor, after implementing in other scenarios.

Firstly, we simulate the effect of total data amount M with some fixed cost parameters α_i, β_i and γ_i. Specifically, we change the value of M from 100 to

290 with the step of 10, and the cost parameters of three workers are the same, i.e., $\alpha_i = \beta_i = \gamma_i = 1.0$, $(i = 1, \cdots, N)$, besides $V = 500$. The results are shown in Fig. 2, where (a), (b), (c) and (d) are indicating the task amount m_i of each worker, price of forwarding per unit of data of each worker p_i, the utility of the requestor and the worker, changing with M. It is clear that all of them are increases with M, which means more data to be delivered, more task and payment of each worker, as well as higher utility of both the requestor and the workers. Note that the cost parameters of three workers are the same, so we use a single legend to represent them.

In the second simulation, we aim to test the influence of the total data amount M and the cost parameters, where $\alpha_1 = \beta_1 = \gamma_1 = 1.0$, $\alpha_2 = \beta_2 = \gamma_2 = 2.0$, $\alpha_3 = \beta_3 = \gamma_3 = 3.0$ and other parameters are the same with the last simulation. Figure 3 displays the simulation results. Note that subgraph (b) shows the total price for the assigned task rather than the unit price to significantly present the difference among all workers. Since the cost of forwarding data is positively correlated with the cost parameters, so it is clear that as the cost increases, all

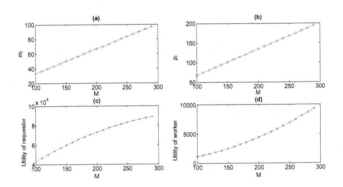

Fig. 2. The workers' assigned tasks, the workers' price, the utility of the requestor and the workers change with M.

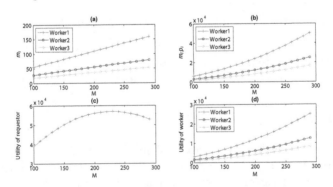

Fig. 3. The workers' assigned tasks, the workers' total price, the utility of the requestor and the workers change with M and α, β, γ.

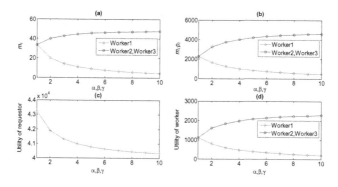

Fig. 4. The workers' assigned tasks, the workers' total price, the utility of the requestor and the workers change with α, β, γ.

the total price are becoming higher, while the requestor rationally chooses the lower-price worker.

Finally, we fix the value of M to 500 and the cost parameters of worker2 and worker3, but change the cost parameters of worker1 from 1 to 10 with the step of 1. Sice the parameters of worker2 and worker3 are equivalent, we use one single curve to present their properties in Fig. 4. We can see that as the increase of the worker1's cost, the quotation is becoming higher, and the requestor tends to assign tasks to the low-cost worker2 and worker3, which is corresponding to the reality. Besides, the utility of the requestor decreases with the cost parameters since the higher cost will reduce the interest of the requestor.

7   Conclusion

Since MON is short of a central node for supervision and management, along with complicated and diverse network services, the pricing for forwarding data is the principal problem to be settled down when some credit based incentive mechanisms are adopted to encourage all the nodes to contribute transmission capability. Considering that the problem of resource scarcity of MON, it is challenging to design an efficient and practicable mechanism for pricing and task assignment. In this paper, we propose a Stackelberg game based incentive mechanism to realize the pricing and task assignment for data forwarding among nodes in MON. By some equilibrium analysis, we prove our proposed scheme to be helpful to guarantee the maximization of the revenue of the requestor and the workers. In the end, we evaluate the effectiveness of our proposed scheme with some simulations.

Acknowledgement. This work has been supported by the National Natural Science Foundation of China (No. 61472044, No. 61272475, No. 61472403, No. 61303243, No. 61003225), and the Fundamental Research Funds for the Central Universities (No. 2014KJJCB32).

References

1. Wang, S., Liu, M., Cheng, X., Li, Z., Huang, J., Chen, B.: Opportunistic routing in intermittently connected mobile p2p networks. IEEE J. Sel. Areas Commun. **31**(9), 369–378 (2013)
2. Wang, S., Liu, M., Cheng, X., Song, M.: Routing in pocket switched networks. Wirel. Commun. IEEE **19**(1), 67–73 (2012)
3. Wang, S., Wang, X., Cheng, X., Huang, J., Bie, R.: The tempo-spatial information dissemination properties of mobile opportunistic networks with levy mobility. In: 2014 Proceedings IEEE ICDCS, pp. 124–133. IEEE (2014)
4. Wang, X., Lin, Y., Zhao, Y., Zhang, L., Liang, J., Cai, Z., A novel approach for inhibiting misinformation propagation in human mobile opportunistic networks. Peer-to-Peer Netw. Appl. 1–18 (2016)
5. Wang, X., Lin, Y., Zhang, L., Cai, Z.: A double pulse control strategy for misinformation propagation in human mobile opportunistic networks. In: Xu, K., Zhu, H. (eds.) WASA 2015. LNCS, vol. 9204, pp. 571–580. Springer, Heidelberg (2015)
6. Resta, G., Santi, P.: A framework for routing performance analysis in delay tolerant networks with application to noncooperative networks. IEEE Trans. Parallel Distrib. Syst. **23**(1), 2–10 (2012)
7. Li, N., Das, S.K., Radon,: reputation-assisted data forwarding in opportunistic networks. In: Proceedings of the Second International Workshop on Mobile Opportunistic Networking, pp. 8–14. ACM (2010)
8. Wei, H., Zhang, Y., Guo, D., Wei, X., Carison,: A community and reputation based incentive scheme for opportunistic networks. In: 2015 Fifth International Conference on Instrumentation and Measurement, Computer, Communication and Control (IMCCC), pp. 1398–1403. IEEE (2015)
9. Shevade, U., Song, H.H., Qiu, L., Zhang, Y.: Incentive-aware routing in DTNs. In: IEEE International Conference on Network Protocols, 2008, ICNP 2008 pp. 238–247. IEEE (2008)
10. Ning, T., Yang, Z., Xie, X., Wu, H.: Incentive-aware data dissemination in delay-tolerant mobile networks. In: 2011 8th Annual IEEE Communications Society Conference on Sensor, Mesh and Ad Hoc Communications and Networks (SECON), pp. 539–547. IEEE (2011)
11. Chen, B., Chan, M.C.: Mobicent: a credit-based incentive system for disruption tolerant network. In: INFOCOM, 2010 Proceedings IEEE, pp. 1 9. IEEE (2010)
12. Cui, Y., Ma, T., Cheng, X.: Multi-hop access pricing in public area wlans. In: INFOCOM, 2011 Proceedings IEEE, pp. 2678–2686. IEEE (2011)

Extensive Form Game Analysis
Based on Context Privacy Preservation
for Smart Phone Applications

Luyun Li[1], Shengling Wang[1(✉)], Junqi Guo[1], Rongfang Bie[1], and Kai Lin[2]

[1] College of Information Science and Technology, Beijing Normal University,
Beijing, China
liluyun1993@mail.bnu.edu.cn, {wangshengling,guojunqi,rfbie}@bnu.edu.cn
[2] Telecommunications Engineering with Management, International School,
Beijing University of Posts and Telecommunications, Beijing, China
827313582@qq.com

Abstract. The sensing capabilities of the smart phones gave birth to context-aware applications, which can provide personalized services based on users' contexts. Since context-aware applications may sell contexts to some malicious third-parties, the exposure of contexts will handicap the development of context-aware applications in large scale. Nevertheless, it is challenging to solve the context privacy issue, because the users of the context-aware applications should trade off between service quality and privacy exposure. Nowadays, most privacy protection techniques for mobile applications neglect the context preservation. Meanwhile, limited work on context privacy doesn't consider the applications' strategies, which are key factors on user's context privacy preservation. In this paper, we make a tradeoff analysis on behaviours of the user, the application and the adversary, and then we use extensive form game to formulate the decision-marking process of these three parties. After constructing payoff functions for them, we solve and analyse their Nash equilibriums. Our study shows that the key of context privacy preservation is to establish a sound reputation mechanism for context-aware applications, through which the issue of context privacy can be eliminated utterly. As a consequence, a trust between users and mobile applications can be built.

Keywords: Context-aware · Privacy protection · Mobile application · Game theory

1 Introduction

Nowadays, almost all mobile devices are equipped with some sensors which can be used to infer users' contexts. For example, a GPS can indicate a user's location, and an accelerometer or a gravity sensor can infer a user's mobility mode, while a light and temperature sensor can perceive a user's surrounding environment. These sensing capabilities gave birth to context-aware applications, which can provide personalized services based on users' contexts.

© Springer International Publishing Switzerland 2016
Q. Yang et al. (Eds.): WASA 2016, LNCS 9798, pp. 389–400, 2016.
DOI: 10.1007/978-3-319-42836-9_35

However, once a context-aware application obtains a user's contexts, the user isn't able to control how the application deals with the user's private information. Since context-aware applications may sell contexts to some malicious third-parties, the exposure of contexts will handicap the development of context-aware applications in large scale.

Nevertheless, it is challenging to solve the context privacy issue, because a user of a context-aware application should trade off between service quality and privacy exposure. In detail, a user may refuse to release its contexts to the application considering privacy protection, but such a practice means abandoning personalized services provided by the application completely, and vice versa.

Nowadays, most privacy protection techniques for mobile applications focus on location protection, neglecting the diversity of user behavior and different degree of users' context sensitivity. Limited work on context privacy protection is *MaskIt* [2,8]. *MaskIt* [2] introduces a technique to filter a user context stream that provably preserves privacy. But it limits that the adversary only takes fixed attack, who can't differentiate strategies according to different context sensitivity. While in the real world, the adversary will adjust its attacking strategies to attain its goal or achieve better profits. For example, the advertisers should push targeted advertisements based on different users' contexts. [2] overcomes this shortcoming and considers a more powerful and realistic adversary in its framework of context privacy preservation. Unfortunately, both [2,8] don't consider the application's strategies.

In fact, whether an adversary can get a user's context privacy depends directly on whether the application leaks it. Although leaking privacy will increase the application's profits, it will also reduce customers' loyalty to the application and the application's reputation. Thus, an optimized strategy of the application is to trade off between maintaining reputation and making a profit by leaking. Once considering the application's strategy, the two-person-game in the existing work needs to be extended to the three-person-game, which leads to different methods analysis and conclusions.

In this paper, we make a tradeoff analysis on behaviours of the user, the application and the adversary, and then we use the game tree to formulate the decision-marking process of the three-parties. After analysing the key impact factors on the payoffs of the three parties, for example, the context sensitivity, the cost of retrieving context and reputation, we construct payoff functions for three parties, based on which we solve and analyse their Nash equilibriums. Our study shows that the key of context privacy preservation is to establish a sound reputation mechanism for context-aware applications, through which the issue of context privacy can be eliminated utterly. As a consequence, a trust between users and mobile applications can be built.

The rest of the paper is organized as follows. Section 2 introduces related work. We then provide problem statement and stochastic game formulations in Sect. 3. Section 4 presents the payoff functions of the players. The solution of the model and the relevant analysis is described in Sect. 5. And then Sect. 6 describes the performance evaluations. Finally, we conclude in Sect. 7.

2   Related Work

As introduced above, there are many work on privacy protection of mobile phone [1,9,11,12], but most researches on context privacy for mobile applications focus on location preservation. To that aim, anonymization and space silencing technique are widely used, of which k-anonymization is the representative. K-anonymization requests there are a certain amount of indistinguishable records in quasi-identifier, so that adversaries are not able to distinguish the specific user, thus protecting individual privacy [3,6,7]. While k-anonymization is not effective in some case, for example, when the k individuals are in a same sensitive location.

Anther important privacy protection method is realized by encryption [4, 5,10]. Encryption is to encode information so that only authorized person can read it, which is widely used to protect data in transit or in storage. While it has high complexity, and needs to consume massive compute and storage resources, which is not applicable for smart phone user.

MaskIt [2,8] are the only work studying the context privacy protection. *MaskIt* [2] is a middleware which can decide wether the user releases current contexts or not for privacy protection. Even when the adversary knows the temporal correlations between contexts, *MaskIt* [2] can prevent it from finding out whether the user is or will be in a sensitive context. [8] constructs a framework of context privacy in the condition that the adversary can adjust attack mode according to the history of contexts. Nevertheless, as we indicate above, both of [2,8] don't consider the application's capability to participate in decision-making process, which stimulates our work.

3   Problem Statement and Game Formulations

3.1   Problem Statement

In this section, we introduce the context sensing system and how mobile phone user, unreliable context-aware application and malicious adversary interact with each other.

Figure 1 illustrates a context sensing system in which a sensor-equipped mobile device runs an unreliable context-aware application. There are three opposing and conflicting participators in the system, namely the user, the application and the adversary. Based on the features of sensor-equipped mobile devices, we know that if the mobile devices are equipped with sensors, they are able to perceive the user's data. And the mobile phone user can decide whether to release this sensing data to the application, because it needs to trade off between personalized services and individual privacy protection. The application firstly receives all the sensing data (if there is any), then analyzes it according to its algorithm to infer the user's contexts, and finally provides the user with corresponding personalized service based on the contexts. During the whole decision process, the application needs to decide whether to expose extracted contexts to the adversary. The leakage of the privacy may harm its reputation but produce

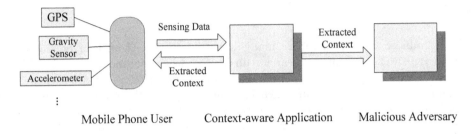

Fig. 1. The context sensing system

profits from the adversary, so the application needs to trade off between maintaining reputation and making a profit by leakage. Due to limited bandwidth used for retrieving contexts and computational constraints, the adversary can't retrieve contexts all the time, which has already been adopted by [8]. Hence, the adversary needs to decide when to retrieve the contexts from the application in order to trade off between lowering the cost of retrieve and obtaining more contexts.

3.2 Extensive Form Game Formulation

In this paper, we use extensive form game theory to analyse the issue of context privacy described above, where the players respectively are the user, the application and the adversary. Ideally, as long as the application receives sensing data from the user, it is bound to infer the user's contexts. Hence, in this paper, we assume that the user decides whether to release contexts rather than the data, so that contexts are the only object on which all the three players focus. According to the problem statement, for the user, his[1] actions are releasing the current context c to the application or not, denoted as α_1 and α_2. Similarly, for the application, its actions are leaking the current context c to the adversary or not, denoted as β_1 and β_2. And for the adversary, her action are retrieving the current context c from the application or not, denoted as γ_1 and γ_2. The actions of the three players are listed as follows: $\{\alpha_1, \alpha_2\}, \{\beta_1, \beta_2\}, \{\gamma_1, \gamma_2\}$.

In our paper, each player's strategy is the probability of taking actions listed above. Because in every round of the game the player decides his/its/her own action according to some other players' actions, hence such a strategy is called an extensive form strategy. We use a game tree, a useful analytical tool for extensive form game, depicted in Fig. 2 to describe each player's strategies.

The game tree can be represented as a three-tuple $\Sigma = (N, A, h)$. $N = \{1, 2, 3\}$ is the numerical representation of $\{user, applicationm, adversary\}$, the players in the game. A is the arc set, indicating the players' actions. $h : \omega_i \to R^n$ is the players' payoffs when reaching the play ω_i. As depicted in the game tree, the user has two choices α_1 and α_2, and if he chooses α_1, the application will

---

[1] In this paper, we use he, it and she to respectively represent the user, the application and the adversary.

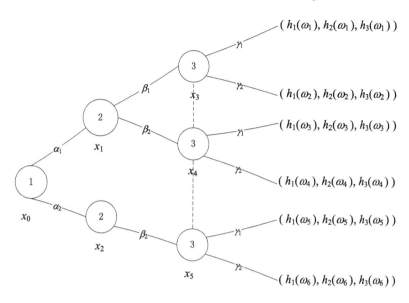

Fig. 2. The game tree of context privacy protection

also have two actions, β_1 and β_2, and so on for the adversary. Finally, there will be six different paths(Note that when the user chooses α_2, the application has to choose β_2, because at that time the application receives nothing from the user), which leads to six kinds of plays ω_i $(i = 1, ...6)$. For example, if the user releases his current context, and the application chooses to leak it, and the adversary doesn't retrieve it, their game will reach the play ω_2, so that their payoffs are $h_1(\omega_2)$, $h_2(\omega_2)$ and $h_3(\omega_2)$ accordingly.

4   Payoff Function

4.1   The User's Payoff Function

In this extensive form game, players' strategies depend on their payoffs. In this section, we define each player's payoffs in detail. Obviously, different contexts have different important degree to a user, based on which we can divide his contexts into two classes, which are sensitive context and non-sensitive context. For example, going to hospital may be a sensitive context to most users, while going to dinner may be a non-sensitive one. Besides, consuming the services provided by the context-aware application will bring the user good experience(payoff) under the risk of context exposure. Since different contexts can carry and reflect different amounts of information, leading to differential degree of loss, we use the following definition to measure the degree of the context privacy loss.

Definition 1 *(Context Sensitivity)[8]. The context sensitivity of contexts c, namely Sens(c), can be calculated as follows: accumulated differences between*

*the prior belief and the posterior one after viewing the user's present context
being in sensitive context from the future perspective. that is,*

$$Sens(c) = \sum_{t=0}^{\infty} \sum_{c^s \in C_s} \gamma^t |P_r[C^t = c_s | C^0 = c] - P_r[C^t = c_s]|, \tag{1}$$

where $0 < \gamma < 1$ is the discount factor of the context privacy, Pr the probability, C^0 the context happening at time 0, and C^t context happening at time t. c_s is a certain sensitive context of the user, and C_s is the set of sensitive contexts.

According to the definition above, the context sensitivity illustrates the amount of privacy information loss. The more context sensitivity is, the more context privacy is lost when the context is retrieved by a adversary. Thus, it is reasonable to use the context sensitivity as the measure of the degree of context privacy loss.

Based on the analysis, when a user releases a context c, which will be leaked by the application and further be sold to the adversary, the user's payoff is

$$U_u(c) = Q(c) - k_1 Sens(c), \tag{2}$$

where $Q(c)$ is the payoff obtained from services provided by the application through releasing context c, and $k_1 > 0$ is the coefficient reflecting the negative impact of the context privacy loss on the user. Obviously, if the user doesn't release context c, his payoff will be 0. And if the application doesn't leak or the adversary doesn't retrieve context c, the user's payoff will be $Q(c)$.

4.2   The Application's Payoff Function

Obviously, the reputation of the application is positively related to its value brought to the user, and negatively related to context privacy loss. Here, when the user releases context c, the application of providing services and successfully selling context c can have the reputation formulated as

$$Rep(c) = Q(c) - k_2 Sens(c), \tag{3}$$

where $k_2 > 0$ is the coefficient reflecting the negative impact of selling context c with $Sens(c)$ on the application's reputation. While when the user doesn't release context c, the application will do nothing, with no services provided to the user and no privacy leaked to the adversary, thus with the result of zero reputation.

If the application leaks a context to a third-party, it will obtain certain profits. And it is obvious that the more valuable the context is, meaning higher context sensitivity, the more profits the application will obtain.

Thus, when the application leaks context c which was released by the user, and will further be retrieved by the adversary, the application's payoff is

$$U_a(c) = Q(c) + (k_3 - k_2) Sens(c), \tag{4}$$

Table 1. The payoff of players in different plays

Play	ω_1	ω_2	ω_3	ω_4	ω_5	ω_6
Action	$(\alpha_1, \beta_1, \gamma_1)$	$(\alpha_1, \beta_1, \gamma_2)$	$(\alpha_1, \beta_2, \gamma_1)$	$(\alpha_1, \beta_2, \gamma_2)$	$(\alpha_2, \beta_2, \gamma_1)$	$(\alpha_2, \beta_2, \gamma_2)$
$h_1(\omega_i)$	$Q(c) - k_1\,Sens(c)$	$Q(c)$	$Q(c)$	$Q(c)$	0	0
$h_2(\omega_i)$	$Q(c) + (k_3 - k_2)\,Sens(c)$	$Q(c)$	$Q(c)$	$Q(c)$	0	0
$h_3(\omega_i)$	$-C + k_4\,Sens(c)$	0	$-C$	0	$-C$	0

where $k_3 > 0$ is coefficient reflecting the positive impact of selling context c with $Senc(c)$ on the application's payoff. But if the application doesn't leak context c, or the adversary chooses not to retrieve, either one will lead to zero context privacy exposure, and thus the application's payoff is $Q(c)$.

4.3 The Adversary's Payoff Function

The adversary's payoff by retrieving context c depends on how valuable the context is, which is proportional to the context sensitivity. Thus, when the adversary retrieves a context, which was released by the user and leaked by the application, the adversary's payoff is

$$U_{ad}(c) = k_4\,Sens(c) - C, \tag{5}$$

where C is the cost of retrieving a context, and $k_4 > 0$ is the coefficient reflecting the positive impact of retrieving context c with $Sens(c)$ on the adversary's payoff. Besides, if the adversary doesn't retrieve context c, her payoff will be 0. And when the application doesn't leaks context c, the payoff of the adversary to retrieve is $-C$.

In conclusion, the payoffs of the players in every play ω_i ($i = 1, 2...6$) are listed in Table 1 below, where $h_1(\omega_i)$, $h_2(\omega_i)$ and $h_3(\omega_i)$ refer to the payoffs of the user, the application and the adversary respectively in the play ω_i.

For example, in play ω_2, the actions of three players are $\alpha_1, \beta_1, \gamma_2$, which means the user releases, the application leaks and the adversary doesn't retrieve context c. And accordingly, their payoffs are $h_1(\omega_2) = Q(c)$, $h_2(\omega_2) = Q(c)$, and $h_3(\omega_2) = 0$.

5 Solving and Analysing the Nash Equilibrium

5.1 The Solution of the Nash Equilibrium

To solve each player's Nash equilibrium, we transform an extensive form game to a strategic one. Let δ, λ and θ respectively denote the probability of the user, the application and the adversary to release, leak and retrieve context c. That to say, δ, λ and θ, the probability of the players' actions, are their strategies. Thus, the probability $s(\omega_i)$ of each play ω_i is the function of δ, λ and θ, which can be calculated in Table 2.

Table 2. The probability of every play

Play	ω_1	ω_2	ω_3	ω_4	ω_5	ω_6
$s(\omega_i)$	$\delta\lambda\theta$	$\delta\lambda(1-\theta)$	$\delta(1-\lambda)\theta$	$\delta(1-\lambda)(1-\theta)$	$(1-\delta)\theta$	$(1-\delta)(1-\theta)$

For example, in play ω_2, where the actions of three players are α_1, β_1 and γ_2, the probability $s(\omega_2)$ of play ω_2 is $\delta\lambda(1-\theta)$. The rest can be deduced by analogy.

Using the players' payoffs $h_j(\omega_i)$ $(j = 1, 2, 3)$ and the probability $s(\omega_i)$ in each play ω_i, the player j's mathematical payoff expectation E_j can be calculated by the equation below:

$$E_j = \sum_{i=1}^{6} s(\omega_i)\, h_j(\omega_i). \tag{6}$$

Thus, with any given context c, the mathematical payoff expectation of the user, the application and the adversary, namely $E(U_u(c))$, $E(U_a(c))$ and $E(U_{ad}(c))$, are as follows:

$$E(U_u(c)) = Q(c)\,\delta - k_1\, Sens(c)\,\delta\,\lambda\,\theta \tag{7}$$

$$E(U_a(c)) = Q(c)\,\delta + (k_3 - k_2)\, Sens(c)\,\delta\,\lambda\,\theta \tag{8}$$

$$E(U_{ad}(c)) = -C\,\theta + k_4\, Sens(c)\,\delta\,\lambda\,\theta. \tag{9}$$

All the players aim to maximize their mathematical payoff expectation by adjusting their strategies. The optimal strategies of these three players can be obtained by solving the following equations.

$$\begin{cases} \dfrac{\partial E(U_u(c))}{\partial \delta} = Q(c) - k_1\, Sens(c)\,\lambda\,\theta = 0 \\[2mm] \dfrac{\partial E(U_a(c))}{\partial \lambda} = (k_3 - k_2)\, Sens(c)\,\delta\,\theta = 0 \\[2mm] \dfrac{\partial E(U_{ad}(c))}{\partial \theta} = -C + k_4\, Sens(c)\,\delta\,\lambda = 0 \end{cases} \tag{10}$$

As a result, we can obtain the following two theorems.

Theorem 1. *When $k_3 > k_2$, the optimal strategies of the user, the application and the adversary are respectively $\delta = \frac{C}{k_4\, Sens(c)}$, $\lambda = 1$ and $\theta = \frac{Q(c)}{k_1\, Sens(c)}$.*

Proof. when $k_3 > k_2$, obviously $\frac{\partial E(U_a(c))}{\partial \lambda} \geq 0$, which means $E(U_a(c))$ is non-monotonic decreasing. Thus, when $\lambda = 1$, $E(U_a(c))$ is maximal, which makes $\delta = \frac{C}{k_4\, Sens(c)}$, $\theta = \frac{Q(c)}{k_1\, Sens(c)}$ can be easily obtained through the other two equations.

Theorem 2. *When $k_3 < k_2$, the optimal strategies of the user, the application and the adversary are respectively $\delta = 1$, $\lambda = 0$ and $\theta = 0$.*

Proof. When $k_3 < k_2$, obviously $\frac{\partial E(U_a(c))}{\partial \lambda} \leq 0$, which means $E(U_a(c))$ is non-monotonic increasing. Thus, when $\lambda = 0$, $E(U_a(c))$ is maximal. Putting $\lambda = 0$ into the other two equations, easily we can get $\delta = 1$ and $\theta = 0$.

Because k_3 reflects the positive impact of selling context c with $Senc(c)$ on the application's payoff, and k_2 reflects the negative one, Theorem 2 indicates that the key of context privacy preservation is to establish a sound reputation mechanism for context-aware applications, through which the issue of context privacy can be eliminated utterly. As a consequence, a trust between users and mobile applications can be built.

6 Numerical Analysis

In this section, we conduct a numerical analysis to verify our analytical framework. According to the definition of context sensitivity, $Sens(c)$ ranges from 0 to 1, and thus we choose this two values 0.3 and 0.7 as representatives. Besides, we choose $Q(c) = 2$, $C = 1.5$. Considering the constraints depicted in (12), we can get the value range of k_1 and k_4, which are $k_1 \geq \frac{Q(c)}{Sens(c)}$ and $k_4 \geq \frac{C}{Sens(c)}$. In fact, we conduct simulations with different range of parameters. Due to the page of limitation, we only give the results under the constraints of above parameters. When the parameters change over the value range, we study how the strategies and payoffs of each player are affected.

When $k_3 < k_2$, establishing a sound reputation mechanism for context-aware applications can preserve context privacy effectively, so there is no need to conduct the simulation for this scenario. Thus, we focus on the results when $k_3 > k_2$. Figures 3, 4, 5, 6, 7, 8, 9 and 10 show when $k_3 > k_2$ and $Sens(c) = 0.3, 0.7$, how

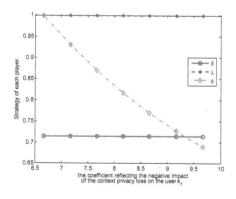

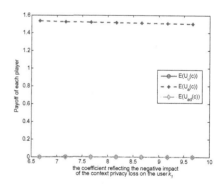

Fig. 3. Impact of k_1 on strategies when $Sens(c) = 0.3$

Fig. 4. Impact of k_1 on payoffs when $Sens(c) = 0.3$

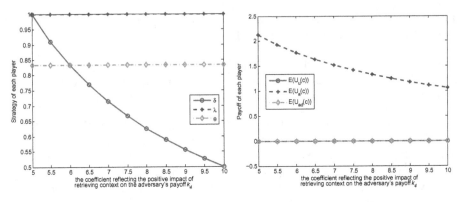

Fig. 5. Impact of k_4 on strategies when $Sens(c) = 0.3$

Fig. 6. Impact of k_4 on payoffs when $Sens(c) = 0.3$

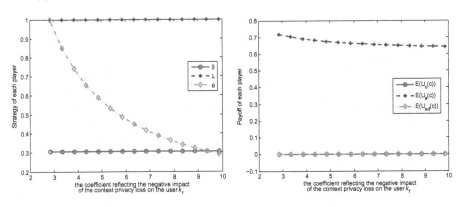

Fig. 7. Impact of k_1 on strategies when $Sens(c) = 0.7$

Fig. 8. Impact of k_1 on payoffs when $Sens(c) = 0.7$

the strategies and payoffs of each player change as k_1 and k_4 change. The results show that the application's strategies are only relevant to k_2 and k_3, which indicates that the application's strategies only depend on how the application weighs its reputation on the user and the profits by leakage. While the user and the adversary are deeply affected by each other. Under the condition of controlling other variables, The probability δ of the user to release a context will decrease as k_4 increases. k_4 reflects the positive impact of retrieving context c with $Sens(c)$ on the adversary's payoff. Thus, increasing k_4 means retrieving context has more positive impact on her payoff, which will promote the action of retrieve, and indirectly restrain the user's action of release. The probability θ of the adversary to retrieve a context will decrease as k_1 increases. k_1 reflects the negative impact of the context privacy loss on the user's payoff. Increasing k_1 means context privacy loss has more negative impact on the user's payoff, which will restrain the action of release, and indirectly restrain the adversary's

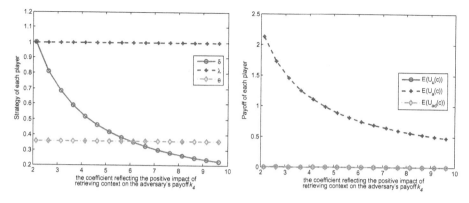

Fig. 9. Impact of k_4 on strategies when $Sens(c) = 0.7$

Fig. 10. Impact of k_4 on payoffs when $Sens(c) = 0.7$

action of retrieve. As to the payoffs of three players, when k_1 and k_4 changes, their variation trend is almost changeless, Because when the optimal strategies are achieved, the players' payoffs tend to constants, so that the players don't have motivation to adjust their strategies any more. This result does reveal the meanings of Nash equilibrium.

7   Conclusion

This paper studies the problem of context privacy protection about the context-aware application. Considering that in context sensing system, mobile phone user, context-aware application and malicious adversary all can adjust their strategies to maximize their payoffs, we use game theory to formulate this problem. Concretely, We use extensive form game to represent their interactions, and formulate their mathematical payoff expectation. Then we obtain the optimal solution by calculating the Nash equilibriums of the stochastic game. The numerical analysis indicates how the players' strategies and payoffs change when relevant parameters change. We can draw the conclusion that reputation mechanism for the context-aware application is crucial, which has great effect on the application's strategy. If reputation mechanism can be designed properly, the application will be willing to preserve the user's privacy by choice of maximizing its profits. Then the adversary doesn't have the chance to retrieve the context privacy, and the user has complete trust to the application, which accords with the requirement of mobile applications' development.

Acknowledgement. This work has been supported by the National Natural Science Foundation of China (No. 61472044, No. 61272475, No. 61571049), and the Fundamental Research Funds for the Central Universities (No. 2014KJJCB32).

References

1. Duan, Z., Yan, M., Cai, Z., Wang, X., Han, M., Li, Y.: Truthful incentive mechanisms for social cost minimization in mobile crowdsourcing systems. Sensors 16(4), 481 (2016)
2. Götz, M., Nath, S., Gehrke, J.: MaskIt: privately releasing user context streams for personalized mobile applications. In: Proceedings of the 2012 ACM SIGMOD International Conference on Management of Data, pp. 289–300. ACM (2012)
3. Groat, M.M., He, W., Forrest, S.: KIPDA: k-indistinguishable privacy-preserving data aggregation in wireless sensor networks. In: INFOCOM, 2011 Proceedings IEEE, pp. 2024–2032. IEEE (2011)
4. Hu, W., Chunqiang, L., Huang, S.: Message in a concealed bottle: achieving query content privacy with accurate location-based services. In: Privacy Enhancing Technologies Symposium (2016, submitted)
5. Narayanan, A., Thiagarajan, N., Lakhani, M., Hamburg, M., Boneh, D.: Location privacy via private proximity testing. In: NDSS (2011)
6. Shin, M., Cornelius, C., Peebles, D., Kapadia, A., Kotz, D., Triandopoulos, N.: Anonysense: a system for anonymous opportunistic sensing. Pervasive Mob. Comput. 7(1), 16–30 (2011)
7. Vu, K., Zheng, R., Gao, L.: Efficient algorithms for k-anonymous location privacy in participatory sensing. In: INFOCOM, 2012 Proceedings IEEE, pp. 2399–2407. IEEE (2012)
8. Wang, W., Zhang, Q.: A stochastic game for privacy preserving context sensing on mobile phone. In: INFOCOM, 2014 Proceedings IEEE, pp. 2328–2336. IEEE (2014)
9. Wang, Y., Cai, Z., Yin, G., Gao, Y., Tong, X., Wu, G.: An incentive mechanism with privacy protection in mobile crowdsourcing systems. Comput. Netw. 102, 157–171 (2016)
10. Westhoff, D., Girao, J., Acharya, M.: Concealed data aggregation for reverse multicast traffic in sensor networks: encryption, key distribution, and routing adaptation. IEEE Trans. Mob. Comput. 5(10), 1417–1431 (2006)
11. Yang, P., Cao, Z., Dong, X., Zia, T.A.: An efficient privacy preserving data aggregation scheme with constant communication overheads for wireless sensor networks. Commun. Lett. IEEE 15(11), 1205–1207 (2011)
12. Zhang, L., Cai, Z., Wang, X.: Fakemask: a novel privacy preserving approach for smartphones

A Novel Delay Analysis for Polling Schemes with Power Management Under Heterogeneous Environments

Li Feng[1], Jiguo Yu[2]([✉]), Jiemin Liang[1], Feng Zhao[3], and Yong Wang[3]

[1] Faculty of Information Technology, Macau University of Science and Technology, Macau, China
lfeng@must.edu.mo, 493494189@qq.com

[2] School of Information Science and Engineering, Qufu Normal University, Rizhao, Shandong 276826, China
jiguoyu@sina.com

[3] Guilin University of Electronic Technology, Guilin 541004, China
{zhaofeng,wang}@guet.edu.cn

Abstract. This paper studies the delay performance of IEEE 802.11 PCF with power saving under heterogeneous environments (particularly the heterogeneous sleeping interval). We propose applying the classic pure limited service queuing system to analyze the mean and variance of the total delay without developing a new analysis model. Compared to the related works, our method is simple and scalable, while our results are general. Simulations show that our analytical results are very accurate for both homogeneous and heterogeneous environments.

Keywords: 802.11 · PCF · Power saving · Queueing analysis

1 Introduction

With the growing popularity of IEEE 802.11 wireless LANs (WLANs), various types of heterogeneous devices (laptops, smartphones, tablets, sensors, actuators etc.) are being deployed wherein. The heterogeneity of these devices implies the heterogeneity of their traffic, their application requirements, and their power saving modes. In this paper, we are concerned with the delay performance of IEEE 802.11 PCF network with power saving [1] under heterogeneous environments (particularly heterogeneous sleeping intervals).

The PCF protocol with power saving is a very basic and important contention-free protocol. It has been widely extended to IEEE 802.11 HCCA [2] and the latest 802.11ah protocol [3]. Despite the growing popularity, the delay performance of PCF with power saving are worth further studying. Most

---

This work is partially supported by Macao Science and Technology Development Fund under Grant (No. 013/2014/A1 and No. 104/2014/A3) and the NSF of China under Grant 61373027 and NSF of Shandong Province under Grant ZR2012FM023.

© Springer International Publishing Switzerland 2016
Q. Yang et al. (Eds.): WASA 2016, LNCS 9798, pp. 401–413, 2016.
DOI: 10.1007/978-3-319-42836-9_36

related works [5,6,9,10] focus on PCF without power saving, assume homogeneous traffic, and evaluate the performance via simulation. The authors in [9] investigated via simulation the throughput performance of PCF. The authors in [10] presented a comparison study via simulation for four polling schemes including PCF. The authors in [5] analyzed the throughput, expected channel access delay, and frame loss for PCF, but ignored the total delay (including the channel access delay, frame transmission time, ACK time, and waiting delay), where the channel access delay of a frame is the time interval between when the frame reaches the head of the MAC queue and when the frame starts being transmitted. Among all related work, [6] is the most relevant to ours. In this study, the author develop an analytical framework to study the total delay for PCF with power saving in homogeneous environments. The same analytical framework is widely used in the author's successive works such as [4,7,11]. However, this analytical framework in [6] is tedious and complicated so that extending it to heterogeneous environments (particularly heterogeneous sleeping intervals) appears to be not easy.

In this paper, we are concerned with heterogeneous environments (i.e., heterogeneous frame arrival rate, frame size, and sleeping interval), and evaluate the frame's total delay of a station by converting the PCF system to an equivalent pure limited vacation system. In comparison with [6], the advantage is that we can borrow all existing formulae for performance evaluation, thereby avoiding reinventing the wheel. For example, employing the classic delay formula, we evaluate the delay jitter performance for variance-sensitive applications such as voice over PCF, while this is not easily done in [6]. Our method is simpler and more scalable than that of [6], while our theoretical results are more general and useful. For example, applying our model to the PCF system (where voice and data traffic coexists), we evaluate the delay performance, and then run simulations and verify that the proposed model is very accurate.

The rest of this paper is organized as follows. Section 2 overviews the PCF protocol with power saving. Section 3 presents the classic pure limited service system with multiple vacations. Section 4 presents the proposed delay model. Section 5 validates our theoretical results via simulation. Section 6 concludes this paper.

2   PCF with Power Management

In 802.11 standard [1], when PCF and DCF coexist, time is divided into a series of repetition intervals with equal length. In each repetition interval, the system runs first in the PCF mode and then in the DCF mode. In the PCF mode, there is a point coordinator (PC) and multiple stations.

PCF defines a power management (PM) scheme to help stations conserve energy. In this scheme, a station alternates between two states: awake and doze states. In the awake state, a station is fully powered and may receive frames at any time. In the doze state, a station is unable to transmit or receive and consumes very low power. A station notifies the PC that its power management

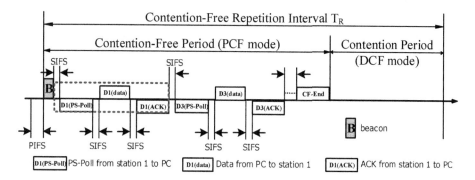

Fig. 1. PCF with power management.

scheme is enabled and sets the listen interval (or sleeping interval) parameter, i.e., the number of the repetition intervals for which the station is in the doze state. Then the PC will buffer frames destined for the station when the station is in the doze state, and deliver one frame to the station for each repetition interval when the station is in the awake state.

With the help of Fig. 1, we explain the operation process of PCF-PM. After a PCF interframe space (PIFS), the PC initializes a contention-free period (CFP) by sending a beacon, marking the beginning of a new repetition interval. The traffic indication map (TIM) field in the beacon contains a list of the stations whose frames have been buffered at the PC. When a station wakes up at the beginning of the repetition interval, it will listen to the TIM beacon. If it finds that its ID is not indicated in the TIM beacon, it will go to sleep immediately for its listen interval. If it finds that its ID is indicated in the TIM beacon, it will keep awake until its turn, and then it begins receiving its buffered frame from the PC by following the pattern: SIFS/PS-Poll/SIFS/Data/SIFS/ACK.

Figure 1 illustrates that after stations 1 and 3 find them appearing in the list sequentially from the beacon, station 1 first waits for a short interframe space (SIFS), and then begins sending a polling frame [D1(PS-Poll)] to the PC. Upon polled, the PC sends one data frame [D1(data)] to station 1 after a SIFS time. Receiving the data frame, station 1 send back an ACK [D1(ACK)] to the PC. The process repeats until all stations in the list has polled the PC. Finally, the PC sends a CF-End control frame (CF-End), marking the end of the current CFP. Hereafter, the system enters the DCF mode, in which the stations in the list can no longer receive data frames until the next repetition interval starts.

3   Classic Pure Limited Service System with Multiple vacations

In this section, we present the classic pure limited service system with multiple vacations [8]. It is a single-server queueing system with infinite buffer. In this

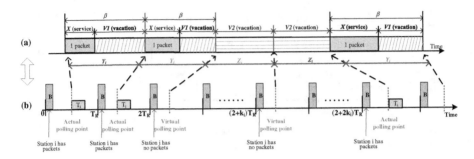

Fig. 2. (a) The classic pure limited service system with multiple vacations, (b) the equivalent PCF-PM system.

system, customers arrive according to a Poisson process with rate λ, and the customer service times have a general distribution.

In this system, the server serves only one customer each time if any and then takes vacation immediately no matter how many customers waiting in the queue. Whenever the server returns from the ongoing vacation and finds no customers waiting in the queue, it will go on a new vacation; and therefore the server is said to take multiple vacations. According to the number of customers served before the server takes vacations, we classify the vacations into two types: type 1 vacation with length V_1 (i.e., the vacation after a customer is served), and type 2 vacation with length V_2 (i.e., the vacation if no customer is served). Figure 2(a) illustrates that the server first takes two type 1 vacations sequentially, and then goes on two type 2 vacations consecutively before it begins serving a new customer.

Assume that customers are served in the order they arrive. Let X be the service time of a customer, let $\beta = X + V_1$, and let W represent the waiting time of a customer before it is served. Let $W^*(s)$, $\beta^*(s)$, and $V_2^*(s)$, respectively, represent the Laplace transforms of the random variables W, β, and V_2. From Sect. 2.6 in [8], $W^*(s)$ is given by

$$W^*(s) = \frac{1 - \lambda E\{\beta\}}{\lambda E\{V_2\}} \cdot \frac{V_2^*(s) - 1}{1 - \frac{s}{\lambda} - \beta^*(s)}. \tag{1}$$

Note that $E\{W^n\} = (-1)^n (W^*(s))_{s=0}^{(n)}$, $E\{\beta^n\} = (-1)^n (\beta^*(s))_{s=0}^{(n)}$, and $E\{V_2^n\} = (-1)^n (V_2^*(s))_{s=0}^{(n)}$ by the basic property of Laplace transform. We can calculate $E\{W\}$ and $E\{W^2\}$ as follows:

$$E\{W\} = f_1(\lambda, \rho, \beta, V_2) \triangleq \frac{\lambda E\{\beta^2\}}{2(1 - \rho)} + \frac{E\{V_2^2\}}{2E\{V_2\}}, \tag{2}$$

and

$$E\{W^2\} = f_2(\lambda, \rho, \beta, V_2) \triangleq \frac{\lambda E\{\beta^3\}}{3(1 - \rho)} + \frac{[\lambda E\{\beta^2\}]^2}{2(1 - \rho)^2} + \frac{\lambda E\{\beta^2\}E\{V_2^2\}}{2(1 - \rho)E\{V_2\}} + \frac{E\{V_2^3\}}{3E\{V_2\}}. \tag{3}$$

where $E\{\cdot\}$ denotes the mean of $\cdot$ and the traffic intensity $\rho = \lambda E\{\beta\}$.

4   The Proposed Delay Model

In this paper, focusing on the downlink traffic from the PC to stations, we study the delay performance of PCF with power management.

Let T_R denote the length of a repetition interval. For each station i $(1 \le i \le n)$, we assume that the downlink traffic is a Poisson process with parameter λ_i, the data frame length is L_i, and the listen interval is $k_i T_R$, where k_i is a positive integer.

Let D_i denote the total delay of a tagged data frame of station i, where the total delay is defined to be the interval between when the tagged data frame arrives at the AP's MAC buffer and when the AP receives the ACK from the station i who receives the tagged frame. Let W_i denote the waiting time of the tagged packet of station i, where the waiting time is defined to be the interval between when the tagged data frame arrives at the AP's MAC buffer and when the AP starts to service station i. Let T_i denote the service time of the tagged data frame of station i, where the service time is defined to be the interval between when the AP starts to service station i (i.e., the instant after which station i first waits for a SIFS time and then sends a PS-Poll message to request its buffered frame from the AP) and when the AP receives the ACK from the station i. Then, D_i is the sum of W_i and T_i, namely,

$$D_i = W_i + T_i, 1 \le i \le n. \tag{4}$$

Note that the service process of a data frame follows the pattern: SIFS/PS-Poll/SIFS/Data/SIFS/ACK, as illustrated in Fig. 1. We can calculate T_i as follows.

$$T_i = 3T_{SIFS} + T_{PS-Poll} + T_{frame,i} + T_{ACK}, \tag{5}$$

where T_{SIFS} denotes the SIFS time, $T_{PS-Poll}$ denotes the PS-Poll time, $T_{frame,i}$ denotes the transmission time of a data frame with length L_i, and T_{ACK} denotes the transmission time of the ACK frame.

Let $E(D_i)$ and $Dev\{D_i\}$ represent the mean and the standard deviation of the delay D_i, respectively. We have

$$E(D_i) = E\{W_i\} + T_i, 1 \le i \le n, \tag{6}$$

$$Dev\{D_i\} = Dev\{W_i\} = \sqrt{E\{W_i^2\} - (E\{W_i\})^2}.$$

The remaining task is to calculate $E\{W_i\}$ and $E\{W_i^2\}$. Below, we first model the PCF-PM system as a pure limited vacation system and then derive the expressions of $E\{W_i\}$ and $E\{W_i^2\}$ from the classic queueing formulas (2) and (3).

4.1   The Equivalent Pure Limited Vacation System

In this section, we will first convert the PCF-PM system into an equivalent pure limited vacation system, and then express $E\{W_i\}$ and $E\{W_i^2\}$ of the PCF-PM system.

We start describing the equivalent relationship from the receiving process that the station receives a frame from the AP. Consider a station i in PCF-PM. Regard station i as a server. Regard the frames (arriving from the AP to station i) as the customers of the server, where frame arrivals follow a Poisson process with parameter λ_i. When station i wakes up, it will receive a frame if it find that its TIM beacon contains its ID, or will not otherwise; equivalently speaking, station i will actually serve a customer for a duration of T_i if it find that its TIM beacon contains its ID, or will virtually serve a customer for a duration of 0 (i.e., station i will not serve a customer) otherwise.

Define the actual (virtual) polling point of a station i, to be the instant that station i begins serving a frame actually (virtually), namely, the instant after the previous $i-1$ stations actually or virtually serve frames. The actual (virtual) polling points are illustrated in Fig. 2(b).

Let Y_i represent the actual polling interval between an actual polling point of station i and its next actual or virtual polling point. According to PCF-PM, a station will receive only one frame in the interval Y_i.

Let Z_i represent the virtual polling interval between a virtual polling point of station i and its next actual or virtual polling point. According to PCF-PM, a station will not receive any frame in the interval Z_i.

Therefore, in an actual or virtual polling interval, station i will receive at most one frame and then it either keeps idle or goes to sleep; equivalently speaking, station i goes on vacations when it either keeps idle or goes to sleep, because it will not receive any frame in that time.

Equivalent pur-limited rules: The instruction in PCF-PM that a station will receive at most one frame in an actual or virtual polling interval, is naturally consistent with the pure-limited rule that the server serves only one customer each time if any.

Equivalent vacation rules: The time in PCF-PM that a station either keeps idle or goes to sleep in an actual or virtual polling interval, is naturally regarded as the vacation time in the pure-limited vacation system, where the serve will not serve any customer once it takes vacation, no matter how many customers waiting in the queue. The fact that a station in PCF-PM will take another vacation if it wakes up and does not find its identify in the received beacon, is naturally consistent with the concept of multiple vacations in the pure-limited vacation system. In addition, the actual polling interval Y_i in PCF-PM (in which station i first serves a frame and then keeps idle) is equivalent to the interval β in the pure limited vacation system; the virtual polling interval Z_i in PCF-PM (in which station i goes to sleep) is equivalent to the interval V_2 in the pure limited vacation system.

In short, from the viewpoint of station i, the PCF-PM system can be regarded as an equivalent pure limited vacation system, where

$$\beta = Y_i, \tag{7}$$
$$V_2 = Z_i.$$

Then, from (2), (3) and (7), we can easily calculate

$$E\{W_i\} = f_1(\lambda_i, \rho_i, Y_i, Z_i)$$

$$E\{W_i^2\} = f_2(\lambda_i, \rho_i, Y_i, Z_i),$$

(8)

where the traffic intensity $\rho_i = \lambda_i E\{Y_i\}$.

To evaluate $E\{W_i\}$ and $E\{W_i^2\}$ in (8), in the next two subsections, we respectively calculate the n-th moment of Y_i and Z_i, where $n = 1, 2, 3$.

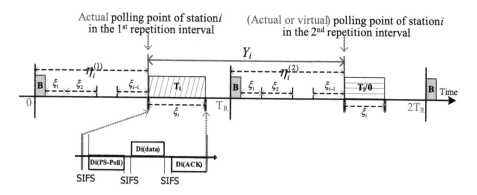

Fig. 3. Actual polling interval.

4.2   Calculation of $E\{Y_i\}$, $E\{Y_i^2\}$ and $E\{Y_i^3\}$

We first express Y_i, with the help of Fig. 3. According to the definition of Y_i, we have

$$Y_i = T_R + \eta_i^{(2)} - \eta_i^{(1)},$$

(9)

where T_R denotes the length of a repetition interval, $\eta_i^{(1)}$ denotes the actual polling point of station i in the first repetition interval, $\eta_i^{(2)}$ denotes the actual or virtual polling point of station i in the second repetition interval.

In our model, $\eta_i^{(1)}$ and $\eta_i^{(2)}$ are independent and identically distributed (i.i.d.) with a generic random variable η_i. We explained the reason as follows. As illustrated in the first repetition interval in Fig. 3, station i begins its service only if station j, $1 \leq j \leq i - 1$, has finished its service. Therefore, we express η_i as follows.

$$\eta_i = T_B + \sum_{j=1}^{i-1} \xi_j,$$

(10)

where T_B is the beacon transmission time and ξ_j ($1 \leq j \leq i - 1$) is a random variable denoting the service time of station j. The duration of ξ_j depends on whether station j is in the awake or doze state. Let $P_{awake,j}$ and $P_{doze,j}$, respectively, represent the probability that station j is in the awake and doze states at any arbitrary instant of time. Since ξ_j is equal to T_j if station j is in the awake state, and 0 if in the doze state, we can write ξ_j as follows.

$$\xi_j = \begin{cases} T_j, \text{ w.p. } P_{awake,j} \\ 0, \text{ w.p. } P_{doze,j}. \end{cases} \tag{11}$$

In (11), we essentially assume that ξ_j in one repetition interval is i.i.d. with that in another repetition interval. In addition, note (i) in each repetition interval, ξ_i is independent of ξ_j for $i \neq j$ since frame arrival to each station is independent, and (ii) the functions of independent random variables are independent as well. We conclude that $\eta_i^{(1)}$ and $\eta_i^{(2)}$ are i.i.d. with η_i.

We then calculate $P_{awake,j}$ and then $P_{doze,j}$, by considering the behavior of station j at every beacon that it receives. Note that station j stays in the awake state for at least T_B to receive a beacon. With probability $\rho_j = \lambda_j E\{Y_j\} = \lambda_j T_R$, station j has packets, and then it stays active for T_R to receive one frame and for another T_B to receive the next beacon. In other words, with probability ρ_j, station j stays in the awake state for $T_R + T_B$. With probability $1-\rho_j$, station j has no packets, and then it goes into sleep and wakes up for every k_j-th beacon. In other words, with probability $1-\rho_j$, station j stays in the awake state for T_B, and stays in the doze state for $k_j T_R - T_B$. Then the fractions of the time that station j spends in the awake and doze states are:

$$P_{awake,j} = \frac{\rho_j[T_R + T_B]}{(1-\rho_j)[k_j T_R - T_B] + \rho_j[T_R + T_B]},$$

$$P_{PS,j} = 1 - P_{awake,j},$$

where $\rho_j = \lambda_j T_R$.

We next calculate the variance of η_i, $Var\{\eta_i\}$. From (11), we have

$$E\{\xi_j\} = T_j P_{awake,j}, \quad E\{\xi_j^2\} = T_j^2 P_{awake,j}, \tag{12}$$
$$Var\{\xi_j\} = E\{(\xi_j)^2\} - (E\{\xi_j\})^2 = (T_j^2 - T_j)P_{awake,j},$$

Since all ξ_js are independent each other, from (10) and (12), we have

$$Var\{\eta_i\} = \sum_{j=1}^{i-1} Var\{\xi_j\} = \sum_{j=1}^{i-1} (T_j^2 - T_j)P_{awake,j} \tag{13}$$

We finally calculate the n-th moment of Y_i, where $n = 1, 2, 3$.

$$E\{Y_i\} = E\{T_R + \eta_i^{(2)} - \eta_i^{(1)}\} = T_R, \tag{14}$$

and

$$E\{Y_i^2\} = E\{(T_R + \eta_i^{(2)} - \eta_i^{(1)})^2\}$$
$$= E\{T_R^2 + 2T_R(\eta_i^{(2)} - \eta_i^{(1)}) + (\eta_i^{(2)} - \eta_i^{(1)})^2\}$$
$$= T_R^2 + E\{(\eta_i^{(2)} - \eta_i^{(1)})^2\}$$
$$= T_R^2 + E\{(\eta_i^{(2)})^2 - 2\eta_i^{(1)}\eta_i^{(2)} + (\eta_i^{(1)})^2\}$$
$$= T_R^2 + 2(E\{\eta_i^2\} - (E\{\eta_i\})^2)$$
$$= T_R^2 + 2Var\{\eta_i\}$$
$$= T_R^2 + 2\sum_{j=1}^{i-1}(T_j^2 - T_j)P_{awake,j}. \qquad (15)$$

$$E\{Y_i^3\} = E\{(T_R + \eta_i^{(2)} - \eta_i^{(1)})^3\}$$
$$= E\{T_R^3 + 3T_R^2(\eta_i^{(2)} - \eta_i^{(1)}) + 3T_R(\eta_i^{(2)} - \eta_i^{(1)})^2 + (\eta_i^{(2)} - \eta_i^{(1)})^3\}$$
$$= E\{T_R^3\} + 3T_R E\{(\eta_i^{(2)} - \eta_i^{(1)})^2\} + E\{(\eta_i^{(2)} - \eta_i^{(1)})^3\}$$
$$= T_R^3 + 3T_R \cdot 2Var\{\eta_i\}$$
$$+ E\{(\eta_i^{(2)})^3 - 3(\eta_i^{(2)})^2\eta_i^{(1)} + 3\eta_i^{(2)}(\eta_i^{(1)})^2 - (\eta_i^{(1)})^3\}$$
$$= T_R^3 + 6T_R Var\{\eta_i\}$$
$$+ E\{(\eta_i)^3\} - 3E\{(\eta_i)^2\}E\{\eta_i\} + 3E\{\eta_i\}E\{(\eta_i)^2\} - E\{(\eta_i)^3\}$$
$$= T_R^3 + 6T_R Var\{\eta_i\}$$
$$= T_R^3 + 6T_R\sum_{j=1}^{i-1}(T_j^2 - T_j)P_{awake,j}. \qquad (16)$$

where we use $E\{(\eta_i^{(2)} - \eta_i^{(1)})^3\} = 0$ in (16).

4.3   Calculation of $E\{Z_i\}$, $E\{Z_i^2\}$ and $E\{Z_i^3\}$

Here, we first express Z_i, with the help of Fig. 4. According to the definition of Z_i, we have

$$Z_i = k_i T_R + \eta_i^{(2)} - \eta_i^{(1)}, \qquad (17)$$

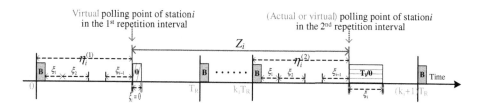

Fig. 4. Virtual polling interval.

where $k_i T_R$ is the listen interval length of station i, $\eta_i^{(1)}$ and $\eta_i^{(2)}$ are defined in (9) and are i.i.d. with η_i in (10).

We then calculate the n-th moment of Z_i, where $n = 1, 2, 3$, following the derivation process in Sect. 4.2.

$$E\{Z_i\} = k_j T_R, \tag{18}$$

$$E\{Z_i^2\} = (k_j T_R)^2 + 2\sum_{j=1}^{i-1}(T_j^2 - T_j)P_{awake,j},$$

$$E\{Z_i^3\} = (k_j T_R)^3 + 6(k_j T_R)\sum_{j=1}^{i-1}(T_j^2 - T_j)P_{awake,j}.$$

5   Model Verification

In this section, we verify our delay model of the PCF-PM system under heterogeneous environments (i.e., heterogeneous traffic arrival rate, frame size, and listen interval). The PCF-PM simulator is written in C++. The default parameter values shown in Table 1 are in accordance with 802.11b, where 1 slot $= T_{slot} = 20$ μs and time is measured in slots, the IP routing header $= 20$ bytes, the length of the frame check sequence (FCS) $= 4$ bytes, and the number of stations $n = 8$. The buffer size for each station and the PC is set to 1000 data frames. Each simulation value is an average over four simulation runs, where each run was for 400 s.

Table 1. Default parameter values.

PHYHeader	= 24 bytes	MACHeader	= 32 bytes
RouteHeader	= 20 bytes	FCS	= 4 bytes
T_{slot}	= 20 μs	T_{SIFS}	= 10 μs
T_R	= 15 ms	n	= 8
R_{data}	= 11 Mbps	R_{basic}	= 1 Mbps
$T_{PS-Poll}$	= (PHYHeader+MACHeader+FCS)/R_{basic}		
T_{header}	= PHYHeader/R_{basic} +(MACHeader+FCS)/R_{data}		
T_{ACK}	= T_{header}	T_B	= 209 μs
$T_{frame,i}$	= T_{header}+(RouteHeader+L_i)/R_{data}		

Table 2. Parameter values for voice traffic [12] and data traffic.

	voice traffic				data traffic			
Station ID	1	2	3	4	5	6	7	8
λ_i(pkts/sec)	16.67	25	33.33	50	20	30	40	50
L_i(bytes)	48	40	50	160	500	600	700	800
$k_i(T_R)$	2	3	4	5	6	7	8	9

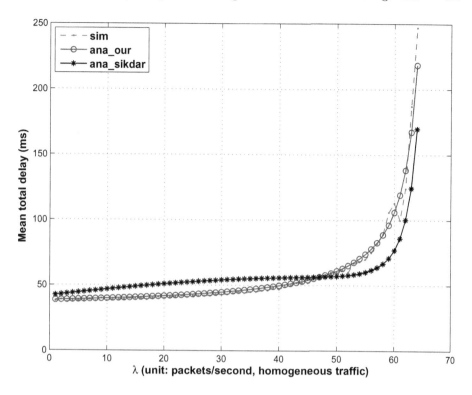

Fig. 5. Mean total delay vs. data frame arrival rate for homogeneous traffic.

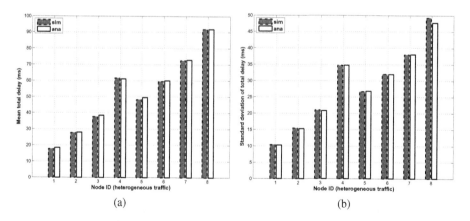

Fig. 6. (a) Mean and (b) standard deviation of total delay vs. station ID for heterogeneous traffic.

We assume Poisson arrivals and run two experiments. In the first experiment, we consider the homogeneous setting, where all stations have the same data frame arrival rate, the same data frame size of 100 bytes, and the same listen interval of $5T_R$. Figure 5 plots the mean total delay of station 8's data frames versus the data frame arrival rate for the homogeneous traffic (note that we obtain very similar results when considering other station's data frame). The dashed curve shows the simulation results, while the solid curve labeled with "ana_our" plots our theoretical result (6) and the solid curve labeled with "ana_sikdar" plots the theoretical result (33) in [6]. From this figure, we can see that our results better match with the corresponding simulation results than those in [6], indicating that our mode is more accurate even for the homogeneous traffic.

In the second experiment, we consider the heterogenous setting. In this experiment, 8 stations are polled by PC, where stations 1 to 4 transmit voice traffic [12] and stations 5 to 8 transmit data traffic at rate 11 Mbps (i.e., $R_{data} = 11$ Mbps), and each station takes a different parameter setting shown in Table 2. Figure 6(a) plots the mean total delay (6) for each station and Fig. 6(b) plots the corresponding standard deviation (6), where the abscissa represents the station ID. The bar with dashed border represents the simulation results, while the bar with solid border represents the theoretical results. Note that the standard deviation of the total delay is same to that of the waiting delay since T_i in (4) is a constant. From Figs. 6(a) and (b), each station has apparently different mean and variance of the delay since each station takes a very different parameter setting. The close match between the theoretical curves and the corresponding simulation curves manifests that our model is very accurate for heterogeneous setting as well.

6   Conclusion

The WLAN traffic is becoming more and more diverse and heterogeneous. In this paper, we first study the delay performance of the PCF network with power saving under heterogeneous environments (particularly the heterogeneous listen interval). In our model, we elegantly convert the PCF network with power saving into an equivalent pure limited vacation system, so that we can borrow existing results to analyze the delay performance without developing new model. Extensive simulations verify that our model is very accurate.

References

1. ANSI/IEEE Std 802.11, Part 11: Wireless LAN Medium Access Control (MAC) and Physical Layer (PHY) Specifications, 1999 Edition (R2003)
2. IEEE Std 802.11e, specific requirements Part 11: Wireless LAN Medium Access Control (MAC) and Physical Layer (PHY) Specifications, Amendment 8: Medium Access Control (MAC) Quality of Service Enhancements (2005)
3. IEEE 802.11ah Task Group, 11/1137r14 Specification Framework for TGah. http://www.ieee802.org/11/Reports/tgah_update.htm
4. Iyengar, R., Sikdar, B.: A queueing model for polled service in WiMAX/IEEE 802.16 networks. IEEE Trans. Commun. 60(7), 1777–1781 (2012)

5. Siddique, M.A.R., Kamruzzaman, J.: Performance analysis of PCF based WLANs with imperfect channel and failure retries. In: Global Telecommunications Conference (GLOBECOM 2010), 2010 IEEE, pp. 1–6, December 2010
6. Sikdar, B.: An analytic model for the delay in IEEE 802.11 PCF MAC-based wireless networks. IEEE Trans. Wireless Commun. **6**(4), 1542–1550 (2007)
7. Sikdar, B.: Queueing analysis of polled service classes in the IEEE 802.16 MAC protocol. IEEE Trans. Wireless Commun. **8**(12), 5767–5772 (2009)
8. Takagi, H.: Queueing analysis, vol. 1, North-Holland Amsterdam (1991)
9. Visser, M., El Zarki, M.: Voice and data transmission over an 802.11 wireless network. In Proceeding IEEE PIMRC, pp. 648–652 (1995)
10. Wu, J., Huang, G.: Simulation study based on QoS schemes for IEEE 802.11. In: 3rd International Conference on Advanced Computer Theory and Engineering (ICACTE), 2010, pp. 534–538, August 2010
11. Yang, H., Sikdar, B.: Queueing analysis of polling based wireless MAC protocols with sleep-wake cycles. IEEE Trans. Commun. **60**(9), 2427–2433 (2012)
12. Zhao, Q.L., Tsang, D.H.K., Sakurai, T.: A simple critical-offered-load-based CAC scheme for IEEE 802.11 DCF networks. IEEE/ACM Trans. Networking **19**(5), 1485–1498 (2011)

Temporal-Spatial Aggregated Urban Air Quality Inference with Heterogeneous Big Data

Xiaorong Lu[✉], Yang Wang, Liusheng Huang, Wei Yang, and Yao Shen

School of CS and Technology, University of Science and Technology of China,
Hefei, China
{ldayy,shenyao}@mail.ustc.edu.cn, {anyang,lshuang,qubit}@ustc.edu.cn

Abstract. Recently air quality information has drawn much attention from public and researchers as deteriorated air quality extremely damages human health. Meanwhile the limiting number of air quality monitor stations and complexity of influencing factors on air quality raise the starving demand on future air quality prediction. In this paper we propose a temporal-spatial aggregated urban air quality inference framework using the heterogeneous temporal and spatial datasets to infer the future air quality. We deeply analyse the influencing factors on air quality in terms of temporal and spatial features and then elaborately design a linear regression-based inference model with offline parameters learning and real time predicting. We not only estimate the parameters for our model itself, but also estimate the correlation parameters of single factor on the air quality in order that the model can make prediction on future air quality precisely. Based on real data sources, we appraise our approach with extensive experiments in Beijing and Suzhou. The results show that with the superior parameters learning, our model overmatches a series of state-of-art and commonly used approaches.

Keywords: Air quality inference · Urban air · Big data · Data management · Urban computing

1 Introduction

Recent years urban air quality prediction has become a challenging and hotspot research area as air quality has deteriorated rapidly in last decades and more extremely related to public health in terms of the concentration of $PM_{2.5}$, PM_{10} and etc. In modern society, air pollutants mainly come from so-called fine particulate matter that is suspended particulate with a diameter less than or equal to 2.5 in the air. The level of air pollutants is quantified by Air Quality Index (AQI) that is reported to public by governmental air quality monitor stations. The higher AQI, the higher concentration of air pollutants is and the more harmful damage to human health.

While real time air quality information is monitored and reported to populace, there are still insufficient air quality monitor stations in a city due to the very expensive cost of constructing and maintaining such a station. For example

© Springer International Publishing Switzerland 2016
Q. Yang et al. (Eds.): WASA 2016, LNCS 9798, pp. 414–426, 2016.
DOI: 10.1007/978-3-319-42836-9_37

there are only 35 monitor stations in Beijing and 8 in Suzhou. Such few stations can not cover the AQI of an entire city area. And worse, air quality is
highly location-dependent and relates to urban dynamics such as traffic follow
and human mobility. All the aforementioned issues make the AQI reports for the
area far from an air monitor stations very difficult and imprecise. Thus future air
quality prediction arises as a starving demand from the government and public
for assessing levels of AQI around the city.

In literature, AQI inference has attracted much attention from researchers
and many a state-of-art have been proposed. Meteorology models are first introduced to further air quality prediction such as spatial interpolation and emission
model. These methods base their assumption on the spatial continuity of air pollutants distribution, which is impractical in real urban region, to examine the
relation between ambient air quality and respiratory health effect. The recently
arising machine learning and big data technic bring a new philosophy to handle
the air quality inference problem and show significant superiority over the classical methods on inference precision. Approaches falling under this category often
leverage a mathematical prediction model to study the influence of temporal and
spatial factors to air quality exploiting the heterogeneous big historical air quality dataset observed from air monitor stations. However, different models have
different assumptions and parameters and may not be applicable to all urban
environments due to the complexity of real temporal and spatial dynamics.

In this paper, we propose a temporal-spatial aggregated urban air quality
inference framework using the heterogeneous big historical air quality datasets
to infer the real time and fine grained AQI throughout a city. In brief our
framework consists of two parts: offline model learning and real time inference.
In contrast with existing work, our proposal overtops the prediction on two
aspects. Firstly, we propose a linear model to solve the non-linear air quality
inference problem. Secondly, using the observed data, we not only estimate the
parameters for the model, but also estimate parameters for temporal and spatial
factors. This kind of elaborate parameter estimation can reflect the influence of
temporal and spatial elements on air quality in a pinpoint extent. We exploit two
cities in China (Beijing and Suzhou) as our testbed to verify the performance of
our model and the experiments show that our approach overmatches the existing
research in terms of inference precision and great applicability in different urban
cities.

2   Related Work

There are different categories of state-of-art in predicting air quality in the past
years. The first category is linear interpolation in terms of spatial division introduced by environmental and public health studies [6,11]. These approaches often
assume that air pollutants have a continuous distribution across the area. However, the prediction precision is quite low for these models as air quality varies
non-linearly in locations.

The type of model belonging to top-down methods relates to satellite remote
sensing which gains popularity from researchers in past years [5,8]. Methods

falling under this type mainly use the high resolution images shot by meteorological satellites to infer air quality. The most representative research introduced in [10] proposes a inference model to estimate $PM_{2.5}$ using the modern resolution imaging spectroradiameter. While these approaches are extremely influenced by weather condition and neglect the influence of urban factors such as traffic flow, human mobility and etc., they have limited predict precision and would not be applicable to different cities.

Recently a large series of air quality inference researches based on machine learning have been proposed by researchers [12,13]. Decision tree [2], SVM [7,9] and ANN(Artificial Neural Network) [4] are widely exploited to make contribution to air quality inference research. And more recently machine learning with big data [14,15] based air quality prediction model has been proposed and shows great outcomes over other methods in terms of air quality inference. However, when the observed dataset is sparse most of the aforementioned models will fail in furnishing a precise predicting result.

3   Framework and Feature Extraction

As depicted in Fig. 1, our air quality inference framework comprises two major parts: offline model learning and realtime air quality inference. In the offline learning phase, we use a variety of observed data from air quality monitor stations including air quality index, meteorology data, urban dynamics and geography data from some public welfare websites to perform feature extraction. Upon that we learn our model parameters based on the extracted features and construct our inference model. While in the realtime inference phase, we infer the AQI of the query grid exploiting its affecting realtime data.

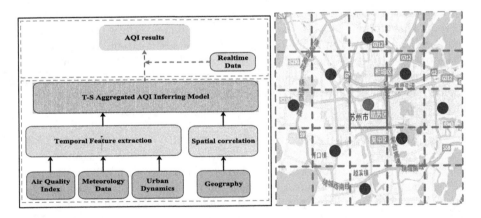

Fig. 1. Temporal-spatial aggregated framework

Fig. 2. Illustration of grid division

3.1   Region Division

For the sake of fine-grained inference, we divide a city into some non-overlapping grids as shown in Fig. 2. In our experiments we define the size of a grid with 1 km × 1 km as most air quality forecast literature do. Here we have an assumption that air quality in any one grid is uniform while different grids may have different air quality index. If an air quality monitor station is located in a grid, then the grid is defined as a labeled grid. While a grid without a station located is a grid to be inferred or an unlabelled grid. As depicted in Fig. 2, the grids with a black dot are labeled grids while others are inferred grids. In addition, the AQI of a grid would mainly be influenced by its historical records and the records of its ambient grids.

3.2   Temporal Feature Extraction

Temporal Features are mainly from three data sources: air quality records, meteorology data and urban dynamics. Air quality records consist of $PM_{2.5}$, PM_{10}, NO_2, CO and SO_2 and are used to calculate the AQI of a region by governments. The classification of AQI levels of health concern is shown in Table 1. We capture these air quality records from public welfare websites[1,2] which publish more than 600 detailed air quality records of 77 cities in each hourly report. Meteorology data comes from some weather forecast websites like nmc[3] and weather[4] which is categorized as temperature, humidity, barometric pressure, wind speed and weather condition (like sunny, cloudy, rainy and snowy). This meteorological data is also collected hourly. The urban dynamics (traffic flow and human mobility) can be widely considered as major culprit to air pollutants that damage air quality [9]. Consequentially we take the urban dynamics into account and extract the features with Bing Map, vehicle trajectories (especially taxicabs) and mobile phones.

3.3   Spatial Feature Extraction

The geographical data (like POI (Points of Interest), road map and urban morphology) is believed as an influence to air quality to some extent. This paper we extract this kind of data from two famous linked spatial data sets named Geoname[5] and DBPedia[6] and regard the data as Spatial feature for our learning model.

---

[1] http://pm25.in.
[2] http://datacenter.mep.gov.cn.
[3] http://www.nmc.cn.
[4] http://www.weather.com.cn.
[5] http://www.geonames.org.
[6] http://dbpedia.org.

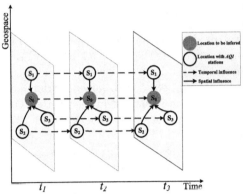

Table 1. *AQI* Levels of Health Concern

AQI Values	Levels of Health Concern	Colors
$0 - 50$	Good	Green
$51 - 100$	Moderate	Yellow
$101 - 150$	Unhealthy for Sensitive Groups	Orange
$151 - 200$	Unhealthy	Red
$201 - 300$	Very Unhealthy	Purple
$301 - 500$	Hazardous	Maroon

Fig. 3. Illustration of inference philosophy (Color figure online)

4   The Proposed Air Quality Inference Method

Intuitively the *AQI* of different grids are correlated with each other in terms of temporal and spatial perspectives. For instance, if the AQI of a grid is in a good condition for the past few hours, then it will be massively more likely to be good currently. However if its neighbor grids' *AQI* deteriorates, then the AQI of the grid itself may tend to be bad. From this point of view we propose our inferring model based on the framework as illustrated in Fig. 1 and the temporal-spatial correlated inference philosophy depicted in Fig. 3. Air quality of a grid depends on its current observation data and that of its previous conditions in temporal aspect denoted as broken black arrows in Fig. 3; meanwhile air quality of that grid is also influenced by its ambient grids in terms of spatial perspective denoted as black solid arrows in Fig. 3. The rest part of this section we will quantify the temporal and spatial features and expatiate on the construction of our proposed inference model.

4.1   Inference Model Construction

Let $\mathbf{x}_{i,t}$ be a dynamic and multi-dimensional vector representing the values of temporal features of the grid i in the time point of t, $\mathbf{s}_i$ be the vector which is the values of spatial features of the grid i and $y_{i,t}$ be the *AQI* level as shown in Table 1. Then a $y_{i,t}$ of a unlabelled grid is determined by the combination of its own historical records $y_{i,t-1}$ and its neighbor grids' $y_{j,t}$ where j represents its neighbors. Denoting $\mathbf{X}_{i,t} = \{\mathbf{x}_{i,t-1}, \cdots, \mathbf{x}_{j,t}\}$ as the observed temporal features and $\mathbf{S}_i = \{\mathbf{s}_i, \cdots, \mathbf{s}_j\}$ as the spatial features where i is the grid to be inferred and j are the neighbor grids. We have the follow inferring formula:

$$y_{i,t} = \pi(\mathbf{X}_{i,t}) + \varepsilon \tag{1}$$

where

$$\pi(\mathbf{X}_{i,t}) = \frac{1}{1 + \exp -(\mathbf{W}^T \Phi(\mathbf{X}_{i,t}) + \mathbf{W}_0)} \qquad (2)$$

$$\Phi(\mathbf{X}_{i,t}) = \alpha \mathbf{X}_{i,t} + \beta \mathbf{S}_i \qquad (3)$$

ε in Formula 1 is a bias on the inference value of $y_{j,t}$ with a Gaussian distribution, i.e., $\varepsilon \sim N(0, \sigma^2)$. $\mathbf{W}$ and $\mathbf{W}_0$ are the regression parameters for Formula 2, α and β are the temporal and spatial correlation coefficient vectors for $\mathbf{X}_{i,t}$ and $\mathbf{S}_i$ with the same dimension to $\mathbf{X}_{i,t}$ and $\mathbf{S}_i$ respectively. Firstly, we deal with the exponent function in Formula 2 utilizing the logistic discrimination method into softmax function [1]. As $y_{j,t}$ is a index value of the AQI of grid i in time t, we define $c_{i,t}$ as a descriptor of the AQI of grid i in time t i.e., $c_{i,t} \in \mathcal{C} = \{G, M, US, U, VU, H\}$ representing the levels of AQI. Here we randomly choose one class like $\mathcal{C}_k$ as a example class descriptor then we have:

$$\log \frac{P(\Phi(\mathbf{X}_{i,t})|\mathcal{C}_j)}{P(\Phi(\mathbf{X}_{i,t})|\mathcal{C}_k)} = \mathbf{W}_j^T \Phi(\mathbf{X}_{i,t}) + \mathbf{W}_{j0}^0 \qquad For \quad j \neq k \qquad (4)$$

And then we get the formula:

$$\frac{P(\mathcal{C}_j|\Phi(\mathbf{X}_{i,t}))}{P(\mathcal{C}_k|\Phi(\mathbf{X}_{i,t}))} = \exp(\mathbf{W}_j^T \Phi(\mathbf{X}_{i,t}) + \mathbf{W}_{j0}) \qquad (5)$$

where

$$\mathbf{W}_{j0} = \mathbf{W}_{j0}^0 + \log \frac{P(\mathcal{C}_j)}{P(\mathcal{C}_k)} \qquad (6)$$

The vitally important matter is that we should get the $P(\mathcal{C}_j|\Phi(\mathbf{X}_{i,t}))$ for grid i in time point of t based on the observed values $\mathbf{X}_{i,t}$ and $\mathbf{S}_i$. Thus after a series of arithmetical operation, we have the following essential formula:

$$\widehat{P}(\mathcal{C}_j|\Phi(\mathbf{X}_{i,t})) = \frac{\exp(\mathbf{W}_j^T \Phi(\mathbf{X}_{i,t}) + \mathbf{W}_{j0})}{\sum\limits_{k=1}^{K} \exp(\mathbf{W}_k^T \Phi(\mathbf{X}_{i,t}) + \mathbf{W}_{k0})} \qquad (7)$$

where K is the size of $\mathcal{C}$ and in this paper it equals to 5. We compute $\widehat{P}(\mathcal{C}_j|\Phi(\mathbf{X}_{i,t}))$ for all k and take the max value to be the class classification probability of grid i at time t, that is:

$$P(\mathcal{C}|\Phi(\mathbf{X}_{i,t})) = \max_{j=1}^{K} \widehat{P}(\mathcal{C}_j|\Phi(\mathbf{X}_{i,t})) \qquad (8)$$

Then combining Formula 4, 5 and 8 we can easily get $\pi(\mathbf{X}_{i,t})$ in Formula 2. And once we know the parameters $\mathbf{W}$, $\mathbf{W}_0$, α and β, we can construct our air quality inference model and commence AQI inference for all the grids to be inferred.

4.2   Regression Parameters Estimation

Empirically it is quite difficult to directly calculate $\mathbf{W}$ and $\mathbf{W}_0$. Thus we take each $P(\mathcal{C}|\Phi(\mathbf{X_{i,t}}))$ as a sample point value for one time multinomial test i.e., $\mathbf{r}^t|\Phi(\mathbf{X}_{i,t}) \sim \mathbf{Mult}_K(1, P(\mathcal{C}|\Phi(\mathbf{X}_{i,t})))$. Then the sample likelihood is:

$$\mathcal{L}(\{\mathbf{W}_i, \mathbf{W}_{i0}\}_i|\Phi(\mathbf{X}_{i,t})) = \prod_t \prod_i (P(\mathcal{C}|\Phi(\mathbf{X}_{i,t})))^{r_i^t} \tag{9}$$

When having a likelihood function required to be maximized, we customarily transform it to the error function of $\boldsymbol{E} = -\log\mathcal{L}$ regarded as cross-entropy of the likelihood. In our problem we get the cross-entropy as follows:

$$\boldsymbol{E}(\{\mathbf{W}_i, \mathbf{W}_{i0}\}_i|\Phi(\mathbf{X}_{i,t})) = -\sum_t \sum_i r_i^t \log P(\mathcal{C}|\Phi(\mathbf{X}_{i,t})) \tag{10}$$

Utilizing the gradient descent method and we get:

$$\frac{\partial P(\mathcal{C}|\Phi(\mathbf{X}_{i,t}))}{\partial \mathbf{W}} = P(\mathcal{C}|\Phi(\mathbf{X}_{i,t}))(\delta_{ij} - P(\mathcal{C}|\Phi(\mathbf{X}_{i,t}))) \tag{11}$$

where δ_{ij} is $Krenecker$ δ equals 1 if $i = j$ while 0 if $i \neq j$. For $j = 1, \cdots, K$, we have the follow update equations:

$$\Delta\mathbf{W}_j = \eta \sum_t \sum_i \frac{r_i^t}{P(\mathcal{C}|\Phi(\mathbf{X}_{i,t}))} P(\mathcal{C}|\Phi(\mathbf{X}_{i,t}))[\delta_{ij} - P(\mathcal{C}|\Phi(\mathbf{X}_{i,t}))]\Phi(\mathbf{X}_{i,t})$$
$$= \eta \sum_t (r_j^t - P(\mathcal{C}_j|\Phi(\mathbf{X}_{i,t})))\Phi(\mathbf{X}_{i,t}) \tag{12}$$

and

$$\Delta\mathbf{W}_{j0} = \eta \sum_t (r_j^t - P(\mathcal{C}_j|\Phi(\mathbf{X}_{i,t}))) \tag{13}$$

where η is the learning rate for updating $\Delta\mathbf{W}_j$ and $\Delta\mathbf{W}_{j0}$.

4.3   Temporal and Spatial Parameters Estimation

As $\boldsymbol{\alpha}$ is temporal correlation coefficient vectors and $\boldsymbol{\beta}$ is the spatial one, we leverage two different methods for the estimation of $\boldsymbol{\alpha}$ and $\boldsymbol{\beta}$ to enhance the inference precision of our model.

Firstly, $\boldsymbol{\alpha}$ is a temporal factor and influenced by temporal features of $\mathbf{X}_{i,t}$. As a consequence we use the Granger-Causality test [3,16] for estimating $\boldsymbol{\alpha}$ based on monofactor estimation. Let r_i and r_j be two different disjointed region, t be the time point, $\mathcal{C}_i$ and $\mathcal{C}_j$ be the class descriptor of AQI of grid r_i and r_j, and $\mathbf{x}_{i,t}$ be the single temporal feature(i.e., $PM_{2.5}$, PM_{10}, NO_2 and etc.) observed historically. Then the Granger-Causality test for $\boldsymbol{\alpha}$ is as follows:

$$Y(\mathcal{C}_i, r_i, t, \mathbf{x}_{i,t-1}) = \sum_{k=1}^{N} a_k Y(\mathcal{C}_i, r_i, t - k, \mathbf{x}_{i,t-k})$$
$$+ \sum_{k=1}^{N} b_k Y(\mathcal{C}_j, r_j, t - k, \mathbf{x}_{i,t-k}) \tag{14}$$

where N is the sample size of observed temporal feature data, a_k and b_k are test coefficient for Granger-Causality test. Iteratively computing based on Formula 14, we can get every element in $\boldsymbol{\alpha}$.

Then for estimation of $\boldsymbol{\beta}$, we use the Pearson Correlation Coefficient test to get every element of vector $\boldsymbol{\beta}$. That is:

$$R = \frac{\sum_{k=1}^{N} \mathbf{s}_i \mathbf{s}_j - \sum_{k=1}^{N} \mathbf{s}_i \sum_{k=1}^{N} \mathbf{s}_j}{\sqrt{N \sum_{k=1}^{N} \mathbf{s}_i^2 - (\sum_{k=1}^{N} \mathbf{s}_i)^2} \sqrt{N \sum_{k=1}^{N} \mathbf{s}_j^2 - (\sum_{k=1}^{N} \mathbf{s}_j)^2}} \tag{15}$$

where N is the sample size of observed spatial feature data.

4.4   Algorithm Flow

The pseudocode of the integrated parameter learning and model inference process are described in Algorithm 1.

Algorithm 1. Temporal-Spatial Aggregated Urban Air Quality Inference

---

Input: A set of grids $\widehat{G}$ with existing AQI monitor stations; A set of grids G to be inferred; A set of features$(\mathbf{X}_{i,t}, \mathbf{S}_i)$ for grids in $\widehat{G}$ and G based on observed historical data; Sample size of N; A threshold θ controlling rounds.
Output: Give a grid G_i, infer the AQI of G_i: AQI_i.
1: **for** $i = 0$ to N **do**
2:     Use Grange-causility and Formula 14 to estimate $\boldsymbol{\alpha}$;
3:     Use Pearson Correlation test and Formula 15 to estimate $\boldsymbol{\beta}$;
4:     $k = 0$;
5:     **repeat**
6:        Use Formula 12 to estimate $\mathbf{W}$;
7:        Use Formula 13 to estimate $\mathbf{W}_0$;
8:     **until** $k \geq \theta$ or ($\mathbf{W}$ and $\mathbf{W}_0$ converge)
9: **end for**
10: Infer $AQI(G_i)$ using Formula 1;
11: **return** $AQI(G_i)$;

---

5 Experiments

In this section, we perform the evaluation of hourly AQI prediction with our proposed method, and compare the inference results with several state-of-art and ground truth.

5.1 Datasets

We collect three category temporal real data and one category spatial data in Beijing and Suzhou detailed as follows and illustrated in Table 2.

Air quality data: We collect real observed AQI with five kinds of air pollutants which are $PM_{2.5}$, PM_{10}, NO_2, CO and SO_2 from the websites which are introduced in Sect. 3. These data are monitored hourly by ground-based air quality monitor stations in the two cities and updated by websites.

Meteorological data: Meteorological data consists of temperature, humidity, barometric pressure, wind speed, wind direction and weather condition. And we collect them from two public weather forecast websites hourly.

Urban dynamics: We collect traffic flow and human mobility as urban dynamics data. The data comes from two parts. One is taxicab trajectory collected by 27 thousands taxis in Beijing and 5 thousand taxcabs in Suzhou as Suzhou is smaller than Beijing in a large extent. The second one is the moving paths from mobile phones equipped by volunteers and some private cars.

City geographical data: City geographical data comprises POI(Points of Interest), road map and urban morphology datasets. We collect these datasets from Google map, Baidu map and two famous linked spatial data sets named GEoname and DBPedia introduced in Sect. 3.

Table 2. Some Details of Four datasets

Datasets		Beijing	Suzhou
Duration		2015/6/1–2016/3/10	
Air quality	stations	35	8
	instances	241,920	55,296
Meteorology	stations	15	7
	instances	103,680	48,384
Urban dynamics	instances	256,047	64,440
City geography	instances	172,428	32,852

5.2 Baselines and Ground Truth

We compare our method with three well-known predicting model: linear interpolation (LI), classical dispersion model (CD) and decision tree (DT) that are presented in Sect. 2. All of the three aforementioned approaches are widely used to compare the precision of air quality inference in most state-of-art. In addition, we predict the air quality of a station from a grid that deliberately removed for the purpose of comparison between the estimation values and real ones as we can get the real readings of the station from its later reports about air quality.

5.3 Results

Overall Results. 70 % of the historical records are used to training our model and the rest are used to evaluate the performance and we use the historical ground truth from Jan. 1, 2016 to Feb. 9, 2016 to verify the prediction of our approach over the contrast methods. Figure 4 and Table 3 shows the overall performance of our model and the three reference model compared with the ground truth in terms of inference precision, where our inference model has a significant precision compared to other methods and closely approximates the ground truth readings.

Results on One Day Prediction. Figure 5 shows the real time one-day prediction of our model at the next 12th hour from $8:00$ to $20:00$ clock hourly against the ground truth in Beijing and Suzhou at Feb. 10, 2016. The one day hourly prediction result exhibits the eminent capacity in tracing the ground truth curves in daytime inference.

Results on Period Prediction. Figures 6 and 7 illustrate the real time period inference curves in contrast to the ground truth from Feb. 10, 2016 to Mar. 10, 2016 in Beijing and Suzhou. There are 720 ground truth hourly records during the one month period and we make the prediction for each hour air quality index. It shows that our model has significant precise prediction ability in long term prediction and is applicable in different cities.

Table 3. Prediciton details of period from Feb.10,2016 to Mar.10 2016

Ground truth	Prediction in Beijing					Prediction in Suzhou				
	G	M	US	U	VU&H	G	M	US	U	VU&H
G	289	37	9	0	0	183	24	0	0	0
M	9	127	12	2	0	24	220	27	6	0
US	2	8	45	7	2	1	13	150	10	4
U	0	0	4	45	7	0	0	2	24	5
VU&H	0	0	4	14	84	0	0	1	2	12

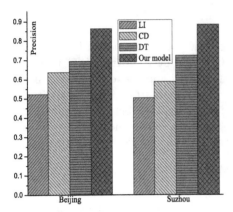

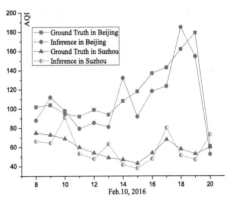

Fig. 4. Overall results of different methods for *AQI* prediction

Fig. 5. 12-h daily prediction curve in Beijing and Suzhou

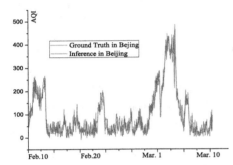

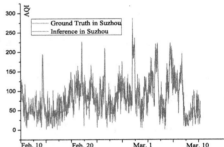

Fig. 6. One-month duration prediction curve in Beijing (Color figure online)

Fig. 7. One-month duration prediction curve in Suzhou (Color figure online)

6   Conclusion

This paper addresses the problem of city-wide air quality inference using a data-driven method with temporal-spatial heterogeneous big data from the combination of the air monitor stations, urban dynamics and city geographical data. In the presented research, we first propose a linear regression model used to infer the future urban air quality. And then we use different methods to analyse all the causalities between spatial-temporal factors and air quality index. Based on the analysis, we assign discriminating weights to different factors to simulate the influence of different issues(air quality factors, meteorological factors, urban dynamics, city geography) on air quality. Finally we make the parameters estimation for our inference model. Extensive contrastive experiments are conducted in two different cities to evaluate the performance of our approach and the results show the significant advantages of our method over a series of state-of-art and commonly used approaches. Future work will focus on the deep learning of the complexity of arch criminal to air pollutants and offering reasonable advices to improve the city-wide air quality from big data perspective.

Acknowledgment. This work was supported by the National Natural Science Foundation of China (No. 61572456, No.61379131) and the Natural Science Foundation of Jiangsu Province of China (No. BK20151241, No. BK20151239).

References

1. Bridle, J.S.: Probabllistic interpretation of feedforward classification network outputs, with relationships to statistical pattern recognition. Neurocomputing. NATO ASI Series, pp. 227–236. Springer, Heidelberg (1990)
2. Burrows, W.R., Benjamin, M., Beauchamp, S., et al.: CART decision-tree statistical analysis and prediction of summer season maximum surface ozone for the Vancouver, Montreal, and Atlantic regions of Canada. J. Appl. Meteorol. **34**(8), 1848–1862 (1995)
3. Granger, C.W.J.Investigating causal relations by econometric models, cross-spectral methods. Econometrica J. Econometric Soc. 424–438 (1969)
4. Hooyberghs, J., Mensink, C., Dumont, G., et al.: A neural network forecast for daily average PM 10 concentrations in Belgium. Atmos. Environ. **39**(18), 3279–3289 (2005)
5. Jiang, Y., Li, K., Tian, L., et al.: MAQS: a personalized mobile sensing system for indoor air quality monitoring. In: Proceedings of the 13th international conference on Ubiquitous computing, pp. 271–280. ACM (2011)
6. Jha, D.K., Sabesan, M., Das, A., et al.: Evaluation of interpolation technique for air quality parameters in Port Blair, India. Univ. J. Environ. Res. Technol. **1**(3), 301–310 (2011)
7. Lu, W.Z., Wang, W.J.: Potential assessment of the support vector machine method in forecasting ambient air pollutant trends. Chemosphere **59**(5), 693–701 (2005)
8. Martin, R.V.: Satellite remote sensing of surface air quality. Atmos. Environ. **42**(34), 7823–7843 (2008)
9. Song, L., Pang, S., Longley, I., et al.: Spatio-temporal PM 2.5 prediction by spatial data aided incremental support vector regression. In: International Joint Conference on Neural Networks (IJCNN), 2014, pp. 623–630. IEEE (2011)
10. Van Donkelaar, A., Martin, R.V., Park, R.J.: Estimating ground-level PM2.5 using aerosol optical depth determined from satellite remote sensing. J. Geophys. Res. Atmos. **111**(D21) (2006)
11. Wong, D.W., Yuan, L., Perlin, S.A.: Comparison of spatial interpolation methods for the estimation of air quality data. J. Exposure Sci. Environ. Epidemiol. **14**(5), 404–415 (2004)
12. Zhang, Y., Bocquet, M., Mallet, V., et al.: Real-time air quality forecasting, part I: history, techniques, and current status. Atmos. Environ. **60**, 632–655 (2012)
13. Zhang, Y., Bocquet, M., Mallet, V., et al.: Real-time air quality forecasting, part II: state of the science, current research needs, and future prospects. Atmos. Environ. **60**, 656–676 (2012)
14. Zheng, Y., Liu, F., Hsieh, H.P.: U-Air: when urban air quality inference meets big data. In: Proceedings of the 19th ACM SIGKDD international conference on Knowledge discovery and data mining, pp. 1436–1444. ACM (2013)

15. Zheng, Y., Yi, X., Li, M., et al.: Forecasting fine-grained air quality based on big data. In: Proceedings of the 21th ACM SIGKDD International Conference on Knowledge Discovery, Data Mining, pp. 2267–2276. ACM (2015)
16. Zhu, J.Y., Sun, C., Li, V.O.K.: Granger-Causality-based air quality estimation with spatio-temporal (ST) heterogeneous big data. In: IEEE Conference on Computer Communications Workshops (INFOCOM WKSHPS), 2015, pp. 612–617. IEEE (2015)

Towards Scheduling to Minimize the Total Penalties of Tardiness of Delivered Data in Maritime CPSs *(Invited Paper)*

Tingting Yang[1,2,3,4(✉)], Hailong Feng[1,2,3,4], Guoqing Zhang[1,2,3,4(✉)], Wenbo Zhang[1,2,3,4], Chengming Yang[1,2,3,4], Ruilong Deng[1,2,3,4], and Zhou Su[1,2,3,4(✉)]

[1] Navigation College, Dalian Maritime University, Dalian, China
yangtingting820523@163.com, zgq_dlmu@163.com, zhousuasagi@gmail.com
[2] School of Naval Architecture, Ocean and Civil Engineering, Shanghai Jiao Tong University, Shanghai, China
[3] Department of Electrical and Computer Engineering, University of Alberta, Edmonton, Canada
[4] School of Mechatronic Engineering and Automation, Shanghai University, Shanghai, China

Abstract. This paper focused on addressing the issue of uploading surveillance videos that vessels generate from the origin port to destination port in maritime Cyber Physical Systems (CPSs). During the period of sailing, the videos should be delivered to the infostations offshore to connect to the Internet. Deadlines are defined respectively to restrict the time domain to finally upload the video packets effectively. Time-capacity mapping method is applied to confront the intermittent infostations scenario. An effective mathematic job-machine scheduling (JMS) problem is represented to minimize the total penalties of tardiness of delivered data considering tardiness and weights of jobs, within each job is expressed with a release time, a deadline, a processing time, and a weight. We develop an offline scheduling algorithm depending on a genetic optimization process comprised with a novel chromosome representation, a heuristic initialization procedure as well as a modified crossover and mutation process. Simulation results demonstrate the effectiveness of the proposed algorithm to solve the (JMS) in maritime CPSs.

Keywords: Job-machine scheduling · Genetic algorithm · Maritime CPSs

1 Introduction

The huge demands of wireless service at sea, brings the strongly requirement to realize broadband communication in maritime scenario. Thus bundles of data with large capacity, such as supervisory controlling videos for vessels especially the important spaces could be uploaded with lower cost, comparing with satellite

© Springer International Publishing Switzerland 2016
Q. Yang et al. (Eds.): WASA 2016, LNCS 9798, pp. 427–439, 2016.
DOI: 10.1007/978-3-319-42836-9_38

communications. The state-of-the-art work on maritime wideband network structures can be summarized as follows. Zhou *et al.* [1] introduced cognitive radio into maritime mesh/ad hoc networks. Worldwide Interoperability for Microwave Access (WiMAX) to carry out wireless-broadband-access for Seaport (WISE-PORT) project in Singapore [2]. The alternative scheme utilized store-carry-and-forward data packet delivery in delay tolerant networks (DTNs) [3] is proposed to meet the intermittent end-to-end path, which is formed by the characteristics of channel on the sea. Our previous work as well as Lin *et al.* [4] is based on the developed the WiMAX-based mesh technology with DTN characteristics. In this paper, the Cyber Physical Systems (CPSs), an emerging research area which incorporate communication, computing and control technology [5], are introduced in maritime scenario to collect data such as monitoring of vessel, compute and deliver it to the maritime authority on land. By analyzing the big data of surveillance videos, ship owners or the other relative personnel on land could intelligently control the vessel navigation, cargo loading and discharging, etc. Therefore, maritime CPSs could potentially provide much more smart, efficient and robust communication and control for maritime society. In our scenario, data delivery can be achieved via infostations shore-side, and a LTE/store-carry-and-forward interworking maritime CPSs are proposed to achieve marine intelligent transportation systems.

In this paper, we only focus on the video data delivery scheduling issue. Videos are partitioned into packets, with respective release time, deadline and weight. The data packets delivered after the deadline is not tolerant enough. We define the tardiness of delivered data with penalty, considering tardiness duration and weights of jobs. The goal of this paper is to minimize the total penalties of tardiness of delivered data. In the literature, although not in maritime scenarios, the land-based vehicle-assisted data delivery has been broadly investigated [6], and the related literatures on land-based network contribute a solid foundation for our work [7–11]. In this paper, time-capacity mapping is applied to convert the initial intermittent connectivity due to intermittent infostations deployment, to a single machine scheduling issue. An offline scheduling algorithm is proposed depending on a genetic optimization process comprised with a novel chromosome representation, a heuristic initialization procedure as well as a modified crossover and mutation process.

The remainder of this paper is organized as follows. System model is given in Sect. 2 and problem formulation is presented in Sect. 3. An offline scheduling algorithm is proposed depending on a genetic optimization process in Sect. 4. In Sect. 5, simulation results are showed to demonstrate the performance of our approach. We conclude this paper in Sect. 6. As many symbols are used in this paper, some important notation definitions are tabulated in Table 1.

2   System Model

This section presents the details of the system model. In this work, we first develop a resource allocation and scheduling problem by considering the spread

Table 1. Notations and definitions.

Symbol	Definition
i, j	The order or index
M_k	The number of vessel (machine)
J_i	The number of Job (operation)
$r_j(d_j)(p_j)(b_j)(e_j)$	The release time(deadline)(processing time)(beginning time)(ending time)of video packet j proceeded on vessel k
A_i	The arrival time of order
D_i	The due date of order, (pre-given)
CP_i	The completion time of order
TD_i	The tardiness of order, $TD_i = \max(0, CP_i - D_i)$
α_i	The weight of tardiness penalty for order, (pre-given)
λ_i	The states if tardiness TD_i of order is greater than 0, $\lambda_i = 1$, else $\lambda_i = 0$
γ_i	The weight of machine M_k processing operation, between 0 and 1.
u	Represent a population size
PPN and QTY	Represent the population and a maximum quantity
CHR_i	An integer string chromosome
PTY	The probability that a machine to process relevant packets
Z	The objective function

of intermittent network connections due to the intermittent infostations shoreside. Our goal is to ensure the quality of video as much as possible. Due to ship routes are relatively stable, the global information in terms of time indices such as release time and deadline, as well as the schedules of vessels. We consider the single vessel scenario, that a vessel generates monitoring videos periodically when sailing from origin port to destination. These videos could be uploaded to content server of administrative agencies by infostations deployed along route line. Network topology is shown in Fig. 1.

A time-capacity mapping technique is used to transform the original scenario with intermittent network connectivity into a virtually continuous scenario [12]. We map the time indices into virtually cumulative capacity values, as shown in Fig. 1. The period $[T_h^o, T_{h+1}^i]$ is defined as the idle period, during which a vessel is not within the coverage of any infostation. For example, t_3 and t_4 moments are in an idle period during which no data is transmitted and thus, corresponding to the same cumulative capacity c_4. On the other hand, t_1 and t_2 are in the coverage of infostations, and are subsequently related to two different cumulative capacity values c_2 and c_3, respectively.

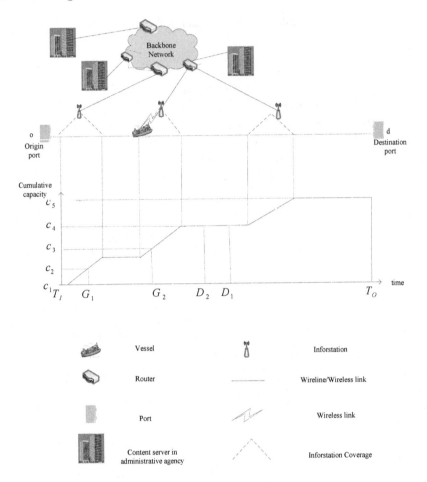

Fig. 1. An illustration of the network topology.

The time-capacity mapping function $f(t) : [T_I, T_o] \rightarrow [0, 1, \cdots \sum_{h=1}^{H} \sum_{k=1}^{K} A_{h,k}]$ is given by

$$f(t) = \begin{cases} \sum_{m=1}^{(t-T_{h_t}^i)/T_F} A_{h_t,m} + \sum_{l=1}^{h_t-1} \sum_{m=1}^{K_l} A_{l,m}, \\ \quad \text{if } h_t \geq 1 \text{ and } T_{h_t}^i \leq t \leq T_{h_t}^o \\ \sum_{l=1}^{h_t} \sum_{m=1}^{K_l} A_{l,m}, \quad \text{otherwise} \end{cases} \tag{1}$$

where $h_t = \arg\max_h \{T_h^i \leq t\}$, if $T_{h_t}^i \leq t \leq T_{h_t}^o$, and $h_t = 0$ otherwise. Based on the time-capacity mapping, the resource allocation issue could be converted from time based scheduling to capacity based scheduling over a continuous horizon [12], such that the job-machine scheduling theory can be applied to solve the resource allocation problem at a low computational complexity.

3   Problem Formulation

With the goal of achieving better video quality, i.e., minimizing the total penalties of tardiness of delivered data considering tardiness and weights of jobs. The offline problem is considered, on the precise of knowing all the global information. A network centralized controller is employed, with the ability to schedule resource allocation problem. In this section, we develop an offline scheduling algorithm depending on a genetic optimization process comprised with a novel chromosome representation, a heuristic initialization procedure as well as a modified crossover and mutation process. These video packets generated by the vessels are just like the genes. These genes are divided in a chromosome, therefore, as the winner to others, these genes have a strong fitness and the character will deliver to next generation. The operation of the genes is the same as the procedure of uploading the videos to ensure the high quality. We take into account of this preemption situation that when one video packet is uploaded, while the other video need to be uploaded immediately. Then the latter video could preempt the band sources of the former, and the former should to stop the operation. When the latter is finished uploading, the former continues the operation.

Therefore, the previous problem will be converted into a new method to solve based on the mathematic method GA. An effective mathematic job-machine scheduling (JMS) problem is represented to minimize the total penalties of tardiness of delivered data considering tardiness and weights of jobs, within each job is expressed with a release time, a deadline, a processing time, and a weight. In the GA, the decision variables in the problem space are represented as individuals of the spatial genetic by the means of coding, it is a genotype data string structure. At the same time, the objective function value will be converted into fitness value, it is used to evaluate the merits of the individual, and as the basis of genetic operations.

3.1   Assumptions

In this work, the model satisfies the following assumptions:

1. Once a job begins, it will stop until finished.
2. Without the distraction of other external factors.
3. Genetic space is empty initially, the algorithm works on the basis of the space.

3.2   Constrains

The actual video packet has many special characteristics and should be subject to some constraints. We describe the characteristics and constraints mathematically in the following context.

1. *Arrival time constrains.* The job can not be started until the arrival of the job.

$$A_i \leq b_i \tag{2}$$

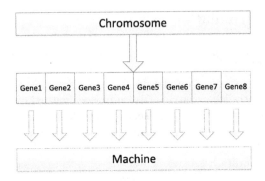

Fig. 2. Sample of the chromosome representation.

2. *Allocation constrains.*state if the packets is uploaded to the machine.

$$x_{jb_j} = \begin{cases} 1, & \text{if job } j \text{ is scheduled at interval } [b_j, b_j + p_j] \\ 0, & \text{otherwise.} \end{cases}$$

3. *Precedence constrains.* The processing time require after the starting time and according to the actual requirement to adjust.
4. *Objective function.* According to the different packets demands, different jobs can adjust on the basis of the above constrains. Every packet has a deadline which is regard as the standards of a job. If the job is accomplished later than the deadline, penalty α_i for each time unit of the delay is demanded. Each job has a starting time and generates appropriate assignment, which is equivalent to minimize the total penalties of tardiness of delivered data considering tardiness and weights of jobs.
   The objective function can be expressed mathematically as follows:

$$\min Z = \sum_{i=1}^{p} (\alpha_i \cdot (CP_i - d_i) \cdot \lambda_i) \tag{3}$$

4   Solution

The genetic algorithm (GA) was first introduced by Holland in 1975 [13]. It is a stochastic heuristics, which encompass semi-random search method whose mechanism is based on the simplifications of evolutionary processes observed in nature. GAs start with an initial population of chromosomes (also called individuals) representing different possible solutions to a problem. A chromosome consists of some genes. GAs work iteratively, each single iteration is called a generation. At each generation, the fitness of each chromosome is evaluated, which is decided by the fitness function, and the chromosome is stochastically selected for the next generation based on its fitness. New chromosomes, called offspring (also called children), are produced by two genetic operators, crossover and mutation. The children are supposed to inherit the excellent genes from their parents, so that the average quality of solutions is better than that in the previous generations. This evolution process is repeated until some termination criteria are met [14]. The following sub-sections describe in detail how the GA is developed to solve the above Job-Machine problem in our scenario.

4.1   Representation

Due to the genetic algorithm (GA) can not deal with the date of the solution space directly, so they must be coded as the spatial genetic genotype data string structure. In constructing the GA, the first thing to solve is to define an appropriate genetic representation (coding). An appropriate representation is the key to all the subsequent steps of the GA. In this paper, we can develop a special chromosome representation. A vessel generates videos during the time sailing from origin port to the destination, and each video can be divided into packets. We define the video packets as the genes. Then each chromosome is a sequence of genes whose length is equal to the capacity of the machine to which packet can be processed. In a chromosome, the weight of each gene contributes the quality of packets which the corresponding machine processes. Fig. 2 presents an example of this representation which considers a problem with 8 packets to be assigned to the appropriate machine.

Initialization. The GA operates on the basis of a population of chromosomes. Due to the Genetic algorithm (GA) group operations require, therefore we must prepare a certain number of initial solution of the initial group for genetic operations. The initial population of each individual is generated by random method. The performance of the GA scheme is corresponding to a random start is better than from the pre-selected starting population. In this study each chromosome is initialized by assigning each packet randomly, with the number of packets 1 to n, to the machine which can deal with it. The initialization process can be described as follows:

- Step 1. Initialize parameters: index $i = 1$, u represent a population size, and the population $PPN = \{\emptyset\}$ and a maximum quantity QTY of packets which the machine can process.
- Step 2. Randomly generate an integer string chromosome CHR_i, $PPN = PPN \cup CHR_i$.
- Step 3. Set $i = i + 1$, If $i > u$, **STOP**, else go to Step 2.

The process for randomly generating a chromosome is detailed as follows:

- Step 1. Set index $j = 1$. For the machine, let $PTY = 1$, where $PTY = 1$ represents the probability that a machine is selected to process relevant packets.
- Step 2. To select the machine which can process packet j.
- Step 3. The machine with greater PTY will be selected with a greater probability to process this operation preferentially.

- Step 4. Assign operation j to selected machines. At the same time, for the selected machine, let $PTY = PTY - \frac{1}{QTY}$.
- Step 5. Set $j = j + 1$. If $j > n$, **STOP**, else go to Step 2.

4.2 Fitness and Selection

Genetic algorithm (GA) in the search process generally do not need other external information, only use fitness value to evaluate the merits of the individual or solution, and as the basis of genetic operation later. Fitness function is defined as the fitness of each chromosome so as to determine which will reproduce and survive into the next generation. It is relevant to the objective function to be optimized. Given a particular chromosome, the value of fitness function, fitness, represents its probability to survive. The greater the fitness of a chromosome is, the greater the probability to survive. In this study, the fitness function fitness is defined as the function of the objective function, which is expressed as follows:

$$fitness = \frac{1}{Z+1} = \frac{1}{\sum\limits_{i=1}^{p} (\alpha_i \cdot (CP_i - d_i) \cdot \lambda_i) + 1} \tag{4}$$

The selection in GAs, based on the natural evolution law of survival of the fittest, is the process in which chromosomes are selected for the next generation in terms of their fitness. Many selection schemes have been put forward. The tournament selection is usually utilized because it is easy to implement and provides appropriate solutions. In this study, this scheme is used and its procedure can be presented as follows:

- Step 1. Set a tournament size s.
- Step 2. Generate a random sequence of the chromosomes in the current population.
- Step 3. Compare the fitness value of the chromosomes listed in the permutation, and select to copy the best one into the next generation. Abandon the strings compared.
- Step 4. If the permutation is disappear, generate another permutation.
- Step 5. Repeat Steps 3 and 4 until no longer need to select the next generation.

The scheme can balance the population diversity and selective pressure by adjusting the tournament size s. The more value of s is large, the more the selective pressure increases while decreasing the population diversity.

4.3 Genetic Operators

Genetic operators are used to combine existing solutions with others methods and ensure the diversity. The former can be carried out by crossover, and the latter can be put into effect by mutation. The detail descriptions of the two operators are as follows.

Crossover. The crossover operation is the main genetic operators in genetic algorithm. Simple crossover can be divided into two steps: first randomly matched for individuals in the population; Second, in matching the individual random set intersections, matching the individual exchange part information. Crossover process used for reproduction of a pair of children from a parent chromosomes cross-validation method. A large number of crossover operators have been proposed. Uniform-order crossover is commonly utilized because it has the advantage of preserving the position of some genes and the relative ordering of the rest. In this study, a modified crossover operator similar to the uniform-order crossover is developed and described in detail.

- Step 1. Randomize generate a bit string with same length as the chromosomes.
- Step 2. Fill in some of the positions in Child 1 by copying the genes from Parent 1 wherever the bit string contains 1. (Now in Child 1, the positions are filled in wherever the bit string contains 1 and positions are left blank wherever the bit string contains 0.)
- Step 3. Make a list of the genes from Parent 1 associated with 0 in the bit string.
- Step 4. Permute the list of genes so that they follow the same order of genes appeared in Parent 2. For the gene with two or more operations, the first operation in Parent 1 is used for permuting the positions of genes of Child 1 following the order of genes of Parent 2. If the number of a gene in the list is more than the number of corresponding genes with same operations in Parent 2, then the sequence of genes in Parent 2 will be duplicated and append to its end.
- Step 5. Fill these permuted genes into the blank positions in Child 1 in the order generated in Step 4.
- Step 6. Child 2 is produced using a similar process as above.

The crossover operation is a stochastic process with a probability of crossover. The probability of a typical crossover operator is between 0.6 and 1.0. For the Job-Machine problem in this study, each operation must be processed on the machine. Genes in the chromosome of the machine, therefore, should be independent and the crossover and mutation operations can only be done among genes with the machine. Therefore, for the genes of the machine, we perform the genetic operation respectively. Figure 3 shows an example of the modified uniform-order crossover operator considering situation of machines.

Mutation. Mutation operation is processed by the bitwise, and mutation operation is also carried out randomly. In general, the mutation probability is small. Mutation genetic operation is very delicate, it needs use with crossover operation, the purpose is to excavate the diversity of the individuals in the group, to overcome the disadvantage of limited to local solution. The mutation operation is critical to the success of the GA since it diversifies the search directions and avoids convergence to local optima conditions. This is a random variation of operation, which is used to convert a chromosome gene. Only some of the

Fig. 3. An example of the modified uniform-order crossover operator considering situation of machines.

children attend the mutation process. The size of this part composed of mutation probability(the typical value is between 0.0015 and 0.03). Many mutation operators have been put forward. In this study, a modified mutation operation similar to inversion mutation operator is developed. The inverse operation first randomly choose between the two genes with a predetermined chromosome mutation probability. According to a appropriate probability (between 0.6 and 1), the gene with two or more operations will then be divided and the separated operations is recombined with its proximate gene.

4.4   Termination Criterion

The GA is controlled by a specified number of children and by using a diversity measure to prevent the algorithm. The diversity of the GA is defined as all the standard deviation of the population fitness value of chromosome in a particular generation. If the two termination condition is met, the GA mechanism shall be terminated.

5   Simulation Results

In order to investigate the effectiveness of the proposed algorithm, the experiment was conducted based on the maritime video packets data transmission from origin port to the destination.

Mode: Only one packet order is processed in the job schedule at any instance of time. Under this mode, if a new packet (packet j) is required to be processed immediately, the current packet (packet i) will be preempted and the new packet

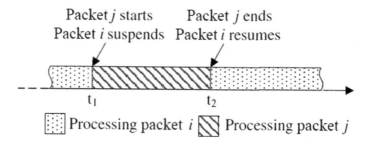

Fig. 4. An illumination of preemption mode of scheduling.

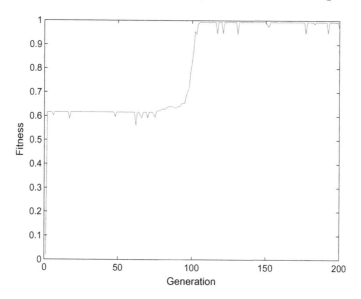

Fig. 5. The evolutionary track of the fitness over generations.

is processed. After the new packet is completed, the current packet is resumed. The preemption mode of video packets is illuminated in Fig. 4.

The genetic optimized results in this study are obtained on the basis of the following setting:

Population size = 20;

Maximum number of generation = 200;

Crossover probability = 0.6;

Mutation probability = 0.01.

According to the results generates from the experiments, the efficiency of the job machine problem could be different with different parameters. In this study, the objective function value is converted into fitness value, it is used to evaluate the merits of the individual, and as the basis of genetic operations. According to the procedure, if we change the deadline or the completion time of the packet, the figure will change into irregular and have no convergence. And the penalty of tardiness of the scheduling result is equal or very close to zero, which makes it become more effective after using this algorithm, in the feasible processes of the experiment, the evolutionary track of the fitness over generations are shown in Fig. 5. From Fig. 5 we find the effectiveness of our proposed GA-based scheduling algorithm.

6   Conclusion

In this paper, an innovative paradigm maritime CPSs is developed. An effective mathematic JMS issue is described to minimize the total penalties of tardiness of delivered data considering tardiness and weights of jobs. And an offline scheduling algorithm based on GA is proposed to optimize the scheduling process. Simulation results demonstrate the effectiveness of the proposed algorithm to solve the JMS issue in maritime CPSs. For future work, we plan to research the modified GA to achieve more convergence rate.

Acknowledgments. This work was supported in part by China Postdoctoral Science Foundation under Grant 2013M530900, Special Financial Grant from the China Postdoctoral Science Foundation under Grant 2015T80238, Natural Science Foundation of China under Grant 61401057, Science and technology research program of Liaoning under Grant L2014213, Dalian science and technology project under Grant 2015A11GX018, NSERC, Canada, Research Funds for the Central Universities 3132016007, China Postdoctoral International Academic Exchange Fund, and also supported by Scientific Research Foundation for the Returned Overseas Chinese Scholars from Ministry of Human Resources and Social Security.

References

1. Zhou, M.T., Harada, H.: Cognitive maritime wireless mesh/ad hoc networks. J. Network Comput Appl. **35**(2), 518–526 (2012)
2. Cellular-news, Maritime WiMAX Network Launched in Singapore (2008). http://www.cellular-news.com/story/29749.php
3. Fall, K.: A delay-tolerant network architecture for challenged internets. In: ACM Conference on Applications, Technologies, Architectures and Protocols for Computer Communications (2003)
4. Lin, H.M., Ge, Y., Pang, A.C., Pathmasuntharam, J.S.: Performance study on delay tolerant networks in maritime communication environments. In: IEEE OCEANS (2010)
5. Kim, K.D., Kumar, P.R.: Cyber-physical systems: a perspective at the centennial. In: IEEE Special Centennial Issue (2012)
6. Cheng, N., Lu, N., Zhang, N., Mark, J.W., Shen, X.: Vehicle-assisted data delivery for smart grid: an optimal stopping approach. In: IEEE ICC (2013)
7. Liu, S., Zhu, H., Du, R., Chen, C., Guan, X.: Location privacy preserving dynamic spectrum auction in cognitive radio network. In: IEEE ICDCS (2013)

8. Ren, J., Zhang, Y., Zhang, N., Zhang, D., Shen, X.: Dynamic channel access to improve energy efficiency in cognitive radio sensor networks. IEEE Trans. Wirel. Commun. **15**(5), 3143–3156 (2016). doi:10.1109/TWC.2016.2517618

9. Deng, R., Zhang, Y., He, S., Chen, J., Shen, X.: Maximizing network utility of rechargeable sensor networks with spatiotemporally-coupled constraints. IEEE J. Sel. Areas Commun. **34**(5), 1307–1319 (2016)

10. Su, Z., Xu, Q., Qi, Q.: Big data in mobile social networks: A QoE oriented framework. IEEE Network **30**(1), 2–57 (2016)

11. Su, Z., Xu, Q., Zhu, H., Wang, Y.: A novel design for content delivery over software defined mobile social networks. IEEE Network **29**(4), 62–67 (2015)

12. Liang, H., Zhuang, W.: Efficient on-demand data service delivery to high-speed trains in cellular/infostation integrated networks. IEEE J. Sel. Areas Commun. **30**(4), 780–791 (2012)

13. Holland, J.H.: Adaptation in Natural and Artificial Systems. University of Michigan Press, Michigan (1975)

14. Guo, Z.X., Wong, W.K., Leung, S.Y.S., Fan, J.T., Chan, S.F.: Mathematical model and genetic optimization for the job shop scheduling problem in a mixed-and multi-product assembly environment: A case study based on the apparel industry. Comput. Indus. Eng. **50**, 202–219 (2006)

Spectrum-Aware Clustering with Proactive Handoff for Distributed Cognitive Radio Ad Hoc Networks

Huyin Zhang[✉], Ning Xu, Fang Xu, and Zhiyong Wang

Department of Computer, Wuhan University, Wuhan, Hubei, China
{zhy2536,davidxn,xf2012,zywang_whu}@whu.edu.cn

Abstract. To improve the transmission performance, cluster structure is constructed for large scale cognitive radio ad hoc networks (CRAHNs). However, dynamic spectrum access (DSA) and blind information environment in CRAHN make the clustering design extremely challenging. To solve this problem, we propose a novel clustering algorithm to construct and maintain the cluster structure. The proposed spectrum-aware clustering algorithm is designed to maximize common channels inside a cluster and to minimize common channels between adjacent clusters. To maintain the cluster architecture, we propose a proactive channel handoff scheme to reduce the interference with PUs. The simulation results show that the constructed clusters have more intra-cluster common channels and less inter-cluster common channels. And the proposed handoff scheme can adjust to the changing PU activities.

Keywords: Cognitive Ad Hoc network · Clustering · Handoff

1 Introduction

In recent years, as the number of wireless devices is growing rapidly, the ISM band is heavily overloaded while a lot of spectrum bands were not efficiently used [1]. Cognitive radio technology is an efficient approach to improve the spectrum efficiency and overcome the shortage of spectrum resource [2]. Secondary Users (SUs) are network nodes equipped with cognitive radios. CRAHN (Cognitive Radio Ad hoc Network) is proposed and has become a hot research topic due to the high flexibility and scalability [1,2].

For Ad Hoc networks, clustering technique is an effective way to improve the efficiency of distributed network, especially in large scale scenario. However, in CRAHNs, SUs have different available channels, thus there is probably no global CCC among SUs. For example, as shown in Fig. 1, five active $PU_1 - PU_5$ and ten SUs $SU_1 - SU_{10}$ are evenly deployed in the network. There are totally 5 licensed channels occupied by the PUs. We can see that there is no CCC available for all the SUs. On the other hand, even if there is a global common channel, SUs have no way to find such channel due to the absence of priori knowledge about the network. Therefore, the clustering design for CRAHNs must not rely on a CCC.

© Springer International Publishing Switzerland 2016
Q. Yang et al. (Eds.): WASA 2016, LNCS 9798, pp. 440–451, 2016.
DOI: 10.1007/978-3-319-42836-9_39

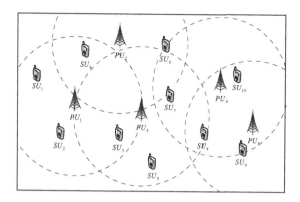

Fig. 1. A CRAHN topology 5 PUs and 10 SUs. There are 5 channels occupied by $PU_1 - PU_5$ respectively.

To maximize the throughput and connectivity inside a cluster, the clustering algorithm should build a structure with more common channels in each clusters. On the other hand, to minimize the interference between adjacent clusters, the clustering method should also minimize the inter-cluster common channels.

Additionally, during the transmission, SUs have to maintain their cluster structure. As the wireless environment is dynamically changing, a PU reappearance may easily interrupt or destroy a cluster. This leads to a worse performance in terms of delay and throughput. Therefore, a cluster maintenance mechanism should be designed to make clusters adapt to the PU activities.

To build a robust cluster structure, we propose a spectrum-aware clustering algorithm. To get rid of the dependence on CCC, we discover the neighbors by rendezvous [3,8,11]. We model the local topology as a simple weighted graph, whose links are weighted by SU similarities. Then, we formulate the clustering design as a graph cut problem. Since it is NP-hard, however, we propose a heuristic greedy algorithm to approximate the optimal solution. To improve the network performance, the clustering algorithm is designed to maximize the intra-cluster common channels and minimizes the inter-cluster common channels. After clustering, we propose a proactive control channel handoff scheme to protect the clusters from frequently reclustering caused by PU activities.

The rest of this paper is organized as follows: The network model is described in Sect. 3. Section 4 presents the spectrum-aware clustering algorithm. Section 5 presents a proactive control channel handoff scheme for cluster maintenance. The performance evaluation is presented in Sect. 6. We summarize our paper in Sect. 7.

2   Related Works

To construct the cluster structure, CogMesh [4] broadcasts beacons on all channels to exchange control information. The first broadcasting SU in the neighborhood will become the cluster head. The random feature cannot guarantee an optimal and stable cluster architecture. To improve CogMesh, Chen et al. [5] optimize the clusters by using minimum dominating set algorithm. However, this method is not spectrum-aware and not suitable for CRAHNs. Zhao et al. [12] propose a neighbor oriented grouping strategy, which maximizes network connectivity. Because of the rendezvous, this method may cause a long delay. Dai et al. [6] adopt a receiver oriented DSA scheme to exchange control information. Clustering is accomplished by LEACH, where reliability and throughput are maximized. However, this method must utilize the geographical information which limits the application scenarios. Lazos et al. formulate the clustering design as a maximum edge biclique problem which is an NP-complete problem [7]. A distributed cluster agreement algorithm called Spectrum-Opportunity Clustering (SOC) is proposed to solve this problem. It makes a tradeoff between coverage and overhead of each cluster. The proposed greedy solution may lead to high overhead and delay. Note that, these methods don't take inter-cluster interference into consideration, which may lead to a low throughput and a long delay.

In this paper, a spectrum-aware clustering scheme is proposed to maximize the intra-cluster channels and to minimize the inter-cluster channels. We also present a proactive handoff scheme, thus the cluster structure is more robust to the PU activities.

3   System Model

There are M non-overlapping channels denoted by $C = \{1, 2, ..., M\}$, where $1, 2, ..., M$ are indexes of the global channels. For simplicity, we ignore the cognitive radio errors. There are K PUs and some SUs evenly distributed in a square area. Both PUs and SUs are running in a time slotted wireless system. All SUs are equipped with two transceivers, one for data transmission and the other for channel monitoring. Additionally, CSMA/CS based protocol is installed in each SU.

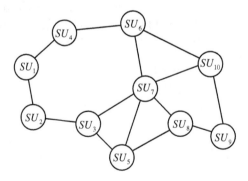

Fig. 2. The origin graph corresponding to the topology in Fig. 1.

We model the CRAHN as a simple connected undirected graph $G(V, E)$, where V denotes the SUs and E denotes the possible communication links between SUs. In this model, an edge exists between two SUs if they can directly communicate with each other. For example, the network topology of Fig. 1 is modeled by a graph in Fig. 2. Given any SU, say SU_i, its one-hop neighborhood is denoted by N_i and its available channel set is denoted by $c_i = (c_i^1, c_i^2, ..., c_i^M)$, where $c_i^j \in \{0, 1\}$ indicates whether the j-th channel is available(1) or not(0).

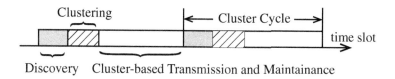

Fig. 3. Cluster cycles for cluster-based CRAHNs.

The network process is made up of multiple cluster cycles. In each cluster cycle, there are three parts: the neighbor discovery period, the clustering period, the transmission and maintenance period, as shown in Fig. 3. First, SUs run discovery protocol to find their one-hop neighbors. Then, a distributed clustering algorithm is adopted to subdivide the network into clusters. After this, each cluster selects their own cluster head and gateways for transmission. During the transmission period, the cluster head maintains the cluster structure and avoids PU interruptions. Lastly, the network enters the next cluster cycle when the transmission period terminates.

4   Spectrum-Aware Clustering

In this section, we propose a novel distributed clustering algorithm to achieve these goals. First of all, we define a hybrid metric to measure the similarity between SUs, where both channel similarity and relative position are taken into consideration. Then, based on the similarity metric, we model the SU local topology as a simple weighted graph and the clustering process is formulated as a graph cut problem. Then, we proposed a greedy heuristic algorithm to obtain a clustering result which compromises between maximum intra-cluster channels and minimum inter-cluster channels.

4.1   Definition of Channel Similarity

Before address the clustering problem, we give the definition of the SU similarity s_{ij} as follow,

$$s_{ij} = \frac{RCC + RPS}{2}. \tag{1}$$

This metric is made up of two components: RCC (ratio of common channels) and RCC (ratio of common channels).

RCC measures the degree of overlap between SUs' channel availabilities. It is computed by

$$RCC_{ij} = \frac{c_i^T c_j}{M}, \tag{2}$$

where c_i, c_j are available channel vectors of SU_i, SU_j respectively, and M is the total number of channels in the network. Their inner product presents the number of common channels.

RPS presents the relative position between two SUs. Assume the wireless radio environment is a free space model, then we have $RSSI_{ij} = RSSI_0 - 10\alpha \lg(d)$, where α is the propagation path loss exponent (free space has $\alpha = 2$ for reference) and $RSSI_0$ is the received signal strength at one meter of distance from SU_i. d is the distance in meters from SU_j to SU_i. Hence, we have $d = 10^{\frac{RSSI_0 - RSSI_{ij}}{10\alpha}}$. After normalization, the relative position similarity is computed by Eq. 3, where d_m is the maximum range of SU_i. Note that a bigger RPS indicates a closer SU.

$$RPS_{ij} = 1 - \frac{d}{d_m}, \tag{3}$$

4.2   Graph Cut Based Clustering

Given a SU, say SU_i, we first construct a weighted graph to represent the local topology of SU_i. The graph is denoted by $G(V, E)$, where V is SU_i's neighbor set and E is data link set. The weight of link between SU_j and SU_k is set to the similarity s_{jk} computed by Eq. 1.

Then, the clustering process for SU_i is to find its cluster memberships or to cut off the link if a SU is not in the same cluster. Thus, we formulate the clustering as a graph cut problem, where the graph cut of G is $(X, \bar{X})$ and $X \subseteq V$ are SUs in the same cluster with SU_i, i.e., the clustering result, while $\bar{X}$ are removed SUs.

Then, the cut cost of cluster X is defined by

$$cut(X) = \sum_{i \in X, j \in \bar{X}} s_{ij}. \tag{4}$$

And the utility of cluster X is defined by

$$u(X) = \sum_{i,j \in X} s_{ij}, \tag{5}$$

where c_i is the channel availability vector of SU_i. A higher cluster utility means a better cluster.

Since the clustering goal is to maximize the intra-cluster similarity and to minimize inter-cluster similarity, the graph cut $(X, \bar{X})$ should minimize

---

Algorithm 1. Spectrum-aware Clustering Algorithm

1: **INPUT**: $G(V, E)$
2: **OUTPUT**: X
3: Compute a starting graph cut X by normalized cut
4: $count = 0$
5: **while** $count <$ MAX_COUNT **do**
6:    **for** each $SU_k \in V$ **do**
7:       **if** $SU_k \in X$ **then**
8:          Compute $\Delta_k = \frac{cut(X)}{u(X)} - \frac{cut(X-\{k\})}{u(X-\{k\})}$
9:       **else**
10:         Compute $\Delta_k = \frac{cut(X)}{u(X)} - \frac{cut(X+\{k\})}{u(X+\{k\})}$
11:      **end if**
12:   **end for**
13:   $\Delta_m = \max\{\Delta_k | SU_k \in V\}$
14:   **if** $\Delta_m < 0$ **then**
15:      **break** //no positive cost reduction.
16:   **else**
17:      **if** $SU_k \in X$ **then**
18:         Remove SU_m from X
19:      **else**
20:         Insert SU_m into X
21:      **end if**
22:   **end if**
23:   $count = count + 1$
24: **end while**
25: **return** X

$cut(X, \bar{X})$ and maximize $u(X)$. Therefore, we can interpret the graph cut as the following optimization problem

$$
\begin{aligned}
\text{minimize } & cut(X)/u(X) \\
\text{subject to } & X \subseteq V
\end{aligned}, \tag{6}
$$

where φ is the tradeoff factor. Unfortunately, this combination optimization problem is NP-hard, which cannot be solved in polynomial time. Therefore, we propose a greedy heuristic Algorithm 1 to approximate the optimal solution.

At the beginning of the clustering, SU_i compute a initial cluster X_i by normalized cut algorithm [9,10]. Note that the normalized cut, which minimizes $\frac{cut(X)}{u(X)} + \frac{cut(X)}{u(\bar{X})}$, gives a good start point to iteratively minimize $\frac{cut(X)}{u(X)}$.

Then, based on this starting point, SU_i iteratively change the cluster by removing or inserting a SU, and then SU_i checks if the objective cost is reduced. Specifically, if SU_k is in X_i, then removing it out of X_i reduces the objective cost by

$$
\Delta_k = \frac{cut(X)}{u(X)} - \frac{cut(X - \{k\})}{u(X - \{k\})} \tag{7}
$$

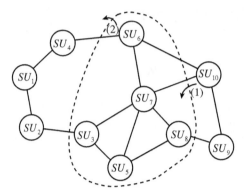

Fig. 4. An example of the proposed clustering algorithm.

If SU_k is out of X_i, then inserting it into X_i reduces the objective by

$$\Delta_k = \frac{cut(X)}{u(X)} - \frac{cut(X + \{k\})}{u(X + \{k\})} \tag{8}$$

In each loop, SU_i computes all the reductions and selects the SU_m with the maximum reduction. If the maximum reduction is greater than 0, then SU_i changes SU_m's cluster and goes on to the next iteration.

For example, the weighted graph in Fig. 4 is constructed by SU_7. SUs in the dashed circle are SU_7's initial cluster memberships generated by spectral clustering algorithm. SU_7 inserts SU_{10} into the cluster in the first loop, and removes SU_6 in the second loop.

If the maximum reduction is less than 0, which indicates that no reduction can be achieved, then SU_i breaks the loop and returns the cluster result X_i. Note that, MAX_COUNT is a predefined number to make sure that the clustering process terminates in finite iterations.

4.3   Cluster Information Coordination

Now, each SU has individually computed its cluster memberships. Note that, however, the memberships are probably different from each other because of the different local topology. Therefore, we propose a synchronization protocol to eliminate this inconsistency. The synchronization protocol contains three steps:

1. SU_i broadcasts its cluster result X_i and receives cluster results from the other SUs.
2. Among all the received cluster results, the optimal cluster, which has the maximum cluster utility and contains SU_i, is selected to be the new cluster of SU_i, denoted by X'_i. Agin, SU_i broadcasts X'_i and exchanges new clusters with the other SUs.
3. For any node $SU_j \in X'_i$, if $SU_i \notin X'_j$, then SU_j is removed from X'_i. Finally, the pruned X'_i, denoted by X''_i is return.

5   Channel Handoff

After clustering, the network starts to transmit based on the cluster structure. To adapt to the changing PU activities, in this section, we present a channel handoff method for each cluster to select and handoff the common channel.

5.1   Cluster Based Transmission

First of all, we briefly introduce a cluster based transmission scheme used in this paper.

The cluster transmission period is made up of three phases: a coordination phase, intra-cluster transmission phase and inter-cluster transmission phase, as shown in Fig. 5.

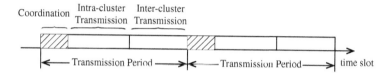

Fig. 5. Transmission period for cluster-based CRAHNs.

In coordination phase, the cluster head receives control messages from gateways and terminal SUs. Since SUs are equipped with two transceivers, they can be scheduled to monitor different channels so that all channel usage statistics can be sensed. Base on the analysis of this information, the cluster head accomplishes tasks like channel selection and handoff. In intra-cluster transmission phase, all SUs transmit data within the cluster, while data out of the cluster will be stored in the gateway nodes instead. In inter-cluster transmission phase, cluster head and terminal SUs can still transmit data inside the cluster, while the gateway nodes start to communicate with gateways from other clusters by rendezvous.

Note that, the details on transmission scheme for cluster based CRAHN are beyond the scope of this paper.

5.2   Handoff Algorithm

Now, we describe the control channel handoff and selection procedure, whose workflow is shown in Fig. 6.

In the coordination period, all SUs update their channel availabilities and send them to the cluster head. After receiving the channel information, the cluster head constructs the common channel list and computes the packet error rate (PER) of each common channel. Next, the cluster head sorts the channel list in descending order by the PER. Based on the sorted channel list, the first channel is selected as the CCC. Then, the cluster head broadcasts the sorted

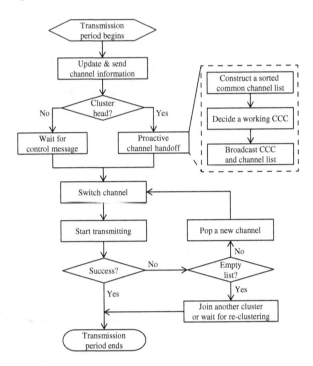

Fig. 6. The workflow diagram of channel handoff.

channel list and the decided CCC to the cluster members. At the end of the coordination period, all cluster members tune to the new CCC.

After receiving the CCC, SUs tune to the new common channel and begin transmitting data packets. If there is no active PU detected, the cluster members successfully enters the next transmission period. If a PU is detected, all cluster members immediately start channel handoff process, switching to the first channel in the list. If the list is empty, which means there is no available common channel left, then SUs would try to join into another cluster or wait for the reclustering.

We can see that, although no PU appears, the cluster might also switch to a new common channel. This proactive feature can effectively improve the cluster robustness to the PU activity.

6   Performance Evaluation

In this section, we evaluate our work by simulations in various scenarios of CRAHN. The simulations are focused on three aspects: the neighbor discovery protocol, the distributed clustering algorithm and the channel handoff scheme.

We randomly distribute 20 PUs in a $100 \times 100\,\mathrm{m}^2$ area, i.e. one PU per $10 \times 10\,\mathrm{m}^2$ on the average. Each PU occupies only one licensed spectrum band and adjacent PUs operate on different channels.

6.1 Clustering Performance

First, we evaluate the cluster structures produced by different clustering methods. During the simulation, the number of licensed channels is set to 30 and the number of PUs is set to 10. For comparison, we implement the following three clustering algorithms: *CogMesh* [5], *VBC* [6] and *SOC* [7].

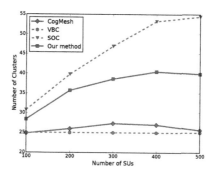

Fig. 7. Number of clusters under different number of SUs with 10 PUs.

In Fig. 7, the PU number is fixed at 10 and the SU number increases from 100 to 500. For CogMesh and VBC, the numbers of clusters are almost unchanged as the SUs increase. For SOC, the cluster number increases fast with the growth of SUs. Because when SUs are increasing, the common channels among SUs decrease. To maintain the intra-cluster common channels, SOC reduces the cluster size, so the number of clusters is increasing. As for our method, the cluster number is lower than SOC and larger than CogMesh, this is because that we consider both intra-cluster and inter-cluster common channels.

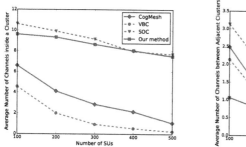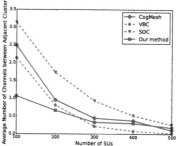

(a) Number of common channels inside a cluster

(b) Number of common channels between clusters

Fig. 8. Common channels under different number of SUs with 10 PUs.

Figure 8 illustrates the common channels of different clustering algorithms. We fix the PU number at 10 and increase the SU number from 50 to 500. In Fig. 8(a) the intra-cluster common channels of CogMesh and VBC stay in a low level. For SOC and our method, the number of intra-cluster common channels keeps a high level due to the optimization of channel characteristics. SOC uses maximum bipartite graph algorithm, only maximizing the intra-cluster channels. Thus, SOC produces more clusters. However, our method also takes the inter-cluster interference into account. Therefore, the cluster number is lower than SOC. This tradeoff is also verified in Fig. 8(b) which shows the average number of common channels between adjacent clusters. The result of our method is always kept in a low level.

6.2 Channel Handoff Performance

Now, we evaluate the performance of the proposed channel handoff scheme. The following two proactive handoff method are adopted for comparison: (1) Random scheme. A SU randomly switches to a new channel when PU activity occurs. (2) Greedy scheme. A SU selects a channel with the maximum channel quality when the handoff occurs.

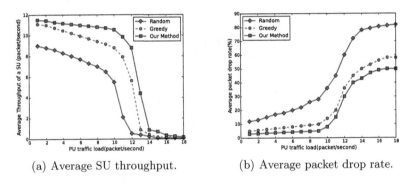

(a) Average SU throughput.   (b) Average packet drop rate.

Fig. 9. Handoff performance under different PU traffics with 20 channels and 200 SUs.

Figure 9 illustrates the handoff performance under different PU traffics, where there are 20 channels and 200 SUs. Figure 9(a) shows that the throughput in greedy method drops fast. As the PU traffic increases, more clusters will switch to the same channel, which leads to a congestion. For random method, channels are randomly selected, thus overload on each channel are lower. Our proposed method have a better performance due to the prediction. Figure 9(b) presents the average packet drop rate of each cluster. Similar with the throughput results, our method is more efficient handoff performance.

7 Conclusion

In this paper, we investigate the cluster structure construction for distributed CRAHNs. To reduce the complexity of large scale CRAHNs, we propose a distributed spectrum-aware clustering method to subdivide the network into non-overlapping clusters, which maximizes the common channels inside a cluster and minimizes the common channels between clusters. Moreover, to adapt to the PU activities, we also propose a proactive handoff scheme to maintenance the cluster. Simulation results show that our work facilitates the transmission performance in large scale CRAHNs.

Acknowledgement. This work is supported by National Natural Science Foundation of China (61272454) and Specialized Research Fund for the Doctoral Program of Higher Education (20130141110022).

References

1. Akyildiz, I.F., Lee, W.Y., Chowdhury, K.R.: Crahns: cognitive radio ad hoc networks. AD Hoc Netw. **7**(5), 810–836 (2009)
2. Akyildiz, I.F., Lee, W.Y., Vuran, M.C., Mohanty, S.: Next generation/dynamic spectrum access/cognitive radio wireless networks: a survey. Comput. Netw. **50**(13), 2127–2159 (2006)
3. Bian, K., Park, J.M., Chen, R.: Control channel establishment in cognitive radio networks using channel hopping. IEEE J. Sel. Areas Commun. **29**(4), 689–703 (2011)
4. Chen, T., Zhang, H., Maggio, G.M., Chlamtac, I.: Cogmesh: a cluster-based cognitive radio network. In: 2nd IEEE International Symposium on New Frontiers in Dynamic Spectrum Access Networks, DySPAN 2007, pp. 168–178. IEEE (2007)
5. Chen, T., Zhang, H., Maggio, G.M., Chlamtac, I.: Topology management in cogmesh: a cluster-based cognitive radio mesh network. In: IEEE International Conference on Communications, ICC 2007, pp. 6516–6521. IEEE (2007)
6. Dai, Y., Wu, J., Xin, C.: Virtual backbone construction for cognitive radio networks without common control channel. In: 2013 Proceedings IEEE INFOCOM, pp. 1456–1464. IEEE (2013)
7. Lazos, L., Liu, S., Krunz, M.: Spectrum opportunity-based control channel assignment in cognitive radio networks. In: 6th Annual IEEE Communications Society Conference on Sensor, Mesh and Ad Hoc Communications and Networks, SECON 2009, pp. 1–9. IEEE (2009)
8. Lin, Z., Liu, H., Chu, X., Leung, Y.W.: Jump-stay based channel-hopping algorithm with guaranteed rendezvous for cognitive radio networks. In: 2011 Proceedings IEEE INFOCOM, pp. 2444–2452. IEEE (2011)
9. Shi, J., Malik, J.: Normalized cuts and image segmentation. IEEE Trans. Pattern Anal. Mach. Intell. **22**(8), 888–905 (2000)
10. Tabatabaei, S.S., Coates, M., Rabbat, M.: Ganc: greedy agglomerative normalized cut for graph clustering. Pattern Recogn. **45**(2), 831–843 (2012)
11. Theis, N.C., Thomas, R.W., DaSilva, L., et al.: Rendezvous for cognitive radios. IEEE Trans. Mob. Comput. **10**(2), 216–227 (2011)
12. Zhao, J., Zheng, H., Yang, G.H.: Distributed coordination in dynamic spectrum allocation networks. In: 2005 First IEEE International Symposium on New Frontiers in Dynamic Spectrum Access Networks, DySPAN 2005, pp. 259–268. IEEE (2005)

A Social Relation Aware Hybrid Service Discovery Mechanism for Intermittently Connected Wireless Network

Dapeng Wu[1,2]($\boxtimes$), Honggang Wang[1,2], and Ruyan Wang[1,2]

[1] Chongqing University of Posts and Telecommunications, Chongiqng 400065, China
[2] University of Massachusetts Dartmouth, Dartmouth 02740, USA
wudapengphd@gmail.com, hwang1@umassd.edu, wangry@cqupt.edu.cn

Abstract. In intermittently connected wireless network, service discovery is utilized to identify the best relay to process packets for the service registration, selection and activation. Since packets are transmitted by intermittently connected nodes, the service discovery is challenging due to the partitioned topology, long delays, and dynamic social feature. To maximize the utilization of limited network resources, in this paper, a hybrid service discovery architecture including Virtual Dictionary Node (VDN) is proposed. According to the historical data of movement, all nodes can discover their relationships with others. Subsequently, according to the node activity, VDN is chosen to facilitate the service registration procedure. Further, the service information outside of a home community can be obtained through Global Active Node (GAN) to support the service selection. To improve the utilization of network resources and provide quality services, a Service Providing Node (SPN) is determined among multiple candidates. Simulation results show that, when compared with other classical service algorithms, the proposed scheme can improve the successful service discovery ratio by 25 % with reduced overheads.

Keywords: Intermittently connected wireless network · Service discovery · Social attribute · Virtual directory node

1 Introduction

To enhance the Quality of Experience (QoE) of Intermittently Connected Wireless Network (ICWN) [1], a service discovery mechanism is essential for users to access the network resources anytime and anywhere. Usually, the service discovery procedure consists of three steps: service registration, service selection and

This work is supported in part by the Natural Science Foundation of China (61371097), Youth Talents Training Project of Chongqing Science & Technology Commission (CSTC2014KJRC-QNRC40001), and US National Science Foundation (award#1401711, #1451629).

© Springer International Publishing Switzerland 2016
Q. Yang et al. (Eds.): WASA 2016, LNCS 9798, pp. 452–463, 2016.
DOI: 10.1007/978-3-319-42836-9_40

service activation. Firstly, SPN should notify other nodes its service information, and this service information is inquired and obtained by Service Demanding Nodes (SDN). Lastly, by selecting the proper SPN from several candidates, packets can be forwarded to SPN to initiate the selected service.

Service discovery mechanisms can be classified into two categories: the centralized and distributed mechanisms. VDNs should be determined with a predefined method for the centralized mechanisms, in which service information is stored. Subsequently, SDN sends the inquiry information to VDN to request a service. Finally, a proper SPN can be selected. Whereas, for distributed mechanisms, the service registration packets and inquiry packets are broadcasted across the network. Consequently, the service information can be obtained by all the nodes in the network, by which SPNs can be selected to complete the service discovery. Two kinds of mechanisms have different advantages at different service discovery stages. Eventually, the conclusion can be drawn that these two kinds of mechanisms are not directly applicable for intermittently connected wireless network, which means a more suitable service discovery mechanism is demanded.

To minimize the overhead and the resource consumption, the service discovery procedure should take advantage of the social features [2–5]. Obviously, the node with high activity degree will encounter more nodes in a given period, and the spreading degree of its carried packets is also large [6]. According to the social theory, there are two kinds of special nodes, Local Active Node (LAN) and Global Active Node (GAN) in the network [7], where LAN is more active in its home community, and GAN is relatively more active within the whole network. Apparently, the performance of service discovery can be improved with the assistance of LAN and GAN.

Aiming at a typical intermittently connected wireless network and combining the advantages of centralized and distributed mechanisms, a hybrid service discovery strategy, Social Attribute aware Service Discovery mechanism (SASD) is proposed in this paper, which fully exploits the relationship between nodes. Firstly, nodes in the network are divided into communities in a distributed manner; meanwhile, node activity degrees are estimated, by which GANs and LANs are selected. During the service registration, VDNs for each community are selected according to their relationships and available buffer resources. Thus the diffusion and update of service registration packets can be restricted into their home community. Subsequently, the service information outside of the home community of a SDN can be provided by GAN for service selection. To guarantee the service availability, the node with the highest service ability is selected as SPN. Finally, the service can be activated between the corresponding SDN and SPN.

For the flexibility and efficiency of the service discovery, nodes with higher local activity degrees and buffer resources are selected as VDNs to maintain the service status; moreover, GANs are utilized to assist the service inquiry targeting at VDNs from other communities. Clearly, only the service registration and service inquiry procedures are assisted by VDNs, and during the service activation, packets are forwarded between SPN and SDN in a distributed manner. Thus, the advantages of centralized and distributed mechanisms can be exploited cleverly.

The remainder of the paper is organized as follows. The nodes relationship evaluation and nodes activity evaluation methods are introduced in Sect. 2, and Sect. 3 respectively. In Sect. 4 the service discovery mechanism is proposed. In Sect. 5 we evaluate the performance of our proposed SASD, and compare it with previous works. Finally, the conclusion is reached in Sect. 6.

2   Nodes Relationship Evaluation

Traditionally, the relationship between nodes can be obtained in the off-line manner, but the realization complexity, discontinuous and distribution features make the task impractical for intermittently connected wireless network. As mentioned above, nodes are socially correlated, and their relationships gradually stabilize along with the operation of the network. Therefore, according to the weak ties theory, the strength of relationship can be reflected by the number of common neighbors. Different from the traditionally defined neighbor, neighbors in intermittently connected wireless network are defined by the average encounter times, as shown in Definition 1. Furthermore, the relationship strength is defined in Definition 2.

Definition 1 (Neighbor Nodes). *The node is viewed as a neighbor of node i while their encounter times is higher than the value of E_{ave}, where E_{ave} is the average encounter times of node i with other nodes. Further, all the nodes meet the above constraint constitute the neighbor node set $\Gamma(i)$ of node i, as shown in (1).*

$$\Gamma(i) = \{v \in V \mid (i,v) \in E\} \tag{1}$$

Definition 2 (Relationship Strength). *The Relationship Strength (RS) between node u and v is determined by two parameters, the number of common neighbors and the total neighbors. The first parameter is utilized to illustrate the relationship between nodes, and the last parameter is utilized to ensure the asymmetric feature of the relationship. The relationship strength from node u to v can be estimated by (2):*

$$b_{u,v} = \frac{|\Gamma(u) \cap \Gamma(v)|}{|\Gamma(u)|} \tag{2}$$

As mentioned above, nodes in intermittently connected wireless network form into communities, and their belongingness for each community is quite different. According to the historical information of movement, the belongingness of a node can be determined by its RS with nodes from the given community, as shown in (3), where $B_C(u)$ is the belongingness of node u to community C, $N_C(u)$ denotes the neighbors of node u sharing the same community label C.

$$B_C(u) = \frac{\sum\limits_{v \in N_C(u)} b_{u,v}}{|N_C(u)|} \qquad (3)$$

Obviously, the relationship between nodes can be evaluated according to the belongingness. Because network resources are limited in intermittently connected wireless network, the belongingness status cannot be diffused in the whole scale of network. According to the social feature, home communities of neighbor nodes are always the same, which means the relationship between nodes and the belongingness for different communities of nodes can be evaluated according to the information of their neighbors.

3   Nodes Activity Evaluation

As mentioned above, the network can be divided into k communities $N = C_1 \cup C_2 \cup C_3 \cdots \cup C_k$. For epoch T, node u records the encounter times with its neighbors, which can be described by $N_{n_1}^u, N_{n_2}^u, N_{n_3}^u \cdots N_{n_i}^u$. Accordingly, the average encounter times N_{ave}^u between node u and its neighbors can be obtained as shown in (4).

$$N_{ave}^u = \frac{\sum\limits_{i=1}^{m} N_{n_i}^u}{m} \qquad (4)$$

Where m is the number of nodes in the home community of node u, and then the active neighbors can be filtered on the basis of the value N_{ave}^u, as shown in (5).

$$\Psi_u(i) = \begin{cases} 1 & N_{n_i}^u \geq N_{ave}^u \\ 0 & N_{n_i}^u < N_{ave}^u \end{cases} \qquad (5)$$

To distinguish the difference between these active neighbors, all nodes in the network evaluate their local activity degree A_{LAN} according to the historical movement status information, as shown in (6). Where C denotes the current community, $|C|$ denotes the node number of community C.

$$A_{LAN}(i) = \frac{\sum\limits_{u \in C} \Psi_u(i)}{|C|} \qquad (6)$$

Different from the local activity degree, the global activity degree describes its relationship with all nodes in the network. The node with higher globe activity degree has closer relationship with nodes outside or inside of its home community.

As can be seen, the globe active nodes are often roaming around, so the globe activity degree $A_{GAN}(i)$ can be evaluated by (7). Obviously, the higher probability of GAN roaming around implies it can provide a wider packet spreading range.

$$A_{GAN}(i) = \frac{N_{roam}^i}{N_{local}^i} \tag{7}$$

Where N_{local}^i is the number of epochs while node i stays in its home community, and N_{roam}^i is the number of epochs while node i is roaming. To determine the node status of each epoch, the home communities of all encountered nodes are maintained locally. While more encountered nodes are from the same home community, the node status of this epoch is local; otherwise, the status is roaming.

For period T, the proportion of N_{local}^i and N_{roam}^i is determined by the probability that the node stays in its home community and roams around, as shown in (8), where $\pi_l^{(i)}$ and $\pi_r^{(i)}$ denotes the probability that the node stays in its home community and roams around for epoch T.

$$\frac{N_{roam}^i}{N_{local}^i} = \frac{\pi_r^{(i)}}{\pi_l^{(i)}} \tag{8}$$

As mentioned above, there are two kinds of status, local and roaming respectively; moreover, the transition between these two kinds of movement status can be described by Markov theory.

Where P_l denotes the probability that a node stays in its home community, and it will remain unchanged in the next epoch; P_r denotes the probability that the node is roaming around, and it will remain roaming around in the next epoch. The stationary equation for $\pi_l^{(i)}$ and $\pi_r^{(i)}$ can be illustrated by (9) and (10).

$$\begin{pmatrix} \pi_l^{(i)} \\ \pi_r^{(i)} \end{pmatrix} = \begin{pmatrix} \pi_l^{(i)} & \pi_r^{(i)} \end{pmatrix} \times \begin{pmatrix} P_l & 1-P_l \\ 1-P_r & P_r \end{pmatrix} \tag{9}$$

$$\pi_l^{(i)} + \pi_r^{(i)} = 1 \tag{10}$$

Further, the expression of $\pi_l^{(i)}$ and $\pi_r^{(i)}$ can be obtained as shown in (11) and (12).

$$\pi_l^{(i)} = \frac{1 - p_r^{(i)}}{2 - p_l^{(i)} - p_r^{(i)}} \tag{11}$$

$$\pi_r^{(i)} = \frac{1 - p_l^{(i)}}{2 - p_l^{(i)} - p_r^{(i)}} \tag{12}$$

Combining (9) to (12), the value of $A_{GAN}(i)$ can be estimated, as shown in (13).

$$A_{GAN}(i) = \frac{1 - p_l^{(i)}}{1 - p_r^{(i)}} \tag{13}$$

According to the above method, each node in the network can evaluate its own global activity degree in a distributed manner.

4   Service Discovery Mechanism

As mentioned previously, neither distributed nor centralized service discovery mechanism is suitable for intermittently connected wireless network. Though the spread degree of service information is higher for the distributed mechanism, its overhead is difficult to control. Comparatively speaking, the centralized mechanism limits the overhead by storing service information in VDN, thus a large number of information should be handled by VDN, resulting in a single point failure problem due to discontinuous connection and energy depletion [8].

To achieve the tradeoff between the spread degree of service information and the overhead of service discovery, a hybrid service discovery mechanism is designed, which consists of the service registration, service inquiry and service activation. Specially, VDN is introduced to handle the registration and the inquiry of service information. In order to reduce overhead, VDNs only provide service for nodes in a finite region. According to the aggregating character of nodes, each community can be regarded as a unit region.

As can be seen, SPNs register their service information to the corresponding VDN in a distributed manner. With the continuous motion of nodes, each VDN can obtain needed service information from other communities in the Best Effort manner; moreover, VDNs are in charge of the service inquiring from SDNs in a centralized manner. Subsequently, by selecting the node with higher service ability as SPN, the reliability of service between SDN and SPN can be guaranteed. Finally, the service activation procedure can be completed by selecting the node with highest encounter frequency to SPN or roaming to the destination community with higher frequency as relay.

4.1   Service Registration and Cancelation

To achieve the ubiquitous computing under the distributed network, SPNs send their service registration information to VDN of the same home community. Apparently, the selection on VDN is one of the most important issues in this stage. Considering about the node relationship within a community, the node with higher $A_{LAN}(i)$ will encounter other nodes more frequently, thus it can help diffuse service registration information to other nodes. Meanwhile, due to the dynamic feature of intermittently connected wireless network, the service status changes constantly and large amount of information should be maintained by VDN, so the buffer capacity is the other factor for VDN selection. Therefore, to register service information and to handle service inquiries cost-efficiently, VDN is selected by jointly considering $A_{LAN}(i)$ and the residual buffer. According to (14), nodes can estimate their suitability as VDNs in a distributed manner. Furthermore, by comparing with each other, the selection on VDN can be accomplished.

$$N_{VDN} = A_{LAN}(i) \times \frac{B_i - B_i^{busy}}{B_i} \tag{14}$$

Where $A_{LAN}(i)$ denotes the local activity degree of node i, B_i denotes the buffer capacity of node i, B_i^{busy} denotes the occupied buffer capacity of node i.

Additionally, when a registered SPN leaves the network or the service information survival time expires, the SPN should send the service cancelation information to VDN. The process of service registration and cancelation is shown in Fig. 1.

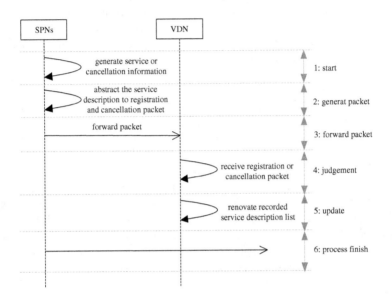

Fig. 1. Service registration procedures

After a service is generated by SPN, the packet containing service description information such as SPN address, service type and survival time is forwarded to VDN of the same home community. Subsequently, VDN stores the received service information until the survival time expires. Additionally, to ensure the validity of services, the service cancelation information should be sent to VDN when the service is unavailable.

4.2 Service Selection

Obviously, the current service information is maintained by VDN, and SDN can obtain the information about available services according to the inquiry results. Obviously, there are probably several SPNs matching the inquiry. As can be seen, the network performance can be improved by selecting the optimal SPN. Due to the distributed feature, the global network status is not perceivable for SDN, so the selection on SPNs cannot be accomplished in a cost-efficient manner.

In order to enhance the successful discovery rate, a service ability aware SPN selection method is introduced. By selecting the node with the highest service

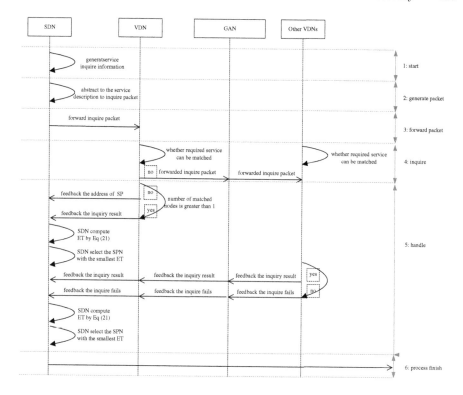

Fig. 2. Service selection procedures

ability as SPN, the results of service inquiry can be replied more quickly, and the relay times can also be reduced. The principle of the proposed service selection method is shown in Fig. 2.

After receiving the service inquiry packet from SDN, VDN searches the related information within its buffer. If the inquired service can be matched by SPN of the same community, the SPN with the highest service ability is selected to provide the service for SDN. Exceptionally, service status outside the community of SDN is often requested. To reduce the resource consumption in this process, the global activity degrees $A_{GAN}(i)$ of all nodes of a given community are compared by VDN, and the node with the highest global activity degree $\max\{A_{GAN}(i_1), A_{GAN}(i_2), \cdots, A_{GAN}(i_n)\}$ is selected to relay service inquiry packets to VDNs of other communities. Subsequently, the service information is checked by VDNs after receiving the service inquiry packets from GAN in a distributed manner, and then the inquired results are replied to GAN. Until GAN encounters VDN matching the inquired service, by repeating the above mentioned local SPN selection procedure, SPN with the highest service ability is selected for the requiring SDN.

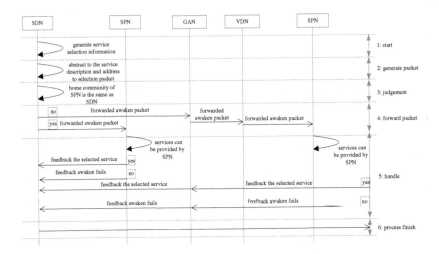

Fig. 3. Service activation procedures

4.3   Service Activation

To exploit the node relationship, the home community of a SPN is checked firstly after the inquiry results are replied by VDN; further, the service activation procedure is executed according to the relationship between SPN and SDN (Fig. 3).

While SDN and SPN belong to the same community, SDN forwards the service activation information to SPN. Generally, packets are forwarded by several relay nodes in intermittently connected wireless network, which is also applied to the transmission of service activation packets.

5   Numerical Results

5.1   Parameter Setting

To compare the performance of our proposed SASD with those of other popular service discovery mechanisms, we establish a simulation environment using ONE (Opportunistic Network Environment) [9], which is a powerful framework for generating different movement models, running simulation with various protocols, visualizing simulations in real time and outputting/post-processing results.

In the simulation, we compare SASD with DSDM [4] and DMBSLP [10]. DSDM is a typical hybrid service discovery mechanism, and multiple VDNs are selected according to distances between VDNs and SPNs, whereas DMBSLP is a typical distributed mechanism, where nodes have identical status.

Along with the change of the node number, four metrics are simulated, and they are SRSProb (Service Register Success Probability), Service Query Success Probability (SQSProb), Service Discovery Success Probability (SDSProb) and Overhead Ratio (OR) respectively.

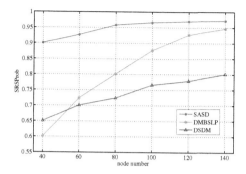

Fig. 4. Service register success probability

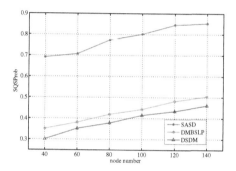

Fig. 5. Service query success probability

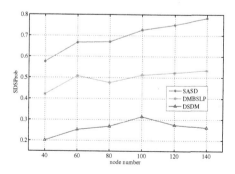

Fig. 6. Service discovery success probability

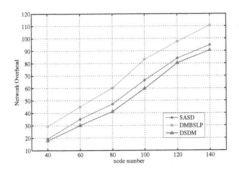

Fig. 7. Overhead ratio

5.2 Network Performance Under Different Node Density

Obviously, the node density of intermittently connected wireless network is lower than that of other wireless networks, and its most important feature is the discontinuous connection between nodes. With higher node density, the encounter interval between nodes can be reduced, and the node encounter times during a given period can be increased. As a result, the network performance can be dramatically affected by node density. The network performance under different node density is shown in Figs. 4, 5, 6 and 7.

From the results shown in Fig. 4 SRSProb for all mechanisms increases with the node density. Our proposed SASD is 28.8 % higher than VDN based DSDM. With the reasonable selection on VDNs, the relationship between nodes is exploited, and the node having the highest meeting frequency with VDN is selected as the relay, so the packet delivery probability can be improved by our proposed SASD. Comparatively speaking, without the support of VDN in DMB-SLP, the service information is spread more widely with the distributed manner, thus SRSProb of SASD is 16.7 % higher than that of DMBSLP.

SQSProb for all mechanisms is illustrated in Fig. 5, SASD has much higher SQSProb than the other two mechanisms. With a higher active degree, the VDN can meet other nodes more frequently, thus its information propagation speed can be enhanced. By selecting the node with the highest service ability as SPN, the service inquiry can be replied more quickly, and the relay times can also be reduced. Therefore, the service query success probability can be improved by SASD.

From the results shown in Fig. 6, SDSProb of SASD is obviously higher than those of other two mechanisms, and the gain is also much higher. With higher SQSProb of SASD, SDNs successfully receive the response information from VDN with higher probability; moreover, service inquiry and service activation packets are carried by better relays or GANs. Meanwhile, SPN can be selected reasonably by SDN, thus SDSProb is improved.

Results in Fig. 7 show that the overhead ratio of DMBSLP is the highest, which is 42.3 % and 22.5 % higher than those of DSDM and SASD. Apparently,

DMBSLP forwards different service information with the distributed manner, and lots of packet copies are flooded into the network, whereas the packet forwarding in SASD and DSDM is assisted by VDNs to control the packet diffusion range.

6 Conclusion

To improve the performance of the service discovery in intermittently connected wireless networks, a new social attribute aware service discovery mechanism is proposed in this paper. Based on the relationships among nodes, a network can be divided into communities logically. Further, LAN and GAN are evaluated according to the information obtained from the historical node movement. Compared with the existing schemes such as DSDM and DMBSLP, SASD can significantly improve the success probability of service discovery and reduce overheads.

References

1. Li, Y., Wang, Z., You, X.H., Liu, Q.L.: NER-DRP: dissemination-based routing protocol with network-layer error control for intermittently connected mobile networks. Mob. Netw. Appl. **17**, 618–628 (2012)
2. Wu, D., Zhang, H., Wang, H.: Quality of Protection (QoP)-driven data forwarding for intermittently connected wireless networks. IEEE Wirel. Commun. **22**, 66–73 (2015)
3. Eyuphan, B., Boleslaw, K.: Exploiting friendship relations for efficient routing in mobile social networks. IEEE Trans. Parallel Distrib. Syst. **23**, 2254–2265 (2012)
4. Sabrina, G., Elena, P., Gian, P.R.: Strangers help friends to communicate in opportunistic networks. Comput. Netw. **55**, 374–385 (2011)
5. Liu, G., Yang, Q., Wang, H., Lin, X.: Assessment of multi-hop interpersonal trust in social networks by Three-Valued Subjective Logic. In: Proceedings of IEEE INFOCOM, pp. 1698–1706 (2014)
6. Luo, C., Min, G., Yu, F.: Energy-efficient distributed relay and power control in cognitive radio cooperative communications. IEEE J. Sel. Areas Commun. **31**, 2442–2452 (2013)
7. Hui, P., Crowcroft, J., Yoneki, E.: BUBBLE rap: social-based forwarding in delay-tolerant networks. IEEE Trans. Mob. Comput. **10**, 1576–1589 (2011)
8. Wu, D., He, J., Wang, H., Wang, C., Wang, R.: A hierarchical packet forwarding mechanism for energy harvesting wireless sensor networks. IEEE Commun. Mag. **8**, 92–98 (2015)
9. Wu, D., Wang, Y., Wang, H., Yang, B., Wang, C., Wang, R.: Dynamic coding control in social intermittent connectivity wireless networks. IEEE Trans. Veh. Technol. doi:10.1109/TVT.2015.2493516
10. Wang, Z., Bulut, E., Boleslaw, S.K.: Service discovery for delay tolerant networks. In: Proceedings of IEEE GLOBECOM, pp. 136–141 (2010)

The Improved Algorithm Based on DFS and BFS for Indoor Trajectory Reconstruction

Min Li[1], Jingjing Fu[1,2], Yanfang Zhang[1(✉)],
Zhujun Zhang[1], and Siye Wang[1,3]

[1] Institute of Information Engineering, CAS, Beijing, China
{limin, fujingjing, zhangyanfang,
zhangzhujun, wangsiye}@iie.ac.cn
[2] University of Chinese Academy of Sciences, Beijing, China
[3] Beijing Jiaotong University, Beijing, China

Abstract. The trajectory of moving objects in large spaces is important, as it enables a range of applications related to security, guidance and so on. Trajectory reconstruction is the process which uses searching algorithms to find a reasonable trajectory. Due to the complexity of indoor environment and the larger area which multi-floor causes, it exits the problem of low searching efficient. To solve the problem, this paper proposes the improved algorithm which combines the Branch and Bound method based on Depth-First-Search (DFS) and Breadth-First-Search(BFS). It helps construct the trajectory quickly on topological map. Experimental results validate the improved algorithm is effective by comparing other algorithms.

1 Introduction

With the development of indoor position technology, people often use trajectory data to find the behavior information of target. Moreover, combining the trajectory data and geography information can help people know the habits of moving targets [1]. The real trajectory is the basement of getting effective message.

There are many ways to reconstruct the trajectory of targets. Using RFID technology to reconstruct [2], it can speculate the room of target at a certain time by history trajectory data. But the trajectory may cross the indoor barrier by connecting the rooms where the target passed. But the trajectory is not reasonable. Using grid map and A* algorithm can get the reasonable trajectory [3]. However, its more storage information [4] make it not be applied for many floors of architecture. The searching efficient is low because of much grids and complex algorithm. Using odometry data from smartphone sensors to find the real trajectory [6], it can identify the trajectory of human. It uses the topological map to construct the indoor environment and DFS algorithm to reconstruct the trajectory. The topological map stores less information than grid map. DFS is simple searching algorithm. But when applying for larger area, it may search many useless nodes and its efficiency is low.

To solve the problem of low efficiency of trajectory reconstruction, this paper proposes the improved algorithm based on topological map [7]. The improved algorithm can apply to larger area or many floors of architecture. The paper improves the

© Springer International Publishing Switzerland 2016
Q. Yang et al. (Eds.): WASA 2016, LNCS 9798, pp. 464–474, 2016.
DOI: 10.1007/978-3-319-42836-9_41

algorithm based on DFS and BFS [9]. DFS and BFS are normal searching algorithm. They are easy to accomplish and don't need a lot of auxiliary conditions. In addition to DFS, BFS, A* algorithm, A*algorithm [5] is complex and needs function to calculate the value. Dijkstra [8] algorithm is also normal algorithm, but Dijkstra algorithm is used for the problem of shortest path.

The paper supposes that there are many monitoring points which are entrances, conference offices and where you want to monitor. When the target passes the monitoring point, we can get the position information of target at the moment. The position information is same with the monitoring point. These information informs the trajectory of the target. We discuss the topological map corresponding to indoor environment has no loop.

This paper first introduces the system model of trajectory reconstruction. Secondly, this paper describes the overview of DFS, BFS and the improved algorithm. The pseudo code of algorithms is given. Thirdly the experiment study is presented. This part display the comparison of DFS, BFS and improved algorithm. The final part is conclusion which introduce the future work.

2 System Model

Trajectory reconstruction contains three aspects. The first part is constructing the topological map of indoor environment. Topological map provides the feasible paths and monitor points corresponding to the real indoor environment. The second part designs the attributes of storage information. It is convenient for querying trajectory information we needed. The third part is using the searching algorithm to get trajectory.

The Topological Map of Indoor Environment. The topological map is the basement of trajectory reconstruction, which combines the normal path and monitoring points. The normal path is area which the monitoring target can move. Monitoring points are

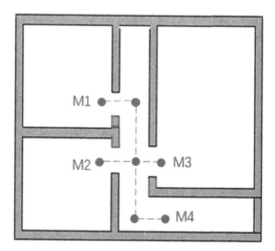

Fig. 1. An example of indoor environment and topological map.

corresponding to some sensitive area. When the target passes these places, they are detected and their information is recorded. Figure 1 presents the example of indoor environment [10] and it's topological map [11, 12]. It is one floor. M1, M2, M3, M4 are monitoring points. Other nodes are auxiliary nodes for trajectory reconstruction.

When the building contains many floors, the topological map can be constructed. In reality, floors are connected by elevators or stairs. We can set these connections as the boundary nodes of topological map. Connect the boundary nodes of adjacent floors. Then, we can construct only one topological map of many floors. Figure 2 presents the connection of topological maps of adjacent floor.

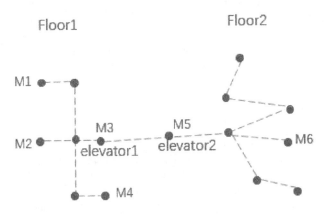

Fig. 2. The topological of Multi-floor

The topology Graph G is defined by (V, E, M, NM), where:

- V is the set of nodes.
- E is the set of undirected edges: $E = \{<v_iv_j> |v_iv_j \in V \wedge v_i \neq v_j$, there is no weigh of edge, because the trajectory is not related to the length of edge.
- M is the set of monitor points: $M \subset V, M \neq \{\}$.
- NM is the set of auxiliary nodes: $NM \subseteq V, NM = V - M$.

The information structure of the node is stored in Table 1.

Table 1. The property of the node

NodeID	The id of node.
X	The horizontal ordinate of node
Y	The vertical ordinate of node
AdjacentNodeNum	The number of adjacent nodes of current node
AdjacentNode	The NodeID of adjacent nodes
Mark	If the node $v_i \in M$, Mark = 1. If the node $v_i \in MN$, Mark = 0.

Trajectory Data. Trajectory data is the input of trajectory reconstruction. When the moving target is detected, the information of target is recorded. The information contains the location of the target. The example of monitor data in Table 2 is presented following. There are six records. The information of record is < Target, Location, T >. Target is the object which is detected. Location is the position which the target is detected. T is the time is when the detection occurred.

Table 2. The record of trajectory

Record	Target	Location	T
1	T1	M1	t_1
2	T2	M1	t_2
3	T1	M3	t_{18}
4	T1	M4	t_{19}
5	T2	M2	t_{24}
6	T3	M4	t_{25}

Trajectory Reconstruction. Reconstruct the trajectory using monitoring data and topological map. Take locations of the target corresponding to the nodes of topological map. Then, use the path searching algorithm to find a reasonable trajectory. For example, the target T1 passes M1, M3, M4 by order. The trajectory displays in Fig. 3.

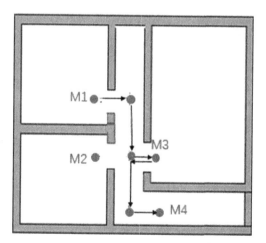

Fig. 3. The trajectory of T1

3   The Improved Algorithm Based on DFS and BFS

As described in Sect. 2, we use the topological map for model indoor environment. The last step is finding the reasonable trajectory by searching algorithms. In this section, we describe the achievement of trajectory reconstruction by DFS and BFS. Then a detail method of improved algorithm is given.

3.1   DFS and BFS

DFS is the classical searching algorithm. The core idea of Depth-First-Search is: Visit one node which has never been visited. Set the value of mark which is corresponding to searching node to 1. Search for adjacent nodes which have never been visited of current. If it exits, then visit the node by above steps until finding the target node.

Algorithm 1 is DFS algorithm to achieve the searching over Topological map.

```
Algorithm 1. DFS(TopologicalMap G,Start S, End E)
INPUT: The topological map G(V,E,M,NM),the start node S,
the end node E ,
OUTPUT: The nodes of path P_{S→E}
Initialization: visit mark Visited←null, stack←null,
1: Push S into stack, visited[s] ←1; currentNode←S;
2: While (stack is not null)
3:   if (currentNode is E)
4:       break;
5:   else
6:       find the first C_{adj} of currentNode.AdjacentNode
which visited[C_{adj}] is 0;
7:           push C_{adj} into stack; visited[C_{adj}] ← 1 ; current-
Node←C_{adj};
8:       if(all adjacent nodes of currentNode have been vis-
ited )
9:           pop currentNode of stack; currentNode ←the top
node of stack
10: P_{S→E} ←stack;
```

BFS is the classical searching algorithm. The core idea of Breadth-First-Search (BFS): Visit node has never been visited. Set the value of Visited[] which is corresponding to searching node to 1. Visit all adjacent nodes have never been visited in order. From these adjacent nodes, visit their adjacent nodes have been not visited in turn. Make sure that "first visited adjacent node" has been visited before "visited adjacent node later" until searching the target node.

Algorithm 2 is BFS algorithm to achieve the path searching over Topological map.

Algorithm 2. BFS(Topological Map G, Start S, End E)
INPUT: The topological map G(V,E,M,NM),the start S, the end E
OUTPUT: The nodes of path $P_{S \to E}$
Initialization: visit mark Visited←null, queue←null;
1:Add S into queue, currentNode←S;
2:**While** (queue is not null)
3:   delete currentNode in queue;
4:   **for** each adjacent node C_{adj} of currentNode do
5:       C_{adj}.parent←currentNode;
6:       **if**(C_{adj} is E)
7:          break;
8:       **else**
9:          add C_{adj} into the tail of queue;
10:   **If**(E has been found)
11:       break;
12:   **else**
13:       currentNode←the head node of queue;
14: $P_{S \to E}$←find all nodes of path by the node of parent;

3.2 The Indoor Trajectory Reconstruction Algorithm Based on DFS and BFS

Indoor Trajectory Reconstruction based on DFS and BFS (ITRBDB) combines DFS and BFS for searching. In the process of searching, it also uses the Branch and Bound method for deleting the impossible paths. Comparing DFS and BFS, ITRBDB can narrow the scope of searching scope and improves efficiency using above method.

ITRBDB is based on DFS because of the structure of topological map. One feature of indoor topological structure is longitudinal extension, such as museums, banks, national important apartment. Topological map is longitudinal extension and each node has no much branches. ITRBDB uses BFS for judging whether the target node is one of adjacent nodes. It doesn't cost a lot of time. Because the adjacent nodes of the current is not too much. The time complexity of ITRBDB remains constant even though in the condition of many branches.

Algorithm 3:ITRBDB (Topological Map G, Start S, End E)
INPUT: The topological map G(V,E,M;NM),the start S, the end E.
OUTPUT: The nodes of path $P_{S \to E}$
Initialization: visit mark Visited←null, stack←null;
1:Push S into stack, currentNode←S; visited[s] ←1;
2:**While**(stack is not null)
3: **for** each adjacent node C_{adj} of currentNode which visited[C_{adj}] is 0 do
4:     **if**(C_{adj} is E)
5:        push C_{adj} into stack; break;
6:     **else**
7:        **if**(C_{adj}.Mark==1 or C_{adj}.AdjacentNodeNum==1)
8:             visited[C_{adj}] ←1;
9:        **else**
10:            push C_{adj} into stack; visited[C_{adj}] ←1; break;
11:    **if**(E has been found)
12:        break;
13:    **else**
14:    **if**(all adjacent nodes of currentNode have been not pushed into stack)
15:        pop currentNode of stack; currentNode ←the top node of stack;
16: $P_{S \to E}$ ←stack;

Firstly, we can delete the adjacent node whose degree is 1. In the process of searching, it can determine whether adjacent nodes of current node is target node. If it is, then end searching. If the degree of adjacent node is 1 and it is not the target node, then give up the search of adjacent node.

Secondly, we can delete the adjacent node which is monitoring point but not the target node. The reason is following: All monitoring points which item passed are saved in p[]. The algorithm searches by segment. Assuming the adjacent node which is the monitoring point is a node of path from p[i] to p[i + 1], then the adjacent node is p [i + 1], If not, the adjacent node is not in the path. In this case, we should give up the path which contain this adjacent node in this segment.

The coal idea of ITRBDB is following: visit the adjacent nodes of current node and judge whether the target node is. If it is, then end searching. Otherwise, if there are location nodes or nodes which their degree is 1, then mark these nodes and give up searching the branch. Select the node which is not marked for searching. If all adjacent nodes have been marked, then return the above node of current. The detail achievement is Algorithm 3.

4   Experimental Result

This paper only discusses the topological map which has no loop. We generate the undirected graph to simulate topological map of indoor environment. The time complexity of three algorithms is $O(n^2)$. To compare the searching efficiency of three algorithms, there are two parameters to vary in experiment. One is the number of important monitoring points, the other is the number of nodes of topological map. We calculate the average of searching nodes of algorithms in the same condition.

$$Ave = \frac{\sum numberofsearchingnodesbetweenadjacentmonitoringpoints}{\sum adjacentmonitoringpoints}$$

Indoor environment is complex and various. So we can generate the topological map randomly. Figure 4 is a topological map generated by Matlab. This graph corresponds as the complex indoor.environment. It contains 100 nodes.

Firstly, we suppose the number of points is fixed and vary the number of monitoring points. The density and positions of monitoring points are determined by actual application and can affect the efficiency of algorithms. So we can change the number of monitoring points by the function randi() of Matlab. The serial number of each important monitoring point is also generated randomly. The array of monitoring points is [6, 13, 24, 33, 65, 40, 53, 79, 92, 94].

The comparing result of three algorithms is followed in Fig. 5. We can see that the ITRBDB algorithm is more efficient than DFS and BFS. The trend of algorithms is consistent. With the increase of monitoring points, the efficient of three algorithms is similar. The reason is when the density of monitoring points is big enough, the Branch and Bound method is invalid. But in actual application, we cannot make every point as the monitoring point because of cost. The number of average searching nodes is

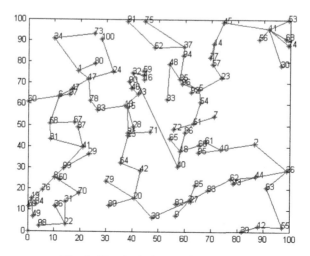

Fig. 4.   Topological map of experiment

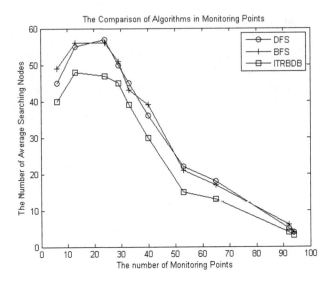

Fig. 5. The result of varying monitoring points

increasing when the number of monitoring points is 20 and 30. One possible reason is the positions of monitoring points generated maybe sparse.

Secondly, we vary the number of nodes of topological map. The points array is [100, 200, 500, 800, 1000]. Set the number of monitoring points for each randomly. Result is displayed in Fig. 6, We can see that ITRBDB algorithm is more efficient than DFS and BFS. When the number of important points is fixed, the ITRBDB will be more efficient with the increase of number of points.

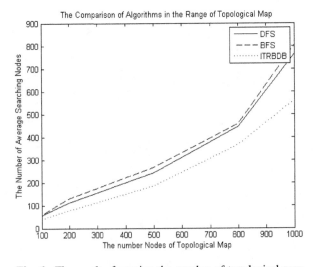

Fig. 6. The result of varying the number of topological map

We have applied the ITRBDB algorithm for our project to monitor items. The trajectory of the item can be reconstructed.

5 Conclusion and Future Work

In this paper, we apply the topological map for indoor trajectory reconstruction and propose improved algorithm to achieve the trajectory of the moving object. But there exits some problems to solve. Firstly, the improved algorithm is only applied in indoor environment whose topological map has no loop. When the indoor environment is complex, in other words, the topological map has loop, there may be many ways between monitoring points. We don't know whether the way is the real trajectory. We should find the real trajectory in some ways. Secondly, the topological map is constructed by labor. How to construct the topological map of indoor environment automatically is worth to research. Finally, we only construct the trajectory but not analysis the trajectory. For example, the motion state of the target. So we can describe the trajectory data in detail by some methods.

Acknowledgement. This work was supported in part by the Innovation Program of Institute of Information Engineering Chinese Academy of Sciences (Grant No. Y5Z0151104).

References

1. Huang, W.Q., Ding, C., Wang, S.Y., Jing, X., Luo, Y.J., Zhang, Y.F., Zhang, Z.J.: An efficient visualization method of RFID indoor positioning data. In: 2nd International Conference on Systems and Informatics (ICSAI), pp. 497–504. IEEE, Shang Hai (2014)
2. Kang, H.Y., Kim, J.S., Li, K.J.: STrack: tracking in indoor symbolic space with RFID sensors. In: Proceedings of the 18th SIGSPATIAL International Conference on Advances in Geographic Information Systems (GIS 2010), pp. 502–505. ACM, San Jose (2010)
3. Yang, M.: The Research and Achievement of Visualization of indoor location data. Shanghai Jiaotong University (2012)
4. Huang, Y., Du, J., Chen, H.: Construct three-dimensional route from blueprint. J. Beijing JiaoTong Univ. Image Build. **34**(2), 80–83 (2010)
5. Li, Z.: The optimization of Trajectory Reconstruction of Indoor Location System. G01C21/32GK102521328SQ201110400719 (2012)
6. Wang, R., Shroff, R., Zha, Y., Seshan, S., Veloso, M.: Indoor trajectory identification: snapping with uncertainty. In: IEEE/RSJ International Conference on Intelligent Robots and Systems (IROS), pp. 4901–4906 (2015)
7. Zheng H, Peng C.: Collaboration and fairness in opportunistic spectrum access. In: IEEE ICC, pp. 3132–3136 (2005)
8. Randria, I., Khelifa, M.M.B., Bouchouicha, M., Abellard, P.: A comparative study of six basic approaches for path planning towards an autonomous navigation. In: 33rd Annual Conference of the IEEE Industrial Electronics Society, IECON 200, pp. 2730–2735. IEEE, Taipei (2007)

9. Lutvica, K., Velagić, J., Kadić, N., Osmić, N., Džampo, G., Muminović, H.: Remote path planning and motion control of mobile robot within indoor maze environment. In: IEEE International Symposium on Intelligent Control, pp. 1596–1601. IEEE, Antibes (2014)

10. Gao, P., Shi, W., Zhou, W., Li, H., Wang, X.: A location predicting method for indoor mobile target localization in wireless sensor networks. Int. J. Distrib. Sens. Netw. **2013**, Article ID 949285, 11pages (2013)

11. Yuan, W., Schneider, M.: iNav: an indoor navigation model supporting length-dependent optimal routing. Geospatial Thinking. Lecture Notes in Geoinformation and Cartography, pp. 299–313. Springer, Heidelberg (2010)

12. Yuan W, Schneider M.: Supporting continuous range queries in indoor space. In: IEEE Eleventh International Conference on Mobile Data Management (MDM 2010), pp. 209–214 (2010)

Feedback Reduction for Multiuser MIMO Broadcast Channel with Zero-Forcing Beamforming

Yu-Lun Tsai, Jin-Hao Li, and Hsuan-Jung Su[✉]

Department of Electrical Engineering, Graduate Institute of Communication
Engineering, National Taiwan University, Taipei, Taiwan
{r97942032,hjs}@ntu.edu.tw, jinghaw2003@gmail.com

Abstract. A multi-user multiple-input multiple-output (MU-MIMO) downlink system with zero-forcing beamforming and semi-orthogonal user selection (SUS) scheduling algorithm is considered in this paper. It is well known that in practical implementation of MU-MIMO, the channel state information (CSI) feedback overhead becomes a limiting factor as the number of users to be supported increases. A novel scheme to reduce the feedback load, in the event of large number of users, by using a threshold-based feedback strategy is proposed and studied in this paper. The key feature of the proposed approach uses the concept of order statistics to construct multiple thresholds on the CSI. This paper also proposes a new modified formulation of the expected signal to interference plus noise ratio (SINR) to address the mismatch of analytical sum rate and simulation results. Simulation results show a significant reduction of feedback load when the scheme is used, while the sum rate performance is not compromised.

Keywords: Multiuser multiple-input multiple-output (MU-MIMO) · Broadcast channel · Zero-forcing beamforming · Feedback reduction

1 Introduction

It is widely known that dirty paper coding (DPC) [1] is a capacity-achieving transmission strategy in multiple input multiple output (MIMO) broadcast channels. However, DPC presents implementation challenges due to its high encoding/decoding complexity. Thus, several practical transmission techniques have been proposed. Downlink linear beamforming [2–6] although suboptimal, has been shown to achieve a large fraction of the DPC capacity, and at the same time exhibiting reduced complexity.

In frequency division duplex (FDD) systems, channel state information (CSI) at the receiver (CSIR) can be obtained through training. However, obtaining

This work was supported by the Ministry of Science and Technology of Taiwan under grants MOST 104-2221-E-002-073-MY2 and 104-2622-8-002-002.

© Springer International Publishing Switzerland 2016
Q. Yang et al. (Eds.): WASA 2016, LNCS 9798, pp. 475–486, 2016.
DOI: 10.1007/978-3-319-42836-9_42

CSI at the transmitter (CSIT) in general requires feedback from the receiver. Because the CSI needs to be fed back from each receiver, the requirement of CSIT in multiuser MIMO (MU-MIMO) downlink places a significant burden in the uplink capacity, especially when the number of users in the system is large. Thus, feedback reduction is an important task for MU-MIMO systems.

A two-stage feedback strategy for the MU-MIMO downlink system with zero-forcing beamforming (ZFBF) was proposed in [7]. In the first stage, each user feeds back a coarsely quantized version of its CSI, and thus the base station (BS) has some information to select the users to be served. Then the BS broadcasts the information about the scheduled user set, and the scheduled users feed back finer CSI to achieve good ZFBF performance. In [8], dynamic feedback bit allocation in the second stage was proposed. A drawback of the two-stage feedback strategy is the delay due to the second stage feedback. In [9], the authors proposed an adaptive channel direction information (CDI) feedback rate control scheme in MIMO broadcast channel with ZFBF. In that work, the users with better channel quality use more bits to quantize their CDI. Threshold-based feedback is another effective feedback reduction strategy [3,10]. In [10], a channel quality threshold is set according to a pre-determined scheduling outage probability for a downlink system using time division multiple access (TDMA). A user does not need to report its CSI when its channel quality is below the threshold. In [3], dual thresholds on channel norm and direction quantization error respectively to constrain the sum feedback rate for the system with opportunistic spatial division multiple access (OSDMA) were considered. In the latter two studies, it has been shown that both threshold-based feedback schemes can preserve a large portion of sum rate and reduce the feedback load dramatically.

In this paper, we extend the results in [11] to MU-MIMO downlink that uses ZFBF. We first propose a new formulation of the approximate sum rate to evaluate the system performance when the semi-orthogonal constraint of the semi-orthogonal user selection (SUS) algorithm is large. We focus on reduction of the feedback load by allowing the user to determine whether to feedback the CSI. The rank of the user in the system is needed, and the concept of order statistics is applied. Furthermore, a multi-threshold scheme in which we construct multiple thresholds on the estimated signal-to-interference-plus-noise-ratio (SINR) to reduce feedback load as well as to be the representative levels for CSI quantization is proposed. The thresholds are derived from the order statistics of the estimated SINR. The receivers whose estimated SINRs are below the smallest threshold do not need to deliver CSI to the transmitter. Through simulation, we demonstrate that the proposed scheme can save a large amount of feedback load and achieve a good sum rate performance.

2 System Model

We consider a single-cell MIMO flat Rayleigh block-fading broadcast channel, where a BS equipped with M antennas is serving K single-antenna user terminals, as shown in Fig. 1. It is assumed that $K > M$, so scheduling is necessary to

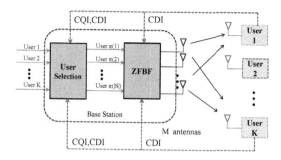

Fig. 1. System model

select users for transmission and maintain reasonable performance. After employing ZFBF to transmit the signal from the BS, the received signal at user k can be written as

$$y_k = \mathbf{h}_k \mathbf{x} + n_k, k = 1, 2, \cdots, K \tag{1}$$

where $\mathbf{x} \in \mathcal{C}^{M \times 1}$ is the transmitted symbol vector obtained from the information symbols of a selected set of users $\mathcal{S} = \{\pi(1), \ldots, \pi(|\mathcal{S}|)\}$, as described below, with an average power constraint $\mathbb{E}[\|\mathbf{x}\|^2] = P$, and $\mathbf{h}_k \in \mathcal{C}^{1 \times M}$ is the channel vector from the BS to user k. The entries of the channel vectors are independent identically distributed (i.i.d.) zero mean and unit variance complex Gaussian random variables. The n_k represents the additive white Gaussian noise (AWGN) with variance σ_n^2 at the k-th user. Therefore, the system average signal to noise ratio (SNR) can be defined as SNR $= P/\sigma_n^2$. For simplicity, we assume that users are homogeneous and experience independent fadings with identical distributions. This assumption corresponds to the situation where users feedback their normalized CSI with respect to their path losses (or short-term average CSI) for the BS to perform proportional fair scheduling.

By using linear beamforming, the transmitted signal $\mathbf{x}$ is given by

$$\mathbf{x} = \sum_{i \in \mathcal{S}} \mathbf{v}_i s_i \tag{2}$$

where $s_i, i \in \mathcal{S}$ is the information symbol of the i-th scheduled user, and $\mathbf{v}_i$ is its beamforming vector determined according to the feedbacks of the users. Then, the received signal at the k-th user via the linear beamforming can be rewritten as

$$y_k = \mathbf{h}_k \mathbf{v}_k s_k + \sum_{j \neq k} \mathbf{h}_k \mathbf{v}_j s_j + n_k, \ k \in \mathcal{S} \tag{3}$$

where $\sum_{j \neq k} \mathbf{h}_k \mathbf{v}_j s_j$ is the interference term. The resulting SINR at user k is

$$SINR_k = \frac{\rho |\mathbf{h}_k \mathbf{v}_k|^2}{1 + \rho \sum_{k \neq j} |\mathbf{h}_k \mathbf{v}_j|^2}, k \in \mathcal{S} \tag{4}$$

where $\rho = P/|\mathcal{S}|$ represents that the symbols of the scheduled users equally share the total power P. Therefore, the sum rate for the scheduled user set $\mathcal{S}$ is given by

$$R(\mathcal{S}) = \sum_{k \in \mathcal{S}} \log_2(1 + SINR_k) \tag{5}$$

To facilitate the scheduling process and the ZFBF design, the CSI report, including both the channel quality indication (CQI) and the CDI, of the users are required.

2.1   Finite Rate Feedback for CDI Quantization

We assume that each user has perfect CSIR of $\mathbf{h}_k$ and quantizes the direction of its (normalized) channel $\tilde{\mathbf{h}}_k = \mathbf{h}_k/\|\mathbf{h}_k\|$ to a unit norm vector $\hat{\mathbf{h}}_k$. The quantization vector is chosen from the codebook $\mathcal{W}_k = \{\hat{\mathbf{h}}_j^c : 1 \leq j \leq 2^{B_D}\}$ according to the minimum distance criterion

$$\hat{\mathbf{h}}_k = \arg \max_{\hat{\mathbf{h}}_j^c : 1 \leq j \leq 2^{B_D}} |\hat{\mathbf{h}}_j^c \tilde{\mathbf{h}}_k^*|. \tag{6}$$

The codebook $\mathcal{W}_k$ is known at both the BS and user k a priori. The user feeds back the index of the codebook to the BS, requiring B_D feedback bits. For simplicity, it is assumed that the feedback is perfect and instantaneous.

2.2   CQI Feedback Model

In addition to the CDI, each user also feeds back B_Q bits to represent its CQI. Due to quantization of the CDI, the eventually received SINR in (4) is unknown at both the transmitter and the receiver. The users estimate their SINR using the expected SINR conditioned on $\tilde{\mathbf{h}}_k$ and $\hat{\mathbf{h}}_k$, given by [5]

$$\mathbb{E}\{SINR_k\} \geq \frac{\rho \|\mathbf{h}_k\|^2 \mathbb{E}\{|\tilde{\mathbf{h}}_k \mathbf{v}_k|^2\}}{1 + \rho \frac{|\mathcal{S}|-1}{M-1} \|\mathbf{h}_k\|^2 \sin^2 \theta_k}$$

$$\geq \frac{\rho \|\mathbf{h}_k\|^2 \cos^2(\theta_k + \phi_k)}{1 + \rho \frac{|\mathcal{S}|-1}{M-1} \|\mathbf{h}_k\|^2 \sin^2 \theta_k} \triangleq \gamma_{k,|\mathcal{S}|}(\phi_k) \tag{7}$$

where θ_k is the direction quantization error, and ϕ_k is the angle between $\hat{\mathbf{h}}_k$ and $\mathbf{v}_k$. Because the quantized channels of the scheduled users may not be orthogonal, there exists a mismatch between $\hat{\mathbf{h}}_k$ and $\mathbf{v}_k$. In [6,12], the CQI feedback $\gamma_{k,M}$ is selected under the semi-orthogonal constraint $\epsilon = 0$

$$\gamma_{k,M} \triangleq \gamma_{k,M}(0). \tag{8}$$

It is noted that (7) is tight when $\epsilon = 0$. As a beginning point, we also use $\gamma_{k,M}$ to represent the estimated SINR, and the distribution of $\gamma_{k,|\mathcal{S}|}$ using the SUS algorithm is given by [5,13]

$$F_{\gamma_{k,|S|}}(x) = \begin{cases} 1 - 2^{B_D} \dfrac{e^{-\frac{x}{\rho}}}{(1+Ax)^{M-1}}, & x \geq \frac{1-\delta}{A\delta} \\ 1 - 2^{B_D} \dfrac{e^{-\frac{x}{\rho}}}{(1+Ax)^{M-1}} + \mathcal{T}, & 0 < x < \frac{1-\delta}{A\delta} \end{cases} \tag{9}$$

where $A = \frac{|S|-1}{M-1}$, $\mathcal{T} = \frac{1}{\Gamma(M-1)}[2^{B_D}\frac{e^{\frac{-x}{\rho}}}{(1+Ax)^{M-1}}(\Gamma(M-1,\delta(Ax+1)v) - \Gamma(M-1,v))]$, $\delta = 2^{-\frac{B_D}{M-1}}$, $v = \frac{x}{\rho(1-\delta-A\delta x)}$ and $\Gamma(a,x)$ is the incomplete gamma function.

2.3 MIMO with ZFBF

In the MIMO broadcast channel using ZFBF, each beamforming vector $\mathbf{v}_j \in \mathcal{C}^{M\times1}$, $j \in S$, should be selected to satisfy the zero-forcing condition $\hat{\mathbf{h}}_i \mathbf{v}_j = 0$ for $i \neq j$, $i \in S$. From $\hat{\mathbf{H}}(S) = ([\hat{\mathbf{h}}^T_{\pi(1)}, \cdots, \hat{\mathbf{h}}^T_{\pi(|S|)}])$, the normalized columns of the pseudo inverse of $\hat{\mathbf{H}}(S)$ defined as $\hat{\mathbf{H}}(S)^\dagger = \hat{\mathbf{H}}(S)^*(\hat{\mathbf{H}}(S)\hat{\mathbf{H}}(S)^*)^{-1}$ can be chosen as the beamforming vectors.

3 Sum Rate with the SUS Algorithm

In the SUS algorithm, the approximate cardinality of the candidate user set $|\mathcal{B}_i|$ at the i-th user selection stage, containing the users which are semi-orthogonal (i.e., with correlation smaller than ϵ) to the previously selected i users, is [14]

$$|\mathcal{B}_i| = \begin{cases} K \triangleq K_0, & i = 0 \\ \lfloor K\alpha_i \rfloor \triangleq K_i, & i = 1, \cdots, M-1 \end{cases} \tag{10}$$

where $\alpha_i = \prod_{k=1}^{i}(1 - (1 - \epsilon^2)^{M-k})$. With the cardinalities of the candidate sets, we can derive the probability P_j that at least j users are selected by the SUS algorithm. According to the process of the SUS algorithm, user k is scheduled at the i-th user scheduling stage only when user k has the largest SINR among the users which satisfy the semi-orthogonal constraint. In order to obtain P_j, we first derive the probability that exactly n users are scheduled, P_{S_n}. Then we will have $P_j = P_{j-1} - P_{S_{j-1}}$. Assume that the users' estimated SINRs are arranged in decreasing order as $\{SINR_{(1)} \geq SINR_{(2)}, \cdots, \geq SINR_{(K)}\}$. The first scheduled user in the zero-th stage of the SUS algorithm is the user with the largest SINR, $SINR_{(1)}$. Since this user can always be found, we have $P_1 = 1$. At the i-th scheduling stage, the probability that a not-yet-selected user satisfies the semi-orthogonal constraint (with respect to the already selected users) is α_i. Taking the first selection stage as an example, if the eventually selected user is the one corresponding to $SINR_{(j)}$, that means that the users corresponding to $SINR_{(2)}, \cdots, SINR_{(j-1)}$ do not satisfy the semi-orthogonal constraint while the user corresponding to $SINR_{(j)}$ does. If, after the entire SUS algorithm finishes and there are exactly two users (corresponding to $SINR_{(1)}$ and $SINR_{(j)}$) selected, that means that the users corresponding to $SINR_{(j+1)}, \cdots, SINR_{(K)}$ do not satisfy the semi-orthogonal constraint at the second scheduling stage. Therefore, the probability of exactly two scheduled users with $SINR_{(1)}, SINR_{(j)}$ is

$$P(SINR_{(1)}, SINR_{(j)}) = (1 - \alpha_1)^{j-2}\alpha_1(1 - \alpha_2)^{K-j}, \ j = 2, 3, \cdots, K. \quad (11)$$

Then, the probability of exactly two scheduled users, P_{S_2}, is

$$P_{S_2} = \sum_{m=0}^{K-2} \alpha_1(1 - \alpha_1)^m (1 - \alpha_2)^{K-2-m}. \quad (12)$$

The probability of exactly n $(n \leq M)$ users scheduled, P_{S_n}, can be similarly derived as

$$P_{S_n} = \sum_{m_1=0}^{K-2} \cdots \sum_{m_{n-1}}^{K-n-Q(n)} \left(\prod_{t=1}^{n-1} \alpha_t(1 - \alpha_t)^{m_t} \right)(1 - \alpha_{m_n})^{K-n-Q(n-1)} \quad (13)$$

where $Q(n) = \sum_{t=1}^{n-1} m_t, n \geq 2$. Therefore, the probability P_j, $j = 1, 2, \cdots, M$ can be obtained as

$$P_j = \begin{cases} 1 & , j = 1 \\ 1 - (1 - \alpha_1)^{K-1} & , j = 2 \\ P_{j-1} - P_{S_{j-1}} & , j = 3, 4, \cdots, M \\ 0 & , otherwise \end{cases} \quad (14)$$

We further define $\gamma_{(K_i),|\mathcal{S}|}$ as the largest random variable among K_i random variables $\{\gamma_{1,|\mathcal{S}|}, \cdots, \gamma_{K_i,|\mathcal{S}|}\}$ with the common CDF in (9) at the i-th user selection stage. Applying the order statistics theorem, the CDF of $\gamma_{(K_i),|\mathcal{S}|}$ is given by

$$F_{\gamma_{(K_i),|\mathcal{S}|}}(x) = F_{\gamma_{K_i,|\mathcal{S}|}}(x)^{K_i}. \quad (15)$$

Then the PDF of $\gamma_{(K_i),|\mathcal{S}|}$ is

$$f_{\gamma_{(K_i),|\mathcal{S}|}}(x) = K_i f_{\gamma_{K_i,|\mathcal{S}|}}(x)(F_{\gamma_{K_i,|\mathcal{S}|}}(x))^{K_i-1}. \quad (16)$$

Applying (14) and (16), the approximate sum rate employing the SUS algorithm with quantized CDI and perfect CQI feedback is given by

$$R \approx \sum_{j=1}^{M}(P_j - P_{j+1})E\left\{ \sum_{i=0}^{j-1} log_2(1 + \gamma_{(K_i),|\mathcal{S}|}) \right\}$$

$$= \sum_{j=1}^{M}(P_j - P_{j+1}) \sum_{i=0}^{j-1} \int_0^\infty log_2(1 + x)f_{\gamma_{(K_i),|\mathcal{S}|}}(x)dx \quad (17)$$

where $(P_j - P_{j+1})$ represents the probability that the total number of scheduled users is j.

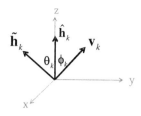

Fig. 2. The average relations among $\hat{\mathbf{h}}_k, \tilde{\mathbf{h}}_k$ and $\mathbf{v}_k$

When we consider the case $\epsilon > 0$, the selected users' channels are no longer perfectly orthogonal, and ϕ_k, the angle between $\hat{\mathbf{h}}_k$ and $\mathbf{v}_k$, in (7) is not zero. In this case, (17) derived by using (9) becomes an upper bound which is loose when ϵ is large. As depicted in Fig. 2, the plane including $\hat{\mathbf{h}}_k$ and $\tilde{\mathbf{h}}_k$ and the plane including $\hat{\mathbf{h}}_k$ and $\mathbf{v}_k$ are orthogonal on average. Thus, the coordinate of $\tilde{\mathbf{h}}_k$ can be expressed as $(\sin\theta_k, 0, \cos\theta_k)$ and the coordinate of $\mathbf{v}_k$ is $(0, \sin\phi_k, \cos\phi_k)$. Taking the inner product between $\tilde{\mathbf{h}}_k$ and $\mathbf{v}_k$, we can show that $\cos\angle(\tilde{\mathbf{h}}_k, \mathbf{v}_k)$ is equal to $\cos\theta_k \cos\phi_k$. Consequently, the expected $SINR_k$ conditioned on $\tilde{\mathbf{h}}_k$ and $\hat{\mathbf{h}}_k$ can be further derived as

$$E\{SINR_k\} \approx \frac{\rho\|\mathbf{h}_k\|^2 \cos^2\theta_k \cos^2\phi_k}{1 + \rho\frac{|\mathcal{S}|-1}{M-1}|\mathbf{h}_k\|^2 \sin^2\theta_k}. \tag{18}$$

Since the exact distribution of $\cos\phi_k$ is difficult to derive, we resorted to obtaining it through simulation. With the distribution of $\cos\phi_k$, the distribution of the modified expected $SINR_k$ can be obtained accordingly, which can then be plugged into (17).

In Fig. 3, it is shown that the theoretical sum rate with this modification matches the simulation result even when the semi-orthogonal constraint ϵ is large.

4   Feedback Reduction Strategy

To facilitate the scheduling operation, the users need to feed back their CSI which include CDI and CQI. The CQI metric derived in Sect. 2.2 provides the estimated SINR which can capture full multiuser diversity gain. Considering that under the maximum sum-rate criterion the users with relatively low estimated SINR are rarely selected, it is reasonable to assume that allowing these users to feed back CSI may not improve the system scheduling performance but on the other hand may increase the feedback load. Consequently, it is proposed in this section division of the range of the estimated SINR into multiple regions. Each of these regions signifies different importance for the SUS algorithm. The proposed multiple-threshold model is shown as Type-I in Fig. 4

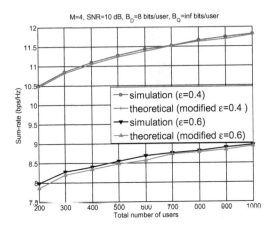

Fig. 3. Simulation and modified theoretical results of sum rate vs. total number of users when $M = 4, SNR = 10, B_D = 10$ bits/user, $B_Q = \infty$ bits/user, $\varepsilon = 0.4, 0.6$.

4.1   Derivation of Multiple Thresholds

From a user's perspective, it has to compete with approximately K_i users and win, if it is to be selected at the ith stage of the SUS scheduling. The higher the user's SINR, the higher the chance that it is selected in an earlier stage. Thus we use $K_i, i = 0, 1, \cdots, M - 1$ to derive the multiple thresholds for CQI feedback.

Let $X_{(1)}, X_{(2)}, \cdots, X_{(K_i)}$, be the order statistic of i.i.d. random variables $\{X_1, X_2, \cdots, X_{K_i}\}$, with common CDF (9) in descending order, i.e., $X_{(1)} \geq X_{(2)} \geq \cdots \geq X_{(K_i)}$. The probability that the estimated SINR of the k-th user r_k is ranked the p-th among the K_i users in set $\mathcal{B}_i$ is shown as follows:

$$P\{X_k = X_{(p)}|X_k = r_k\} = \frac{(K_i - 1)!\{F_{\gamma_{k,|S|}}(r_k)\}^{K_i - p}\{1 - F_{\gamma_{k,|S|}}(r_k)\}^{p-1}}{(K_i - p)!}.$$

For example, when the k-th user has estimated SINR r_k, the probability that user k has the highest SINR value among all K_i users is

$$\frac{P\{r_k = X_{(1)}\}}{P\{X_k = r_k\}} = (F_{\gamma_{k,|S|}}(r_k))^{K_i - 1}. \tag{19}$$

In addition, (19) also satisfies

$$\sum_{p=1}^{K_i} P\{X_k = X_{(p)}|X_k = r_k\} = 1. \tag{20}$$

With the estimated SINR r_k, the k-th user can judge its most possible rank among the K_i users in $\mathcal{B}_i$ according to

$$rank_i(r_k) = arg \max_{p=1,\cdots,K_i} P\{X_k = X_{(p)}|X_k = r_k\}. \tag{21}$$

With the SUS algorithm, the BS selects the i-th user whose estimated SINR is the highest among the K_{i-1} users in $\mathcal{B}_{i-1}$. Based on this process, we can construct M thresholds to reduce feedback and use these thresholds as quantization levels of CQI. For simplicity, we use $r_{k,M}$ in (8) to derive the thresholds. The first (highest) threshold $\gamma_{th,1}$ is set to allow the potential winners of the 0th SUS stage to feedback. With the i.i.d. CQI assumption, $\gamma_{th,1}$ is the same for all users such that

$$\text{when } \gamma_{k,M} \in [\gamma_{th,1}, \infty), \; rank_0(\gamma_{k,M}) = 1. \tag{22}$$

Similarly, the other thresholds can be set to allow the potential winners of the following SUS stages to feedback:

$$\text{when } \gamma_{k,M} \in [\gamma_{th,i}, \infty), \; rank_{i-1}(\gamma_{k,M}) = 1, i = 2, \cdots, M. \tag{23}$$

All thresholds can be computed off-line as long as the number of users, the semi-orthogonal constraint ϵ and the fading statistics are known. The values of the thresholds can be updated periodically as part of the system configuration broadcast from the BS. When a user's estimated SINR is higher than $\gamma_{th,M}$, it feeds back the index of the highest threshold its estimated SINR is above. Otherwise it does not feedback.

4.2   Feedback Load Analysis

With the way the lowest threshold $\gamma_{th,M}$ is set, i.e., letting the user with the highest SINR among K_{M-1} i.i.d. users feedback, it can be easily derived that the feedback probability of each users is $1/K_{M-1}$. As a result, given a total number of feedback bits $B_T = B_D + B_Q$ per user, the total feedback load for the proposed scheme can be derived to be

$$L_{fbk} = \begin{cases} KB_T, & 0 < K \leq \frac{1}{\lfloor \alpha_{M-1} \rfloor} \\ \frac{B_T K}{K_{M-1}} = \frac{B_T}{\lfloor \alpha_{M-1} \rfloor}, & K > \frac{1}{\lfloor \alpha_{M-1} \rfloor} \end{cases}. \tag{24}$$

The total feedback load becomes fixed when the total number of users in the system $K > \frac{1}{\lfloor \alpha_{M-1} \rfloor}$. On the other hand, it increases linearly with the number of users when the total number of users is smaller than $\frac{1}{\lfloor \alpha_{M-1} \rfloor}$.

5   Numerical Results

In this section, we compare the sum rate performance and total feedback load of our proposed scheme with other feedback strategies. In the simulation, we assume that the transmitter is equipped with $M = 4$ antennas, and there are K single antenna users. The semi-orthogonal constraint is set to $\varepsilon = 0.4$ in the SUS scheduling algorithm. Each user feeds back $B_T = B_Q + B_D$ bits to represent the CQI and CDI to the BS to facilitate the scheduling operation. The feedback models considered are shown in Fig. 4. The Type-I feedback model is

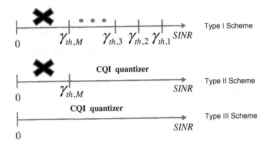

Fig. 4. Different feedback models with CQI quantization.

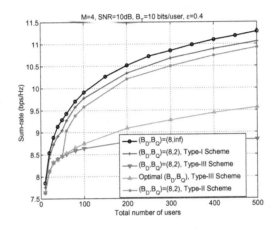

Fig. 5. Sum-rate vs. total number of users when $M = 4$, SNR $= 10$ dB, $B_T = 10$ and $\varepsilon = 0.4$.

the proposed multiple-threshold model with the CQI quantization levels equal to the thresholds. In the Type-II model, a user feeds back when its SINR is greater than the threshold $r_{th,M}$, and the CQI feedback is uniformly quantized in the region $(r_{th,M}, \infty)$ using B_Q bits. For Type-III, no matter what the SINR is, a user uniformly quantizes CQI in $(0, \infty)$ using B_Q bits and feeds back.

Figure 5 compares the sum rate performance of different feedback schemes. For Type-III, the optimal bit combination (B_D, B_Q) still results in significant sum rate loss due to inefficient quantization in region $(0, \infty)$. Quantizing only in $(r_{th,M}, \infty)$ instead of $(0, \infty)$, the Type-II scheme is able to achieve higher sum rate than the Type-III scheme. When the total number of users is small ($0 \le K \le \frac{1}{\lfloor \alpha_{M-1} \rfloor}$), the threshold $r_{th,M}$ becomes zero, and the sum rate performance of Type-II is the same as that of Type-III. The proposed Type-I scheme on the other hand has better CQI quantization, and achieves higher sum rate than Type-II.

In Fig. 6, the overall feedback load of different schemes are compared. Type-I and Type-II schemes can efficiently feedback CSI to the BS and keep the overall

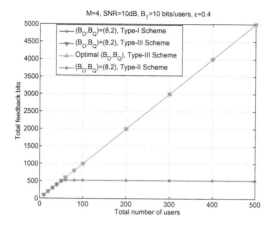

Fig. 6. Total feedback load vs. total number of users when $M = 4$, SNR $= 10$ dB, $B_T = 10$ and $\varepsilon = 0.4$.

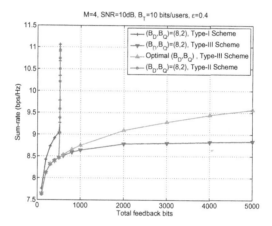

Fig. 7. Sum-rate vs. total feedback load when $M = 4$, SNR $= 10$ dB, $B_T = 10$ and $\varepsilon = 0.4$.

feedback load as a constant. As shown in Fig. 7, Type-I and Type-II schemes can achieve the multiuser diversity gain with a small amount of feedback load. Because the overall number of feedback bits is a constant, the sum rate can be increased without increasing the feedback load.

6   Conclusion

A MU-MIMO broadcast channel with ZFBF and limited feedback has been analyzed and evaluated through simulation in this paper. Starting with the distribution of estimated SINR and the approximate cardinality of the candidate sets in the SUS algorithm, an approximation of sum rate for the system with both quantized CDI and perfect CQI feedback is derived. The angle between the channel vector and beamforming vector, ϕ_k, is also taken into account to provide a realistic sum-rate estimation. We further proposed a new multi-threshold scheme to reduce a large amount of feedback load as well as to quantize the CQI. The proposed scheme maintains a constant feedback overhead as the number of users in the system increases beyond $K > \frac{1}{\lceil \alpha_{M-1} \rceil}$. Extensive simulation has been conducted to show that the proposed scheme can efficiently reduce the feedback load while achieving good sum-rate performance.

References

1. Costa, M.: Writing on dirty paper. IEEE Trans. Inf. Theory **29**(3), 439–441 (1983)
2. Jindal, N.: MIMO broadcast channels with finite-rate feedback. IEEE Trans. Inf. Theory **52**(11), 5045–5060 (2006)
3. Huang, K., Heath, R.W., Andrews, J.G.: Space division multiple access with a sum feedback rate constraint. IEEE Trans. Signal Process. **55**(7), 3879–3891 (2007)
4. Sharif, M., Hassibi, B.: On the capacity of MIMO broadcast channels with partial side information. IEEE Trans. Inf. Theory **51**(2), 506–522 (2005)
5. Yoo, T., Jindal, N., Goldsmith, A.: Multi-antenna downlink channels with limited feedback and user selection. IEEE J. Select. Areas Commun. **25**(7), 1478–1491 (2007)
6. Trivellato, M., Boccardi, F., Tosato, F.: User selection schemes for MIMO broadcast channels with limited feedback. In: Proceedings of IEEE Vehicular Technology Conference (VTC), pp. 2089–2093, April 2007
7. Zakhour, R., Gesbert, D.: A two-stage approach to feedback design in multi-user MIMO channels with limited channel state information. In: Proceedings of IEEE Personal, Indoor and Mobile Radio Communication (PIMRC), pp. 1–5, September 2007
8. Sohn, I., Park, C.S., Lee, K.B.: Dynamic channel feedback control for limited-feedback multi-user MIMO systems. In: Proceedings of IEEE International Conference Communication (ICC), June 2009
9. Zakhour, R., Gesbert, D.: Adaptive feedback rate control in MIMO broadcast systems. In: Proceedings of IEEE Information Theory Workshop (ITW), pp. 440–444, May 2008
10. Gesbert, D., Alouini, M.-S.: How much feedback is multi-user diversity really worth? In: Proceedings of IEEE International Conference Communication (ICC), vol. 1, pp. 234–238, June 2004
11. Li, J.-H., Su, H.-J.: Opportunistic feedback reduction for multiuser mimo broadcast channel with orthogonal beamforming. IEEE Trans. Wirel. Commun. **13**(3), 1321–1333 (2014)
12. Yoo, T., Goldsmith, A.: On the optimality of multiantenna broadcast scheduling using zero-forcing beamforming. IEEE J. Sel. Areas Commun. **24**, 528–541 (2006)
13. Kountouris, M.: Multiuser multi-antenna systems with limited feedback. Ph.D. dissertation, EURECOM Institute (2008)
14. Shao, Y., Yuan, J.: A lower bound to the sum-rate of MIMO broadcast channels with limited-rate feedback. In: Proceedings of IEEE International Conference Communication (ICC), pp. 3674–3678, May 2008

MPBSD: A Moving Target Defense Approach for Base Station Security in Wireless Sensor Networks

Tommy Chin[1(✉)] and Kaiqi Xiong[2(✉)]

[1] Department of Computing Security,
Rochester Institute of Technology, Rochester, NY 14623, USA
txc9627@rit.edu
[2] Florida Cyber Security Center, University of South Florida, Tampa, FL 33620, USA
xiongk@usf.edu

Abstract. This paper addresses one major concern on how to secure the location information of a base station in a compromised Wireless Sensor Network (WSN). In this concern, disrupting or damaging the wireless base station can be catastrophic for a WSN. To aid in the mitigation of this challenge, we present Moving Proximity Base Station Defense (MPBSD), a Moving Target Defense (MTD) approach to concealing the location of a base station within a WSN. In this approach, we employ multiple base stations to serve a WSN where one of the multiple base stations is elected to serve the WSN in a specific period of time. Specifically, our approach periodically changes the designation over a period of time to provide obscurity in the location information of the base station. We further evaluate MPBSD using a real-world testbed environment utilizing Wi-Fi frequencies. Our results show that MPBSD is an effective MTD approach to securing base stations for a WSN in term of sensory performance such as end-to-end delay.

Keywords: Wireless Sensor Network · Moving Target Defense · Security

1 Introduction

Sensory-based infrastructures including Internet of Things (IoT) and Wireless Sensor Networks (WSN) provide many methods for data accessibility such as localization tracking, smart homes, and metric evaluation. Although IoT and WSN make significant impacts on various fields of use, the base station—in which each sensory node communicates to—can be manipulated or subdued to adverse cyber attacks. There have been numerous approaches to identifying and securing a base station such as the implementation of an Intrusion Detection Systems (IDS) [1], an approach to increasing the anonymity of a base station [2], and an intrusion-tolerant routing solution (INSENS) [3]. Yet none, to the best of our knowledge, has examine Moving Target Defense (MTD) for securing a WSN base station.

© Springer International Publishing Switzerland 2016
Q. Yang et al. (Eds.): WASA 2016, LNCS 9798, pp. 487–498, 2016.
DOI: 10.1007/978-3-319-42836-9_43

To mitigate adverse threats in locating the WSN base station, we present a novel approach to periodically changing its location using an election process between multiple active and inactive base stations within a given proximity. We call our approach Moving Proximity Base Station Defense (MPBSD), which is inspired by previous studies in [2,4,5] to enhance security in WSN. The designation of an active base station is done through an election process amongst all the base stations to be the sole receiving and transmitting base station for the WSN. Inactive base stations will transmit spoof data within the given region to mask the location of the active base station in aims to hinder localization methods for the subdue sensor node. Our approach periodically changes the roles of each base station from active to inactive state and vice-versa over a given timeframe utilizing a combination of heartbeat messaging and election processes. Our implementation demonstrates the capability of our approach through our experiments.

To implement our MPBSD approach, we utilize Global Environment for Network Innovation (GENI) [6] and specifically—the Orbit Lab Grid testbed [7] and the w-iLab.t testbed [8] to conduct experiments. Using a pool of 400 wireless sensors, we randomly select a minimal of two scaling upwards to five sensors as base stations for our WSN. We conduct multiple experiments to measure performance impacts and localization constraints for a compromised sensor node to locate the base station. Additionally, if an adverse user has the ability to compromise a single sensor node, other nodes are also at risk, therefore—we examined constraints for multiple sensor nodes.

We summarize the contributions of this paper as follows:

- We propose and implement our MPBSD as an approach to obscuring the location of a base station when a sensor node is compromised in a WSN. Our approach utilizes a number of features of heartbeat messaging, falsifies data transmission, and involves multiple base stations that change states of active and inactive state.
- We examine the impacts of convergence for MPBSD when a base station transitions from active to inactive state. Our examination focuses on the performance of sensor communication with respect to end-to-end delay.
- Our implementation using a real-world testbed solution demonstrates the effectiveness of MPBSD as a viable solution to enhance the security of a base station by obscuring the physical location. We provide evaluation of the challenges and give results of the accuracy to locate a base station.

The rest of this paper is organized as follows. In Sect. 2 we state our research problem and describe challenges to our approach. Section 3 provides some related work. Architectural designs and our election algorithm are described in Sect. 4. In Sect. 5 we provide our experimental results to our proposed design and implementation. Lastly, in Sect. 6 we conclude our paper and present future work.

2   Problem Statement

In this section, we summarize background knowledge on localization problems in wireless networks and provide motivation and research challenges for our work.

2.1   Background on Localization Challenges

A common method to locate a wireless device within a given region is through the use of Received-Signal-Strength-Indicator (RSSI). A major constraint to the use of RSSI as a localization method is that RSSI is subdue to environmental factors. Essentially, many of the localization methods utilize a relationship of RSSI values and correlates the metric to distance. The accuracy of RSSI is heavily influenced by obstructions such as walls, piping, and water, etc., causing negligible localization measurements. The inaccuracy of using RSSI is a common issue, and we will fully utilize this weakness as an enhancement in our MPBSD approach.

2.2   Research Challenge and Motivation

A completely secure environment in a WSN would be a dream case scenario by many, but the increase in new attack vectors for adverse users provides a grand challenge to address. Locating the base station from a physical perspective can be devastating for a WSN as adverse users can manipulate or destroy the functionality of the base station. Specifically, an adverse user can modify a base station to manipulate data transmission from sensor nodes to the base station such that data processing or post processing information can be skewed or altered affecting end goals of a WSN. This presents a number of challenges.

In order to outline the challenges in this work, we provide a brief description as follows:

– How can we determine what state should be switched to not only enhance security but also significantly does not influence the performance of sensor nodes with respect to network and power?
– RSSI as a localization method has negligible accuracy in locating a target. How can we utilize these inaccuracies as an enhancement to secure the base station
– Utilizing heartbeat methods between base stations can be easily manipulated or replayed by an adverse user. How can we address the security of our MPBSD's heartbeat method to prevent or reduce the vulnerability of an adverse attack?

To address such challenges, related work will be examined for characteristics or traits that provide an aid to our proposed MPBSD solution.

3   Related Work

The implementation of an IDS [1] in a WSN has been examined in which researchers positioned numerous IDSs within a WSN where cluster heads inherit a cooperative infrastructure-wide detection model while sensors within a cluster gain independent of a local variant IDS. Although detection methods were discussed, a major weakness to the use of an IDS approach focuses towards increase energy consumption and computational resource stress. To alleviate stress on sensors within a WSN with security in mind, Acharya and Younis [2] proposed an increase anonymity approach where the base station transmits false data within the region to mimic a sensory device. Additionally, they proposed a moving base station approach where the position becomes difficult to locate when the base station moves to another area within the WSN. Comparatively, MPBSD periodically cycles positions using randomization functions over Acharya and Younis approach [2]. Although location and obscure methods can be used to increase security, Deng et al. [3] examined routing approaches to securing a WSN when a sensory device becomes compromised. Additionally, routing concepts are common addressing security in a WSN. Such management has been examined with a trusted system approach [9–11] and replication attack detection [4], and outlined with a survey of best practices [5].

4   Design

To address and identify challenges that we previously describe in enhancing the security of a WSN base stations from being located, we present a detailed overview of the proposed base station enhancement method—MPBSD.

4.1   System Architecture

MPBSD provides three major characteristics to enhance WSN base station security to prevent localization threats from adverse users. Those characteristics are:

- Multiple base stations utilizing state based methods of active and inactive states where inactive base stations transmit falsified data to further obscure the active base station.
- A heartbeat method to intercommunicate base stations to change states of being active and inactive based on an election model and a decision algorithm.
- Utilizes RSSI localization inaccuracies as an enhancement method to further obscure the position of the base station.

The state of base stations utilizing the active and inactive state plays a significant role in MPBSD. In order to describe our approach, we provide a model of states for base stations in Fig. 1.

As described in Fig. 1, a base station initiates itself under the *initialize* state. Under this process, network addresses are established, and an election process occurs to determine the state of the base station. In Subsect. 4.2, we describe the election algorithm in detail where the algorithm undergoes to determine the state of a base station. If the base station is determined to be in an *active* state, data will be transmitted and received from the various sensor nodes in the WSN. If the base station is in the *inactive* state, falsify data is transmitted to the WSN region to obscure and mask the active base station in the MPBSD process. To be specific, the falsified data transmitted will be spoofed header information that mimic existing data on the WSN. The falsified data will have no receiving

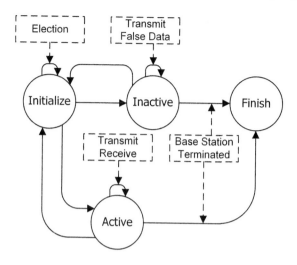

Fig. 1. A logic diagram of base station roles utilizing MPBSD where the active state is the designated base station within a WSN to transmit and receive data from sensor nodes while the inactive state aim to further mask the location of the active base station. The change of a base stations' state is determined by MPBSD's election process and wait timers.

client to transmit to and will simply transmit in the airspace to obscure the location of the base station. Additionally, inactive base stations will vary the transmitting antenna power level to further confuse values of RSSI in order to obscure localization methods from an adverse user. Lastly, the *finish* state is a result if an issue on a base station occurs leading to termination.

4.2   Election Method: Decision Algorithm and Heartbeat

The election process for MPBSD determines the state of a base station within a WSN given a period of time. The state of the base station changes periodically to reduce the footprint markings of its location. In our MPBSD approach, the election process begins with a predetermined set δ of base stations at the initialization of the WSN. The set δ is ordered by the base stations' mac-addresses from low to high. We select $\rho \in \delta$ ($\rho > 0$) as the active base station where ρ is a random integer variable following the discrete uniform distribution over the set δ and the remaining elements of the set as inactive base stations. Once an election occurs, MPBSD operates over a period of time before a re-election occurs. This period of time for the MPBSD operation is given by the value α ($\alpha > 0$), a random integer variable following the discrete uniform distribution over the minimal range β and the maximum bound γ. We determine the values of β and γ through analysis from experimentation as the interval in which a base station changes states can influence network performance for sensor nodes. To clarify our process, Fig. 2 demonstrates a diagram of the election process.

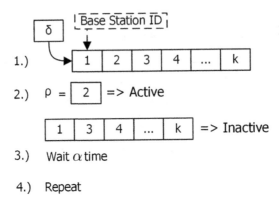

Fig. 2. A step process to the election method in MPBSD to select the state of a base station over the operational time of the WSN. For Line 2, ρ is an example and does not reflect any static value.

In step 4 of Fig. 2, we express that the election process repeats itself over a period of time. Step 2 demonstrates a potential change of states for a base station, but the time for a sensor node to re-establish communication can be devastating with regards to network performance. Our experiments will provide analysis to the potential hazards of this step in aims to optimize this constraint. To synchronize the communication between each base station, we utilize a heartbeat mechanism.

Although each base station undergoes an election process to change their operational states from active and inactive, a heartbeat mechanism is utilize to maintain the membership each base station for the election. Additionally, the heartbeat mechanism triggers the election process once the operational period α expires. Communication-wise, each heartbeat message will be transmitted on the infrastructural side of the WSN—that is, each heartbeat message will be transmitted on the wired interface of each base station to reduce security threats within the wireless portion.

4.3 Inaccuracies of RSSI as an Enhancement Suite

Environmental influences become a significant constraint to localization methods using RSSI, and specifically—the accuracy of the tracking system. Using previous work [12], we use the relationship of RSSI-to-Distance (RtD) as the method to locate the base station from varying quantity of compromised sensor nodes. Specifically, Eq. (1) represents our tracking estimation for RtD where r represents values of RSSI measured in dBm and x represents the distance of the target in meters.

$$r = -42.98x^{0.1534} \tag{1}$$

Although Eq. (1) was constructed through pre-examined measurements and curve fitted on a graph, this method was not examined in the Orbit Lab Grid [7].

To present the ambiguity an adverse user may experience when compromising a WSN of unknown constraints, we use this method as an estimation to locate the base station. Additionally, if an adverse user were to subdue a sensor node with a WSN, then the potential to compromise remaining nodes can also be a viable direction. Using Eq. (2), an adverse user can obtain samples from three or more sensor nodes in an attempt to locate the active base station where x, y represent sensor location and d represents distance using RtD. Secondly, the accuracy to locate the target using RSSI can be negligible due to real-time changes within the environment when tracking the base station. Lastly, depending on the adverse user, the position of the wireless sensor may be unknown to the attacker. For our analysis, we treat the adverse user having knowledge of the wireless sensor location for examination purposes.

$$2(x_i - x_{i+1})x + 2(y_i - y_{i+1})y - (d_{i+1}^2 - d_i^2) = (x_i^2 - x_{i+1}^2) + (y_i^2 - y_{i+1}^2) \quad (2)$$

The use of RSSI's negligible tracking metric as an enhancement suite for MPBSD has presentable areas of examination. Under the MPBSD approach, inactive base stations transmit falsified data within the WSN to obscure the position of the active base station. Using this falsified data approach, we fluctuate the transmitting power of each inactive base station to alter the values of RSSI that can be potentially seen by an adverse user on a compromise sensor node. Although a base station broadcasts a network for sensor nodes to communicate with each other, a compromise sensor node can capture data within the WSN region to determine its own location with respect to the WSN in addition to determining the number of neighboring sensor devices.

5 Evaluation

We analyzed the effects of our MPBSD approach through experiments outlined by our methodology. In this section, we provide detailed results of MPBSD, the effects to sensory node performance and evaluate troubled areas that were noticed during our experimental evaluation.

5.1 Implementation and Preliminary Problems

In our preliminary configuration of MPBSD, we deployed our approach on a small-scale topology of three base stations and five sensor nodes as expressed in Fig. 3. Our configuration had each base station broadcast the respective SSID for the WSN when elected as an active base station. We chose this approach to identify any preliminary challenges that MPBSD produces from our designed model. In our preliminary experiment, we had each sensor node ping the active base station over a period of time. Our configuration had all base stations sharing the same IP address on the network topology that interfaces with each sensor node. Inactive base stations, although having a similar IP address, would have their interface switched to promiscuous mode—losing its ability to communicate to the network and remove the problem for the IP to conflict. The first problem

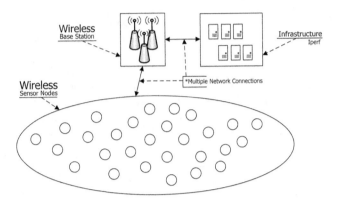

Fig. 3. A topology design outlining the infrastructure used for our experiments. Note, quantity of items in this figure do not project or reflect our experiments, but purely a representation of how our infrastructure was deployed and configured.

that was identified from this approach was mac-address. Although each base station shares the same IP address, mac-addresses would also need to be the same to remove layer 2 problems in the OSI model. It was noticed that every time a base station broadcast the shared SSID on the WSN, different mac-addresses would be used per base station causing each sensor node to transmit a new ARP Request due to inconsistent entries in their ARP table. To solve such issue, we fixed the mac-address value for each base station's wireless interface to reduce sensor node confusion. Upon correcting such problem, we began to execute various experiments to examine the effects of MPBSD.

5.2 Convergence Delay Problems: Overhead

One of our main concerns for our MPBSD approach is when base stations switch roles from active to inactive state. Specifically, we wanted to examine our role switching behavior to see whether our approach would create or inflect any communication problems for each sensor node with respect to convergence. To conduct such experiments, we measure the delay that was the time that a base station switches role from sensor nodes using ping as a fundamental method. Although the distance between each sensor node and a base station can affect the network performance with respect to delay, we initially base line the average delay for each sensor node prior to the role switch to measure the delay at the point of switch. In Fig. 4, we depict the delay that was produced during time of convergence where the delay was the time for a base station to switch from active to inactive state.

As expressed in Fig. 4, during the examination of MPBSD, it was noticed that for each time a base station switched roles from active to inactive, sensor nodes would see an average delay ranging from ∼3 ms upwards to ∼18 ms delay. Some critical points had a more notable area of delay as signified by the spikes in

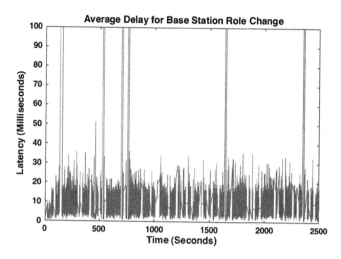

Fig. 4. Average network delay for sensor nodes to communicate to a base station during the MPBSD process when base station roles change occurs. Notably, results in this graph project the direct increase of delay for sensor nodes when a base station changes roles. Specifically, we took the increase delay value and subtract a base line value to project the average delay measurement.

the graph. The highest recorded delay was roughly ∼2000 ms, but we determine that those results were due to data retransmission from our delay measurements.

5.3 Security Metric: Hunting the Base Station

The key component to this researched work is to increase the difficulty to locate a wireless base station. Using methods of localization from previous work [12], we attempt to track the base station from a compromise sensor node. In our first attempt to locate the wireless base station, we measured the RSSI values that were presented from the active base station. Specifically, we wanted to identify the minimal amount of time needed (β) to switch roles for a base station to increase the ambiguity from being located. Although finding β allowed us to determine the minimal time needed to switch roles for a base station, we wanted to identify the maximum time allowed (γ) to reduce the predictability for a compromised sensor node from knowing the time interval for a role change. In Fig. 5, we present results for locating the base station from a compromised sensor node.

As expressed in Fig. 5, we examined a single node locating the active base station using MPBSD. The line *Actual* represents an active base station from the perspective of the sensor node. In this experiment, there were three base stations positioned at various distances away from the sensor node in our analysis. Notably, the base station that was the closest to the sensor node at an approximately ∼6 m was more distinguishable using RSSI localization methods. Although further away, the two other base stations were not easily determined by the sensor node located ∼25 m and ∼36 m away. Additionally, some variations

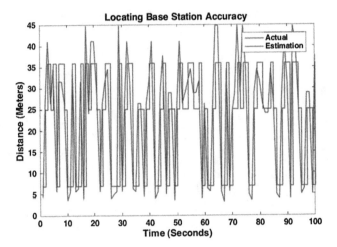

Fig. 5. A compromised sensor node attempting to locate the active base station within the given WSN. This figure projects an experiment to find the minimal time β for a base station to change role. The width of *Actual* with respect to X represents time a base station remained active using MPBSD. Lastly, the angle can not be determined from the sensor node to the active base station. (Color figure online)

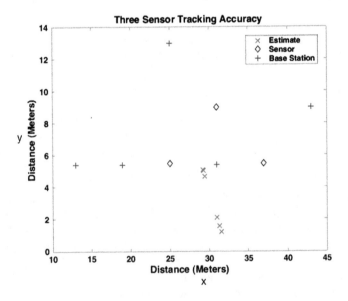

Fig. 6. Multiple compromised sensor nodes attempt to locate the active base station within the WSN using MPBSD. Additionally, this experiment demonstrated the use of five base stations using MPBSD to service the WSN while only three compromised sensor nodes were used to locate. The location of each Base Station was undetermined due to the safeguard of MPBSD and that the threat actor could assume only five Base Stations are present in the WSN. (x, y) represents the location of a sensor or a Base Station, or the estimated location of a sensor.

of the measurements had a significant decrease in signal quality from the active base station. This decrease in signal strength was observed as a behavior of using RSSI as a localization method. Lastly, although the *Actual* and *Estimation* were very close to one another, we did not determine the angle of the active base station with respect to the compromise sensor due to the constraint of having a single sensor. Therefore, we can only determine an approximate area for the base station.

To demonstrate localization constraints for multiple compromised sensor nodes, we present our experiment of using three sensor nodes to locate the active base station in Fig. 6. There were a total of five base stations within the WSN area positioned at varying distances to service sensor nodes. It was demonstrated that the base stations of near proximity to one another using MPBSD created more ambiguity in determining the location of the active base station. Additionally, each base station had equal amount of turns to be the active base station for the WSN. Lastly, this experiment was conducted numerous times where multiple sample sets were taken. It was apparent that the estimation determined five distinguishable points for base stations within the area, the actual positions were still concealed using MPBSD.

6   Conclusion

In this paper, we proposed MPBSD to obscure the location of a wireless base station from a compromised sensor node by using concepts of MTD. We expressed that our approach increased the difficulty to locate a wireless base station using localization methods of RSSI. It was stated that each base station inherits two roles, active and inactive, through an election process. We identified areas of increase network delay when a base station changes roles from active to inactive and vice-versa. Lastly, we demonstrated the difficulties a compromised wireless sensor node experienced in locating the active wireless base station using localization methods of RSSI. Our evaluations demonstrated MPBSD as a viable solution to obscure the location of wireless base stations with minimal overhead depending on distance from sensor to base station.

In the future, we plan to examine MPBSD in a more thorough analysis with varying types of data transfer, and specifically—UDP traffic. Other network characteristics such as packet loss, jitter, and varying types of network performance concerns will also be examined. Since data corruption is a significant concern with regards to changing roles of a base station, we will examine in further detail the effects of MPBSD to improve handling data transfer. Lastly, we examined the effects of how an adverse user—if given access—can attempt to locate an active base station, but we did not examine the effects of network-based security attacks. We plan to also examine the effects of MPBSD when under a threat of adverse attacks within the WSN.

Acknowledgment. We acknowledge the National Science Foundation (NSF) to partially sponsor this research under grants #1633978, #1620871, #1303382, #1431265, and BBN/GPO project #1936 through NSF/CNS grant. We would like to thank Pieter Becue, Brecht Vermeulen, Vincent Sercu, and Bart Jooris for their diligent work in maintaining and supporting the w-iLab.t testbed that has made possible to conduct the real-world experiments in this paper. Additionally, we would like to thank the members of Winlab at Rutgers University for maintaining the Orbit Lab testbed. Lastly, the views and conclusions contained herein are those of the authors and should not be interpreted as necessarily representing the official policies, either expressed or implied of the NSF.

References

1. Butun, I., Morgera, S.D., Sankar, R.: A survey of intrusion detection systems in wireless sensor networks. IEEE Commun. Surv. Tutorials **16**(1), 266–282 (2014)
2. Acharya, U., Younis, M.: Increasing base-station anonymity in wireless sensor networks. Ad Hoc Netw. **8**(8), 791–809 (2010)
3. Deng, J., Han, R., Mishra, S.: Insens: intrusion-tolerant routing for wireless sensor networks. Comput. Commun. **29**(2), 216–230 (2006)
4. Zhu, W.T., Zhou, J., Deng, R.H., Bao, F.: Detecting node replication attacks in wireless sensor networks: a survey. J. Netw. Comput. Appl. **35**(3), 1022–1034 (2012)
5. Lopez, J., Roman, R., Agudo, I., Fernandez-Gago, C.: Trust management systems for wireless sensor networks: best practices. Comput. Commun. **33**(9), 1086–1093 (2010)
6. Berman, M., Chase, J.S., Landweber, L., Nakao, A., Ott, M., Raychaudhuri, D., Ricci, R., Seskar, I.: Geni: a federated testbed for innovative network experiments. Comput. Netw. **61**, 5–23 (2014). Special issue on Future Internet Testbeds Part I
7. Raychaudhuri, D., Seskar, I., Ott, M., Ganu, S., Ramachandran, K., Kremo, H., Siracusa, R., Liu, H., Singh, M.: Overview of the orbit radio grid testbed for evaluation of next-generation wireless network protocols. In: IEEE Wireless Communications and Networking Conference, vol. 3, pp. 1664–1669. IEEE (2005)
8. Bouckaert, S., Vandenberghe, W., Jooris, B., Moerman, I., Demeester, P.: The w-iLab.t testbed. In: Magedanz, T., Gavras, A., Thanh, N.H., Chase, J.S. (eds.) TridentCom 2010. LNICST, vol. 46, pp. 145–154. Springer, Heidelberg (2011)
9. Yu, Y., Li, K., Zhou, W., Li, P.: Trust mechanisms in wireless sensor networks: attack analysis and countermeasures. J. Netw. Comput. Appl. **35**(3), 867–880 (2012)
10. Camtepe, S.A., Yener, B.: Key distribution mechanisms for wireless sensor networks: a survey, Rensselaer Polytechnic Institute, Troy, New York, pp. 5–7. Technical Report (2005)
11. Omar, M., Challal, Y., Bouabdallah, A.: Reliable and fully distributed trust model for mobile ad hoc networks. Comput. Secur. **28**(3), 199–214 (2009)
12. Chin, T., Xiong, K., Blasch, E.: Nonlinear target tracking for threat detection using rssi and optical fusion. In: 18th International Conference on Information Fusion (Fusion), pp. 1946–1953, July 2015

Toward Exposing Timing-Based Probing Attacks in Web Applications

Jian Mao[1,3]($\boxtimes$), Yue Chen[1], Futian Shi[1], Yaoqi Jia[2], and Zhenkai Liang[2,3]

[1] School of Electronic and Information Engineering,
BeiHang University, Beijing, China
maojian@buaa.edu.cn
[2] School of Computing, National University of Singapore, Singapore, Singapore
[3] Department of Computer Science,
George Washington University, Washington, DC, USA

Abstract. Timing attacks in web applications have been known for over a decade. Recently, new attacks have been reported to exploit timing techniques to probe sensitive information from web applications. In this paper, we present a tool to detect timing-based probing attacks in web applications. The main idea of our approach is to monitor the browser behaviors and identify anomalous timing behaviors. We prototyped our approach in the Google Chrome browser, and demonstrated its effectiveness.

1 Introduction

In web applications, the same origin policy (SOP) [1] prevents a web application from directly accessing information belonging to other web applications. Since the web application share the same browser environment with web applications under other origins, it may *indirectly* figure out information from other web applications through analyzing the shared states in the browser environment [5,7,9,11,14–16]. For example, attackers can infer whether a website has been visited by the user via checking the color of a link to the site, as demonstrated in the browser-history sniffing attack [10]. Using this technique, via including a list of links pointing to a list of websites, a malicious website can obtain a user's browsing history by checking the color of the links[1]. This example shows that an attacker can steal users' information indirectly, i.e., inferring the information about another site by checking the browser states that are affected by visiting the website.

Observation. Compared to direct access to users' private information in the browser environment, this type of inference attack can only obtain limited information in each attempt. For example, the browser history inference is obtained

---

[1] Traditional ways to do this is by calling "getComputedStyle" method, but this method has already been modified to prevent this kind of misuse. However, there are still other ways to check the links colors [13,18].

© Springer International Publishing Switzerland 2016
Q. Yang et al. (Eds.): WASA 2016, LNCS 9798, pp. 499–510, 2016.
DOI: 10.1007/978-3-319-42836-9_44

site-by-site. In other words, the "data rate" of information leakage in such attacks is low. In order to obtain a significant amount of information, attackers have to *repeatedly* check and infer information from the other origin. We call them *browser probing attacks*, and the repetitive nature of browser probing attacks forms the basis to detect them.

We focus on timing-based probing attacks [8,12,13,17] in this paper, which are a popular browser probing attacks. They indirectly access sensitive information, such as cryptographic keys and states from other virtual machines [2,4]. They rely on the variations in the time taken by the systems to process different inputs [8,13]. This type of attacks has been adopted to exploit web applications. In a timing-based probing attack, a malicious web application check the time required to perform various tasks that can be affected by other websites.

Our approach. In this paper, we present a tool to detect timing-based probing attacks in web applications. The main idea of our approach is to monitor a web application's runtime behaviors, and identify anomalous timing operations to detect timing probing attacks. We summarize behavior patterns for timing-based probing attacks, and our approach detects timing probing attacks by matching monitored behaviors with such behavior patterns. Our approach alarms users with the potential risk of the privacy leakage to the website, and shows users the suspicious behaviors embedded in a malicious web page.

We prototype our approach in the Google Chrome browser. We evaluate the effectiveness of our approach using malicious probing applications built from known attacks.

Contributions. Our contribution is as follows.

- *New understanding of the timing-based probing attack.* We studied common timing probing attacks and define a general behavior model to describe the timing probing attacks. Based on the proposed model, we generate behavior patterns corresponding to different timing probing attacks respectively.
- *Light-weight approach to expose and limit the timing-based probing attack.* We propose an extention-based approach that monitors web application's behaviors and detect timing probing attacks, based on the repeat rate of sturctured-probing-behavior patterns. Our approach makes the timing-base probing attacks more difficult to succeed.
- *System prototype and evaluation.* We prototyped our approach as an extension of Google Chrome. Our evaluation demonstrates the effectiveness of our approach.

2   Overview

In this section, we discuss the threat from timing-based probing attacks and analyze their core features that can be used as the basis for detecting them.

2.1   Background

In this paper, we assume the adversary to be a web attacker. That is, the attacker controls a website, and is able to run JavaScript in the victim's browser. But the attacker cannot run native code in the victim's system, nor can the attacker exploit vulnerabilities in the victim's system or browser. The attacker aims to infer the victim user's private information in the browser environment through timing probing attacks.

Timing-Based Probing Attacks. Felten and Schneider [8] introduces a timing attack to web applications. This attack measures the time required to load a web resource. As the time needed to load a web resource is affected by the resource's cache status, the attacker can learn the resource's cache status, and then infer the user's browsing history.

From this example, we generalize *timing-based probing attacks* as follows. The attacker first retrieves time from the system, which is either to record system time or to start a timer. We refer to this activity as T_1 and the time obtained as the starting time t_1. It then starts a workload W, such as loading resources or perform a computation. Once W is finished, the attacker immediately takes another time measurement. We refer to this activity as T_2 and the time obtained as the ending time t_2. The time difference $t = t_2 - t_1$ is the time spent on W. If W depends on browser states that cannot be directly accessed by attackers, t reveals information about such states.

Properties of Timing Probing Attacks. Timing-based probing attacks are usually invisible to users. Since they are launched to indirectly infer other users' sensitive data with the presence of strong security mechanisms in browsers, each probing attempt typically infer only limited information. For example, in the above attack, every time the attacker can only infer whether a web resource is cached, among tens of thousands of resources that may reveal users' privacy. In other words, the "data rate" of leaked information in such probing attacks is very low. Due to the limited information accessible through probing, attackers/malicious websites need a large amount of repetitive operations to extract enough information for inferring a small amount of users' privacy. For example, to probe users' browsing history, the attacker must prepare a list of URLs, and check each of them repeatedly (using the behavior sequence (T_1, W, T_2)). In addition, the result of a practical timing based probing will differ depending on the speed of the hardware on which the browser is running. To achieve accurate time-based measurement results, attackers have to repeat time measurement operations to achieve the desired calibration.

Challenge. Though timing-based probing attacks do require repetitive behaviors of accessing time and carrying out the workload, benign web applications also have legitimate reasons to frequently access time and perform regular activities. Simply repeating such behaviors cannot be considered as the distinguished feature to identify the timing based probing attacks. We need to distinguish benign repeated timing behaviors from malicious ones.

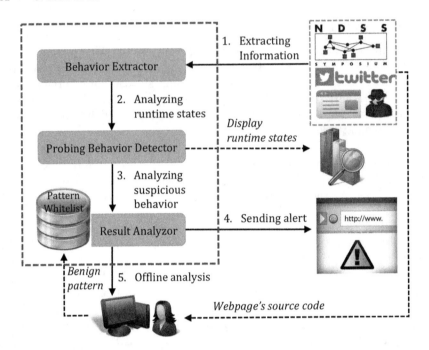

Fig. 1. Architecture of our approach(Color figure online)

2.2   Approach

The overall architecture of our approach is illustrated in Fig. 1. It monitors a web application's behaviors for abnormal patterns of timing-related events to alert the user of potential timing-based probing attacks. Our approach consists of three kernel components: *Behavior Extractor*, *Probing Behavior Detector*, and *Result Analyzer*.

In particular, the *Behavior Extractor* component monitors the web application and extracts its runtime execution information; the *Probing Behavior Detector* analyzes the runtime states gathered by the *Behavior Extractor* and detects suspicious timing-based probing behaviors; According to the knowledge in *Pattern Whitelist*, *Result Analyzer* analyzes the suspicious behaviors detected by *Probing Behavior Detector*; once a malicious behavior is confirmed, it displays *Alert* to the browser user. The intercepted behaviors and detection results are made available to an *Offline Analysis* component, where analysts identifies benign repetitive timing behaviors and update the *Pattern Whitelist*, so that such benign behaviors will not be flagged as attacks in the future.

Extracting Runtime Behaviors. Behavior extraction is the basis of our approach. Since most of a web application's dynamic behaviors are carried by JavaScript, our tool intercepts JavaScript API calls to represent the behavior of a web application. The behavior extractor module records the API together with its parameters. To help understand the behavior and distinguish APIs used under different scenarios, the behavior extractor also extracts the runtime JavaScript stack of the API.

In order to extract these runtime behaviors without modifying the browser, we build our tool as a browser extension. Though our focus is mainly on the timing-related behaviors, the interception mechanism is flexible to allow users to specify general JavaScript APIs to monitor. It intercepts JavaScript behaviors of web applications through rewriting JavaScript functions. Our extension preloads the rewriting JavaScript code before any code in the web application is loaded. It then takes a list of APIs to be hooked, which is specified by the users, and interpose the APIs to output them in a log of JavaScript behaviors, which records the functions' names, the arguments, and the functions' call stack information.

While obtaining API call information is straightforward, getting JavaScript call stack information needs more effort. We take the advantage of an error-handling feature of JavaScript, which reports the call stack information.

Detecting Probing Behaviors. Timing-related APIs are commonly used in benign web applications. To distinguish benign usage of timing APIs from probing attacks, the probing behavior detector adopts a two-level detection mechanism to expose probing behaviors. First, it flags suspicious timing behaviors based on the *frequency pattern*, i.e., the frequency of timing behaviors and their distribution over time. It serves as the first-level detector. To further prevent mistakenly reporting benign timing behaviors as probing attacks, the detector analyzes the *structure* of timing behaviors, and performs detection based on structured timing behavior pattern.

Distribution-based probing behavior pattern. The first-level detection is based on the distribution of timing-behaviors. We gather statistics on how many times timing functions are called over a period of time.

At this level, our approach provides light-weight real-time attack detection. Taking the cache timing attack explained above as example, our approach displays statistics for monitored JavaScript APIs. The user can pay particular attention to the *getTime* API. Once the frequency exceeds a certain threshold, the user can be alarmed about possible timing attack on the website he is visiting. To further increase the detection accuracy, we use another level detection via structure information of web application's timing behavior.

Structure-based probing behavior pattern. Timing probing attacks always contain two operations of obtaining system time value T_1 and T_2, as well as a workload in the middle W, which is the operation to be timed. So it forms the following pattern:

1. A *get-time* activity T_1 (such as a *Date.getTime* API call or a *set-timer* event);
2. One or several workload operations, such as loading an image or drawing a frame. We refer to the collection of such operations[2] as W;
3. Another *get-time* operation T_2.

---

[2] Note that the behaviors in W might not always be shown as the form of a function call (e.g. when loading an image, it's just an assignment to the src attribute of the image element).

Due to the asynchronous nature of the JavaScript language, T_1 and T_2 often appear in completely different program locations and contexts. However, in many timing probing attacks, W is carried out by an asynchronous operation, where T_2 can only be obtained in the callback functions of the asynchronous operation. When T_2 is executed, it is difficult to decide the corresponding T_1 and W. Moreover, in actual timing attacks, the (T_1, W, T_2) pattern may repeat multiple times consecutively, making T_2 of one iteration the T_1 of later iterations, making the following pattern $(T_1, W, T_2, W', T_2', ...)$. In this case, we can use the connection between the last two operations as our pattern for the timing attack, and treat abnormal amount of repeated pattern as indicator of a timing attack.

Some attacks that have distinguishing features that can be identified inside the behavior log can be detected automatically. Take the cache timing attack as an example. This attack always contains two system time acquire operations (normally by calling *Date.getTime* function), one before an resource (often an image) begins to load and another after the resource is loaded (i.e., being called inside the *onload* function of the resource). For this attack, the connection between T_2 and W is the *Date.getTime* function call for T_2 is inside an *onload* function of an *HTMLImageELement* for W. This connection, between the second system time acquire operation T_2 and the image loading operation W, plays an important role in distinguishing benign behaviors from probing behaviors in websites in our experiment.

3   Evaluation

We have prototyped our tool as an extension to the Google Chrome browser. Our prototype is based on the 64-bit Chrome browser. We have evaluated our approach from the following aspects. We used recent timing probing attacks and showed that our approach can successfully detect them. We then analyzed the performance overhead of our approach.

3.1   Timing-Based Probing Attack Detection

To evaluate the effectiveness of our approach, we used recent timing probing attacks in web applications. We implemented the attacks according to their technical descriptions. We first introduce the attacks and then describe how they are exposed by our approach.

Web Caching Based Probing Attack

Attack Mechanism. Web browsers use caching to speed up the access to the recently visited files/resources. A web-cache-based probing attack may make use of this functionality by measuring the time required to access a particular file belongs to another origin. If that file is in the user's cache, the access must be faster. According to the time cost for accessing, the attacker may infer whether the file is in the browser's cache, and whether the user has accessed the target origin as well (deducing the users' browsing history indirectly). We illustrate

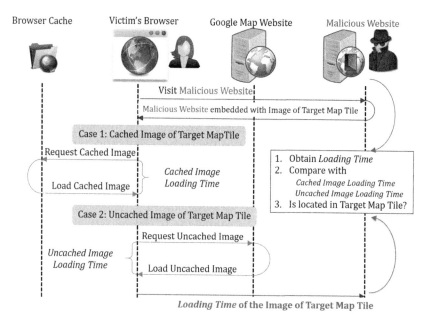

Fig. 2. Web caching based timing probing Attack(Color figure online)

the basic principle of the cache-based probing attack in Fig. 2. To evaluate the effectiveness on web caching based attack, we use the attack proposed by Jia et al. [12] as the test case.

Effectiveness. In Jia's attack, malicious webpage needs to measure the loading time of image files, so it is required to call *Date.getTime* function after image is loaded. The corresponding behavior pattern is *calling* Date.getTime *function inside* onload *function of* HTMLImageElement *element.* The pattern matching can be done by searching for lines containing both string *Date.getTime* and regular expression `HTMLImageElement \ .[^]*\.onload` inside function call stack data.

function call count or element access count in time intervals(in seconds)

document.createTextNode
document.createAttribute
document.getElementById
document.getElementsByName

• • •

XMLHttpRequest.prototype.send
Date.prototype.getTime
requestAnimationFrame

• • •

element_removeEventListener
element_getAttribute
element_setAttribute
element_removeAttribute

Fig. 3. Real-time function call and element access chart(Color figure online)

Figure 3 illustrates the real-time function call and element access chart (first-level detection), as well as key behavior log of the web caching based timing probing attacks (second-level detection).

Pixel-Based Attacks. Kotcher et al. [13] proposed another timing probing attacks, which allows the attacker to "see" the target website.

The shader inside browsers often takes different time to draw pixels of different color. So theoretically by measuring the time taken to draw a pixel, attackers can know the color of this pixel. And by traversing all pixels inside a target region of the target website, the attacker can get an image of this region, i.e. "seeing" this region of the target website.

Then attackers will measure the webpage's drawing time to infer the color of the pixels, which can be done by measuring the refreshing rate of the web page. By consecutively calling *requestAnimationFrame* function until certain amount of frames have been drawn, and measuring the time required to draw these frames, attackers can know the web page's refreshing rate, which is mostly influenced by the drawing speed of pixels of different color. By checking the web page's refreshing rate, the attackers can know the color of the current targeting pixel.

The attack needs to measure the frame rate of websites, which need to call *Date.getTime* function after a frame is drawn. And the function used as *requestAnimationFrame* function's argument will be called after a frame is drawn. so the pattern used to indicate this attack is *calling* Date.getTime *function inside functions that are used as* requestAnimationFrame *function's argument*. The pattern matching can be done by first searching for regular expression ^ `requestAnimationFrame:function` [^ (]*(inside function call data and get the argument function's names, and then searching for lines containing both string *Date.getTime* and the argument function's names, inside function call stack data.

Repainting-Based Attacks. Stone [17] proposed a way to check the visit status of web links and sniff the browsing history by measuring the web page's repainting time.

According to the synchronizing property of the Chrome browser, when the browser found a link's target URL has changed, it will check whether this link's visit status has change too, i.e., from unvisited to visited or the other way around. If the visit status has changed, the Chrome browser will repaint this link element, while doing nothing if the visit status remains the same. The repainting operation may be inferred by measuring the drawing time of the web page.

This attack needs to measure the frame drawing time of a certain frame, which needs to call the *Date.getTime* function after a frame is drawn, the same as the last attack. Also note that the function used as *requestAnimationFrame* function's argument will be called after a frame is drawn. so the pattern used to indicate this attack is still *calling* Date.getTime *function inside functions that are used as* requestAnimationFrame *function's argument*. The pattern matching can be done the same way as in the last attack. The pattern distribution is the same as in that of the last attack, too.

3.2   Performance

We evaluate the performance overhead of our tool. We test the average time cost of *baidu.com* under different configurations. The result is shown in Table 1.

Table 1. Time cost on different configurations

Performance Test Environment	
CPU: Intel®Core™i5-4570	
Memory: 4 Gigabyte	
Operating system: Linux 12.04.2 (64-bit)	
Browser: Chrome, Version 42.0.2311.90 (64-bit)	
Enabled Functionalities	**Time Cost**
None	241 ms
Write function name to console	454 ms
Write function call stack to console	1420 ms
Write function name to console	1583 ms
Write function call stack to console	
Draw real-time behavior chart	310 ms
Warn attack(white list enabled)	1180 ms
Draw real-time behavior chart	1193 ms
Warn attack(white list enabled)	

The first three configurations are for offline behavior analysis. The additional overhead only affects the speed of evaluating a large amount of websites, which can be optimized by our automatic website parallel testing method. The last three configurations are for real-time behavior analysis. Drawing the real-time behavior chart causes neglectable overhead. And with warning functionality enabled, the time cost only increases to approximately 1 second. This is only the starting phase of visiting a website, after the website has been loaded and stabilized, the difference can be neglected too, users will not feel any difference.

4   Related Work

Previous work has discovered several classic browser probing attacks, along with some detection and prevention methods.

Kotcher et al. [13] discovered two timing probing attacks using CSS default filters. The first attack can check whether a user has an account with a website by exploiting the DOM rendering time difference. And the second attack can sniff user browsing history or read text token by stealing pixels on the user's screen. They conducted evaluations of their attacks, and proved the attacks' feasibility.

Felten et al. [8] described a class of timing attacks used to sniff browsing history too, but their attacks focus on operations whose time consumption depends on the cache status. They also proposed *web cookies*, which are a series of traditional cached files used as one traditional cookie. Using Web Cookies in attacks can make them harder to be detected. To prevent these attacks, one can turn off caching or alter the hit or miss performance of the cache, but both will make caching lack of usefulness.

Weinberg et al. [18] proposed a way to sniff browsing history. The traditional way to do this is secretly checking the status of the browser environment. But since browsing history will affect the appearance of the display to the user, the attacker can trick the user to tell him what the user has seen on the screen, which can be used to infer the user's browsing history. The links are disguised as CAPTCHAs, so that while the user is finishing the CAPTCIIAs, hc is actually telling the attacker his browsing history. They also come up with a way to "see" the user's screen by monitoring the reflection of the screen using the user's web camera. They proved that this is also a practical way to sniff the user's browsing history.

Bansal et al. [3] exploited the Web Worker APIs to make the cache probing operation parallel, which speeds up the traditional cache probing attacks. They also proposed the idea of canceling resource requests once the attacker can confirm that the resource being probed is from browser cache. In this way, the attacker can avoid polluting the cache. They applied their improved cache timing attack on four scenarios, including attacks on web environment and operating systems. At the end of their paper, they discussed potential countermeasures, such as separating cache among different operating system components, and setting no-cache headers to private data. However, their improved attacks doesn't reduce the number of probes that the attacker requires, so our approach can still detect these attacks.

Chen [6] found a vulnerability in four web applications that can leak users sensitive information. The base of this vulnerability is that, since the application needs to provide different contents according to the user's choices, different user inputs will result in different network traffic sizes. Furthermore, usually the possible user input at one application state is very few, making it easy to guess the user's input. The authors also use history traffic data to aid the process of guessing the user's input. In their opinion, in order to effectively and efficiently mitigate the impact of this vulnerability, the method has to be application-specific.

5   Conclusion

In this paper, we studied common browser probing attacks and develop a solution to detect such attacks based on generalized behavior patterns. We present a browser-extension-based tool to detect browser probing attacks. Our approach enables users to be aware of the potential risk of the privacy leakage during their surfing, and exposes the suspicious behaviors embedded in a malicious web page.

Acknowledgment. This work was supported in part by the National Natural Science Foundation of China (No. 61402029), the National Key Basic Research Program (NKBRP) (973 Program) (No. 2012CB315905), the National Natural Science Foundation of China (No. 61370190), Beijing Natural Science Foundation (No4162020), Singapore Ministry of Education under NUS grant R-252-000-539-112.

References

1. Same-origin policy. http://en.wikipedia.org/wiki/Same-origin_policy
2. Agrawal, D., Archambeault, B., Rao, J.R., Rohatgi, P.: The EM side—channel(s). In: Kaliski, B.S., Koç, Ç.K., Paar, C. (eds.) Cryptographic Hardware and Embedded Systems - CHES 2002. LNCS, vol. 2523, pp. 29–45. Springer, Heidelberg (2003)
3. Bansal, C., Preibusch, S., Milic-Frayling, N.: Cache timing attacks revisited: efficient and repeatable browser history, OS and network sniffing. In: Federrath, H., Gollmann, D., Chakravarthy, S.R. (eds.) SEC 2015. IFIP AICT, vol. 455, pp. 97–111. Springer, Heidelberg (2015). doi:10.1007/978-3-319-18467-8_7
4. Brier, E., Joye, M.: Weierstraß elliptic curves and side-channel attacks. Public Key Cryptography. Springer, Heidelberg (2002)
5. Cabuk, S., Brodley, C.E., Shields, C.: IP covert timing channels: design and detection. In: Proceedings of the 11th ACM Conference on Computer and Communications Security (2004)
6. Chen, S., Wang, R., Wang, X., Zhang, K.: Side-channel leaks in web applications: A reality today, a challenge tomorrow. In: Proceedings of the IEEE Symposium on Security and Privacy. IEEE (2010)
7. Chevallier-Mames, B., Ciet, M., Joye, M.: Low-cost solutions for preventing simple side-channel analysis: Side-channel atomicity. IEEE Trans. Comput. **53**(6), 760–768 (2004)
8. Felten, E.W. Schneider, M.A.: Timing attacks on web privacy. In: Proceedings of the 7th ACM Conference on Computer and Communications Security (2000)
9. Irazoqui, G., Eisenbarth, T., Sunar, B.: S$a: A shared cache attack that works across cores and defies VM sandboxingand its application to AES. In: Proceedings of the 36th IEEE Symposium on Security and Privacy (2015)
10. Jackson, C., Bortz, A., Boneh, D., Mitchell, J.C.: Protecting browser state from web privacy attacks. In: Proceedings of the 15th International Conference on World Wide Web (2006)
11. Janc, A., Olejnik, L.: Feasibility and real-world implications of web browser history detection. In: Proceedings of Web 2.0 Security and Privacy Workshopp (2010)
12. Jia, Y., Dong, X., Liang, Z., Saxena, P.: I know where you've been: Geo-inference attacks via the browser cache. Internet Comput. IEEE **19**(1), 44–53 (2015)
13. Kotcher, R., Pei, Y., Jumde, P., Jackson, C.: Cross-origin pixel stealing: timing attacks using CSS filters. In: Proceedings of the ACM Conference on Computer and Communications Security (2013)
14. Lee, S., Kim, H., Kim, J.: Identifying cross-origin resource status using application cache (2015)
15. Liu, F., Yarom, Y., Ge, Q., Heiser, G., Lee, R.B.: Last-level cache side-channel attacks are practical. In: Proceedings of the 36th IEEE Symposium on Security and Privacy (2015)
16. Oren, Y., Kemerlis, V.P., Sethumadhavan, S., Keromytis, A.D.: The spy in the sandbox: Practical cache attacks in Javascript. In: Proceedings of the 22nd ACM SIGSAC Conference on Computer and Communications Security (2015)

17. Stone, P.: Pixel perfect timing attacks with html5. Context Information Security(White Paper) (August 2013)
18. Weinberg, Z., Chen, E.Y., Jayaraman, P.R., Jackson, C.: I still know what you visited last summer: Leaking browsing history via user interaction and side channel attacks. In: Proceedings of the IEEE Symposium on Security and Privacy (2011)

Collaborative Outsourced Data Integrity Checking in Multi-Cloud Environment

Jian Mao[1,2(✉)], Jian Cui[1], Yan Zhang[1], Hanjun Ma[1], and Jianhong Zhang[3]

[1] School of Electronic and Information Engineering,
Beihang University, Beijing, China
maojian@buaa.edu.in
[2] Department of Computer Science, George Washington University,
Washington, DC, USA
[3] School of Science, North China University of Technology, Beijing, China

Abstract. Cloud storage has been widely used to in services such as data outsourcing and resource sharing due to its convenience, low cost and flexibility. However, users will lose the physical control of their data after outsourcing; consequently, ensuring the integrity of their outsourced data becomes an important security requirement of multi-cloud storage applications. In this paper, we present a collaborative multi-cloud data integrity audition scheme, which is based on BLS (Boneh-Lynn-Shacham) signatures and homomorphic tags. According to the proposed scheme, users can audit their outsourced data in a one-round challenge-response process with low performance overhead. Our scheme also enables public verification and supports dynamic data maintenance. The theoretical analysis and experiment results illustrate that our scheme is provably secure and efficient.

1 Introduction

Cloud storage has been widely used in services like data outsourcing and resource sharing due to its convenience, low cost and flexibility. Nowadays, online service providers, such as Amazon [1], Yahoo, Google [2], Baidu [3], operate large data centers and offer "infinite" storage capacity for users to relief their burden of local data management and maintenance [4,5]. In addition, cloud storage enables universal data access in any place. However, users lose the physical control of their outsourced data and the cloud storage service provider is not always trustworthy. Dishonest service providers may conceal the fact that users' data have been damaged due to some mis-operations or unexpected accidents. Even worse, malicious service providers also might delete the data seldom accessed by users to gain more benefits. How to ensure the integrity of their remotely outsourced data becomes a great concern of the users selecting cloud storing service.

Traditional hash-function-based data integrity verification solutions [6,7] are obviously impractical to audit cloud data remotely due to their unacceptable communication overhead to retrieve the oursourced files. To check the remote data integrity effectively without retrieving the whole outsourced document,

© Springer International Publishing Switzerland 2016
Q. Yang et al. (Eds.): WASA 2016, LNCS 9798, pp. 511–523, 2016.
DOI: 10.1007/978-3-319-42836-9_45

Ateniense et al. present the first probabilistic verification model called "*provable data possession*" (PDP) based on homomorphic cryptography algorithm and "*sampling*" techniques [8]. Taking the public verifiability into account, Ateniense et al. improve their approach [9]; Wang et al. also propose a publicly verifiable cloud data audit scheme that supports dynamic data maintenance by using Merkle Hash Tree data structure [10]. Juels et al. introduce error correcting coding techniques and propose *Proof of Retrievability* (POR) mechanisms to audit cloud data and ensure data correction if data corruption happened.

Most of these previous work mainly targets at the problem of data integrity audition in a single cloud storage environment rather than a heterogeneous cloud infrastructure that collaborates multiple internal (private) and/or external (public) cloud resources [11,12]. In the multi-cloud environment, users split their data, duplicate file blocks and outsource them to different CSP servers; accordingly, the solutions above cannot enforce the data integrity checking efficiently in such an environment where data spread over multiple servers. Zhu et al. propose a cooperative provable data possession (CPDP) scheme [11,13] in the multi-cloud scenario. However, in the CPDP scheme, the security parameter π' is independent of other parameters; and thus servers can bypass the authentication by forging the parameter π' in the response sequence. Moreover, in the process of third-party public verification, the third party needs to know where every data block is exactly stored, which poses a threat to user data. Therefore, it is significant to develop an efficient and effective data integrity verification scheme for the multi-cloud storage.

In this paper, we present a collaborative multi-cloud data integrity audition scheme which is based on BLS signature and homomorphic tags. According to proposed scheme, users can audit their outsourced data in one-round challenge-response process with low communication cost. Our scheme also enables public verification and supports dynamic data maintenance that users can modify; delete the data with low performance overhead. The contributions made by this paper are summarized as follows.

- We propose an effective collaborative multi-cloud data audition scheme enabling users to conduct data integrity checking among multiple CPS server simultaneously in one round challenge-response procedure.
- The proposed scheme supports public verification and dynamic data maintenance efficiently.
- We prototype our scheme and conduct system evaluation. The theoretical analysis and experiment results illustrate that our scheme is provably secure and efficient.

2   Approach Overview

2.1   System Framework

As shown in Fig. 1, the general multi-cloud storage system includes three network entities:

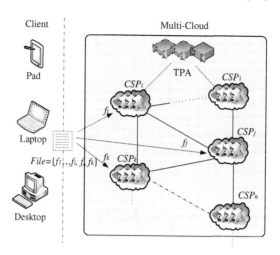

Fig. 1. Overall architecture of the multicolud environment

- *Clients/Users*[1]: Clients outsource data to reduce local storage overhead and make use of the computation resources provided by the cloud service providers in mulit-cloud storage system.
- *Cloud Service Providers (CSPs)*: CSPs that possess a large quantity of hardware and software resources are clustered to provide remote data storing services. We assume that there is an organizer in the CSP cluster, a mediation node that interacts with users and other CSPs.
- *Third Party Authority (TPA)*: TPA is an optional entity being partially trusted in the multi-cloud scenario.

In the multi-cloud storage system shown in Fig. 1, the user splits her/his documents into several file blocks. The file blocks will be distributed the cloud storage servers belonging to different cloud service provider. In addition, to promote the access efficiency and ensure the data retrievability, users might also duplicate the file blocks and spread the copies to several cloud servers.

2.2 Challenges and Goals

As the CSPs in the multi-cloud system cannot always be trustworthy, it is necessary for users to establish the integrity audition mechanism that ensures their outsourced data are stored correctly without unauthorized access by CSP servers or other entities. To make the audition more efficient, another challenge of data integrity audition in the multi-cloud environment is to conduct parallel checking, which means to verify the integrity of block files stored in different CSP servers simultaneously. Moreover, supporting secure dynamic maintenance is also a major concern of the multi-cloud data audition.

---

[1] We use the term *user* and *client* exchangeably in this paper.

Aiming at addressing the above challenges, the goal of this paper is to propose an effective multi-cloud data integrity audition mechanism satisfying the following requirements.

- *Correctness*: benign servers will prove themselves successfully and none of the misbehaved servers can bypass the checking.
- *Batch verification*: the client can simultaneously verify the integrity of the file blocks distributed in different CSP servers without retrieving the file.
- *Stateless and unbounded checking*: the audition procedure is stateless and supports unlimited challenge-response interactions.

2.3   Collaborative Data Integrity Audition Model

Our collaborative data audition model consists of three stages, preprocessing, challenge-response, user authentication. Additionally, it also designates a sub-procedure to support dynamic maintenance. The procedure of our scheme is shown in Fig. 2.

Stage I: Initialization and Preprocessing. Stage I consists of steps (1)–(2) in Fig. 2. In step (1), the user selects system parameters and generates keys for BLS algorithm used in the successive steps. Meanwhile, the user splits the file F into file block set and each file block m_{ij} consists of several file sectors. Then the user computes the homomorphic tags σ_{ij} corresponding to the file sectors. After preprocessing the outsourced file, the user distributes the file blocks with the metadata for audition into the cloud servers belonging to the different CSPs and keeps the secret parameter locally.

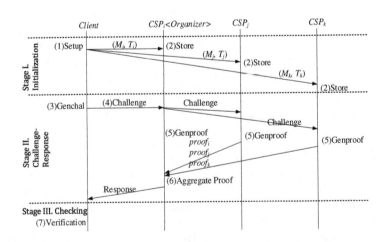

Fig. 2. The procedure of our scheme

Stage II: Challenge-Response. Stage II includes steps (3)–(6) in Fig. 2. When the user wants to audit her/his outsourced file, she/he computes a challenge sequence corresponding to the file blocks under test. The user sends *organizer* the challenge sequence and *organizer* will forward the challenges to the aimed CSP servers that contain the user's file blocks. CSP servers calculate and return their proofs to *organizer*. *Organizer* aggregates the proof received and reply the user the aggregated value as response.

Stage III: Integrity Checking. Based on the received response from *organizer* the user verifies the data integrity in step (7) shown in Fig. 2. If data are stored correctly, the algorithm outputs *"TRUE"*; otherwise, outputs *"FALSE"*, which means there exists misbehaved CSP servers.

Dynamic maintenance: When users need to conduct dynamic operations on their outsourced data, they re-create tags corresponding to the new file sectors and send them to the organizer for updating.

3   Collaborative Multi-cloud Data Integrity Audition Scheme

In this section, we present our collaborative multi-cloud data integrity audition scheme in detail. The notations and concepts employed in our work are listed below.

- $\pi = (p, G, G_T, e, g)$ is the system parameter. p is a big prime number and is the order of the cyclic group G; $e : G \times G \to G_T$ is a non-degenerate bilinear map. g is the generator of G.
- l is the number of the CSPs, represented as $\{CSP_1, CSP_2, \ldots, CSP_l\}$
- F is user's file and F_n is the file name. The file F is separated into n blocks, each of which contains s sectors, $F = \{m_{ij}\}_{n \times s}$, where $m_{ij} \in Z_p$.
- Q is the challenge generated by users.
- $H : \{0,1\}^* \to G$ is a hash function.

    As shown in Fig. 2, our scheme includes three entities, a *user*, *CSP* servers and an *organizer*, which is also one of the CSP servers. The integrity checking scheme is fulfilled by the following eight steps.

Step 1: User Setup.

(1) **KeyGen** $KeyGen(1^\lambda) \to \{sk, pk\}$

   The user selects secure parameter λ and system parameters π and H. She/he randomly selects an $\alpha \in Z_p^*$ to be the private key. The public key is $v \leftarrow g^\alpha \in G$. Then we get $pk = \{v, g\}, sk = \{\alpha\}$.

(2) **File Preprocessing** $F \rightarrow \{m_{ij}\}_{n \times s}$

The user splits the file F into n blocks, each of which contains s parts. File F is represented as follows.

$$F = \begin{bmatrix} m_1 \\ m_2 \\ \vdots \\ m_n \end{bmatrix} = \begin{bmatrix} m_{11} & m_{12} & \cdots & m_{1s} \\ m_{21} & m_{22} & \cdots & m_{2s} \\ \vdots & \vdots & \cdots & \vdots \\ m_{n1} & m_{n2} & \cdots & m_{ns} \end{bmatrix}, m_{ij} \in Z_p$$

Assume $num_i(i = 1 \ldots n)$ is the total number of copies corresponding to each data block $m_i(i = 1 \ldots n)$ stored in different CSPs, and $V_i(i = 1 \ldots n)$ represents how many times each data is updated. The initial value of $V_i(i = 1 \ldots n)$ is 0 for all the elements. We use $\chi_i = i \parallel num_i \parallel V_i(i = 1, \ldots, n)$ to represent it. $\parallel$ represents concatenation.

(3) **TagGen** $TagGen(sk, pk, F) \rightarrow \{\sigma\}$ The user randomly selects s parameters $u_1, \ldots, u_s \in G$ and computes the tags $\sigma_{ik} \leftarrow (H(F_n \parallel i \parallel k \parallel V_i) \cdot \prod_{j=1}^{s} u_j^{m_{ij}}))^{\alpha}$ for $k = 1, \ldots, num_i$ corresponding to each data block $m_i(i = 1 \ldots n)$ and thus the set of all lables is obtained. As is shown in Fig. 3, $m_i(i = 1 \ldots n)$ represents data blocks from files; each block is separated into s parts and every part of a block is represented as $m_{ij}(i = 1 \ldots n; j = 1 \ldots s)$; $\sigma_{ik}(i = 1 \ldots n; k = 1 \ldots num_i)$ represent num_i tags corresponding to m_i.

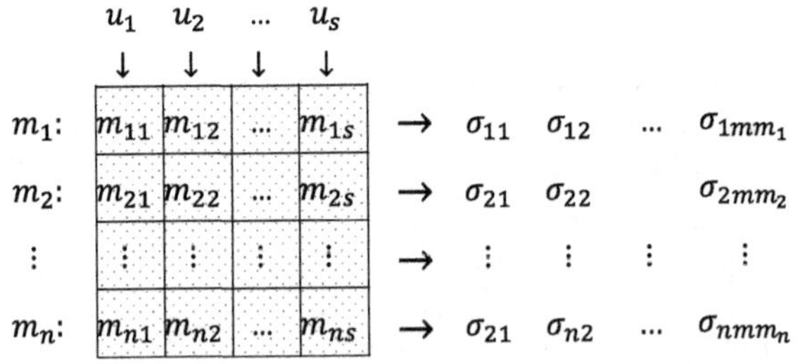

Fig. 3. Sketch of label generating

Step 2: Data Outsourcing. The user sends the file F and corresponding tags to the organizer, and the organizer distributes data blocks with corresponding tags to different CSP servers. If a data block is stored with several copies, every copy of the file block has a tag. For instance, data block $m_i(i = 1, \ldots, n)$ is stored with num_i copies, then there are num_i tags, which means the CSPs should store data m_i along with the tag $\sigma_{ik}(k \in [1..num_i])$ from the num_i labels. Users compute the public parameter $\psi = (u, \chi)$ $(u = \{u_1, \ldots, u_s\}, \chi = \{\chi_1, \ldots, \chi_n\})$ and send it to the trusted third party for storage. The user keeps the private key locally.

Step 3: Challenge Creation: $Challenge(chal)$. When a user wants to audit the outsourced data, he or she compute a challenge, $chal = Q = \{(i_j, a_j), j = 1 \ldots c, i_j \in [1, n], a_j \in Z_p\}$, and sends it to the organizer.

Step 4: Challenge Delivery: $Forward(chal)$. The organizer forwards the received challenge $chal = Q$ to the CSP servers, $CSP_k(k \in [1..l])$. Without losing the generality, assume there are t CSP servers that store the blocks challenged by the user.

Step 5: Proof Creation and Delivery: $GenProof(pk, Q, m_i, \sigma_{ix}) \to \{P_k\}$. The service provider $CSP_k(k \in [1..l])$ computes the evidence according to the Formula (1) and (2).

$$p_{1kj} = \sum_{m_i \in CSP_k} a_i m_{ij} \mod p(j = 1 \ldots s) \tag{1}$$

$$p_{2k} \leftarrow \prod_{m_i \in CSP_k} \sigma_{ix}^{a_i} \in G \tag{2}$$

The user returns the proofs shown in Eq. (3) and (4) to the organizer.

$$P_k = \{p_{1k}, p_{2k}\} \tag{3}$$

$$p_{1k} = \{p_{1k1}, p_{1k2}, \ldots, p_{1ks}\} \tag{4}$$

Step 6: Proof Aggregation and Response. $Aggregation(pk, Q, P_1, P_2, \ldots, P_t) \to \{P\}$. The organizer computes $P_{1j} = \sum_{k=1}^{t} P_{1kj} \mod p(j = 1, 2, \ldots, s), P_2 \leftarrow \prod_{k=1}^{t} P_{2k} \in G$. Then the organizer returns the aggregated proof $P, P = \{P_1, P_2\}$, to the user, where $P_1 = \{P_{11}, P_{12}, \ldots, P_{1s}\}$.

Step 7: User Verification. After the user received the data $P = \{P_1, P_2\}$ sent by the organizer, she/he gets the parameter $\psi = (u, \chi)$ from trusted third party and verify the response according to the Formula (5):

$$e(P_2, g) = e\left(\prod_{(i, a_i) \in Q} \prod_{k=1}^{num_i} H(F_n \| i \| k \| V_i)^{a_i} \prod_{j=1}^{s} u_j^{p_{1j}}, v \right) \tag{5}$$

If Formula (5) holds, it means the outsourced data are stored correctly and the output is "*TRUE*"; otherwise, the output is "*FALSE*".

Dynamic Update When users need to update data $m_i \rightarrow m'$, they should make a modification $V_i = V_i + 1$ from $\chi_i = i \parallel num_i \parallel V_i$, compute the new label $new\_\sigma_{ik} \leftarrow (H(F_n \parallel i \parallel k \parallel V_i) \cdot \prod_{j=1}^{s} u_j^{m'_j}))^\alpha, for(k = 1, \dots, num_i)$ and then send the updated χ_i along with the corresponding label $\sigma_{ik}(k = 1, \dots, num_i)$ to the organizer. After that, the organizer only needs to conduct a distributed storage. Due to the relevance between the label and the sequence of the data, the scheme could only realize part of the update operations, namely data modification and deletion.

4   Evaluation

4.1   Security Analysis

In this section, we prove two properties to ensure data integrity under our scheme.

Theorem 1. *Correctness. If all CSP servers keep user's data correctly, they can successfully pass the challenge-response verification procedure initiated by the user.*

Proof. To verify the data correctness, according to step (7), the use computes $e(P_2, g)$. It can be noticed in step (5)–(6) that $P_{1j} = \sum_{k=1}^{t} P_{1kj} \mod p(j = 1, 2, \dots, s)$ and $P_2 = \prod_{k=1}^{t} P_{2k}$, where $p_{1kj} = \sum_{m_i \in CSP_k} a_i m_{ij} \mod p(j = 1 \dots s)$ and $p_{2k} \leftarrow \prod_{m_i \in CSP_k} \sigma_{ix}^{a_i} \in G$.

According to the bilinear property of the weil-paring function, we get

$$e(P_2, g) = e(\prod_{k=1}^{t} P_{2k}, g)$$

$$= e(\prod_{k=1}^{t}(\prod_{m_i \in CSP_k} \sigma_{ix}^{a_i}), g)$$

$$= e(\prod_{k=1}^{t}(\prod_{m_i \in CSP_k} (H(F_n \parallel i \parallel k \parallel V_i) \cdot \prod_{j=1}^{s} u_j^{m_{ij}}))^{a_i \alpha}), g)$$

$$= e(\prod_{k=1}^{t}(\prod_{m_i \in CSP_k} H(F_n \parallel i \parallel k \parallel V_i) \cdot \prod_{j=1}^{s} u_j^{m_{ij}})^{a_i}), g^\alpha)$$

$$= e(\prod_{(i,a_i) \in Q} \prod_{k=1}^{num_i} H(F_n \parallel i \parallel k \parallel V_i)^{a_i} \prod_{j=1}^{s} u_j^{\sum_{k=1}^{t} \sum_{m_i \in CSP_k} a_i m_{ij}}, v)$$

$$= e(\prod_{(i,a_i) \in Q} \prod_{k=1}^{num_i} H(F_n \parallel i \parallel k \parallel V_i)^{a_i} \prod_{j=1}^{s} u_j^{p_{1j}}, v)$$

This completes our proof.

Theorem 2. *Soundness. If the one-way hash function is secure and the computational Deffie-hellman (CDH) assumption holds, in the random oracle model, no adversary (e.g., CSP_j) against the soundness of our scheme can ever (except with negligible probability) cause the user to accept the response.*

4.2 Performance Analysis

We prototyped our algorithm and the evaluation is conducted on a desktop with IntelR-Core(TM)2 Duo CPU @2.66 GHz Oracle VM VirtualBox Version 4.2.10 2 GB memory Ubuntu 10.10, and adopted PBC library to implement the crypto primitives. The security parameter of the bilinear pairing function is configured as 80, which means the prime number p is 160 bits. In the evaluation, we set the file size as 80 KB, 160 KB, 320 KB, respectively. The result of evaluation is illustrated in Table 1.

Table 1. Evaluation results of our approach

Size (bits)	Blocks (#)	Sectors (#)	Challenge Blocks (#)	Preprocessing Time (s)	Generating Challenge (us)	Generating Proof (ms)	Verifying Proof (ms)
80	64	64	32	24.223	20	3121	1063
80	32	128	16	23.326	15	154	1223
80	16	256	8	25.352	18	81	1414
320	128	128	64	84.337	29	927	1671
320	64	256	32	81.216	19	512	2085
320	32	512	16	84.164	16	305	2847
1280	256	256	128	330	44	4950	3289
1280	128	512	64	336	119	9110	6761

The experiment results shown in Fig. 1 show that for the time cost of preprocessing and challenge generating will not be influenced by the number of file blocks. The time cost of proof generating decreases with the decline of N, the number of file blocks; in contrast the time cost of verification will increase when N decreases. The time cost of preprocessing increases proportionally with the increase of file size. When file size increases, the challenge generation time cost almost remains unchanged and the time cost of proof generating and verification increases.

5   Related Work

Static Data Integrity Verification. Deswarte et al. [14] propose the first remote data integrity verification model and propose two solutions based on hash function and RSA signature respectively. Filho et al. [15] develop a remote audition scheme based on RSA signature with hash function techniques, which supports unlimited checking operation. But the verification requires the whole file retrieval and its computational overhead is very high. Ateniese et al. [8,16] propose a probabilistic remote data integrity checking scheme called "*Provable Data Possession*" (PDP) by using homomorphic verification tags and "*sampling*" technique.

The schemes above could only detect on whether data is properly stored but cannot recover the damaged data. Juels et al. [17] combine data possession checking with error correction coding techniques and propose a model called "*Proof of Retrievability*" (POR) for remote data checking and recovery. Shacham et al. [18] proposed two types of POR schemes, one is a public authentication scheme based on BLS signature, the other is private authentication on the basis of pseudo random function and both of the schemes have low interactions and computations. Boweres et al. [19,20] introduced POR scheme in distributed static data storage system and realized as well as practiced it. Naor and Rothblum [21] introduce message authentication code (MAC) combined with error-correction code to check the cloud data integrity and realize error localization and data recovery as well. Xu et al. [22] proposed a highly efficient POR scheme, in which data block is involved with s group elements and L child data blocks, the storage overhead is $\frac{1}{S}$ of the file block and computational costs is $O(s)$. Wang et al. [23] proposed scheme that supports public authentication and privacy preservation based on zero-knowledge mechanism.

Integrity Verification that Supports Dynamic Data Operation. In most situation, because of the flexibility of cloud storage service, users may need to modify, delete or update the stored data. It is necessary to do research on integrity authentication that support dynamic data operation. Erway et al. [24] propose the Dynamic PDP (DPDP) scheme using memory detection [25] and skip-lists [26] technique. They prove that under the standard model, their solution is more sound and robust than the PDP solutions based on random oracle model. Its computing overhead and communication overhead are both $o(\log n)$. Wang et al. propose a solution in the work [10], which supports data modification, deletion and appending. They proposed an improved solution based on bilinear pairing BLS signature [27] and Merkle Hash tree technique [28]. Hao et al. [29] propose a privacy protected solution that supports dynamic data operations. In this solution, the interaction data size is $o(1)$ while both the local saved data size and the server computing overhead are $o(n)$.

Privacy Preserving in Cloud Data Checking. Ensuring the data auditing without any unnecessary information leakage is a critical concern in the practical application. Yu et al. [30] introduce the term, *zero-knowledge privacy*, to define the goal of privacy preserving in data integrity verification, which ensures that the TPA cannot obtain any additional information of file content from all the auxiliary verification information available. Fan et al. [31] propose an indistinguishability-game-based definition, *IND-Privacy*, to evaluate the cloud data privacy preserving. They point out that many approaches are not theoretically secure according to the IND-Privacy definition. They also present their example protocol that ensures content-integrity checking and satisfies the IND-Privacy.

Integrity Verification on Multicloud. By the extensive use of cloud storage, people start to consider saving their data on more than one cloud service providers. The integrity verification of multicloud becomes especially important [13]. Zhu et al. [12] propose a CPDP module that can achieve the integrity authentication of multicloud. This CPDP module is based on the HIH and HVR and the security of this module is based on zero-knowledge proof system. It has the validity and zero-knowledge characteristics. The verifier does not connect directly with CSPs, but connect to the organizer. This can reduce the communication overhead and computing flexibility of the verifier. Huaqun Wang et al. [32] find that the protocol presented by Yan Zhu et al. [12] exists vulnerability. Any malicious CSP or organizer can generate response that can pass the authentication even it has already deleted all the data. It means that this module does not have the soundness characteristic. To reduce the clients' cost in multi-cloud remote data verification, Wang [33] presents ID-DPDP (identity-based distributed provable data possession) scheme. Under the standard CDH problem assumption, the scheme is provably secure and can support regular verification, delegate verification and public verification as well.

6   Conclusion

In this paper, we present a collaborative multi-cloud data integrity audition scheme, which is based on BLS signatures and homomorphic tags. Based on the proposed scheme, users can audit their outsourced data in a one-round challenge-response process. Our scheme also enables public verification and supports dynamic data maintenance (e.g., data modification, insertion, deletion, etc.). The theoretical analysis demonstrates the effectiveness of our scheme and the probability that the dishonest CSP server can bypass the checking successfully is neglectable if the one-way hash function is collision-resistant and the computational Deffie-hellman (CDH) assumption holds.

Acknowledgment. This work was supported in part by the National Natural Science Foundation of China (No. 61402029), the National Key Basic Research Program (NKBRP) (973 Program) (No. 2012CB315905), the National Natural Science Foundation of China (No. 61370190), Beijing Natural Science Foundation (No. 4162020), Singapore Ministry of Education under NUS grant R-252-000-539-112.

References

1. Amazon.com. Amazon web service. http://aws.amazon.com
2. Google.com. http://www.google.com
3. Baidu.com. http://www.baidu.com
4. Yu, L., Chen, L., Cai, Z., Shen, H., Liang, Y., Pan, Y.: Stochastic load balancing for virtual resource management in datacenters. IEEE Trans. Cloud Comput. **PP**(99), 1–1 (2016)
5. Yu, L., Cai, Z.: Dynamic scaling of virtual clusters with bandwidth guarantee in cloud datacenters. In: Proceedings of the 35rd Annual IEEE Internationa Conference on Computer Communications (INFOCOM) (2016)
6. Deswarte, Y., Quisquater, J.J., Saidane, A.: Remote integrity checking. In: Proceedings of Conference on Integrity and Iternal Control in Information Systems 2003 (2003)
7. Filho, D.L.G., Baretto, P.: Demonstrating data possession and uncheatable data transfer. IACR ePrint archive, Report /150 (2006)
8. Ateniese, G., Burns, R., Curtmola, R., Herring, J., Kissner, L., Peterson, Z., Song, D.: Provable data possession at untrusted stores. In: Proceedings of the 14th ACM Conference on Computer and Communications Security, pp. 598–609. ACM (2007)
9. Ateniese, G., Kamara, S., Katz, J.: Proofs of storage from homomorphic identification protocols. In: Matsui, M. (ed.) ASIACRYPT 2009. LNCS, vol. 5912, pp. 319–333. Springer, Heidelberg (2009)
10. Wang, Q., Wang, C., Ren, K., Lou, W., Li, J.: Enabling public auditability and data dynamics for storage security in cloud computing. Parallel Distrib. Syst. IEEE Trans. **22**(5), 847–859 (2011)
11. Zhu, Y., Hu, H., Ahn, G.-J., Han, Y., Chen, S.: Collaborative integrity verification in hybrid clouds. In: 7th International Conference on Collaborative Computing,: Networking, Applications and Worksharing (CollaborateCom), pp. 191–200. IEEE (2011)
12. Zhu, Y., Hu, H., Ahn, G.-J., Yu, M.: Cooperative provable data possession for integrity verification in multicloud storage. Parallel Distrib. Syst. IEEE Trans. **23**(12), 2231–2244 (2012)
13. Zheng, Q., Xu, S.: Fair and dynamic proofs of retrievability. In: Proceedings of the First ACM Conference on Data and Application Security and Privacy, pp. 237–248. ACM (2011)
14. Deswarte, Y., Quisquater, J.-J., Saïdane, A.: Remote integrity checking. Proc. IICIS **140**, 1–11 (2003)
15. Gazzoni Filho, D.L., Barreto, P.S.L.M.: Demonstrating data possession and uncheatable data transfer. IACR Cryptology ePrint Arch. **2006**, 150 (2006)
16. Ateniese, G., Burns, R., Curtmola, R., Herring, J., Khan, O., Kissner, L., Peterson, Z., Song, D.: Remote data checking using provable data possession. ACM Trans. Inf. Syst. Secur. (TISSEC) **14**(1), 12 (2011)
17. Juels, A., Kaliski Jr., B.S.: Pors,: Proofs of retrievability for large files. In: Proceedings of the 14th ACM Conference on Computer and Communications Security, pp. 584–597. ACM (2007)
18. Shacham, H., Waters, B.: Compact proofs of retrievability. J. Cryptology **26**(3), 442–483 (2013)
19. Bowers, K.D., Juels, A., Oprea, A.: Proofs of retrievability: Theory and implementation. In: Proceedings of the ACM Workshop on Cloud Computing Security, pp. 43–54. ACM (2009)

20. Bowers, K.D.: Hail: a high-availability and integrity layer for cloud storage. In: Proceedings of the 16th ACM Conference on Computer and Communications Security, pp. 187–198. ACM (2009)

21. Naor, M., Rothblum, G.N.: The complexity of online memory checking. In: 46th Annual IEEE Symposium on Foundations of Computer Science, FOCS 2005, pp. 573–582. IEEE (2005)

22. Xu, J., Chang, E.-C.: Towards efficient proofs of retrievability. In: Proceedings of the 7th ACM Symposium on Information, Computer and Communications Security, pp. 79–80. ACM (2012)

23. Wang, C., Wang, Q., Ren, K., Lou, W.: Privacy-preserving public auditing for data storage security in cloud computing. In: INFOCOM: Proceedings IEEE, pp. 1–9. IEEE (2010)

24. Erway, C.C., Küpçü, A., Papamanthou, C., Tamassia, R.: Dynamic provable data possession. ACM Trans. Inf. Syst. Secur. (TISSEC) 17(4), 15 (2015)

25. Clarke, D., Devadas, S., van Dijk, M., Gassend, B., Suh, G.E.: Incremental multiset hash functions and their application to memory integrity checking. In: Laih, C.-S. (ed.) ASIACRYPT 2003. LNCS, vol. 2894, pp. 188–207. Springer, Heidelberg (2003)

26. Goodrich, M.T., Tamassia, R., Schwerin, A.: Implementation of an authenticated dictionary with skip lists and commutative hashing. In: DARPA Information Survivability Conference and Exposition II: DISCEX 2001. Proceedings, vol. 2, pp. 68–82. IEEE (2001)

27. Boneh, D., Lynn, B., Shacham, H.: Short signatures from the weil pairing. In: Boyd, C. (ed.) ASIACRYPT 2001. LNCS, vol. 2248, p. 514. Springer, Heidelberg (2001)

28. Merkle, R.C.: Protocols for public key cryptosystems. In: null, p. 122. IEEE (1980)

29. Hao, Z., Zhong, S., Yu, N.: A privacy-preserving remote data integrity checking protocol with data dynamics and public verifiability. Knowl. Data Eng. IEEE Trans. 23(9), 1432–1437 (2011)

30. Yu, Y., Au, M.H., Yi Mu, S.T., Ren, J., Susilo, W., Dong, L.: Enhanced privacy of a remote data integrity-checking protocol for secure cloud storage. Int. J. Inf. Secur. 14, 307–318 (2015)

31. Fan, X., Yang, G., Mu, Y., Yu, Y.: On indistinguishability in remote data integrity checking. Comput. J. 58, 823–830 (2015)

32. Wang, H., Zhang, Y.: On the knowledge soundness of a cooperative provable data possession scheme in multicloud storage. Parallel Distrib. Syst. IEEE Trans. 25(1), 264–267 (2014)

33. Wang, H.: Identity-based distributed provable data possession in multicloud storage. IEEE Trans. Serv. Comput. 8(2), 328–340 (2015)

An Adaptive Beaconing Scheme Based on Traffic Environment Parameters Prediction in VANETs

Jin Qian[1]([✉]), Tao Jing[1], Yan Huo[1], Hui Li[1], Liran Ma[2], and Yanfei Lu[1]

[1] School of Electronics and Information Engineering,
Beijing Jiaotong University, Beijing, China
12111020@bjtu.edu.cn
[2] Department of Computer Science,
Texas Christian University, Fort Worth, USA

Abstract. In Vehicular Ad Hoc Networks (VANETs), it is common for vehicles to inform their current states such as position, direction and speed to their neighboring vehicles by broadcasting beacon messages periodically. Choosing a suitable beaconing scheme has been considered an important challenge since we need to balance the trade-off between the information accuracy and the channel congestion. In this paper, we propose a new adaptive beaconing scheme based on the short-term traffic environment prediction. By using our adaptive beaconing scheme, vehicles can effectively reduce the channel congestion and enhance the utilization of the limited channel resource. This paper introduces the ARIMA model based prediction method in details, and gives a description of the beaconing adaption method which combined the transmission power adaption and the beacon generation rate adaption together. The analysis and simulation demonstrate the performance of our adaptive beaconing scheme.

Keywords: VANETs · Beaconing scheme · Traffic environment prediction · ARIMA model

1 Introduction

VANETs hold great potential in enhancing vehicle safety and improving traffic efficiency [4,7,17]. In VANETs, each vehicle is equipped with a wireless communication system to exchange information among each other. One of the main information exchange methods in VANETs is beaconing. Based on IEEE 802.11p, beacon messages are broadcasted periodically on the control channel (CCH) by vehicles to inform their current states such as position, direction and speed. These beacon messages can be used by the neighboring vehicles to detect their traffic environment as well as preventing the potential traffic accidents [6,9,15].

The bandwidth of the CCH is 10 MHz. Channel load will sharply increase in scenarios with high traffic density. High channel load causes the channel congestion between vehicles, resulting in a high degree of performance degradation of VANETs. In recent years, some researchers have studied the adaptive beaconing

© Springer International Publishing Switzerland 2016
Q. Yang et al. (Eds.): WASA 2016, LNCS 9798, pp. 524–535, 2016.
DOI: 10.1007/978-3-319-42836-9_46

schemes to reduce the channel congestion. Two main adaptation approaches have been proposed: the beacon generation rate adaptation [2,3,5,11] and the beacon transmission power adaptation [8,10,13]. While most of these researchers just focus on studying one of these two approaches. Through analysis we believe separately adapting the transmission power or adapting the beacon generation rate can not satisfy the requirement of all the scenarios in VANETs. For example, in the highway scenario, due to the high speed of vehicles, to ensure the neighboring vehicles have enough distance to react the potential collision, we have to make sure the beaconing power can transmit the beacon message far enough. As another example, in the congested scenario where the vehicle density is high and the distance between two vehicle is short, we need a high beacon generation rate to ensure the real-time message exchange between vehicles. The other problem we find in existing works is that all the researchers adapt the future beaconing scheme based on the current parameters. As the traffic environment is changing, we believe this kind of beaconing adaption is delayed and inaccurate, especially when the vehicle beacon generation rate is low.

Different from existing works, we propose a new adaptive beaconing scheme based on the short-term traffic environment prediction in this paper. In our new scheme, to reduce the channel congestion, we combine the beacon transmission power adaptation and the beacon generation rate adaption in a certain way and order. In addition, according to the continuous change of the short-term traffic environment, we use the current and historical traffic environment parameters including the traffic density and the vehicle velocity to predict the future vehicle environment parameters. Based on these predicted parameters, we can adapt the beaconing scheme in advance. One important contribution is that we use the Auto Regressive Integrated Moving Average (ARIMA) model [12] based prediction method to guarantee the efficiency and accuracy of our prediction. To the best of our knowledge, this is the first paper to use the parameters prediction to improve the beaconing scheme.

The rest of this paper is organized as follows. In Sect. 2, we briefly present some existing works about the adaptive beaconing scheme. In Sect. 3, we introduce the system structure and give some assumptions used in this paper. In Sect. 3, we describe the online part of our adaptive beaconing scheme. The offline part is described in Sect. 4. In Sect. 5, we make evaluation of the performance of our Scheme. The conclusion is finalized in Sect. 6.

2   Related Works

As stated earlier in the previous section, some works have been proposed to improve the adaptive beaconing schemes. In [11], the authors propose an adaptive beaconing scheme which reduces the beacon generation rate based on two key metrics: message utility and channel quality. The scheme proposed [2] computes the beacon generation rate based on the bandwidth sharing information of the neighboring vehicles. A fuzzy logic approach is used in [5] to classify the moving states of vehicles, and vehicles adapt the beacon generation rate based on the moving states. The author in [3] consider beacon generation rate based on the fairness utilization of the bandwidth resource. [13] selects the beacon transmission power according to the utility of the beacon to be transmitted. In [8], the authors randomly select the beacon transmission power following a given probability distribution. In [10], authors discuss multi-tradeoffs in beacon transmission power adaption. All these works do not consider the combination of the beacon transmission power adaption and the beacon generation rate adaption together, and they adapt the future beaconing scheme based on the current parameters. To cover the shortage of these, we propose the adaptive beaconing scheme based on traffic environment parameters prediction in VANETs.

3   System Description

The basic idea of our proposed scheme is that the vehicle adapts the beaconing scheme based on the predicted traffic environment parameters. To build up a complete adaptive beaconing scheme, we also need to consider when to initiate the adaption, and how we adapt the beaconing scheme.

In Fig. 1, we present the system diagram of our scheme. There are two main parts in our scheme, an offline part and an online part. In the offline part, based on the large numbers of the historical traffic environment data, we built several historical traffic patterns. The completed historical traffic patterns can be pre-stored in all the vehicles. It means one vehicle has no need to repeat the building process individually. The vehicle enters the online part when it is driving on the road. The online part is further divided into two phases, the detection phase and the adaption phase. In the detection phase, the vehicle continuously monitors the channel state to consider whether to initiate a beaconing scheme adaption or not. If not, it goes on monitoring the channel, otherwise it enters the beaconing scheme adaption phase. In the adaption phase, to identify the current traffic pattern, we use the pattern matching mechanism. The vehicle can quickly predict the traffic environment parameters with the last sets of the traffic environment data. Then based on the predicted parameters, it adapts the future beaconing scheme.

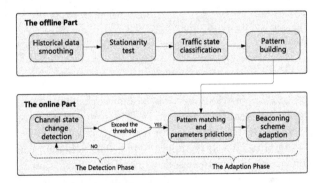

Fig. 1. The system diagram of our scheme

There are some assumptions in this paper. The first and also the most important assumption is that all the vehicles adapt their beacon transmission power and beacon generation rates using the same scheme. They have a fair share of the available bandwidth. Therefore, at the same time, the nearby vehicles have the similar beaconing states. The second assumption is that the vehicle can collect its own velocity and location in real time, and it can obtain the velocity and location of the neighboring vehicles from the received beacon messages. The third assumption is that the radio channel is ideal, the bit errors are not considered in this paper. To help understanding our adaptive beaconing scheme, we will introduce the online part first.

4   The Online Part in the Adaptive Beaconing Scheme

4.1   The Detection Phase

Before we adapt the beaconing scheme, we need to detect and confirm the necessity of the adaption. Since the channel congestion is the result of a considerable amount of the data exchange between vehicles which exceeds the network capacity. It is a simple but effective way to judge whether to initiate the adaption or not based on the number of the neighboring vehicles. In many researches, they calculated the number through counting the number of the received beacons. However, we think the beacon-based estimation is not accurate due to the collision of packets especially in congestion-related situations. The collision of packets is the ad-hoc nature of vehicular networks, and it is unavoidable. To tackle this problem, in our scheme, we choose the number of the received packets and the number of the collision packets to estimate the number of the vehicles. These two parameters are easy to collect and they do not need additional information exchange between vehicles. In this subsection, we will introduce our estimation method first. And then we give the judgement standard for initiating the channel scheme adaption.

Estimating the Number of Neighbors. To estimate the number of the neighboring vehicles, the estimation model is shown in Fig. 2. In this paper, we denote that all the vehicle B, C and D within the interference range are the neighboring nodes of vehicle A. Vehicle B and vehicle C are in the communication range of vehicle A. Vehicle D is in the interference range of vehicle A. All vehicles broadcast the beacon messages periodically. The beacon messages sent by vehicle D cannot be decoded by vehicle A and will be considered as collisions by vehicle A. The vehicle monitors the channel state periodically and continuously. Generally, each period takes one second. At the end of each period, we make a statistical analysis of the channel state. In period i, we can obtain the total number of the collisions packets which is denoted as n_{i_cp}, and we can obtain the total number of the received packets which is denoted as n_{i_rp}. Based on the received beacons, we define R_{i_avg} as the average beaconing rate of neighbors. When one neighbor vehicle is in the interference range, the beacon packets from it are decodable. We

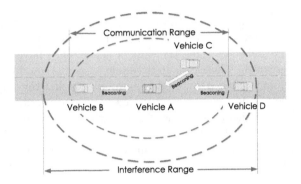

Fig. 2. Neighbor number estimation model

define n_{i_ndp} as the number of this kind of collision packet. When two neighbor vehicle are both in the communication range of the receiver. If they broadcast the beacon packets at the same time, the beacon packets will collide. We define n_{i_rcp} as the number of this kind of collision packet. Then we have:

$$n_{i\_cp} = n_{i\_ncp} + n_{i\_rcp}. \tag{1}$$

In [1], the author has described that the percentage of n_{i_rcp} in n_{i_cp} can be considered as a constant parameter. It is denoted as θ in this paper. We have:

$$n_{i\_rcp} = n_{i\_cp} \cdot \theta, \tag{2}$$

and

$$n_{i\_rcp} = n_{i\_ncp} \cdot (1 - \theta). \tag{3}$$

As the assumption in the estimation model, the situation that three or more packets colliding at a same time is negligible. For one vehicle in period i, we define the number of neighboring vehicles within the interference range as N_i. It can be estimated as follows:

$$
\begin{aligned}
N_i &= \frac{(n_{i\_rcp} + n_{i\_ncp} + 2 \cdot n_{i\_rcp})}{R_{i\_avg}} \\
&= \frac{(n_{i\_rcp} + (1 + \theta) \cdot n_{i\_cp})}{R_{i\_avg}}
\end{aligned}
\tag{4}
$$

Making the Judgement. At the end of each detection phase, we can obtain the number of the neighboring vehicles. The number of the last period is denoted as N_{i-1}. With this two parameters we can make the judgement on whether to initiate a beaconing scheme adaption or not. The following is the judgement process. We have the variable T expressed the change of the the number of the neighboring vehicles:

$$C = |N_i - N_{i-1}|. \tag{5}$$

We define C_t as the threshold of the change. It can be calculated as follows:

$$C_t = \varepsilon \cdot N_{i-1},\tag{6}$$

where ε is a constant which we defined in the system. If C exceeds threshold C_t, the vehicle judges that it should initiate the beaconing scheme adaption. Then the vehicle finishes the judgement process.

Obtaining the Parameters Used in the Adaption Phase. At every end of the monitoring periods, the vehicle should recalculate C and C_t. To realize the pattern matching prediction in the adaption phase, besides the above parameters, the vehicle acquire another two parameters. The first is the velocity of the vehicle itself denoted as v_i which can be directly collected from the vehicle. The second is the traffic density denoted as d_i. Generally in vehicle environment, the traffic density is described as the number of vehicles in every kilometre. Defining $R_{inter f}$ as the interference range of the vehicle, d_i can be calculated based on N_i and $R_{inter f}$. The formula is expressed as follows:

$$d_i = \frac{N_i}{2R_{inter f}}.\tag{7}$$

And we can calculate the interference range as follows:

$$R_{inter f} = \frac{\lambda}{4\pi\theta} \cdot \sqrt{\frac{G \cdot P_i^t}{P_{rmin}}},\tag{8}$$

where G is the antenna gain, P_i^t is the transmission power, P_{rmin} is the minimal received power which can successfully decode the message, λ is the wavelength.

4.2 The Adaption Phase

Different from other researches, we use the predicted parameters to do the beaconing scheme adaption. In the end of the detection phase, we have obtained the parameters v_i and d_i which can reflect the traffic environment.

The future parameters can be quickly predicted with the current and historical parameters by using the pattern matching mechanism. In this paper, based on the ARIMA model, we build the traffic patterns. The pattern building process is presented in the next section. Here, we introduce the pattern matching and the prediction process.

Pattern Matching. The target of the pattern matching process is to select a pattern from the historical traffic patterns which is most similar to the current traffic conditions. According to the description in [16], we extract the second-order autoregressive parameters of the current traffic data firstly. And then we apply the Euclid Distance to estimate the similarity between the historical and the identified current traffic patterns. The formula is expressed as follows:

$$D_E^2(\phi_T, \phi_R) = (\phi_T - \phi_R)^T (\phi_T - \phi_R), \tag{9}$$

where ϕ_R and ϕ_T denote the autoregressive parameters of the historical pattern and the identified pattern, respectively.

Future Parameters Prediction. After matching the traffic pattern, combining with the current parameters, the future parameters v_{i+1} and d_{i+1} can be quickly obtained by one-step or multistep prediction shown in Eq. 10.

$$\hat{x}_t(l) = \begin{cases} \phi_0 + \sum_{i=1}^p (\phi_i \, \dot{x}_{i-1}(l)) - \sum_{j=1}^q (\theta_i \, c_{i+l-j}) & 1 \leq q, \\ \phi_0 + \sum_{i=1}^p (\phi_i \, \hat{x}_{i-1}(l)) & 1 \geq q. \end{cases} \tag{10}$$

where $\phi_i, i = 1, 2, \ldots, p$ is the autoregressive parameter, $\theta_j, j = 1, 2, \ldots, q$ are the moving average parameters, p is the order of autoregressive parameters, q is the order of moving average parameters, ε_t are variances of the residual series and l is the step-size of the backward prediction. By using the predicted traffic parameters, we can avoid some channel congestion caused by the delayed beaconing scheme adaption.

Beaconing Scheme Adaption. We present our beaconing scheme adaption method in this subsection. In the introduction of this paper, we have introduced the disadvantages of separately adapting the transmission power and separately adapting the beacon generation rate. Fortunately, the situation that high density of vehicles driving with a high speed dose not exist. So it is possible to design a beaconing adaption method to satisfy the requirement of all the scenarios in VANETs.

In our scheme, we combine the transmission power adaption and the beacon generation rate adaption together. This is also one of the main contributions of this paper. The adaption method can be summarized as: we adapt the beacon generation rate until it reaches the minimum beacon transmission power, and then we adapt the beacon generation rate. The minimum beacon transmission power denoted as P_{i+1}^{tmin} is calculated based on the current vehicle velocity. We have

$$P_{i+1}^{tmin} = \frac{64\pi^2 v_{i+1}{}^2 P_{rmin}}{G\lambda^2}. \tag{11}$$

The core idea of our adaption method is to make our best effort to maintain the beacon generation rate. We believe that most of the safety applications enquire a high beaconing rate. Frequently reducing the beaconing rate will affect the vehicle safey. While reducing the transmission power only means reducing the number of vehicles in the communication range, the most important vehicles relating to the safey are these nearest ones, the slight adaption on the transmission power will not affect these vehicles. So adapting the beaconing transmission power before the beacon generation rate is appropriate. At the same time, the calculated minimum beacon transmission power can ensure that the nearest vehicles are in the awareness region. We believe the proposed beaconing scheme adaption method can satisfy various requirements of VANETs.

5   The Offline Part in the Adaptive Beaconing Scheme

In the offline part, using the historical traffic environment data, the vehicle builts the historical traffic patterns based on the ARIMA model. The ARIMA model is a common used model for time series analysis which is also known as the famous Box-Jenkins model. In our scheme, the pattern building have 4 steps:

Step1: Data smoothing. In our scheme, the historical traffic environment data mainly include the number of neighboring vehicles and vehicle velocity in different areas and at different times. It is unavoidable that there are some error or inaccurate data. For the time series, these data are noises and will affect the quality of the pattern building. Hence, it is necessary to smooth the date. In this paper, due to the features of simplicity and high efficiency, we use the exponential smoothing method to smooth the data.

Step2: Stationarity test. Since the modeling process require the stationarity of the time series, we need to do the stationarity test. If one series shows the evidence of non-stationarity, we can use the difference method to reduce the non-stationarity. Sometimes, the second-difference is also needed.

Step3: Traffic state classification. In the research of the paper [14], the author has proved that the traffic state classification can improve the modeling accuracy. In our paper, based on the velocity-density relation, we classify the traffic states into three states, the free flowing state, the high traffic state and the congested state. Before building the traffic patterns, all the historical traffic environment data are classified based on the three states.

Step4: Pattern building. After finish the above data preprocessing steps, we can formally start building the traffic patterns. In this step, we will do the model recognition, the parameter estimation, the model diagnostics, and the patterns storage. According to [16], the ARIMA (p, d, q) model of the time series $\{X_1, X_2, \ldots, X_t\}$ can be defined as:

$$X_t = \phi_1 X_{t-1} + \phi_2 X_{t-2} + \cdots + \phi_p X_{t-p} + a_t - \theta_1 a_{t-1} - \theta_2 a_{t-2} - \cdots - \theta_q a_{t-q} \tag{12}$$

X_t is obtained by differencing the original time series d times, a_t is the white noise component at t, $\phi_i, i = 1, 2 \ldots p$ are the autoregressive parameters, $\theta_j, j = 1, 2 \ldots q$ are the moving average parameters, p is the order of autoregressive parameters and q is the order of moving average parameters.

According to the different characters of these historical traffic environment data, we can choose a suitable ARIMA model for these data. The model recognition process is equivalent to the process that determining the value of p, d, and q. The parameter estimation process is equivalent to process that determining the value of the parameters in Eq. 12. In this paper, we use the maximum likelihood estimation method to obtain all the value of these parameters. The model diagnostics phase, we test the estimated parameters in the model, and diagnose whether the residual series error is white noise or not. In [12], they have given the detailed explanations and computing methods of the ARIMA model. So we do not repeat them here. Based on the diagnosis, we can know the appropriateness of the model. After all the processes, we can store the builded historical traffic patterns and they will be used in the online part.

6   Performance Evaluation

In this section we evaluate the performance of our adaptive beaconing scheme. The simulation is based on the IEEE 802.11p Medium Access Control model (MAC) with 10 MHz wide channels. All simulation results are averaged from 100 different simulation tries.

Figures 3 and 4 show the relationship between the actual density time-series and the future density parameters used in the beaconing scheme adaption. The future density parameters in Fig. 4 are the predicted parameters after the ARIMA model based prediction, and the future density parameters in Fig. 3 are calculated just according to the current traffic density. Figure 5 shows the collision rate with these two kinds parameters to do the beaconing scheme adaption. We can find that, the beaconing scheme with predicted parameters has better performance than the other beaconing scheme. Especially when the traffic environment has a large change, the beaconing scheme without parameters prediction cause a obvious increase in beaconing collision rate. The simulation proves the advantage of our adaptive beaconing scheme based on traffic environment parameters prediction. With the pattern matching technology, our beaconing scheme can adapt in advance to avoid the channel congestion.

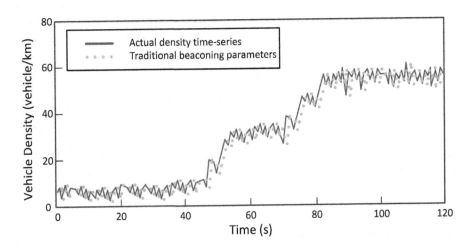

Fig. 3. The traditional parameters used to adapt the beaconing scheme

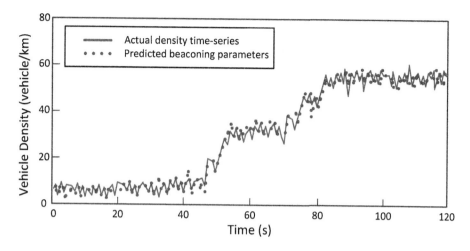

Fig. 4. The predicted parameters used to adapt the beaconing scheme

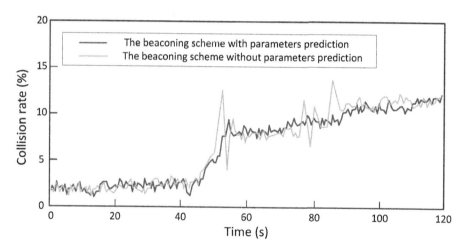

Fig. 5. The collection rate of different beaconing scheme (Color figure online)

We analyze the relationship between the packets collision rate and the vehicle density of different adaption methods in Fig. 6. We can find that, when the vehicle density is more than 50 vehicles per kilometer, there is a obvious increase in the collision rate of the beaconing scheme which separately adapting the transmission power or adapting the beacon generation rate. Since we combine the beacon transmission power adaptation and the beacon generation rate adaption together in our adaption methods, we have a distinct advantage in the collision rate especially when the vehicle density is high. We also analyze the relationship between the number of the average received beacons and the vehicle density of different adaption methods in Fig. 7. Similarly, our combined scheme has a

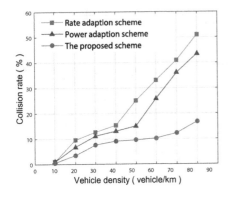

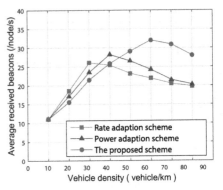

Fig. 6. Packets collision rate   **Fig. 7.** Average received beacons

distinct advantage in number of the average received beacons when the vehicle density is high. From these simulations, we can find that the ARIMA model based prediction method and the combined beaconing adaption method are effective to reduce the channel congestion and enhance the utilization of the limited channel resource.

7   Conclusion

In this paper, we study the problem of how to adapt the beaconing scheme. We propose an adaptive beaconing scheme based on traffic environment parameters prediction. The ARIMA model based prediction method is used to do the prediction. And we combine the beacon transmission power adaptation and the beacon generation rate adaption in our adaption method. Simulation results confirm the benefits of our scheme. In our future research, we plan to study the relationship between the beaconing scheme adaption and the contentiom window adaptation.

Acknowledgements. The authors would like to thank the support from the National Natural Science Foundation of China (Grant No. 61471028, 61371069 and 61272505).

References

1. Chaabouni, N., Hafid, A., Sahu, P.K.: A collision-based beacon rate adaptation scheme(cba) for vanets. In: IEEE ANTS, pp. 1–6, December 2013
2. Djahel, S., Ghamri-Doudane, Y.: A robust congestion control scheme for fast and reliable dissemination of safety messages in vanets. In: IEEE WCNC, pp. 2264–2269, April 2012
3. Egea-Lopez, E., Marino, P.P.: Distributed and fair beaconing rate adaptation for congestion control in vehicular networks. IEEE TMC **PP**(99), 1 (2016)
4. Guan, X., Huang, Y., Cai, Z., Ohtsuki, T.: Intersection-based forwarding protocol for vehicular ad hoc networks. Telecommun. Syst. **62**(1), 1–10 (2015)

5. Hassan, A., Ahmed, M.H., Rahman, M.A.: Adaptive beaconing system based on fuzzy logic approach for vehicular network. In: IEEE PIMRC, pp. 2581–2585, September 2013
6. Huang, Y., Chen, M., Cai, Z., Guan, X., Ohtsuki, T., Zhang, Y.: Graph theory based capacity analysis for vehicular ad hoc networks. In: 2015 IEEE Global Communications Conference (GLOBECOM), pp. 1–5, December (2015)
7. Huang, Y., Guan, X., Cai, Z., Ohtsuki, T.: Multicast capacity analysis for social-proximity urban bus-assisted vanets. In: 2013 IEEE International Conference on Communications (ICC), pp. 6138–6142, June 2013
8. Kloiber, B., Harri, J., Strang, T.: Dice the TX power-improving awareness quality in vanets by random transmit power selection. In: IEEE VNC, pp. 56–63, November 2012
9. Lim, J.H., Kim, W., Naito, K., Yun, J.H., Cabric, D., Gerla, M.: Interplay between tvws and dsrc: optimal strategy for safety message dissemination in vanet. IEEE JSAC 32(11), 2117–2133 (2014)
10. Mussa, S.A.B., Manaf, M., Ghafoor, K.Z.: Beaconing and transmission range adaptation approaches in vehicular ad hoc networks: trends & research challenges. In: ICCST. pp. 1–6, August 2014
11. Sommer, C., Tonguz, O.K., Dressler, F.: Traffic information systems: efficient message dissemination via adaptive beaconing. IEEE Commun. Mag. 49(5), 173–179 (2011)
12. Tan, M.C., Wong, S.C., Xu, J.M., Guan, Z.R., Zhang, P.: An aggregation approach to short-term traffic flow prediction. IEEE Trans. Intell. Transp. Syst. 10(1), 60–69 (2009)
13. Torrent-Moreno, M., Mittag, J., Santi, P., Hartenstein, H.: Vehicle-to-vehicle communication: fair transmit power control for safety-critical information. IEEE TVT 58(7), 3684–3703 (2009)
14. Vlahogianni, E., Karlaftis, M., Golias, J., Kourbelis, N.: Pattern-based short-term urban traffic predictor. In: IEEE ITSC, pp. 389–393, September 2006
15. Wang, X., Guo, L., Ai, C., Li, J., Cai, Z.: An urban area-oriented traffic information query strategy in VANETs. In: Ren, K., Liu, X., Liang, W., Xu, M., Jia, X., Xing, K. (eds.) WASA 2013. LNCS, vol. 7992, pp. 313–324. Springer, Heidelberg (2013)
16. Yang, J., Zhang, L., Chen, Y.: Pattern-based short-term traffic forecasting under urban heterogeneous conditions. In: Tenth International Conference of Chinese Transportation Professionals (ICCTP) (2010)
17. Zheng, X., Cai, Z., Li, J., Gao, H.: An application-aware scheduling policy for real-time traffic. In: 2015 IEEE 35th International Conference on Distributed Computing Systems (ICDCS), pp. 421–430, June 2015

OSim: An OLAP-Based Similarity Search Service Solver for Dynamic Information Networks

Xiaoguang Niu[1,2(✉)], Yihao Zhang[1,2],
Ting Huang[1,2], and Xiaoping Wu[1,2]

[1] State Key Laboratory of Software Engineering,
Wuhan University, Wuhan, China
{xgniu,yihaozhang,jieyuth,xpwu}@whu.edu.cn
[2] School of Computer Science, Wuhan University, Wuhan, China

Abstract. Similarity search service has always been one of the most popular topics in data mining. In recent years similarity search has been embedded in a more comprehensive framework and the semantic meanings behind meta paths play a crucial role in measuring similarity in heterogeneous information networks. PathSim has been considered one of the state-of-art models to find peer objects in the network. However, it only conducts similarity search in a global setting and the object attributes are not taken into consideration. In this paper, we propose OSim, a novel OLAP-based similarity search service solver. OSim is an attribute-enriched meta path-based measure to capture similarity based on object connectivity, visibility and features. A set of common attribute dimensions are defined across different types of objects and each dimension forms a hierarchical attribute tree. A path on the tree is represented by a node vector, pointing from the highest to a lowest level node. An object therefore can be described by a set of such node vectors. Online Analytical Processing techniques are further utilized in this framework to provide analysis in multiple resolutions and to improve search efficiency. Experiments show that our approaches improve search efficiency without compromising effectiveness.

Keywords: Similarity search service · Relational structure · Data mining · Dynamic heterogeneous information network

1 Introduction

News data is one of the most proliferous sources of data in existence. Information and knowledge that can be explored, extracted and analyzed from dynamic news data is often intuitive yet beyond the expectation of general public; one can make incredible conclusions on certain statistics for personal, educational, business and many other uses. Data mining researchers are aware that latent information has been hidden behind the massive amount of data due to its unstructured nature. It is a promising topic in the sense that different categories of operation functions can be further explored both individually and jointly. Also, since dynamic heterogeneous information network involves multiple types of objects and links, searching in such network efficiently is an

© Springer International Publishing Switzerland 2016
Q. Yang et al. (Eds.): WASA 2016, LNCS 9798, pp. 536–547, 2016.
DOI: 10.1007/978-3-319-42836-9_47

important research topic. Tao proposed a news mining system NewsNetExplorer which can perform the automatic construction and exploration of dynamic information network [1]. NewsNetExplorer can construct a semi-structured news information network NewsNet, which builds the foundation for further exploration and data mining.

This paper proposes OSim, an attribute-enriched meta path and OLAP-based similarity search service solver for dynamic heterogeneous information networks. There are two layers in OSim, which are user-based layer OLAP and network-based layer. For the user-based layer OLAP, we need to analyze the semantic meaning of each input sentence or phrase and find related topics. And for the network-based layer, we firstly construct the hierarchy network based on current nodes and links. Then, a revised similarity search technique OLAP-based attribute-enriched meta path similarity measure is developed to find most similar objects based on a specific query. In addition, when the search area is specified, our algorithm can drill down to that area and implement local search instead of global search. By leveraging the hierarchal organization of the heterogeneous network, granularity of our results is better tuned. To conclude, by combining both layers, we can use the algorithm to find the answer but unlimited to Who is Jiawei Han most similar with? As well as Who is Jiawei Han most similar to within Data Mining?

2 Problem Definition

In a dynamic information network, where multiple types of objects and their links among each other comprise a much larger and more complex graph than in a homogeneous network, a couple of meta path-based similarity measures have been previously defined. However, none of these measures considers object attributes, which can be very informative and without which significant information loss harm to user interest is possible. This is especially true when different types of objects share a certain common dimensions. In such a setting, relationships between objects are reflected not only on the way by which they connect to each other, but also on the similarity of their characteristics. For example, consider the news network consisting of people, events, organizations, topics and their three common dimensions, year, location and area. People who have stronger connectivity and share similar characteristics, e.g. those who are active around 1990–2000, are more likely to be similar to each other. In another example, where the heterogeneous network is constructed on the relations in DBLP database, authors that are frequently connected to each other and have common features tend to be more similar. An author who focuses mostly in machine learning is more likely to be similar to someone who is also in this field. This paper introduces an attribute-enriched meta path-based framework for similarity search and applies a well-defined similarity measure, PathSim [7], in an OLAP setting.

2.1 Heterogeneous Information Network and Network Scheme

The heterogeneous information network in this paper consists of a directed graph contains multiple types of objects and the links among them. In addition, each object type share a set of common dimensions whose attribute values are an inherent part of the model.

Definition 1. Heterogeneous Information Network. A heterogeneous information network is represented by a directed graph $G = (V, E)$ with an object type mapping function $\phi: V \rightarrow A$ and a link type mapping function $\Psi: E \rightarrow R$, where each object $v \in V$ belongs to one particular object type $\phi(v) \in A$ and each link $e \in E$ belongs to one particular relation $\Psi(e) \in R$. Note that both $|A|$ and $|R|$ are greater than 1 in such a network.

Each object is described by certain characteristics and therefore has a set of dimensions. Each dimension is further represented by a hierarchical attribute tree similar to those defined in Topic Cube and OLAP. To incorporate attributes of multiple types of objects in a heterogeneous information network context, the following definition is proposed.

Definition 2. Object Feature Dimensions. Each object $v \in V$, despite of its object type $\phi(v) \in A$, has a common set of informational dimension $(d_1, d_2,...,d_Q)$.

One main difference between our paper and previous works in dimension representation is that we use a set of hierarchical attribute trees and their corresponding attribute paths instead of single attribute values to describe each dimension. Also note that since the Q dimensions are commonly shared by all object types, only attributes having potential influence on similarity search are included in the model and irrelevant attributes can be pruned efficiently.

Definition 3. Hierarchical Attribute Tree. Suppose each dimension of an object has M possible finest attribute values, a hierarchical attribute tree T is a hierarchy as such; each node on the hierarchy, n_{ij} contains a subset of such attributes, with i denoting hierarchy level $i = \{0, 1, 2,...,I\}$, 0 representing the apex level while I the lowest level, j denoting the jth node within a given level. n_0 is the apex level having only one node and contains all M attributes. n_I is the lowest level and has M leaf nodes. A node in the ith level has multiple subsets which are exclusive of each other and form the $1 + i^{th}$ level children nodes, $U_j n_{ij} = M$. A path in the hierarchical attribute tree ζ is defined as a vector of I nodes $= (n_0, n_{1j1}, n_{2j2},...,n_{Ijl})^T$. Each dimension d_q of an object $v \in V$ is therefore represented by a corresponding path ζ_q.

Given the definition and nature of tree path, once a lower level node is determined, all its higher level nodes can be specified. To summarize definition 1–3, $\forall v \in V$, $v(d_1, d_2,...,d_Q)$, $d_q:\zeta_q = (n_0, n_{1j1}, n_{2j2},...,n_{Ijl})^T$ and $n's \in T_q$. Therefore, an object can be represented by a set of Q dimension attribute vectors, each vector has I_q elements. Note that I_q might take different values, depending on the specific characteristics of each dimension. Each of the objects in the news information network, despite of object types, shares three common dimensions, year, location and area. Each of the three dimensions forms a hierarchical attribute tree as shown in Fig. 1. Suppose we are interested in an Italian politician active in 1950s, three dimension tree paths can be used to describe the characteristics of this person; (all years, 1900 to 2000, 1950 to 2000), (world, Europe, Southern Europe, Italy), (all area, Music).

To better capture the underneath structure and relationships in a heterogeneous network, a network schema is drawn to outline the meta level structural information.

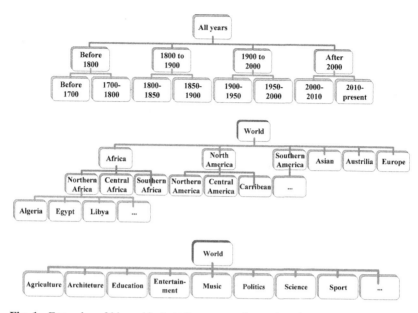

Fig. 1. Examples of hierarchical attribute trees of year, location and area dimensions

Definition 4. Network schema. The network schema, $S_G = (A, R)$, for a heterogeneous information network $G = (V, E)$ is a directed graph to define the relations R among objects $v \in V$, $\phi(v) \in A$.

2.2 Attribute-Enriched Meta Path-Based Similarity Measure

As discussed in [7], two objects in the heterogeneous information network can be connected through different metapaths and have different corresponding relationships.

Definition 5. Meta Path. A meta path P is defined on the network schema of a graph $S_G = (A, R)$ and has form: $A_1 \xrightarrow{R_1} A_2 \xrightarrow{R_2} \ldots \xrightarrow{R_l} A_{l+1}$. A path instance p following a specific path P is $(a_1 a_2 \ldots a_{l+1}), \forall i, \phi(a_i) \in A_i$, where a_i is an object $v(d_1, d_2, \ldots, d_Q)$ of the ith object type.

Other meta-path related concepts, such as reverse meta path and reverse path instance, are defined similarly as in [7]. Since similarity search is conducted between two objects of the same type, only paths with $A_1 = A_{l+1}$ is considered. Furthermore, the underlying principle of OSim, relation of peer, indicates a symmetric meta path, therefore all paths in our model are in a symmetric form $P = (P_l P_l^{-1})$ with A_l denoting the midpoint of such a path.

Definition 6. PathSim. A meta path-based similarity measure between two objects x and y considering object attributes is as follow:

$$\frac{2 \times \left|\{p_{x \to y} : p_{x \to y} \in \mathrm{P}\}\right|}{\left|\{p_{x \to x} : p_{x \to x} \in \mathrm{P}\}\right| + \left|\{p_{y \to y} : p_{y \to y} \in \mathrm{P}\}\right|} \qquad (1)$$

where x and $y \in A_i$, $x(d_1, d_2,\ldots, d_Q) = x(\zeta_1, \zeta_2,\ldots, \zeta_Q)$ and $y(\zeta'_{10}, \zeta'_{20},\ldots, \zeta'_{Q0})$. $p_{x \to y}$ is a path instance between x and y, $p_{x \to x}$ a path instance looping back to x, $p_{y \to y}$ a path instance looping back to y.

Definition 7. Commuting Matrix. Given a meta path $P = (A_1 A_2,\ldots,A_l)$, its commuting matrix $M = W_{A1A2} W_{A2A3}\cdots W_{Al-1Al}$ where W_{Ai-1Ai} is the adjacency matrix between object type A_{i-1} and A_i. $M(i, j)$ calculates the number of path instances between object $x_i \in A_1$ and $y_j \in A_1$ under such meta path P.

The concept of commuting matrix is constructed to efficiently compute the number of path instances between two objects following a specific path. The OSim measure can therefore be computed with matrices multiplication: $s(x_i, y_j) = (2M_{ij})/(M_{ii} + M_{jj})$.

2.3   User Query

Note that commuting matrix M is a $|A_1| \times |A_l|$ matrix, each row representing a type A_1 object and each column a type A_l object. Since each object, no matter what object type it be-longs to, has a common dimension set $(d_1, d_2,\ldots,d_Q)$, information on object similarity may be revealed after using certain techniques to further explore attributes in the Q dimensions and the efficiency of matrix computation may be enhanced.

Definition 8. User Query. We assume that a user query is in this form: find top-k objects x_j that are most similar to x_i, where x_i ($\zeta_1, \zeta_2, \zeta_Q$), $x_j \in A_l$ and x_j ($\zeta'_1(n_{i1})$, $\zeta'_2(n_{i2})$, $\zeta'_Q(n_{iQ})$), where n_{iq} denotes a i-th level node in the qth dimension tree path that is specified by user.

Note that once we make a query on a certain object x_i, the Q full dimension tree paths are known. The query also specifies a node for each of x_js Q dimensions. In a very extreme case where all specified n_{iq}'s are from the highest level, which means only $x_j(\zeta'_1(n_{01})$, $\zeta'_2(n_{02}),\ldots,\zeta'_Q(n_{0Q}))$ is specified by user, it is essentially a global query that requests similarity search over the entire information network. On the other extreme where all n_{iq}'s are from the lowest level, a very specific requirement is set on x_j and only very few objects are searched. In this situation, available data might be very sparse and a similarity search could be less robust.

When $0 < i < I$ for all dimensions. Once n_{iq}'s are specified by users, the higher level nodes n_{iq}'s on each attribute tree paths are known, which means the Q tree paths are automatically partially materialized.

Intuitively, both x_i and x_j belong to the same object type, meaning $A_1 = A_1$, and the attribute tree paths of x_i, $(\zeta_1, \zeta_2,\ldots, \zeta_Q)$ should be similar to the ones of x_j (even though the full tree paths might be unknown at this point).

3   OSim: OLAP-Based Similarity Service Search Solver

In [7], a partial materialization framework is used. Given a certain symmetric meta path $P = (P_l P_l^{-1})$, with $P_l = (A_1 A_2 ... A_l)$, the commuting matrix of P is $M = M_p M_p^T$, M_P and M_P^T respectively denoting the commuting matrix of P_l and P_l^{-1}. Pre-compute $M_P^T = (W_{A1A2} \ W_{A2A3} ... W_{Al-1Al})^T$, as well as the diagonal of M, $D = (M_{11}, M_{22}, .., M_{nn})$, where $M_{ii} = M_P(i,:) \ M_P(i,:)^T$. Two methods are utilized to perform matrix computation based on the pre-computed statistic.

3.1   Baseline Method

Given the pre-computed commuting matrix $M_P^T = (W_{A1A2} \ W_{A2A3} ... W_{Al-1Al})^T$ and diagonal of M, the following three steps to compute similarity measure between x_i and x_j is straightforward:

(1) Multiple the ith row vector of M_P by M_P^T to get the ith row of M, $M(i,:) = M_P(i,:) \ M_P^T$. $M_P(i,:)$ is also the ith column of M_P^T.
(2) The OSim measure between x_i and any x_j of the same object type is $s(x_i, x_j) = (2M_{ij})/(M_{ii} + M_{jj})$. However, it is not necessary to calculate such measure for all x_j. Recall the definition of user query, nodes on the Q dimension ($C'_1(n_{i1}), C'_2(n_{i2}), ..., C'_Q(n_{iQ})$) and their partially materialized attribute tree paths are automatically designated as the user query is input. Therefore, only x_js satisfying such requirements are considered and their OSim measures with x_i are calculated. Depending on structures of the Q hierarchical attribute trees and combination of the Q nodes, the actual number of measures to be calculated may vary significantly. Furthermore, we can filter x_js by whether they are orthogonal to x_i in the vector form. If they are not within a 2-step neighborhood of x_i, they are not promising candidates and can therefore be pruned.
(3) Sort $s(x_i, x_j)$ to generate a top-k list.

3.2   Pruning Method

In [7] a greedy KL-divergence based co-clustering method is first applied to cluster target objects and feature objects. In our model, such clustering is unnecessary since the Q dimensions of objects already naturally partition all objects into groups with additional advantage of providing a multiple granularity view.

Suppose we consider only one of the Q dimensions. We first arrange the M finest nodes of the hierarchical attribute tree in such a way that the first M_{I1} nodes consist of the first $I-1$ level node $n_{(I-1)1}$, the $(M_{I1+1})^{th}$ to $(M_{I1} + M_{I2})^{th}$ nodes consist of the second $I-1$ level node, etc., $\sum_i M_{Ii} = M$. And the first $M_{(I-1)1}$ $(I-1)$-level nodes are from the first $(I-2)$-level node, $(M_{(I-1)1} +1)^{th}$ to $(M_{(I-1)1} + M_{(I-1)2})^{th}$ nodes belong to the second $(I-1)$-level node, etc., $P_i \ M_{(I-1)i} = M$.

Since each object belongs to exactly one of the M finest node, its straightforward to see that objects can be partitioned into M such node in the hierarchical tree T. And then for each object type, we can arrange the objects in such a way that the first $|n_{I1}|$ of them are from the first group, the second $|n_{I2}|$ from the second group, etc. Accordingly, the first $| n_{I1}| + |n_{I2}| + \dots + |n_{Im1}|$ objects form a super-group that correspond to the first $(I-1)$-level node. Repeat the process until all objects are arranged. Such an arrangement provides a multiple granularity view of objects. As shown in Fig. 2, each square represents an object, squares in the same color represents objects belonging to the same finest node (level-I), represents a level-$(I-1)$node while it represents a level-$(I-2)$ node. In this way, different resolutions can be obtained by changing the range of observations.

Fig. 2. Illustration of object rearrangement

Conduct such arrangement for each type of objects and we can decompose the commuting matrix into disjoint blocks. The idea is similar to what is discussed in [7] but here we use the natural arrangement based on object attributes instead of other clustering methods. The commuting matrix M_P^T with each element representing the path instance between an object from type A_1 and an object from type A_l therefore has the following properties. The first $|n_{I1}|$ rows and columns of the matrix correspond to the path instances connecting type A_1 and type A_l objects that are both in the first finest group. The second $|n_{I2}|$ rows and $|n_{I1}|$ columns, for example, model the connectivity of type A_1 objects in the first group and type A_l object in the second group. Similar to the way we view a single object type with different granularities, the commuting matrix can be decomposed into blocks in multi-level resolutions. To facilitate computation, for each finest block, the following necessary statistical information is pre-computed and stored, with U as row block and V as column block.

1. Element sum of each block $T^{\{U \times V\}} : t_{uv} = \sum_{(i \in U)} \sum_{(j \in V)} M_P^T(i,j)$.

2. Sum of row vectors $T_1^{\{U \times M\}} : t_{(uv,1)}(j) = \sum_{(i \in U)} M_P^T(i,j)$, for $j \in V$.

3. Square root of sum of square of row vectors (2-norm of each column vector)
   $TT_1^{\{U \times M\}} t_{(uv,1)}^2(j) = \sqrt{\sum_{(i \in U)} (M_P^T(i,j))^2}$, for $j \in V$.

4. Sum of column vectors (1-norm of each row vector) $T_2^{\{n \times V\}} t_{(uv,2)}(i) = \sum_{(i \in V)} M_P^T(i,j)$,

   for $i \in U$.

5. Square root of sum of square of column vectors (2-norm of each row vector)
   $TT_2^{\{n \times V\}} : t_{(uv,2)}^2(i) = \sqrt{\sum_{j \in V} (M_P^T(i,j))^2}$ for $i \in U$. The query vector is compressed to

   align with the block-based commuting matrix.

As discussed above, the user query specifies requirements for target objects in the form of a node on each of the Q dimension tree paths $(C'_1(n_{i1}), C'_2(n_{i2}),\dots, C'_Q(n_{iQ}))$.

For the one dimension that we are currently considering, a node n_{iq} is inputted and only the objects having such feature are considered and their OSim measures with x_i might be calculated. Therefore, certain column blocks in the commuting matrix M_P^T can be initially pruned with efficiency.

In addition, one of the principle philosophies we follow is that objects (of the same type) are more likely to be similar when they share certain relevant attributes. From the way we arrange objects, it essentially means that objects that are closer to each other in the arrangement have a higher chance of being similar to each other in terms of this dimension. Therefore, a certain area of the commuting matrix is more likely to contain information on the ground truth, i.e. columns around the ith one have a higher probability of covering the top-k most similar objects to x_i.

To quantify this intuition, upper-bounds for similarity between object x and a finest column block V, as well as similarity between x and candidate $y \in V$, are estimated.

Upperbound1. $\forall y \in V$, $s(x, y) \leq s(x, nv) = \sum\limits_{y \in V} s(x, y) \leq \frac{2x_1^T T(:,v)}{D(x)+1} Z$, where $T(:, v)$ is the sum of element sums of blocks related to V. And x_T^1 is the transpose of the compressed query vector given the grouping of objects, where $(x_1)(u) = max_{j \in U}\{x(j)\}$.

Upperbound2. $\forall y \in V$, $s(x, y) \leq \frac{2x_2^T TT_1(:,y)}{D(x)+D(y)} Z$, where $x_2^T(u) = \sqrt{\sum\limits_{j \in U} x(j)^2}$.

Upperbound1 can be calculated for all remaining blocks after initial pruning and sorted in decreasing order. High **Upperbound1** suggests a higher chance of containing similar objects to x. The most promising groups are spotted in this way and the least ones are further pruned. Then within the remaining groups of candidates, **Upperbound2** can be used to further prune target objects that are less likely to be similar to x. So far only one dimension is discussed and the candidate range has already greatly narrowed down. Apply similar procedures with the 2nd dimension, and candidate set can be reduced to a low level. At last, exact similarity measure can be computed to find the top-k candidates.

4   Experimental Performance Evaluation

For the experiments, we use a bibliographic sub network extracted from DBLP to test the correctness and effectiveness of our algorithm. The data contains more than 28,000 authors, 28,000 papers, and only 20 conferences. From those papers, we extracted over 13,000 terms. There are 4 area groups, which are data mining (DM), database (DB), machine learning (ML) and information retrieval (IR). At the same time, we have five organization groups that hold the 20 conferences, which are ACM, IEEE, SIAM, AAAI and other, respectively. Those area groups and organization groups are designed for similarity search with specified hierarchy.

Our relation heterogeneous network is built according to the relation.txt file which gives all relationships between different types of objects. There are four types of objects in the experiment network, which are author, paper, conference and term. Each object in the file has a global identification. For example, there is a link from 42141 to 3572, which means the paper Implementation of Integrity Constraints and Views by Query Modification contains term query.

Based on the constructed heterogeneous network, both OSim and other two similarity search algorithms, P-PageRank and SimRank, are tested. Top-K results will be compared among the three algorithms. And we will test the efficiency and correctness based on different meta-paths. Similarity score is also calculated both in global search and local search to test the effectiveness of embedding hierarchy in our OSim.

We conducted a case study of similarity measures on query 46477, which is the global identification of Jiawei Han. By global searching, Table 1 shows top-5 most similar author to Jiawei Han, where there is a comparison among OSim, SimRank and P-PageRank). For OSim, the result is generated by using meta-path A-P-T-P-A in global search. From the Table 1, we can see that three different similarity search measures have significant differences in the top-5 results. The results of SimRank and P-PageRank are similar, while the results calculated by OSim using a meta path of Author-Paper-Term-Paper-Author are quite different. The authors that are ranked in the top five by SimRank and P-PageRank do not show up in the top 5 results of OSim, however if the list is extended to include more results, the names SimRank and P-PageRank ranked in the top five will show up. This shows that OSim puts emphasis on a different set of values then SimRank and P-PageRank. SimRank and P-PageRank are developed for homogeneous networks, while OSim is for heterogeneous networks.

Table 1. Top-5 authors similar with Jiawei Han in OSim, SimRank and P-PageRank

Rank	OSim	SimRank	P-PageRank
1	Philip S.Yu	Jiong Yang	Feida Zhu
2	Wei Wang	Feida Zhu	Yiwen Yin
3	Jian Pei	David W.Cheung	Xianghong Jasmine Zhou
4	Charu C.Aggarwal	Xianghong Jasmine Zhou	Petre Tzvetkov
5	Hongjun Lu	Yifan Li	Cheong Youn

In OSim, the user can also specify a meta path. Each meta path used has a different semantic meaning associated with it. For example, meta path of Author-Paper-Author implies the similarity should calculated only based on co-authorship similarity. While a meta of Author-Paper-Term-Paper-Author or Author-Paper-Conference-Paper Author suggests a similarity search calculation is based on similar area of research.

Based on different meta-paths, the top-5 similarity rank in global search is also quite different. Table 2 demonstrates different top-5 rank computed based on meta-path A-P-A, A-P-T-P-A and A-P-C-P-A. Along with the author name is the related score. By comparing the scores in the same rank among three meta-paths, we can conclude that the longer meta-path will generate higher similarity score, which implies the more similar that author is with Jiawei Han. The top five ranks for A-P-T-P-A and A-P-C-P-A may be the same, but if the rank list is extended the results will show the difference. The reason A-P-T-P-A and A-P-C-P-A are so similar is due to the synonymous semantic meanings

Table 2. Top-5 authors similar with Jiawei Han based on different meta-path

Rank	A-P-A (author, score)		A-P-T-P-A (author, score)		A-P-C-P-A (author, score)	
1	Xifeng Yan	0.4274	Philip S.Yu	0.8243	Philip S.Yu	0.9540
2	Dong Xin	0.2881	Wei Wang	0.7248	Wei Wang	0.8034
3	Hong Cheng	0.2542	Jian Pei	0.6965	Jian Pei	0.7351
4	Philip S.Yu	0.2500	Charu C.Aggarwal	0.5532	Charu C.Aggarwal	0.6435
5	Xiaolei Li	0.2456	Hongjun Lu	0.5460	Hongjun Lu	0.6311

that these two paths imply. Both A-P-T-P-A and A-P-C-PA implies similarity based on the closeness of the area of research two authors are in.

When the user specifies the detailed area they want to search, which is the local search in our method, the OSim in global search and local search will generate different results. Table 3 shows the exact rank in each area: database, machine learning, data mining and information retrieval.

Table 3. Top-5 rank authors similar with Jiawei Han in areas:DB, ML, DM, IR

Rank	DB	ML	DM	IR
1	Philip S.Yu	Lawrence J. Henschen	Jian Pei	ChengXiang Zhai
2	Wei Wang	Yixin Chen	Charu C. Aggarwal	Qiaozhu Mei
3	Haixun Wang	Daniel P. Huttenlocher	Ke Wang	Xuehua Shen
4	Hongjun Lu	Thomas S.huang	Jiong Yang	Xiaofei He
5	Laks V.S. Lakshmanan	Yunbe Pan	Martin Ester	Deng Cai

5 Related Works

Traditional OLAP techniques have previously been proven to be very successful in handling structured data, and research efforts have been shifting to its applications in unstructured text data during recent years. The Text Cube model in [5] constructs two concept hierarchies, dimension hierarchy which is similar to those in traditional OLAP and term hierarchy, a newly introduced hierarchy to explore the semantic levels of text terms.

In [2], Topic Cube is proposed to integrate OLAP with Probability Latent Semantic Analysis techniques so that data mining in structure data and unstructured text can be performed simultaneously within a unified framework. However, neither of these works considers the links among individual data tuples and information loss is very likely. Graph OLAP [10] outperforms its previous work such that it uses the graph theory for data representation and provides a framework for multi-dimension and multi-level navigation. A graph cube is constructed based on informational dimensions and each cell in the cube corresponds to an aggregated graph which serves as a primary measure of the cell. In contrast to overlaying corresponding snapshots of the graph, Graph Cube in [6] mainly utilizes Topological-OLAP so that relation-ships between different entity groups can be explored. In [8, 9], similar researches to Graph Cube are conducted independently to enable graph summarization based on user-selected node attributes.

On the other hand, similarity search is another popular research domain. In [3], SimRank compares two objects based on their neighborhood similarity. Personalized PageRank [4] proposes an asymmetrical measure to quantify the probability of having a path from one object to the other. These two methods are mostly based on homogeneous information network and a more novel similarity search model, PathSim [7] is constructed for applications in a heterogeneous network. PathSim proposes the concept of peers; objects that are strongly connected to each other and have similar visibility. Also, it respects the distinct semantic meanings behind different meta paths and enables user to interpret similarity in various context.

However, PathSim only performs similarity search in global setting while more specific user-defined search range is possible in reality. To address the limitations of PathSim and to incorporate OLAP for the purpose of multi-granularity navigation, our OSim model has two primary goals: (1) Consider object attributes in similarity search, and (2) construct hierarchical attribute/dimension trees to provide views in different resolutions.

6   Conclusions

In this paper, we design an attribute-enriched metapath and OLAP-based service, namely OSim, to capture similarity based on object connectivity, visibility and features in dynamic heterogeneous information networks. A set of common attribute dimensions are defined across different types of objects. Each dimension forms a hierarchical attribute tree. A path on the tree points from the highest to a lowest level node. An object therefore can be described by a set of such node vectors. It's an innovative method to conduct similarity searches for object for different levels in a hierarchy tree. By scrolling along the hierarchy tree, we can find top K similar objects not only in the whole network but also within sub-networks. Further, OLAP are utilized in this framework to provide analysis in multiple resolutions and to improve search efficiency. Experiments show that OSim can improve both search efficiency and result granularity.

Acknowledgments. This work was partially supported by the Program for Changjiang Scholars and Innovative Research Team in University (Grant No. IRT1278), the National Natural Science Foundation of China NSFC (Grant No. 41127901-06, 61572370), Development Program of China "863 Project" (Grant No. 2015AA016004), the Natural Science Foundation of Hubei Province of China (Grant No. 2014CFB191).

References

1. Tao, F., Han, J., Ji, H., Brova, G., Wang, C., Kishky, A., Liu, J.: NewsNetExplorer: automatic construction and exploration of news information networks. In: Proceedings of SigMOD, pp. 1091–1094 (2014)
2. Zhang, D., Zhai, C., Han, J., Srivastava, A., Oza, N.: Topic modeling: for OLAP on multidimensional text databases: topic cube and its applications. Stat. Anal. Data Min. 2(5), 378–395 (2009)
3. Jeh, G., Widom, J.: SimRank: a measure of structural context similarity. In: Proceedings of KDD, pp. 538–543 (2002)
4. Jeh, G., Widom, J.: Scaling personalized web search. In: Proceedings of WWW, pp. 271–279 (2003)
5. Lin, C., Ding, B., Han, J., Zhu, F., Zhao, B.: Text cube: computing IR measures for multidimensional text database analysis. In: Proceedings of ICDM, pp. 905–910 (2008)
6. Zhao, P., Li, X., Xin, D., Han, J.: Graph cube: on warehousing and OLAP multidimensional networks. In: Proceedings of ACM SigMOD, pp. 853–864 (2011)
7. Sun, Y., Han, J., Yan, X., Yu, P., Wu, T.: PathSim: meta path-based Top-K similarity search in heterogeneous information networks. In: Proceedings of VLDB, pp. 992–1003 (2011)
8. Tian, Y., Hankins, R., Patel, J.: Efficient aggregation for graph summarization. In: Proceedings of SigMOD, pp. 567–580 (2008)
9. Zhang, N., Tian, Y., Patel, J.: Discovery-driven graph summarization. In: Proceedings of ICDE, pp. 880–891 (2010)
10. Chen, C., Yan, X., Zhu, F., Han, J., Yu, P.: Graph OLAP: towards online analytical processing on graphs. In: Proceedings of ICDM, pp. 103–112 (2008)

Planning Roadside Units for Information Dissemination in Urban VANET

Junyu Zhu[1,2], Chuanhe Huang[1,2(✉)], Xiying Fan[1,2], and Bin Fu[3]

[1] State Key Lab of Software Engineering, Computer School,
Wuhan University, Wuhan 430072, China
{2011,huangch,wow}@whu.edu.cn
[2] Collaborative Innovation Center of Geospatial Technology,
Wuhan University, Wuhan 430072, China
[3] Department of Computer Science,
The University of Texas Rio Grande Valley, Edinburg, TX 78539, USA
bin.fu@utrgv.edu

Abstract. With the development of vehicular ad hoc network (VANET), data dissemination has been widely studied and its performance is expected to be greatly improved. Research on data dissemination generally focuses on how to utilize road infrastructures, such as roadside units (RSUs), to facilitate the dissemination. In this paper, we consider a VANET where a given number of RSUs are available for disseminating information in an urban area. We formulate the problem as to minimize the number of RSUs selected from the available RSUs to cover a specific region. The paper proposes a c-street model and a city model. Then we develop a greedy polynomial time covering algorithm under the c-street model and a polynomial time approximation scheme is proposed under the city model based on shifting strategy. By evaluating the proposed solution in realistic urban environment, our simple greedy algorithm is implemented and some simulation results are provided.

Keywords: VANET · RSU · Data dissemination · Polynomial time · Approximation

1 Introduction

Wireless communication for intelligent transportation system is intended for the support of traffic safety and efficiency, as well as commercial applications [1]. Vehicular ad hoc network (VANET) is a modern intelligent transportation system. A particularly important technical interest in VANET is data dissemination [2]. An important functionality of RSUs is to inform vehicles about the real

C. Huang—This work is supported by the National Science Foundation of China (No. 61373040, No. 61173137), The Ph.D. Programs Foundation of Ministry of Education of China (20120141110073). This research was supported in part by National Science Foundation Early Career Award 0845376 and Bensten Fellowship of the University of Texas - Rio Grande Valley.

© Springer International Publishing Switzerland 2016
Q. Yang et al. (Eds.): WASA 2016, LNCS 9798, pp. 548–559, 2016.
DOI: 10.1007/978-3-319-42836-9_48

time traffic status such that the vehicles can respond in time to avoid accidents. Current research in data dissemination mainly focuses on how to fully utilize the RSUs to facilitate the dissemination, particularly in urban areas [3].

In this paper, we study a fundamental data dissemination problem, to tackle the important issue of deploying an intelligent transportation system in a specific urban area, which can improve the dissemination efficiency.

To maximize the number of vehicles that drive under the coverage of one or more RSUs in the area, this paper aims to fulfill a full coverage of the area. According to this, the paper proposes the following problem: assume in an urban area with a given number of RSU locations to choose, what is the best deployment strategy to fulfill the coverage over the area while select the minimum number of RSUs? We formulate our problem as to minimize the number of RSU selected, and our goal is to take advantage of the minimum number of RSUs deployed to cover the area. Fewer RSUs can reduce redundant traffic information while it also reduces system overhead.

To tackle the problem, we first introduce a c-street model, in which each RSU covers at most c streets and it covers at most one interval in each of the c streets. To cover a specific region, we propose a greedy polynomial time algorithm to obtain the RSU deployment. The key idea is to use the minimum number of RSUs to cover all the streets in the target area.

Second, to represent more geometric characteristics of urban areas, we introduce a $(r, d, f(.), g(.,.))$-city model, where r indicates RSUs' transmission range, d is an integer, $f(.)$, $g(.,.)$ respectively denote the number of street intersections and RSUs. Based on the shifting strategy developed by Hochbaum and Maass [4], a polynomial time approximation scheme is proposed. The scheme uses the divide-and-conquer approach by dividing the target region into different kinds of partitions. Then it obtains the approximate optimal RSU deployment for each partition. Finally, select the most favorable resulting solution.

The remainder of this paper is organized as follows. Section 2 introduces the network scenario and RSU deployment problem. Section 3 proposes a c-street model and a greedy polynomial time algorithm. Section 4 proposes a city model and a polynomial time approximation algorithm. Section 5 describes the simulation environment and the results. Section 6 introduces the previous related work. Section 7 concludes the paper.

2   Network Scenario and Covering Problem

In this section, we describe the network scenario and formulate the problem that needs to be solved.

Here, the general system model of data dissemination in the VANETs is considered, where RSUs are the data resources, and vehicles are the receivers. Assume in the area, RSUs are denoted by the set $R = \{R_1, R_2, \cdots, R_n\}$. Each RSU R_i covers an area $D(R_i)$. In this paper, we use a set of street intervals $\{I_{i,1}, I_{i,2}, \cdots, I_{i,t}\}$ to represent the region $D(R_i)$, where each $I_{i,j}$ is a continuous part of a street. Therefore, here we have $D(R_i) = \{I_{i,1}, I_{i,2}, \cdots, I_{i,k}\}$. For the set R of RSUs, the covered region is defined as $C(R)$, which is the union $\cup_{R_i \in R} D(R_i)$.

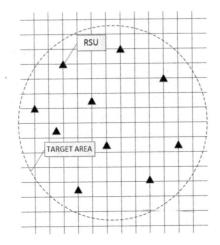

Fig. 1. An example of the geographic area

Besides, we assume that all the streets are on a plane to form a planar graph, where each intersection is considered as a node. An example of the geographical area can be shown as Fig. 1. The region inside the circle represents the target area while the triangles represent the available RSU locations.

Consider an urban area B. Assume there are a set of RSUs R available in B, which are randomly located. Our goal is to choose a minimum number of RSUs to realize the coverage of the area.

3   Bounded Number of Street Intervals

In this section, we present a greedy-based algorithm. A street S can be defined as one dimensional curve $C(t) : [a, b] \rightarrow (-\infty, +\infty) \times (-\infty, +\infty)$ on a two dimensional plane, where $C(.)$ is a one-one smooth function. An interval of a street S is a continuous area of the curve $C(.)$ with $t \in [a', b'] \subseteq [a, b]$ for some $a \leq a' < b' \leq b$. In this model, each RSU R_i covers a finite number of streets intervals $\{I_{i,1}, I_{i,2}, \cdots, I_{i,k}\}$.

The street coverage is transformed into interval coverage. Let $I_1, I_2, \cdots, I_m$ be a list of intervals, interval I_i has the longest leftmost coverage for interval $I = [a, b]$ if $a \in I_i$ and $I_i \cap I$ is the longest among $\{I_t \cap I : a \in I_t, 1 \leq t \leq m\}$. For a interval $I = [a, b]$, define $\text{Left}(I) = a$, and $\text{Right}(I) = b$.

We let Algorithm 1 be embedded in Algorithm 2 to give optimal coverage for each street. Algorithm 2 shows the global covering solution.

3.1   Bounded Streets for Each RSU

In this section, we assume that each RSU covers at most c streets with at most one interval in each of the c streets. It is called the c-street model.

Algorithm 1. Interval covering algorithm

1: Input: an interval $I = [a, b]$ to be covered and a list of intervals $I_1, I_2, \cdots, I_n$ with $I \subseteq I_1 \cup I_2 \cup \cdots I_n$, which is used to cover I.
2: Output: a sublist $I_{k_1}, I_{k_2}, \cdots, I_{k_m}$ of intervals from $I_1, I_2, \cdots, I_n$ such that $I \subseteq I_{k_1} \cup I_{k_2} \cup \cdots I_{k_m}$.
3: Let $C = \emptyset$;
4: Let Uncovered $= I$;
5: Repeat
6:    Find I_j that covers the longest leftmost of Uncovered interval (Left(Uncovered) $\in I_j$, and ($I_j \cap$ Uncovered) is the largest);
7:    Let Uncovered $=$ Uncovered $- I_j$;
8:    Let $C = C \cup \{I_j\}$;
9: Until Uncovered $= \emptyset$;
10: Output C as a covering solution.
11: **End of Algorithm**

Algorithm 2. Covering algorithm

1: Input: a set of RSUs R and a set of streets S to be covered.
2: Output: a set of RSUs R', contains a minimum number of RSUs that can cover the streets.
3: Let $s_1, s_2, \cdots, s_m$ be the list of the streets in S to be covered.
4: Let Uncovered$_i = s_i$ for $i = 1, 2, \cdots, m$;
5: Let $C_i = \emptyset$;
6: for($i = 1, 2, \cdots, m$)
7:    Repeat
8:       Find $R_j \in R$ that covers the longest leftmost of Uncovered$_i$;
9:       Let Uncovered$_i =$ Uncovered$_i - D(R_j)$;
10:       Let $C_i = C_i \cup \{R_j\}$;
11:    Until Uncovered$_i = \emptyset$;
12: Output $C_1 \cup C_2 \cup \cdots \cup C_m$ as a covering solution for the streets.
13: **End of Algorithm**

Lemma 1. *There is a $O(n \log n)$ time algorithm for the one dimensional interval covering problem, where n is the number of intervals in the input.*

Proof. The algorithm is described in Algorithm 1. Sort the intervals by left boundaries of all intervals. It takes $O(n \log n)$ steps using merge sorting. Use the greedy method. Cover the points with intervals from left to right. Every time we pick up an interval that touches the leftmost uncovered point and covers the maximal uncovered area. The total time is $O(n \log n)$. The correctness of the algorithm is based on a simple induction. We claim that the first k selected intervals produces the largest left coverage for the interval I among all k intervals from the list. In other words, the following conditions are satisfied for the first k sets $I_{j_1}, I_{j_2}, \cdots, I_{j_k}$ generated by the algorithm.

1. $I_{j_1} \cup I_{j_2} \cup \cdots \cup I_{j_k}$ is an interval.
2. $a \in I_{j_1} \cup I_{j_2} \cup \cdots \cup I_{j_k}$, where $I = [a, b]$.

3. $|I \cap (I_{j_1} \cup I_{j_2} \cup \cdots \cup I_{j_k})|$ is the largest among all k sets that satisfy conditions (1) and (2).

It is trivial when $k = 1$ since it follows from the Algorithm 1 at line 6. Assume that first k selected intervals by Algorithm 1 satisfy conditions (1), (2), and (3). Consider the case $k + 1$. Let $I_{u_1}, I_{u_2}, \cdots, I_{u_{k+1}}$ be a set of $k + 1$ intervals that produces the largest left coverage for I by satisfying conditions (1), (2), and (3). Let $I_{j_1}, I_{j_2}, \cdots, I_{j_k}$ be the first k intervals generated by the algorithm. By inductive hypothesis, they satisfy conditions (1), (2), and (3). We have $I \cap (I_{u_1} \cap I_{u_2} \cap \cdots \cap I_{u_k}) \subseteq I \cap (I_{j_1} \cap I_{j_2} \cap \cdots \cap I_{j_k})$. Thus, $I_{j_1} \cup I_{j_2} \cup \cdots \cup I_{j_k} \cup I_{u_{k+1}}$ is an interval.

If $\mathrm{Right}(I \cap (I_{j_1} \cup I_{j_2} \cup \cdots \cup I_{j_k})) \notin I_{u_{k+1}}$, then $I \cap (I_{j_1} \cup I_{j_2} \cup \cdots \cup I_{j_k} \cup I_{u_{k+1}}) = I \cap (I_{j_1} \cup I_{j_2} \cup \cdots \cup I_{j_k})$.

If $\mathrm{Right}(I \cap (I_{j_1} \cup I_{j_2} \cup \cdots \cup I_{j_k})) \in I_{u_{k+1}}$, then $I \cap (I_{j_1} \cup I_{j_2} \cup \cdots \cup I_{j_k} \cup I_{u_{k+1}}) \subseteq I \cap (I_{j_1} \cup I_{j_2} \cup \cdots \cup I_{j_k} \cup I_{j_{k+1}})$.

Thus, when $I_{j_{k+1}}$ is selected by the algorithm, we have $|I \cap (I_{j_1} \cup I_{j_2} \cup \cdots \cup I_{j_k} \cup I_{j_{k+1}})| \geq |I \cap (I_{u_1} \cup I_{u_2} \cup \cdots \cup I_{u_k} \cup I_{u_{k+1}})|$. Therefore, $I_{j_1}, I_{j_2}, \cdots, I_{j_k}, I_{j_{k+1}}$ satisfy conditions (1), (2), and (3).

Theorem 1. *Under the c-street model, there is a polynomial time c-approximation algorithm for the region covering problem.*

Proof. Let $s_1, s_2, \cdots, s_m$ be all of the streets to be covered. Let C_i be an optimal covering for s_i for $i = 1, 2, \cdots, m$. Let $C_1 \cup C_2 \cup \cdots \cup C_m$ be the approximate solution to be output.

Let C^* be an optimal covering, and let C_i^* be the RSUs in C^* to cover s_i. We have the following inequalities:

$$|C_1 \cup C_2 \cup \cdots \cup C_m| \leq |C_1| + |C_2| + \cdots + |C_m| \tag{1}$$
$$\leq |C_1^*| + |C_2^*| + \cdots + |C_m^*| \tag{2}$$
$$\leq c|C_1^* \cup C_2^* \cup \cdots \cup C_m^*| \tag{3}$$
$$\leq c|C^*| \tag{4}$$

As we know, C_i is an optimal covering for s_i, and C_i^* is the local covering for S_i in a global optimal covering. So, we have the transition from (1) to (2). The transition from (2) to (3) is because of the condition that each RSU can touch at most c different streets.

3.2   NP-Hardness

We have Theorem 2 to show that the area covering problem is still NP-hard when each RSU covers three streets.

Let X, Y and Z be three finite, disjoint sets, and let T be a subset of $X \times Y \times Z$. That is, T is a set of triples (x, y, z) such that $x \in X, y \in Y$ and $z \in Z$. Now $M \subseteq T$ is a 3-dimensional matching if the following holds: for any two distinct triples $(x_1, y_1, z_1) \in M$ and $(x_2, y_2, z_2) \in M$, we have $x_1 \neq x_2, y_1 \neq y_2$ and $z_1 \neq z_2$.

The 3-matching problem is to determine if $T \subseteq X \times Y \times Z$ with $m = |X| = |Y| = |Z|$ has a 3-dimensional matching M of size m. This is one of the classical NP-complete problems [12].

Theorem 2. *The covering problem in the c-street model is NP-hard for $c \geq 3$ and there are only 3 streets.*

Proof. Reduce 3-matching problem to it. Let T be a set of triples in $X \times Y \times Z$. Consider three streets S_1, S_2 and S_3. Partition each S_i $(i = 1, 2, 3)$ into m regions $I_{i,1}, I_{i,2}, \cdots, I_{i,m}$, where $m = |X| = |Y| = |Z|$. Let $X = \{x_1, x_2, \cdots, x_m\}$, $Y = \{y_1, y_2, \cdots, y_m\}$, and $Z = \{z_1, z_2, \cdots, z_m\}$. For each $(x_a, y_b, z_c) \in T$, construct a RSU R_{x_a, y_b, z_c} that covers $I_{1,a}, I_{2,b}$ and $I_{3,c}$. It is easy to see that there is a 3-matching solution if and only if there are m RSUs to cover the streets. Furthermore, it is impossible to have a covering solution with less than m RSUs since each of the three streets has m regions and each RSU can only cover one of the m regions in one street.

4   A Polynomial Time Approximation Scheme

In this section, we will show a polynomial time approximation scheme. The scheme is based on the shifting strategy developed by Hochbaum and Maass [4].

To represent more geometric properties of urban area, we introduce a city model for the covering problem. Here, we formally present some definitions used in the model.

Definition 1. *Assume that C is a city with some RSUs.*

- *A street graph for the city C is a planar graph such that every node in the graph is the intersection of two streets in city C, and every edge (u, v) in G is the part of streets connecting u and v.*
- *For path $p = v_1 v_2 \cdots v_k$ on a street graph $G(V, E)$, an initial part q of p is that for some node $v_i (1 \leq i \leq k)$, q is the union of $v_1 v_2 \cdots v_i$ and $v_i u$, where u is a point on the street $v_i v_{i+1}$.*
- *If there are at most k paths $p_1, \cdots, p_k$ $(k \leq d)$ through v in $G(V, E)$, we call there is a d-star through node v. RSU R's coverage has the d-star property if there is a d-star of k paths $p_1, \cdots, p_k$ $(k \leq d)$ each starts from v in G, and R only covers a union of initial parts of $p_1, \cdots, p_k$.*

City Model: Let $r > 0$, d be an integer, $f(.)$ be a function $N \rightarrow N$, and $g(.,.)$ be a function $N \times N \rightarrow N$. Let $l > 0$ be the integer parameter to control the accuracy of approximation. In this $(r, d, f(.), g(.,.))$-*city model*, assume the following conditions:

1. Each RSU covers a region within a radius bounded by r.
2. There are at most $f(l)$ street intersections within a $2lr \times 2lr$ square region.
3. Each RSU has the d-star property for its coverage.
4. Each $2lr \times 2lr$ square region has at most $g(l, n)$ $(g(l, n) \leq n)$ RSUs deployed, where n is the total number of $RSUs$.

4.1   Shifting Strategy

We consider the $(r, d, f(.), g(., .))$-*city model* in this section. The shifting strategy [4] used in our algorithm is described.

To solve the covering problem using shifting strategy, the specific target region is subdivided into vertical strips of width $2r$. Groups of l consecutive strips, resulting in strips of width $2r \cdot l$ each, are considered. Each partition can be derived from the previous one by shifting to right with a distance $2r$. Repeating the shift l times, we end up with the same partition we start from. The l distinct shifting partitions are represented by $P_i, i = 1 \cdots l$. In each partition, we use a local algorithm to find out the deployment strategy in this partition. We repeat the process to find the global deployment solution for the l partitions. Choose the partition which can be mostly covered by utilizing the minimum number of RSUs. It should be the approximate optimal solution.

According to the shifting strategy, region B is partitioned into vertical strips of width $2r$, denoted by $B_1, B_2, \cdots, B_k$. Group every l consecutive strips into a wider strip of width $2r \cdot l$. Each wider strip is $L_i = B_i \cup B_{i+1} \cup \cdots \cup B_{i+l-1}$ for $i = 1, \cdots, k - l + 1$, and $L_i = B_i \cup B_{i+1} \cup \cdots \cup B_k$ for $i = k - l + 2, \cdots, k$. We also define $L_i^0 = B_1 \cup B_2 \cup \cdots \cup B_{i-1}$, which is the union of first $i - 1$ blocks. The i-th shifting case has a set of wider strips $P_i = \{L_i^0, L_i, L_{i+l}, L_{i+2l}, \cdots, L_{i+tl}\}$, forming a partition for B $(B = L_i^0 \cup L_i \cup L_{i+l} \cup \cdots L_{i+tl})$. We can get a simple shifting conception from an example shown in Fig. 2.

Based on the shifting strategy, we propose a polynomial time approximation algorithm. It is described as Algorithm 3. The i-th vertical partition P_i for B is denoted by $P_V(B, i)$. The 0-th strip of $P_V(B, i)$ is L_i^0, denoted by $P_V(B, i, 0)$. The j-th strip of $P_V(B, i)$ is L_i^j for $j \geq 1$, denoted by $P_V(B, i, j)$. Similarly, we define $P_H(B, i)$ and $P_H(B, i, j)$.

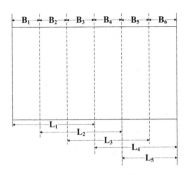

Fig. 2. An example of a partition of Region B, assume $k = 6, l = 3$, B is partitioned into vertical strips $B_1, B_2, \cdots, B_6$

Define $opt_P(B)$ to be the set of the RSUs in an optimal solution for covering the intervals of the set P in the region B. Let $d_i = \sum_{L \in P_i} |opt_P(L)|$. The crucial property of the shifting method [4] is that $\sum_{i=1}^{l} d_i \leq (1 + l)|opt_P(B)|$. This implies that $\min_{1 \leq i \leq l} d_i \leq (1 + \frac{1}{l})|opt_P(B)|$. Assume we have a local algorithm A for solving each local area L_i with approximation ratio P_A. The solution of the algorithm A for the partition P_i is $s_i = \sum_{L \in P_i} A(L) \leq P_A \cdot d_i$. The shifting method SA applies the algorithm A for each partition P_i, $1 \leq i \leq l$, and outputs the result $SA(B) = \min_{i=1}^{l} s_i$. Therefore, $SA(B) \leq (1 + \frac{1}{l}) \cdot P_A \cdot opt_P(B)$. This discussion proves Lemma 2.

Lemma 2. *Assume that a local algorithm A has an approximation ratio P_A for the covering problem. Then, the approximation ratio P_{SA} of the shifting method utilizing A satisfies $P_{SA} \leq (1 + \frac{1}{l})P_A$.*

Our result has some differences with the standard disc covering problem, in which the disc positions are not fixed in the input. In the covering problem, the RSU locations are given from the input.

5   Performance Evaluation

In this section, we first introduce the simulation environment, then present the compared algorithms and performance metrics for performance evaluation of the proposed algorithm. Finally, we give the experimental results.

5.1   Simulation Environment

To evaluate the performance of the proposed greedy polynomial time algorithm, extensive simulations have been done.

For the performance evaluation, here, we evaluate the performance of the algorithm in the regular generated urban maps. Without loss of generality, the urban areas which the algorithm will be applied to should be some representative downtown areas, so we construct an evaluation scenario which is equal to a $3 \, \text{km} \times 4 \, \text{km}$ regional area. Each road segment has bidirectional traffic.

We conduct four sets of simulations. In the first set, the scenario is from New York city, USA. We choose this area for it is a typical urban area with intersections and most of its faces contain four vertices. For the second set, we choose Shanghai, China. Without loss of generality, we also extract the maps of the areas of Zurich and Winterthur, Switzerland, which are typical for their irregular street shape.

5.2   Compared Algorithms

We compare the proposed algorithm with several alternative algorithms. The evaluation metric is the coverage ratio, i.e., the size of area covered by selected RSUs over the size of the entire target regional area.

The optimal algorithm (Optimal). The algorithm can always select the optimal RSU locations from the candidate locations by exhaustive search.

The proposed greedy polynomial time c-factor algorithm (Greedy-c).

Algorithm 3. Polynomial time approximation scheme

1: Input: target region B, the set of street intervals P, a set of RSUs R, a local algorithm A
2: Output: a set $SA(B)$ of RSUs that covers the intervals of streets.
3: Partition B into vertical strips $B_1, B_2, \cdots$, of width $2r$;
4: Form the vertical partitions $P_V(B, 1), P_V(B, 2), \cdots, P_V(B, m)$;
5: Form the horizontal partitions $P_H(P_V(B, i, j))$ for each strip $P_V(B, i, j)$.
6: Find an optimal covering $a_{i,j,s,t}$ for each square $P_H(P_V(B, i, j), s, t)$ of size $2rl \times 2rl$;
7: **for** all i, j, s **do**
8:     Compute $a_{i,j,s} = \sum_t a_{i,j,s,t}$;
9: **end for**
10: **for** all i, j **do**
11:     Compute $a_{i,j} = \min_s a_{i,j,s}$;
12: **end for**
13: **for** all i, **do**
14:     let $a_i = \sum_j a_{i,j}$.
15: **end for**
16: $SA(B) = \min a_i$
17: **End of Algorithm**

The uniform deployment algorithm (Uniform). With this algorithm, the whole region is divided into grids of identical size. The algorithm deploys base stations on grid points.

Random algorithm (Random). This algorithm needs a large number of RSUs to be deployed in order to provide one contact or more to each vehicle.

5.3   Evaluation Results

We run the proposed polynomial time algorithm and the compared algorithms on the four generated road topologies. In the simulation, we set up a relative small number of candidate locations from 15 to 60.

The coverage ratio achieved by the different compared algorithms for each street layout in New York is described as Fig. 3, and the other three regions Shanghai, Zurich and Winterthur is respectively shown as Figs. 4, 5, and 6. For the proposed deployment algorithm and the compared algorithms, the coverage ratio is recorded versus the number of allowed RSUs k. The performance of greedy-c is better than Uniform and Random while its coverage efficiency is slightly inferior to Optimal. As expected, the coverage ratio increases as the number of RSUs increases. The variability in the percentages above is due to the different scenarios that we have considered.

As it can be easily seen, when the complexity of the road topology in the downtown regions increases, it can possibly result in lower coverage ratios, especially in the case that there is just a few RSUs available in the region. It is also obvious to see that in the regular downtown region, just a few RSUs may be sufficient to cover most of the target region. We can easily come to a conclusion that, in a smaller urban region, it is easier to cover a specific area by deploying

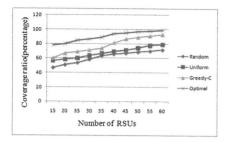

Fig. 3. New York

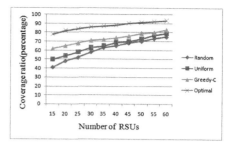

Fig. 4. Shanghai

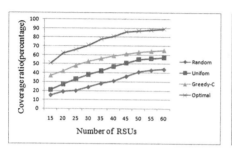

Fig. 5. Zurich

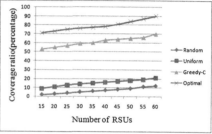

Fig. 6. Winterthur

just a few RSUs at strategic locations. Therefore, in large downtown areas, it is much harder to cover the specific area with a limited number of RSUs.

6 Related Work

Extensive research has been conducted in data dissemination through vehicle-to-vehicle communication with the help of roadside stations. Minimum required transmission time was considered in [5] when planning roadside infrastructures, whereas Liang et al. made a tradeoff between the number of hops in inter-vehicle communication and the number of installed access points [6]. To improve driving convenience, Lee aimed to maximize the connectivity of the network [7]. Given the number of access points, the communication range and the collected vehicle traces, the proposed algorithm calculated the locations to install access points to cover most of the vehicle traces. An adapted generic algorithm was proposed in [8] to select a minimum number of positions along the road to install access points, such that the whole road was covered and any wireless device on the road could communicate with one of the access points. To tackle the broadcast storm and network partition problems simultaneously, Akabane et al. [9] proposed a suitable multi-hop broadcast protocol named as TURBO to deliver messages under dense and sparse networks. Yan et al. [10] formulated the intersection selection problem and provided the adapted-bipartite-based heuristics

(ABS). Mukherjee et al. [11] proposed a publish-subscribe based event notification framework that used RSUs to deliver events to vehicles that subscribed to them.

As mentioned before, coverage is considered as an important metric of communication quality. Most research has been done in terms of coverage. Trullols et al. [13] proposed a maximum coverage approach to solve the problem of information dissemination in intelligent transportation systems. Zhu et al. [14] considered the critical problem of base stations for maximizing delay-constrained coverage of an urban area achieved by the vehicular network. The authors formulated a new objective of maximizing the expected sensing coverage. They took random vehicle mobility into account and exploited the regularity in vehicle mobility. Yoon and Kim [15] studied the maximum coverage deployment problem in wireless sensor networks and proposed an efficient genetic algorithm. Lin and Rubin [16] proposed a Vehicular Backbone Network (VBN) protocol and developed an analytical model to characterize the maximum throughput rate.

7   Conclusion

To address the crucial problem of RSUs deployment to cover a specific urban area, we formulate the region covering problem, which is proved to be NP-hardness. We present a c-street model and then propose a novel greedy-based polynomial time factor-c algorithm under the c-street model. To be more realistic, we also introduce a $(r, d, f(.), g(.,.))$-city model which can represent more geometric properties of the modern cities. According to the model, a polynomial time approximation scheme is proposed based on the shifting method [4]. Finally, the proposed simple greedy-based algorithm is implemented and some simulation results are provided.

Acknowledgements. The authors are very grateful to the anonymous reviewers for their helpful comments on an earlier version of this paper.

References

1. Chen, W., Guha, R.K., Kwon, T.J., Lee, J., Hsu, Y.Y.: A survey and challenges in routing and data dissemination in vehicular ad hoc networks. Wirel. Commun. Mobile Comput. **11**(7), 787–795 (2011)
2. Dubey, B.B., Chauhan, N., Pant, S.: Effect of position of fixed infrastructure on data dissemination in VANETs. IJRRCS **2**(2), 482–486 (2011)
3. Yan, T., Zhang, W., Wang, G.: DOVE: data dissemination to a desired number ofreceivers in VANET. IEEE Trans. Veh. Technol. **63**(4), 1903–1916 (2014)
4. Hochbaum, D.S., Maass, W.: Approximation schemes for covering and packing problems in image processing and VLSI. J. ACM(JACM) **32**(1), 130–136 (1985)
5. Cavalcante, E.S., Aquino, A.L., Pappa, G.L., Loureiro, A.A.: Roadside unit deployment for information dissemination in a VANET: An evolutionary approach. In: Proceedings of the 14th Annual Conference Companion on Genetic and Evolutionary Computation, pp. 27–34. ACM (2012)

6. Liang, Y., Liu, H., Rajan, D.: Optimal placement and configuration of roadside units in vehicular networks. In: Vehicular Technology Conference (VTC Spring), pp. 1–6, Yokohama (2012)
7. Lee, J.: Design of a network coverage analyzer for roadside-to-vehicle telematics networks. In: Ninth ACIS International Conference on Software Engineering, Artificial Intelligence, Networking, and Parallel/Distributed Computing, vol. 13(12), pp. 201–205 (2008)
8. Ghaffarian, H., Soryani, M., Fathy, M.: Planning VANET infrastructures to improve safety awareness in curved roads. J. Zhejiang Univ. Sci. C **13**(12), 918–928 (2012)
9. Akabane, A.T., Villas, L.A., Madeira, M., Roberto, E.: An adaptive solution for data dissemination under diverse road traffic conditions in urban scenarios. In: IEEE Wireless Communications and Networking Conference (WCNC), pp. 1654–1659, New Orleans (2015)
10. Yan, T., Zhang, W., Wang, G., Zhang, Y.: Access points planning in urban area for data dissemination to drivers. IEEE Trans. Veh. Technol. **63**(1), 390–402 (2014)
11. Mukherjee, J.C., Gupta, A., Sreenivas, R.C.: Event Notification in VANET With Capacitated Roadside Units. IEEE Trans. Intell. Transp. Syst. **pp**(99), 1–13 (2016)
12. Karp, R.M.: Reducibility among combinatorial problems. In: Miller, R.E., Thatcher, J.W., Bohlinger, J.D. (eds.) Complexity of Computer Computations, pp. 85–103. Springer, US (1972)
13. Trullols, O., Fiore, M., Casetti, C., Chiasserini, C.F., Ordinas, J.B.: Planning roadside infrastructure for information dissemination in intelligent transportation systems. Comput. Commun. **33**(4), 432–442 (2010)
14. Zhu, Y., Bao, Y., Li, B.: On maximizing delay-constrained coverage of urban vehicular networks. IEEE Sel. Areas Commun. **30**(4), 804–817 (2012)
15. Yoon, Y., Kim, Y.H.: An efficient genetic algorithm for maximum coverage deployment in wireless sensor networks. IEEE Trans. Cybern. **43**(5), 1473–1483 (2013)
16. Lin, Y., Rubin, I.: Throughput maximization under guaranteed dissemination coverage for VANET systems. In: Information Theory and Applications Workshop (ITA), pp. 313–318 (2015)

Channel Assignment with User Coverage Priority and Interference Optimization for Multicast Routing in Wireless Mesh Networks

Feng Zeng[1][✉], Nan Zhao[1], Zhigang Chen[1], Hui Liu[2], and Wenjia Li[3][✉]

[1] School of Software, Central South University, Changsha, China
{fengzeng,czg}@csu.edu.cn
[2] Department of Computer Science, Missouri State University, Springfield, USA
HuiLiu@MissouriState.edu
[3] Department of Computer Science, New York Institute of Technology, New York, USA
wli20@nyit.edu

Abstract. In order to improve multicast performance in wireless mesh networks, we consider both multicast tree construction and channel assignment in this paper. To maximize the possibility of providing good service to the users, we treat the user coverage of each destination as the top priority in channel assignment. In addition, we propose the multicast tree constructing algorithm (namely CIOMT) and channel assignment algorithm with the name CIOCA. In the CIOMT algorithm, each destination selects the minimum interference path to the constructing tree and joins into the constructing tree. For QoS consideration, the source-to-destination hop count is up bounded. In the CIOCA algorithm, the nodes are assigned the sending channels by the descending order of priority. During the channel assignment process, the channel with minimum interference to the whole tree will be selected and assigned to the corresponding interfaces. Simulation results have shown that the proposed solution outperforms the other existing algorithms.

Keywords: Wireless mesh network · Multicast · Channel assignment · Interference

1 Introduction

Wireless Mesh Network (WMN) is an important technology for "last mile" Internet access [1]. In the WMNs, there are three types of nodes, namely client, mesh router and gateway. The mesh routers and gateways are often static and form a wireless mesh backbone. The clients access the wireless mesh backbone through its associated mesh router, and visit the Internet via gateways finally. Consequently, in a WMN, wireless mesh backbone plays a key role in packets transmission directed to/from the Internet, and has an important impact on the network performance.

Traditionally, in wireless mesh backbone, each node has one radio, and all nodes share and compete for only one channel. Due to the interference among links transmitting simultaneously, the capacity and QoS of the network are severely limited [2].

© Springer International Publishing Switzerland 2016
Q. Yang et al. (Eds.): WASA 2016, LNCS 9798, pp. 560–570, 2016.
DOI: 10.1007/978-3-319-42836-9_49

To solve this issue, an effective approach is to equip each node with multiple interfaces, and the nodes could transmit packets simultaneously with multiple channels. With appropriate channel assignment, interference can be greatly reduced [3].

As we all know, multicast is a useful technology in Internet, especially to some network applications such as online video, p2p transmission and so on. Due to the importance of multicast and the effectiveness of multi-interface multi-channel technology, we should develop the proper channel assignment strategy for multicast in WMNs, and improve the multicast performance.

In this paper, we study channel assignment for multicast in multi-interface multi-channel WMNs. More specifically, we consider both multicast tree construction and channel assignment to reduce interference in multicast routing. By this means, we could provide high quality multicast service to the users as much as possible.

2   Related Work

There are some works on channel assignment for multicast in WMNs. In [4], Zeng et al. proposed a Multi-Channel Multicast (MCM) algorithm to optimize throughput for multi-channel and multi-interface mesh networks. In MCM, channel assignment started from the root of multicast tree, and the channel with minimum interference would be selected. The total interference of each node was calculated from the interference caused by its neighbouring nodes within one hop. However, due to the effect of hidden nodes, the measurement accuracy of the channel interference will be con-strained if we only consider one-hop interferences. To this end, Nguyen et al. [5] proposed a channel assignment algorithm called M4, which eliminated the hidden channel problem by adding to the optimization function the channel information of the two hop neighbours of a node.

Elaheh [6] et al. proposed an algorithm based on genetic algorithm to build a delay constrained minimum cost multicast tree with minimum interference. Farzinvash [7] et al. proposed an optimal cross-layer model aiming to maximize the total number of obtained layers by the receivers, and network coding was used to improve multicast capacity. Network coding was also used in the work of Ning [8] to increase the utilization of spectrum resource and improve network throughput.

Yang [9, 10] et al. proposed the channel assignment algorithm BBF, in which back-tracking and best first search strategies were developed to find channel assignment with minimum interference. Tan [11] et al. converted the channel assignment problem into a binary integer-programming model. Then, an algorithm was presented to find the optimized multicast routing and channel assignment. Kumar [12] et al. proposed a learning-automata-based channel assignment with topology preservation.

Unlike the aforementioned works, in this paper, we study both multicast tree construction and channel assignment problems together to reduce the interference and improve the network throughput. Moreover, we also take user priority of receiving multicast service into consideration. In some cases, we may want to provide good multicast service for users as much as possible, and provide the users who have higher priority with better service. Our work would make it possible to address both of these two issues.

3   System Description

3.1   Network Model

The wireless backbone in a WMN can be modeled as an undirected graph $G(V, E)$, where V is the set of nodes, $n = |V|$ is the total number of nodes. E is the set of edges. Each node has the same fixed communication range r. For a node v_i, we assume that p_i is its position. Then, the distance of node v_i and v_j can be denoted as $d_{ij} = |p_i - p_j|$. Therefore, if $d_{ij} \leq r$, then $e_{ij} \in E$, where e_{ij} is the link between v_i and v_j. In a multi-interface and multi-channel WMN, each node can be equipped with some Network Interface Cards (NICs), and these NICs could be tuned to different and non-overlapping channels, which allow the node to perform more concurrent transmissions. Moreover, we also assume that each node has two NICs, one is for sending multicast packets to its child nodes, and the other is for receiving multicast packets from its parent node.

3.2   Multicast Routing Tree

In a mesh backbone $G(V, E)$, a gateway would be the multicast source, and some mesh routers are multicast destinations. Each destination is associated with many end users, which is called user coverage in this paper. For a mesh router $v \in V$, the number of users covered by v is defined as $u(v)$. Consequently, if $v \in V$ and $u(v) > 0$, then the node v must be one of multicast destinations, and the set of multicast destinations can be denoted as $M = \{v \mid u(v) > 0, v \in V\}$. For multicast in a WMN, we must construct a routing tree, which is rooted at a gateway and covers all destinations.

3.3   Channel Assignment

As is shown in previous research, assigning non-overlapping (orthogonal) channels to neighboring links is the best solution to reduce the interference among wireless links. However, the number of non-overlapping channels is limited, and the interfered links may be more than the non-overlapping channels. Therefore, we should make use of the overlapping channels.

All channels in IEEE 802.11 b/g are shown in Fig. 1. As shown from the figure, the spectrum separation of non-overlapping channels is at least 30 Hz, and consequently there are 3 non-overlapping channels at most, which are channel 1, 6 and 11. To the channels c_1 and c_2, if and only if $|c_1 - c_2| \geq 5$, they don't overlap with each other.

In experiments, it was found that the interfering distance between two links depends on their channel separation. In [8], the authors found that given the interfering distance I_c, and channel separation c, the relation of I_c/r and c is shown in Table 1 at 2 M, 5.5 M and 11 M sending rate, where r is the communication range of nodes. The data in Table 1 shows that I_c decreases with the increase of c.

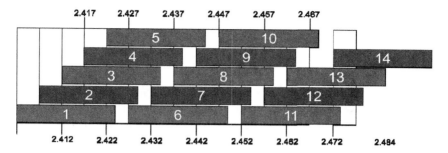

Fig. 1. Channel bandwidth of IEEE 802.11 b/g (GHz)

Table 1. I_c/r vs. c [8]

c	0	1	2	3	4	>=5
2Mbits/s	2.5	1.6	1.2	0.9	0.5	0.0
5.5Mbits/s	2.2	1.5	1.0	0.8	0.3	0.0
11Mbits/s	2.0	1.2	0.7	0.5	0.2	0.0

3.4 Problem Description

We denote the multicast tree as a directed graph $T(V_T, E_T)$, where V_T is the set of nodes in multicast tree, and E_T is the set of edges. In V_T, each node is equipped with two NICs, which are assigned with two channels for sending and receiving packets respectively. There are h available channels for assignment, and the channel set is denoted as $C = \{c_1, c_2, \ldots, c_h\}$. For a node v_i, its sending and receiving channels are denoted as cs_i and cr_i respectively with $cs_i \in C$ and $cr_i \in C$. If v_j is one of child nodes of v_i, there must be a directed edge $e_{ij} \in E_T$. It is supposed that the link e_{ij} is assigned channel c_{ij}, then $cs_i = cr_j = c_{ij}$, that is, the receiving channel of a non-root node is the same as the sending channel of its parent node. To a node v_i, its child and offspring nodes sets are separately denoted as $CH(v_i)$ and $OP(v_i)$, then we have $CH(v_i) \subseteq OP(v_i)$. If v_j and v_k are two child nodes of v_i, that is $\{v_j, v_k\} \subseteq CH(v_i)$, then two links e_{ij} and e_{ik} should have the same channel assigned, i.e. $c_{ij} = c_{ik}$. We assume that the binary variable x_i represents whether v_i is interfered by other nodes, $x_i = 1$ for true, while $x_i = 0$ for false, as is shown in Eq. (1). In Eq. (2), w_i is the number of users covered by v_i and its offspring nodes, and called downstream user coverage of v_i. In Eq. (3), $Int(T)$ is the interference of multicast tree $T(V_T, E_T)$.

$$x_i = \begin{cases} 1 & \exists v_j \in V_T, d_{ij} \leq I_{|cs_i-cs_j|} \text{ or } d_{ij} \leq I_{|cr_i-cs_j|} \\ 0 & \text{otherwise} \end{cases} \tag{1}$$

$$w_i = u(v_i) + \sum_{v_j \in OP(v_i)} u(v_j) \tag{2}$$

$$Int(T) = \sum_{v_i \in V_T} w_i x_i \tag{3}$$

In this paper, the problem is to construct a multicast tree T and minimize $Int(T)$ through channel assignment. Since the existing works have proved that the similar problem is NP-Hard, we propose the heuristic algorithms to find the effective solution of the problem.

4   User Coverage and Interference Optimization for Multicast

Our solution includes two stages. The first stage is to construct multicast tree, and the second stage is to assign channels to the nodes in multicast tree.

4.1   Multicast Tree Construction

For each receiver, the shorter distance to source could ensure better service. Therefore, the hop count between source and receiver has an upper bound in our multicast tree construction process. In tree $T(V_T, E_T)$, the hop count between a destination v and the root s is denoted as $Hop_T(v, s)$, which satisfies the inequality (4). In order to ensure multicast tree covering all destination nodes, the constant Δ is defined as the maximum hop count of all shortest paths between each destination and source in $G(V, E)$, as is shown in Eq. (5), where $MinHop_G(v, s)$ is the hop count of the shortest path between v and s in G.

$$Hop_T(v, s) \leq \Delta \tag{4}$$

$$\Delta = Max_{v \in M}\{MinHop_G(v, s)\} \tag{5}$$

Furthermore, we aim to ensure that as many users as possible to have good multicast service. For each user, the shorter distance to source means the better service. On the whole, the sum of all distances could be used to measure the multicast QoS, and a smaller sum represents the better multicast QoS.

In addition, the structure of routing tree also has a significant impact on the interference among links. As is shown in Fig. 2, node 4, 5 and 6 are multicast destinations. The original network is demonstrated in Fig. 2 (a), whereas two multicast trees are shown in Fig. 2 (b) and (c), respectively. According to the positions of node 1, 2 and 3, link 1 -> 4, 1 -> 5, 2 -> 5 and 2 -> 6 may be interfered with each other, while link 3 -> 6 having no interference with 1 -> 4 and 1 -> 5. For interference optimization, multicast tree B is better than A.

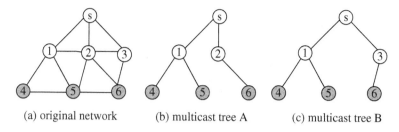

(a) original network   (b) multicast tree A   (c) multicast tree B

Fig. 2. Interference relieved tree structure

Based on the above analysis, during the tree construction process, we set the following goals: (1) high level link sharing, (2) up bounded hop count between each destination and root, (3) most users having good service, and (4) interference relieved tree structure. To achieve these goals, we propose a greedy algorithm CIOMT for the construction of Coverage and Interference Optimization Multicast Tree. Taking original network $G(V, E)$ as algorithm input, CIOMT is described as follows, and a multicast tree $T(V_T, E_T)$ will be algorithm output.

Step 1 - Parameters Setting: Set $V_T = \{s\}$, $E_T = \{\}$, $M_T = M$. Find all shortest paths from all destinations to source in $G(V, E)$, set Δ is the maximum hop count of all shortest paths.

Step 2 - Tree Initialization: Scan each node in M_T, if the node v has the only path with hop count not more than Δ to s in $G(V, E)$, then this only path joins into tree $T(V_T, E_T)$. To each destination node v which has joined into T, update $M_T = M_T - \{v\}$.

Step 3 - End Condition Checking: If M_T is empty, **the algorithm ends,** and $T(V_T, E_T)$ is the expected multicast tree. Otherwise, go to Step 4.

Step 4 - Candidate Nodes and Paths Selecting: Find at most k shortest paths from nodes in M_T to the constructing tree T, and supposed these paths are $Path_1$, $Path_2$, ..., $Path_k$. The paths must meet the following pattern: each $Path_i$ $(1 \leq i \leq k)$ can be denoted by $v_1 v_2 \dots v_x$, where $v_1 \in M_T$, $v_x \in V_T$, and the intermediate node $v_j \notin M_T$ and $v_j \notin V_T$ $(1 < j < x)$.

Step 5 - Tree updating: For at most k paths, based on Eq. (6), compute the interference of the paths to the constructing tree T, and denoted as $Inf_T(Path_1)$, $Inf_T(Path_2)$, ..., $Inf_T(Path_k)$. Supposed $Path_x$ has the minimum interference to the constructing tree T. $Path_x$ joins into tree T, and the destination node in $Path_x$ removes from M_T. Go to Step 3.

$$Inf_T\left(v_1 v_2 \dots v_x\right) = \sum_{i=2}^{x-1} N_T(v_i) \tag{6}$$

In Eq. (6), the interference of a path $v_1 v_2 \dots v_x$ to tree T is denoted as Inf_T $(v_1 v_2 \dots v_x)$. Since the interfered nodes can be similarly considered as the neighboring nodes of the path, the interference is defined as the number of all nodes in T interfered by the path. $N_T(v_i)$ is the number of neighboring nodes of v_i in the tree T.

In CIOMT, a parameter k is used for trade-off between link sharing and interference relieving. If k is 1, the shortest path will be selected to join into the tree. If k is large enough, the path with minimum interference to tree will join into the tree.

For the tree construction process shown in Fig. 2, nodes s, 1, 4 and 5 have been in the tree. If node 6 is going to join into the tree, there are two paths 6-2-s and 6-3-s between node 6 and the tree with $\Delta = 2$. For node 2 and 3 have 2 and 1 neighboring nodes in the tree respectively, the path 6-3-s has less interference to the tree than path 6-2-s. Therefore, path 6-3-s joins into the tree, as is shown in Fig. 2 (c).

4.2   Channel Assignment with User Coverage Priority

We define the priority $P_r \subset [0, 1]$ of each node for channel assignment, which is shown in Eq. (7) where w_{root} and w_i are the related user numbers of root and v_i in a multicast tree T respectively, according to Eq. (2).

$$\Pr(v_i) = \frac{w_i}{w_{root}} \tag{7}$$

We propose the channel assignment algorithm for Coverage and Interference Optimization Channel Assignment, with the name CIOCA. In channel assignment, the nodes are assigned channels in descending order of their priorities. In order to ensure a node to have higher priority than its child nodes, the user coverage is assumed to be 0.5 for the nodes with none user coverage. Thus, in the priority queue, a node is always ahead of its offspring nodes, and the root has the highest priority among the nodes in a multicast tree. CIOCA is described as the following four steps. Multicast tree $T(V_T, E_T)$ and channel set $C = \{1, 2, ..., 12\}$ are algorithm inputs.

Step 1 - Initialization: Set initial multicast tree as $T(V_T, E_T)$, channel set as $C = \{1, 2, ..., 12\}$. Set all links in T with channel 1. That is, each node's sending and receiving channels are 1. The nodes except the root in multicast tree T enter into a queue *node_queue1* in the descending order of their priorities. Moreover, create a backup of *node_queue1* as *node_queue2*. Go to step 2.

Step 2 - Channel Assignment: Assume that the first node in *node_queue1* is v_i. Its receiving channel is assigned to the same channel as its parent node's sending channel. If v_i is a leaf node, it does not need to be assigned a sending channel. Otherwise, its sending channel cs_i is set to the channel with minimum tree interference $Inf(T)$ based on Eqs. (1), (2) and (3). It is supposed that c_{min} is the sending channel for v_i with the minimum tree interference $Inf(T)$, which is shown in Eq. (8). Then, let $cs_i = c_{min}$. After channel assignment for v_i is completed, v_i is removed from *node_queue1*. Go to step 3.

$$Inf_{cs_i = c_{min}}(T) = \min\left\{ Inf_{cs_i = c_j}(T) \mid c_j \in C \right\} \tag{8}$$

Step 3 - Iterating Condition: If *node_queue1* is not empty, go to step 2. Otherwise, go to step 4.

Step 4 - Optimization: According the order of nodes in *node_queue2*, we find the minimum interference sending channel c_{min} of each non-root and non-leaf node v_i. If $cs_i \neq c_{min}$, then set it's sending channel cs_i and its child nodes' receiving channels as c_{min}. Optimization runs until *Inf(T)* is fixed. **Algorithm ends.**

For the example shown in Fig. 3, node 4, 5 and 6 are destinations, and all nodes' w values are denoted on their upper right direction. The root (s) has highest priority for channel assignment, and its sending channel and receiving channel of node 1 are both assigned to be channel 1. Then, the sending channel of node 1 and its child nodes' receiving channels are assigned to channel 6, which is non-overlapping with channel 1. Since node 2 has higher priority than node 3, channel 11 is assigned to the sending NIC of node 2. So far, the only 3 non-overlapping channels (channel 1, 6 and 11) are assigned to the related nodes. Based on Eq. (1), we can find out whether or not there exists a channel assigned to node 3 with no interference to its neighboring nodes. If there exists no non-interference channel for node 3, channel 11 would be assigned to the sending NIC of node 3. As we can see from Fig. 3, within all of its neighboring nodes, node 5 has minimum w value, and for minimizing the number of users affected by wireless interference, node 3 with channel 11 as sending channel would only interfere with node 5 in this case.

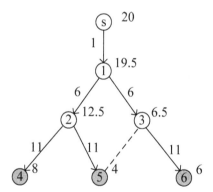

Fig. 3. Channel assignment example

5   Simulation

We implement the proposed multicast routing and channel assignment algorithms in NS-2 simulator, and evaluate CIOCA by performance comparison with MCM [4] and M4 [5] from the following metrics:

Throughput: The throughput is the average number of packets each multicast destination receives during a time unit.

Delay: The delay is the average time it takes for a packet to reach the destination after it leaves the source.

User Satisfaction Degree (USD): It is assumed that the destinations $\{v_1, v_2, ..., v_m\}$ have the user coverage $\{a_1, a_2, ..., a_m\}$, the numbers of packets they received are $\{b_1, b_2, ..., b_m\}$, and the total number of packets sent by source node is b. The USD of multicast tree T is defined as Eq. (9). From the definition of USD, if all destinations can receive the total b packets, the USD is 1, which means all users are satisfied. Otherwise, the higher the USD value is, the more the users are satisfied.

$$USD(T) = \frac{\sum_{i=1}^{m} a_i \frac{b_i}{b}}{\sum_{i=1}^{m} a_i} = \frac{\sum_{i=1}^{m} a_i b_i}{b \sum_{i=1}^{m} a_i} \tag{9}$$

From Fig. 4 (a), when the multicast group size is small, the three algorithms have similar performance. With the increase of multicast group size, CIOCA has better performance than M4 and MCM with average packet receiving rate increased by 6.8 % and 14.1 % respectively. From Fig. 4 (b), compared with M4 and MCM, CIOCA has the average source-to-destination delay decreased by 3.4 % and 6.7 % respectively.

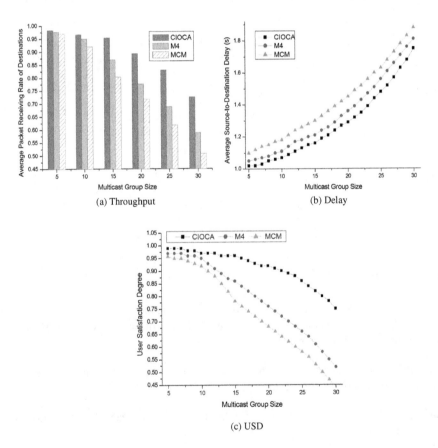

(a) Throughput

(b) Delay

(c) USD

Fig. 4. Simulation results

Based on USD definition Eq. (9) and the above experiment data, we can calculate out average USD of the three algorithms with various multicast group sizes. The result is shown in Fig. 4 (c). CIOCA has much better user satisfaction than M4 and MCM with the USD increased by 23.7 % and 35.3 %.

6   Conclusion

In this paper, we focus on interference reduction and QoS improvement in multicast routing. We take both multicast tree construction and channel assignment problems into consideration, and treat the user coverage of each destination as a top priority for channel assignment. Simulation results have shown that the proposed solution outperforms the existing two widely used algorithms in the literature. In particular, the proposed solution has much better performance than other algorithms in term of user satisfaction.

Acknowledgement. This work is supported in part by the National Science Foundation of China (Grant No. 61379057) and the Research Foundation of Central South University (Grant No. 2014JSJJ019).

References

1. Akyildiz, I.F., Wang, X.: A survey on wireless mesh networks. IEEE Commun. Mag. **43**(9), 23–30 (2005)
2. Gupta, P., Kumar, P.R.: The capacity of wireless networks. IEEE Trans. Inf. Theory **46**(2), 388–404 (2000)
3. Kyasanur, P., Vaidya, N.H.: Capacity of multi-channel wireless networks: impact of number of channels and interfaces. In: The 11th Annual International Conference on Mobile Computing and Networking, pp. 43–57. ACM Press, Cologne (2005)
4. Guokai, Z., Bo, W., Yong, D.: Multicast algorithms for multi-channel wireless mesh networks. In: IEEE International Conference on Network Protocols, pp. 1–10. IEEE Press, Beijing (2007)
5. Lan, N.H., Trang, N.U.: Minimum interference channel assignment for multicast in multi-radio wireless mesh networks. In: International Wireless Communications and Mobile Computing Conference, pp. 626–631. IEEE Press, Crete (2008)
6. Vaezpour, E., Dehghan, M.: A multi-objective optimization approach for joint channel assignment and multicast routing in multi-radio multi-channel wireless mesh networks. Wireless Pers. Commun. **77**(2), 1055–1076 (2014)
7. Farzinvash, L., Dehghan, M.: A cross-layer approach for multi-layer multicast routing in multi-channel multi-radio wireless mesh networks. Int. J. Ad Hoc Ubiquitous Comput. **21**(1), 26–40 (2016). doi:10.1504/IJAHUC.2016.074387
8. Ning, Z., Song, Q., Guo, L., Kong, X.: A novel adaptive spectrum allocation scheme for multi-channel multi-radio wireless mesh networks. J. Netw. Comput. Appl. **56**(10), 19–27 (2015)
9. Wen-Lin, Y., Wan-Ting, H.: Backtracking and best-first based channel assignment strategy for multicast in multi-radio wireless mesh networks. In: International Conference on Multimedia Technology, pp. 2984–2987. IEEE Press, Hangzhou (2011)

10. Yang, W., Wei-Tsung, H.: The study of interference-free multicast using non-orthogonal channels for multi-radio and multi-channel wireless mesh networks. In: International Computer Symposium, pp. 547–552. IEEE Press, Tainan (2010)
11. Tan, X., Wen, H., He, X.: Channel assignment strategy in multi-channel multi-radio wireless mesh networks based on improved binary integer programming. In: The 31st Chinese Control Conference, pp. 6550–6555. Hefei, China (2012)
12. Kumar, N., Lee, J.-H.: Collaborative-learning-automata-based channel assignment with topology preservation for wireless mesh networks under QoS constraints. IEEE Syst. J. 9(3), 675–685 (2015)

Performance Evaluation of Vehicular Ad Hoc Networks for Rapid Response Traffic Information Delivery

Isaac J. Cushman[1], Danda B. Rawat[1], Lei Chen[1(✉)], and Qing Yang[2]

[1] Georgia Southern University, Statesboro, GA 30560, USA
{ic00214,drawat,lchen}@georgiasouthern.edu
[2] Montana State University, Bozeman, MT 59717, USA
Qing.yang@cs.montana.edu

Abstract. Vehicular transportation has received rapid growth in many areas thanks to the increase in population density and massive city expansion. Such advancement however leads to the loss of time, money and human lives due to many reasons including driver distraction and serious roadway conditions. Recent trends have shown improvement of vehicular safety on account of design and manufacturing innovations such as additional airbags and pre-collision detection and warning using sensors. Nonetheless, the national averages of fatality, injuries, and property damages due to roadway vehicular crashes still remain at high levels. For the purpose of saving lives, reducing fuel costs and travel time on road, it is demanded to have a vehicular communication system that rapidly learns about the environment and promptly respond and notify drivers for decision making. Our research in this paper aims to design a system that utilizes the communications among vehicles in a Vehicular Ad Hoc Network (VANET) and roadside infrastructure-based devices. Our design and analysis indicate that such system can be applied to assist drivers in adjusting their driving for better safety and making route decisions to save time and fuel costs.

1 Introduction

The data released by the National Highway Traffic Safety Administration (NHTSA) in 2014 shows a total number of 32,675 fatal crashes in the United States. It can also be found in the same set of data that 2.3 million injuries from vehicle accidents were reported in the same year [1]. In addition to lives and injuries, two other major losses on road are time and cost of fuel, which are typical in cities and metropolitan areas where commuters loose great amount of time due to traffic congestions and road conditions during peak time for their weekday commuting. A study released in 2015 by the Texas A&M Transportation Institute indicates that annually the U.S. suffers a loss of $140 million due to time and fuel wasted in traffic congestions, and on average each commuter spends an extra 42 h and wastes 19 gallons of fuel caused by traffic and road conditions [2].

The Vehicular Ad Hoc Networks (VANETs) are designed and implemented primarily for improving road safety and driving efficiency. A VANET can be comprised of a mixture of two network topologies: infrastructure-based and infrastructure-less (ad hoc). In contrast to an infrastructure-based network such as the backbone

© Springer International Publishing Switzerland 2016
Q. Yang et al. (Eds.): WASA 2016, LNCS 9798, pp. 571–579, 2016.
DOI: 10.1007/978-3-319-42836-9_50

telecommunication networks on the roadside, an ad hoc network allows a vehicular communication device to quickly join and exit the network. Example technologies that can be utilized for such network topology include Bluetooth, Wi-Fi and cellular, which is embedded in every smart phone carried by a driver or passenger in a vehicle. In a similar way, a vehicular system can also have the same functions of transmitting and receiving vital roadway and traffic updates based on their current travel route and information received from surrounding vehicles and roadside units. VANETs are quickly becoming critical for road safety thanks to its ability to quickly adapt, expand and exchange information through a network formed using existing communication technologies. With a VANET created with systems installed and running on multiple vehicles that share traffic and driving related information such as driving speed and road side conditions, such abilities can make key contribution to improving road safety and driving efficiency.

To support the aforementioned infrastructure-based and ad hoc network topologies, the Dedicated Short Range Communication (DSRC) enabled IEEE 802.11p technology allows On Board Units (OBUs) and Roadside Units (RSUs) for vehicle-to-vehicle (V2V), Vehicle-to-Infrastructure (V2I) as well as Infrastructure-to-Infrastructure (I2I) communications. While I2I communications are often considered beyond the scope of VANETs and therefore are not further addressed here, V2I communications enable nodes (communication devices on moving vehicles) to connect to the infrastructure network through DSRC, cellular or Wi-Fi networks. V2V communication occurs over a pure ad hoc network as all devices connected to one another are located in (moving) vehicles without any stationary infrastructure. In contrast to V2I communications, V2V may not always provide reliable direct path from one node to another. However, satisfactory connections can be expected in within the communication range under normal weather and road conditions. Research has been conducted and solutions exist for enhancing reliable and secure VANET communications borrowing mechanisms from Mobile Ad-Hoc Networks (MANETs) and Wireless Local Area Networks (WLANs) [3], however problems still exist in current VANET systems due to the changing volume of connected devices and environment constraints.

In this paper, we investigate how much time can be saved by propagating the upcoming traffic information to vehicles that are approaching the congested area with an aim of avoiding traffic accidents as well as reducing congestion time and fuel consumption because of traffic congestions.

The rest of this paper is organized as follows: Sect. 2 introduces the proposed VANET system by discussing its design concept, design of VANET, and analyzing the probability of Over- and Under-Crowded of the proposed system. Section 3 concludes the research and plans for future research. References are listed at the end of this paper.

2   Proposed VANET System

We introduce the proposed VANET system in this section, starting with the design concept for vehicular communication.

2.1   Design Concept

One of the major causes of congested traffic is a sudden decrease of drivable pathways for the volume of moving vehicles on the road. In order to accurately and promptly exchanging information among vehicles and save time and costs, we postulate and examine the probability of drivers being able and willing to take a detour from their original route when the projected time for passing through the traffic via original route is greater than that of the detour. As the number of surrounding vehicles increases, the expected time to be spent by the drivers for slowly moving and/or completely stopping will gradually increase. It can be modeled using Fig. 1 where vehicles on the road can be divided into multiple groups or clusters, in this case groups A, B, and C, based on how close they are approaching to an event or incident on road. In this scenario, group A is the front group and is closest to the incident and is expected to experience the least of travel time among all groups, while group C at the end of the growing queue is expected to see longer travel time through the traffic ahead.

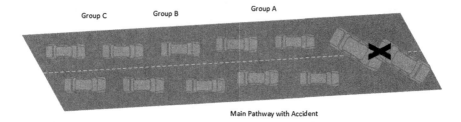

Fig. 1. Roadway with variable number of vehicles with event blocking pathway

Based on the above modeling, we present the traffic scenario as an "inch worm". During traffic peak time, and in the event or incident such as sports events and traffic accidents, the queue of vehicles can be observed as multiple groups A, B, C, D, etc. The number of vehicles in a group can be random, unless constraints exist, e.g. same queue divided into more groups may potentially increase the amount of communication in the VANET. In the figure, at the instant of stopped traffic (e.g. around vehicle Group A), there will be a ripple motion causing all vehicles in Groups A through C to slow down, leading to the happening of the "inch worm" effect. Consequently each forthcoming vehicle group will slow down and all groups have to wait until they slowly move and pass the root cause point of the traffic. It can be assumed that Group A will be close enough to the incident that any amount of detour time will not be beneficial to them, while groups behind A will be increasingly beneficial by detouring as farther away from the start of the queue. In the case that some drivers in any groups decide to reroute and take the detour (when such detouring exist), all vehicles behind them will have a more open route while vehicles ahead of them will still be moving through the obstruction in the case when rerouting is not worthwhile for these vehicles. By enforcing rerouting as soon as changes to the queue occur, it is expected that all recent incoming traffic will only slightly be or not be slowed down at all by the event.

Here we give an example scenario to further explain how making decision of detouring may affect the overall travel time. Suppose the travel time for vehicles in Groups B and C extends to 30 min due to congestion, while the detour only takes 20 min. In this case it is possible some of the drivers may decide to take the detour but the others may not. In the scenario that most would take the detour, the traffic ahead of a new Group D may see an update with reduced travel time, e.g. from 45~60 min down to 20~30 min. This is illustrated in Fig. 2, where Groups B and C take the detour and free up the traffic in the main pathway where the accident happened, and Group D will expect reduced travel time due to the detour of vehicles ahead of it.

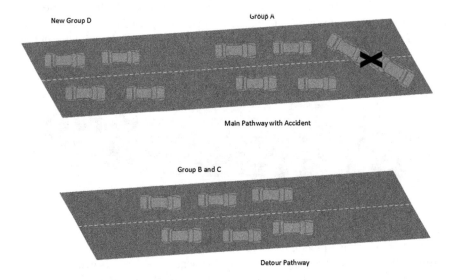

Fig. 2. Roadway where available detour is taken by Groups C and B

2.2 Analysis and Performance Evaluation

To evaluate the above design concept, we analyze the time delay that each group of vehicle will expect in VANET using following mathematical expression

$$(TE_N) = TE + \sum TE_{N-1} \tag{1}$$

where TE_N is the total delay time for the Nth group directly affected by the accident. The time taken by the incident to clear the road block is TE. We plotted the variation of average time that each vehicle cluster would take to cross the accident area (100 m) vs. the distance as shown in Fig. 3. Each cluster has its average time to get to a given distance when there is no accidents. This time increases when there is delay because of an accident/congestion as shown in Fig. 3. Traffic event occurs for group A at 40 m away from 100 m (i.e., 60 m in Fig. 3) and then 50 and 60 m for groups B and C (i.e., 50 and 40 m in Fig. 3), respectively. When there is no alternative route, the delay time is added to the original estimated time to get to the destination. Note that when there is no alternative route for all clusters, the delay time due to event is 5 min (average) for the first/closest cluster and therefore Groups A, B, and C will have 5, 10, and 15 min delay respectively. Delays for clusters B and C are increased since they need to cross the longer distance with slower speeds.

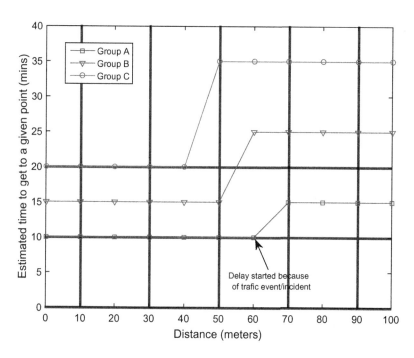

Fig. 3. Variation of traffic delay with no alternative route for vehicle clusters/groups A, B and C considered in our analysis.

Next, we considered another scenario plotted the variation of estimated time vs the distance as shown in Fig. 4 where Group B has an alternative route to save 5 min without having to wait in the congested traffic, then they would only be delayed by half of the amount of staying to pass the event in the previous scenario. Likewise, Group C would be able to save roughly 10 min of the travel time if they are promptly informed about an alternative route. This trend would continue to all vehicles or clusters/group needing to pass through the traffic event that is blocking the lanes of traffic.

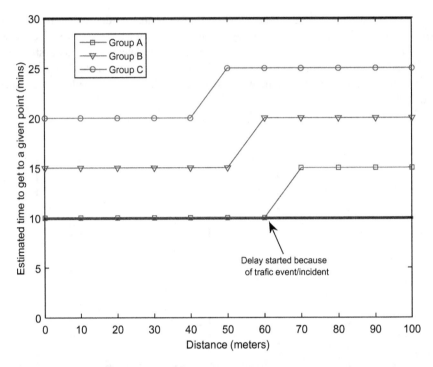

Fig. 4. Variation of traffic delay with an alternative route for vehicle clusters/groups B and C considered in our analysis.

2.3   VANET Communications

In order to reliably exchange critical information such as accidents and road/weather conditions, V2V and V2I networks must be properly connected. We look at the time duration available for V2V communication for given relative speed and transmission range of 1000 m (using $t = 1000/v$) as shown in Fig. 5 for different technologies (ZigBee takes 30 ms for association, Wi-Fi takes about 550 ms for association, Bluetooth takes about 1 to 4 s for association). ZigBee technology is not suitable for relative speed greater than 10 mph, Wi-Fi is not good for relative speed greater than 90 mph as there is no time left for actual message transfer as shown in Fig. 5.

V2V and V2I communications use different technologies and protocols for information delivery [4]. Furthermore, the vehicle-assisted data delivery allows for low delays in packet forwarding [5]. The time left for communication in Fig. 5 is used to exchange information in VANET based on relative speed and association me used technologies. The amount of information exchanged depends on the data rate that vehicles use to exchange their information and time left in Fig. 5 for given relative speed. Note that when vehicle travel in same direction, they will have low (or zero) relative speed and thus they will have longer time to communicate.

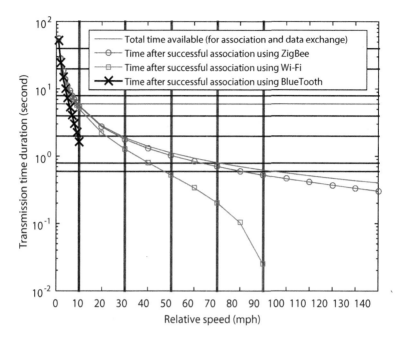

Fig. 5. Variation of time duration vs the relative speed for different relative speed for information exchange using V2V communications.

2.4 Probability of Over- and Under- Crowded for Connectivity

At any given time, the number of vehicles connected in VANET may range from one to thousands. Two basic scenarios are considered: (1) when there is very limited number of vehicles in the network, and (2) there are many vehicles in the network. Based on the work in [6], it can be estimated that the probability of network connectivity (at least two devices are within the communication range of each other), in regards to vehicle density on highway, is around 3 %, 68 %, and 98 % with corresponding vehicle density of 3.9, 26, and 44.9 vehicles per kilometer respectively. Similar techniques described in [7] can be adapted to increase the probability of connectivity. In the scenario that a group of vehicles all travelling together, they can keep a stable and constant communication as long as the distance among them are within the transmission range of each other. When vehicles are assumed to be distributed according to a Poisson distribution, the probability that the group of vehicles in a given density are all part of the network can be expressed as

$$P_c = [(1 - p)(1 - e^{-\rho R_1}) + p(1 - e^{-\rho R_2})]^{N-1} \tag{2}$$

where $p = M / (K + M)$ and is the ratio between network vehicle (M) and regular vehicle (K); P_c is the probability of connectivity, and ρ is the traffic density (vehicles/meter); R_1 is the distance across all of the networked vehicles and R_2 is the network coverage for the system. This equation gives the probability of connectivity compared to traffic density, when the coverage area for regular vehicle (R_1) is variable.

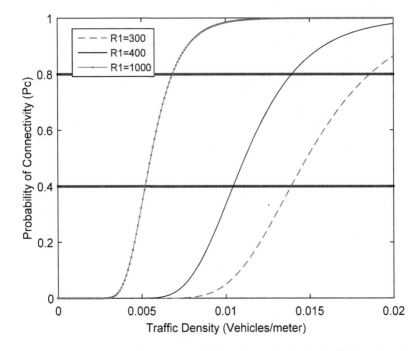

Fig. 6. Variation of probability of connectivity vs the traffic density for different R_1 values

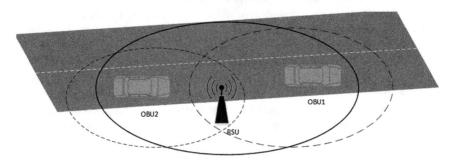

Fig. 7. A typical Scenario for vehicle (onboard unit or OBU) to road side unit (RSU) communications

We consider that $M = 40$, $K = 60$, and $R_2 = 800$ m to see the probability connectivity as shown in Fig. 6. It can be seen in Fig. 5 that as the traffic density increases, the distance the vehicles span across the network increases. This helps to increase the ability of vehicles to communicate with other vehicles. The probability of connectivity higher for higher R_1 as shown in Fig. 6.

In the case of over-crowded, each vehicle may have to adjust the transmission range to reduce the broadcast storm problem. However when there are no sufficient vehicle on the road (low vehicle density), each vehicle can carry the message until another vehicle is found or we need to road side unit (RSU) as illustrated in Fig. 7. The RSU can aggregate messages to avoid redundant transmissions and overloading the VANET.

3   Conclusion

In this paper, we have presented an analysis about how much time can be saved by propagating upcoming traffic information in VANET. When options are available for drivers they can reroute and save the drive time in case of congestion. This reduction in time results in reduction in lost productive work hours and fuel consumptions.

All in all, VANET is emerging as a technology to save time, money and human lives as well as reduce fatality, injuries, and property damages caused by traffic accidents and congestions.

References

1. Traffic Safety Facts, 1st edn. NHTSA's National Center for Statistics and Analysis, Washington (2015)
2. Lomax, T., Schrank, D., Eisele, B.: Urban Mobility Scorecard, 1st edn. The Texas A&M Transportation Institute and INRIX, Kirkland (2015)
3. Azogu, I., Ferreira, M., Larcom, J., Liu, H.: A new anti-jamming strategy for VANET metrics-directed security defense. IEEE GLOBECOM Workshops (2013)
4. Das, D., Misra, R.: Efficient vehicle to vehicle communication protocol for VANET. Recent Advances in Engineering and Computational Sciences (RAECS) (2014)
5. Chen, L., Tang, H., Wang, J.: Analysis of VANET security based on routing protocol information. In: Fourth International Conference on Intelligent Control and Information Processing (ICICIP) (2013)
6. Monteiro, R., Sargento, S., Viriyasitavat, W., Tonguz, O.: Improving VANET protocols via network science. In: IEEE Vehicular Network Conference (VNC) (2012)
7. Shao, C., Leng, S., Zhang, Y., Vinel, A., Jonsson, M.: Analysis of connectivity probability in platoon-based vehicular Ad Hoc networks. In: International Wireless Communications and Mobile Computing Conference (IWCMC) (2014)

Author Index

Printed in the United States
By Bookmasters